Charles Dickens

The Old Curiosity Shop

A Tale of Two Cities

– Charles Dickens –

THE OLD CURIOSITY SHOP

A TALE OF TWO CITIES

© EDIMAT BOOKS Ltd. London
is an affiliate of Edimat Libros S.A.
C/ Primavera, 35 Pol. Ind. El Malvar
Arganda del Rey - 28500 (Madrid) Spain
E-mail: edimat@edimat.es

ISBN: 84-9794-041-5
Legal Deposit: M-48879-2004

PRINTED IN SPAIN

THE OLD
CURIOSITY SHOP

PREFACE

(TO THE FIRST CHEAP EDITION)

IN April, 1840, I issued the first number of a new weekly publication, price threepence, called MASTER HUMPHREY'S CLOCK. It was intended to consist, for the most part, of detached papers, but was to include one continuous story, to be resumed from time to time, with such indefinite intervals between each period of resumption as might best accord with the exigencies and capabilities of the proposed Miscellany.

The first chapter of this tale appeared in the fourth number of MASTER HUMPHREY'S CLOCK, when I had already been made uneasy by the desultory character of that work, and when, I believe, my readers had throroughly participated in the feeling. The commencement of a story was a great satisfaction to me, and I had reason to believe that my readers participated in this feeling too. Hence, being pledged to some interruptions and some pursuit of the original design, I cheerfully set about disentangling myself from those impediments as fast as I could; and, that done, from that time until its completion THE OLD CURIOSITY SHOP was written and published from week to week, in weekly parts.

When the story was finished, that it might be freed from the incumbrance of associations and interruptions with which it had no kind of concern, I caused the few sheets of MASTER HUMPHREY'S CLOCK, which had been printed in connexion with it, to be cancelled; and, like the unfinished tale of the windy night and the notary in The Sentimental Journey, they became the property of the trunk-maker and butterman. I was especially unwilling, I confess, to enrich those respectable trades with the paper of the abandoned design, in which MASTER HUMPHREY described himself and his manner of life. Though I now affect to make the confession philosophically, as referring to a bye-gone emotion, I am conscious that my pen winces a little even while I write these words. But it was done, and wisely done, and MASTER HUMPHREY'S CLOCK, as originally constructed, became one of the lost books of the earth—which, we all know, are far more precious than any than can be read for love or money.

In reference to the tale itself, I desire to say very little here. The many friends it has won me, and the many hearts it has turned to me when they were full of private sorrow, invest it with an interest, in my mind, which is not a public one, and the rightful place of which appears to be "a more removed ground."

I will merely observe, therefore, that, in writing the book, I had it always in my fancy to surround the lonely figure of the child with grotesque and wild, but not impossible companions, and to gather about her innocent face and pure intentions, associates as strange and uncongenial as the grim objects that are about her bed when her history is first fore-shadowed.

MASTER HUMPHREY (before his devotion to the trunk and butter business) was originally supposed to be the narrator of the story. As it was constructed from the beginning, however, with a view to separate publication when completed, his demise has not involved the necessity of any alteration.

I have a mournful pride in one recollection associated with "little Nell." While she was yet upon her wanderings, not then concluded, there appeared in a literary journal, an essay of which she was the principal theme, so earnestly, so eloquently, and tenderly appreciative of her, and of all her shadowy kith and kin, that it would have been insensibility in me, if I could have read it without an unusual glow of pleasure and encouragement. Long afterwards, and when I had come to know him well, and to see him, stout of heart, going slowly down into his grave, I knew the writer of that essay to be THOMAS HOOD.

LONDON, September, 1848.

CHAPTER I

NIGHT is generally my time for walking. In the summer I often leave home early in the morning, and roam about fields and lanes all day, or even escape for days or weeks together, but saving in the country I seldom go out until after dark, though, Heaven be thanked, I love its light and feel the cheerfulness it sheds upon the earth, as much as any creature living.

I have fallen insensibly into this habot, both because it favours my infirmity and because it affords me greater opportunity of speculating on the characters and occupations of those who fill the streets. The glare and hurry of broad noon are not adapted to idle pursuits like mine; a glimpse of passing faces caught by the light of a street lamp or a shop window is often better for my purpose than their full revelation in the daylight, and, if I muct add the truth, night is kinder in this respect than day, which too often destroys an air-built castle at the moment of its completion, without the smallest ceremony or remorse.

That constant pacing to and fro, that never-ending restlessness, that incessant tread of feet wearing the rough stones smooth and glossy—is it not a wonder how the dwellers in narrow ways can bear to hear it! Think of a sick man in such a place as Saint Martin's Court, listening to the footsteps, and in the midst of pain and weariness obliged, despite himself (as though it were a task he must perform) to detect the child's step from the man's, the slipshod beggar from the booted exquisite, the lounging from the busy, the dull heel of the sauntering outcast from the quick tread of an expectant pleasure-seeker—think of the hum and noise being always present to his senses, and of the stream of life that will not stop, pouring on, on, on, through all his restless dreams, as if he were condemned to lie dead but conscious, in a noisy churchyard, and had no hope of rest for centuries to come.

Then the crowds for ever passing and repassing on the bridges (on those which are free of toll at least) where many stop on fine evenings looking listlessly down upon the water with some vague idea that by-and-by it runs between green banks which grow wider and wider until at last it joins the broad vast sea—where some halt to rest from heavy loads and think as they look over the parapet pon a hot tarpaulin, in a dull slow sluggish barge, must be happiness unalloyed—and where some, and a very different class, pause with heavier loads than they, remembering to have heard or read in some old time that drowning was not a hard death, but of all means of suicide the easiest and best.

Covent Garden Market at sunrise too, in the spring or summer, when the fragrance of sweet flowers is in the air, overpowering even the unwholesome streams of last night's debauchery, and driving the dusky thrush, whose cage has hung outside a garret window all night long, half mad with joy! Poor bird! The only neighbouring thing at all akin to the other little captives, some of whom, shrinking from the hot hands of drunken purchasers, lie drooping on the path already, while others, soddened by close contact, await the time when they shall be watered and freshened up to please more sober company, and make old clerks who pass them on their road to business, wonder what has filled their breasts with visions of the country.

But my present purpose is not to expatiate upon my walks. An adventure which I am about to relate, and to which I shall recur at intervals, arose out of one of these rambles, and thus I have been led to speak of them by way of preface.

One night I had roamed into the City, and was walking slowly on in my usual way, musing upon a great many things, when I was arrested by an inquiry, the purport of which did not reach me, but which seemed to be addressed to myself, and was preferred in a soft sweet voice that struck me very pleasantly. I turned hastily round and found at my elbow a pretty little girl, who begged to be directed to a certain street at a considerable distance, and indeed in quite another quarter of the town.

"It is a very long way from here," said I, "my child."

"I know that, sir," she replied timidly. "I am afraid it is a very long way, for I came from there to-night."

"Alone?" said I, in some surprise.

"Oh yes, I don't mind that, but I am a little frightened now, for I have lost my road."

"And what made you ask it of me? Suppose I should tell you wrong."

"I am sure you will not do that," said the little creature, "you are such a very old gentleman, and walk so slow yourself."

I cannot describe how much I was impressed by this appeal and the energy with which it was made, which brought a tear into the child's clear eye, and made her slight figure tremble as she looked up into my face.

"Come," said I, "I'll take you there."

She put her hand in mine as confidingly as if she had known me from her cradle, and we trudged away together: the little creature accomodating her pace to mine, and rather seeming to lead and take care of me than I to be protecting her. I observed that every now and then she stole a curious look at my face as if to make quite sure that I was not deceiving her, and that these glances (very sharp and keen they were too) seemed to increase her confidence at every repetition.

For my part, my curiosity and interest were at least equal to the child's, for child she certainly was, although I thought it probable from what I could make out, that her very small and delicate frame imparted a peculiar youthfulness to her appearance. Though more scantily attired than she might have been she was dressed with perfect neatness, and betrayed no marks of poverty or neglect.

"Who has sent you so far by yourself?" said I.

"Somebody who is very kind to me, sir."

"And what have you been doing?"

"That, I must not tell," said the child firmly.

There was something in the manner of this reply which caused me to look at the little creature with an involuntary expression of surprise; for I wondered what kind of errand it might be that occasioned her to be prepared for questioning. Her quick eye seemed to read my thoughts, for as it met mine she added that there was no harm in what she had been doing, but it was a great secret—a secret which she did not even known herself.

This was said with no appearance of cunning or deceit, but with an unsuspicious frankness that bore the impress of truth. She walked on as before, growing more familiar with me as we proceeded and talking cheerfully by the way, but she said no more about her home, beyond remarking that we were going quite a new road and asking if it were a short one. While we were thus engaged, I revolved in my mind a hundred different explanations of the riddle and rejected them every one. I really felt ashamed to take advantage of the ingenuousness or grateful feeling of the child for the purpose of gratifying my curiosity. I love these little people; and it is not a slight thing when they, who are so fresh from God, love us. As I had felt pleased at first by her confidence I determined to deserve it, and to so credit to the nature which had prompted her to repose it in me.

There was no reason, however, why shoul refrain from seeing the person who had inconsiderately sent her to so great a distance by night and alone, and as it was not improbable that if she found herself near home she might take farewell of me and deprive me of the opportunity, I avoided the most frequented ways and took the most intricate, and thus it was not until we arrived in the street itself that she knew where we were. Clapping her hands with pleasure and running on before me for a short distance, my little acquaintance stopped at a door and remaining on the step till I came up knocked at it when I joined her.

A part of this door was of glass unprotected by any shutter, which I did not observe at first, for all was very dark and silent within, and I was anxious (as indeed the child was also) for an answer to our summons. When she had knocked twice or thrice there was a noise as if some person were moving inside, and at length a faint light appeared through the glass which, as it approached very slowly, the bearer having to make his way through a great many scattered articles, enabled me to see both what kind of person it was who advanced and what kind of place it was through which he came.

It was a little old man with long grey hair whose face and figure as he held the light above his head and looked before him as he approached, I could plainly see. Though much altered by age, I fancied I could recognise in his spare and slender form something of that delicate mould which I had noticed in the child. Their bright blue eyes were certainly alike, but his face was so deeply furrowed and so very full of care, that here all resemblance ceased.

The place through which he made his way at leisure was one of those receptacles for old and curious things which seem to crouch in odd corners of this town and to hide their musty treasures from the public eye in jealousy and distrust. There were suits of mail standing like ghosts in armour here and there, fantastic carvings brought from monkish cloisters, rusty weapons of various kinds, distorted figures in china and wood and iron and ivory: tapestry and strange furniture that might have been designed in dreams. The haggard aspect of the little old man was wonderfully suited to the place; he might have groped among old churches and tombs and deserted houses and gathered all the spoils with his own hands. There was nothing in the whole collection but was in keeping with himself; nothing that looked older or more worn than he.

As he turned the key in the lock, he surveyed me with some astonishment which was not diminished when he looked from me to my companion. The door being opened, the child addressed him as grandfather, and told him the little story of our companionship.

"Why bless thee, child," said the old man patting her on the head, "how couldst thou miss thy way? What if I had lost thee, Nell!"

"I would have found my way back to *you*, grandfather," said the child boldly; "never fear."

The old man kissed her, then turning to me and begging me to walk in, I did so. The door was closed and locked. Preceding me with the light, he led me through the place I had already seen from without, into a small sitting-room behind, in which was another door opening into a kind of closet, where I saw a little bed that a fairy might have slept in, it looked so very small and was so prettily arranged. The child took a candle and tripped into his little room, leaving the old man and me together.

"You must be tired, sir," said he as he placed a chair near the fire, "how can I thank you?"

"By taking more care of your grandchild another time, my good friend," I replied.

"More care!" said the old man in a shrill voice, "more care of Nelly! Why, who ever loved a child as I love Nell?"

He said this with such evident surprise that I was perplexed what answer to make, and the more so because coupled with something feeble and wandering in his manner, there were in his face marks of deep and anxious thought which convinced me that he could not be, as I had been at first inclined to suppose, in a state of dotage or imbecility.

"I don't think you consider"— I began.

"I don't consider!" cried the old man interrupting me, "I don't consider her! Ah, how little you know of the truth! Little Nelly, little Nelly!"

It would be impossible for any man, I care not what his form of speech might be, to express more affection that the dealer in curiosities did, in these four words. I waited for him to speak again, but he rested his chin upon his hand and shaking his head twice of thrice fixed his eyes upon the fire.

While we were sitting thus in silence, the door of the closet opened, and the child returned, her light brown hair hanging loose about her neck, and her face flushed with the haste she had made to rejoin us. She busied herself immediately in preparing supper, and while she was thus engaged I remarked that the old man took an opportunity of observing me more closely than he had done yet. I was surprised to see that all this time everything was done by the child, and that there appeared to be no other persons but ourselves in the house. I took advantage of a moment when she was absent to venture a hint on this point, to which the old man replied that there were few grown persons as trustworty or as careful as she.

"It always grieves me," I observed, roused by what I took to be his selfishness, "it always grieves me to contemplate the initiation of children into the ways of life, when they are scarcely more than infants. It checks their confidence and simplicity—two of the best qualities that Heaven gives them—and demands that they share our sorrows before they are capable of entering into our enjoyments."

"It will never check hers," said the old man looking steadily at me, "the springs are too deep. Besides, the children of the poor know but few pleasures. Even the cheap delights of childhood must be bought and paid for."

"But—forgive me for saying this—you are surely not so very poor"— said I.

"She is not my child, sir," returned the old man. "Her mother was, and she was poor. I save nothing—not a penny—though I live as you see, but"—he laid his hand upon my arm and leant forward to whisper—"she shall be rich one of these days, and a fine lady. Don't you think ill of me, because I use her help. She gives it cheerfully as you see, and it would break her heart if she knew that I suffered anybody else to do for me what her little hands could undertake. I don't consider!"—he cried with sudden querulousness, "why, God knows that this one child is the thought and object of my life, and yet he never prospers me—no, never!"

At this juncture, the subject of our conversation again returned, and the old man motioning to me to approach the table, broke off, and said no more.

We had scarcely begun our repast when there was a knock at the door by which I had entered, and Nell bursting into a hearty laugh, which I was rejoiced to hear, for it was childlike and full of hilarity, said it was no doubt dear old Kit come back at last.

"Foolish Nell!" said the old man fondling with her hair. "She always laughs at poor Kit."

The child laughed again more heartily than before, and I could not help smiling from pure sympathy. The little old man took up a candle and went to open the door. When he came back, Kit was at his heels.

Kit was a shock-headed shambling awkward lad with an uncommonly wide mouth, very red cheeks, a turned-up nose, and certainly the most comical expression of face I ever saw. He stopped short at the door on seeing a stranger, twirled in his hand a perfectly round old hat without any vestige of a brim, and resting himself now on one leg and now on the other and changing them constantly, stood in the doorway, looking into the parlour with the most extraordinary leer I ever beheld. I entertained a grateful feeling towards the boy from that minute, for I felt that he was the comedy of the child's life.

"A long way, wasn't it, Kit?" said the little old man.

"Why then, it was a goodish stretch, master," returned Kit.

"Did you find the house easily?"

"Why then, not over and above easy, master," said Kit.

"Of course you have come back hungry?"

"Why then, I do consider myself rather so, master," was the answer.

The lad had a remarkable manner of standing sideways as he spoke, and thrusting his head forward over his shoulder, as if he could not get at his voice without that accompanying action. I think he would have amused one anywhere, but the child's exquisite enjoyment of his oddity, and the relief it was to find that there was something she associated with merriment in a place that appeared so unsuited to her, were quite irresistible. It was a great point too that Kit himself was flattered by the sensation he created, and after several efforts to preserve his gravity, burst into a loud roar, and so stood with his mouth wide open and his eyes nearly shut, laughing violently.

The old man had again relapsed into his former abstraction and took no notice of what passed, but I remarked that when her laugh was over, the child's bright eyes were dimmed with tears, called forth by the fulness of heart with which she welcomed her uncouth favourite after the little anxiety of the night. As for Kit himself (whose laugh had been all the time one of that sort which very little would change into a cry) he carried a large slice of bread and meat and a mug of beer into a corner, and applied himself to disposing of them with great voracity.

"Ah!" said the old man turning to me with a sigh as if I had spoken to him but that moment, "you don't know what you say when you tell me that I don't consider her."

"You must not attach too great weight to a remark founded on first appearances, my friend," said I.

"No," returned the old man thoughtfully, "no. Come hither, Nell." The little girl hastened from her seat, and put her arm about his neck. "Do I love thee, Nell?" said he. "Say—do I love thee, Nell, or no?"

The child only answered by her caresses, and laid her head upon his breast.

"Why dost thou sob," said the grandfather pressing her closer to him and glancing towards me. "Is it because thou know'st I love thee, and dost not like that I should seem to doubt it by my question? Well, well—then let us say I love thee dearly."

"Indeed, indeed you do," replied the child with great earnestness, "Kit knows you do."

Kit, who in despatching his bread and meat had been swallowing two thirds of his knife at every mouthful with the coolness of a juggler, stopped short in his operations on being thus appealed to, and bawled "Nobody isn't such a fool as to say he doosn't," after which he incapacitated himself for further conversation by taking a most prodigious sandwich at one bite.

"She is poor now"—said the old man patting the child's cheek, "but I say again that the time is coming, but it must come at last; a very long time, but it surely must come. It has come to other men who do nothing but waste and riot. When *will* it come to me!"

"I am very happy as I am, grandfather," said the child.

"Tush, tush!" returned the old man, "thou dost not know—how should'st thou!" Then he muttered again between his teeth, "The time must come, I am very sure it must. It will be all the better for coming late;" and then he sighed and fell into his former musing state, and still holding the child between his knees appeared to be insensible to everything around him. By this time it wanted but a few minutes of midnight and I rose to go, which recalled him to himself.

"One moment, sir," he said. "Now, Kit—near midnight, boy, and you still here! Get home, get home, and be true to your time in the morning, for there's work to do. Good night! There, bid him good night, Nell, and let him be gone!"

"Good night, Kit," said the child, her eyes lighting up with merriments and kindness.

"Good night, Miss Nell," returned the boy.

"And thank this gentleman," interposed the old man, "but for whose care I might have lost my little girl to-night."

"No, no, master," said Kit, "that won't do, that won't do."

"What do you mean?" cried the old man.

"I'd have found her, master," said Kit, "I'd have found her. I'd bet that I'd find her if she was above ground, I would, as quick as anybody, master. Ha ha ha!"

Once more opening his mouth and shutting his eyes, and laughing like a stentor, Kit gradually backed to the door, and roared himself out.

Free of the room, the boy was not slow in taking his departure; when he had gone, and the child was occupied in clearing the table, the old man said:

"I haven't seemed to thank you, sir, enough for what you have done to-night, but I do thank you humbly and heartily, and so does she, and her thanks are better worth than mine. I should be sorry that you went away and thought I was unmindful of your goodness, or careless of her—I am not indeed."

I was sure of that, I said, from what I had seen. "But," I added, "may I ask you a question?"

"Ay, sir," replied the old man, "what is it?"

"This delicate child," said I, "with so much beauty and intelligence—has she nobody to care for her but you? Has she no other companion or adviser?"

"No," he returned looking anxiously in my face, "no, and she wants no other."

"But are you not fearful," said I, "that you may misunderstand a charge so tender? I am sure you mean well, but are you quite certain that you know how to execute such a trust as this? I am an old man, like you, and I am actuated by an old man's concern in all that is young and promising. Do you not think that what I have seen of you and this little creature to-night must have an interest not wholly free from pain?"

"Sir," rejoined the old man after a moment's silence, "I have no right to feel hurt at what you say. It is true that in many respects I am the child, and she the grown person—that you have seen already. But walking or sleeping, by night or day, in sickness or health, she is the one object of my care, and if you knew of how much care, you would look on me with different eyes, you would indeed. Ah! it's a weary life for an old man—a weary, weary life—but there is a great end to gain and that I keep before me."

Seeing that he was in a state of excitement and impatience, I turned to put on an outer coat which I had thrown off on entering the room, purposing to say no more. I was surprised to see the shild standing patiently by with a cloak upon her arm, and in her hand a hat and stick.

"Those are not mine, my dear," said I.

"No," returned the child quietly, "they are grandfather's."

"But he is not going out to-night."

"Oh yes he is," said the child, with a smile.

"And what becomes of you, my pretty one?"

"Me! I stay here of course. I always do."

I looked in astonishment towards the old man, but he was, or feigned to be, busied in the arrangement of his dress. From him I looked back to the slight gentle figure of the child. Alone! In that gloomy place all the long, dreary night.

She evinced no consciousness of my surprise, but cheerfully helped the old man with his cloak, and when he was ready took a candle to light us out. Finding that we did not follow as she expected, she looked back with a smile and waited for us. The old man showed by his face that he plainly understood the cause of my hesitation, but he merely signed to me with an inclination of the head to pass out of the room before him, and remained silent. I had no resource but to comply.

When we reached the door, the child setting down the candle, turned to say good night and raised her face to kiss me. Then she ran to the old man, who folded her in his arms and bade God bless her.

"Sleep soundly, Nell," he said in a low voice, "and angels guard thy bed! Do not forget thy prayers, my sweet."

"No indeed," answered the child fervently, "they make me feel so happy!"

"That's well; I know they do; they should," said the old man. "Bless thee a hundred times! Early in the morning I shall be home."

"You'll not ring twice," returned the child. "The bell wakes me, even in the middle of a dream."

With this, they separated. The child opened the door (now guarded by a shutter which I had heard the boy put up before he left the house) and with another farewell whose clear and tender note I have recalled a thousand times, held it until we had passed out. The old man paused a moment while it was gently closed and fastened on the inside, and, satisfied that this was done, walked on at a slow pace. At the street-corner he stopped, and regarding me with a troubled countenance said that our ways were widely different and that he must take his leave. I would have spoken, but summoning up more alacrity than might have been expected in one of his appearance, he hurried away. I could see that twice or thrice he looked back as if to ascertain if I were still watching him, or perhaps to assure himself that I was not following at a distance. The obscurity of the night favoured his disappearance, and his figure was soon beyond my sight.

I remained standing on the spot where he had left me, unwilling to depart, and yet unknowing why I should loiter there. I looked wistfully into the street we had lately quitted, and after a time directed my steps that way. I passed and repased the house, and stopped and listened at the door; all was dark, and silent as the grave.

Yet I lingered about, and could not tear myself away, thinking of all possible harm that might happen to the child—of fires and robberies and even murder—and feeling as if some evil must ensue if I turned my back upon the place. The closing of a door or window in the street brought me before the curiosity-dealer's once more; I crossed the road and looked up at the house to assure myself that the noise had not come from there. No, it was black, cold, and lifeless as before.

There were few passengers astir; the street was sad and dismal, and pretty well my own. A few stragglers from the theatres hurried by, and now and then I turned aside to avoid some noisy drunkard as he reeled homewards, but these interruptions were not frequent and soon, promising myself that every time should be the last, and breaking faith with myself on some new plea as often as I did so.

The more I thought of what the old man had said, and of his looks and bearing, the less I could account for what I had seen and heard. I had a strong misgiving that his nightly absence was for no good purpose. I had only come to know the fact through the innocence of the child, and though the old man was by at the time, and saw my undisguised surprise, he had preserved a strange mystery upon the subject and offered no word of explanation. These reflections naturally recalled again more strongly than before his haggard face, his wandering manner, his restless anxious looks. His affection for the child might not be inconsistent with villany of the worst kind; even that very affection was in itself an extraordinary contradiction, or how could he leave her thus? Disposed as I was to think badly of him, I never doubted that his love for her was real. I could not admit the thought, remembering what had passed between us, and the tone of voice in which he had recalled her by her name.

"Stay here of course," the child had said in answer to my question, "I always do!" What could take him from home by night, and every night! I called up all the strange tales I had ever heard of dark and secret deeds committed in great towns and escaping detection for a long series of years; wild as many of these stories were, I could not find one adapted to this mystery, which only became the more impenetrable, in proportion as I sought to solve it.

Occupied with such thoughts as thee, and a crowd of others all tending to the same point, I continued to pace the street for two long hours; at length the rain began to descend heavily, and then overpowered by fatigue though no less interested than I had been at first, I engaged the nearest coach and so got home. A cheerful fire was blazing on the hearth, my lamp burnt brightly, my clock received me with its old familiar welcome; everything was quiet warm and cheering, and in happy contrast to the gloom and darkness I had quitted.

But all that night, waking or in my sleep, the same thoughts recurred and the same images retained possession of my brain. I had ever before me the old dark murky rooms—the gaunt suits of mail witht their ghostly silent air—the faces all awry, grinning from wood and stone—the dust and rust and worn that lives in wood—and alone in the midst of all this lumber and decay and ugly age, the beautiful child in her gentle slumber, smiling through her light and sunny dreams.

CHAPTER II

AFTER combating, for nearly a week, the feeling which impelled me to revisit the place I had quitted under the circumstances already detailed, I yielded to it at length; and determining that this time I would present myself by the light of day, bent my steps thither early in the afternoon.

I walked past the house, and took several turns in the street, with that kind of hesitation which is natural to a man who is conscious that the visit he is about to pay is unexpected, and may not be very acceptable. However, as the door of the shop was shut, and it did not appear likely that I should be recognised by those within, if I continued merely to pass up and down before it, I soon conquered this irresolution, and found myself in the Curiosity Dealer's warehouse.

The old man and another person were together in the back part, and there seemed to have been high words between them, for their voices which were raised to a very loud pitch suddenly stopped on my entering, and the old man advancing hastily towards me, said in a tremulous tone that he was very glad I had come.

"You interrupted us at a critical moment," he said, pointing to the man whom I had found in company with him; "this fellow will murder me one of these days. He would have done so, long ago, if he had dared."

"Bah! You would swear away my life if you could," returned the other, after bestowing a stare and a frown on me; "we all know that!"

"I almost think I could," cried the old man, turning feebly upon him. "If oaths, or prayers, or words, could rid me of you, they should. I would be quit of you, and would be relieved if you were dead."

"I know it," returned the other. "I said so, didn't I? But neither oaths, nor prayers, nor words, *will* kill me, and therefore I live, and mean to live."

"And his mother died!" cried the old man, passionately clasping his hands and looking upward; "and this is Heaven's justice!"

The other stood laughing with his foot upon a chair, and regarded him with a contemptuous sneer. He was a young man of one-and-twenty or thereabouts; well made, and certainly handsome, though the expression of his face was far from prepossessing, having in common with his manner and even his dress, a dissipated, insolent air which repelled one.

"Justice or no justice," said the young fellow, "here I am and here I shall stop till such time as I think fit to go, unless you send for assistance to put me out—which you won't do, I know. I tell you again that I want to see my sister."

"*Your* sister!" said the old man bitterly.

"Ah! You can't change the relationship," returned the other. "If you could, you'd have done it long ago. I want to see my sister, that you keep cooped up here, poisoning her mind with your sly secrets and pretending an affection for her that you may work her to death, and add a few scraped shillings every week to the money you can hardly count. I want to see her; and I will."

"Here's a moralist to talk of poisoned minds! Here's a generous spirit to scorn scraped-up shillings!" cried the old man, turning from him to me. "A profligate, sir, who has forfeited every claim not only upon those who have the misfortune to be of his blood, but upon society which knows nothing of him but his misdeeds. A liar too," he added, in a lower voice as he drew closer to me, "who knows how dear she is to me, and seeks to wound me even there, because there is a stranger by."

"Strangers are nothing to me, grandfather," said the young fellow catching at the word, "nor I to them, I hope. The best they can do, is to keep an eye to their business and leave me to mine. There's a friend of mine waiting outside, and as it seems that I may have to wait some time, I'll call him in, with your leave."

Saying this, he stepped to the door, and looking down the street beckoned several times to some unseen person, who, to judge from the air of impatience with which these signals were accompanied, required a great quantity of persuasion to induce him to advance. At length there sauntered up, on the opposite side of the way—with a bad pretence of passing by accident—a figure conspicuous for its dirty smartness, which after a great many frowns and jerks of the head, in resistance of the invitation, ultimately crossed the road and was brought into the shop.

"There. It's a Dick Swiveller," said the young fellow, pushing him in. "Sit down, Swiveller."

"But is the old min agreeable?" said Mr. Swiveller in an under tone.

"Sit down," repeated his companion.

Mr. Swiveller complied, and looking about him with a propitiatory smile, observed that last week was a fine week for the dust; he also observed that whilst standing by the post at the street-corner, he had observed a pig with a straw in his mouth issuing out of the tobacco-shop, from which appearance he augured that another fine week for the ducks was approaching, and that rain would certainly ensue. He furthermore took occasion to apologise for any negligence that might be perceptible in his dress, on the ground that last night he had had "the sun very strong in his eyes;" by which expression he was understood to convey to his hearers in the most delicate manner possible, the information that he had been extremely drunk.

"But what," said Mr. Swiveller with a sigh, "what is the odds so long as the fire of soul is kindled at the taper of conwiviality, and the wing of friendship never moults a feather! What is the odds so long as the spirit is expanded by means of rosy wine, and the present moment is the least happiest of our existence!"

"You needn't act the chairman here," said his friend, half aside.

"Fred!" cried Mr. Swiveller, tapping his nose, "a word to the wise is sufficient for them—we may be good and happy without riches, Fred. Say not another syllable. I know my cue; smart is the word. Only one little whisper, Fred—is the old min friendly?"

"Never you mind," replied his friend.

"Right again, quite right," said Mr. Swiveller, "caution is the word, and caution is the act." With that, he winked as if in preservation of some deep secret, and folding his arms and leaning back in his chair, looked up at the ceiling with profound gravity.

It was perhaps not very unreasonable to suspect from what had already passed, that Mr. Swiveller was not quite recovered from the effects of the powerful sunlight to which he had made allusion; but if no such suspicion had been awakened by his speech, his wiry hair, dull eyes, and sallow face, would still have been strong witnesses against him. His attire was not, as he had himself hinted, remarkable for the nicest arrangement, but was in a state of disorder which strongly induced the idea that he had gone to bed in it. It consisted of a brown body-coat with a great many brass buttons up the front and one behind, a bright check neckerchief, a plaid waistcoat, soiled white trousers, and a very limp hat, worn with the wrong side foremost, to hide a hole in the brim. The breast of his coat was ornamented with an outside pocket from which there peeped forth the cleanest end of a very large and very ill-favoured handkerchief; his dirty wristbands were pulled down as far as possible and ostentatiously folded back over his cuffs; he displayed no gloves, and carried a yellow cane having at the top a bone hand with the semblance of a ring on its little finger and a black ball in its grasp. With all these personal advantages (to which may be added a strong savour of tobacco-smoke and a prevailing greasiness of appearance) Mr. Swiveller leant back in his chair with his eyes fixed on the ceiling, and occasionally pitching his voice to the needful key, obliged the company with a few bars of an intensely dismal air, and then, in the middle of a note, relapsed into his former silence.

The old man sat himself down in a chair, and, with folded hands, looked sometimes at his grandson and sometimes at his strange companion, as if he were utterly powerless and had no resource but to leave them to do as they pleased. The young man reclined against a table at no great distance from his friend, in apparent indifference to everything that had passed; and I—who felt the difficulty of any interference, notwithstanding that the old man had appealed to me, both my words and looks—made the best feint I could of being occupied in examining some of the goods that were disposed for sale, and paying very little attention to the persons before me.

The silence was not of long duration, for Mr. Swiveller, after favouring us with several melodious assurances that his heart was in the Highlands, and that he wanted but his Arab steed as a preliminary to the achievement of great feats of valour and loyalty, removed his eyes from the ceiling and subsided into prose again.

"Fred," said Mr. Swiveller, stopping short as if the idea had suddenlt occurred to him, and speaking in the same audible whisper as before, "*is* the old men friendly?"

"What does it matter?" returned his friend peevishly.

"No, but *is* he?" said Dick.

"Yes, of course. What do I care whether he is or not."

Emboldened as it seemed by this reply to enter into a more general conversation, Mr. Swiveller plainly laid himself out to captivate our attention.

He began by remarking that soda-water, though a good thing in the abstract, was apt to lie cold upon the stomach unless qualified with ginger, or a small infusion of brandy, which latter article he held to be preferable in all cases, saving for the one consideration of expense. Nobody venturing to dispute these positions, he proceeded to observe that the human hair was a great retainer of tobacco-smoke, and that the young gentlemen of Westminster and Eton, after eating vast quantities of apples to conceal any scnet of cigars from their anxious friends, were usually detected in consequence of their heads possessing this remarkable property; whence he concluded that if the Royal Society would turn their attention to the circumstance, and endeavour to find in the resources of science a means of preventing such untoward revelations, they might indeed be looked upon as benefactors to mankind. These opinions being equally incontrovertible with those he had already pronounced, he went on to inform us that Jamaica rum, though unquestionably an agreeable spirit of great richness and flavour, had the drawback of remaining constantly present to the taste next day; and nobody being venturous enough to argue this point either, he increased in confidence and became yet more companionable and communicative.

"It's a devil of a thing, gentlemen," said Mr. Swiveller, "when relations fall out and disagree. If the wing of friendship should never moult a feather, the wing of relationship should never be clipped, but be always expanded and serene. Why should a grandson and grandfather peg away at each other with mutual wiolence when all might be bliss and concord? Why not join hands and forgit it?"

"Hold your tongue," said his friend.

"Sir," replied Mr. Swiveller, "don't you interrupt the chair. Gentlemen, how does the case stand, upon the present occasion? Here is a jolly old grandfather—I say it with the utmost respect—and here is a wild young grandson. The jolly old grandfather says to the wild young grandson, 'I have brought you up and educated you, Fred; I have put you in the way of getting on in life; you have bolted a little out of the course, as young fellows often do; and you shall never have another chance, nor the ghost of half a one.' The wild young grandson makes answe to this and says. 'You're as rich as rich can be; you have been at no uncommon expense on my account, you're saving up piles of money for my little sister that lives with you in a secret, stealthy, hugger-muggering kind of way and with no manner of enjoyment—why can't you stand a trifle for your grown-up relation?' The jolly old grandfather unto this, retorts, not only that he declines to fork out with that cheerful readiness which is always so agreeable and pleasant in a gentleman of his time of life, but that he will blow up, and call names, and make reflections whenever they meet. Then the plain question is, an't it a pity that this state of things should continue, and how much better would it be for the old gentleman to hand over a rasonable amount of tin, and make it all right and comfortable?"

Having delivered this oration with a great many waves and flourishes of the hand, Mr. Swiveller abruptly thrust the head of his cane into his mouth as if to prevent himself from impairing the effect of his speech by adding one other word.

"Why do you hunt and persecute me, God help me!" said the old man turning to his grandson. "Why do you bring your profligate companions here? How often am I to tell you that my life is one of care and self-denial, and that I am poor?"

"How often am I to tell you," returned the other, looking coldly at him, "that I know better?"

"You have chosen your own path," said the old man. "Follow it. Leave Nell and me to toil and work."

"Nell will be a woman soon," returned the other, "and bred in your faith, she'll forget her brother unless he shows himself sometimes."

"Take care," said the old man with sparkling eyes, "that she does not forget you whn you would have her memory keenest. Take care that the day don't come when you walk barefoot in the streets, and she rides by in a gay carriage of her own."

"You mean when she has your money?" retorted the other. "How like a poor man he talks!"

"And yet," said the old man dropping his voice and speaking like one who thinks aloud, "how poor we are, and what a life it is! The cause is a young child's, guiltless of all harm or wrong, but nothing goes well with it! Hope and patience, hope and patience!"

These words were uttered in too low a tone to reach the ears of the young men. Mr. Swiveller appeared to think that they implied some mental struggle consequent upon the powerful effect of his address, for he poked his friend with his cane, and whispered his conviction that he had administered "a clincher," and that he expected a comission on the prosfits. Discovering his mistake after a while, he appeared to grow rather sleepy and discontened, and more than once suggested the propriety of an immediate departure, when the door opened, and the child herself appeared.

CHAPTER III

THE child was closely followed by an elderly man of remarkably hard features and forbidding aspect, and so low in stature as to be quite a dwarf, though his head and face were large enough for the body of a giant. His black eyes were restless, sly, and cunning; his mouth and chin, bristly with the stubble of a coarse hard beard; and his complexion was one of that kind which never looks clean or wholesome. But what added most to the grotesque expression of his face, was a ghastly smile, which, appearing to be the mere result of habit and to have no connexion with any mirthful or com-placent feeling, constantly revealed the few discoloured fangs that were yet scattered in his mouth, and gave him the aspect of a panting dog. His dress consisted of a large high-crowned hat, a worn dark suit, a pair of capacious shoes, and a dirty white neckerchief sufficiently limp and crumpled to dis-close the greater portion of his wiry throat. Such hair as he had, was of a grizzled black, cut short and straight upon his temples, and hanging in a frowsy fringe about his ears. His hands, which were of a rough coarse grain, were very dirty; his finger-nails were crooked, long, and yellow.

There was ample time to note these particulars, for besides that they were sufficiently obvious without very close observation, some moments elapsed before any one broke silence. The child advanced timidly towards her brother and put her hand in his, the dwarf (if we may call him so) glanced keenly at all present, and the curiosity-dealer, who plainly had not expected his uncouth visitor, seemed disconcerted and embarrassed.

"Ah!" said the dwarf, who with his hand stretched out above his eyes had been surveying the young man attentively, "that should be your grand-son, neighbour!"

"Say rather that he should not be," replied the man. "But he is."

"And that?" said the dwarf, pointing to Dick Swiveller.

"Some friend of his, as welcome here as he," said the old man.

"And that?" inquired the dwarf wheeling round and pointing straight at me.

"A gentleman who was so good as to bring Nell home the other night when she lost her way, coming from your house."

The little man turned to the child as if to chide her or express his won-der, but as she was talking to the young man, held his peace, and bent his head to listen.

"Well, Nelly," said the young fellow aloud. "Do they teach you to hate me, eh?"

"No, no. For shame. Oh, no!" cried the child.

"To love me, perhaps?" pursued her brother with a sneer.

"To do neither," she returned. "They never speak to me about you. Indeed they never do."

"I dare be bound for that," he said, darting a bitter look at the grand-father. "I dare be bound for that, Nell. Oh! I believe you there!"

"But I love you dearly, Fred," said the child.

"No doubt!"

"I do indeed, and always will," the child repeated with great emotion, "but oh! if you would leave off vexing him and making him unhappy, then I could love you more."

"I see! said the young man, as he stooped carelessly over the child, and having kissed her, pushed her from him: "There—get you away now you have said your lesson. You needn't whimper. We part good friends enoug, if that's the matter."

He remained silent, following her with his eyes, until she had gained her little room and closed the door; and then turning to the dwarf, said abruptly,

"Harkee, Mr.—"

"Meaning me?" returned the dwarf. "Quilp is my name. You might re-member. It's not a long one—Daniel Quilp."

"Harkee, Mr. Quilp, then," pursued the other. "You have some influ-ence with my grandfather there."

"Some," said Mr. Quilp, then," pursued the other. "You have some in-fluence with my grandfather there."

"Some," said Mr. Quilp emphatically.

"And are in a few of his mysteries and secrets."

"A few," replied Quilp, with equal dryness.

"Then let me tell him once for all, through you, that I will come into and go out of this place as often as I like, so long as he keeps Nell here; and that if he wants to be quit of me, he must first be quit of her. What have I done to be made a bugbear of, and to be shunned and dreaded as if I brought the plague? He'll tell you that I have no natural affection; and that I care no more for Nell, for her own sake, than I do for him. Let him say so. I care for the whim, then, of coming to and fro and reminding her of my existence. I *will* see her when I please. That's my point. I came here to-day to maintain it, and I'll come here again fifty times with the same object and always with the same success. I said I would stop till I had gained it. I have done so, and now my visit's ended. Come, Dick."

"Stop!" cried Mr. Swiveller, as his companion turned towards the door. "Sir!"

"Sir, I am your humble servant," said Mr. Quilp, to whom the monosyllable was addressed.

"Before I leave the gay and festive scene, and halls of dazzling light, sir," said Mr. Swiveller, "I will, with your permission, attempt a slight remark. I came here, sir, this day, under the impression that the old min was friendly."

"Proceed, sir," said Daniel Quilp; for the orator had made a sudden stop.

"Inspired by this idea and the sentiments it awakened, sir, and feeling as a mutual friend that badgering, baiting, and bullying, was not the sort of thing calculated to expand the souls and promote the social harmony of the contending parties, I took upon myself to suggest a course which is *the* course to be adopted on the present occasion. Will you allow me to whisper half a syllable, sir?"

Without waiting for the permission he sought, Mr. Swiveller stepped up to the dwarf, and leaning on his shoulder and stooping down to get at his ear, said in a voice which was perfectly audible to all present,

"The watch-word to the old men is—fork."

"Is what?" demanded Quilp.

"Is fork, sir, fork," replied Mr. Swiveller slapping his pocket. "You are awake, sir?"

The dwarf nodded. Mr. Swiveller drew back and nodded likewise, then drew a little further back and nodded again, and so on. By these means he in time reached the door, where he gave a great cough to attract the dwarf's attention and gain an opportunity of expressing in dumb show, the closest confidence and most inviolable secrecy. Having performed the serious pantomime that was necessary for the due conveyance of these ideas, he cast himself upon his friend's track, and vanished.

"Humph!" said the dwarf with a sour look and a shrug of his shoulders, "so much for dear relations. Thank God I acknowledge none! Nor need you either," he added, turning to the old man, "if you were not as weak as a reed, and nearly as senseless."

"What would you have me do?" he retorted in a kind of helpless desperation. "It is easy to talk and sneer. What would you have me do?"

"What would *I* do if I was in your case?" said the dwarf.

"Something violent, no doubt."

"You're right there," returned the little man, highly gratified by the compliment. For such he evidently considered it; and grinning like a devil as he rubbed his dirty hands together. "Ask Mrs. Quilp, pretty Mrs. Quilp, obedient, timid, loving Mrs. Quilp. But that remainds me—I have left her all alone, and she will be anxious and know not a moment's peace till I return. I know she's always in that condition when I'm away, though she doesn't dare to say so, unless I lead her on and tell her she may speak freely and won't be angry with her. Oh! well-trained Mrs. Quilp!"

The creature appeared quite horrible with his monstrous head and little body, as he rubbed his hands slowly round, and round, and round again—with something fantastic even in his manner of performing this slight action—and, dropping his shaggy brows and cocking his chin in the air, glanced upward with a stealthy look of exultation that an imp might have copied and appropriated to himself

"Here," he said, putting his hand into his breast and sidling up to the old man as he spoke; "I brought it myself for fear of accidents, as, being in gold, it was something large and heavy for Nell to carry in her bag. She need be accustomed to such loads betimes though, neighbour, for she will carry weight when you are dead."

"Heaven send she may! I hope so," said the old man with something like a groan.

"Hope so!" echoed the dwarf, approaching close to his ear;" neighbour, I would I knew in what good investment all these supplies are sunk. But you are a deep man, and keep your secret close."

"My secret!" said the other with a haggard look. "Yes, you're right—I—I—keep it close."

He said no more, but taking the money turned away with a slow uncertain step, and pressed his hand upon his head like a weary and dejected man. The dwarf watched him sharply, while he passed into the little sitting-room and locked it in an iron safe above the chimney-piece; and after musing for a short space, prepared to take his leave, observing that unless he made good haste, Mrs. Quilp would certainly be in fits on his return.

"And so, neighbour," he added, "I'll turn my face homewards, leaving my love for Nelly and hoping she may neevr lose her way again, though her doing so *has* procured me an honour I didn't expect." With that he bowed and leered at me, and with a keen glance around which seemed to comprehend every object within his range of vision, however small or trivial, went his way.

I had several times essayed to go myself, but the old man had always opposed it and entreated me to remain. As he renemwed his entreaties on our being left alone, and adverted with many thanks to the former occasion of our being together, I willingly yielded to his persuasions, and sat down, pretending to examine some curious miniatures and a few old medals which he had placed before me. It needed no great pressing to induce me to stay, for if my curiosity had been excited on the occasion of my first visit, it certainly was not disminished now.

Nell joined us before long, and bringing some needle-work to the table, sat by the old man's side. It was pleasant to observe the fresh flowers in the room, the pet bird with a green bough shading his little cage, the breath of freshness and youth which seemed to rustle through the dull old house and hover round the child. It was curious, but not so plesant, to turn from the beauty and grace of the girl, to the stooping figure, care-worn face, and jaded aspect of the old man. As he grew weaker and more feeble, what would become of this lonely little creature; poor protector as he was, say that he died—what would her fate be, then?

The old man almost answered my thoughts, as he laid his hand on hers, and spoke aloud.

"I'll be of better cheer, Nell," he said; "there must be good fortune in store for thee—I do not ask it for myself, but thee. Such miseries must fall on thy innocent head without it, that I cannot believe but that, being tempted, it will come at last!"

She looked cheerfully into his face, but made no answer.

"When I think," said he, "of the many years—many in thy short life— that thou hast lived alone with me; of thy monotonous existence, knowing no companions of thy own age nor any childish pleasures; of the solitude in which thou hast grown to be what thou art, and in which thou hast lived apart from nearly all thy kind but one old man; I sometimes fear I have dealt hardly by thee, Nell."

"Grandfather!" cried the child in unfeigned surprise.

"Not in intention—no no," said he. "I have ever looked forward to the time that should enable thee to mix among the gayest and prettiest, and take thy station with the best. But I still look forward, Nell, I still look forward, and if I should be forced to elave thee, meanwhile, how have I fitted thee for struggles with the world? The poor bird yonder is as well qualified to en- counter it, and be turned adrift upon its mercies—Hark! I hear Kit outside. Go to him, Nell, go to him."

She rose, and hurrying away, stopped, turned back, and put her arms about the old man's neck, then left him and hurried away again—but faster this time, to hide her falling tears.

"A word in your ear, sir," said the old man in a hurried whisper. "I have been rendered uneasy by what you said the other night, and can only plead that I have done all for the best—that it is too late to retract, if I could (though I cannot)—and that I hope to triumph yet. All is for her sake. I have borne great poverty myself, and would spare her the sufferings that poverty carries with it. I would spare her the miseries that brought her mother, my own dear child, to an early grave. I would leave her—not with resources which could be easily spent or squandered away, but with what would place her beyond the reach of want for ever. You mark me, sir? She shall have no pittance, but a fortune—Hush! I can say no more than that, now or at any other time, and she is here again!"

The eagerness with which all this was poured into my ear, the trem- bling of the hand with which he clasped my arm, the strained and starting eyes he fixed upon me, the wild vehemence and agitation of his manner, filled me with amazement. All that I had heard and seen, and a great part of what he had said himself, led me to suppose that he was a wealthy man. I could form no comprehension of his character, unless he were one of those miserable wretches who, having made gain the sole end and object of their lives and having succeeded in amassing great riches, are constantly tortured by the dread of poverty, and beset by fears of loss and ruin. Many things he had said which I had been at a loss to understand, were quite reconcileable with the idea thus presented to me, and at length I concluded that beyond all doubt he was one of this unhappy race.

The opinion was not the result of hasty consideration, for which indeed there was no opportunity at that time, as the child came back directly, and soon occupied herself in preparations for giving Kit a writing lesson, of which it seemed he had a couple every week, and one regularly on that evening, to the great mirth and enjoyment both of himself and his instructress. To relate how it was a long time before his modesty could be so far prevailed upon as to admit of his sitting down in the parlour, in the presence of an unknown gentleman—how, when he did sit down, he tucked up his sleeves and squared his elbows and put his face close to the copy-book and squinted horribly at the lines—how, from the very first moment of having the pen in his hand, he began to wallow in blots, and to daub himself with ink up to the very roots of his hair—how, if he did by accident form a letter properly, he immediately smeared it out again with his arm in his preparations to make another—how, at every fresh mistake, there was a fresh burst of merriment from the child and a louder and not less hearty laugh from poor Kit himself—and how there was all the way through, notwithstanding, a gentle wish on her part to teach, and an anxious desire on his to learn—to relate all these particulars would no doubt occupy more space and time that they deserve. It will be sufficient to say that the lesson was given—that evening passed and night came on—that the old man again grew restless and impatient—that he quitted the house secretly at the same hour as before—and that the child was once more left alone within its gloomy walls.

And now, that I have carried this history so far in my own character and introduced these personages to the reader, I shall for the convenience of the narrative detach myself from its further course, and leave those who have prominent and necessary parts in it to speak and act for themselves.

CHAPTER IV

MR. and Mrs. Quilp resided on Tower Hill; and in her bower on Tower Hill Mrs. Quilp was left to pine the absence of her lord, when he quitted her on the business which he has been already seen to transact.

Mrs. Quilp could scarcely be said to be of any particular trade or calling, though his pursuits were diversified and his occupations numerous. He collected the rents of whole colonies of filthy streets and alleys by the waterside. Advanced money to the seamen and petty officers of merchant vessels, had a share in the ventures of divers mates of East Indiamen, smoked his smuggled cigars under the very nose of the Custom House, and made appointments on 'Change with men in glazed hats and round jackets pretty well every day. On the Surrey side of the river was a small rat-infested dreary yard called "Quilp's Wharf," in which were a little wooden counting-house burrowing all awry in the dust as if it had fallen from the clouds and ploughed into the ground; a few fragments of rusty anchors; several large irong rings; some piles of rotten wood; and two or three heaps of old sheet copper, crumpled, cracked, and battered. On Quilp's Wharf, Daniel Quilp was a ship-breaker, yet to judge from these appearances he must either have been a ship-breaker on a very small scale, or have broken his ships up very small indeed. Neither did the place present any extraordinary aspect of life or activity, as its only human occupant was an amphibious boy in a canvas suit, whose sole change of occupation was from sitting on the head of a pile and throwing stones into the mud when the tide was out, to standing with his hands in his pockets gazing listlessly on the motion and on the bustle of the river at high-water.

The dwarf's lodging on Tower Hill comprised, besides the needful accommodation for himself and Mrs. Quilp, a small sleeping-closet for that lady's mother, who resided with the couple and waged perpetual was with Daniel; of whom, notwithstanding, she stood in no slight dread. Indeed, the ugly creature contrived by some means or other—whether by his ugliness or his ferocity or his natural cunning is no great matter—to impress with a wholesome fear of his anger, most of those with whom he was brought into daily contact and communication. Over nobody had he such complete ascendancy as Mrs. Quilp herself—a pretty little, mild-spoken, blue-eyed woman, who having allied herself in wedlock to the dwarf in one of those strange infatuations of which examples are by no means scarce, performed a sound practical penance for her folly, every day of her life.

It has been said that Mrs. Quilp was pining in her bower. In her bower she was, but not alone, for besides the old lady her mother of whom mention has recently been made, there were present some half-dozen ladies of the neighbourhood who had happened by a strange accident (and also by a little understanding among themselves) to drop in one after another, just about tea-time. This being a season favourable to conversation, and the room being a cool, shady, lazy kind of place, with some plants at the open window shutting out the dust, and interposing pleasantly enough between the tea table within and the old Tower without, it is no wonder that the ladies felt an inclination to talk and linger, especially when there are taken into account the additional inducements of fresh butter, new bread, shrimps, and water-cresses.

Now, the ladies being together under these circumstances, it was extremely natural that the discourse should turn upon the propensity of mankind to tyrannise over the weaker sex, and the duty that devolved upon the weaker sex to resist that tyranny and assert their rights and dignity. It was natural for four seasons: firstly, because Mrs. Quilp being a young woman and notoriously under the dominion of her husband ought to be excited to rebel; secondly, because Mrs. Quilp's parent was known to be laudably shrewish in her disposition and inclined to resist male authority; thirdly, because each visitor wished to show for herself how superior she was in this respect to the generality of her sex; and fourthly, because the company being accustomed to scandalise each other in pairs, were deprived of their usual subject of conversation now that they were all assembled in close friendship, and had consequently no better employment than to attack the common enemy.

Moved by these considerations, a stout lady opened the proceedings by inquiring, with an air of great concern and sympathy, how Mr. Quilp was; whereunto Mr. Quilp's wife's mother replied sharply, "Oh! he was well enough—nothing much was ever the matter with him—and ill weeds were sure to thrive." All the ladies then sighed in concert, shook their heads gravely, and looked at Mrs. Quilp as at a martyr.

"Ah!" said the spokeswoman, "I wish you'd give her a little of your advice, Mrs. Jiniwin"—Mrs. Quilp had been a Miss Jiniwin it should be observed—"nobody knows better than you, ma'am, what us women owe to ourselves."

"Owe indeed, ma'am!" replied Mrs. Jiniwin. "When my poor husband, her dear father, was alive, if he had ever ventur'd a cross word to *me*, I'd have—"the good old lady did not finish the sentence, but she twisted off the head of a shrimp with a vindictiveness which seemed to imply that the action was in some degree a substitute for words. In this light it was clearly understood by the other party, who immediately replied with a great approbation, "You quite enter into my feelings, ma'am, and it's jist what I'd do myself."

"But you have no call to do it," said Mrs. Jiniwin. "Luckily for you, you have no more occasion to do it than I had."

"No woman need have, if she was true to herself," rejoined the stout lady.

"Do you hear that, Betsy?" said Mrs. Jiniwin, in a warning voice. "How often have I said the very same words to you, and almost gone down on my knees when I spoke 'em!"

Poor Mrs. Quilp, who had looked in a state of helplessness from one face of condolence to another, coloured, smiled, and shook her head doubtfully. This was the signal for a general clamour, which beginning in a low murmur gradually swelled into a great noise in which everybody spoke at once, and all said that she being a young woman had no right to set up her opinions against the experiences of those who knew so much better; that it was very wrong of her not to take the advice of people who had nothing at heart but her good; that it was next door to being downright ungrateful to conduct herself in that manner; that if she had no respect for herself she ought to have some for other women, all of whom she compromised by her meekness; and that if she had no respect for other women would have no respect for her; and she would be very sorry for that, they could tell her. Having dealt out these admonitions, the ladies fell to a more powerful assault than they had yet made upon the mixed tea, new bread, fresh butter, shrimps, and water-cresses, and said that their vexation was so great to see her going on like that, that they could hardly bring themselves to eat a single morsel.

"It's all very fine to talk," said Mrs. Quilp with much simplicity, "but I know that if I was to die to-morrow, Quilp could marry anybody he pleased—now that he could, I know!"

There was quite a scream of indignation at this idea. Marry whom he pleased! They would like to see him dare to think of marrying any of them; they would like to see the faintest approach to such a thing. One lady (a widow) was quite certain she should stab him if he hinted at it.

"Very well," said Mrs. Quilp, nodding her head, "as I said just now, it's very easy to talk, but I say again that I know—that I'm sure—Quilp has such a way with him when he likes, that the best-looking woman here couldn't refuse him if I was dead, and she was free, and he chose to make love to her. Come!"

Everybody bridled up at this remark, as much as to say "I know you mean me. Let him try—that's all." And yet for some hidden reason they were all angry with the widow, and each lady whispered in her neighbour's ear that it was very plain the said widow thought herself the person referred to, and what a puss she was!

"Mother knows," said Mrs. Quilp, "that what I say is quite correct, for she often said so before we were married. Didn't you say so, mother?"

This inquiry involved the respected lady in rather a delicate position, for she certainly had been an active party in making her daughter Mrs. Quilp, and, besides, it was not supporting the family credit to encourage the idea that she had married a man whom nobody else would have. On the other hand, to exaggerate the captivating qualities of her son-in-law would be to weaken the cause of revolt, in which all her energies were deeply engaged. Beset by these opposing considerations, Mrs. Jiniwin admitted the powers of insinuation, but denied the right to govern, and with a timely compliment to the stout lady brought back the discussion to the point from which it had strayed.

"Oh! It's a sensible and proper thing indeed, what Mrs. George has said!" exclaimed the old lady. "If women are only true to themselves!—But Betsy isn't, and more's the shame and pity."

"Before I'd let a man order me about as Quilp orders her," said Mrs. George; "before I'd consent to stand in awe of a man as she does of him, I'd—I'd kill myself, and write a letter first to say he did it!"

This remark being loudly commended and approved of, another lady (from the Minories) put in her word:

"Mr. Quilp may be a very nice man," said this lady, "and I suppose there's no doubt he is, because Mrs. Quilp says he is, and Mrs. Jiniwin says he is, and they ought to know, or nobody does. But still he is not quite a—what one calls a handsome man, nor quite a young man neither, which might be a little excuse for him if anything could be; whereas his wife is young, and is good-looking, and is a woman—which is the great thing after all."

This last clause being delivered with extraordinary pathos, elicited a corresponding murmur from the hearers, stimulated by which the lady went on to remark that if such a husband was cross and unreasonable with such a wife, then—

"If he is!" interposed the mother, putting down her tea-cup and brushing the crumbs out of her lap, preparatory to making a solemn declaration. "If he is! He is the greatest tyrant that ever lived, she daren't call her soul her own, he makes her tremble with a word and even with a look, he frightens her to death, and she hasn't the spirit to give him a word back, no, not a single word."

Notwithstanding that the fact had been notorious beforehand to all the tea-drinkers, and had been discussed and expatiated on at every tea-drinking in the neighbourhood for the last twelve months, this official communication was no sooner made than they all began to talk at once and to vie with each other in vehemence and volubility. Mrs. George remarked that people would talk, that people had often said this to her before, that Mrs. Simmons then and there present had told her so twenty times, that she had always said, "No, Henrietta Simmons, unless I see it with my own eyes and hear it with my own ears, I never will believe it." Mrs. Simmons corroborated this testimony and added strong evidence of her own. The lady from the Minories recounted a succesful course of treatment under which she had placed her own husband, who, from manifesting one month after marriage unequivocal symptoms of the tiger, had by this means become subdued into a perfect lamb. Another lady recounted her own personal struggle and final triumph, in the course of whereof she had found it necessary to call in her mother and two aunts, and to weep incessantly night and day for six weeks. A third, who in the general confusion could secure no other listener, fastened herself upon a young woman still unmarried who happened to be amongst them, and conjured her as she valued her own peace of mind and happiness to profit by this solemn occasion, to take example from the weakness of Mrs. Quilp, and from that time forth to direct her whole thoughts to taming and subduing the rebellious spirit of man. The noise was at its height, and half the company had elevated their voices into a perfect shriek in order to drown the voices of the other half, when Mrs. Jiniwin was seen to change colour and shake her forefinger stealthily, as if exhorting them to silence. Then, and not until then, Daniel Quilp himself, the cause and occasion of all this clamour, was observed to be in the room, looking on and listening with profound attention.

"Go on, ladies, go on," said Daniel. "Mrs. Quilp, pray ask the ladies to stop to supper, and have a couple of lobsters and something light and palatable."

"I—I—didn't ask them to tea, Quilp," stammered his wife. "It's quite an accident."

"So much the better, Mrs. Quilp; these accidental parties are always the pleasantest," said the dwarf, rubbing his hands so hard that he seemed to be engaged in manufacturing, of the dirt with which they were encrusted, little charges for popguns. "What! Not going, ladies, you are not going, surely!"

His fair enemies tossed their heads slightly as they sought their respective bonnets and shawls, but left all verbal contention to Mrs. Jiniwin, who finding herself in the position of champion, made a faint struggle to sustain the character.

"And why *not* stop to supper, Quilp," said the old lady, "if my daughter had a mind?"

"To be sure," rejoined Daniel. "Why not?"

"There's nothing dishonest or wrong in a supper, I hope?" said Mrs. Jiniwin.

"Surely not," returned the dwarf. "Why should there be? Nor anything unwholesome either, unless there's lobster-salad or prawns, which I'm told are not good for digestion."

"And you wouldn't like *your* wife to be attacked with that, or anything else that would make her uneasy, would you?" said Mrs. Jiniwin.

"Not for a score of worlds," replied the dwarf with a grin. "Not even to have a score of mothers-in-law at the same time—and what a blessing that would be!"

"My daughter's your wife, Mrs. Quilp, certainly," said the old lady with a giggle, meant for satirical and to imply that he needed to be reminded of the fact; "your wedded wife."

"So he is, certainly. So he is," observed the dwarf.

"And she has a right to do as she likes, I hope, Quilp," said the old lady trembling, partly with anger and partly with a secret fear of her impish son-in-law.

"Hope she has!" he replied. "Oh! Don't you know she has? Don't you know she has, Mrs. Jiniwin?"

"I know she ought to have, Quilp, and would have, if she was of my way of thinking."

"Why an't you of your mother's way of thinking, my dear? She's the ornament of her sex—your father said so every day of his life. I am sure he did."

"Her father was a blessed creetur, Quilp, and worth twenty thousand of some people," said Mrs. Jiniwin; "twenty hundred million thousand."

"I should like to have known him," remarked the dwarf. "I dare say he was a blessed creature then; but I'm sure he is now. It was a happy release. I believe he had suffered a long time?"

The old lady gave a gasp, but nothing came of it; Quilp resumed, with the same malice in his eye and the same sarcastic politeness on his tongue.

"You look ill, Mrs. Jiniwin; I know you have been exciting yourself too much—talking perhaps, for it is your weakness. Go to bed. Do go to bed."

"I shall go when I please, Quilp, and not before."

"But please to go now. Do please to go now," said the dwarf.

The old woman looked angrily at him, but retreated as he advanced, and falling back before him, suffered him to shut the door upon her and bolt her out among the guests, who were by this time crowding down stairs. Being left alone with his wife, who sat trembling in a corner with her eyes fixed upon the ground, the little man planted himself before her, and folding his arms looked steadily at her for a long time without speaking.

"Mrs. Quilp," he said at last.

"Yes, Quilp," she replied meekly.

Instead of pursuing the theme he had in his mind, Quilp folded his arms again, and looked at her more sternly than before, while she averted her eyes and kept them on the ground.

"Mrs. Quilp."

"Yes, Quilp."

"If ever you listen to these beldames again, I'll bite you."

With this laconic threat, which he accompanied with a snarl that gave him the appearance of being particularly in earnest, Mr. Quilp bade her clear the teaboard away, and bring the rum. The spirit being set before him in a huge case-bottle, which had originally come out of some ship's locker, he ordered cold water and the box of cigars; and these supplied, he settled himself in an armchair with his large head and face squeezed up against the back, and his little legs planted on the table.

"Now, Mrs. Quilp," he said; "I feel in a smoking humour, and shall probably blaze away all night. But sit where you are, if you please, in case I want you."

His wife returned no other reply than the customary "Yes, Quilp," and the small lord of the creation took his first cigar and mixed his first glass of grog. The sun went down and the stars peeped out, the Tower turned from its own proper colours to grey and from grey to black, the room became perfectly dark and the end of the cigar a deep fiery red, but still Mr. Quilp went on smoking and drinking in the same position, and staring listlessly out of the window with the dog-like smile always on his face, save when Mrs. Quilp made some involuntary movement of restlessness or fatigue; and then it expanded into a grin of delight.

CHAPTER V

WHETHER Mr. Quilp took any sleep by snatches of a few winks at a time, or whether he sat with his eyes wide open all night long, certain it is that he kept his cigar alight, and kindled every fresh one from the ashes of that which was nearly consumed, without requiring the assistance of a candle. Nor did the striking of the clocks, hour after hour, appear to inspire him with any sense of drowsiness or any natural desire to go to rest, but rather to increase his wakefulness, which he showed, at every such indication of the progress of the night, by a suppressed cackling in his throat, and a motion of his shoulders, like one who laughs heartily but at the same time slyly and by stealth.

At length the day broke, and poor Mrs. Quilp, shivering with the cold of early morning and harassed by fatigue and want of sleep, was discovered sitting patiently on her chair, raising her eyes at intervals in mute appeal to the compassion and clemency of her lord, and gently reminding him by an occasional cough that she was still unpardoned and that her penance had been of long duration. But her dwarfish spouse still smoked his cigar and drank his rum without heeding her; and it was not until the sun had some time risen, and the activity and noise of city day were rife in the street, that he deigned to recognise her presence by any word or sign. He might not have done so even then, but for certain impatient tappings at the door which seemed to denote that some pretty hard knuckles were actively engaged upon the other side.

"Why dear me!" he said looking round with a malicious grin, "it's day! Open the door, sweet Mrs. Quilp!"

His obedient wife withdrew the bolt, and her lady mother entered.

Now, Mrs. Jiniwin bounced into the room with great impetuosity; for, supposing her son-in-law to be still a-bed, she had come to relieve her feelings by pronouncing a strong opinion upon his general conduct and character. Seeing that he was up and dressed, and that the room appeared to have been occupied ever since she quitted it on the previous evening, she stopped short, in some embarrassment.

Nothing escaped the hawk's eye of the ugly little man, who, perfectly understanding what passed in the old lady's mind, turned uglier still in the fulness of his satisfaction, and bade her good morning, with a leer of triumph.

"Why, Betsy," said the old woman, "you haven't been a—you don't mean to say you've been a—"

"Sitting up all night?" said Quilp, supplying the conclusion of the sentence. "Yes she has!"

"All night!" cried Mrs. Jiniwin.

"Ay, all night. Is the dear old lady deaf?" said Quilp, with a smile of which a frown was part. "Who says man and wife are bad company? Ha ha! The time has flown."

"You're a brute!" exclaimed Mrs. Jiniwin.

"Come come," said Quilp, wilfully misunderstanding her, of course, "you mustn't call her names. She's married now, you know. And though she *did* beguile the time and keep me from my bed, you must not be so tenderly careful of me as to be out of humour with her. Bless you for a dear old lady. Here's your health!"

"I am *much* obligued to you," returned the old woman, testifying by a certain restlessness in her hands a vehement desire to shake her matronly fist at her son-in-law. "Oh! I'm very much obliged to you!"

"Grateful soul!" cried the dwarf. "Mrs. Quilp."

"Yes, Quilp," said the timid sufferer.

"Help your mother to get breakfast, Mrs. Quilp. I am going to the wharf this morning—the earlier, the better, so be quick."

Mrs. Jiniwin made a faint demonstration of rebellion by sitting down in a chair near the door and folding her arms as if in a resolute determination to do nothing. But a few whispered words from her daughter, and a kind inquiry from her son-in-law whether she felt faint, with a hint that there was abundance of cold water in the next apartment, routed these symptoms effectually, and she applied herself to the prescribed preparations with sullen diligence.

While they were in progress, Mr. Quilp withdrew to the adjoining room, and, turning back his coat-collar, proceeded to smear his countenance with a damp towel of very unwholesome appearance, which made his complexion rather more cloudy than it was before. But, while he was thus engaged, his caution and inquisitiveness did not forsake him, for with a face as sharp and cunning as ever, he often stopped, even in this short process, and stood listening for any conversation in the next room, of which he might be the theme.

"Ah!" he said after a short effort of attention, "it was not the towel over my ears, I thought it wasn't. I'm a little hunchy villain and a monster, am I, Mrs. Jiniwin? Oh!"

The pleasure of this discovery called up the old doglike smile in full force. When he had quite done with it, he shook himself in a very doglike manner, and rejoined the ladies.

Mr. Quilp now walked up to the front of a looking-glass, and was standing there putting on his neckerchief, when Mrs. Jiniwin, happening to be behind him, could not resist the inclination she felt to shake her fist at her tyrant son-in-law. It was the gesture of an instant, but as she did so and accompanied the action with a menacing look, she met his eye in the glass, catching her in the very act. The same glance at the mirror conveyed to her the reflection of a horribly grotesque and distorted face with the tongue lolling out; and the next instant the dwarf, turning about with a perfectly bland and placid look, inquired in a tone of great affection,

"How are you now, my ear old darling?"

Slight and ridiculous as the incident was, it made him appear such a little fiend, and withal such a keen and knowing one, that the old woman felt too much afraid of him to utter a single word, and suffered herself to be led with extraordinary politeness to the breakfast-table. Here he by no means diminished the impression he had just produced, for he ate hard eggs, shell and all, devoured gigantic prawns with the heads and tails on, chewed tobacco and water-cresses at the same time and with extraordinary greediness, drank boiling tea without winking, bit his fork and spoon till they bent again, and in short performed so many horrifying and uncommon acts that the women were nearly frightened out of their wits, and began to doubt if he were really a human creature. At last, having gone through these proceedings and many others which were equally a part of his system, Mr. Quilp left them, reduced to a very obedient and humbled state, and betook himself to the river-side, where he took boat for the wharf on which he had bestowed his name.

It was flood tide when Daniel Quilp sat himself down in the wherry to cross to the opposite shore. A fleet of barges were coming lazily on, some sideways, some head first, some stern first; all in a wrong-headed, dogged, obstinate way, bumping up against the larger craft, running under the bows of steamboats, getting into every kind of nook and corner where they had no business, and being crunched on all sides like so many walnut-shells; while each with its pair of long sweeps struggling and splashing in the water looked like some lumbering fish in pain. In some of the vessels at anchor all hands were busily engaged in coiling ropes, spreading out sails to dry, taking in or discharging their cargoes; in others no life was visible but two or three tarry boys, and perhaps a barking dog running to and fro upon the deck or scrambling up to look over the side and bark the louder for the view. Coming slowly on through the forests of masts was a great steam ship, beating the water in short impatient strokes with her heavy paddles as though she wanted room to breathe, and advancing in her huge bulk like a sea monster among the minnows of the Thames. On either hand were long black tiers of colliers; between them vessels slowly working out of harbour with sails glistening in the sun, and creaking noise on board, re-echoed from a hundred quarters. The water and all upon it was in active motion, dancing and buoyant and bubbling up; while the old grey Tower and piles of building on the shore, with many a church-spire shooting up between, looked coldly on, and seemed to disdain their chafing, restless neighbour.

Daniel Quilp, who was not much affected by a bright morning save in so far as it spared him the trouble of carrying an umbrella, caused himself to be put ashore hard by the wharf, and proceeded thither through a narrow lane which, partaking of the amphibious character of its frequenters, had as much water as mud in its composition, and a very liberal supply of both. Arrived at his destination, the first object that presented itself to his view was a pair of very imperfectly shod feet elevated in the air with the soles upwards, which remarkable appearance was referable to the boy, who being of an eccentric spirit and having a natural taste for tumbling, was now standing on his head and contemplating the aspect of the river under these uncommon circumstances. He was speedily brought on his heels by the sound of his master's voice, and as soon as his head was in its right position, Mr. Quilp, to speak expressively in the absence of a better verb, "punched it" for him.

"Come, you let me alone," said the boy, parrying Quilp's hand with both his elbows alternately. "You'll get something you won't like if you don't, and so I tell you."

"You dog," snarled Quilp, "I'll beat you with an iron rod, I'll scratch you with a rusty nail, I'll pinch your eyes, if you talk to me—I will."

With these threats he clenched his hand again, and dexterously diving in between the elbows and catching the boy's head as it dodged from side to side, gave it three or four good hard knocks. Having now carried his point and insisted on it, he left off.

"You won't do it again," said the boy, nodding his head and drawing back, with the elbows ready in case of the worst; "now—"

"Stand still, you dog," said Quilp. "I won't do it again, because I've done it as often as I want. Here. Take the key."

"Why don't you hit one of your size?" said the boy approaching very slowly.

"Where is there one of my size, you dog?" returned Quilp. "Take the key, or I'll brain you with it"—indeed he gave him a smart tap with the handle as he spoke. "Now, open the counting-house."

The boy sulkily complied, muttering at first, but desisting when he looked round and saw that Quilp was following him with a steady look. And here it may be remarked, that between this boy and the dwarf there existed a strange kind of mutual linking. How born or bread, or how nourished upon blows and threats on one side, and retorts and defiances on the other, is not to the purpose. Quilp would certainly suffer nobody to contradict him but the boy, and the boy would assuredly not have submitted to be so knocked about by anybody but Quilp, when he had the power to run away at any time he chose.

"Now," said Quilp, passing into the wooden counting-house, "you mind the wharf. Stand upon your head again, and I'll cut one of your feet off."

The boy made no answer, but directly Quilp shut himself in, stood on his head before the door, then walked on his hands to the back and stood in his head there, and then to the opposite side and repeated the performance. There were indeed four sides to the counting-house, but he avoided that one where the window was, deeming it probable that Quilp would be looking out of it. This was prudent, for in point of fact the dwarf, knowing his disposition, was lying in wait at a little distance from the sash armed with a large piece of wood, which, being rough and jagged and studded in many parts with broken nails, might possibly have hurt him.

It was a dirty little box, this counting-house, with nothing in it but an old ricketty desk and two stools, a hat-peg, an ancient almanack, an inkstand with no ink and the stump of one pen, and an eight-day clock which hadn't gone for eighteen years at least, and of which the minute-hand had been twisted off for a tooth-pick. Daniel Quilp pulled his hat over his brows, climbed on to the desk (which had a flat top), and stretching his short length upon it went to sleep with the ease of an old practitioner; intending, no doubt, to compensate himself for the deprivation of last night's rest, by a long and sound nap.

Sound it might have been, but long it was not, for he had not been asleep a quarter of an hour when the boy opened the door and thrust in his head, which was like a bundle of badly-picked oakum. Quilp was a light sleeper and started up directly.

"Here's somebody for you," said the boy.

"Who?"

"I don't know."

"Ask!" said Quilp, seizing the trifle of wood before mentioned and throwing it at him with such dexterity that it was well the boy disappeared before it reached the spot on which he had stood. "Ask, you dog."

Not caring to venture within range of such missiles again, the boy discreetly sent in his stead the first cause of the interruption, who now presented herself at the door.

"What, Nelly!" cried Quilp.

"Yes,"—said the child, hesitating whether to enter or retreat, for the dwarf just roused, with his dishevelled hair hanging all about him and a yellow handkerchief over his head, was something fearful to behold; "it's only me, sir."

"Come in," said Quilp, without getting off the desk. "Come in. Stay. Just look out into the yard, and see whether there's a boy standing on his head."

"No, sir," replied Nell. "He's on his feet."

"You're sure he is?" said Quilp. "Well. Now, come in and shut the door. What's your message, Nelly?"

The child handed him a letter; Mr. Quilp, without changing his position further than to turn over a little more on his side and rest his chin on his hand, proceeded to make himself acquainted with its contents.

CHAPTER VI

LITTLE Nell stood timidly by, with her eyes raised to the countenance of Mr. Quilp as he read the letter, plainly showing by her looks that while she entertained some fear and distrust of the little man, she was much inclined to laugh at his uncouth appearance and grotesque attitude. And yet there was visible on the part of the child a painful anxiety for his reply, and a consciousness of his power to render it disagreeable or distressing, which was strongly at variance with this impulse and restrained it more effectually than she could possibly have done by any efforts of her own.

That Mr. Quilp was himself perplexed, and that in no small degree, by the contents of the letter, was sufficiently obvious. Before he had got through the first two or three lines he began to open his eyes very wide and to frown most horribly, the next two or three caused him to scratch his head in an uncommonly vicious manner, and when he came to the conclusion he gave a long dismal whistle indicative of surprise and dismay. After folding and laying it down beside him, he bit the nails of all his ten fingers with extreme voracity; and taking it up sharply, read it again. The second perusal was to all appearance as unsatisfactory as the first, and plunged him into a profound reverie from which he awakened to another assault upon his nails and a long stare at the child, who with her eyes turned towards the ground awaited his further pleasure.

"Halloa here!" he said at length, in a voice, and with a suddenness, which made the child start as though a gun had been fired off at her ear. "Nelly?"

"No, sir!"

"Are you sure, quite sure, quite certain, upon your soul?"

"Quite sure, sir."

"Do you wish you may die if you do know, hey?" said the dwarf.

"Indeed I don't know," returned the child.

"Well!" muttered Quilp as he marked her earnest look. "I believe you.

Humph! Gone already? Gone in four-and-twenty hours! What the devil has he done with it, that's the mystery!"

This reflection set him scratching his head and biting his nails once more. While he was thus employed his features gradually relaxed into what was with him a cheerful smile, but which in any other man would have been a ghastly grin of pain, and when the child looked up again she found that he was regarding her with extraordinary favour and complacency.

"You look very pretty to-day, Nelly, charmingly pretty. Are you tired, Nelly?"

"No, sir. I'm in a hurry to get back, for he will be anxious while I am away."

"There's no hurry, little Nell, no hurry at all," said Quilp. "How should you like to be my number two, Nelly?"

"To be what, sir?"

"My number two, Nelly, my second, my Mrs. Quilp," said the dwarf.

The child looked frightened, but seemed not to understand him, which Mr. Quilp observing, hastened to explain his meaning more distinctly.

"To be Mrs. Quilp the second, when Mrs. Quilp the first is dead, sweet Nell," said Quilp, wrinkling up his eyes and luring her towards him with his bent forefinger, "to be my wife, my little cherry-cheeked, red-lipped wife Say that Mrs. Quilp lives five years, or only four, you'll be just the proper age for me. Ha ha! Be a good girl, Nelly, a very good girl, and see if one of these days you don't come to be Mrs. Quilp of Tower Hill."

So far from being sustained and stimulated by this delightful prospect, the child shrank from him in great agitation, and trembled violently. Mr. Quilp, either because frightening anybody afforded him a constitutional delight, or because it was pleasant to contemplate the death of Mrs. Quilp number one, and the elevation of Mrs. Quilp number two to her post and title, or because he was determined for purposes of his own to be agreeable and good-humoured at that particular time, only laughed and feigned to take no heed of her alarm.

"You shall come with me to Tower Hill, and see Mrs. Quilp that is, directly," said the dwarf. "She's very fond of you, Nell, though not so fond as I am. You shall come home with me."

"I must go back indeed," said the child. "He told me to return directly I had the answer."

"But you haven't it, Nelly," retorted the dwarf, "and won't have it, and can't have it, until I have been home, so you see that to do your errand you must go with me. Reach me yonder hat, my dear, and we'll go directly." With that, Mr. Quilp suffered himself to roll gradually off the desk until his short legs touched the ground, when he got upon them and led the way from the counting-house to the wharf outside, when the first objects that presented themselves were the boy who had stood on his head and another young gentleman of about his own stature, rolling in the mud together, locked in a tight embrace, and cuffing each other with mutual heartiness.

"It's Kit!" cried Nelly, clasping her hands, "poor Kit who came with me! oh pray stop them, Mr. Quilp!"

"I'll stop 'em," cried Quilp, diving into the little counting-house and returning with a thick stick. "I'll stop 'em. Now, my boys, fight away. I'll fight you both. I'll take both of you, both together, both together!"

With which defiances the dwarf flourished his cudgel, and dancing round the combatants and treading upon them and skipping over them, in a kind of frenzy, laid about him, now on one and now on the other, in a most desperate manner, always aiming at their heads and dealing such blows as none but the veriest little savage would have inflicted. This being warmer work than they had calculated upon, speedily cooled the courage of the belligerents, who scrambled to their feet and called for quarter.

"I'll beat you to a pulp, you dogs," said Quilp, vainly endeavouring to get near either of them for a parting blow. "I'll bruise you till you're copper-coloured, I'll break your faces till you haven't a profile between you, I will."

"Come, you drop that stick or it'll be worse for you," said his boy, dodging round him and watching an opportunity to rush in; "you drop that stick."

"Come a little nearer, and I'll drop it on your skull, you dog," said Quilp with gleaming eyes; "a little nearer—nearer yet."

But the boy declined the invitation until his master was apparently a little off his guard, when he darted in and seizing the weapon tried to wrest it from his grasp. Quilp, who was as strong as a lion, easily kept his hold until the boy was tugging at it with his utmost power, when he suddenly let it go and sent him reeling backwards, so that he fell violently upon his head. The success of this manœuvre tickled Mr. Quilp beyond description, and he laughed and stamped upon the ground as at a most irresistible jest.

"Never mind," said the boy, nodding his head and rubbing it at the same time; "you see if ever I offer to strike anybody again because they say you're a uglier dwarf than can be seen anywheres for a penny, that's all."

"Do you mean to say, I'm not, you dog?" returned Quilp.

"No!" retorted the boy.

"Then what do you fight on my wharf for, you villain?" said Quilp.

"Because he said so," replied the boy, pointing to Kit, "not because you an't."

"Then why did he say," bawled Kit, "that Miss Nelly was ugly, and that she and my master was obliged to do whatever his master liked? Why did he say that?"

"He said what he did because he's fool, and you said what you did because you're very wise and clever—almost too clever to live, unless you're very careful of yourself, Kit," said Quilp, with great suavity in his manner, but still more of quiet malice about his eyes and mouth. "Here's sixpence for you, Kit. Always speak the truth. At all times, Kit, speak the truth. Lock the counting-house, you dog, and bring me the key."

The other boy, to whom this order was addressed, did as he was told, and was rewarded for his partianship in behalf of his master, by a dexterous rap on the nose with the key, which brought the water into his eyes. Then Mr. Quilp departed with the child and Kit in a boat, and the boy revenged himself by dancing on his head at intervals on the extreme verge of the wharf, during the whole time they crossed the river.

There was only Mrs. Quilp at home, and she, little expecting the return of her lord, was just composing herself for a refreshing slumber when the sound of his footsteps roused her. She had barely time to seem to be occupied in some needle-work, when he entered, accompanied by the child; having left Kit down stairs.

"Here's Nelly Trent, dear Mrs. Quilp," said her husband. "A glass of wine, my dear, and a biscuit, for she has had a long walk. She'll sit with you, my soul, while I write a letter."

Mrs. Quilp looked tremblingly in her spouse's face to know what this unusual courtesy might portend, and obedient to the summons she was in his gesture, followed him into the next room.

"Mind what I say to you," whispered Quilp. "See if you can get out of her anything about her grandfather, or what they do, or how they live, or what he tells her. I've my reasons for knowing, if I can. You women talk more freely to one another than you do to us, and you have a soft, mild way with you that'll win upon her. Do you hear?"

"Yes, Quilp."

"Go, then. What's the matter now?"

"Dear Quilp," faltered his wife, "I love the child—if you *could* do without making me deceive her—"

The dwarf muttering a terrible oath looked round as if for some weapon with which to inflict conding punishment upon his disobedient wife. The submissive little woman hurriedly entreated him not to be angry, and promised to do as he bade her.

"Do you hear me," whispered Quilp, nipping and pinching her arm; "worm yourself into her secrets; I know you can. I'm listening, recollect. If you're not sharp enough I'll creak the door, and woe betide you if I have to creak it much. Go!"

Mrs. Quilp departed according to order, and her amiable husband, ensconcing himself behind the partly opened door, and applying his ear close to it, began to listen with a face of great craftiness and attention.

Poor Mrs. Quilp was thinking, however, in what manner to begin or what kind of inquiries she could make; and it was not until the door, creaking in a very urgent manner, warned her to proceed without further consideration, that the sound of her voice was heard.

"How very often you have come backwards and forwards lately to Mr. Quilp, my dear."

"I have said so to grandfather, a hundred times," returned Nell innocently.

"And what has he said to that?"

"Only seighed, and dropped his head, and seemed so sad and wretched that if you could have seen him I am sure you must have cried; you could not have helped it more than I, I know. How that door creaks!"

"It often does," returned Mrs. Quilp, with an uneasy glance towards it. "But your grandfather—he used not to be so wretched?"

"Oh no!" said the child eagerly, "so different! we were once so happy and he so cheerful and contented! You cannot think what a sad change has fallen on us since."

"I am very, very sorry, to hear you speak like this, my dear!" said Mrs. Quilp. And she spoke the truth.

"Thank you," returned the child, kissing her cheek, "you are always kind to me, and it is a pleasure to talk to you. I can speak to no one else about him, but poor Kit. I am very happy still, I ought to feel happier perhaps than I do, but you cannot think how it grieves me sometimes to see him alter so."

"He'll alter again, Nelly," said Mrs. Quilp, "and be what he was before."

"Oh, if God would only let that come about!" said the child with streaming eyes; "but it is a long time now, since he first began to—I thought I saw that door moving!"

"It's the wind," said Mrs. Quilp faintly. "Began to—?"

"To be so thoughtful and dejected, and to forget our old way of spending the time in the long evenings," said the child. "I used to read to him by the fireside, and he sat listening, and when I stopped and we began to talk, he told me about my mother, and how she once looked and spoke just like me when she was a little child. Then, he used to take me on his knee, and try to make me understand that she was not lying in her grave, but had flown to a beautiful country beyond the sky, where nothing died or ever grew old—we were very happy once!"

"Nelly, Nelly!"—said the poor woman, "I can't bear to see one as young as you, so sorrowful. Pray don't cry."

"I do so very seldom," said Nell, "but I have kept this to myself a long time, and I am not quite well, I think, for the tears come into my eyes and I cannot keep them back. I don't mind telling you my grief, for I know you will not tell it to any one again."

Mrs. Quilp turned away her head and made no answer.

"Then," said the child, "we often walked in the fields and among the green trees, and when we came home at night, we liked it better for being tired, and said what a happy place it was. And if it was dark and rather dull, we used to say, what did it matter to us, for it only made us remember our last walk with greater pleasure, and look forward to our next one. But now we never have these walks, and though it is the same house it is darker and much more gloomy than it used to be, indeed!"

She paused here, but though the door creaked more than once, Mrs. Quilp said nothing.

"Mind you don't suppose," said the child earnestly, "that grandfather is less kind to me than he was. I think he loves me better every day, and is kinder and more affectionate than he was the day before. You do not know how fond he is of me!"

"I am sure he loves you dearly," said Mrs. Quilp.

"Indeed, indeed he does!" cried Nell, "as dearly as I love him. But I have not told you the greatest change of all, and this you must never breathe again to any one. He has no sleep or rest, but that which he takes by day in his easy chair; for every night and nearly all night long he is away from home."

"Nelly!"

"Hush!" said the child, laying her finger on her lip and looking round. "When he comes home in the morning, which is generally just before day, I let him in. Last night he was very late, and it was quite light. I saw that his face was deadly pale, that his eyes were bloodshot, and that his legs trembled as he walked. When I had gone to bed again, I heard him groan. I got up and ran back to him, and heard him say, before he knew that I was there, that he could not bear his life much longer, and if it was not for the child, would wish to die. What shall I do! Oh! what shall I do!"

The fountains of her heart were opened; the child, overpowered by the weight of her sorrows and anxieties, by the first confidence she had ever shown, and the sympathy with which her little tale had been received, hid her face in the arms of her helpless friend, and burst into a passion of tears.

In a few moments Mr. Quilp returned, and expressed the utmost surprise to find her in this condition, which he did very naturally and with admirable effect, for that kind of acting had been rendered familiar to him by long practice, and he was quite at home in it.

"She's tired, you see, Mrs. Quilp," said the dwarf, squinting in a hideous manner to imply that his wife was to follow his lead. "It's a long way from her home to the wharf, and then she was alarmed to see a couple of young scoundrels fighting, and was timorous on the water besides. All this together has been too much for her. Poor Nell!"

Mr. Quilp unintentionally adopted the very best means he could have devised for the recovery of his young visitor, by patting her on the head. Such an application from any other hand might not have produced a remarkable effect, but the child shrank so quickly from his touch and felt such an instinctive desire to get out of his reach, that she rose directly and declared herself ready to return.

"But you'd better wait, and dine with Mrs. Quilp and me," said the dwarf.

"I have been away too long, sir, already," returned Nell, drying her eyes.

"Well," said Mr. Quilp, "if you will go, you will, Nelly. Here's the note. It's only to say that I shall see him to-morrow or maybe next day, and that I couldn't do that little business for him this morning. Good-bye, Nelly. Here, you sir; take care of her, d'ye hear?"

Kit, who appeared at the summons, deigned to make no reply to so needless an injunction, and after staring at might not have been the cause of Nelly shedding tears, and felt more than half-disposed to revenge the fact upon him on the mere suspicion, turned about and followed his young mistress, who had by this time taken her leave of Mrs. Quilp and departed.

"You're a keen questioner, an't you, Mrs. Quilp?" said the dwarf, turning upon her as soon as they were left alone.

"What more could I do?" returned his wife timidly

"What more could you do?" sneered Quilp, "couldn't you have done something less? couldn't you have done what you had to do, without appearing in your favourite part of the crocodile, you minx?"

"I am very sorry for the child, Quilp," said his wife. "Surely I've done enough. I've led her on to tell her secret when she supposed we were alone; and you were by, God forgive me."

"You led her on! You did a great deal truly!" said Quilp. "What did I tell you about making me creak the door? It's lucky for you that from what she let fall, I've got the clue I want, for if I hadn't, I'd have visited the failure upon you, I can tell you."

Mrs. Quilp being fully persuaded of this, made no reply. Her husband added with some exultation,

"But you may thank your fortunate stars—the same stars that made you Mrs. Quilp—you may thank them that I'm upon the old gentleman's track, and have got a new light. So let me hear no more about this matter now or at any other time, and don't get anything too nice for dinner, for I shan't be home to it."

So saying, Mr. Quilp put his hat on and took himself off, and Mrs. Quilp, who was afflicted beyond measure by the recollection of the part she had just acted, shut herself up in her chamber, and smothering her head in the bed-clothes bemoaned her fault more bitterly than many less tender-hearted persons would have mourned a much greater offence; for, in the majority of cases, conscience is an elastic and very flexible article, which will bear a deal of stretching and adapt itself to a great variety of circumstances. Some people by prudent management and leaving it off piece by piece like a flannel waistcoat in warm weather, even contrive, in time, to dispense with it altogether; but there be others who can assume the garment and throw it off at pleasure; and this, being the greatest and most convenient improvement, is the one most in vogue.

CHAPTER VII

"FRED," said Mr. Swiveller, "remember the once popular melody of 'Begone dull care;' fan the sinking flame of hilarity with the wing of friendship; and pass the rosy wine."

Mr. Richard Swiveller's apartments were in the neighbourhood of Dury Lane, and in addition to this conveniency of situation had the advantage of being over a tobacconist's shop, so that he was enabled to procure a refreshing sneeze at any time by merely stepping out upon the staircase, and was saved the trouble and expense of maintaining a snuff-box. It was in these apartments that Mr. Swiveller made use of the expressions above recorded for the consolation and encouragement of his desponding friend;

and it may not be uninteresting or improper to remark that even these brief observations partook in a double sense of the figurative and poetical character of Mr. Swiveller's mind, as the rosy wine was in fact represented by one glass of cold gin-and-water, which was replenished as occasion required from a bottle and jug upon the table, and was passed from one to another, in a scarcity of tumblers which, as Mr. Swiveller's was a bachelor's establishment, may be acknowledged without a blush. By a like pleasant fiction his single chamber was always mentioned in the plural number. In its disengaged times, the tobacconist had announced it in his window as apartments for a single gentleman, and Mr. Swiveller, following up the hint, never failed to speak of it as his rooms, his lodgings, or his chambers, conveying to his hearers a notion of indefinite space, and leaving their imaginations to wander through long suites of lofty halls, at pleasure.

In this flight of fancy, Mr. Swiveller was assisted by a deceptive piece of furniture, in reality a bedstead, but in semblance a bookcase, which occupied a prominent situation in his chamber and seemed to defy suspicion and challenge inquiry. There is no doubt that by day Mr. Swiveller firmly believed this secret convenience to be a bookcase and nothing more; that he closed his eyes to the bed, resolutely denied the existence of the blankets, and spurned the bolster from his thoughts. No word of its real use, no hint of its mighty service, no allusion to its peculiar properties, had ever passed between him and his most intimate friends. Implicit faith in the deception was the first article of his creed. To be the friend of Swiveller you must reject all circumstantial evidence, all reason, observation, and experience, and repose a blind relief in the bookcase. It was his pet weakness, and he cherished it.

"Fred!" said Mr. Swiveller, finding that his former adjuration had been productive of no effect. "Pass the rosy."

Young Trent with an impatient gesture pushed the glass towards him, and fell again into the moody attitude from which he had been unwillingly roused.

"I'll give you, Fred," said his friend, stirring the mixture, "a little sentiment appropriate to the occasion. Here's May the—"

"Pshaw!" interposed the other. "You worry me to death with your chattering. You can be merry under any circumstances."

"Why, Mr. Trent," returned Dick, "there is a proverb which talks about being merry and wise. There are some people who can be merry and can't be wise, and some who can be wise (or think they can) and can't be merry. I'm one of the first sort. If the proverb's a good 'un, I suppose it's better to keep to half of it than none; at all events I'd rather be merry and not wise, than like you, neither one nor t'other."

"Bah!" muttered his friend, peevishly.

"With all my heart," said Mr. Swiveller. "In the polite circles I believe this sort of thing isn't usually said to a gentleman in his own apartments, but never mind that. Make yourself at home." Adding to this retort an observation to the effect that his friend appeared to be rather "cranky" in point of temper, Richard Swiveller finished the rosy and applied himself to the composition of another glassful, in which, after tasting it with great relish, he proposed a toast to an imaginary company.

"Gentlemen, I'll give you, if you please, Success to the ancient family of the Swivellers, and good luck to Mr. Richard in particular—Mr. Richard, gentlemen," said Dick with great emphasis, "who spends all his money on his friends and is *Bah!'d* for his pains. Hear, hear!"

"Dick!" said the other, returning to his seat after having paced the rooms twice or thrice, "will you talk seriously for two minutes, if I show you a way to make your fortune with very little trouble?"

"You've shown me so many," returned Dick; "and nothing has come on any one of 'em but empty pockets—"

"You'll tell a different story of this one, before a very long time is over," said his companion drawing his chair to the table. "You saw my sister Nell?"

"What about her?" returned Dick.

"She has a pretty face, has she not?"

"Why, certainly," replied Dick, "I must say for her that there's not any very strong family likeness between her and you."

"Has she a pretty face?" repeated his friend impatiently.

"Yes," said Dick, "she has a pretty face, a very pretty face. What of that?"

"I'll tell you," returned his friend. "It's very plain that the old man and I will remain at daggers-drawn to the end of our lives, and that I have nothing to expect from him. You see that, I suppose?"

"A bat might see that, with the sun shining," said Dick.

"It's equally plain that the money which the old flint—rot him—first taught me to expect that I should share with her at his death, will all be hers, is it not?"

"I should say it was," replied Dick; "unless the way in which I put the case to him, made an impression. It may have done so. It was powerful, Fred. 'Here is a jolly old grandfather'—that was strong, I thought—very friendly and natural. Did it strike you in that way?"

"It didn't strike *him*," returned the other, "so we needn't discuss it. Now look here. Nell is nearly fourteen."

"Fine girl of her age, but small," observed Richard Swiveller parenthetically.

"If I am to go on, be quite for one minute," returned Trent, fretting at the very slight interest the other appeared to take in the conversation. "Now I'm coming to the point."

"That's right," said Dick.

"The girl has strong affections, and brought up as she has been, may, at her age, be easily influenced and persuaded. If I take her in hand, I will be bound by a very little coaxing and threatening to bend her to my will. Not to beat about the bush (for the advantages of the scheme would take a week to tell) what's to prevent your marrying her?"

Richard Swiveller, who had been looking over the rim of the tumbler while his companion addressed the foregoing remarks to him with great energy and earnestness of manner, no sooner heard these words than he evinced the utmost consternation, and with difficulty ejaculated the monosyllable.

"What!"

"I say, what's to prevent," repeated the other with a steadiness of manner, of the effect of which upon his companion he was well assured by long experience, "what's to prevent your marrying her?"

"And she's 'nearly fourteen'!" cried Dick.

"I don't mean marrying her now"—returned the brother angrily; "say in two years' time, in three, in four. Does the old man look like a long-liver?"

"He don't look like it," said Dick shaking his head, "but these old people—there's no trusting 'em, Fred. There's an aunt of mine down in Dorsetshire that was going to die when I was eight years old, and hasn't kept her word yet. They're so aggravating, so unprincipled, so spiteful—unless there's apoplexy in the family, Fred, you can't calculate upon 'em, and even then they deceive you just as often as not."

"Look at the worst side of the question then," said Trent as steadily as before, and keeping his eyes upon his friend. "Suppose he lives."

"To be sure," said Dick. "There's the rub."

"I say," resumed his friend, "suppose he lives, and I persuaded, or if the word sounds more feasible, forced Nell to a secret marriage with you. What do you think would come of that?"

"A family and an annual income of nothing, to keep 'em on," said Richard Swiveller after some reflection.

"I tell you," returned the other with an increased earnestness, which, whether it were real or assumed, had the same effect on his companion, "that he lives for her, that his whole energies and thoughts are bound up in her, that he would no more disinherit her for an act of disobedience than he would take into his favour again for any act of obedience or virtue that I could possibly be guilty of. He could not do it. You or any other man with eyes in his head may see that, if he chooses."

"It seems improbable certainly," said Dick, musing.

"It seems improbable because it is improbable," his friend returned. "If you would furnish him with an additional inducement to forgive you, let there be an irreconcileable breach, a most deadly quarrel, between you and me—let there be a pretence of such a thing, I mean, of course—and he'll do so fast enough. As to Nell, constant dropping will wear away a stone; you know you may trust to me as far as she is concerned. So, whether he lives or dies, what does it come to? That you become the sole inheritor of the wealth of this rich old hunks, that you and I spend it together, and that you get into the bargain a beautiful young wife."

"I suppose there's no doubt about his being rich"—said Dick.

"Doubt! Did you hear what he let fall the other day when we were there? Doubt! What will you doubt next, Dick?"

It would be tedious to pursue the conversation through all its artful windings, or to develop the gradual approaches by which the heart of Richard Swiveller was gained. It is sufficient to know that vanity, interest, poverty, and every spendthrift consideration urged him to look upon the proposal with favour, and that where all other inducements were wanting, the habitual carelessness of his disposition stepped in and still weighed down the scale on the same side. To these impulses must be added the complete ascendancy which his friend had long been accustomed to exercise over him—an ascendancy exerted in the beginning sorely at the expense of the unfortunate Dick's purse and prospects, but still maintained without the slightest relaxation, notwithstanding that Dick suffered for all his friend's vices, and was in nine cases out of ten looked upon as his designing tempter when he was indeed nothing but his thoughtless light-headed tool.

The motives on the other side were something deeper than any which Richard Swiveller entertained or understood, but these being left to their own development, require no present elucidation. The negotiation was concluded very pleasantly, and Mr. Swiveller was in the act of stating in flowery terms that he had no insurmountable objection to marrying anybody plentifully endowed with money or moveables, who could be induced to take him, when he was interrupted in his observations by a knock at the door, and the consequent necessity of crying "Come in."

The door was opened, but nothing came in except a soapy arm and a strong gush of tobacco. The gush of tobacco came from the shop down stairs, and the soapy arm proceeded from the body of a servant girl, who being then and there engaged in cleaning the stairs had just drawn it out of a warm pail to take in a letter, which letter she now held in her hand, proclaiming aloud with that quick perception of surnames peculiar to her class that it was for Mister Snivelling.

Dick looked rather pale and foolish when he glanced at the direction, and still more so when he came to look at the inside, observing that this was one of the inconveniences of being a lady's man, and that it very easy to talk as they had been talking, but he had quite forgotten her.

"*Her*. Who?" demanded Trent.

"Sophy Wackles," said Dick.

"Who's she?"

"She's all my fancy painted her, sir, that's what she is," said Mr. Swiveller, taking a long pull at "the rosy" and looking gravely at his friend. "She is lovely, she's divine. You know her."

"I remember," said his companion carelessly. "What of her?"

"Why, sir," returned Dick, "between Miss Sophia Wackles and the humble individual who has now the honour to address you, warm and tender sentiments have been engendered, sentiments of the most honourable and inspiring kind. The Goddess Diana, sir, that calls aloud for the chace, is not more particular in her behaviour than Sophia Wackles; I can tell you that."

"Am I to believe there's anything real in what you say?" demanded his friend; "you don't mean to say that any love-making has been going on?"

"Love-making, yes. Promising, no," said Dick. "There can be no action for breach, that's one comfort. I've never committed myself in writing, Fred."

"And what's in the letter, pray?"

"A reminder, Fred, for to-night—a small party of twenty, making two hundred light fantastic toes in all, supposing every lady and gentleman to have the proper complement. I must go, if it's only to begin breaking off the affair—I'll do it, don't you be afraid. I should like to know whether she left this herself. If she did, unconscious of any bar to her happiness, it's affecting, Fred."

To solve this question, Mr. Swiveller summoned the handmaid and ascertained that Miss Sophy Wackles had indeed left the letter with her own hands; and that she had come accompanied, for decorum's sake no doubt, by a younger Miss Wackles; and that on learning that Mr. Swiveller was at home and being requested to walk up stairs, she was extremely shocked and professed that she would rather die. Mr. Swiveller heard this account with a degree of admiration not altogether consistent with the project in which he had just concurred, but his friend attached very little importance to his behaviour in this respect, probably because he knew that he had influence sufficient to control Richard Swiveller's proceedings in this or any other matter, whenever he deemed it necessary, for the advancement of his own purpose, to exert it.

CHAPTER VIII

BUSINESS disposed of, Mr. Swiveller was inwardly reminded of its being near dinner-time, and to the intent that his health might not be endangered by longer abstinence, despatched a messenger to the nearest eating-house requiring an immediate supply of boiled beef and greens for two. With this demand, however, the eating-house (having experience of its customer) declined to comply, churlishly sending back for answer that if Mr. Swiveller stood in need of beef perhaps he would be so obliging as to come there and eat it, bringing with him, as grace before meat, the amount of a certain small account which had been long outstanding. Not at all intimidated by this rebuff, but rather sharpened in wits and appetite, Mr. Swiveller forwarded the same message to another and more distant eating-house, adding to it by way of rider that the gentleman was induced to send so far, not only by the great fame and popularity its beef had acquired, but in consequence of the extreme toughness of the beef retailed at the obdurate cook's shop, which rendered it quite unfit not merely for gentlemanly food but for any human consumption. The good effect of this politic course was demonstrated by the speedy arrival of a small pewter pyramid, curiously constructed of platters and covers, whereof the boiled-beef-plates formed the base, and a foaming quart-pot the apex; the structure being resolved into its component part afforded all things requisite and necessary for a hearty meal, to which Mr. Swiveller and his friend applied themselves with great keenness and enjoyment.

"May the present moment," said Dick, sticking his fork into a large carbuncular potato, "be the worst of our lives! I like this plan of sending 'em with the peel on; there's a charm in drawing a potato from its native element (if I may so express it) to which the rich and powerful are strangers. Ah! 'Man wants but little here below, nor wants that little long!' How true that is!—after dinner."

"I hope the eating-house keeper will want but little and that *he* may not want that little long," returned his companion; "but I suspect you've no means of paying for this!"

"I shall be passing presently, and I'll call," said Dick, winking his eye significantly. "The waiter's quite helpless. The goods are gone, Fred, and there's an end of it."

In point of fact, it would seem that the waiter felt this wholesome truth, for when he returned for the empty plates and dishes and was informed by Mr. Swiveller with dignified carelessness that he would call and settle when he should be passing presently, he displayed some perturbation of spirit, and muttered a few remarks about "payment on delivery," and "no trust," and another unpleasant subjects, but was fain to content himself with inquiring at what hour it was likely the gentleman would call, in order that being personally responsible for the beef, greens, and sundries, he might take care to be in the way at the time. Mr. Swiveller, after mentally calculating his engagements to a nicety, replied that he should look in at from two minutes before six to seven minutes past; and the man disappearing with this feeble consolation, Richard Swiveller took a greasy memorandum-book from his pocket and made an entry therein.

"Is that a reminder, in case you should forget to call?" said Trent, with a sneer.

"Not exactly, Fred," replied the imperturbable Richard, continuing to write with a business-like air, "I enter in this little book the names of the streets that I can't go down while the shops are open. This dinner to-day closes Long Acre. I bought a pair of boots in Great Queen Street last week, and made that no throughfare too. There's only one avenue to the Strand left open now, and I shall have to stop up that to-night with a pair of gloves. The roads are closing so fast in every direction, that in about a month's time, unless my aunt sends me a remittance, I shall have to go three or four miles out of town to get over the way."

"There's no fear of her failing, in the end?" said Trent.

"Why, I hope not," returned Mr. Swiveller, "but the average number of letters it takes to soften her is six, and this time we have got as far as eight without any effect at all. I'll write another to-morrow morning. I mean to blot it a good deal and shake some water over it out of the pepper-castor, to make it look penitent. 'I'm in such a state of mind that I hardly know what I write'—blot—'if you could see me at this minute shedding tears for my past misconduct'—pepper-castor—'my hand tembles when I think'—blot again—if that don't produce the effect, it's all over."

By this time Mr. Swiveller had finished his entry, and he now replaced his pencil in its little sheath and closed the book, in a perfectly grave and serious frame of mind. His friend discovered that it was time for him to fulfil some other engagement, and Richard Swiveller was accordingly left alone, in company with the rosy wine and his own meditations touching Miss Sophy Wackles.

"It's rather sudden," said Dick shaking his head with a look of infinite wisdom, and running on (as he was accustomed to do) with scraps of verse as if they were only prose in a hurry; "when the heart of a man is depressed with fears, the mist is dispelled when Miss Wackles appears: she's a very nice girl. She's like the red red rose that's newly sprung in June—there's no denying that—she's also like a melody that's sweetly played in tune. It's really very sudden. Not that there's any need, on account of Fred's little sister, to turn cool directly, but it's better not to go too far. If I being to cool at all I must begin at once, I see that. There's the chance of an action for breach, that's one reason. There's the chance of Sophy's getting another husband, that's another. There's the chance of—no, there's no chance of that, but it's as well to be on the safe side."

This undeveloped consideration was the possibility, which Richard Swiveller sought to conceal even from himself, of his not being proof against the charms of Miss Wackles, and in some unguarded moment, by linking his fortunes to hers for ever, of putting it out of his own power to further the notable scheme to which he had so readily become a party. For all these reasons, he decided to pick a quarrel with Miss Wackles without delay, and casting about for a pretext determined in favour of groundless jealousy. Having made up his mind on this important point, he circulated the glass (from his right hand to his left, and back again) pretty freely, to enable him to act his part with greater discretion, and then, after making some slight improvements in his toilet, bent his steps towards the spot hallowed by the fair object of his meditations.

This spot was Chelsea, for there Miss Sophia Wackles resided with her widowed mother and two sisters, in conjunction with whom she maintained a very small day-school for young ladies of proportionate dimensions; a circumstance which was made known to the neighbourhood by an oval board over the front first-floor window, whereon appeared in circumambient flourishes the words "Ladies' Seminary;" and which was further published and proclaimed at intervals between the hours of half-past nine and ten in the morning, by a straggling and solitary young lady of tender years standing on the scraper on the tips of her toes and making futile attempts to reach the knocker with a spelling-book. The several duties of instruction in this establishment were thus discharged. English grammar, composition, geography, and the use of the dumb-bells, by Miss Melissa Wackles; writing, arithmetic, dancing, music, and general fascination, by Miss Sophy Wackles; the art of needle-work, marking, and samplery, by Miss Jane Wackles; corporal punishment, fasting, and other tortures and terrors, by Mrs. Wackles. Miss Melissa Wackles was the eldest daughter, Miss Sophy the next, and Miss Jane the youngest. Miss Melissa might have seen five-and-thirty summers or thereabouts, and verged on the autumnal; Miss Sophy was a fresh, good-humoured, buxom girl of twenty; and Miss Jane numbered scarcely sixteen years. Mrs. Wackles was an excellent but rather venomous old lady of three-score.

To this Ladies' Seminary, then, Richard Swiveller hied, with designs obnoxious to the peace of the fair Sophia, who, arrayed in virgin white, embellished by no ornament but one blushing rose, received him on his arrival, in the midst of very elegant not to say brilliant preparations; such as the embellishment of the room with the little flower-pots which always stood on the window-sill outside, save in windy weather when they blew into the area; the choice attire of the day-scholars who were allowed to grace the festival; the unwonted curls of Miss Jane Wackles who had kept her head during the whole of the preceding day screwed up tight in a yellow play-bill; and the solemn gentility and stately bearing of the old lady and her eldest daughter, which struck Mr. Swiveller as being uncommon but made no further impression upon him.

The truth is—and, as there is no accounting for tastes, even a taste so strange as this may be recorded without being looked upon as a wilful and malicious invention—the truth is that neither Mrs. Wackles nor her eldest daughter had at any time greatly favoured the pretensions of Mr. Swiveller, being accustomed to make slight mention of him as "a gay young man" and to sigh and shake their heads ominously whenever his name was mentioned. Mr. Swiveller's conduct in respect to Miss Sophy having been of that vague and dilatory kind which is usually looked upon as betokening no fixed matrimonial intentions, the young lady herself began in course of time to deem it highly desirable, that it should be brought to an issue one way or other. Hence she had at last consented to play off against Richard Swiveller a stricken market-gardener known to be ready with his offer on the smallest encouragement, and hence—as this occasion has been specially assigned for the purpose—that great anxiety on her part for Richard Swiveller's presence which had occasioned her to leave the note he has been seen to receive. "If he has any expectations at all or any means of keeping a wife well," said Mrs. Wackles to her eldest daughter, "he'll state 'em to us now or never."— "If he really cares about me," thought Miss Sophy, "he must tell me so, to-night."

But all these sayings and doings and thinkings being unknown to Mr. Swiveller, affected him not in the least; he was debating in his mind how he could best turn jealous, and wishing that Sophy were for that occasion only far less pretty than she was, or that she were her own sister, which would have served his turn as well, when the company came, and among them the market-gardener, whose name was Cheggs. But Mr. Cheggs came not alone or unsupported, for he prudently brought along with him his sister, Miss Cheggs, who making straight to Miss Sophy and taking her by both hands, and kissing her on both cheeks, hoped in an audible whisper that they had not come too early.

"Too early, no!" replied Miss Sophy.

"Oh my dear," rejoined Miss Cheggs in the same whisper as before, "I've been so tormented, so worried, that it's a mercy we were not here at four o'clock in the afternoon. Alick has been in *such* a state of impatience to come! You'd hardly believe that he was dressed before dinner-time and has been looking at the clock and teasing me ever since. It's all your fault, you naughty thing."

Hereupon Miss Sophy blushed, and Mr. Cheggs (who was bashful before ladies) blushed too, and Miss Sophy's mother and sisters, to prevent Mr. Cheggs from blushing more, lavished civilities and attentions upon him, and left Richard Swiveller to take care of himself. Here was the very thing he wanted, here was good cause reason and foundation for pretending to be angry; but having this cause reason and foundation which he had come expressly to see, not expecting to find, Richard Swiveller was angry in sound earnest, and wondered what the devil Cheggs meant by his impudence.

However, Mr. Swiveller had Miss Sophy's hand for the first quadrille (country-dances being low, were utterly proscribed) and so gained an advantage over his rival, who sat despondingly in a corner and contemplated the glorious figure of the young lady as she moved through the mazy dance. Nor was this the only start Mr. Swiveller had of the market-gardener, for determining to show the family what quality of man they trifled with, and influenced perhaps by his late libations, he performed such feats of agility and such spins and twirls as filled the company with astonishment, and in particular caused a very long gentleman who was dancing with a very short scholar, to stand quite transfixed by wonder and admiration. Even Mrs. Wackles forgot for the moment to snub three small young ladies who were inclined to be happy, and could not repress a rising thought that to have such a dancer as that in the family would be a pride indeed.

At this momentous crisis, Miss Cheggs proved herself a vigorous and useful ally, for not confining herself to expressing by scornful smiles a contempt for Mr. Swiveller's accomplishments, she took every opportunity of whispering into Miss Sophy's ear expressions of condolence and sympathy on her being worried by such a ridiculous creature, declaring that she was frightened to death lest Alick should fall upon, and beat him, in the fulness of his wrath, and entreating Miss Sophy to observe how the eyes of the said Alick gleamed with love and fury; passions, it may be observed, which being too much for his eyes rushed into his nose also, and suffused it with a crimson glow.

"You must dance with Miss Cheggs," said Miss Sophy to Dick Swiveller, after she had herself danced twice with Mr. Cheggs and made great show of encouraging his advances. "She's such a nice girl—and her brother's quite delightful."

"Quite delightful is he?" muttered Dick. "Quite delighted too, I should say, from the manner in which he's looking this way."

Here Miss Jane (previously instructed for the purpose) interposed her many curls and whispered her sister to observe how jealous Mr. Cheggs was.

"Jealous! Like his impudence!" said Richard Swiveller.

"His impudence, Mr. Swiveller!" said Miss Jane, tossing her head. "Take care he don't hear you, sir, or you may be sorry for it."

"Oh pray, Jane—" said Miss Sophy.

"Nonsense!" replied her sister. "Why shouldn't Mr. Cheggs be jealous if he likes? I like that, certainly. Mr. Cheggs has as good a right to be jealous as anybody else has, and perhaps he may have a better right soon if he hasn't already. You know best about that, Sophy!"

Though this was a concerted plot between Miss Sophy and her sister, originating in humane intentions and having for its objects the inducing Mr. Swiveller to declare himself in time, it failed in its effect; for Miss Jane being one of those young ladies who are prematurely shrill and shrewish, gave such undue importance to her part that Mr. Swiveller retired in didgeon, resigning his mistress to Mr. Cheggs and conveying a defiance into his looks which that gentleman indignantly returned.

"Did you speak to me, sir?" said Mr. Cheggs, following him into a corner. "Have the kindness to smile, sir, in order that we may not be suspected. Did you speak to me, sir?"

Mr. Swiveller looked with a supercilious smile at Mr. Chegg's toes, then raised his eyes from them to his ankle, from that to his shin, from that to his knee, and so on very gradually, keeping up his right leg, until he reached his waistcoat, when he raised his eyes from button to button until he reached his chin, and travelling straight up the middle of his nose came at last to his eyes, when he said abruptly.

"No, sir, I didn't."

"Hem!" said Mr. Cheggs, glancing over his shoulder, "have the goodness to smile again, sir. Perhaps you wished to speak to me, sir."

"No, sir, I didn't do that, either."

"Perhaps you may have nothing to say to me *now*, sir," said Mr. Cheggs fiercely.

At these words Richard Swiveller withdrew his eyes from Mr. Chegg's face, and travelling down the middle of his nose and down his waistcoat and down his right leg, reached his toes again, and carefully surveyed them; this done, he crossed over, and coming up the other leg and thence approaching by the waistcoat as before, said when he had got to his eyes, "No, sir, I haven't."

"Oh indeed sir!" said Mr. Cheggs. "I'm glad to hear it. You know where I'm to be found, I suppose, sir, in case you *should* have anything to say to me?"

"I can easily inquire, sir, when I want to know."

"There's nothing more we need say, I believe, sir?"

"Nothing more, sir."—With that they closed the tremendous dialogue by frowning mutually. Mr. Cheggs hastened to tender his hand to Miss Sophy, and Mr. Swiveller sat himself down in a corner in a very moody state.

Hard by this corner, Mrs. Wackles and Miss Wackles were seated, looking on at the dance; and unto Mrs. and Miss Wackles, Miss Cheggs occasionally darted when her partner was occupied with his share of the figure, and made some remark or other which was gall and wormwood to Richard Swiveller's soul. Looking into the eyes of Mrs. and Miss Wackles for encouragement, and sitting very upright and uncomfortable on a couple of hard stools, were two of the day-scholars; and when Miss Wackles smiled, and Mrs. Wackles smiled, the two little girls on the stools sought to curry favour by smiling likewise, in gracious acknowledgment of which attention the old lady frowned them down instantly, and said that if they dared to be guilty of such an impertinence again, they should be sent under convoy to their respective homes. This threat caused one of the young ladies, she being of a weak and trembling temperament, to shed tears, and for this offence they were both filed off immediately, with a dreadful promptitude that struck terror into the souls of all the pupils.

"I've got such news for you," said Miss Cheggs approaching once more, "Alick has been saying such things to Sophy. Upon my word, you know, it's quite serious and in earnest, that's clear."

"What's he been saying, my dear?" demanded Mrs. Wackles.

"All manner of things," replied Miss Cheggs, "you can't think how out he has been speaking!"

Richard Swiveller considered it advisable to hear no more, but taking advantage of a pause in the dancing, and the approach of Mr. Cheggs to pay his court to the old lady, swaggered with an extremely careful assumption of extreme carelessness towards the door, passing on the way Miss Jane Wackles, who in all the glory of her curls was holding a flirtation (as good practice when no better was to be had) with a feeble old gentleman who lodged in the parlour. Near the door sat Miss Sophy, still fluttered and confused by the attentions of Mr. Cheggs, and by her side Richard Swiveller lingered for a moment to exchange a few parting words.

"My boat is on the shore and my bark is on the sea, but before I pass this door I will say farewell to thee," murmured Dick, looking gloomily upon her.

"Are you going?" said Miss Sophy, whose heart sank within her at the result of her stratagem, but who affected a light indifference notwithstanding.

"Am I going!" echoed Dick bitterly. "Yes, I am. What then?"

"Nothing, except that it's very early," said Miss Sophy; "but you are your own master, of course."

"I would that I had been my own mistress too," said Dick, "before I had ever entertained a thought of you. Miss Wackles, I believed you true, and I was blest in so believing, but now I mourn that e'er I knew, a girl so fair yet so deceiving."

Miss Sophy bit her lip and affected to look with great interest after Mr. Cheggs, who was quaffing lemonade in the distance.

"I came here," said Dick, rather oblivious of the purpose with which he had really come, "with my bosom expanded, my heart dilated, and my sentiments of corresponding description. I go away with feelings that may be conceived but cannot be described, feeling within myself the desolating truth that my best affections have experienced this night a stifler!"

"I am sure I don't know what you mean, Mr. Swiveller," said Miss Sophy with downcast eyes. "I'm very sorry if—"

"Sorry, ma'am!" said Dick, "sorry in the possession of a Cheggs! But I wish you a very good night, concluding with this slight remark, that there is a young lady growing up at this present moment for me, who has not only great personal attractions but great wealth, and who has requested her next of kin to propose for my hand, which having a regard for some members of her family, I have consented to promise. It's a gratifying circumstance which you'll be glad to hear, that a young and lovely girl is growing into a woman expressly on my account, and is now saving up for me. I thought I'd mention it. I have now merely to apologise for trespassing so long upon your attention. Good night."

"There's one good thing springs out of all this," said Richard Swiveller to himself when he had reached home and was hanging over the candle with the extinguisher in his hand, "which is, that I now go heart and soul, neck and heels, with Fred in all his scheme about little Nelly, and right glad he'll be to find me so strong upon it. He shall know all about that to-morrow, and in the meantime, as it's rather late, I'll try and get a wink or two of the balmy."

"The balmy" came almost as soon as it was courted. In a very few minutes Mr. Swiveller was fast asleep, dreaming that he had married Nelly Trent and come into her property, and that his first act of power was to lay waste the market-garden of Mr. Cheggs and turn it into a brick-field.

CHAPTER IX

THE child, in her confidence with Mrs. Quilp, had but feebly described the sadness and sorrow of her thoughts, or the heaviness of the cloud which overhung her home, and cast dark shadows on its hearth. Besides that it was very difficult to impart to any person not intimately acquainted with the life she led, an adequate sense of its gloom and loneliness, a constant fear of in some way committing or injuring the old man to whom she was so tenderly attached, had restrained her even in the midst of her heart's overflowing, and made her timid of allusion to the main cause of her anxiety and distress.

For, it was not the monotonous day unchequered by variety and uncheered by pleasant companionship, it was not the dark dreary evenings or the long solitary nights, it was not the absence of every slight and easy pleasure for which young hearts beat high, or the knowing nothing of childhood but its weakness and its easily wounded spirit, that had wrung such tears from Nell. To see the old man struck down beneath the pressure of some hidden grief, to mark his wavering and unsettled state, to be agitated at times with a dreadful fear that his mind was wandering, and to trace in his words and looks the dawning of despondent madness; to watch and wait and listen for confirmation of these things day after day, and to feel and know that, come what might, they were alone in the world with no one to help or advise or care about them—these were causes of depression and anxiety that might have sat heavily on an older breast with many influences at work to cheer and gladden it, but how heavily on the mind of a young child to whom they were ever present, and who was constantly surrounded by all that could keep such thoughts in restless action!

And yet, to the old man's vision, Nell was still the same. When he could for a moment disengage his mind from the phantom that haunted and brooded on it always, there was his young companion with the same smile for him, the same earnest words, the same merry laugh, the same love and care that sinking deep into his soul seemed to have been present to him through his whole life. And so he went on, content to read the book of her heart from the page first presented to him, little dreaming of the story that lay hidden in its other leaves, and murmuring within himself that at least the child was happy.

She had been once. She had gone singing through the dim rooms, and moving with gay and lightsome step among their dusty treasures, making them older by her young life, and sterner and more grim by her gay and cheerful presence. But now the chambers were cold and gloomy, and when she left her own little room to while away the tedious hours, and sat in one of them, she was still and motionless as their inanimate occupants, and had no heart to startle the echoes—hoarse from their long silence—with her voice.

In one of these rooms was a window looking into the street, where the child sat, many and many a long evening, and often far into the night, alone and thoughtful. None are so anxious as those who watch and wait, and at these times, mournful fancies came flocking on her mind in crowds.

She would take her station here at dusk, and watch the people as they passed up and down the street, or appeared at the windows of the opposite houses, wondering whether those rooms were as lonesome as that in which she sat, and whether those people felt it company to see her sitting there, as she did only to see them look out and draw in their heads again. There was a crooked stack of chimneys on one of the roofs, in which by often looking at them she had fancied ugly faces that were frowning over at her and trying to peer into the room, and she felt glad when it grew too dark to make them out, though she was sorry too, when the man came to light the lamps in the street, for it made it late, and very dull inside. Then she would draw in her head to look round the room and see that everything was in its place and hadn't moved; and looking out into the street again, would perhaps see a man passing with a coffin on his back, and two or three others silently following him to a house where somebody lay dead, which made her shudder and think of such things until they suggested afresh the old man's altered face and manner, and a new train of fears and speculations. If he were to die—if sudden illness had happened to him, and he were never to come home again, alive—if, one night, he should come home, and kiss and bless her as usual, and after she had gone to bed and had fallen asleep and was perhaps dreaming pleasantly, and smiling in her sleep, he should kill himself and his blood come creeping, creeping, on the ground to her own bedroom door! These thoughts were too terrible to dwell upon, and again she would have recourse to the street, now trodden by fewer feet and darker and more silent than before. The shops were closing fast, and lights began to shine from the upper windows, as the neighbours went to bed. By degrees these dwindled away and disappeared, or were replaced here and there by a feeble rush-candle which was to burn all night. Still there was one late shop at no great distance which sent forth and ruddy glare upon the pavement even yet, and looked bright and companionable. But in a little time this closed, the light was extinguished, and all was gloomy and quiet, except when some stray footsteps sounded on the pavement, or a neighbour, out later than his wont, knocked lustily at his house-door to rouse the sleeping inmates.

When the night had worn away thus far (and seldom now until it had) the child would close the window, and steal softly down stairs, thinking as she went that if one of those hideous faces below, which often mingled with her dreams, were to meet her by the way, rendering itself visible by some strange light of its own, how terrified she would be. But these fears vanished before a well-trimmed lamp and the familiar aspect of her own room. After praying fervently and with many bursting tears for the old man, and the restoration of his peace of mind and the happiness they had once enjoyed, she would lay her head upon the pillow and sob herself to sleep, often starting up again, before the daylight came, to listen for the bell, and respond to the imaginary summons which had roused her from her slumber.

One night, the third after Nelly's interview with Mrs. Quilp, the old man, who had been weak and ill all day, said he should not leave home. The child's eyes sparkled at the intelligence, but her joy subsided when they reverted to his worn and sickly face.

"Two days," he said, "two whole, clear, days have passed, and there is no reply. What *did* he tell thee, Nell?"

"Exactly what I told you, dear grandfather, indeed."

"True," said the old man, faintly. "Yes. But tell me again, Nell. My head fails me. What was it that he told thee? Nothing more that that he would see me to-morrow or next day? That was in the note."

"Nothing more," said the child. "Shall I go to him again to-morrow, dear grandfather? Very early? I will be there and back, before breakfast."

The old man shook his head, and sighing mournfully, drew her towards him.

"Twould be of no use, my dear, no earthly use. But if he deserts me, Nell, at this moment—if he deserts me now, when I should, with his assistance, be recompensed for all the time and money I have lost, and all the agony of mind I have undergone, which makes me what you see, I am ruined, and—worse, far worse than that—have ruined thee, for whom I ventured all. If we are beggars—!"

"What if we are?" said the child boldly. "Let us be beggars, and be happy."

"Beggars—and happy!" said the old man. "Poor child!"

"Dear grandfather," cried the girl with an energy which shone in her flushed face, trembling voice, and impassioned gesture, "I am not a child in that I think, but even if I am, oh hear me pray that we may beg, or work in open roads or fields, to earn a scanty living, rather than live as we do now."

"Nelly!" said the old man.

"Yes, yes, rather than live as we do now," the child repeated, more earnestly than before. "If you are sorrowful, let me know why and be sorrowful too; if you waste away and are paler and weaker every day, let me be your nurse to try to comfort you. If you are poor, let us be poor together, but let me be with you, do not let me see such change and not know why, or I shall break my heart and die. Dear grandfather, let us leave this sad place tomorrow, and beg our way from door to door."

The old man covered his face with his hands, and hid it in the pillow of the couch on which he lay.

"Let us be beggars," said the child passing an arm round his neck, "I have no fear but we shall have enough, I am sure we shall. Let us walk through country places, and sleep in fields and under trees, and never think of money again, or anything that can make you sad, but rest at nights, and have the sun and wind upon our faces in the day, and thank God together. Let us never set foot in dark rooms or melancholy house any more, but wander up and down wherever we like to go, and when you are tired, you shall stop to rest in the pleasantest place that we can find, and I will go and beg for both."

The child's voice was lost in sobs as she dropped upon the old man's neck; nor did she weep alone.

These were not words for other ears, nor was it a scene for other eyes. And yet other ears and eyes were there and greedily taking in all that passed, and moreover they were the ears and eyes of no less a person than Mr. Daniel Quilp, who, having entered unseen when the child first place herself at the old man's side, refrained—actuated, no doubt, by motives of the purest delicacy—from interrupting the conversation, and stood looking on with his accustomed grin. Standing, however, being a tiresome attitude to a gentleman already fatigued with walking, and the dwarf being one of that kind of persons who usually make themselves at home, he soon cast his eyes upon a chair into which he skipped with uncommon agility, and perching himself on the back with his feet upon the seat, was thus enabled to look on and listen with greater comfort to himself, besides gratifying at the same time that taste for doing something fantastic and monkey-like, which on all occasions had strong possession of him. Here, then, he sat, one leg cocked carelessly over the other, his chin resting on the palm of his hand, his head turned a little on one side, and his ugly features twisted into a complacent grimace. And in this position the old man, happening in course of time to look that way, at length chanced to see him, to his unbounded astonishment.

The child uttered a suppressed shriek on beholding this agreeable figure; in their first surprise both she and the old man, not knowing what to say, and half doubting its reality, looked shrinkingly at it. Not at all disconcerted by this reception, Daniel Quilp preserved the same attitude, merely nodding twice or thrice with great condescension. At length the old man pronounced his name, and inquired how he came there.

"Through the door," said Quilp pointing over his shoulder with his thumb. "I'm not quite small enough to get through key-holes. I wish I was.

I want to have some talk with, particularly, and in private—with nobody present, neighbour. Good-bye, little Nelly."

Nell looked at the old man, who nodded to her to retire, and kissed her cheek.

"Ah!" said the dwarf, smacking his lips, "what a nice kiss that was—just upon the rosy part. What a capital kiss!"

Nell was one the slower in going away, for this remark. Quilp looked after her with an admiring leer, and when she had closed the door, fell to complimenting the old man upon her charms.

"Such a fresh, blooming, modest little bud, neighbour," said Quilp, nursing his short leg, and making his eyes twinkle very much; "such a chubby, rosy, cosy, little Nell!"

The old man answered by a forced smile, and was plainly struggling with a feeling of the keenest and most exquisite impatience. It was not lost upon Quilp, who delighted in torturing him, or indeed anybody else when he could.

"She's so," said Quilp, speaking very slowly, and feigning to be quite absorbed in the subject, "so small, so compact, so beautifully modelled, so fair, with such blue veins and such transparent skin, and such little feet, and such winning ways,—but bless me, you're nervous! Why neighbour, what's the matter? I swear to you," continued the dwarf dismounting from the chair and sitting down in it, with a careful slowness of gesture very different from the rapidity with which he had sprung up upheard, "I swear to you that I ahd no idea old blood ran so fast or kept so warm. I thought it was sluggish in its course, and cool, quite cool. I am pretty sure it ought to be. Yours must be out of order, neighbour."

"I believe it is," groaned the old man, clasping his head with both hands. "There's burning fever here, and something now and then to which I fear to give a name."

The dwarf said never a word, but watched his companion as he paced restlessly up and down the room, and presently returned to his seat. Here he remained, with his head bowed upon his breast for some time, and then suddenly raising it, said,

"Once, and once for all, have you brought me any money?"

"No!" returned Quilp.

"Then," said the old man, clenching his hands desperately, and looking upward, "the child and I are lost!"

"Neighbour;" said Quilp glancing his hands desperately, and looking upward, "the child and I are lost!"

"Neighbour," said Quilp glancing sternly at him, and beating his hand twice or thrice upon the table to attract his wandering attention, "let me be plain with you, and play a fairer game than when you held all the cards, and I saw but the backs and nothing more. You have no secret from me now."

The old man looked up, trembling.

"You are surprised," said Quilp. "Well, perhaps that's natural. You have no secret from me now, I say; no, not one. For now I know that all those sums of money, that all those loans, advances, and supplies that you have had from me, have found their way to—shall I say the word?"

"Ay!" replied the old man, "say it, if you will."

"To the gaming-table," rejoined Quilp, "your nightly haunt. This was the precious scheme to make your fortune, was it; this was the secret certain source of wealth in which I was to have sunk my money (if I had been the fool you took me for); this was your inexhaustible mine of gold, your El Dorado, eh?"

"Yes," cried the old man, turning upon him with gleaming eyes, "it was. It is. It will be till I die."

"That I should have been blinded," said Quilp looking contemptuously at him, "by a mere shallow gambler!"

"I am no gambler," cried the old man fiercely. "I call Heaven to witness that I never played for gain of mine, or love of play; that at every piece I staked, I whispered to myself that orphan's name and called on Heaven to bless the venture, which it never did. Whom did it prosper? Who were those with whom I played? Men who lived by plunder, profligacy, and riot, squandering their gold in doing ill and propagating vice and evil. My winnings would have been from them, my winnings would have been bestowed to the last farthing on a young sinless child whose life they would have sweetened and made happy. What would they have contracted? The means of corruption, wretchedness, and misery. Who would not hoped in such a cause—tell me that; now who would not have hoped as I did?"

"When did you first begin this mad career?" asked Quilp, his taunting inclination subdued for a moment by the old man's grief and wildness.

"When did I first begin?" he rejoined, passing his hand across his brow. "When *was* it, that I first began? When should it be, but when I began to think how little I had saved, how long a time it took to save at all, how short a time I might have at my age to live, and how she would be left to the rough mercies of the world, with barely enough to keep her from the sorrows that wait on poverty; then it was that I began to think about it."

"After you first came to me to get your precious grandson packed off to sea?" said Quilp.

"Shortly after that," replied the old man. "I thought of it a long time, and had it in my sleep for months. Then I began. I found no pleasure in it, I expected none. What has it ever brought to me but anxious days and sleepless nights, but loss of health and peace of mind, and gain of feebleness and sorrow!"

"You lost what money you had laid by, first, and then came to me. While I thought you were making your fortune (as you said you were) you were making yourself a beggar, eh? Dear me! And so it comes to pass that I hold every security you could scrape together, and a bill of sale upon the—upon the stock and property," said Quilp standing up and looking about him, as if to assure himself that none of it had been taken away. "But did you never win?"

"Never!" groaned the old man. "Never won back my loss!"

"I thought," sneered the dwarf, "that if a man played long enough he was sure to win at last, or at the worst not to come off a loser."

"And so he is," cried the old man, suddenly rousing himself from his state of despondency, and lashed into the most violent excitement, "so he is;

I have felt that from the first, I have always known it, I've seen it, I never felt it half so strongly as I feel it now. Quilp, I have dreamed three nights of winning the same large sum, I never could dream that dream before, though I have often tried. Do not desert me now I have this chance. I have no resource but you, give me some help, let me try this one last hope."

The dwarf shrugged his shoulders and shook his head.

"See, Quilp, good tender-hearted Quilp," said the old man, drawing some scraps of paper from his pocket with a trembling hand, and clasping the dwarf's arm, "only see here. Look at these figures, the result of long calculation, and painful and hard experience. I *must* win. I only want a little help once more, a few pounds, but two score pounds, dear Quilp."

"The last advance was seventy," said the dwarf; "and it went in one night."

"I know it did," answered the old man, "but that was the very worst fortune of all, and the time had not come then. Quilp, consider, consider," the old man cried, trembling so much the while that the papers in his hand fluttered as if they were shaken by the wind, "that orphan child. If I were alone, I could die with gladness—perhaps even anticipate that doom which is dealt out so unequally, coming as it does on the proud and happy in their strength, and shunning the needy and afflicted and all who court it in their despair—but what I have done, has been for her. Help me fore her sake I implore you—not for mine, for hers!"

"I'm sorry I've got an appointment in the City," said Quilp, looking at his watch with perfect self-possession, "or I should have been very glad to have spent half an hour with you while you composed yourself—very glad."

"Nay, Quilp, good Quilp," gasped the old man, catching at his skirts— "you and I have talked together more than once for her poor mother's story. The fear of her coming to poverty has perhaps been bred in me by that. Do not be hard upon me, but take that into account. You are a great gainer by me. Oh spare me the money for this one last hope!"

"I couldn't do it really," said Quilp with unusual politeness, "though I tell you what—and this is a circumstance worth bearing in mind as showing how the sharpest among us may be taken in sometimes—I was so deceived by the penurious way in which you lived, alone with Nelly—"

"All done to save money for tempting fortune, and make her triumph greater," cried the old man.

"Yes yes, I understand that now," said Quilp; "but I was going to say, I was so deceived by that, your miserly way, the reputation you had among those who knew you of being rich, and your repeated assurances that you would make of my advances treble and quadruple the interest you paid me, that I'd have advanced you even now what you want, on your simple note of hand, though I had been led to suspect something wrong, if I hadn't unexpectedly become acquainted with your secret way of life."

"Who is it," retorted the old man desperately, "that notwithstanding all my caution, told you that? Come. Let me know the name—the person."

The crafty dwarf, bethinking himself that his giving up the child would lead to the disclosure of the artifice he had employed, which, as nothing was to be gained by it, it was as well to conceal, stopped short in his answer and said, "Now, who do you think?"

"It was Kit, it must have been the boy; he played the spy and you tampered with him?" said the old man.

"How came you to think of him?" said the dwarf in a tone of great commiseration. "Yes, it was Kit. Poor Kit!"

So saying, he nodded in a friendly manner, and took his leave, stopping when he had passed the outer door a little distance, and grinning with extraordinary delight.

"Poor Kit!" muttered Quilp. "I think it was Kit who said I was an uglier dwarf than could be seen anywhere for a penny, wasn't it. Ha ha ha! Poor Kit!"

And with that he went his way, still chuckling as he went.

CHAPTER X

DANIEL Quilp neither entered nor left the old man's house, unobserved. In the shadow of an archway nearly opposite, leading to one of the many passages which diverged from the main street, there lingered one who having taken up his position when the twilight first came on, still maintained it with undiminished patience, and leaning against the wall with the manner of one who had a long time to wait, and being well used to it was quite resigned, scarcely changed his attitude for the hour together.

This patient lounger attracted little attention from any of those who passed, and bestowed as little upon them. His eyes were constantly directed towards one object, the window at which the child was accustomed to sit. If he withdrew them for a moment, it was only to glance at a clock in some neighbouring shop, and then to strain his sight once more in the old quarter with increased earnestness and attention.

It has been remarked that this personage evinced no weariness in his place of concealment, nor did he, long as his waiting was. But as the time went on, he manifested some anxiety and surprise, glancing at the clock more frequently and at the window less hopefully than before. At length the clock was hidden from his sight by some envious shutters, then the church steeples proclaimed eleven at night, then the quarter past, and then the conviction seemed to obtrude itself upon his mind that it was of no use tarrying there any longer.

That the conviction was an unwelcome one, and that he was by no means willing to yield to it, was apparent from his reluctance to quit the spot; from the tardy steps with which he often left it, still looking over his shoulder at the same window, and from the precipitation with which he as often returned, when a fancied noise or the changing and imperfect light induced him to suppose it had been softly raised. At length he gave the matter up as hopeless for that night, and suddenly breaking into a run as though to force himself away, scampered off at his utmost speed, nor once ventured to look behind him lest he should be tempted back again.

Without relaxing his pace or stopping to take breath, this mysterious individual dashed on through a great many alleys and narrow ways until he at length arrived in a square paved court, when he subsided into a walk, and making for a small house from the window of which a light was shining, lifted the latch of the door and passed in.

"Bless us!" cried a woman turning sharply round, "who's that? Oh! It's you, Kit!"

"Yes, mother, it's me."

"Why, how tired you look, my dear!"

"Old master an't gone out to-night," said Kit; "and so she hasn't been at the window at all." With which words, he sat down by the fire and looked very mournful and discontented.

The room in which Kit sat himself down in this condition was an extremely poor and homely place, but with that air of comfort about it, nevertheless, which—or the spot must be a wretched one indeed—cleanliness and order can always impart in some degree. Late as the Dutch clock showed it to be, the poor woman was still hard at work at an ironing-table; a young child lay sleeping in a cradle near the fire; and another, a sturdy boy of two or three years old, very wide awake, with a very tight night-cap on his head, and a night-gown very much too small for him on his body, was sitting bolt upright in a clothes-basket, staring over the rim with his great round eyes, and looking as if he had thoroughly made up his mind never to go to sleep any more; which, as he had already declined to take his natural rest and had been brought out of bed in consequence, opened a cheerful prospect for his relations and friends. It was rather a queer-looking family; Kit, his mother, and the children, being all strongly alike.

Kit was disposed to be out of temper, as the best of us are too often—but he looked at the youngest child who was sleeping soundly, and from him to his other brother in the clothes-basket, and from him to their mother, who had been at work without complaint since morning, and thought it would be a better and kinder thing to be good-humoured. So he rocked the cradle with his foot, made a face at the rebel in the clothes-basket, which put him in high good-humoured. So he rocked the cradle with his foot, made a face at the rebel in the clothes-basket, which put him in high good-humour directly, and stoutly determined to be talkative and make himself agreeable.

"Ah mother!" said Kit, taking out his clasp-knife and falling upon a great piece of bread piece of bread and meat which she had had ready for him, hours before, "what a one you are! There an't many such as you, I know."

"I hope there are many a great deal better, Kit," said Mrs. Nubbles; "and that there are, or ought to be, accordin' to what the parson at chapel says."

"Much *he* knows about it," returned Kit contemptuously. "Wait till he's a widder and works like you do, and gets as little, and does as much, and keeps his spirits up the same, and then I'll ask him what's o'clock and trust him for being right to half a second."

"Well," said Mrs. Nubbles, evading the point, "your beer's down there by the fender, Kit."

"I see," replied her son, taking up the porter pot, "my love to you, mother. And the parson's health too if you like. I don't bear him any malice, not I!"

"Did you tell me just now that your master hadn't gone out to-night?" inquired Mrs. Nubbles.

"Yes," said Kit, "worse luck."

"You should say better luck, I think," returned his mother, "because Miss Nelly won't have been left alone."

"Ah!" said Kit, "I forgot that. I said worse luck, because I've been watching ever since eight o'clock, and seen nothing of her."

"I wonder what she'd say," cried his mother, stopping in her work and looking round, "if she knew that every night, when she—poor thing—is sitting alone at that window, you are watching in the open street for fear any harm should come to her, and that you never leave the place or come home to your bed though you're ever so tired, till such time as you think she's safe in hers."

"Never mind what she'd say," replied Kit, with something like a blush on his uncouth face; "she'll never know nothing, and consequently, she'll never say nothing."

Mrs. Nubbles ironed away in silence for a minute or two, and coming to the fireplace for another iron, glanced stealthily at Kit while she rubbed it on a board and dusted it with a duster, but said nothing until she had returned to her table again, when holding the iron at an alarmingly short distance from her cheek, to test its temperature, and looking round with a smile, she observed:

"I know what some people would say, Kit—"

"Nonsense," interposed Kit with a perfect apprehension of what was to follow.

"No, but they would indeed. Some people would say that you'd fallen in love with her, I know they would."

To this Kit only replied by bashfully bidding his mother "get out," and forming sundry strange figures with his legs and arms, accompanied by sympathetic contortions of his face. Not deriving from these means the relief which he sought, he bit off an immense mouthful from the bread and meat, and took a quick drink of the porter, by which artificial aids he choked himself and effected a diversion of the subject.

"Speaking seriously though, Kit," said his mother taking up the theme afresh, after a time, "for of course I was only in joke just now, it's very good and thoughtful, and like you, to do this, and never let anybody know it, though some day I hope she may come to know it, for I'm sure she would be very grateful to you, and feel it very much. It's a cruel thing to keep the dear child shut up there. I don't wonder that the old gentleman wants to keep it from you."

"He don't think it's cruel, bless you," said Kit, "and don't mean it to be so, or he wouldn't do it—I do consider, mother, that he wouldn't do it for all the gold and silver in the world. No, no, that he wouldn't. I know him better than that."

"Then what does he do it for, and why does he keep it so close from you?" said Mrs. Nubbles.

"That I don't know," returned her son. "If he hadn't tried to keep it so close though, I should never have found it out, for it was his getting me away at night and sending me off so much earlier than he used to, that first made me curious to know what was going on. Hark! what's that?"

"It's only somebody outside."

"It's somebody crossing over here"—said Kit, standing up to listen, "and coming very fast too. He can't have gone out after I left, and the house caught fire, mother!"

The boy stood for a moment, really bereft, by the apprehension he had conjured up, of the power to move. The footsteps drew nearer, the door was opened with a hasty hand, and the child herself, pale and breathless, and hastily wrapped in a few disordered garments, hurried into the room.

"Miss Nelly! What is the matter!" cried mother and son together.

"I must not stay a moment," she returned, "grandfather has been taken very ill, I found him in a fit upon the floor—"

"I'll run for a doctor"—said Kit, seizing his brimless hat. "I'll be there directly, I'll—"

"No, no," cried Nell, "there is one there, you're not wanted you—you—you—must come near us any more!"

"What!" roared Kit.

"Never again," said the child. "Don't ask me why, for I don't know. Pray don't ask me why, pray don't be sorry, pray don't be vexed with me, I have nothing to do with it indeed!"

Kit looked at her with his eyes stretched wide, and opened and shut his mouth a great many times, but couldn't get out one word.

"He complains and raves of you," said the child, "I don't know what you have done, but I hope it's nothing very bad."

"*I* done!" roared Kit.

"He cries that you're the cause of all his misery," returned the child with tearful eyes; "he screamed and called for you, they say you must not come near him or he will die. You must not return to us any more. I came to tell you. I thought it would be better that I should come than somebody quite strange. Oh, Kit, what *have* you done? You, in whom I trusted so much, and who were almost the only friend I had!"

The unfortunate Kit looked at his young mistress harder and harder, and with eyes growing wider and wider, but was perfectly motionless and silent.

"I have brought his money for the week," said the child, looking to the woman and laying it on the table— "and—and—a little more, for he was always good and kind to me. I hope he will be sorry and do well some-where else and not take this to heart too much. It grieves me very much to part with him like this, but there is no help. It must be done. Good night!"

With the tears streaming down her face, and her slight figure trem-bling with the agitation of the scene she had left, the shock she had received, the errand she had just discharged, and a thousand painful and affectionate feelings, the child hastened to the door, and disappeared as rapidly as she had come.

The poor woman, who had no cause to doubt her son, but every rea-son for relying on his honesty and truth, was staggered, notwithstanding, by his not having advanced one word in his defence. Visions of gallantry, knavery, robbery; and of the nightly absences from home for which he had accounted so strangely, having been occasioned by some unlawful pursuit; flocked into her brain and rendered her afraid to question him. She rocked herself upon a chair, wringing her hands and weeping bitterly, but Kit made no attempt to comfort her and remained quite bewildered. The baby in the cradle woke up and cried, the boy in the clothes-basket fell over on his back with the basket upon him and was seen no more, the mother wept louder yet and rocked faster, but Kit, insensible to all the din and tumult, remained in a state of utter stupefaction.

CHAPTER XI

QUIET and solitude were destined to hold uninterrupted rule no longer, beneath the roof that sheltered the child. Next morning the old man was in a raging fever accompanied with delirium, and sinking under the influence of this disorder he lay for many weeks in imminent peril of his life. There was watching enough now, but it was the watching of strangers who made of it a greedy trade, and who, in the intervals of their attendance upon the sick man, huddled together with a ghastly good-fellowship, and ate and drank and made merry; for disease and death were their ordinary household gods.

Yet in all the hurry and crowding of such a time, the child was more alone than she had ever been before; alone in spirit, alone in her devotion to him who was wasting away upon his burning bed; alone in her unfeigned sorrow, and her unpurchased sympathy. Day after day, and night after night, found her still by the pillow of the unconscious sufferer, still antici-pating his every want, and still listening to those repetitions of her name and those anxieties and cares for her, which were ever uppermost among his feverish wanderings.

The house was no longer theirs. Even the sick chamber seemed to be retained on the uncertain tenure of Mr. Quilp's favour. The old man's ill-ness had not lasted many days when he took formal possession of the premises and all upon them, in virtue of certain legal powers to that effect, which few understood and none presumed to call in question. This important step secured, with the assistance of a man of law whom he brought with him for the purpose, the dwarf proceeded to establish himself and his coadjutor in the house, as an assertion of his claim against all comers; and then set about making his quarters comfortable after his own fashion.

To this end, Mr. Quilp encamped in the back parlour, having first put an effectual stop to any further business by shutting up the shop. Having looked out from among the old furniture the handsomest and most commodious chair he could possibly find, which he reserved for his own use, and an especially hideous and uncomfortable one, which he considerately appropriated to the accommodation of his friend, he caused them to be carried into this room and took up his position in great state. The apartment was very far removed from the old man's chamber, but Mr. Quilp deemed it prudent, as a precaution against infection from fever, and a means of wholesome fumigation, not only to smoke himself without cessation, but to insist upon it that his legal friend did the like. Moreover, he sent an express to the wharf for the tumbling boy, who arriving with all despatch was enjoined to sit himself down in another chair just inside the door, continually to smoke a great pipe which the dwarf had provided for the purpose, and to take it from his lips under any pretence whatever, were it only for one minute at a time, if he dared. These arrangements completed, Mr. Quilp looked around him with chuckling satisfaction, and remarked that he called that comfort.

The legal gentleman, whose melodious name was Brass, might have called it comfort also but for two drawbacks, one was that he could by no exertion sit easily in his chair, the seat of which was very hard, angular, slippery, and sloping; the other that tobacco-smoke always caused him great internal discomposure and annoyance. But as he was quite a creature of Mr. Quilp'a and had a thousand reasons for conciliating his good opinion, he tried to smile, and nodded his acquiescence with the best grace he could assume.

This Brass was an attorney of no very good repute from Bevis Marks in the City of London; he was a tall, meagre man, with a nose like a wen, a protuding forehead, retreating eyes, and hair of a deep red. He wore a long black surtout reaching nearly to his ankles, short black trousers, high shoes, and cotton stockings of a bluish grey. He had a cringing manner but a very harsh voice, and his blandest smiles were so extremely forbidding, that to have had his company under the least repulsive circumstances, one would have wished him to be out of temper that he might only scowl.

Quilp looked at his legal adviser, and seeing that he was winking very much in the anguish of his pipe, that he sometimes shuddered when he happened to inhale its full flavour, and that he constantly fanned the smoke from him, was quite overjoyed and rubbed his hands with glee.

"Smoke away, you dog," said Quilp turning to the boy; "fill your pipe again and smoke it fast, down to the boy; fill your pipe again and smoke it fast, down to the last whiff, or I'll put the sealing-waxed end of it in the fire and rub it red hot upon your tongue."

Luckily the boy was case-hardened, and would have smoked a small lime-kiln if anybody had treated him with it. Wherefore he only muttered a brief defiance of his master, and did as he was ordered. "Is it good, Brass, is it nice, is it fragant, do you feel like the Grand Turk?" said Quilp.

Mr. Brass thought that if he did, the Grand Turk's feelings were by no means to be envied, but he said it was famous, and he had no doubt he felt very like that Potentate.

"This is the way to keep off fever," said Quilp, "this is the way to keep off every calamity of life. We'll never leave off all the time we stop here—smoke away, you dog, or you shall swallow the pipe."

"Shall we stop here long, Mr. Quilp?" inquired his legal friend, when the dwarf had given his boy this last gentle admonition.

"We must stop, I suppose, till the old gentleman up stairs is dead," returned Quilp.

"He he he!" laughed Mr. Brass, "oh! very good!"

"Smoke away!" cried Quilp. "Never stop! you can talk as you smoke. Don't lose time."

"He he he!" cried Brass faintly, as he again applied himself to the odious pipe. "But if he should get better, Mr. Quilp?"

"Then we shall stop till he does, and no longer," returned the dwarf.

"How kind it is of you, sir, to wait till then!" said Brass. "Some people, sir, would have sold or removed the goods—oh dear, the very instant the law allowed 'em. Some people, sir, would have been all flintiness and granite. Some people, sir, would have—"

"Some people would have spared themselves the jabbering of such a parrot as you," interposed the dwarf.

"He he he!" cried Brass. "You have *such* spirits!"

The smoking sentinel at the door interposed in this place, and without taking his pipe from his lips, growled,

"Here's the gal a comin' down."

"The what, you dog?" said Quilp.

"The gal," returned the boy. "Are you deaf?"

"Oh!" said Quilp, drawing in his breath with great relish as if he were taking soup, "you and I will have such a settling presently; there's such a scratching and bruising in store for you, my dear young friend. Aha! Nelly! How is he now, my duck of diamonds?"

"He's very bad," replied the weeping child.

"What a pretty little Nell!" cried Quilp.

"Oh beautiful, sir, beautiful indeed," said Brass. "Quite charming!"

"Has she come to sit upon Quilp's knee," said the dwarf, in what he meant to be a soothing tone, "or is she going to bed in her own little room inside here—which is poor Nelly going to do?"

"What a remarkable pleasant way he has with children" muttered Brass, as if in confidence between himself and the ceiling; "upon my word it's quite a treat to hear him."

CHARLES DICKENS

"I'm not going to stay at all," faltered Nell. "I want a few things out of that room, and then I—I—won't come down here any more."

"And a very nice little room it is!" said the dwarf looking into it as the child entered. "Quite a bower. You're sure you're not going to use it, you're sure you're not coming back, Nelly?"

"No," replied the child, hurrying away, with the few articles of dress she had come to remove; "never again, never again."

"She's very sensitive," said Quilp, looking after her. "Very sensitive; that's a pity. The bedstead is much about my size. I think I shall make it *my* little room."

Mr. Brass encouraging this idea, as he would have encouraged any other emanating from the same source, the dwarf walked in to try the effect, which he did by throwing himself on his back upon the bed with his pipe in his mouth, and then kicking up his legs and smoking violently. Mr. Brass applauding this picture very much, and the bed being soft and comfortable, Mr. Quilp determined to use it, both as a sleeping place by night and as a kind of divan by day, and in order that it might be converted to the latter purpose at once, remained where he was and smoked his pipe out. The legal gentleman being by this time rather giddy and perplexed in his ideas (for this was one of the operations of the tobacco upon his nervous system), took the opportunity of slinking away into the open air where in course of time he recovered sufficiently to return with a countenance of tolerable composure. He was soon led on by the malicious dwarf to smoke himself into a relapse, and in that state stumbled upon a settee where he slept till morning.

Such were Mr. Quilp's first proceedings on entering upon his new property. He was for some days restrained by business from performing any particular pranks, as his time was pretty well occupied between taking, with the assistance of Mr. Brass, a minute inventory of all the goods in the place, and going abroad upon his other concerns which happily engaged him for several hours at a time. His avarice and caution being now thoroughly awakened, however, he was never absent from the house one night, and his eagerness for some termination, good or bad, to the old man's disorder, increasing rapidly as the time passed by, soon began to vent itself in open murmurs and exclamations of impatience.

Nell shrank timidly from all the dwarf's advances towards conversation and fled from the very sound of his voice, nor were the lawyer's smiles less terrible to her than Quilp's grimaces. She lived in such continual dread and apprehension of meeting one or other of them upon the stairs or in the passages if she stirred from her grandfather's chamber, that she seldom left it for a moment until late at night, when the silence encouraged her to venture forth and breathe the purer air of some empty room.

One night she had stolen to her usual window and was sitting there very sorrowfully, for the old man had been worse that day, when she thought that she heard her name pronounced by a voice in the street, and looking down, recognised Kit, whose endeavours to attract her attention had roused her from her sad reflections.

"Miss Nell!" said the boy in a low voice.

"Yes," replied the child, doubtful whether she ought to hold any communication with the supposed culprit, but inclining to her old favourite still, "what do you want?"

"I have wanted to say a word to you for a long time," the boy replied, "but the people below have driven me away and wouldn't let me see you. You don't believe—I hope you don't really believe—that I deserve to be cast off as I have been; do you, miss?"

"I must believe it," returned the child. "Or why would grandfather have been so angry with you?"

"I don't know," replied Kit. "I'm sure I've never deserved it from him, no, nor from you. I can say that with a true and honest heart any way. And then to be driven from the door, when I only came to ask how old master was—!"

"They never told me that," said the child. "I didn't know it indeed. I wouldn't have had them do it for the world."

"Thank'ee, miss," returned Kit, "it's comfortable to hear you say that. I said I never would believe that it was your doing."

"That was right!" said the child eagerly.

"Miss Nell," cried the boy, coming under the window and speaking in a lower tone, "there are new masters down stairs. It's a change for you."

"It is indeed," replied the child.

"And so it will be for him when he gets better," said the boy, pointing towards the sick room.

"—If he ever does," added the child, unable to restrain her tears.

"Oh, he'll do that, he'll do that," said Kit, "I'm sure he will. You mustn't be cast down, Miss Nell. Now don't be, pray."

These words of encouragement and consolation were few and roughly said, but they affected the child and made her for the moment weep the more.

"He'll be sure to get better now," said the boy anxiously, "if you don't give way to low spirits and turn ill yourself, which would make him worse and throw him back just as he was recovering. When he does, say a good word—say a kind word for me, Miss Nell."

"They tell me I must not even mention your name to him for a long, long time," rejoined the child. "I dare not; and even if I might, what good would a kind word do you, Kit? We shall be very poor. We shall scarcely have bread to eat."

"It's not that I may be taken back," said the boy, "that I ask the favour of you. It isn't for the sake of food and wages that I've been waiting about so long in hopes to see you. Don't think that I'd come in a time of trouble to talk of such things as them."

The child looked gratefully and kindly at him, but waited that he might speak again.

"No, it's not that," said Kit hesitating, "it's something very different from that. I haven't got much sense I know, but if he could be brought to believe that I'd been a faithful servant to him, doing the best I could, and never meaning harm, perhaps he mightn't—"

Here Kit faltered so long that the child entreated him to speak out, and quickly, for it was very late, and time to shut the window.

"Perhaps he mightn't think it over venturesome of me to say—well then, to say this,"—cried Kit with sudden boldness. "This home is gone from you and him. Mother and I have got a poor one, but that's better than this with all these people here; and why not come there, till he's had time to look about and find a better!"

The child did not speak. Kit, in the relief of having made his proposition, found his tongue loosened, and spoke out in its favour with his utmost eloquence.

"You think," said the boy, "that it's very small and inconvenient. So it is, but it's very clean. Perhaps you think it would be noisy, but there's not a quieter court than ours in all the town. Don't be afraid of the children; the baby hardly ever cries, and the other one is very good—besides, I'd mind 'em. They wouldn't vex you much, I'm sure. Do try, Miss Nell, do try. The little front room up stairs is very pleasant. You can see a piece of the church-clock through the chimneys and almost tell the time; mother says it would be just the thing for you, and so it would, and you'd have her to wait upon you both, and me to run of errands. We don't want money, bless you; you're not to think of that. Will you try him, Miss Nell? Only say you'll try him. Do try to make old master come, and ask him first what I have done—will you only promise that, Miss Nell?"

Before the child could reply to this earnest solicitation, the street-door opened, and Mr. Brass thrusting out his night-capped head called in a surly voice, "Who's there!" Kit immediately glided away, and Nell, closing the window softly, drew back into the room.

Before Mr. Brass had repeated his inquiry many times, Mr. Quilp, also embellished with a night-cap, emerged from the same door and looked carefully up and down the street, and up at all the windows of the house from the opposite side. Finding that there was nobody in sight he presently returned into the house with his legal friend, protesting (as the child heard from the staircase) that there was a league and plot against him, that he was in danger of being robbed and plundered by a band of conspirators who prowled about the house at all seasons, and that he would delay no longer but take immediate steps for disposing of the property and returning to his own peaceful roof. Having growled forth these and a great many other threats of the same nature, he coiled himself once more in the child's little bed, and Nell crept softly up the stairs.

It was natural enough that her short and unfinished dialogue with Kit should leave a strong impression on her mind, and influence her dreams that night and her recollections for a long, long time. Surrounded by unfeeling creditors, and mercenary attendants upon the sick, and meeting in the height of her anxiety and sorrow with little regard or sympathy even from the women about her, it is not surprising that the affectionate heart of the child should have been touched to the quick by one kind and generous spirit, however uncouth the temple in which it dwelt. Thank Heaven that the temples of such spirits are not made with hands, and that they may be more worthily hung with poor patchwork than with purple and fine linen!

CHAPTER XII

AT length the crisis of the old man's disorder was past, and he began to mend. By very slow and feeble degrees his consciousness came back, but the mind was weakened and its functions were impaired. He was patient, and quiet; often sat brooding, but not despondently, for a long space; was easily amused, even by a sunbeam on the wall or ceiling; made no complaint that the days were long or the nights tedious; and appeared indeed to have lost all count of time and every sense of care or weariness. He would sit for hours together with Nell's small hand in his, playing with the fingers and stopping sometimes to smooth her hair or kiss her brow; and when he saw that tears were glistening in her eyes would look, amazed, about him for the cause, and forget his wonder even while he looked.

The child and he rode out: the old man propped up with pillows, and the child beside him. They were hand in hand as usual. The noise and motion in the streets fatigued his brain at first, but he was not surprised, or curious, or pleased, or irritated. He was asked if he remembered this, or that. "Oh yes," he said, "quite well—why not?" Sometimes he turned his head and looked with earnest gaze and outstretched neck, after some stranger in the crowd, until he disappeared from sight; but, to the question why he did this, he answered not a word.

He was sitting in his easy chair one day, and Nell upon a stool beside him, when a man outside the door inquired if he might enter. "Yes," he said without emotion, "it was Quilp, he knew. Quilp was master there. Of course he might come in." And so he did.

"I'm glad to see you well again at last, neighbour," said the dwarf, raising his voice, for the old man's senses were duller than they had been; "but, as soon as you *can* arrange your future proceedings, the better."

"Surely," said the old man. "The better for all parties."

"You see," pursued Quilp after a short pause, "the goods being once removed, this house would be uncomfortable; uninhabitable in fact."

"You say true," returned the old man. "Poor Nell, too, what would *she* do?"

"Exactly," bawled the dwarf nodding his head; "that's very well observed. Then will you consider about it neighbour?"

"I will certainly," replied the old man. "We shall not stop here."

"So I supposed," said the dwarf. "I have sold the things. They have not yielded quite as much as they might have done, but pretty well—pretty well. To-day's Tuesday. When shall they be moved? There's no hurry—shall we say this afternoon?"

"Say Friday morning," returned the old man.

"Very good," said the dwarf. "So be it,—with the understanding that I can't go beyond that day, neighbour, on any account."

"Good," returned the old man. "I shall remember it."

Mr. Quilp seemed rather puzzled by the strange, even spiritless way in which all this was said; but as the old man nodded his head and repeated "on Friday morning. I shall remember it," he had no excuse for dwelling upon the subject any further, and so took a friendly leave with many expressions of good-will and many compliments to his friend on his looking so remarkably well; and went below stairs to report progress to Mr. Brass.

All that day, and all the next, the old man remained in this state. He wandered up and down the house and into and out of the various rooms, as if with some vague intent of bidding them adieu, but he referred neither by direct allusions nor in any other manner to the interview of the morning or the necessity of finding some other shelter. An indistinct idea he had, that the child was desolate and in want of help, for he often drew her to his bosom and bade her be of good cheer, saying that they would not desert each other; but he seemed unable to contemplate their real position more distinctly, and was still the listless, passionless creature, that suffering of mind and body had left him.

We call this a state of childishness, but it is the same poor hollow mockery of it, that death is of sleep. Where, in the dull eyes of doating men, are the laughing light and life of childhood, the gaiety that has known no check, the frankness that has felt no chill, the hope that has never withered, the joys that fade in blossoming? Where, in the sharp lineaments of rigid and unsightly death, is the calm beauty of slumber, telling of rest for the waking hours that are past, and the gentle hopes and loves for those which are to come? Lay death and sleep down, side by side, and say who shall find the two akin. Send forth the child and childish man together, and blush for the pride that libels our own old happy state, and gives its little to an ugly and distorted image.

Thursday arrived, and there was no alteration in the old man. But, a change came upon him that evening, as he and the child sat silently together.

In a small dull yard below his window, there was a tree—green and flourishing enough, for such a place—and as the air stirred among its leaves, it threw a rippling shadow on the white wall. The old man sat watching the shadows as they trembled in this patch of light until the sun went down, and when it was night and the moon was slowly rising he still sat in the same spot.

To one who had been tossing on a restless bed so long, even these few green leaves and this tranquil light, although it languished among chimneys and house-tops, were pleasant things. They suggested quiet places afar off, and rest, and peace.

The child thought more than once that he was moved, and had forborne to speak. But now he shed tears—tears that it lightened her aching heart to see—and making as though he would fall upon his knees, besought her to forgive him.

"Forgive you—what?" said Nell, interposing to prevent his purpose. "Oh grandfather, what should *I* forgive?"

"All that is past, all that has come upon thee, Nell, all that was done in that uneasy dream," returned the old man.

"Do not talk so," said the child. "Pray do not. Let us speak of something else."

"Yes, yes, we will," he rejoined. "And it shall be of what we talked of long ago—many months—months is it, or weeks, or days? which is it, Nell?"

"I do not understand you," said the child.

"It has come back upon me to-day, it has all come back since we have been sitting here. I bless thee for it, Nell!"

"For what, dear grandfather?"

"For what you said when we were first made beggars, Nell. Let us speak softly. Hush! for if they knew our purpose down stairs, they would cry that I was mad and take thee from me. We will not stop here another day. We will go far away, from here."

"Yes, let us go," said the child earnestly. "Let us begone from this place, and never turn back or think of it again. Let us wander barefoot through the world, rather than linger here."

"We will," answered the old man, "we will travel afoot through fields and woods, and by the side of rivers, and trust ourselves to God in the places where He dwells. It is far better to lie down at night beneath an open sky like that yonder—see how bright it is—than to rest in close rooms which are always full of care and weary dreams. Thou and I together, Nell, may be cheerful and happy yet, and learn to forget this time, as if it had never been."

"We will be happy," cried the child. "We never can be here."

"No, we never can again—never again—that's truly said," rejoined the old man. "Let us steal away tomorrow morning—early and softly, that we may not be seen or heard—and leave no trace or track for them to follow by. Poor Nell, thy cheek is pale and thy eyes are heavy with watching and weeping—with watching and weeping for me—I know—for me; but thou wilt be well again, and merry too, when we are far away. To-morrow morning, dear, we'll turn our faces from this scene of sorrows, and be as free and happy as the birds."

And then the old man clasped his hands above her head, and said in a few broken words that from that time forth they would wander up and down together, and never part more until Death took one or other of the twain.

The child's heart beat high with hope and confidence. She had no thought of hunger or cold, or thirst, or suffering. She saw in this, but a return of the simple pleasures they had once enjoyed, a relief from the gloomy solitude in which she had lived, an escape from the heartless people by whom she had been surrounded in her late time of trial, the restoration of the old man's health and peace, and a life of tranquil happiness. Sun, and stream, and meadow, and summer days, shone brightly in her view, and there was no dark tint in all the sparkling picture.

The old man had slept for some hours soundly in his bed, and she was yet busily engaged in preparing for their flight. There were a few articles of clothing for herself to carry, and a few for him; old garments, such as became their fallen fortunes, laid out to wear; and a staff to support his feeble steps, put ready for his use. But this was not all her task, for now she must visit the old rooms for the last time.

And how different the parting with them was from any she had expected, and most of all from that which she had oftenest pictured to herself. How could she ever have thought of bidding them farewell in triumph, when the recollection of the many hours she had passed among them rose to her swelling heart, and made her feel the wish a cruelty, lonely and sad though many of those hours had been! She sat down at the window where she had spent so many evenings—darker far than this—and every thought of hope or cheerfulness that had occurred to her in that place came vividly upon her mind, and blotted out all its dull and mournful associations in an instant.

Her own little room, too, where she had so often knelt down and prayed at night—prayed for the time which she hoped was dawning now—the little room where she had slept so peacefully, and dreamed such pleasant dreams—it was hard not to be able to glance round it once more, and to be forced to leave it without one kind look or grateful tear. There were some trifles there—poor useless things—that she would have liked to take away; but that was impossible.

This brought to mind her bird, her poor bird, who hung there yet. She wept bitterly for the loss of this little creature—until the idea occurred to her—she did not know how or why it came into her head—that it might by some means fall into the hands of Kit who would keep it for her sake, and think perhaps that she had left it behind in the hope that he might have it, and as an assurance that she was grateful to him. She was calm and comforted by the thought, and went to rest with a lighter heart.

From many dreams of rambling through light and sunny places, but with some vague object unattained which ran indistinctly through them all, she awoke to find that it was yet night, and that the stars were shining brightly in the sky. At length the day began to glimmer, and the stars to grow pale and dim. As soon as she was sure of this, she arose, and dressed herself for the journey.

The old man was yet asleep, and as she was unwilling to disturb him, she left him to slumber on until the sun rose. He was anxious that they should leave the house without a minute's loss of time, and was soon ready.

The child then took him by the hand, and they trod lightly and cautiously down the stairs, trembling whenever a board creaked, and often stopping to listen. The old man had forgotten a kind of wallet which contained the light burden he had to carry, and the going back a few steps to fetch it seemed an interminable delay.

At last they reached the passage on the ground floor, where the snoring of Mr. Quilp and his legal friend sounded more terrible in their ears than the roars of lions. The bolts of the door were rusty, and difficult to unfasten without noise. When they were all drawn back it was found to be locked, and, worst of all, the key was gone. Then the child remembered for the first time one of the nurses having told her that Quilp always locked both the house-doors at night, and kept the keys on the table in his bedroom.

It was not without great fear and trepidation that little Nell slipped off her shoes and gliding through the store-room of old curiosities, where Mr. Brass—the ugliest piece of goods in all the stock—lay sleeping on a mattress, passed into her own little chamber.

Here she stood for a few moments quite transfixed with terror at the sight of Mr. Quilp, who was hanging so far out of bed that he almost seemed to be standing on his head, and who, either from the uneasiness of this posture or in one of his agreeable habits, was gasping and growling with his mouth wide open, and the whites (or rather the dirty yellows) of his eyes distinctly visible. It was no time, however, to ask whether anything ailed him, so possessing herself of the key after one hasty glance about the room, and repassing the postrate Mr. Brass, she rejoined the old man in safety. They got the door open without noise, and passing into the street, stood still.

"Which way?" said the child.

The old man looked, irresolutely and helplessly, first at her, then to the right and left, then at her again, and shook his head. It was plain that she was thenceforth his guide and leader. The child felt it, but had no doubts or misgiving, and putting her hand in his, led him gently away.

It was the beginning of a day in June; the deep blue sky unsullied by a cloud, and teeming with brilliant light. The streets were as yet nearly free from passengers, the houses and shops were closed, and the healthful air of morning fell like breath from angels, on the sleeping town.

The old man and the child passed on through the glad silence, elate with hope and pleasure. They were alone together once again; every object was bright and fresh; nothing reminded them, otherwise than by contrasts, of the monotony and constraint they had left behind; church towers and steeples, frowning and dark at other times, now shone and dazzled in the sun; each humble nook and corner rejoiced in light; and the sky, dimmed by excessive distance, sheds its placid smile on everything beneath.

Forth from the city, while it yet slumbered, went the two poor adventurers, wandering they knew not whither.

CHAPTER XIII

DANIEL Quilp of Tower Hill, and Sampson Brass of Bevis Marks in the city of London, Gentleman, one of her Majesty's attornies of the Courts of King's Bench and Common Pleas at Westminster and a solicitor of the High Court of Chancery, slumbered on unconscious and unsuspicious of any mischance, until a knocking at the street-door, often repeated and gradually mounting up from a modest single rap into a perfect battery of knocks, fired in long discharged with a very short interval between, caused the said Daniel Quilp to struggle into a horizontal position, and to stare at the ceiling with a drowsy indifference, betokening that he heard the noise and rather wondered at the same, but couldn't be at the trouble of bestowing any further thought upon the subject.

As the knocking, however, instead of accomodating itself to his lazy state, increased in vigour and became more importunate, as if in earnest remonstrance against his falling asleep again now that he had once opened his eyes, Daniel Quilp began by degrees to comprehend the possibility if there being somebody at the door, and thus he gradually came to recollect that it was Friday morning, and he had ordered Mrs. Quilp to be in waiting upon him at an early hour.

Mr. Brass, and often twisting his face and eyes into an expression like that which is usually produced by eating gooseberries very early in the season, was by this time awake also, and seeing that Mr. Quilp invested himself in his every-day garments, hastened to do the like, putting on his shoes before his stockings, and thrusting his legs into his coat sleeves, and making such other small mistakes in his toilet as are not uncommon to those who dress in a hurry, and labour under the agitation of having been suddenly roused.

While the attorney was thus engaged, the dwarf was groping under the table, muttering desperate imprecations upon himself and mankind in general and all inanimate objects to boot, which suggested to Mr. Brass the question "what's the matter?"

"The key," said the dwarf, looking viciously at him, "the door-key,—that's the matter. D'ye know anything of it?"

"How should I know anything of it, sir?" returned Mr. Brass.

"How should you?" repeated Quilp with a sneer. "You're a nice lawyer, an't you. Ugh, you idiot!"

Not caring to represent to the dwarf in his present humour, that the loss of a key by another person could scarcely be said to affect his (Brass's) legal knowledge in any material degree, Mr. Brass humbly suggested that it must have been forgotten over night, and was doubtless at that moment in its native key-hole. Notwithstanding that Mr. Quilp had a strong conviction to the contrary, founded on his recollection of having carefully taken it out, he was fain to admit that this was possible, and therefore went grumbling to the door where, sure enough, he found it.

Now, just as Mr. Quilp laid his hand upon the lock and saw with great astonishment that the fastenings were undone, the knocking came again with most irritating violence, and the daylight which had been shining through the key-hole was intercepted on the outside by a human eye. The dwarf was very much exasperated, and wanting somebody to wreak his ill-humour upon, determined to dart out suddenly and favour Mrs. Quilp with a gentle acknowledgment of her attention in making that hideous uproar.

With this view he drew back the lock very silently and softly, and opening the door all at once, pounced out upon the person on the other side, who had at that moment raised the knocker for another application, and at whom the dwarf ran head first, throwing out his hands and feet together, and biting the air in the fulness of his malice.

So far, however, from rushing upon somebody who offered no resistance and implored his mercy, Mr. Quilp was no sooner in the arms of the individual whom he had taken for his wife than he found himself complimented with two staggering blows on the head, and two more, of the same quality, in the chest, and closing with his assailant, such a shower of buffets rained down upon his person as sufficed to convince him that he was in skilful and experienced hands. Nothing daunted by this reception, he clung tight to his opponent, and bit and hammered away with such good-will and heartiness, that it was at least a couple of minutes before he was dislodged. Then, and not until then, Daniel Quilp found himself, all flushed and dishevelled, in the middle of the street, with Mr. Richard Swiveller performing a kind of dance round him and requiring to know "whether he wanted any more?"

"There's plenty more of it at the same shop," said Mr. Swiveller, by turns advancing and retreating in a threatening attitude, "a large and extensive assortment always on hand—country orders executed with promptitude and despatch—will you have a little more, sir—don't say no, if you'd rather not."

"I thought it was somebody else," said Quilp rubbing his shoulders, "why didn't you say who you were?"

"Why didn't you say who *you* were?" returned Dick, "instead of flying out of the house like a Bedlamite?"

"It was you that—that knocked," said the dwarf, getting up with a short groan, "was it?"

"Yes, I am the man," replied Dick. "That lady had begun when I came, but she knocked too soft, so I relieved her." As he said this, he pointed towards Mrs. Quilp, who stood trembling at a little distance.

"Humph!" muttered the dwarf, darting an angry look at his wife, "I thought it was your fault! And you, sir—don't you know there has been somebody ill here, that you knock as if you'd beat the door down?"

"Damme!" answered Dick, "that's why I did it. I thought there was somebody dead here."

"You came for some purpose, I suppose," said Quilp. "What is it you want?"

"I want to know how the old gentleman is," rejoined Mr. Swiveller, "and to hear from Nell herself, with whom I should like to have a little talk. I'm a friend of the family, sir,—at least I'm the friend of one of the family, and that's the same thing."

"You'd better walk in then," said the dwarf. "Go on, sir, go on. Now, Mrs. Quilp—after you, ma'am."

Mrs. Quilp hesitated, but Mr. Quilp insisted. And it was not a contest of politeness, or by any means a matter of form, for she knew very well that her husband wished to enter the house in this order, that he might have a favourable opportunity of inflicting a few pinches on her arms, which were seldom free from impressions of his fingers in black and blue colours. Mr. Swiveller, who was not in the secret, was a little surprised to hear a suppressed scream, and, looking round, to see Mrs. Quilp following him with a sudden jerk; but he did not remark on these appearances, and soon forgot them.

"Now, Mrs. Quilp," said the dwarf when they had entered the shop, "go you upstairs, if you please, to Nelly's room, and tell her that she's wanted."

"You seem to make yourself at home here," said Dick, who was acquainted with Mr. Quilp's authority.

"I *am* at home, young gentleman," returned the dwarf.

Dick was pondering what these words might mean, and still more what the presence of Mr. Brass might mean, when Mrs. Quilp came hurrying down stairs, declaring that the rooms above were empty.

"Empty, you fool!" said the dwarf.

"I give you my word, Quilp," answered his trembling wife, "that I have been into every room and there's not a soul in any of them."

"And that," said Mr. Brass, clapping his hands once, with an emphasis, "explains the mystery of the key!"

Quilp looked frowningly at him, and frowningly at his wife, and frowningly at Richard Swiveller; but, receiving no enlightenment from any of them, hurried up stairs, whence he soon hurried down again, confirming the report which had been already made.

"It's a strange way of going," he said, glancing at Swiveller, "very strange not to communicate with me who am such a close and intimate friend of his! Ah! he'll write to me no doubt, or he'll bid Nelly write—yes, yes, that's what he'll do. Nelly's very fond of me. Pretty Nell!"

Mr. Swiveller looked, as he was, all open-mouthed astonishment. Still glancing furtively at him, Quilp turned to Mr. Brass and observed with assumed carelessness, that this need not interfere with the removal of the goods.

"For indeed," he added, "we knew that they'd go away to-day, but not that they'd go so early or so quietly. But they have their reasons, they have their reasons."

"Where in the devil's name are they gone?" said the wondering Dick.

Quilp shook his head and pursued up his lips, in a manner which implied that he knew very well, but was not at liberty to say.

"And what," said Dick, looking at the confusion about him, "what do you mean by moving the goods?"

"That I have bought 'em sir," rejoined Quilp. "Eh? What then?"

"Has the sly old fox made his fortune then, and gone to live in a tranquil cot in a pleasant spot with a distant view of the changing sea?" said Dick, in great bewilderment.

"Keeping his place of retirement very close, that he may not be visited too often by affectionate grandsons and their devoted friends, eh?" added the dwarf, rubbing his hands hard; "*I* say nothing, but is that your meaning, sir?"

Richard Swiveller was utterly aghast at this unexpected alteration of circumstances, which threatened the complete overthrow of the project in which he bore so conspicuous a part, and seemed to nip his prospects in the bud. Having only received from Frederick Trent, late on the previous night, information of the old man's illness, he had come upon a visit of condolence and inquiry to Nell, prepared with the first instalment of that long train of fascinations which was to fire her heart at last. And here, when he had been thinking of all kinds of graceful and insinuating approaches, and meditating on the fearful retaliation which was slowly working against Sophy Wackles—here were Nell, the old man, and all the money gone, melted away, decamped he knew not whither, as if with a fore-knowledge of the scheme and a resolution to defeat it in the very outset, before a step was taken.

In his secret heart, Daniel Quilp was both surprised and troubled by the flight which had been made. It had not escaped his keen eye that some indispensable articles of clothing were gone with the fugitives, and knowing the old man's weak state of mind, he marvelled what that course of proceeding might be in which he had so readily procured the concurrence of the child. It must not be supposed (or it would be a gross injustice to Mr. Quilp) that he was tortured by any disinterested anxiety on behalf of either. His uneasiness arose from a misgiving that the old man had some secret store of money which he had not suspected, and the bare idea of its escaping his clutches, overwhelmed him with mortification and self-reproach.

In this frame of mind, it was some consolation to him to find that Richard Swiveller was, for different reasons, evidently irritated and disappointed by the same cause. It was plain, thought the dwarf, that he had come there on behalf of his friend to cajole or frighten the old man out of some small fraction of that wealth of which they supposed him to have an abundance. Therefore it was a relief to vex his heart with a picture of the riches the old man hoarded, and to expatiate on his cunning in removing himself even beyond the reach of importunity.

"Well," said Dick, with a blank look, "I suppose it's of no use my staying here."

"Not the least in the world," rejoined the dwarf.

"You'll mention that I called, perhaps?" said Dick.

Mr. Quilp nodded, and said he certainly would, the very first time he saw them.

"And say," added Mr. Swiveller, "say, sir, that I was wafted here upon the pinions of concord; that I came to remove, with the rake of friendship, the seeds of mutual wiolence and heart-burning, and to sow in their place, the germs of social harmony. Will you have the goodness to charge yourself with that commission, sir?"

"Certainly!" rejoined Quilp.

"Will you be kind enough to add to it, sir," said Dick, producing a very small limp card, "that *that* is my address, and that I am to be found at home every morning. Two distinct knocks, sir, will produce the slavey at any time. My particular friends, sir, are accustomed to sneeze when the door is opened, to give her to understand that they *are* my friends and have no interested motives in asking if I'm at home. I beg your pardon; will you allow me to look at that card again?"

"Oh! by all means," rejoined Quilp.

"By a slight and not unnatural mistake, sir," said Dick, substituting another in its stead, "I had handed you the pass-ticket of a select convival circle called the Glorious Apollers, of which I have the honour to be Perpetual Grand. That is the proper document, sir. Good morning."

Quilp bade him good day; the Perpetual Grand Master of the Glorious Apollers, elevating his hat in honour of Mrs. Quilp, dropped it carelessly on the side of his head again, and disappeared with a flourish.

By this time certain vans had arrived for the conveyance of the goods, and divers strong men in carpet caps were balancing chests of drawers and other trifles of that nature upon their heads, and performing muscular feats which heightened their complexions considerably. Not to be behind-hand in the bustle, Mr. Quilp went to work with surprising vigour; hustling and driving the people about, like an evil spirit; setting Mrs. Quilp upon all kinds of arduous and impracticable tasks; carrying great weights up and down with no apparent effort; kicking the boy from the wharf whenever he could get near him; and inflicting with his loads a great many sly bumps and blows upon the shoulders of Mr. Brass, as he stood upon the door-steps to answer all the inquiries of curious neighbours, which was his department. His presence and example diffused such alacrity among the persons employed, that in a few hours the house was emptied of everything, but pieces of matting, empty porter-pots, and scattered fragments of straw.

Seated, like an African chief, on one of these pieces of matting, the dwarf was regaling himself in the parlour with bread and cheese and beer, when he observed, without appearing to do so, that a boy was prying in at the outer door. Assured that it was Kit, though he saw little more than his nose, Mr. Quilp hailed him by his name; whereupon Kit came in and demanded what he wanted.

"Come here, you sir," said the dwarf. "Well, so your old master and young mistress have gone?"

"Where?" rejoined Kit, looking round.

"Do you mean to say you don't know where?" answered Quilp sharply. "Where have they gone, eh?"

"I don't know," said Kit.

"Come," retorted Quilp, "let's have no more of this! Do you mean to say that you don't know they went away by stealth, as soon as it was light this morning?"

"No," said the boy, in evident surprise.

"You don't know that?" cried Quilp. "Don't I know that you were hanging about the house the other night, like a thief, eh? Weren't you told then?"

"No," replied the boy.

"You were not?" said Quilp. "What were you told then; what were you talking about?"

Kit, who knew no particular reason why he should keep the matter secret now, related the purpose for which he had come on that occasion, and the proposal he had made.

"Oh!" said the dwarf after a little consideration. "Then, I think they'll come to you yet."

"Do you think they will?" cried Kit eagerly.

"Ay, I think they will," returned the dwarf. "Now, when they do, let me know; d'ye hear? Let me know, and I can't do 'em a kindness unless I know where they are. You hear what I say?"

Kit might have returned some answer which would not have been agreeable to his irascible questioner, if the boy from the wharf, who had been skulking about the room in search of anything that might have been left about by accident, had not happened to cry, "Here's a bird! What's to be done with this?"

"Wring its neck," rejoined Quilp.

"Oh no, don't do that," said Kit, stepping forward. "Give it to me."

"Oh yes, I dare say," cried the other boy. "Come! You let the cage alone, and let me wring its neck, will you? He said I was to do it. You let the cage alone, will you?"

"Give it here, give it to me, you dogs," roared Quilp. "Fight for it, you dogs, or I'll wring its neck myself!"

Without further persuasion, the two boys fell upon each other tooth and nail, while Quilp, holding up the cage in one hand, and chopping the ground with his knife in an ecstasy, urged them on by his taunts and cries to fight more fiercely. They were a pretty equal match, and rolled about together, exchanging blows which were by no means child's play, until at length Kit, planting a well-directed hit in his adversary's chest, disengaged himself, sprang nimbly up, and snatching the cage from Quilp's hands made off with his prize.

He did not stop once until he reached home, where his bleeding face occasioned great consternation, and caused the elder child to howl dreadfully.

"Goodness gracious, Kit, what is the matter, what have you been doing?" cried Mrs. Nubbles.

"Never you mind, mother," answered her son, wiping his face on the jack-towel behind the door. "I'm not hurt, don't you be afraid for me. I've been a fightin' for a bird and won him, that's all. Hold your noise, little Jacob. I never see such a naughty boy in all my days!"

"You have been fighting for a bird!" exclaimed his mother.

"Ah! Fightin' for a bird!" replied Kit, "and here he is—Miss Nelly's bird, mother, that they was a goin' to wring the neck of! I stopped that though—ha ha ha! They wouldn't wring his neck and me by, no no. It wouldn't do, mother, it wouldn't do at all. Ha ha ha!"

Kit laughed so heartily, with his swoln and bruised face looking out of the towel, made little Jacob laugh, and then his mother laughed, and then the baby crowed and kicked with great glee, and then they all laughed in concert, partly because of Kit's triumph, and partly because they were very fond of each other. When this fit was over, Kit exhibited the bird to both children, as a great and precious wall for an old nail, made a scaffolding of a chair and table and twisted it out with great exultation.

"Let me see," said the boy, "I think I'll hang him in the winder, because it's more light and cheerful, and he can see the sky there, if he looks up very much. He's such a one to sing, I can tell you!"

So, the scaffolding was made again, and Kit, climbing up with the poker for a hammer, knocked in the nail and hung up the cage, to the immeasurable delight of the whole family. When it had been adjusted and straightened a good many times, and he had walked backwards into the fireplace in his admiration of it, the arrangement was pronounced to be perfect.

"And now, mother," said the boy, "before I rest any more, I'll go out and see if I can find a horse to hold, and then I can buy some birdseed, and a bit of something nice for you, into the bargain."

CHAPTER XIV

AS it was very easy for Kit to persuade himself that the old house was in his way, his way being anywhere, he tried to look upon his passing it once more as a matter of imperative and disagreeable necessity, quite apart from any desire of his own, to which he could not choose but yield. It is uncommon for people who are much better fed and taught that Christopher Nubbles had ever been, to make duties of their inclinations in matters of more doubtful propriety, and to take great credit for the self-denial with which they gratify themselves.

There was no need of any caution this time and no fear of being detained by having to play out a return match with Daniel Quilp's boy. The place was entirely deserted, and looked as dusty and dingy as if it had been so for months. A rusty padlock was fastened on the door, ends of discoloured blinds and curtains flapped drearily against the half-opened upper windows, and the crooked holes cut in the closed shutters below, were black with the darkness of the inside. Some of the glass in the window he had so often watched, had been broken in the rough hurry of the morning, and that room looked more deserted and dull than any. A group of idle urchins had taken possession of the door-steps; some were plying the knocker and listening with delighted dread to the hollow sounds it spread through the dismantled house; others were clustered about the key-hole, watching half in jest and half in earnest for "the ghost," which an hour's gloom, added to the mystery that hung about the late inhabitants, had already raised. Standing all alone in the midst of the business and bustle of the street, the house looked a picture of cold desolation; and Kit, who remembered the cheerful fire that used to burn there on winter's night and the no less cheerful laugh that made the small room ring, turned quite mournfully away.

It must be specially observed in justice to poor Kit that he was by no means of a sentimental turn, and perhaps had never heard that adjective in all his life. He was only a soft-hearted grateful fellow, and had nothing genteel or polite about him; consequently instead of going home again in his grief to kick the children and abuse his mother (for when you finely strung people are out of sorts they must have everybody else unhappy likewise), he turned his thoughts to the vulgar expedient of making them more comfortable if he could.

Bless us, what a number of gentlemen of horseback there were riding up and down, and how few of them wanted their horses held! A good city speculator or a parliamentary commissioner could have told to a fraction, from the crowds that were cantering about, what sum of money was realised in London in the course of a year, by holding horses alone. And undoubtedly it would have been a very large one, if only a twentieth part of the gentlemen without grooms had had occasion to alight; but they hadn't; and it is often an ill-natured circumstance like this, which spoils the most ingenious estimate in the world.

Kit walked about, now with quick step and now with slow; now lingering as some rider slackened his horse's pace and looked about him; and now darting at full speed up a bye-street as he caught a glimpse of some distant horseman going lazily up the shady side of the road, and promising to stop, at every door. But on they all went, one after another, and there was not a penny stirring. "I wonder," thought the boy, "if one of these gentlemen knew there was nothing in the cupboard at home, whether he'd stop on purpose, and make believe that he wanted to call somewhere, that I might earn a trifle?"

He was quite tired out with pacing the streets, to say nothing of repeated disappointments, and was sitting down upon a step to rest, when there approached towards him a little clattering jingling four-wheeled chaise, drawn by a little obstinate-looking rough-coated pony, and driven by a little fat placid-faced old gentleman. Beside the little old gentleman sat a little old lady, plump and placid like himself, and the pony was coming along at his own pace and doing exactly as he pleased with the whole concern. If the old gentleman remonstrated by shaking the reins, the pony replied by shaking his head. It was plain that the utmost the pony would consent to do, was to go in his own way up any street that the old gentleman particularly wished to traverse, but that it was an understanding between them that he must do this after his own fashion or not at all.

As they passed where he sat Kit looked so wistfully at the little turn-out that the old gentleman looked at him, and Kit rising and putting his hand to his hat, the old gentleman intimated to the pony that he wished to stop, to which proposal the pony (who seldom objected to that part of his duty) graciously acceded.

"I beg your pardon, sir," said Kit. "I'm sorry you stopped, sir. I only meant did you want your horse minded."

"I'm going to get down in the next street," returned the old gentleman. "If you like to come on after us, you may have the job."

Kit thanked him, and joyfully obeyed. The pony ran off at a sharp angle to inspect a lamp-post on the opposite side of the way, and then went off at a tangent to another lamp-post on the other side. Having satisfied himself that they were of the same pattern and materials, he came to a stop, apparently absorbed in meditation.

"Will you go on, sir?" said the old gentleman, gravely, "or are we to wait here for you till it's too late for our appointment?"

The pony remained immoveable.

"Oh you naughty Whisker," said the old lady. "Fie upon you! I'm ashamed of such conduct."

The pony appeared to be touched by this appeal to his feelings, for he trotted on directly, though in a sulky manner, and stopped no more until he came to a door whereon was a brass plate with the words "Witherden—Notary." Here the old gentleman got out and helped out the old lady, and then took from under the seat a nosegay resembling in shape and dimensions a full-seized warming-pan with the handle cut short off. This, the old lady carried into the house with a staid and stately air, and the old gentleman (who had a club-foot) followed close upon her.

They went, as it was easy to tell from the sound of their voices, into the front parlour, which seemed to be a kind of office. The day being very warm and the street a quiet one, the windows were wide open, and it was easy to hear through the Venetian blinds all that passed inside.

At first there was a great shaking of hands and shuffling of feet, succeeded by the presentation of the nosegay, for a voice, supposed by the listener to be that of Mr. Witherden the Notary, was heard to exclaim a great many times, "oh, delicious!" "oh, fragrant, indeed!" and a nose, also supposed to be the property of that gentleman, was heard to inhale the scent with a snuffle of exceeding pleasure.

"I brought it in honour of the occasion, sir," said the old lady.

"Ah! an occasion indeed, ma'am; an occasion which does honour to me, ma'am, honour to me," rejoined Mr. Witherden the Notary. "I have had many a gentleman articled to me, ma'am, many a one. Some of them are now rolling in riches, unmindful of their old companion and friend, ma'am, others are in the habit of calling upon me to this day and saying, 'Mr. Witherden, some of the pleasantest hours I ever spent in my life were spent in this office—were spent, sir, upon this very stool;' but there was never one among the number, ma'am, attached as I have been to many of them, of whom I augured such bright things as I do of your only son."

"Oh dear!" said the old lady. "How happy you do make us when you tell us that, to be sure!"

"I tell you, ma'am," said Mr. Witherden, "what I think as an honest man, which, as the poet observes, is the noblest work of God. I agree with the poet in every particular, ma'am. The mountainous Alps on the one hand, or a humming-bird on the other, is nothing, in point of workmanship, to an honest man—or woman—or woman."

"Anything that Mr. Witherden can say of me," observed a small quiet voice, "I can say with interest of him, I am sure."

"It's a happy circumstance, a truly happy circumstance," said the Notary, "to happen too upon his eight-and-twentieth birthday, and I hope I know how to appreciate it. I trust, Mr. Garland, my dear sir, that we may mutually congratulate each other upon this auspicious occasion."

To this the old gentleman replied that he felt assured they might. There appeared to be another shaking of hands in consequence, and when it was over, the old gentleman said that, though he said it who should not, he believed no son had ever been a greater comfort to his parents than Abel Garland had been to his.

"Marrying as his mother and I did, late in life, sir, after waiting for a great many years, until we were well enough off—coming together when we were no longer young, and then being blessed with one child who has always been dutiful and affectionate—why, it's source of great happiness to us both, sir."

"Of course it is, I have no doubt of it," returned the Notary in a sympathising voice. "It's the contemplation of this sort of thing, that makes me deplore my fate in being a bachelor. There was a young lady once, sir, the daughter of an outfitting warehouse of the first respectability—but that's a weakness. Chuckster, bring in Mr. Abel's articles."

"You see, Mr. Witherden," said the old lady, "that Abel has not been brought up like the run of young men. He has always had a pleasure in our society, and always been with us. Abel has never been absent from us, for a day; has he, my dear?"

"Never, my dear," returned the old gentleman, "except when he went to Margate one Saturday with Mr. Tomkinley that had been a teacher at that school he went to, and came back upon the Monday; but he was very ill after that, you remember, my dear; it was quite a dissipation."

"He was not used to it, you know," said the old lady, "and he couldn't bear it, that's the truth. Besides he had no comfort in being there without us, and had nobody to talk to or enjoy himself with."

"That was it, you know," interposed the same small quiet voice that had spoken once before. "I was quite abroad, mother, quite desolate, and to think that the sea was between us—oh, I never shall forget what I felt when I first thought that the sea was between us!"

"Very natural under circumstances," observed the Notary. "Mr. Abel's feelings did credit to his nature, and credit to your nature, ma'am, and his father's nature, and human nature. I trace the same current now, flowing through all his quiet and unobtrusive proceedings.—I am about to sign my name, you observe, at the foot of the articles which Mr. Chuckster will witness; and, placing my finger upon this blue wafer with the vandyked corners, I am constrained to remark in a distinct tone of voice—don't be alarmed, ma'am, it is merely a form of law—that I deliver this, as my act and deed. Mr. Abel will place his name against the other wafer, repeating the same cabalistic words, and the business is over. Ha ha ha! You see how easily these things are done!" ,

There was a short silence, apparently, while Mr. Abel went through the prescribed form, and then the shaking of hands and shuffling of feet were renewed, and shortly afterwards there was a clinking of wine-glasses and a great talkativeness on the part of everybody. In about a quarter of an hour Mr. Chuckster (with a pen behind his ear and his face inflamed with wine) appeared at the door, and condescending to address Kit by the jocose appellation of "Young Snob," informed him that the visitors were coming out.

Out they came forthwith; Mr. Witherden, who was short, chubby, fresh-coloured, brisk, and pompous, leading the old lady with extreme politeness, and the father and son following them, arm in arm. Mr. Abel, who had a quaint old-fashioned air about him, looked nearly of the same age as his father, and bore a wonderful resemblance to him in face and figure, though wanting something of his full, round cheerfulness, and substituting in its place, a timid reserve. In all other respects, in the neatness of the dress, and even in the club-foot, he and the old gentleman were precisely alike.

Having seen the old lady safely in her seat, and assisted in the arrangement of her cloak and a small basket which formed an indispensable portion of her equipage, Mr. Abel got into a little box behind which had evidently been made for his express accommodation, and smiled at everybody present by turns, beginning with his mother and ending with the pony. There was then a great to-do to make the pony hold up his head that the bearing-rein might be fastened; at last even this was effected; and the old gentleman, taking his seat and the reins, put his hand in his pocket to find a sixpence for Kit.

He had no sixpences, neither had the old lady, nor Mr. Abel, nor the Notary, nor Mr. Chuckster. The old gentleman thought a shilling too much, but there was no shop in the street to get change at, so he gave it to the boy.

"There," he said jokingly, "I'm coming here again next Monday at the same time, and mind you're here, my lad, to work it out."

"Thank you, sir," said Kit. "I'll be sure to be here."

He was quite serious, but they all laughed heartily at his saying so, especially Mr. Chuckster, who roared outright and appeared to relish the joke amazingly. As the pony, with a presentiment that he was going home, or a determination that he would not go anywhere else (which was the same thing), trotted away pretty nimbly, Kit had no time to justify himself, and went his way also. Having expended his treasure in such purchases as he knew would be most acceptable at home, not forgetting some seed for the wonderful bird, he hastened back as fast as he could, so elated with his success and great fortune, that he more than half expected Nell and the old man would have arrived before him.

CHAPTER XV

OFTEN, while they were yet pacing the silent streets of the town on the morning of their departure, the child trembled with a mingled sensation of hope and fear as in some far-off figure imperfectly seen in the clear distance, her fancy traced a likeness to honest Kit. But although she would gladly have given him her hand and thanked him for what he had said at their last meeting, it was always a relief to find, when they came nearer to each other, that the person who approached was not he, but a stranger; for even if she had not dreaded the effect which the sight of him might have wrought upon her fellow-traveller, she felt that to bid farewell to anybody now, and most of all to him who had been so faithful and so true, was more than she could bear. It was enough to leave dumb things behind, and objects that were insensible both to her love and sorrow. To have parted from her only other friend upon the threshold of that wild journey, would have wrung her heart indeed.

Why is it that we can better bear to part in spirit than in body, and while we have the fortitude to act farewell have not the nerve to say it? On the eve of long voyages or an absence of many years, friends who are tenderly attached will separate with the usual look, the usual pressure of the hand, planning one final interview for the morrow, while each well knows that it is but a poor feint to save the pain of uttering that one word, and that the meeting will never be. Should possibilities be worse to bear than certainties? We do not shun our dying friends; the not having distinctly taken leave of one among them, whom we left in all kindness and affection, will often embitter the whole reminder of a life.

The town was glad with morning light; places that had shown ugly and distrustful all night long, now wore a smile; and sparkling sunbeams dancing on chamber windows, and twinkling through blind and curtain before sleepers' eyes, shed light even into dreams, and chased away the shadows of the night. Birds in hot rooms, covered up close and dark, felt it was morning, and chafed and grew restless in their little cells; bright-eyed mice crept back to their tiny homes and nestled timidly together; the sleek house-cat, forgetful of her prey, sat winking at the rays of sun starting through key-hole and cranny in the door, and longed for her stealthy run and warm sleek bask outside. The nobler beasts confined in dens stood motionless behind their bars, and gazed on fluttering boughs and sunshine peeping through some little window, with eyes in which old forests gleamed—then trod impatiently the track their prisoned feet had worn—and stopped and gazed again. Men in their dungeons stretched their cramp cold limbs and cursed the stone that no bright sky could warm. The flowers that sleep by night, opened their gentle eyes and turned them to the day. The light, creation's mind, was everywhere, and all things owned its power.

The two pilgrims, often pressing each other's hands, or exchanging a smile or cheerful look, pursued their way in silence. Bright and happy as it was, there was something solemn in the long deserted streets, from which like bodies without souls all habitual character and expression had departed, leaving but one dead uniform repose, that made them all alike. All was so still at that early hour, that the few pale people whom they met seemed as much unsuited to the scene, as the sickly lamp which had been here and there left burning was powerless and faint in the full glory of the sun.

Before they had penetrated very far into the labyrinth of men's abodes which yet lay between them and the outskirts, this aspect began to melt away, and noise and bustle to usurp its place. Some straggling carts and coaches rumbling by, first broke the charm, then others came, then others yet more active, then a crowd. The wonder was at first to see a tradesman's window open, but it was a rare thing soon to see one closed; then smoke rose slowly from the chimneys, and sashes were thrown up to let in air, and doors were opened, and servant-girls, looking lazily in all directions but their brooms, scattered brown clouds of dust into the eyes of shrinking passengers, or listened disconsolately to milkmen who spoke of country fairs, and told of waggons in the mews, with awnings and all things complete and gallant swains to boot, which another hour would see upon their journey.

This quarter passed, they came upon the haunts of commerce and great traffic, where many people were resorting, and business was already rife. The old man looked about him with a startled and bewildered gaze, for these were places that he hoped to shun. He pressed his finger on his lip, and drew the child along by narrow courts and winding ways, nor did he seem at ease until they had left it far behind, often casting a backward look towards it, murmuring that ruin and self-murder were crouching in every street, and would follow if they scented them; and that they could not fly too fast.

Again this quarter passed, they came upon a straggling neighbourhood, where the mean houses parcelled off in rooms, and window patched with rags and paper, told of the populous poverty that sheltered there. The shops sold goods that only poverty could buy, and sellers and buyers were pinched and griped alike. Here were poor streets where faded gentility essayed with scanty space and shipwrecked means to make its last feeble stand, but tax-gatherer and creditor came there as elsewhere, and the poverty that yet faintly struggled was hardly less squalid and manifest than that which had long ago submitted and given up the game.

This was a wide, wide track—for the humble followers of the camp of wealth pitch their tents round about it for many a mile—but its character was still the same. Damp rotten houses, many to let, many yet building, many half-built and mouldering away lodgings, where it would be hard to tell which needed pity most, those who let or those who came to take—children, scantily fed and clothed, spread over every street, and sprawling in the dust—scolding mothers, stamping their slipshod feet with noisy threats upon the pavements—shabby fathers, hurrying with dispirited looks to the occupation which brought them "daily bread" and little more—mangling-women, washerwomen, cobblers, tailors, chandlers, driving their trades in parlours and kitchens and back rooms and garrets, and sometimes all of them under the same roof—brick-fields, skirting gardens paled with staves of old casks, or timber pillaged from houses burnt down and blackened and blistered by the flames—mounds of dockweed, nettles, coarse grass and oyster-shells, heaped in rank confusion—small Dissenting chapels to teach, with no lack of illustration, the miseries of Earth, and plenty of new churches, erected with a little superfluous wealth, to show the way to Heaven.

At length these streets, becoming more straggling yet, dwindled and dwindled away, until there were only small garden patches bordering the road, with many a summer-house innocent of paint and built of old timber or some fragments of a boat, green as the tough cabbage-stalks that grew about it, and grottoed at the seams with toad-stools and tight-sticking snails. To these succeeded pert cottages, two and two with plots of ground in front, laid out in angular beds with stiff box borders and narrow paths between, where footstep never strayed to make the gravel rough. Then came the public-house, freshly painted in green and white, with tea-gardens and a bowling-green, spurning its old neighbour with the horse-trough where the waggons stopped; then fields; and then some houses, one by one, of goodly size with lawns, some even with a lodge where dwelt a porter and his wife. Then came a turnpike; then fields again with trees and haystacks; then a hill; and on the top of that the traveller might stop, and— looking back at old Saint Paul's looming through the smoke, its cross peeping above the cloud (if the day were clear), and glittering in the sun; and casting his eyes upon the Babel out of which it grew until he traced it down to the furthest outposts of the invading army of bricks and mortar whose station lay for the present nearly at his feet—might feel at last that he was clear of London.

Near such a spot as this, and in a pleasant field, the old man and his little guide (if guide she were, who knew not wither they were bound) sat down to rest. She had had the precaution to furnish her basket with some slices of bread and meat, and there they made their frugal breakfast.

The freshness of the day, the singing of the birds, the beauty of the waving grass, the deep green leaves, the wild flowers, and the thousand exquisite scents and sounds that floated in the air,—deep joys to most of us, but most of all to those whose life is in the bucket of a human well,—sank into their breasts and made them very glad. The child had repeated her artless prayers once that morning, more earnestly perhaps than she had ever done in all her life, but as she felt all this, they rose to her lips again. The old man took off his hat—he had no memory for the words—but he said amen, and that they were very good.

There had been an old copy of the Pilgrim's Progress, with strange plates, upon a shelf at home, over which she had often pored whole evenings, wondering whether it was true in every word, and where those distant countries with the curious names might be. As she looked back upon the place they had left, one part of it came strongly on her mind.

"Dear grandfather," she said, "only that this place is prettier and a great deal better than the real one, if that in the books is like it, I feel as if we were both Christian, and laid down on this grass all the cares and troubles we brought with us; never to take them up again."

"No—never to return—never to return"—replied the old man, waving his hand towards the city. "Thou and I are free of it now, Nell. They shall never lure us back."

"Are you tired?" said the child, "are you sure you don't feel ill from this long walk?"

"I shall never feel ill again, now that we are once away," was his reply. "Let us be stirring, Nell. We must be further away—a long, long way further. We are too near to stop, and be at rest. Come!"

There was a pool of clear water in the field, in which the child laved her hands and face, and cooled her feet before setting forth to walk again. She would have the old man refresh himself in this way too, and making him sit down upon the grass, cast the water on him with her hands, and dried it with her simple dress.

"I can do nothing for myself, my darling," said the grandfather, "I don't know how it is, I could once, but the time's gone. Don't leave me, Nell; say thou'lt not leave me. I loved thee all the while, indeed I did. If I lose thee too, my dear, I must die!"

He laid his head upon her shoulder and moaned piteously. The time had been, and a very few days before, when the child could not have restrained her tears and must have wept with him. But now she soothed him with gentle and tender words, smiled at his thinking they could ever part, and rallied him cheerfully upon the jest. He was soon calmed and fell asleep, singing to himself in a low voice, like a little child.

He awoke refreshed, and they continued their journey. The road was pleasant, lying between beautiful pastures and fields of corn, above which, posed high in the clear blue sky, the lark trilled out her happy song. The air came laden with the fragrance it caught upon its way, and the bess, upborne upon its scented breath, hummed forth their drowsy satisfaction as they floated by.

They were now in the open country; the houses were very few and scattered at long intervals, often miles apart. Occasionally they came upon a cluster of poor cottages, some with a chair or low board put across the open door to keep the scrambling children from the road, others shut up close while all the family were working in the fields. These were often the commencement of a little village: and after an interval came a wheelwright's shed or perhaps a blacksmith's forge; then a thriving farm with sleepy cows lying about the yard, and horses peering over the low wall and scampering away when harnessed horses passed upon the road, as though in triumph at their freedom. There were dull pigs too, turning up the ground in search of dainty food, and grunting their monotonous grumblings as they prowled about, or crossed each other in their quest; plump pigeons skimming round the roof or strutting on the eaves; and ducks and geese, far more graceful in their own conceit, waddling awkwardly about the edges of the pond or sailing glibly on its surface. The farm—yard passed, then came the little inn; the humbler beer-shop; and the village tradesman's; then the lawyer's and the parson's, at whose dread names the beer-shop trembled; the church then peeped out modestly from a clump of trees; then there were a few more cottages; then the cage, and pound, and not unfrequently, on a bank by the way-side, a deep old dusty well. Then came the trim-hedged fields on either hand, and the open road again.

They walked all day, and slept that night at a small cottage where beds were let to travellers. Next morning they were afoot again, and though jaded at first, and very tired, recovered before long and proceed briskly forward.

They often stopped to rest, but only for a short space at a time, and still kept on, having had but slight refreshment since the morning. It was nearly five o'clock in the afternoon, when, drawing near another cluster of labourers' huts, the child looked wistfully in each, doubtful at which to ask for permission to rest awhile, and buy a draught of milk.

It was not easy to determine, for she was timid and fearful of being repulsed. Here was a crying child, and there a noisy wife. In this, the people seemed too poor; in that, too many. At length she stopped at one where the family were seated round the table—chiefly because there was an old man sitting in a cushioned chair beside the hearth, and she thought he was a grandfather and would feel for hers.

There were besides, the cottagers and his wife, and three young sturdy children, brown as berries. The request was no sooner preferred, than granted. The eldest boy ran out to fetch some milk, the second dragged two stools towards the door, and the youngest crept to his mother's gown, and looked at the strangers from beneath his sunburnt hand.

"Good save you, master," said the old cottager in a thin piping voice; "are you travelling far?"

"Yes, sir, a long way" replied the child; for her grandfather appealed to her.

"From London?" inquired the old man.

The child said yes.

Ah! He had been in London many a time used to go there often once, with waggons. It was nigh two-and-thirty year since he had been there last, and he did hear say there were great changes. Like enough! He had changed, himself, since then. Two-and-thirty year was a long time and eighty-four a great age, though there was some he had known that had lived to very hard upon a hundred and not hearty as he, neither no, nothing like it.

"Sit thee down, master, in the elbow chair," said the old man, knocking his stick upon the brick floor, and trying to do so sharply. "Take a pinch out o' that box; I don't take much myself, for it comes dear, but I find it wakes me up sometimes, and ye're but a boy to me. I should have a son pretty nigh as old as you if he'd lived, but they listed to him for a so'gerhe come back home though, for all he had but one poor leg. He always said he'd buried near the sun—dial he used to climb upon when he was a baby, did my poor boy, and his words come true you can see the place with your own eyes; we've kept the turf up, ever since."

He shook his head, and looking at his daughter with watery eyes, said she needn't be afraid that he was going to talk about that any more. He didn't wish to trouble nobody, and if he had troubled anybody by what he said, he asked pardon, that was all.

The milk arrived, and the child producing her little basket and selecting its best fragments for her grandfather, they made a hearty meal. The furniture of the room was very homely of course—a few rough chairs and a table, a corner cupboard with their little stock of crockery and delf, a gaudy tea-tray, representing a lady in bright red, walking out with a very blue parasol, a few common, coloured Scripture subjects in frames upon the wall and chimney, an old dwarf clothes-press and an eight-day clock, with a few bright saucepans and a kettle, comprised the whole. But everything was clean and neat, and as the child glanced round, she felt a tranquil air of comfort and content to which she had long been unaccustomed.

"How far is it to any town or village?" she asked of the husband.

"A matter of good five mile, my dear," was the reply, "but you're not going on to-night?"

"Yes yes, Nell," said the old man hastily, urging her too by signs. "Further on, further on, darling, further away if we walk till midnight."

"There's a good barn hard by, master," said the man, "or there's travellers' lodgings, I know, at the Plow an' Harrer. Excuse me, but you do seem a little tired, and unless you're very anxious to get on—"

"Yes yes, we are," returned the old man fretfully. "Further away, dear Nell, pray further away."

"We must go on, indeed," said the child, yielding to his restless wish. "We thank you very much, but we cannot stop so soon. I'm quite ready, grandfather."

But the woman had observed, from the young wanderer's gait, that one of her little feet was blistered and sore, and being a woman and a mother too, she would not suffer her to go until she had washed the place and applied some simple remedy, which she did so carefully and with such a gentle hand—rough-grained and hard though it was, with work—that the child's heart was too full to admit of her saying more than a fervent "God bless you!" nor could she look back nor trust herself to speak, until they had left the cottage some distance behind. When she turned her head, she saw that the whole family, even the old grandfather, were standing in the road watching them as they went, and so, with many waves of the hand, and cheering nods, and on one side at lest not without tears, they parted company.

They trudged forward, more slowly and painfully than they had done yet, for another mile or thereabouts, when they heard the sound of wheels behind them, and looking round observed an empty cart approaching pretty briskly. The driver on coming up to them stopped his horse and looked earnestly at Nell.

"Didn't you stop to rest at a cottage yonder?" he said.

"Yes, sir," replied the child.

"Ah! They asked me to look out for you," said the man. "I'm going your way. Give me your hand—jump up, master."

This was a great relief, for they were very much fatigued and could scarcely crawl along. To them the jolting cart was a luxurious carriage, and the ride the most delicious in the world. Nell had scarcely settled herself on a little heap of straw in one corner, when she fell asleep, for the first time that day.

She was awakened by the stopping of the cart, which was about to

turn up a bye-lane. The driver kindly got down to help her out, and pointing to some trees at a very short distance before them, said that the town lay
there, and that they had better take the path which they would see leading
through the churchyard. Accordingly, towards this spot they directed their
weary steps.

CHAPTER XVI

THE sun was setting when they reached the wicket-gate at which the
path began, and as the rain falls upon the just and unjust alike, it shed its
warm tint even upon the resting-places of the dead, and bade them be of
good hope for its rising on the morrow. The church was old and grey, with
ivy clinging to the walls, and round the porch. Shunning the tombs, it crept
about the mounds, beneath which slept poor humble men, twining for them
the first wreaths they had ever won, but wreaths less liable to wither and far
more lasting in their kind, than some which were graven deep in stone and
marble, and told in pompous terms of virtues meekly hidden for many a
year, and only revealed at last to executors and mourning legatees.

The clergyman's horse, stumbling with a dull blunt sound among the
graves, was cropping the grass; at once deriving orthodox consolation from
the dead parishioners, and enforcing last Sunday's text that this was what all
flesh came to; a lean ass who had sought to expound it also, without being
qualified and ordained, was pricking his ears in an empty pound hard by, and
looking with hungry eyes upon his priestly neighbour.

The old man and the child quitted the gravel path, and strayed among
the tombs; for there the ground was soft, and easy to their tired feet. As they
passed behind the church, they heard voices near at hand, and presently
came on those who had spoken.

They were two men who were seated in easy attitudes upon the grass,
and so busily engaged as to be at first unconscious of intruders. It was not
difficult to divine that they were of a class of itinerant showmen—exhibitors
of the freaks of Punch—for, perched cross-legged upon a tombstone behind them, was a figure of that hero himself, his nose and chin as hooked and
his face as beaming as usual. Perhaps his imperturbable character was never
more strikingly developed, for he preserved his usual equable smile notwithstanding that his body was dangling in a most uncomfortable position, all
loose and limp and shapeless, while his long peaked cap, unequally balanced against his exceedingly slight legs, threatened every instant to bring
him toppling down.

In part scattered upon the ground at the feet of the two men, and in
part jumbled together in a long flat box, were the other persons of the
Drama. The hero's wife and one child, the hobby-horse, the doctor, the
foreign gentleman who not being familiar with the language is unable in

the representation to express his ideas otherwise than by the utterance of the word "Shallabalah" three distinct times, the Radical neighbour who will by no means admit that a tin bell is an organ, the executioner, and the Devil, were all here. Their owners had evidently come to that spot to make some needful repairs in the stage arrangements, for one of them was engaged in binding together a small gallows with thread, while the other was intent upon fixing a new black wig, with the aid of a small hammer and some tacks, upon the head of the Radical neighbour, who had been beaten bald.

They raised their eyes when the old man and his young companion were close upon them, and pausing in their work, returned their looks of curiosity. One of them, the actual exhibitor no doubt, was a little merry-faced man with a twinkling eye and a red nose, who seemed to have unconsciously imbibed something of his hero's character. The other—that was he who took the money—had rather a careful and cautious look, which perhaps inseparable from his occupation also.

The merry man was the first to greet strangers with a nod; and following the old man's eyes, he observed that perhaps that was the first time he had ever seen a Punch off the stage. (Punch, it may be remarked, seemed to be pointing with the tip of his cap to a most flourishing epitaph, and to be chuckling over it with all his heart.)

"Why do you come here to do this?" said the old man, sitting down beside them, and looking at the figures with extreme delight.

"Why you see," rejoined the little man, "we're putting up for to-night at the public-house yonder, and it wouldn't do to let 'em see the present company undergoing repair."

"No!" cried the old man, making signs to Nell to listen, "why not, eh? Why not?"

"Because it would destroy all the delusion, and take away all the interest, wouldn't it?" replied the little man. "Would you care a ha'penny for the Lord Chancellor if you know'd him in private and without his wig—certainly not."

"Good!" said the old man, venturing to touch one of the puppets, and drawing away his hand with a shrill laugh. "Are you going to show 'em to-night? are you?"

"That is my intention, governor," replied the other, "and unless I'm much mistaken, Tommy Codlin is a calculating at this minute what we've lost through your coming upon us. Cheer up, Tommy, it can't be much."

The little man accompanied these latter words with a wink, expressive of the estimate he had formed of the traveller's finances.

To this Mr. Codlin, who had a surly, grumbling manner, replied, as the twitched Punch off the tombstone and flung him into the box,

"I don't care if we haven't lost a farden, but you're too free. If you stood in front of the curtain and see the public's faces as I do, you'd know human natur' better."

"Ah" it's been the spoiling of you, Tommy, your taking to that branch," rejoined his companion. "When you played the ghost in the reg'lar drama in the fairs, you believed in everything—except ghosts. But now you're a universal mistruster. *I* never see a man so changed."

"Never mind," said Mr. Codlin, with the air of a discontented philosopher. "I know better now, and p'raps I'm sorry for it."

Turning over the figures in the box like one who knew and despised them, Mr. Codlin drew one forth and held it up for the inspection of his friend:

"Look here; here's all this Judy's clothes falling to pieces again. You haven't got a needle and thread I suppose?"

The little man shook his head, and scratched it ruefully as he contemplated this severe indisposition of a principal performer. Seeing that they were at a loss, the child said timidly:

"I have a needle, sir, in my basket, and thread too. Will you let me try to mend it for you? I think I can do it neater than you could."

Even Mr. Codlin had nothing to urge against a proposal so seasonable. Nelly, kneeling down beside the box, was soon busily engaged in her task, and accomplishing it to a miracle.

While she was thus engaged, the merry little man looked at her with an interest which did not appear to be diminished when he glanced at her helpless companion. When she had finished her work he thanked her, and inquired whither they were travelling.

"N—no further to-night, I think," said the child, looking towards her grandfather.

"If you're wanting a place to stop at," the man remarked, "I should advise you to take up at the same house with us. That's it—the long, low, white house there. It's very cheap."

The old man, notwithstanding his fatigue, would have remained in the churchyard all night if his new acquaintance had stayed there too. As he yielded to this suggestion a ready and rapturous assent, they all rose and walked away together; he keeping close to the box of puppets in which he was quite absorbed, the merry little man carrying it slung over his arm by a strap attached to it for the purpose, Nelly having hold of her grandfather's hand, and Mr. Codlin sauntering slowly behind, casting up at the church tower and neighbouring trees such looks as he was accustomed in town-practice to direct to drawing-room and nursery windows, when seeking for a profitable spot on which to plant the show.

The public-house was kept by a fat old landlord and landlady who made no objection to receiving their new guests, but praised Nelly's beauty and were at one prepossessed in her behalf. There was no other company in the kitchen but the two showmen, and the child felt very thankful that they had fallen upon such good quarters. The landlady was very astonished to learn that they had come all the way from London, and appeared to have no little curiosity touching their farther destination. The child parried her enquiries as well as she could, and with no great trouble, for finding that they appeared to give her pain, the old lady desisted.

"These two gentlemen have ordered supper in an hour's time," she said, taking her into the bar; "and your best plan will be to sup with them.

Meantime you shall have a little taste of something that'll do you good, for I'm sure you must want it after all you've gone through to-day. Now, don't look after the old gentleman, because when you've drunk that, he shall have some too."

As nothing could induce the child to leave him alone, however, or to touch anything in which he was not the first and greatest sharer, the old lady was obliged to help him first. When they had been thus refreshed, the whole house hurried away into an empty stable where the show stood, and where, by the light of a few flaring candles stuck round a hoop which hung by a line from the ceiling, it was to be forthwith exhibited.

And now Mr. Thomas Codlin, the misanthrope, after blowing away at the Pan's pipes until he was intensely wretched, took his station on one side of the checked drapery which concealed the mover of the figures, and putting his hands in his pockets prepared to reply to all questions and remarks of Punch, and to make a dismal feint of being his most intimate private friend, of believing in him to the fullest and most unlimited extent, of knowing that he enjoyed day and night a merry and glorious existence in that temple, and that he was at all times and under every circumstance the same intelligent and joyful person that the spectators then beheld him. All this Mr. Codlin did with the air of a man who had made up his mid for the worst and was quite resigned; his eye slowly wandering about during the briskest repartee to observe the effect upon the audience, and particularly the impression made upon the landlord and landlady, which might be productive of every important results in connexion with the supper.

Upon this head, however, he had no cause for any anxiety, for the whole performance was applauded to the echo, and voluntary contributions were showered in with a liberality which testified yet more strongly to the general delight. Among the laughter none was more loud and frequent than the old man's. Nell's was unheard, for she, poor child, with her head dropping on his shoulder, had fallen asleep, and slept too soundly to be roused by any of his efforts to awaken her to a participation in his glee.

The supper was very good, but she was too tired to eat, and yet would not leave the old man until she had kissed him in his bed. He, happily insensible to every care and anxiety, sat listening with a vacant smile and admiring face to all that his new friends said; and it was not until they retired yawning to their room, that he followed the child up stairs.

It was but a loft partitioned into two compartments, where they were to rest, but they were well pleased with their lodging and had hoped for none so good. The old man was uneasy when he had lain down, and begged Nell would come and sit at his bedside as she had done for so many nights. She hastened to him, and sat there till he slept.

There was a little window, hardly more than a chink in the wall, in her room, and when she felt him, she opened it, quite wondering at the silence. The sight of the old church and the graves about it in the moonlight, and the dark trees whispering among themselves, made her more thoughtful than before. She closed the window again, and sitting down upon the bed, thought of the life that was before them.

She had a little money, but it was very little, and when that was gone, they must begin to beg. There was one piece of gold among it, and an emergency might come when its worth to them would be increased a hundred fold. It would be best to hide this coin, and never produce it unless their case was absolutely desperate, and no other resource was left them.

He resolution taken, she sewed the piece of gold into her dress, and going to bed with a lighter heart sank into a deep slumber.

CHAPTER XVII

ANOTHER bright day shining in through the small casement, and claiming fellowship with the kindred eyes of the child, awoke her. At sight of the strange room and its unaccustomed objects she started up in alarm, wondering how she had been moved from the familiar chamber in which she seemed to have fallen asleep last night, and whither she had been conveyed. But another glance around called to her mind all that had lately passed, and she sprang from her bed, hoping and trustful.

It was yet early, and the old man being still asleep, she walked out into the churchyard, brushing the dew from the long grass with her feet, and often turning aside into places where it grew longer than in others, that she might not tread upon the graves. She felt a curious kind of pleasure in lingering among these houses of the dead, and read the inscriptions on the tombs of the good people (a great number of good people were buried there), passing on from one to another with increasing interest.

It was a very quiet place, as such a place should be, save for the cawing of the rooks who had built their nests among the branches of some tall old trees, and were calling to one another, high up in the air. First one sleek bird, hovering near his ragged house as it swung and dangled in the wind, uttered his hoarse cry, quite by chance as it would seem, and in a sober tone as though he were but talking to himself. Another answered, and he called again, but louder than before; then another spoke and then another; and each time the first, aggravated by contradiction, insisted on his case more strongly. Other voices, silent till now, struck in from boughs lower down and higher up and midway, and to the right and left, and from the tree-tops; and others, arriving hastily from the grey church turrets and old belfry window, joined the clamour which arose and fell, and swelled and dropped again, and still went on; and all this noisy contention amidst a skimming to and fro, and lighting on fresh branches, and frequent change of place, which satirised the old restlessness of those who lay so still beneath the moss and turf below, and the useless strife in which they had worn away their lives.

Frequently raising her eyes to the trees whence these sounds came down, and feeling as though they made the place more quiet than perfect silence would have done, the child loitered from grave to grave, now stopping to replace with careful hands the bramble which had started from some green mound it helped to keep in shape, and now peeping through one of the low latticed windows into the church, with its worm-eaten books upon the desks, and baize of whitened-green mouldering from the pew sides and leaving the naked wood to view. There were the seats where the poor old people sat, worn spare, and yellow like themselves; the rugged font where children had their names, the homely altar where they knelt in after life, the plain black tressels that bore their weight on their last visit to the cool old shady church. Everything told of long use and quiet slow decay; the very bell-rope in the porch was frayed into a fringe, and hoary with old age.

She was looking at a humble stone which told of a young man who had died at twenty-three years old, fifty-five years ago, when she heard a faltering step approaching, and looking round saw a feeble woman bent with the weight of years who tottered to the foot of that same grave and asked her to read the writing on the stone. The old woman thanked her when she had done, saying that she had had the words by heart for many a long, long year, but could not see them now.

"Were you his mother?" said the child.

"I was his wife, my dear."

She the wife of a young man of three-and-twenty" Ah, true! It was fifty-five years ago.

"You wonder to hear me say that," remarked the old woman, shaking her head. "You're not the first. Older folk that you have wondered at the same thing before now. Yes, I was his wife. Death doesn't change us more than life, my dear."

"Do you come here often?" asked the child.

"I sit here very often in the summer time," she answered; "I used to come here once to cry and mourn, but that was a weary while ago, bless God!"

"I pluck the daisies as they grow, and take them home," said the old woman after a short silence. "I like no flowers so well as these, and haven't for five-and-fifty year. It's a long time, and I'm getting very old!"

Then growing garrulous upon a theme which was new to one listener though it were but a child, she told her how she had wept and moaned and prayed to die herself, when this happened; and how when she first came to that place, a young creature strong in love and grief, she had hoped that her heart was breaking as it seemed to be. But that time passed by, and although she continued to be sad when she came there, still she could bear to come, and so went on until it was plain no longer, but a solemn pleasure, and a duty she had learned to like. And now that five-and-fifty years were gone, she spoke of the dead man as if he had been her son or grandson, with a kind of pity for his youth, growing out of her own old age, and an exalting of his strength and manly beauty as compared with her own weakness and decay; and yet she spoke about him as her husband too, and thinking of herself in connexion with him, as she used to be and not as she was now, talked of their meeting in another world as if he were dead but yesterday, and she, separated from her former self, were thinking of the happiness of that comely girl who seemed to have died with him.

The child left her gathering the flowers that grew upon the grave, and thoughtfully retraced her steps.

The old man was by this time up and dressed. Mr. Codlin, still doomed to contemplate the harsh realities of existence, was packing among his linen the candle-ends which had been saved from the previous night's performance; while his companion received the compliments of all the loungers in the stable-yard, who, unable to separate him from the master-mind of Punch, set him down as next in importance to that merry outlaw, and loved him scarcely less. When he had sufficiently acknowledged his popularity he came in to breakfast, at which meal they all sat down together.

"And where are you going to-day?" said the little man, addressing himself to Nell.

"Indeed I hardly know,—we have not determined yet," replied the child.

"We're going on to the races," said the little man. "If that's your way and you like to have us for company, let us travel together. If you prefer going alone, only say the word and you'll find that we shan't trouble you."

"We'll go with you," said the old man, "Nell,—with them, with them."

The child considered for a moment, and reflecting that she must shortly beg, and could scarcely hope to do so at a better place than were crowds of rich ladies and gentlemen were assembled together for purposes of enjoyment and festivity, determined to accompany these men so far. She therefore thanked the little man for his offer, and said, glancing timidly towards his friend, that if there was no objection to their accompanying them as far as the race town—

"Objection!" said the little man. "Now be gracious for once, Tommy, and say that you'd rather they went with us. I know you would. Be gracious, Tommy."

"Trotters," said Mr. Codlin, who talked very slowly and eat very greedily, as is not uncommon with philosophers and misanthropes; "you're too free."

"Why, what harm can it do?" urged the other.

"No harm at all in this particular case, perhaps," replied Mr. Codlin; "but the principle's a dangerous one, and you're too free I tell you."

"Well, are they to go with us or not?"

"Yes, they are," said Mr. Codlin; "but you might have made a favour of it, mightn't you?"

The real name of the little man was Harris, but it had gradually merged into the less euphonious one of Trotters, which with the prefatory adjective, Short, had been conferred upon him by reason of the small size of his legs. Short Trotters, however, being a compound name, inconvenient of use in friendly dialogue, the gentleman on whom it had better bestowed was known among his intimates either as "Short," or "Trotters," and was seldom accosted at full length as Short Trotters, except in formal conversations and on occasions of ceremony.

Short, then, or Trotters, as the reader pleases, returned unto the remonstrance of his friend Mr. Tomas Codlin a jocose answer calculated to turn aside his discontent; and applying himself with great relish to the cold boiled beef, the tea, and bread and butter, strongly impressed upon his companions that they should do the like. Mr. Codlin indeed required no such persuasion, as he had already eat as much as he could possibly carry and was now moistening his clay with strong ale, whereof he took deep draughts with a silent relish and invited nobody to partake,—thus again strongly indicating his misanthropical turn of mind.

Breakfast being at length over, Mr. Codlin called the bill, and charging the ale to the company generally (a practice also savouring of misanthropy) divided the sum-total into two fair and equal parts, assigning one moiety to himself and friend, and the other to Nelly and her grandfather. These being duly discharged and all things ready for their departure, they took farewell of the landlord and landlady and resumed their journey.

And here Mr. Codlin's false position in society and the effect it wrought upon his wounded spirit, were strongly illustrated; for whereas he had been last night accosted by Mr. Punch as "master," and had by inference left the audience to understand that he maintained that individual for his own luxurious entertainment and delight, here he was, now, painfully walking beneath the burden of that same Punch's temple, and bearing it bodily upon his shoulders on a sultry day and along a dusty road. In place of enlivening his patron with a constant fire of wit or the cheerful rattle of his quarter-staff on the heads of his relations and acquaintance, here was that beaming Punch utterly devoid of spine, all slack and drooping in a dark box, with his legs doubled up round his neck, and not one of his social qualities remaining.

Mr. Codlin trudged heavily on, exchanging a word or two at intervals with Short, and stopping to rest and growl occasionally. Short led the way; with the flat box, the private luggage (which was not extensive) tied up in a bundle, and a brazen trumpet slung from his shoulder-blade. Nell and her grandfather walked next him on either hand, and Thomas Codlin brought up the rear.

When they came to any town or village, or even to a detached house of good appearance, Short blew a blast upon the brazen trumpet and carolled a fragment of a song in that hilarious tone common to Punches and their consorts. If people hurried to the windows, Mr. Codlin pitched the temple, and hastily unfurling the drapery and concealing Short therewith, flourished hysterically on the pipes and performed an air. Then the entertainment began as soon as might be; Mr. Codlin having the responsibility of deciding on its length and of protracting or expending the time for the hero's final triumph over the Enemy of mankind, according as he judged that the after-crop of halfpence would be plentiful or scant. When it had been gathered in to the last farthing, he resumed his load and on they went again.

Sometimes they played out the toll across a bridge or ferry, and once exhibited by particular desire at a turnpike, where the collector, being drunk in his solitude, paid down a shilling to have it to himself. There was one small place of rich promise in which their hopes were blighted, for a favourite character in the play having gold-lace upon his coat and being a meddling wooden-headed fellow was held to be a libel on the beadle, for

which reason the authorities enforced a quick retreat; but they were generally well received, and seldom left a town without a troop of ragged children
shouting at their heels.

They made a long day's journey, despite these interruptions, and
were yet upon the road when the moon was shining in the sky. Short beguiled the time with songs and jests, and made the best of everything that
happened Mr. Codlin on the other hand, cursed his fate, and all the hollow things of earth (but Punch especially), and limped along with the theatre on his back, a prey to the bitterest chagrin.

They had stopped to rest beneath a finger-post where four roads met,
and Mr. Codlin in his deep misanthropy had let down the drapery and
seated himself in the bottom of the show, invisible to mortal eyes and disdainful of the company of his fellow-creatures, when two monstrous shadows were seen stalking towards them from a turning in the road by which
they had come. The child was at first quite terrified by the sight of these
gaunt giants—for such they looked as they advanced with lofty strides
beneath the shadow of the trees—but Short, telling her there was nothing
to fear, blew a blast upon the trumpet, which was answered by a cheerful
shout.

"It's Grinder's lot, an't it?" cried Mr. Short in a loud key.

"Yes," replied a couple of shrill voices.

"Come on then," said Short. "Let's have a look at you. I thought it
was you."

Thus invited, "Grinder's lot" approached with redoubled speed and
soon came up with the little party. Mr Grinder's company, familiarly
termed a lot, consisted of a young gentleman and a young lady on stilts,
and Mr. Grinder himself, who used his natural legs for pedestrian purposes and carried at his back a drum. The public costume of the young people
was of the Highland kind, but the night being damp and cold, the young
gentleman wore over his kilt a man's pea jacket reaching to his ankles, and
a glazed hat; the young lady too was muffled in an old cloth pelisse and
had a handkerchief tied about her head. Their Scotch bonnets, ornamented
with plumes of jet black feathers, Mr. Grinder carried on his instrument.

"Bound for the races, I see," said Mr. Grinder coming up out of
breath. "So are we. How are you, Short?" With that they shook hands in
a very friendly manner. The young people being too high up for the ordinary salutations, saluted Short after their own fashion. The young gentleman twisted up his right stilt and patted him on the shoulder, and the
young lady rattled her tambourine.

"Practice?" said Short, pointing to the stilts.

"No," returned Grinder. "It comes either to walkin' in 'em or car-
ryin' of 'em, and they like walkin' in 'em best. It's weary pleasant for the
prospects. Which road are you takin'? We go the nightest."

"Why, the fact is," said Short, "that we were going the longest way, because then we could stop for the night, a mile and a half on. But three or four
mile gained to-night is so many saved to-morrow, and if you keep on, I
think our best way is to do the same."

"Where's your partner?" inquired Grinder.

"Here he is," cried Mr. Thomas Codlin, presenting his head and face in the proscenium of the stage, and exhibiting an expression of countenance not often seen there; "and he'll see *his* partner boiled alive before he'll go on to-night. That's what *he* says."

"Well, don't say such things as them, in a spear which is dewoted to something pleasanter," urged Short. "Respect associations, Tommy, even if you do cut up rough."

"Rough or smooth," said Mr. Codlin, beating his hand on the little footboard where Punch, when suddenly struck with the symmetry of his legs and their capacity for silk stockings, is accustomed to exhibit them to popular admiration, "rough or smooth, I won't go further than the mile and a half to-night. I put up at the Jolly Sandboys and nowhere else. If you like to come there, come there. If you like to go on by yourself, go on by yourself, and do without me if you can."

So saying, Mr. Codlin disappeared from the scene and immediately presented himself outside the theatre, took it on his shoulders at a jerk, and made off with most remarkable agility.

Any further controversy being now out of the question, Short was fain to part with Mr. Grinder and his pupils and to follow his morose companion. After lingering at the finger-post a few minutes to see the stilts frisking away in the moonlight and the bearer of the drum toiling slowly after them, he blew a few notes upon the trumpet as a parting salute, and hastened with all speed to follow Mr. Codlin. With this view he gave his unoccupied hand to Nell, and bidding her be of good cheer as they would soon be at the end of their journey for that night, and stimulating the old man with a similar assurance, led them at a pretty swift pace towards their destination, which he was the less unwilling to make for, as the moon was now overcast and the clouds were threatening rain.

CHAPTER XVIII

THE Jolly Shadow was a small road-side inn of pretty ancient date, with a sign representing three Sandboys increasing their jollity with as many jugs of ale and bags of gold, creaking and swinging on its post on the opposite side of the road. As the travellers had observed that day many indications of their drawing nearer and nearer to the race town, such as gipsy camps, carts laden with gambling booths and their appurtenances, itinerant showmen of various kinds, and beggars and trampers of every degree, all wending their way in the same direction, Mr. Codlin was fearful of finding the accommodations forestalled; this fear increasing as he diminished the distance between himself and the hostelry, he quickened his pace, and notwithstanding the burden he had to carry, maintained a round trot until he reached the threshold. Here he had the gratification of finding that his fears were without foundation, for the landlord was leaning against the door-post looking lazily at the rain, which had by this time begun to descend heavily, and no tinkling of cracked bell, nor boisterous shout, nor noisy chorus, gave note of company within.

"All alone?" said Mr. Codlin, putting down his burden and wiping his forehead.

"All alone as yet," rejoined the landlord, glancing at the sky, "but we shall have more company to-night I expect. Here one of you boys, carry that show into the barn. Make haste in out of the wet, Tom; when it came on to rain I told 'em to make the fire up, and there's a glorious blaze in the kitchen, I can tell you."

Mr. Codlin followed with a willing mind, and soon found that the landlord had not commended his preparations without good reason. A mighty fire was blazing on the hearth and roaring up the wide chimney with a cheerful sound, which a large iron cauldron, bubbling and simmering in the heat, lent its pleasant aid to swell. There was a deep red ruddy blush upon the room, and when the landlord stirred the fire, sending the flames skipping and leaping up—when he took off the lid of the iron pot and there rushed out a savoury smell, while the bubbling sound grew deeper and more rich, and an unctuous steam came floating out, hanging in a delicious mist above their heads—when he did this, Mr. Codlin's heart was touched. He sat down in the chimney-corner and smiled.

Mr. Codlin sat smiling in the chimney-corner, eyeing the landlord as with roguish look he held the cover in his hand, and, feigning that his doing so was needful to the welfare of the cookery, suffered the delightful steam to tickle the nostrils of his guest. The glow of the fire was upon the land-lord's bald head, and upon his twinkling eye, and upon his watering mouth, and upon his pimpled face, and upon his round fat figure. Mr. Codlin drew his sleeve across his lips, and said in a murmuring voice, "What is it?"

"It's a stew of tripe," said the landlord smacking his lips, "and cow-heel," smacking them again, "and bacon," smacking them once more, "and steak," smacking them for the fourth time, "and peas, cauliflowers, new potatoes, and sparrow-grass, all working up together in one delicious gravy." Having come to the climax, he smacked his lips a great many times, and taking a long hearty sniff of the fragrance that was hovering about, put on the cover again with the air of one whose toils on earth were over.

"At what time will it be ready?" asked Mr. Codlin faintly.

"It'll be done to a turn," said the landlord looking up at the clock—and the very clock had a colour in its fat white face, and looked a clock for Jolly Sandboys to consult—"it'll be done to a turn at twenty-two minutes before eleven."

"Then," said Mr. Codlin, "fetch me a pint of warm ale, and don't let anybody bring into the room even so much as a biscuit till the time arrives."

Nodding his approval of this decisive and manly course of procedure, the landlord retired to draw the beer, and presently returning with it, applied himself to warm the same in a small tin vessel shaped funnel-wise, for the convenience of sticking it far down in the fire and getting at the bright places. This was soon done, and he handled it over to Mr. Codlin with that creamy froth upon the surface which is one of the happy circumstances attendant upon mulled malt.

Greatly softened by this soothing beverage, Mr. Codlin now bethought him on his companions, and acquainted mine host of the Sandboys that their arrival might be shortly looked for. The rain was rattling against the windows and pouring down in torrents, and such was Mr. Codlin's extreme amiability of mind, that he more than once expressed his earnest hope that they would not be so foolish as to get wet.

At length they arrived, drenched with the rain and presenting a most miserable appearance, notwithstanding that Short had sheltered the child as well as he could under the skirts of his own coat, and they were nearly breathless from the haste they had made. But their steps were no sooner heard upon the road than the landlord, who had been at the outer door anxiously watching for their coming, rushed into the kitchen and took the cover off. The effect was electrical. They all came in with smiling faces, though the wet was dripping from their clothes upon the floor, and Short's first remark was, "What a delicious smell!"

It is not very difficult to forget rain and mud by the side of a cheerful fire, and in a bright room. They were furnished with slippers and such dry garments as the house or their own bundles afforded, and ensconcing themselves, as Mr. Codlin had already done, in the warm chimney-corner, soon forgot their late troubles or only remembered them as enhancing the delights of the present time. Overpowered by the warmth and comfort and the fatigue they had undergone, Nelly and the old man had not long taken their seats here, when they fell asleep.

"Who are they?" whispered the landlord.

Short shook his head, and wished he knew himself.

"Don't *you* know?" asked the host, turning to Mr. Codlin.

"Not I," he replied. "They're no good, I suppose."

"They're no harm," said Short. "Depend upon that. I tell you what–it's plain that the old man an't in his right mind—"

"If you haven't got anything newer than that to say," growled Mr. Codlin, glancing at the clock, "you'd better let us fix our minds upon the supper, and not disturb us."

"Hear me out, won't you?" retorted his friend. "It's very plain to me, besides, that they're not used to this way of life. Don't tell me that that handsome child has been in the habit of prowling about as she's done these last twp or three days. I know better."

"Well, who *does* tell you she has?" growled Mr. Codlin, again glancing at the clock and from it to the cauldron, "can't you think of anything more suitable to present circumstances than saying things and then contradicting 'em?"

"I wish somebody would give you your supper," returned Short, "for there'll be no peace till you've got it. Have you seen how anxious the old man is to get on—always wanting to be furder away—furder away. Have you seen that?"

"Ah! what then?" muttered Thomas Codlin.

"This, then," said Short. "He has given his friends the slip. Mind what I say,—he has given his friends the slip, and persuaded this delicate young creetur all along of her fondness for him to be his guide and travelling companion—where to, he knows no more than the Man in the Moon. Now, I'm not a going to stand that."

"*You're* not a going to stand that!" cried Mr. Codlin, glancing at the clock again and pulling his hair with both hands in a kind of frenzy, but whether occasioned by his companion's observation or the tardy pace of Time, it was difficult to determine. "Here's a world to live in!"

"I," repeated Short emphatically and slowly, "am not a going to stand it. I am not a going to see this fair young child a falling into bad hands, and getting among people that she's no more fit for, than they are to get among angels as their ordinary chums. Therefore when they dewelope an intention of parting company from us, I shall take measures for detaining of 'em, and restoring 'em to their friends, who I dare say have had their disconsolation pasted up on every wall in London by this time."

"Short," said Mr. Codlin, who with his head upon his hands, and his elbow on his knees, had been shaking himself impatiently from side to side up to this point and occasionally stamping on the ground, but who now looked up with eager eyes; "it's possible that there may be uncommon good sense in what you've said. If there is, and there should be a reward, Short, remember that we're partners in everything!"

His companion had only time to nod a brief assent to this position, for the child awoke at the instant. They had drawn close together during the previous whispering, and now hastily separated and were rather awkwardly endeavouring to exchange some casual remarks in their usual tone, when strange footsteps were heard without, and fresh company entered.

These were no other than four very dismal dogs, who came pattering in one after the other, headed by an old bandy dog of particularly mournful aspect, who, stopping when the last of his followers had got as far as the door, erected himself upon his hind legs and looked round at his companions, who immediately stood upon their hind legs, in a grave and melancholy row. Nor was this the only remarkable circumstance about these dogs, for each of them wore a kind of little coat of some gaudy colour trimmed with tarnished spangles, and one of them had a cap upon his head, tied very carefully under his chin, which had fallen down upon his nose and completely obscured one eye; add to this, that the gaudy coats were all wet through and discoloured with rain, and that the wearers were splashed and dirty, and some idea may be formed of the unusual appearance of these new visitors to the Jolly Sandboys. '

Neither Short nor the landlord nor Thomas Codlin, however, were the least surprised, merely remarking that these were Jerry's dogs and that Jerry could not be far behind. So there the dogs stood, patiently winking and gaping and looking extremely hard at the boiling pot, until Jerry himself appeared, when they all dropped down at once and walked about the room in their natural manner. This posture it must be confessed did not much improve their appearance, as their own personal tails and their coat tails—both capital things in their way—did not agree together.

Jerry, the manager of these dancing dogs, was a tall black-whiskered man in a velveteen coat, who seemed well known to the landlord and his guests and accosted them with great cordiality. Disencumbering himself of a barrel organ which he placed upon a chair, and retaining in his hand a small whip wherewith to awe his company of comedians, he came up to the fire to dry himself, and entered into conversation.

"Your people don't usually travel in character, do they?" said Short, pointing to the dresses of the dogs. "It must come expensive if they do?"

"No," replied Jerry, "no, it's not the custom with us. But we've been playing a little on the road to-day, and we come out with a new wardrobe at the races, so I didn't think it worth while to stop to undress. Down, Pedro!"

This was addressed to the dog with the cap on, who being a new member of the company and not quite certain of his duty, kept his unobscured eye anxiously on his master, and was perpetually starting upon his hind legs when there was no occasion, and falling down again.

"I've got a animal here," said Jerry, putting his hand into the capacious pocket of his coat, and diving into one corner as if he were feeling for a small orange or an apple or some such article, "a animal here, wot I think you know something of, Short."

"Ah!" cried Short, "let's have a look at him."

"Here he is," said Jerry, producing a little terrier from his pocket. "He was once a Toby of yours, warn't he!"

In some versions of the great drama of Punch there is a small dog—a modern innovation—supposed to be the private property of that gentleman, whose name is always Toby. This Toby has been stolen in youth from another gentleman, and fraudulently sold to the confiding hero, who having no guile himself has no suspicion that it lurks in others; but Toby, entertaining a grateful recollection of his old master, and scorning to attach himself to any new patrons, not only refuses to smoke a pipe at the bidding of Punch, but to mark his old fidelity more strongly, seizes him by the nose and wrings the same with violence, at which instance of canine attachment the spectators are deeply affected. This was the character which the little terrier in question had once sustained; if there had been any doubt upon the subject he would speedily have resolved it by his conduct; for not only did he, on seeing Short, give the strongest tokens of recognition, but catching sight of the flat box he barked so furiously at the pasteboard nose which he knew was inside, that his master was obliged to gather him up and put him into his pocket again, to the great relief of the whole company.

The landlord now busied himself in laying the cloth, in which process Mr. Codlin obligingly assisted by setting forth his own knife and fork in the most convenient place and establishing himself behind them. When everything was ready, the landlord took off the cover for the last time, and then indeed there burst forth such a goodly promise of supper, that if he had offered to put it on again or had hinted at postponement, he would certainly have been sacrificed on his own hearth.

However, he did nothing of the kind, but instead thereof assisted a stout servant girl in turning the contents of the cauldron into a large tureen; a proceeding which the dogs, proof against various hot splashes which fell upon their noses, watched with terrible eagerness. At length the dish was lifted on the table, and mugs of ale having been previously set round, little Nell ventured to say grace, and supper began.

At this juncture the poor dogs were standing on their hind legs quite surprisingly; the child, having pity on them, was about to cast some morsels of food to them before she tasted it herself, hungry though she was, when their master interposed.

"No, my dear, no, not an atom from anybody's hand but mine if you please. That dog," said Jerry, pointing out the old leader of the troop, and speaking in a terrible voice, "lost a halfpenny to-day. *He* goes without his supper."

The unfortunate creature dropped upon his fore-legs directly, wagged his tail, and looked imploringly at his master.

"You must be more careful, sir," said Jerry, walking coolly to the chair where he had placed the organ, and setting the stop. "Come here. Now, sir, you play away at that, while we have supper, and leave off if you dare."

The dog immediately began to grind most mournful music. His master having shown him the whip resumed his seat and called up the others, who, at his directions, formed in a row, standing upright as a file of soldiers.

"Now, gentlemen," said Jerry, looking at them attentively. "The dog whose name's called eats. The dogs whose names an't called, keep quiet. Carlo!"

The lucky individual whose name was called, snapped up the morsel thrown towards him, but none of the others moved a muscle. In this manner they were fed at the discretion of their master. Meanwhile the dog in disgrace ground hard at the organ, sometimes in quick time, sometimes in slow, but never leaving off for an instant. When the knives and forks rattled very much, or nay of his fellows got an unusually large piece of fat, he accompanied the music with a short howl, but he immediately checked it on his master looking round, and applied himself with increasing diligence to the Old Hundredth.

CHAPTER XIX

SUPPER was not yet over, when there arrived at the Jolly Sandboys two more travellers bound for the same haven as the rest, who had been walking in the rain for some hours, and came in shining and heavy with water. One of these was the proprietor of a giant, and a little lady without legs or armsm who had jogged forward in a van; the other, a silent gentleman who earned his living by showing tricks upon the cards, and who had rather deranged the natural expression of his countenance by putting small leaden lozenges into his eyes and bringing them out at his mouth, which was one of his professional accomplishments. The name of the first of these new-comers was Vuffin; the other, probably as a pleasant satire upon his ugliness, was called Sweet William. To render them as comfortable as he could, the landlord bestirred himself nimbly, and in a very short time both gentlemen were perfectly at their ease.

"How's the Giant?" said Short, when they all sat smoking round the fire.

"Rather weak upon his legs," returned Mr. Vuffin. "I begin to be afraid he's going at the knees."

"That's a bad look-out," said Short.

"Ay! Bad indeed," replied Mr. Vuffin, contemplating the fire with a sigh. "Once get a giant shaky on his legs, and the public care no more about him than they do for a dead cabbage-stalk."

"What becomes of the old giants?" said Short, turning to him again after a little reflection.

"They're usually kept in a carawans to wait upon the dwarfs," said Mr. Vuffin.

"The maintaining of 'em must come expensive when they can't be shown, eh?" remarked Short, eyeing him doubtfully.

"It's better that, than letting 'em go upon the parish or about the streets," said Mr. Vuffin. "Once make a giant common and giants will never draw again. Look at wooden legs. If there was only one man with a wooden leg what a property *he'd* be!"

"So he would!" observed the landlord and Short both together. "That's very true."

"Instead of which," pursued Mr. Vuffin, "if you was to advertise Shakespeare played entirely by wooden legs, it's my belief you wouldn't draw a sixpence."

"I don't suppose you would," said Short. And the landlord said so too.

"This shows, you see," said Mr. Vuffin, waving his pipe with an argumentative air, "this shows the policy of keeping the used-up giants still in the carawans, where they get food and lodging for nothing, all their lives, and in general very glad they are to stop there. There was one giant—a black 'un—as left his carawan some year ago and took to carrying coach-bills about London, making himself as cheap as crossing-sweepers. He died. I make no insinuation against anybody in particular," said Mr. Vuffin, looking solemnly round, "but he was ruining the trade;—and he died."

The landlord drew his breath hard, and looked at the owner of the dogs, who nodded and said gruffly that *he* remembered.

"I know you do, Jerry," said Mr. Vuffin with profound meaning. "I know you remember it, Jerry, and the universal opinion was, that it served him right. Why, I remember the time when the old Maunders as had three-and-twenty wans—I remember the time when old Maunders had in his cottage in Spa Fields in the winter time when the season was over, eight male and female dwarfs setting down to dinner every day, who was waited on by eight old giants in green coats, red smalls, blue cotton stockings, and high-lows: and there was one dwarf as had grown elderly and wicious who whenever his giant wasn't quick enough to please him, used to stick pins in his legs, not being able to reach up any higher. I know that's a fact, for Maunders told it me himself."

"What about the dwarfs, when *they* get old?" inquired the landlord.

"The older dwarf is, the better worth he is," returned Mr. Vuffin; "a great-headed dwarf, well wrinkled, is beyond all suspicion. But a giant weak in the legs and not standing upright!—keep him in the carawan, but never show him, never show him, for any persuasion that can be offered."

While Mr. Vuffin and his two friends smoked their pipes and beguiled the time with such conversation as this, the silent gentleman sat in a warm corner, swallowing, or seeming to swallow, sixpennyworth of halfpence for practice, balancing a feather upon his nose, and rehearsing other feats of dexterity of that kind, without paying any regard whatever to the company, who in their turn left him utterly unnoticed. At length the weary child prevailed upon her grandfather to retire, and they withdrew, leaving the company yet seated round the fire, and the dogs fast asleep at a humble distance.

After bidding the old man good night, Nell retired to her poor garret, but had scarcely closed the door, when it was gently tapped at. She opened it directly, and was a little startled by the sight of Mr. Thomas Codlin, whom she had left, to all appearance, fast asleep down stairs.

"What is the matter?" said the child.

"Nothing's the matter, my dear," returned her visitor. "I'm your friend. Perhaps you haven't thought so, but it's me that's your friend—not him."

"Not who?" the child inquired.

"Short, my dear. I tell you what," said Codlin, "for all his having a kind of way with him that you'd be very apt to like, I'm the real, open-hearted man. I mayn't look it, but I am indeed."

The child began to be alarmed, considering that the ale had taken effect upon Mr. Codlin, and that commendation of himself was the consequence.

"Short's very well, and seems kind," resumed the misanthrope, "but he overdose it. Now I don't."

Certainly if there were any fault in Mr. Codlin's usual deportment, it was that he rather underdid his kindness to those about him, than overdid it. But the child was puzzled, and could not tell what to say.

"Take my advice," said Codlin; "don't ask me why, but take it. As long as you travel with us, keep as near me as you can. Don't offer to leave us—not on any account—but always stick to me and say that I'm your friend. Will you bear that in mind, my dear, and always say that it was me that was your friend?"

"Say so where,—and when?" inquired the child innocently.

"Oh, nowhere in particular," replied Codlin, a little put out as it seemed by the question; "I'm only anxious that you should think me so, and do me justice. You can't think what an interest I have in you. Why didn't you tell me your little history—that about you and the poor old gentleman? I'm the best adviser that ever was, and so interested in you—so much more interested in you than Short. I think they're breaking up down stairs; you needn't tell Short, you know, that we've had this little talk together. God bless you. Recollect the friend. Codlin's the friend, not Short. Short's very well as far as he goes, but the real friend is Codlin—not Short."

Eking out these professions with a number of benevolent and protecting looks and great fervour of manner, Thomas Codlin stole away on tiptoe, leaving the child in a state of extreme surprise. She was still ruminating upon his curious behaviour, when the floor of the crazy stairs and landing cracked beneath the tread of the other travellers who were passing to their beds. When they had all passed, and the sound of their footsteps had died away, one of them returned, and after a little hesitation and rustling in the passage, as if he were doubtful what door to knock at, knocked at hers.

"Yes?" said the child from within.

"It's me—Short"—a voice called through the key-hole. "I only wanted to say that we must be off early to-morrow morning, my dear, because unless we get the start of the dogs and conjuror, the villages won't be worth a penny. You'll be sure to be stirring early and go with us? I'll call you."

The child answered in the affirmative, and returning his "good night" heard him creep away. She felt some uneasiness at the anxiety of these men, increased by the recollection of their whispering together down stairs and their slight confusion when she awoke, nor was she quite free from a misgiving that they were not the fittest companions she could have stumbled on. Her uneasiness, however, was nothing, weighed against her fatigue; and she soon forgot it in sleep.

Very early next morning Short fulfilled his promise, and knocking softly at her door, entreated that she would get up directly, as the proprietor of the dogs was still snoring, and if they lost no time they might get a good deal in advance both of him and the conjuror, who was talking in his sleep, and from what he could be heard to say, appeared to be balancing a donkey in his dreams. She started from her bed without delay, and roused the old man with so much expedition that they were both ready as soon as Short himself, to that gentleman's unspeakable gratification and relief.

After a very unceremonious and scrambling breakfast, of which the staple commodities were bacon and bread, and beer, they took leave of the landlord and issued from the door of the Jolly Sandboys. The morning was fine and warm, the ground cool to the feet after the late rain, the hedges gayer and more green, the air clear, and everything fresh and healthful. Surrounded by these influences, they walked on pleasantly enough.

They had not gone very far, when the child was again struck by the altered behaviour of Mr. Thomas Codlin, who instead of plodding on sulkily by himself as he had theretofore done, kept close to her, and when he had an opportunity of looking at her unseen by his companion, warned her by certain wry faces and jerks of the head not to put any trust in Short, but to reserve all confidences for Codlin. Neither did he confine himself to looks and gestures, for when she and her grandfather were walking on beside the aforesaid Short, and that little man was talking with his accustomed cheerfulness on a variety of indifferent subjects, Thomas Codlin testified his jealousy and distrust by following close at her heels, and occasionally admonishing her ankles with the legs of the theatre in a very abrupt and painful manner.

All these proceedings naturally made the child more watchful and suspicious, and she soon observed that whenever they halted to perform outside a village alehouse or other place, Mr. Codlin while he went through his share of the entertainments kept his eye steadily upon her and the old man, or with a show of great friendship and consideration invited the latter to lean upon his arm, and so held him tight till the representation was over and they again went forward. Even Short seemed to change in this respect, and to mingle with his good nature something of a desire to keep them in safe custody. This increased the child's misgivings, and made her yet more anxious and uneasy.

Meanwhile, they were drawing near the town where the races were to begin next day; for, from passing numerous groups of gipsies and trampers on the road, wending their way towards it, and straggling out from every by-way and cross-country lane, they gradually fell into a stream of people, some walking by the side of covered carts, others with horses, others with donkeys, others toiling on with heavy loads upon their backs, but all tending to the same point. The public-houses by the wayside, from being empty and noiseless as those in the remoter parts had been, now sent out boisterous shouts and clouds of smoke; and, from the misty windows, clusters of broad red faces looked down upon the road. On every piece of waste or common ground, some small gambler drove his noisy trade, and bellowed to the idle passers-by to stop and try their chance; the crowd grew thicker and more noisy; gilt gingerbread in blanket-stalls exposed its glories to the dust; and often a four-horse carriage, dashing by, obscured all objects in the gritty cloud it raised, and left them, stunned and blinded, far behind.

It was dark before they reached the town itself, and long indeed the few last miles had been. Here all was tumult and confusion; the streets were filled with throngs of people—many strangers were there, it seemed, by the looks they cast about—the church-bells rang out their noisy peals, and flags streamed from windows and house-tops. In the large inn-yards waiters flitted to and fro and ran against each other, horses clattered on the uneven stones, carriage steps fell rattling down, and sickening smells from many dinners came in a heavy lukewarm breath upon the sense. In the smaller public-houses, fiddles with all their might and main were squeaking out the tune to staggering feet; drunken men, oblivious of the burden of their song, joined in a senseless howl, which drowned the tinkling of the feeble bell and made them savage for their drink; vagabond groups assembled round the doors to see the stroller woman dance, and add their uproar to the shrill flageolet and deafening drum.

Through this delirious scene the child, frightened and repelled by all she saw, led on her bewildered charge, clinging close to her conductor, and trembling lest in the press she should be separated from him and left to find her way alone. Quickening their steps to get clear of all the roar and riot, they at length passed through the town and made for the race-course, which was upon an open heath, situated on an eminence, a full mile distant from its furthest bounds.

Although there were many people here, none of the best favoured or best clad, busily erecting tents and driving stakes into the ground, and hurrying to and fro with dusty feet and many a grumbled oath—although there were tired children cradled on heaps of straw between the wheels of carts, crying themselves to sleep—and poor lean horses and donkeys just turned loose, grazing among the men and women, and pots and kettles, and half-lighted fires, and ends of candles flaring and wasting in the air—for all this, the child felt it an escape from the town and drew her breath more freely. After a scanty supper, the purchase of which reduced her little stock so low, that she had only a few halfpence with which to buy a breakfast on the morrow, she and the old man lay down to rest in a corner of a tent, and slept, despite the busy preparations that were going on around them all night long.

And now they had come to the time when they must beg their bread. Soon after sunrise in the morning she stole out from the tent, and rambling into some fields at a short distance, plucked a few wild roses and such humble flowers, purposing to make them into little nosegays and offer them to the ladies in the carriages when the company arrived. Her thoughts were not idle while she was thus employed; when she returned and was seated beside the old man in one corner of the tent, tying her flowers together, while the two men lay dozing in another corner, she plucked him by the sleeve, and slightly glancing towards them, said in a low voice—

"Grandfather, don't look at those I talk of, and don't seem as if I spoke of anything but what I am bout. What was that you told me before we left the old house? That if they knew what we were going to do, they would say that you were mad, and part us?"

The old man turned to her with an aspect of wild terror; but she checked him by a look, and bidding him hold her flowers while she tied them up, and so bringing her lips closer to his ear, said—

"I know that was what you told me. You needn't speak, dear. I recollect it very well. It was not likely that I should forget it. Grandfather, these men suspect that we have secretly left our friends, and mean to carry us before some gentleman and have us taken care of and sent back. If you let your hand tremble so, we can never get away from them, but if you're only quiet now, we shall do so, easily."

"How?" muttered the old man. "Dear Nelly, how? They will shut me up in a stone room, dark and cold, and chain me up to the wall, Nell—flog me with whips, and never let me see thee more!"

"You're trembling again," said the child. "Keep close to me all day. Never mind them, don't look at them, but me. I shall find a time when we can steal away. When I do, I mind you come with me, and do not stop or speak a word. Hush! That's all."

"Halloa! what are you up to, my dear?" said Mr. Codlin, raising his head, and yawning. Then observing that his companion was fast asleep, he added in an earnest whisper, "Codlin's the friend, remember—not Short."

"Making some nosegays," the child replied; "I am going to try and sell some, these three days of the races. Will you have one—as a present I mean?"

Mr. Codlin would have risen to receive it, but the child hurried towards him and placed it in his hand. He stuck it in his buttonhole with an air of ineffable complacency for a misanthrope, and leering exultingly at the unconscious Short, muttered, as he laid himself down again, "Tom Codlin's the friend by G—!"

As the morning wore on, the tents assumed a gayer and more brilliant appearance, and long lines of carriages came rolling softly on the turf. Men who had lounged about all night in smock-frocks and leather leggings, came out in silken vests and hat and plumes, as jugglers or mountebanks; or in gorgeous liveries as soft-spoken servants at gambling booths; or in sturdy yeoman dress as decoys at unlawful games. Black-eyes gipsy girls, hooded in showy handkerchiefs, sallied forth to tell fortunes, and pale slender women with consumptive faces lingered upon the footsteps of ventriloquists and conjurors, and counted the sixpences with anxious eyes long before they were gained. As many of the children as could be kept within bounds, were stowed away, with all the other signs of dirt and poverty, among the donkeys, carts, and horses; and as many as could not be thus disposed of ran in and out in all intricate spots, crept between people's legs and carriage wheels, and came forth unharmed from under horses' hoofs. The dancing-dogs, the stilts, the little lady and the tall man, and all the other attractions, with organs out of number and bands innumerable, emerged from the holes and corners in which they had passed the night, and flourished boldly in the sun.

Along the uncleared course, Short led his party, sounding the brazen trumpet and revelling in the voice of Punch; and at his heels went Thomas Codlin, bearing the show as usual, and keeping his eye on Nelly and her grandfather, as they rather lingered in the rear. The child bore upon her arm the little basket with her flowers, and sometimes stopped, with timid and modest looks, to offer them at some gay carriage; but alas! there were many bolder beggars there, gipsies who promised husbands, and other adepts in their trade, and although some ladies smiled gently as they shook their heads, and others cried to the gentlemen beside them "See what a pretty face!" they let the pretty face pass on, and never thought that it looked tired or hungry.

There was but one lady who seemed to understand the child, and she was one who sat alone in a handsome carriage, while two young men in dashing clothes, who had just dismounted from it, talked and laughed loudly at a little distance, appearing to forget her, quite. There were many ladies all around, but they turned their backs, or looked another way, or at the two young men (not unfavourably at *them*), and left her to herself. She motioned away a gipsy-woman urgent to tell her fortune, saying that it was told already and had been for some years, but called the child towards her, and taking her flowers put money into her trembling hand, and bade her go home and keep at home for God's sake.

Many a time they went up and down those long, long lines, seeing everything but the horses and the race; when the bell rang to clear the course, going back to rest among the carts and donkeys, and not coming out again until the heat was over. Many a time, too, was Punch displayed in the full zenith of his humour, but all this while the eye of Thomas Codlin was upon them, and to escape without notice was impracticable.

At length, in the day, Mr. Codlin pitched the show in a convenient spot, and the spectators were soon in the very triumph of the scene. The child, sitting down with the old man close behind it, had been thinking how strange it was that horses who were such fine honest creatures should seem to make vagabonds of all the men that drew about them, when a loud laugh at some extemporaneous witticism of Mr. Short's, having allusion to the circumstances of the day, roused her from her meditation and caused her to look around.

If they were ever to get away unseen, that was the very moment. Short was plying the quarter-staves vigorously and knocking the characters in the fury of the combat against the sides of the show, the people were looking on with laughing faces, and Mr. Codlin had relaxed into a grim smile as his roving eye detected hands going into waistcoat pockets and groping secretly for sixpences. If they were ever to get away unseen, that was the very moment. They seized it and fled.

They made a path through booths and carriages and throngs of people, and never once stopped to look behind. The bell was ringing and the course was cleared by the time they reached the ropes, but they dashed across it insensible to the shouts and screeching that assailed them for breaking in upon its sanctity, and creeping under the brow of the hill at a quick pace, made for the open fields.

CHAPTER XX

DAY after day as he bent his steps homeward, returning from some new effort to procure employment, Kit raised his eyes to the window of the little room he had so much commended to the child, and hoped to see some indication of her presence. His own earnest wish, coupled with the assurance he had received from Quilp, filled him with the belief that she would yet arrive to claim the humble shelter he had offered, and from the death of each day's hope, another hope sprang up to live to-morrow.

"I think they must certainly come to-morrow, eh mother?" said Kit, laying aside his hat with a weary air and sighing as he spoke. "They have been gone a week. They surely couldn't stop away more than a week, could they now?"

The mother shook her head, and reminded him how often he had been disappointed already.

"For the matter of that," said Kit, "you speak true and sensible enough, as you always do, mother. Still, I do consider that a week is quite long enough for 'em to be rambling about; don't you say so?"

"Quite long enough, Kit, longer than enough, but they may not come back for all that."

Kit was for a moment disposed to be vexed by this contradiction, and not the less so from having anticipated it in his own mind and knowing how just it was. But the impulse was only momentary, and the vexed look became a kind one before it had crossed the room.

"Then what do you think, mother, has become of 'em? You don't think they've gone to sea, anyhow?"

"Not gone for sailors, certainly," returned the mother with a smile. "But I can't help thinking that they have gone to some foreign country."

"I say," cried Kit with a rueful face, "don't talk like that, mother."

"I am afraid they have, and that's the truth," she said. "It's the talk of all the neighbours, and there are some even that know of their having been seen on board ship, and can tell you the name of the place they've gone to, which is more than I can, my dear, for it's a very hard one."

"I don't believe it," said Kit. "Not a word of it. A set of idle chatter-boxes, how should they know!"

"They may be wrong of course," returned the mother, "I can't tell about that, though I don't think it's at all unlikely that they're in the right, for the talk is that the old gentleman had put by a little money that nobody knew of, not even that ugly little man you talk to me about—what's his name—Quilp; and that he and Miss Nell have gone to live abroad where it can't be taken from them, and they will never be disturbed. That don't seem very far out of the way now, do it?"

Kit scratched his head mournfully, in reluctant admission that id did not, and clambering up to the old nail took down the cage and set himself to clean it and to feed the bird. His thoughts reverting from his occupation to the little old gentleman who had given him the shilling, he suddenly recollected that that was the very day—nay, nearly the very hour—at which the little old gentleman had said he should be at the notary's house again. He no sooner remembered this, than he hung up the cage with great precipitation, and hastily explaining the nature of his errand, went off at full, speed to the appointed place.

It was some two minutes after the time when he reached the spot, which was a considerable distance from his home, but by great good luck the little old gentleman had not yet arrived; at least there was no pony-chaised to be seen, and it was not likely that he had come and gone again in so short a space. Greatly relieved to find that he was not too late, Kit leant against a lamp-post to take breath, and waited the advent of the pony and his charge.

Sure enough, before long the pony came trotting round the corner of the street, looking as obstinate as a pony might, and picking his steps as if he were spying about for the cleanest places, and would by no means dirty his feet or hurry himself inconveniently. Behind the pony sat the little old lady, carrying just such a nosegay as she had brought before.

The old gentleman, the old lady, the pony, and the chaise, came up the street in perfect unanimity, until they have arrived within some half a dozen doors of the notary's house, when the pony, deceived by a brass-plate beneath a tailor's knocker, came to a halt, and maintained by a sturdy silence, that that was the house they wanted.

"Now, sir, will you have the goodness to go on; this is *not* the place," said the old gentleman.

The pony looked with great attention into a fire-plug which was near him, and appeared to be quite absorbed in contemplating it.

"Oh dear, such a naughty Whisker!" cried the old lady. "After being so good too, and coming along so well! I am quite ashamed of him. I don't know what we are to do with him, I really don't."

The pony having thoroughly satisfied himself as to the nature and properties of the fire-plug, looked into the air after his old enemies the flies, and as there happened to be one of them tickling his ear at that moment he shook his head and whisked his tail, after which he appeared full of thought but quite comfortable and collected. The old gentleman having exhausted his powers of persuasion, alighted to lead him; whereupon the pony, perhaps because he held this to be a sufficient concession, perhaps because he happened to catch sight of the other brass-plate, or perhaps because he was in a spiteful humour, darted off with the old lady and stopped at the right house, leaving the old gentleman to come panting on behind.

It was then that Kit presented himself at the pony's head, and touched his hat with a smile.

"Why, bless me," cried the old gentleman, "the lad *is* here! My dear, do you see?"

"I said I'd be here, sir," said Kit, patting Whisker's neck. "I hope you've had a pleasant ride, sir. He's a very nice little pony."

"My dear," said the old gentleman. "This is an uncommon lad; a good lad, I'm sure."

"I'm sure he is," rejoined the old lady. "A very good lad, and I'm sure he is a good son."

Kit acknowledged these expressions of confidence by touching his hat again and blushing very much. The old gentleman then handed the old lady out, and after looking at him with an approving smile, they went into the house—talking about him as they went, Kit could not help feeling. Presently Mr. Witherden, smelling very hard at the nosegay, came to the window and looked at him, and after that Mr. Abel came and looked at him, and after that the old gentleman and lady came and looked at him again, and after that they all came and looked at him together, which Kit, feeling very much embarrassed by, made a pretence of not observing. Therefore he patted the pony more and more; and this liberty the pony most handsomely permitted.

The faces had not disappeared from the window many moments, when Mr. Chuckster in his official coat, and with his hat hanging on his head just as it happened to fall from its peg, appeared upon the pavement, and telling him he was wanted inside, bade him go in and he would mind the chaise the while. In giving him this direction Mr. Chuckster remarked that he wished he might be blessed if he could make out whether he (Kit) was "precious raw" or "precious deep," but intimated by a distrustful shake of the head, that he inclined to the latter opinion.

Kit entered the office in a great tremor, for he was not used to going among strange ladies and gentlemen, and the tin boxes and bundles of dusty papers had in his eyes an awful and venerable air. Mr. Witherden too was a bustling gentleman who talked loud and fast, and all eyes were upon him, and he was very shabby.

"Well, boy," said Mr. Witherden, "you came to work out that shilling;—not to get another, hey?"

"No indeed, sir," replied Kit, taking courage to look up. "I never thought of such a thing."

"Father alive?" said the notary.

"Dead, sir."

"Mother?"

"Yes, sir."

"Married again—eh?"

Kit made answer, not without some indignation, that she was a widow with three children, and that as to her marrying again, if the gentleman knew her he wouldn't think of such a thing. At this reply Mr. Witherden buried his nose in the flowers again, and whispered behind the nosegay to the old gentleman that he believed the lad was as honest a lad as need be.

"Now," said Mr. Garland when they had made some further inquiries of him, "I am not going to give you anything——"

"Thank you, sir," Kit replied; and quite seriously too, for this announcement seemed to free him from the suspicion which the notary had hinted.

"—But," resumed the old gentleman, "perhaps I may want to know something more about you, so tell me where you live and I'll put it down in my pocket-book."

Kit told him, and the old gentleman wrote down the address with his pencil. He had scarcely done so, when there was a great uproar in the street, and the old lady hurrying to the window cried that Whisker had run away. Upon which Kit darted out to the rescue, and the others followed.

It seemed that Mr. Chuckster had been standing with his hands in his pockets looking carelessly at the pony, and occasionally insulting him with such admonitions as "Stand still,"—"Be quiet,"—"Woa-a-a," and the like, which by a pony of spirit cannot be borne. Consequently, the pony being deterred by no considerations of duty or obedience, and not having before him the slightest fear of the human eye, had at length started off, and was at that moment rattling down the street,—Mr. Chuckster, with his hat off and a pen behind his ear, hanging on in the rear of the chaise and making futile attempts to draw it the other way, to the unspeakable admiration of all beholders. Even in running away, however, Whisker was perverse, for he had not gone very far when he suddenly stopped, and before assistance could be rendered, commenced backing at nearly as quick a pace as he had gone forward. By these means Mr. Chuckster was pushed and hustled to the office again, in a most inglorious manner, and arrived in a state of great exhaustion and discomfiture.

The old lady then stepped into her seat, and Mr. Abel (whom they had come to fetch) into his. The old gentleman, after reasoning with the pony on the extreme impropriety of his conduct, and making the best amends in his power to Mr. Chuckster, took his place also, and they drove away, waving a farewell to the notary and his clerk, and more than once turning to nod kindly to Kit as he watched them from the road.

CHAPTER XXI

KIT turned away and very soon forgot the pony, and the chaise, and the little old lady, and the little old gentleman, and the little young gentleman to boot, in thinking what could have become of his late master and his lovely grandchild, who were the fountain-head of all his meditations. Still casting about for some plausible means of accounting for their non-appearance, and of persuading himself that they must soon return, he bent his steps towards home, intending to finish the task which the sudden recollection of his contract had interrupted, and then to sally forth once more to seek his fortune for the day.

When he came to the corner of the court in which he lived, lo and behold there was the pony again! Yes, there he was, looking more obstinate than ever; and alone in the chaise, keeping a steady watch upon his every wink, sat Mr. Abel, who, lifting up his eyes by chance and seeing Kit pass by, nodded to him as though he would have nodded his head off.

Kit wondered to see the pony again, so near his own home too, but it never occurred to him for what purpose the pony might have come there, or where the old lady and the old gentleman had gone, until he lifted the latch of the door, and walking in, found them seated in the room in conversation with his mother, at which unexpected sight he pulled off his hat and made his best bow in some confusion.

"We are here before you, you see, Christopher," said Mr. Garland smiling.

"Yes, sir," said Kit; and as he said it he looked towards his mother for an explanation of the visit.

"The gentleman's been kind enough, my dear," said she, in reply to this mute interrogation, "to ask me whether you were in a good place, or in any place at all, and when I told him no, you were not in any, he was so good as to say that—"

"That we wanted a good lad in our house," said the old gentleman and the old lady both together, "and that perhaps we might think of it, if we found everything as we would wish it to be."

As this thinking of it, plainly meant the thinking of engaging Kit, he immediately partook of his mother's anxiety and fell into a great flutter; for the little old couple were very methodical and cautious, and asked so many questions that he began to be afraid there was no chance of his success.

"You see, my good woman," said Mrs. Garland to Kit's mother, "that it's necessary to be very careful and particular in such a matter as this, for we're only three in family, and are very quiet, regular folks, and it would be a sad thing if we made any kind of mistake, and found things different from what we hoped and expected."

To this, Kit's mother replied, that certainly it was quite true, and quite right, and quite proper, and Heaven forbid that she should shrink, or have cause to shrink, from any inquiry into her character or that of her son, who was a very good son though she was his mother, in which respect, she was bold to say, he took after his father, who was not only a good son though she was his mother, in which respect, she was bold to say, he took after his father, who was not only a good son to *his* mother, but the best of husbands and the best of fathers besides, which Kit could and would corroborate she knew, and so would little Jacob and the baby likewise if they were old enough, which unfortunately they were not, though as they didn't know what a loss they had had, perhaps it was a great deal better that they should be as young as they were; and so Kit's mother wound up a long story by wiping her eyes with her apron, and patting little Jacob's head, who was rocking the cradle and staring with all his might at the strange lady and gentleman.

When Kit's mother had gone speaking, the old lady struck in again, and said that she was quite sure she was a very honest and very respectable person or she never would have expressed herself in that matter, and that certainly the appearance of the children and the cleanliness of the house deserved great praise and did her the utmost credit, whereat Kit's mother dropped a curtsey and became consoled. Then the good woman entered into a long and minute account of Kit's life and history from the earliest period down to that time, not omitting to make mention of his miraculous fall out of a back-parlour window when an infant of tender years, or his uncommon sufferings in a state of measles, which were illustrated by correct imitations of the plaintive manner in which he called for toast and water, day and night, and said "don't cry, mother, I shall soon be better;" for proof of which statements reference was made to Mrs. Green, lodger, at the cheesemonger's round the corner, and divers other ladies and gentlemen in various parts of England and Wales (and one Mr. Brown who was supposed to be then a corporal in the East Indies, and who could of course be found with very little trouble), within whose personal knowledge the circumstances had occurred. This narration ended, Mr. Garland put some questions to Kit respecting his qualifications and general acquirements, while Mrs. Garland noticed the children, and hearing from Kit's mother certain remarkable circumstances which had attended the birth of her own son, Mr. Abel, from which it appeared that both Kit's mother and herself had been, above and beyond all other women of what condition or age soever, peculiarly hemmed in with perils and dangers. Lastly, inquiry was made into the nature and extent of Kit's wardrobe, and a small advance being made to improve the same, he was formally hired at an annual income of Six Pounds, over and above his board and lodging, by Mr. and Mrs. Garland, of Abel Cottage, Finchley.

It would be difficult to say which party appeared most pleased with this arrangement, the conclusion of which was hailed with nothing but pleasant looks and cheerful smiles on both sides. It was settled that Kit should repair to his new adobe on the next day but one, in the morning; and finally, the little old couple, after bestowing a bright half-crown on little Jacob and another on the baby, took their leaves; being escorted as far as the street by their new attendant, who held the obdurate pony by the bridle while they took their seats, and saw them drive away with a lightened heart.

"Well, mother," said Kit, hurrying back into the house, "I think my fortune's about made now."

"I should think it was indeed, Kit," rejoined his mother. "Six pound a year! Only think!"

"Ah!" said Kit, trying to maintain the gravity which the consideration of such a sum demanded, but grinning with delight in spite of himself. "There's a property!"

Kit drew a long breath when he had said this, and putting his hands deep into his pockets as if there were one year's wages at least in each, looked at his mother, as though he saw through her, and down an immense perspective of sovereigns beyond.

"Please God we'll make such a lady of you for Sundays, mother! such a scholar of Jacob, such a child of the baby, such a room of the one up stairs! Six pound a year!"

"Hem!" croaked a strange voice. "What's that about six pound a year? What about six pound a year?" And as the voice made this inquiry, Daniel Quilp walked in with Richard Swiveller at his heels.

"Who said he was to have six pound a year?" said Quilp, looking sharply round. "Did the old man say it, or did little Nell say it? And what's he to have it for, and where are they, eh?"

The good woman was so much alarmed by the sudden apparition of this unknown piece of ugliness, that she hastily caught the baby from its cradle and retreated into the furthest corner of the room; while little Jacob, sitting upon his stool with his hands on his knees, looked full at him in a species of fascination, roaring lustily all the time. Richard Swiveller took an easy observation of the family over Mr. Quilp's head, and Quilp himself, with his hands in his pockets, smiled in an exquisite enjoyment of the commotion he occasioned.

"Don't be frightened, mistress," said Quilp, after a pause; "Your son knows me; I don't eat babies; I don't like 'em. It will be as well to stop that young screamer though, in case I should be tempted to do him a mischief. Holloa, sir! Will you be quiet?"

Little Jacob stemmed the course of two tears which he was squeezing out of his eyes, and instantly subsided into a silent horror.

Mind you don't break out again, you villain," said Quilp, looking sternly at him, "or I'll make faces at you and throw you into fits, I will. Now you sir, why haven't you been to me as you promised?"

"What should I come for?" retorted Kit. "I hadn't any business with you, no more than you had with me."

"Here, mistress," said Quilp, turning quickly away, and appealing from Kit to his mother. "When did his old master come or send here last? Is he here now? If not, where's he gone?"

"He has not been here at all," she replied. "I wish we knew where they have gone, for it would make my son a good deal easier in his mind, and me too. If you're the gentleman named Mr. Quilp, I should have thought you'd have known, and so I told him only this very day."

"Humph!" muttered Quilp, evidently disappointed to believe that this was true. "That's what you tell this gentleman too, is it?"

"If the gentleman comes to ask the same question, I can't tell him anything else, sir; and I only wish I could, for our own sakes," was the reply.

Quilp glanced at Richard Swiveller, and observed that having met him on the threshold, he assumed that he had come in search of some intelligence of the fugitives. He supposed he was right?

"Yes," said Dick, "that was the object of the present expedition. I fancied it possible - but let us go ring fancy's knell. I'll begin it."

"You seem disappointed," observed Quilp.

"A baffler, sir, a baffler, that's all," returned Dick. "I have enterred upon a speculation Which has proved a baffler; and a Being of brightness and beauty will be offered up a sacrifice at Cheggs's altar. That's all, sir."

The dwarf eyed Richard with a sarcastic smile, but Richard, who had been taking a rather strong lunch with a friend, observed him not, and continued to deplore his fate with mournful and despondent looks. Quilp plainly discerned that there was some secret reason for this visit and his uncommon disappointment, and, in the hope that there might be means of mischief lurking beneath it, resolved to worm it out. He had no sooner adopted this resolution, than he conveyed as much honesty into his face as it was capable of expressing, and sympathised with Mr. Swiveller exceedingly.

"I am disappointed myself," said Quilp, "out of mere friendly feeling for them; but you have real reasons, private reasons I have no doubt, for your disappointment, and therefore it comes heavier than mine."

"Why, of course it does," Dick observed, testily.

"Upon my word, I'm very sorry, very sorry. I'm rather cast down myself. As we are companions in adversity, shall we be companions in the surest way of forgetting it? If you had no particular business, now, to lead you in another direction," urged Quilp, plucking him by the sleeve and looking slyly up into his face out of the corners of his eyes, "there is a house by the waterside where they have some of the noblest Schiedam-reputed to be smuggled, but that's between ourselves-that can be got in all the world. The landlord knows me. There's a little summer-house over-looking the river, where we might take a glass of this delicious liquor with a whiff of the best tobacco—it's in this case, and of the rarest quality, to my certain knowledge-and be perfectly snug and happy, could we possibly contrive it; or is there any very particular engagement that peremptorily takes you another way, Mr. Swiveller, eh?"

As the dwarf spoke, Dick's face relaxed into a compliant smile, and his brows slowly unbent. By the time he had finished, Dick was looking down at Quilp in the same sly manner as Quilp was looking up at him, and there re-mained nothing more to be done but to set out for the house in question. This they did, straightway. The moment their backs were turned, little Jacob thawed, and resumed his crying from the point where Quilp had frozen him.

The summer-house of which Mr. Quilp had spoken was a, rugged wooden box, rotten and bare to see, which overhung the river's mud, and threatened to slide down into it. The tavern to which it belonged was a crazy building, sapped and undermined by the rats, and only upheld by great bars of wood which were reared against its walls, and had propped it up so long that even they were decaying and yielding with their load, and of a windy night might be heard to creak and crack as if the whole fabric were about to come toppling down. The house stood-if anything so old and feeble could be said to stand-on a piece of waste ground, blighted with the unwhole-some smoke of factory chimneys, and echoing the clank of iron wheels and rush of troubled water. Its internal accommodations amply fulfilled the promise of the outside. The rooms were low and damp, the clammy walls were pierced with chinks and holes, the rotten floors had sunk from their level, the very beams started from their places and warned the timid stranger from their neighbourhood.

To this inviting spot, entreating him to observe its beauties as they passed along, Mr. Quilp led Richard Swiveller, and on the table of the sum-mer-house, scored deep with many a gallows and initial letter, there soon ap-peared a wooden keg, full of the vaunted liquor. Drawing it off into the glasses with the skill of a practised hand, and mixing it with about a third part of water, Mr. Quilp assigned to Richard Swiveller his portion, and light-ing his pipe from an end of a candle in a very old and battered lantern, drew himself together upon a seat and puffed away.

"Is it good?" said Quilp, as Richard Swiveller smacked his lips, "is it strong and fiery? Does it make you wink, and choke, and your eyes water, and your breath come short-does it?"

Does it?" cried Dick, throwing away part of the contents of his glass, and filling it up with water, "why, man, you don't mean to tell me that you drink such fire as this?"

"No!" rejoined Quilp. "Not drink it! Look here. And here. And here again. Not drink it!"

"As he spoke, Daniel Quilp drew off and drank three small glassfuls of the raw spirit, and then with a horrible grimace took a great many pulls at his pipe, and swallowing the smoke, discharged it in a heavy cloud from his nose. This feat accomplished he drew himself together in his former posi-tion, and laughed excessively.

"Give us a toast!" cried Quilp, rattling on the table in a dexterous man-ner with his fist and elbow alternately, in a kind of tune, "a woman, a beau-ty. Let's have a beauty for our toast and empty our glasses to the last drop. Her name, come!"

"If you want a name," said Dick, "here's Sophy Wackles."

"Sophy Wackles," screamed the dwarf, "Miss Sophy Wackles that is-Mrs. Richard Swiveller that shall be-that shall be-ha ha ha!"

"Ah!" said Dick, "you might have said that a few weeks ago, but it won't do now, my buck. Immolating herself upon the shrine of Cheggs-",

"Poison Cheggs, cut Cheggs's ears off," rejoined Quilp. "I won't hear of Cheggs. Her name is Swiveller or nothing. I'll drink her health again, and her father's and her mother's; and to all her sisters and brothers-the glorious family of the Wackleses-all the Wackleses in one glass-down with it to the dregs!"

"Well," said Richard Swiveller, stopping short in the act of raising the glass to his lips and looking at the dwarf in a species of stupor as he flourished his arms and legs about: "you're a jolly fellow, but of all the jolly fellows I ever saw or heard of, you have the queerest and most extraordinary way with you, upon my life you have."

This candid declaration tended rather to increase than restrain Mr. Quilp's eccentricities, and Richard Swiveller, astonished to see him in such a roystering vein, and drinking not a little himself, for company,-began imperceptibly to become more companionable and confiding, so that, being judiciously led on by Mr. Quilp, he grew at last very confiding indeed. Having once got him into this mood, and knowing now the key-note to strike whenever he was at a loss, Daniel Quilp's task was comparatively an easy one, and he was soon in possession of the whole details of the scheme contrived between the easy Dick and his more designing friend.

"Stop!" said Quilp. "That's the thing, that's the thing. It can be brought about, it shall be brought about. There's my hand upon it; I am your friend from this minute."

"What! do you think there's still a chance?" inquired Dick, in surprise at this encouragement.

"A chance!" echoed the dwarf, "a certainty! Sophy Wackles may become a Cheggs or anything else she likes, but not a Swiveller. Oh you lucky dog! He's richer than any Jew alive; you're a made man. I see in you now nothing but Nelly's husband, rolling in gold and silver. I'll help you. It shall be done. Mind my words, it shall be done."

"But how?" said Dick.

"There's plenty of time," rejoined the dwarf, "and it shall be done. We'll sit down and talk it over again all the way through. Fill your glass while I'm gone. I shall be back directly-directly."

With these hasty words, Daniel Quilp withdrew into a dismantled skittle-ground behind the public-house, and, throwing himself upon the ground, actually screamed and rolled about in the most uncontrollable delight.

"Here's sport!" he cried, "sport ready to my hand, all invented and arranged, and only to be enjoyed. It was this shallow-pated fellow who made my bones ache t'other day, was it? It was his friend and fellow-plotter, Mr. Trent, that once made eyes at Mrs. Quilp, and leered and looked, was it? After labouring for two or three years in their precious scheme, to find that they've got a beggar at last, and one of them tied for life. Ha ha ha! He shall marry Nell. He shall have her, and I'll be the first man, when the knot's tied hard and fast, to tell 'em what they've gained and what I've helped 'em to. Here will be a clearing of old scores, here will be a time to remind 'em what a capital friend I was, and how I helped 'em to the heiress. Ha ha ha!"

In the height of his ecstasy, Mr. Quilp had like to have met with a dis-agreeable check, for, rolling very near a broken dog-kennel, there leapt forth a large fierce dog, who, but that his chain was of the shortest, would have given him a disagreeable salute. As it was, the dwarf remained upon his back in perfect safety, taunting the dog with hideous faces, and triumphing over him in his inability to advance another inch, though there were not a couple of feet between them.

"Why don't you come and bite me, why don't you come and tear me to pieces, you coward?" said Quilp, hissing and worrying the animal till he was nearly mad. "You're afraid, you bully, you're afraid, you know you are."

The dog tore and strained at his chain with starting eyes and furious bark, but there the dwarf lay, snapping his fingers with gestures of defiance and contempt. When he had sufficiently recovered from his delight, he rose, and with his arms a-kimbo, achieved a kind of demon-dance round the ken-nel, just without the limits of the chain, driving the dog quite wild. Having by this means composed his spirits and put himself in a pleasant train, he returned to his unsuspicious companion, whom he found looking at the tide with exceeding gravity, and thinking of that same gold and silver which Mr. Quilp had mentioned.

CHAPTER XXII

THE remainder of that day and the whole of the next were a busy time for the Nubbles family, to whom everything connected with Kit's outfit and departure was a matter of as great moment as if he had been about to penetrate into the interior of Africa, or to take a cruise round the world. It would be difficult to suppose that there ever was a box which was opened and shut so many times within four-and- twenty hours, as that which con-tained his wardrobe and necessaries; and certainly there never was one which to two small eyes presented such a mine of clothing, as this mighty chest with its three shirts and proportionate allowance of stockings and pocket-handkerchiefs, disclosed to the astonished vision of little Jacob. At last it was conveyed to the carrier's, at whose house at Finchley Kit was to find it next day; and the box being gone, there remained but two questions for consider-ation: firstly, whether the carrier would lose, or dishonestly feign to lose, the box upon the road; and secondly, whether Kit's mother perfectly understood how to take care of herself in the absence of her son.

"I don't think there's hardly a chance of his really losing it, but carriers are under great temptation to pretend they lose things, no doubt," said Mrs. Nubbles apprehensively, in reference to the first point.

"No doubt about it," returned Kit, with a serious look; "upon my word, mother, I don't think it was right to trust it to itself. Somebody ought to have gone with it, I'm afraid."

"We can't help it now," said his mother; "but it was foolish and wrong. People oughtn't to be tempted."

Kit inwardly resolved that he would never tempt a carrier any more, save with an empty box; and having formed this Christian determination, he turned his thoughts to the, second question.

"You know you must keep up your spirits, mother, and not be lonesome because I'm not at home. I shall very often be able to look in when I come into town I dare say, and I shall send you a letter sometimes, and when the quarter comes round, I can get a holiday of course; and then see if we don't take little Jacob to the play, and let him know what oysters means."

"I hope plays mayn't be sinful, Kit, but I'm a'most afraid," said Mrs. Nubbles.

"I know who has been putting that in your head," rejoined her son disconsolately; "that's Little Bethel again. Now I say, mother, pray don't take to going there regularly, for if I was to see your good-humoured face that has always made home cheerful, turned into a grievous one, and the baby trained to look grievous too, and to call itself a young sinner (bless its heart) and a child of the devil (which is calling its dead father names); if I was to see this, and see little Jacob looking grievous likewise, I should so take it to heart that I'm sure I should go and list for a soldier, and run my head on purpose against the first cannon-ball I saw coming my way."

"Oh, Kit, don't talk like that."

"I would, indeed, mother, and unless you want to make me feel very wretched and uncomfortable, you'll keep that bow on your bonnet, which you'd more than half a mind to pull off last week. Can you suppose there's any harm in looking as cheerful and being as cheerful as our poor circumstances will permit? Do I see anything in the way I'm made, which calls upon me to be a snivelling, solemn, whispering chap, sneaking about as if I couldn't help it, and expressing myself in a most unpleasant snuffle? on the contrairy, don't I see every reason why I shouldn't? Just hear this! Ha ha ha! An't that as nat'ral as walking, and as good for the health? Ha ha ha! An't that as nat'ral as a sheep's bleating, or a pig's grunting, or a horse's neighing, or a bird's singing? Ha ha ha! Isn't it, mother?"

There was something contagious in Kit's laugh, for his mother, who had looked grave before, first subsided into a smile, and then fell to joining in it heartily, which occasioned Kit to say that he knew it was natural, and to laugh the more. Kit and his mother, laughing together in a pretty loud key, woke the baby, who, finding that there was something very jovial and agreeable in progress, was no sooner in its mother's arms than it began to kick and laugh, most vigorously. This new illustration of his argument so - tickled Kit, that he fell backward in his chair in a state of exhaustion, pointing at the baby and shaking his sides till he rocked again. After recovering twice or thrice, and as, often relapsing, he wiped his eyes and said grace; and a very cheerful meal their scanty supper was.

With more kisses, and hugs, and tears, than many young gentlemen who start upon their travels, and leave well-stocked homes behind them would deem within the bounds of probability (if matter so low could be herein set down), Kit left the house at an early hour next morning, and set out to walk to Finchley; feeling a sufficient pride in his appearance to have warranted his excommunication from Little Bethel from that time forth, if he had ever been one of that mournful congregation.

Lest anybody should feel a curiosity to know how Kit was clad, it may be briefly remarked that he wore no livery, but was dressed in a coat of pepper-and-salt with waistcoat of canary colour, and nether garments of iron-grey; besides these glories, he shone in the lustre of a new pair of boots and an extremely stiff and shiny hat, which on being struck anywhere with the knuckles, sounded like a drum. And in this attire, rather wondering that he attracted so little attention, and attributing the circumstances to the insensibility of those who got up early, he made his way towards Abel Cottage.

Without encountering any more remarkable adventure on the road, than meeting a lad in a brimless hat, the exact counterpart of his old one, on whom he bestowed half the sixpence he possessed, Kit arrived in course of time at the carrier's house, where, to the lasting honour of human nature, he found the box in safety. Receiving from the wife of this immaculate man, a direction to Mr. Garland's, he took the box upon his shoulder and repaired thither directly.

To be sure, it was a beautiful little cottage with a thatched roof and little spires at the gable-ends, and pieces of stained glass in some of the windows, almost as large as pocket-books. On one side of the house was a little stable, just the size for the pony, with a little room over it, just the size for Kit. White curtains were fluttering, and birds, in cages that looked as bright as if they were made of gold, were singing at the windows; plants were arranged on either side of the path, and clustered about the door; and the garden was bright with flowers in full bloom, which shed a sweet odour all round, and had a charming and elegant appearance. Everything, within the house and without, seemed to be the perfection of neatness and order. In the garden there was not a weed to be seen, and to judge from some dapper gardening-tools, a basket, and a pair of gloves which were lying in one of the walks, old Mr. Garland had been at work in it that very morning.

Kit looked about him, and admired, and looked again, and this a great many times before he could make up his mind to turn his head another way and ring the bell. There was abundance of time to look about him again though, when he had rung it, for nobody came, so after ringing twice or thrice he sat down upon his box and waited.

He rang the bell a great many times, and yet nobody came. But at last, as he was sitting upon the box thinking about giants' castles, and princesses tied up to pegs by the hair of their heads, and dragons bursting out from behind gates, and other incidents of the like nature, common in story-books to youths of low degree on their first visit to strange houses, the door was gently opened, and a little servant-girl, very tidy, modest, and demure, but very pretty too, appeared.

"I suppose you're Christopher, sir," said the servant- girl.

Kit got off the box, and said yes, he was.

"I'm afraid you've rung a good many times perhaps," she rejoined, "but we couldn't hear you, because we've been catching the pony."

Kit rather wondered what this meant, but as he couldn't stop there, asking questions, he shouldered the box again and followed the girl into the hall, where through a back- door he descried Mr. Garland leading Whisker in triumph up the garden, alter that self-willed pony had (as he after wards learned) dodged the family round a small paddock in the rear, for one hour and three quarters.

The old gentleman received him very kindly and so did the old lady, whose previous good opinion of him was greatly enhanced by his wiping his boots on the mat until the soles of his feet burnt again. He was then taken into the parlour to be inspected in his new clothes; and when he had been surveyed several times, and had afforded by his appearance unlimited satisfaction, he was taken into the stable (where the pony received him with uncommon complaisance); and thence into the little chamber he had already observed, which was very clean and comfortable; and thence into the garden, in which the old gentleman told him he would be taught to employ himself, and where he told him, besides, what great things he meant to do to make him comfortable, and happy, if he found he deserved it. All these kindnesses, Kit acknowledged with various expressions of gratitude, and so many touches of the new hat, that the brim suffered considerably. When the old gentleman had said all he had to say in the way of promise and advice, and Kit had said all he had to say in the way of assurance and thankfulness, he was handed over again to the old lady, who, summoning the little servant-girl (whose name was Barbara) instructed her to take him down stairs and give him something to eat and drink, after his walk.

Down stairs, therefore, Kit went; and at the bottom of the stairs there was such a kitchen as was never before seen or heard of out of a toy-shop window, with everything in it as bright and glowing, and as precisely ordered too, as Barbara herself. And in this kitchen, Kit sat himself down at a table as white as a tablecloth, to eat cold meat, and drink small ale, and use his knife and fork the more awkwardly, because there was an unknown Barbara looking on and observing him.

It did not appear, however, that there was anything remarkably tremendous about this strange Barbara, who having lived a very quiet life, blushed very much and was quite as embarrassed and uncertain what she ought to say or do, as Kit could possibly be. When he had sat for some little time, attentive to the ticking of the sober clock, he ventured to glance curiously at the dresser, and there, among the plates and dishes, were Barbara's little work box with a sliding lid to shut in the balls of cotton, and Barbara's prayer-book, and Barbara's hymn-book, and Barbara's Bible. Barbara's little looking-glass hung in a good light near the window, and Barbara's bonnet was on a nail behind the door. From all these mute signs and tokens of her presence, he naturally glanced at Barbara herself, who sat as mute as they, shelling peas into a dish; and just when Kit was looking at her eyelashes and wondering-quite in the simplicity of his heart-what colour her eyes might be, it perversely happened that Barbara raised her head a little to look at him, when both pair of eyes were hastily withdrawn, and Kit leant over his plate, and Barbara over her pea-shells, each in extreme confusion at having been detected by the other.

CHAPTER XXIII

MR. Richard Swiveller wending homewards from the Wilderness (for such was the appropriate name of Quilp's choice retreat), after a sinuous and corkscrew fashion, with many checks and stumbles; after stopping suddenly and staring about him, then as suddenly running forward for a few paces, and as suddenly halting again and shaking his head; doing everything with a jerk and nothing by pre-meditation; -Mr. Richard Swiveller wending his way home-wards after this fashion, which is considered by evil-minded men to be symbolical of intoxication, and is not held by such persons to denote that state of deep wisdom and reflection in which the actor knows himself to be, began to think that possibly he had misplaced his confidence and that the dwarf might not be precisely the sort of person to whom to entrust a secret of such delicacy and importance. And being led and tempted on by this remorseful thought into a condition which the evil-minded class before referred to would term the maudlin state of stage of drunkenness, it occurred to Mr. Swiveller to cast his hat upon the ground, and moan, crying aloud that he was an unhappy orphan, and that if he had not been an unhappy orphan things had never come to this.

"Left an infant by my parents, at an early age," said Mr. Swiveller, bewailing his hard lot, "cast upon the world in my tenderest period, and thrown upon the mercies of a deluding dwarf, who can wonder at my weakness! Here's a miserable orphan for you. Here," said Mr. Swiveller raising his voice to a high pitch, and looking sleepily round, "is a miserable orphan!"

"Then," said somebody hard by, "let me be a father to you."

Mr. Swiveller swayed himself to and fro to preserve his balance, and, looking into a kind of haze which seemed to surround him, at last perceived two eyes dimly twinkling through the mist, which he observed after a short time were in the neighbourhood of a nose and mouth. Casting his eyes down towards that quarter in which, with reference to a man's face, his legs are usually to be found, he observed that the face had a body attached; and when he looked more intently he was satisfied that the person was Mr. Quilp, who indeed had been in his company all the time, but whom he had some vague idea of having left a mile or two behind.

"You have deceived an orphan, sir," said Mr. Swiveller solemnly.

"I! I'm a second father to you," replied Quilp.

"You my father, sir!" retorted Dick. "Being all right myself, sir, I request to be left alone-instantly, sir."

"What a funny fellow you are!" cried Quilp.

"Go, sir," returned Dick, leaning against a post and waving his hand. "Go, deceiver, go, some day, sir, p'r'aps you'll waken, from pleasure's dream to know, the grief of orphans forsaken. Will you go, sir?"

The dwarf taking no heed of this adjuration, Mr. Swiveller advanced with the view of inflicting upon him condign chastisement. But forgetting his purpose or changing his mind before he came close to him, he seized his hand and vowed eternal friendship, declaring with an agreeable frankness that from that time forth they were brothers in everything but personal appearance. Then he told his secret all over again, with the addition of being pathetic on the subject of Miss Wackles, who, he gave Mr. Quilp to understand, was the occasion of any slight incoherency he might observe in his speech at that moment, which was attributable solely to the strength of his affection and not to rosy wine or other fermented liquor. And then they went on arm in arm, very lovingly together.

"I'm as sharp," said Quilp to him, at parting, "as sharp as a ferret, and as cunning as a weasel. You bring Trent to me; assure him that I'm his friend though I fear he a little distrusts me (I don't know why, I have not deserved it); and you've both of you made your fortunes— in perspective."

"That's the worst of it," returned Dick. "These fortunes in perspective look such a long way off."

"But they look smaller than they really are, on that account," said Quilp pressing his arm. "You'll have no conception of the value of your prize until you draw close to it. Mark that."

"D'ye think not?" said Dick.

"Ay, I do; and I am certain of what I say, that's better," returned the dwarf. "You bring Trent to me. Tell him I am his friend and yours-why shouldn't I be?"

"There's no reason why you shouldn't, certainly," replied Dick, "and perhaps there are a great many why you should-at least there would be nothing strange in your wanting to be my friend, if you were a choice spirit, but then you know you're *not* a choice spirit."

"I not a choice spirit!" cried Quilp.

"Devil a bit, sir," returned Dick. "A man of your appearance couldn't be. If you're any spirit at all, sir, you're an evil spirit. Choice spirits," added Dick, smiting himself on the breast, "are quite a different looking sort of people, you may take your oath of that, sir."

Quilp glanced at his free-spoken friend with a mingled expression of cunning and dislike, and wringing his hand almost at the same moment, declared that he was an uncommon character and had his warmest esteem. With that they parted; Mr. Swiveller to make the best of his way home and sleep himself sober; and Quilp to cogitate upon the discovery he had made, and exult in the prospect of the rich field of enjoyment and reprisal it opened to him.

It was not without great reluctance and misgiving that Mr. Swiveller, next morning, his head racked by the fumes of the renowned Schiedam, repaired to the lodging of his friend Trent (which was in the roof of an old house in an old ghostly inn), and recounted by very slow degrees what had yesterday taken place between him and Quilp. Nor was it without great surprise and much speculation on Quilp's probable motives, nor without many bitter comments on Dick Swiveller's folly, that his friend received the tale.

"I don't defend myself, Fred," said the penitent Richard; "but the fellow has such a queer way with him and is such an artful dog, that first of all he set me upon thinking whether there was any harm in telling him, and while I was thinking, screwed it out of me. If you had seen him drink and smoke, as I did, you couldn't have kept anything from him. He's a salamander you know, that's what he is."

Without inquiring whether salamanders were of necessity good confidential agents, or whether a fire-proof man was as a matter of course trustworthy, Frederick Trent threw himself into a chair, and, burying his head in his hands, endeavoured to fathom the motives which had led Quilp to insinuate himself into Richard Swiveller's confidence;- for that the disclosure was of his seeking, and had not been spontaneously revealed by Dick, was sufficiently plain from Quilp's seeking his company and enticing him away.

The dwarf had twice encountered him when he was endeavouring to obtain intelligence of the fugitives. This, perhaps, as he had not shown any previous anxiety about them, was enough to awaken suspicion in the breast of a creature so jealous and distrustful by nature, setting aside any additional impulse to curiosity that he might have derived from Dick's incautious manner. But knowing the scheme they had planned, why should he offer to assist it? This was a question more difficult of solution; but as knaves generally overreach themselves by imputing their own designs to others, the idea immediately presented itself that some circumstances of irritation between Quilp and the old man, arising out of their secret transactions and not unconnected perhaps with his sudden disappearance, now rendered the former desirous of revenging himself upon him by seeking to entrap the sole object of his love and anxiety into a connexion of which he knew he had a dread and hatred. As Frederick Trent himself, utterly regardless of his sister, had this object at heart, only second to the hope of gain, it seemed to him the more likely to be Quilp's main principle of action. Once investing the dwarf with a design of his own in abetting them, which the attainment of their purpose would serve, it was easy to believe him sincere and hearty in the cause; and as there could be no doubt of his proving a powerful and useful auxiliary, Trent determined to accept his invitation and go to his house that night, and if what he said and did confirmed him in the impression he had formed, to let him share the labour of their plan, but not the profit.

Having revolved these things in his mind and arrived at this conclusion, he communicated to Mr. Swiveller as much of his meditations as he thought proper (Dick would have been perfectly satisfied with less), and giving him the day to recover himself from his late salamandering, accompanied him at evening to Mr. Quilp's house.

Mightily glad Mr. Quilp was to see them, or mightily glad he seemed to be; and fearfully polite Mr. Quilp was to Mrs. Quilp and Mrs. Jiniwin; and very sharp was the look he cast on his wife to observe how she was affected by the recognition of young Trent. Mrs. Quilp was as innocent as her own mother of any emotion, painful or pleasant, which the sight of him awakened, but as her husband's glance made her timid and confused, and uncertain what to do or what was required of her, Mr. Quilp did not fail to assign her embarrassment to the cause he had in his mind, and while he chuckled at his penetration was secretly exasperated by his jealousy.

Nothing of this appeared, however. On the contrary, Mr. Quilp was all blandness and suavity, and presided over the case-bottle of rum with extraordinary open-heartedness.

"Why, let me see," said Quilp. "It must be a matter of nearly two years since we were first acquainted."

"Nearer three, I think," said Trent.

"Nearer three!" cried Quilp. "How fast time flies. Does it seem as long as that to you, Mrs. Quilp?"

"Yes, I think it seems full three years, Quilp," was the unfortunate reply.

"Oh indeed, ma'am," thought Quilp, "you have been pining, have you? Very good, ma'am."

"It seems to me but yesterday that you went out to Demerara in the Mary Anne," said Quilp; "but yesterday, I declare. Well, I like a little wildness. I was wild myself once."

Mr. Quilp accompanied this admission with such an awful wink, indicative of old rovings and backslidings, that Mrs. Jiniwin was indignant, and could not forbear from remarking under her breath that he might at least put off his confessions until his wife was absent; for which act of boldness and insubordination Mr. Quilp first stared her out of countenance and then drank her health ceremoniously.

"I thought you'd come back directly, Fred. I always thought that," said Quilp setting down his glass. "And when the Mary Anne returned with you on board, instead of a letter to say what a contrite heart you had, and how happy you were in the situation that had been provided for you, I was amused-exceedingly amused. Ha ha ha!"

The young man smiled, but not as though the theme were the most agreeable one that could have been selected for his entertainment; and for that reason Quilp pursued it.

"I always will say," he resumed, "that when a rich relation having two young people-sisters or brothers, or brother and sister-dependent on him, attaches himself exclusively to one, and casts off the other, he does wrong."

The young man made a movement of impatience, but Quilp went on as calmly as if he were discussing some abstract question in which nobody present had the slightest personal interest.

"It's very true," said Quilp, "that your grandfather urged repeated forgiveness, ingratitude, riot, and extravagance, and all that; but as I told him 'these are common faults.' 'But he's a scoundrel,' said he. 'Granting that,' said I (for the sake of argument of course), 'a great many young noblemen and gentlemen are scoundrels too!' But he wouldn't be convinced."

"I wonder at that, Mr. Quilp," said the young man sarcastically.

"Well, so did I at the time," returned Quilp, "but he was always obstinate. He was in a manner a friend of mine, but he was always obstinate and wrong-headed. Little Nell is a nice girl, a charming girl, but you're her brother, Frederick. You're her brother after all; as you told him the last time you met, he can't alter that."

"He would if he could, confound him for that and all other kindnesses," said the young man impatiently. "But' nothing can come of this subject now, and let us have done with it in the Devil's name."

"Agreed," returned Quilp, "agreed on my part, readily. Why have I alluded to it? Just to show you, Frederick, that I have always stood your friend. You little knew who was your friend, and who your foe; now did you? You thought I was against you, and so there has been a coolness between us; but it was all on your side, entirely on your side. Let's shake hands again, Fred."

With his head sunk down between his shoulders, and a hideous grin overspreading his face, the dwarf stood up and stretched his short arm across the table. After a moment's hesitation, the young man stretched out his to meet it; Quilp clutched his fingers in a grip that for the moment stopped the current of the blood within them, and pressing his other hand upon his lip and frowning towards the unsuspicious Richard, released them and sat down.

This action was not lost upon Trent, who, knowing that Richard Swiveller was a mere tool in his hands and knew no more of his designs than he thought proper to communicate, saw that the dwarf perfectly understood their relative position, and fully entered into the character of his friend. It is something to be appreciated, even in knavery. This silent homage to his superior abilities, no less than a sense of the power with which the dwarf's quick perception had already invested him, inclined the young man towards that ugly worthy, and determined him to profit by his aid.

It being now Mr. Quilp's cue to change the subject with all convenient expedition, lest Richard Swiveller in his heedlessness should reveal anything which it was inexpedient for the women to know, he proposed a game at four-handed cribbage; and partners being cut for, Mrs. Quilp fell to Frederick Trent, and Dick himself to Quilp. Mrs. Jiniwin being very fond of cards was carefully excluded by her son-in-law from any participation in the game, and had assigned to her the duty of occasionally replenishing the glasses from the case-bottle; Mr. Quilp from that moment keeping one eye constantly upon her, lest she should by any means procure a taste of the same, and thereby tantalising the wretched old lady (who was as much attached to the case-bottle as the cards) in a double degree and most ingenious manner.

But it was not to Mrs. Jiniwin alone that Mr. Quilp's attention was restricted, as several other matters required his constant vigilance. Among his various eccentric habits he had a humorous one of always cheating at cards, which rendered necessary on his part, not only a close observance of the game, and a sleight-of-hand in counting and scoring, but also involved the constant correction, by looks, and frowns, and kicks under the table, of Richard Swiveller, who being bewildered by the rapidity with which his cards were told, and the rate at which the pegs travelled down the board, could not be prevented from sometimes expressing his surprise and incredulity. Mrs. Quilp too was the partner of young Trent, and for every look that passed between them, and every word they spoke, and every card they played, the dwarf had eyes and ears; not occupied alone with what was passing above the table, but with signals that might be exchanging beneath it, which he laid all kinds of traps to detect; besides often treading on his wife's toes to see whether she cried out or remained silent under the infliction, in which latter case it would have been quite clear that Trent had been treading on her toes before. Yet, in the midst of all these distractions, the one eye was upon the old lady always, and if she so much as stealthily advanced a tea-spoon towards a neighbouring glass (which she often did), for the purpose of abstracting but one sup of its contents, Quilp's hand would overset it in the very moment of her triumph, and Quilp's mocking voice implore her to regard her precious health. And in any one of these his many cares, from first to last, Quilp never flagged nor faltered.

At length, when they had played a great many rubbers and drawn pretty freely upon the case-bottle, Mr. Quilp warned his lady to retire to rest, and that submissive wife complying, and being followed by her indignant mother, Mr. Swiveller fell asleep. The dwarf beckoning his remaining companion to the other end of the room, held a short conference with him in whispers.

"It's as well not to say more than one can help before our worthy friend," said Quilp, making a grimace towards the slumbering Dick. "Is it a bargain between us, Fred? Shall he marry little rosy Nell by-and-by?"

"You have some end of your own to answer, of course," returned the other.

"Of course I have, dear Fred," said Quilp, grinning to think how little he suspected what the real end was. "It's retaliation perhaps; perhaps whim, I have influence, Fred, to help or oppose. Which way shall I use it? There are a pair of scales, and it goes into one."

"Throw it into mine then," said Trent.

"It's done, Fred," rejoined Quilp, stretching out his clenched hand and opening it as if he had let some weight fall out. "It's in the scale from this time, and turns it, Fred. Mind that."

"Where have they gone?" asked Trent.

Quilp shook his head, and said that point remained to be discovered, which it might be, easily. When it was, they would begin their preliminary advances. He would visit the old man, or even Richard Swiveller might visit him, and by affecting a deep concern in his behalf, and imploring him to settle in some worthy home, lead to the child's remembering him with gratitude and favour. Once impressed to this extent, it would be easy, he said, to win her in a year or two, for she supposed the old man to be poor, as it was a part of his jealous policy (in common with many other misers) to feign to be so, to those about him.

"He has feigned it often enough to me, of late," said Trent.

"Oh! and to me too!" replied the dwarf. "Which is more extraordinary, as I know how rich he really is."

"I suppose you should," said Trent.

"I think I should indeed," rejoined the dwarf; and in that, at least, he spoke the truth.

After a few more whispered words, they returned to the table, and the young man rousing Richard Swiveller informed him that he was waiting to depart. This was welcome news to Dick, who started up directly. After a few words of confidence in the result of their project had been exchanged, they bade the grinning Quilp good night.

Quilp crept to the window as they passed in the street below, and listened. Trent was pronouncing an encomium upon his wife, and they were both wondering by what enchantment she had been brought to marry such a mis-shapen wretch as he. The dwarf after watching their retreating shadows with a wider grin than his face had yet displayed, stole softly in the dark to bed.

In this hatching of their scheme, neither Trent nor Quilp had had one thought about the happiness or misery of poor innocent Nell. It would have been strange if the careless profligate, who was the butt of both, had been harassed by any such consideration; for his high opinion of his own merits and deserts rendered the project rather a laudable one than otherwise; and if he had been visited by so unwonted a guest as reflection, he would-being a brute only in the gratification of his appetites-have soothed his conscience with the plea that he did not mean to beat or kill his wife, and would therefore, after all said and done, be a very tolerable, average husband.

CHAPTER XXIV

IT was not until they were quite exhausted and could no longer maintain the pace at which they had fled from the race-ground, that the old man and the child ventured to stop, and sit down to rest upon the borders of a little wood. Here, though the course was hidden from their view, they could yet faintly distinguish the noise of distant shouts, the hum of voices, and the beating of drums. Climbing the eminence which lay between them and the spot they had left, the child could even discern the fluttering flags and white tops of booths; but no person was approaching towards them, and their resting-place was solitary and still.

Some time elapsed before she could reassure her trembling companion, or restore him to a state of moderate tranquility. His disordered imagination represented to him a crowd of persons stealing towards them beneath the cover of the bushes, lurking in every ditch, and peeping from the boughs of every rustling tree. He was haunted by apprehensions of being led captive to some gloomy place where he would be chained and scourged, and worse than all, where Nell would never come to see him, save through iron bars and gratings in the wall. His terrors affected the child. Separation from her grandfather was the greatest evil she could dread; and feeling for the time as though, go where they would, they were to be hunted down, and could never be safe but in hiding, her heart failed her, and her courage drooped.

In one so young, and so unused to the scenes in which she had lately moved, this sinking of the spirit was not surprising. But, Nature often enshrines gallant and noble hearts in weak bosoms-oftenest, God bless her, in female breasts-and when the child, casting her tearful eyes upon the old man, remembered how weak he was, and how destitute and helpless he would be if she failed him, her heart swelled within her, and animated her with new strength and fortitude.

"We are quite safe now, and have nothing to fear indeed, dear grandfather," she said.

"Nothing to fear!" returned the old man. "Nothing to fear if they took me from thee! Nothing to fear if they parted us! Nobody is true to me. No, not one. Not even Nell!"

"Oh! do not say that," replied the child, "for if ever anybody was true at heart, and earnest, I am. I am sure you know I am."

"Then how," said the old man, looking fearfully round, "how can you bear to think that we are safe, when they are searching for me everywhere, and may come here, and steal upon us, even while we're talking?"

"Because I'm sure we have not been followed," said the child. "Judge for yourself, dear grandfather; look round, and see how quiet and still it is. We are alone together, and may ramble where we like. Not safe! Could I feel easy-did I feel at ease-when any danger threatened you?"

"True, true," he answered, pressing her hand, but still looking anxiously about. "What noise was that?"

"A bird," said the child, "flying into the wood, and leading the way for us to follow. You remember that we said we would walk in woods and fields, and by the side of rivers, and how happy we would be-you remember that? But here, while the sun shines above our heads, and everything is bright and happy, we are sitting sadly down, and losing time. See what a pleasant path and there's the bird -the same bird-now he flies to another tree, and stays to sing. Come!"

When they rose up from the ground, and took the shady track which led them through the wood, she bounded on before, printing her tiny footsteps in the moss, which rose elastic from so light a pressure and gave it back as mirrors throw off breath; and thus she lured the old man on, with many a backward look and merry beck, now pointing stealthily to some lone bird as it perched and twittered on a branch that strayed across their path, now stopping to listen to the songs that broke the happy silence, or watch the sun as it trembled through the leaves, and stealing in among the ivied trunks of stout old trees, opened long paths of light. As they passed onward, parting the boughs that clustered in their way, the serenity which the child had first assumed, stole into her breast in earnest; the old man cast for longer fearful looks behind, but felt at ease and cheerful, for the further they passed into the deep green shade, the more they felt that the tranquil mind of God was there, and shed its peace on them.

At length, the path becoming clearer and less intricate, brought them to the end of the wood, and into a public road. Taking their way along it for a short distance, they came to a lane, so shaded by the trees on either hand that they met together overhead, and arched the narrow way. A broken finger-post announced that this led to a village three miles off; and thither they resolved to bend their steps.

The miles appeared so long that they sometimes thought they must have missed their road. But at last, to their great joy, it led downward in a steep descent, with overhanging banks over which the footpaths led; and the clustered houses of the village peeped out from the woody hollow below.

It was a very small place. The men and boys were playing at cricket on the green; and as the other folk were looking on, they wandered up and down, uncertain where to seek a humble lodging. There was but one old man in the little garden before his cottage, and him they were timid of approaching, for he was the schoolmaster, and had "School" written up over his window in black letters on a white board. He was a pale, simple-looking man, of a spare and meager habit, and sat among his flowers and beehives, smoking his pipe, in the little porch before his door.

"Speak to him, dear," the old man whispered.

"I am almost afraid to disturb him," said the child timidly. "He does not seem to see us. Perhaps if we wait a little, he may look this way."

They waited, but the schoolmaster cast no look towards them, and still sat, thoughtful and silent, in the little porch. He had a kind face. In his plain old suit of black, he looked pale and meager. They fancied, too, a lonely air about him and his house, but perhaps that was because the other people formed a merry company upon the green, and he seemed the only solitary man in all the place.

They were very tired, and the child would have been bold enough to address even a schoolmaster, but for something in his manner which seemed to denote that he was uneasy or distressed. As they stood hesitating at a little distance, they saw that he sat for a few minutes at a time like one in a brown study, then laid aside his pipe and took a few turns in his garden, then approached the gate and looked towards the green, then took up his pipe again with a sigh, and sat down thoughtfully as before.

As nobody else appeared and it would soon be dark, Nell at length took courage, and when he had resumed his pipe and seat, ventured to draw near, leading her grandfather by the hand. The slight noise they made in raising the latch of the wicket-gate, caught his attention. He looked at them kindly but seemed disappointed too, and slightly shook his head.

Nell dropped a curtsey, and told him they were poor travellers who sought a shelter for the night which they would gladly pay for, so far as their means allowed. The schoolmaster looked earnestly at her as she spoke, laid aside his pipe, and rose up directly.

"If you could direct us anywhere, sir," said the child, "we should take it very kindly."

"You have been walking a long way," said the schoolmaster.

"A long way, sir," the child replied.

"You're a young traveller, my child," he said, laying his hand gently on her head. "Your grandchild, friend?"

"Ay, sir," cried the old man, "and the stay and comfort of my life."

"Come in," said the schoolmaster.

Without further preface he conducted them into his little schoolroom, which was parlour and kitchen likewise, and told them they were welcome to remain under his roof till morning. Before they had done thanking him, he spread a coarse white cloth upon the table, with knives and platters; and bringing out some bread and cold meat and a jug of beer, besought them to eat and drink.

The child looked round the room as she took her seat. There were a couple of forms, notched and cut and inked all over; a small deal desk perched on four legs, at which no doubt the master sat; a few dog's-eared books upon a high shelf; and beside them a motley collection of peg-tops, balls, kites, fishing-lines, marbles, half-eaten apples, and other confiscated property of idle urchins. Displayed on hooks upon the wall in all their terrors, were the cane and ruler; and near them, on a small shelf of its own, the dunce's cap, made of old newspapers and decorated with glaring wafers of the largest size. But, the great ornaments the walls were certain moral sentences fairly copied in good round text, and well-worked sums in simple addition and multiplication, evidently achieved by the same hand, which were plentifully pasted all round the room: for the double purpose, as it seemed, of bearing testimony to the excellence of the school, and kindling a worthy emulation in bosoms of the scholars.

"Yes," said the old schoolmaster, observing that her attention was caught by these latter specimens. "That's beautiful writing, my dear."

"Very, sir," replied the child modestly, "is it yours?"

"Mine!" he returned, taking out his spectacles and putting them on, to have a better view of the triumphs so dear to his heart. "I couldn't write like that, now-a-days. No. They're all done by one hand; a little hand it is, not so old as yours, but a very clever one."

As the schoolmaster said this, he saw that a small blot of ink had been thrown on one of the copies, so he took a penknife from his pocket, and going up to the wall, carefully scraped it out. When he had finished, he walked slowly backward from the writing, admiring it as one might contemplate a beautiful picture, but with something of sadness in his voice and manner which quite touched the child, though she was unacquainted with its cause.

"A little hand indeed," said the poor schoolmaster.

"Far beyond all his companions, in his learning and his, sports too, how did he ever come to be so fond of me! That I should love him is no wonder, but that he should love me -" and there the schoolmaster stopped, and took off his spectacles to wipe them, as though they had grown dim.

"I hope there is nothing the matter, sir," said Nell anxiously.

"Not much, my dear," returned the schoolmaster. "I hoped to have seen him on the green to-night. He was always foremost among them. But he'll be there to- morrow."

"Has he been ill?" asked the child, with a child's quick sympathy.

"Not very. They said he was wandering in his head yesterday, dear boy, and so they said the day before. But that's a part of that kind of disorder; it's not a bad sign-not at all a bad sign."

The child was silent. He walked to the door, and looked wistfully out. The shadows of night were gathering, and all was still.

"If he could lean upon anybody's arm, he would come to me, I know," he said, returning into the room. "He always came into the garden to say good night. But perhaps his illness has only just taken a favourable turn, and it's too late for him to come out, for it's very damp and there's a heavy dew. It's much better he shouldn't come to-night."

The schoolmaster lighted a candle, fastened the window shutter, and closed the door. But after he had done this, and sat silent a little time, he took down his hat, and said he would go and satisfy himself, if Nell would sit up till ho returned. The child readily complied, and he went out.

She sat there half an hour or more, feeling the place very strange and lonely, for she had prevailed upon the old man to go to bed, and there was nothing to be heard but the ticking of an old clock, and the whistling of the wind among the trees. When he returned, he took his seat in the chimney-corner, but remained silent for a long time. At length he turned to her, and speaking very gently, hoped she would say a prayer that night for a sick child.

"My favourite scholar!" said the poor schoolmaster, smoking a pipe he had forgotten to light, and looking mournfully round about the walls. "It is a little hand to have done all that, and waste away with sickness. It is a very, very little hand!"

CHAPTER XXV

AFTER a sound night's rest in a chamber in the thatched roof, in which it seemed the sexton had for some years be en a lodger, but which he had lately deserted for a wife and a cottage of his own, the child cose early in the morning and descended to the room where she had supped last night. As the schoolmaster had already left his bed and gone out, she bestirred her-self to make it neat and comfortable, and had just finished its arrangement when the kind host returned.

He thanked her many times, and said that the old dame who usually did such offices for him had gone to nurse the little scholar whom he had told her of. The child asked how he was, and hoped he was better.

"No," rejoined the schoolmaster shaking his head sorrowfully, "No better. They even say he is worse."

"I am very sorry for that, sir," said the child.

The poor schoolmaster appeared to be gratified by her earnest manner, but yet rendered more uneasy by it, for he added hastily that anxious people often magnified an evil and thought it greater than it was; "for my part," he said, in his quiet, patient way, "I hope it's not so. I don't think he can be worse."

The child asked his leave to prepare breakfast, and her grandfather coming down stairs, they all three partook of it together. While the meal was in progress, their host remarked that the old man seemed much fatigued, and evidently stood in need of rest.

"If the journey you have before you is a long one," he said, "and don't press you for one day, you're very welcome to pass another night here. I should really be glad if you would, friend."

He saw that the old man looked at Nell, uncertain whether to accept or decline his offer; and added,

"I shall be glad to have your young companion with me for one day. If you can do a charity to a lone man, and rest yourself at the same time, do so. If you must proceed upon your journey, I wish you well through it, and will walk a little way with you before school begins."

"What are we to do, Nell?" said the old man irresolutely, "say what we're to do, dear."

It required no great persuasion to induce the child to answer that they had better accept the invitation and remain. She was happy to show her gratitude to the kind schoolmaster by busying herself in the performance of such household duties as his little cottage stood in need of. When these were done, she took some needle-work from her basket, and sat herself down upon a stool beside the lattice, where the honeysuckle and woodbine entwined their tender stems, and stealing into the room filled it with their delicious breath. Her grandfather was basking in the sun outside, breathing the perfume of the flowers, and idly watching the clouds as they floated on before the light summer wind.

As the schoolmaster, alter arranging the two forms in due order, took his seat behind his desk and made other preparations for school, the child was apprehensive that she might be in the way, and offered to withdraw to her little bedroom. But this he would not allow, and as he seemed pleased to have her there, she remained, busying herself with her work.

"Have you many scholars, sir?" she asked.

The poor schoolmaster shook his head, and said that they barely filled the two forms.

"And are the others clever, sir?" asked the child, glancing at the trophies on the wall.

"Good boys," returned the schoolmaster, "good boys enough, my dear, but they'll never do like that."

A small white-headed boy with a sunburnt face appeared at the door while he was speaking, and stopping there to make a rustic bow, came in and took his seat upon one of the forms. The white-headed boy then put an open book astonishingly dog's-eared, upon his knees, and thrusting his hands into his pockets began counting the marbles with which they were filled; displaying in the expression of his face a remarkable capacity of totally abstracting his mind from the spelling on which his eyes were fixed. Soon afterwards another white-headed little boy came straggling in, and alter him a red-headed lad, and alter him two more with white heads, and then one with a flaxen poll, and so on until the forms were occupied by a dozen boys or there abouts, with heads of every colour but grey, and ranging in their ages from four years old to fourteen years or more; for the legs of the youngest were a long way from the floor when he sat upon the form, and the eldest was a heavy good-tempered foolish fellow, about half a head taller than the schoolmaster.

At the top of the first form-the post of honour in the school-was the vacant place of the little sick scholar, and at the head of the rows of pegs on which those who came in hats or caps were wont to hang them up, one was left empty. No boy attempted to violate the sanctity of seat or peg, but many a one looked from the empty spaces to the schoolmaster, and whispered his idle neighbour behind his hand.

Then began the hum of conning over lessons and getting them by heart, the whispered jest and stealthy game, and all the noise and drawl of school; and in the midst of the din sat the poor schoolmaster, the very image of meekness and simplicity, vainly attempting to fix his mind upon the duties of the day, and to forget his little friend. But the tedium of his office reminded him more strongly of the willing scholar, and his thoughts were rambling from his pupils-it was plain.

None knew this better than the idlest boys, who, growing holder with impunity, waxed louder and more daring; playing odd-or-even under the master's eye, eating apples openly and without rebuke, pinching each other in sport or malice without the least reserve, and cutting their autographs in the very legs of his desk. The puzzled dunce, who stood beside it to say his lesson out of book, looked no longer at the ceiling for forgotten words, but drew closer to the master's elbow and boldly cast his eye upon the page; the wag of the little troop squinted and made grimaces (at the smallest boy of course), holding no book before his face, and his approving audience knew no constraint in their delight. If the master did chance to rouse himself and seem alive to what was going on, the noise subsided for a moment and no eyes met his but wore a studious and a deeply humble look; but the instant he relapsed again, it broke out afresh, and ten times louder than before.

Oh! how some of those idle fellows longed to be outside, and how they looked at the open door and window, as if they half meditated rushing violently out, plunging into the wood, and being wild boys and savages from that time forth. What rebellious thoughts of the cool river, and some shady bathing-place beneath willow trees with branches dipping in the water, kept tempting and urging that sturdy boy, who, with his shirt-collar unbuttoned and flung back as far as it could go, sat fanning his flushed face with a spelling-book, wishing himself a whale, or a tittlebat, or a fly, or anything but a boy at school on that hot, broiling day! Heat! ask that other boy, whose seat being nearest to the door gave him opportunities of gliding out into the garden and driving his companions to madness by dipping his face into the bucket of the well and then rolling on the grass-ask him if there were ever such a day as that, when even the bees were diving deep down into the cups of flowers and stopping there, as if they had made up their minds to retire from business and be manufacturers of honey no more. The day was made for laziness, and lying on one's back in green places, and staring at the sky till its brightness forced one to shut one's eyes and go to sleep; and was this a time to be poring over musty books in a dark room, slighted by the very sun itself? Monstrous!

Nell sat by the window occupied with her work, but attentive still to all that passed, though sometimes rather timid of the boisterous boys. The lessons over, writing time began; and there being but one desk and that the master's, each boy sat at it in turn and laboured at his crooked copy, while the master walked about. This was a quieter time; for he would come and look over the writer's shoulder, and tell him mildly to observe how such a letter was turned in such a copy on the wall, praise such an upstroke here and such a down-stroke there, and bid him take it for his model. Then he would stop and tell them what the sick child had said last night, and how he had longed to be among them once again; and such was the poor school master's gentle and affectionate manner, that the boys seemed quite remorseful that they had worried him so much, and were absolutely quiet; eating no apples, cutting no names, inflicting no pinches, and making no grimaces, for full two minutes afterwards.

"I think, boys," said the schoolmaster when the clock struck twelve, "that I shall give an extra half-holiday this afternoon."

At this intelligence, the boys, led on and headed by the tall boy, raised a great shout, in the midst of which the master was seen to speak, but could not be heard. As he held up his hand, however, in token of his wish that they should be silent, they were considerate enough to leave off, as soon as the longest-winded among them were quite out of breath.

"You must promise me first," said the schoolmaster, "that you'll not be noisy, or at least, if you are, that you'll go away and be so-away out of the village I mean. I'm sure you wouldn't disturb your old playmate and companion."

There was a general murmur (and perhaps a very sincere one, for they were but boys) in the negative; and the tall boy, perhaps as sincerely as any of them, called those about him to witness that he had only shouted in a whisper.

"Then pray don't forget, there's my dear scholars," said the schoolmaster, "what I have asked you, and do it as a favour to me. Be as happy as you can, and don't be unmindful that you are blessed with health. Good-bye all!"

"Thank'ee, sir," and, "good-bye, sir," were said a great many times in a variety of voices, and the boys went out very slowly and softly. But there was the sun shining and there were the birds singing, as the sun only shines and the birds only sing on holidays and half-holidays; there were the trees waving to all free boys to climb and nestle among their leafy branches; the hay, entreating them to come and scatter it to the pure air; the green corn, gently beckoning towards wood and stream; the smooth ground, rendered smoother still by blending lights and shadows, inviting to runs and leaps, and long walks God knows whither. It was more than boy could bear, and with a joyous whoop the whole cluster took to their heels and spread themselves about, shouting and laughing as they went.

"It's natural, thank Heaven!" said the poor schoolmaster looking after them. "I'm very glad they didn't mind me!"

It is difficult, however, to please everybody, as most of us would have discovered, even without the fable which bears that moral; and in the course of the afternoon several mothers and aunts of pupils looked in to express their entire disapproval of the schoolmaster's proceeding. A few confined themselves to hints, such as politely inquiring what red-letter day or saint's day the almanack said it was; a few (these were the profound village politicians) argued that it was a slight to the Throne and an affront to Church and State, and savoured of revolutionary principles, to grant a half-holiday upon any lighter occasion than the birthday of the Monarch; but the majority expressed their displeasure on private grounds and in plain terms, arguing that to put the pupils on this short allowance of learning was nothing but an act of downright robbery and fraud: and one old lady, finding that she could not inflame or irritate the peaceable schoolmaster by talking to him, bounced out of his house and talked at him for half an hour outside his own window, to another old lady, saying that of course he would deduct this half-holiday from his weekly charge, or of course he would naturally expect to have an opposition started against him; there was no want of idle chaps in that neighbourhood (here the old lady raised her voice), and some chaps who were too idle even to be schoolmasters, might soon find that there were other chaps put over their heads, and so she would have them take care, and look pretty sharp about them. But all these taunts and vexations failed to elicit one word from the meek schoolmaster, who sat with the child by his side,- a little more dejected perhaps, but quite silent and uncomplaining.

Towards night and old woman came tottering up the garden as speedily as she could, and meeting the schoolmaster at the door, said he was to go to Dame West's directly, and had best run on before her. He and the child were on the point of going out together for a walk, and without relinquishing her hand, the schoolmaster hurried away, leaving the messenger to follow as she might.

They stopped at a cottage-door, and the schoolmaster knocked softly at it with his hand. It was opened without loss of time. They entered a room where a little group of women were gathered about one, older than the rest, who was crying very bitterly, and sat wringing her hands and rocking herself to and fro.

"Oh dame!" said the schoolmaster, drawing near her chair, "is it so bad as this?"

"He's going fast," cried the old woman; "my grandson's dying. It's all along of you. You shouldn't see him now, but for his being so earnest on it. This is what his learning has brought him to. Oh dear, dear, dear, what can I do!"

"Do not say that I am in any fault," urged the gentle schoolmaster. "I am not hurt, dame. No, no you are in great distress of mind, and don't mean what you say. I am sure you don't."

"I do," returned the old woman. "I mean it all. If he hadn't been poring over his books out of fear of you, he would have been well and merry now, I known he would."

The schoolmaster looked round upon the other women as if to entreat some one among them to say a kind word for him, but they shook their heads, and murmured to each other that they never thought there was much good in learning, and that this convinced them. Without saying a word in reply, or giving them a look of reproach, he followed the old woman who had summoned him (and who had now rejoined them) into another room, where his infant friend, half-dressed, lay stretched upon a bed.

He was a very young boy; quite a little child. His hair still hung in curls about his face, and his eyes were very bright; but their light was of Heaven, not earth. The schoolmaster took a seat beside him, and stooping over the pillow, whispered his name. The boy sprang up, stroked his face with his hand, and threw his wasted arms around his neck, crying out that he was his dear kind friend.

"I hope I always was. I meant to be, God knows," said the poor schoolmaster.

"Who is that?" said the boy, seeing Nell. "I am afraid to kiss her, lest I should make her ill. Ask her to shake hands with me."

The sobbing child came closer up, and took the little languid hand in hers. Releasing his again after a time, the sick boy laid him gently down.

"You remember the garden, Harry," whispered the schoolmaster, anxious to rouse him, for a dulness seemed gathering upon the child, "and how pleasant it used to be in the evening time? You must make haste to visit it again, for I think the very flowers have missed you, and are less gay than they used to be. You will come soon, my dear, very soon now,-won't you?"

The boy smiled faintly-so very, very faintly-and put his hand upon his friend's grey head. He moved his lips too, but no voice came from them; no, not a sound.

In the silence that ensued, the hum of distant voices borne upon the evening air came floating through the open window. "What's that?" said the sick child, opening his eyes.

"The boys at play upon the green."

He took a handkerchief from his pillow, and tried to wave it above his head. But the feeble arm dropped power less down.

"Shall I do it?" said the schoolmaster.

"Please wave it at the window," was the faint reply.

"Tie it to the lattice. Some of them may see it there. Perhaps they'll think of me, and look this way."

He raised his head, and glanced from the fluttering signal to his idle bat, that lay with slate and book and other boyish property upon a table in the room. And then he laid him softly down once more, and asked if the little girl were there, for he could not see her.

She stepped forward, and pressed the passive hand that lay upon the coverlet. The two old friends and companions for such they were, though they were man and child held each other in a long embrace, and then the little scholar turned his face towards the wall, and fell asleep.

The poor schoolmaster sat in the same place, holding the small cold hand in his, and chafing it. It was but the hand of a dead child. He felt that; and yet he chafed it still, and could not lay it down.

CHAPTER XXVI

ALMOST broken-hearted, Nell withdrew with the schoolmaster from the bedside and returned to his cottage. In the midst of her grief and tears she was yet careful to conceal their real cause from the old man, for the dead boy had been a grandchild, and left but one aged relative to mourn his premature decay.

She stole away to bed as quickly as she could, and when she was alone, gave free vent to the sorrow with which her breast was overcharged. But the sad scene she had witnessed, was not without its lesson of content and gratitude; of content with the lot which left her health and freedom; and gratitude that she was spared to the one relative and friend she loved, and to live and move in a beautiful world, when so many young creatures-as young and full of hope as she-were stricken down and gathered to their graves. How many of the mounds in that old churchyard where she had lately strayed, grew green above the graves of children! And though she thought as a child herself, and did not perhaps sufficiently consider to what a bright and happy existence those who die young are borne, and how in death they lose the pain of seeing others die around them, bearing to the tomb some strong affection of their hearts (which makes the old die many times in one long life), still she thought wisely enough, to draw a plain and easy moral from what she had seen that night, and to store it, deep in her mind.

Her dreams were of the little scholar: not coffined and covered up, but mingling with angels, and smiling happily. The sun darting his cheerful rays into the room, awoke her; and now there remained but to take leave of the poor schoolmaster and wander forth once more.

By the time they were ready to depart, school had begun. In the dark-

ened room, the din of yesterday was going on again: a little sobered and softened down, perhaps, but only a very little, if at all. The schoolmaster rose
from his desk and walked with them to the gate.

It was with a trembling and reluctant hand, that the child held out to
him the money which the lady had given her at the races for her flowers:
faltering in her thanks as she thought how small the sum was, and blushing
as she offered it. But he bade her put it up, and stooping to kiss her cheek,
turned back into his house.

They had not gone half a dozen paces when he was at the door again;
the old man retraced his steps to shake hands, and the child did the same.

"Good fortune and happiness go with you!" said the poor schoolmaster. "I am quite a solitary man now. If ever you pass this way again, you'll
not forget the little village-school."

"We shall never forget it, sir," rejoined Nell; "nor ever forget to be
grateful to you for your kindness to us."

"I have heard such words from the lips of children very often," said the
schoolmaster, shaking his head and smiling thoughtfully, "but they were
soon forgotten. I had attached one young friend to me, the better friend for
being young-but that's over-God bless you!"

They bade him farewell very many times, and turned away, walking
slowly and often looking back, until they could see him no more. At length
they had left the village far behind, and even lost sight of the smoke among
the trees. They trudged onward now, at a quicker pace, resolving to keep the
main road, and go wherever it might lead them.

But main roads stretch a long, long way. With the exception of two or
three inconsiderable clusters of cottages which they passed, without stopping, and one lonely roadside public-house where they had some bread and
cheese, this highway had led them to nothing-late in the afternoon-and still
lengthened out, far in the distance, the same dull, tedious, winding course,
that they had been pursuing all day. As they had no resource, however, but
to go forward, they still kept on, though at a much slower pace, being very
weary and fatigued.

The afternoon had worn away into a beautiful evening, when they arrived at a point where the road made a sharp turn and struck across a common. On the border of this common, and close to the hedge which divided
it from the cultivated fields, a caravan was drawn up to rest; upon which, by
reason of its situation, they came so suddenly that they could not have
avoided it if they would.

It was not a shabby, dingy, dusty cart, but a smart little house upon
wheels, with white dimity curtains festooning the windows, and window-
shutters of green picked out with panels of a staring red, in which happily-
contrasted colours the whole concern shone brilliant. Neither was it a poor
caravan drawn by a single donkey or emaciated horse, for a pair of horses in
pretty good condition were released from the shafts and grazing on the
frowzy grass. Neither was it a gipsy caravan, for at the open door (graced
with a bright brass knocker) sat a Christian lady, stout and comfortable to
look upon, who wore a large bonnet trembling with bows. And that it was

not an unprovided or destitute caravan was clear from this lady's occupation, which was the very pleasant and refreshing one of taking tea. The tea-things, including a bottle of rather suspicious character and a cold knuckle of ham, were set forth upon a drum, covered with a white napkin; and there, as if at the most convenient round-table in all the world, sat this roving lady, taking her tea and enjoying the prospect.

It happened that at that moment the lady of the caravan had her cup (which, that everything about her might be of a stout and comfortable kind, was a breakfast cup) to her lips, and that having her eyes lifted to the sky in her enjoyment of the full flavour of the tea, not unmingled possibly with just the slightest dash or gleam of something out of the suspicious bottle-but this is mere speculation and not distinct matter of history-it happened that being thus agreeably engaged, she did not see the travellers when they first came up. It was not until she was in the act of setting down the cup, and drawing a long breath after the exertion of causing its contents to disappear, that the lady of the caravan beheld an old man and a young child walking slowly by, and glancing at her proceedings with eyes of modest but hungry admiration.

"Hey I" cried the lady of the caravan, scooping the crumbs out of her lap and swallowing the same before wiping her lips. "Yes, to be sure-Who won the Helter-Skelter Plate, child?"

"Won what, ma'am?" asked Nell.

"The Helter-Skelter Plate at the races, child-the plate that was run for on the second day."

"On the second day, ma'am?"

"Second day! Yes, second day," repeated the lady with an air of impatience. "Can't you say who won the Helter-Skelter Plate when you're asked the question civilly?"

"I don't know, ma'am."

"Don't know!" repeated the lady of the caravan; "why, you were there. I saw you with my own eyes."

Nell was not a little alarmed to hear this, supposing that the lady might be intimately acquainted with the firm of Short and Codlin; but what followed tended to reassure her.

"And very sorry I was," said the lady of the caravan, "to see you in company with a Punch; a low, practical, wulgar wretch, that people should scorn to look at."

"I was not there by choice," returned the child; "we didn't know our way, and the two men were very kind to us, and let us travel with them. Do you-do you know them, ma'am?"

"Know 'em, child!" cried the lady of the caravan in a sort of shriek. "Know *them!* But you're young and inexperienced, and that's your excuse for asking sich a question. Do I look as if I know'd 'em, does the caravan look as if it know'd 'em?"

"No, ma'am, no," said the child, fearing she had committed some grievous fault. "I beg your pardon."

It was granted immediately, though the lady still appeared much ruffled and discomposed by the degrading supposition. The child then explained that they had left the races on the first day, and were travelling to the next town on that road, where they purposed to spend the night. As the countenance of the stout lady began to clear up, she ventured to inquire how far it was. The reply-which the stout lady did not come to, until she had thoroughly explained that she went to the races on the first day in a gig, and as an expedition of pleasure, and that her presence there had no connexion with any matters of business or profit-was, that the town was eight miles off.

This discouraging information a little dashed the child, who could scarcely repress a tear as she glanced along the darkening road. Her grandfather made no complaint, but he sighed heavily as he leaned upon his staff, and vainly tried to pierce the dusty distance.

The lady of the caravan was in the act of gathering her tea equipage together preparatory to clearing the table, but noting the child's anxious manner she hesitated and stopped. The child curtseyed, thanked her for her information, and giving her hand to the old man had already got some fifty yards or so away, when the lady of the caravan called to her to return.

"Come nearer, nearer still"-said she, beckoning to her to ascend the steps. "Are you hungry, child?"

"Not very, but we are tired, and it's-it is a long way-"

"Well, hungry or not, you had better have some tea," rejoined her new acquaintance. "I suppose you are agree able to that, old gentleman?"

The grandfather humbly pulled off his hat and thanked her. The lady of the caravan then bade him come up the steps likewise, but the drum proving an inconvenient table for two, they descended again, and sat upon the grass, where she handed down to them the tea-tray, the bread and butter, the knuckle of ham, and in short everything of which she had partaken herself, except the bottle which she had already embraced an opportunity of slipping into her pocket.

"Set 'em out near the hind wheels, child, that's the best place" said their friend, superintending the arrangements from above. "Now hand up the teapot for a little more hot water, and a pinch of fresh tea, and then both of you eat and drink as much as you can, and don't spare anything; that's all I ask of you."

They might perhaps have carried out the lady's wish, if it had been less freely expressed, or even if it had not been expressed at all. But as this direction relieved them from any shadow of delicacy or uneasiness, they made a hearty meal and enjoyed it to the utmost.

While they were thus engaged, the lady of the caravan alighted on the earth, and with her hands clasped behind her, and her large bonnet trembling excessively, walked up and down in a measured tread and very stately manner, surveying the caravan from time to time with an air of calm delight, and deriving particular gratification from the red panels and the brass knocker. When she had taken this gentle exercise for some time, she sat down upon the steps and called "George:" whereupon a man in a carter's frock, who had been so shrouded in a hedge up to this time as to see everything that passed without being seen himself, parted the twigs that concealed him, and appeared in a sitting attitude, supporting on his legs a baking-dish and a half-gallon stone bottle, and bearing in his right hand a knife, and in his left a fork.

"Yes, missus" -said George.

"How did you find the cold pie, George?"

"It warn't amiss, mum."

"And the beer," said the lady of the caravan, with an appearance of being more interested in this question than the last; "is it passable, George?"

"It's more flatterer than it might be," George returned, "but it an't so bad for all that."

To set the mind of his mistress at rest, he took a sip (amounting in quantity to a pint or thereabouts) from the stone bottle, and then smacked his lips, winked his eye, and nodded his head. No doubt with the same amiable desire, he immediately resumed his knife and fork, as a practical assurance that the beer had wrought no bad effect upon his appetite.

The lady of the caravan looked on approvingly for some time, and then said,

"Have you nearly finished?"

"Wery nigh, mum." And indeed, after scraping the dish all round with his knife and carrying the choice brown morsels to his mouth, and after taking such a scientific pull at the stone bottle that, by degrees almost imperceptible to the sight, his head went further and further back until he lay nearly at his full length upon the ground, this gentleman declared himself quite disengaged, and came forth from his retreat.

"I hope I haven't hurried you, George," said his mistress, who appeared to have a great sympathy with his late pursuit.

"If you have," returned the follower, wisely reserving himself for any favourable contingency that might occur, "we must make up for it next time, that's all."

"We are not a heavy load, George?"

"That's always what the ladies say," replied the man, looking a long way round, as if he were appealing to Nature in general against such monstrous propositions. "If you see a woman a driving, you'll always perceive that she never will keep her whip still; the horse can't go fast enough for her. If cattle have got their proper load, you never can persuade a woman that they'll not bear something more. What is the cause of this here?"

"Would these two travellers make much difference to the horses, if we took them with us?" asked his mistress; offering no reply to the philosophical inquiry, and pointing to Nell and the old man, who were painfully preparing to resume their journey on foot.

"They'd make a difference in course," said George doggedly.

"Would they make much difference?" repeated his mistress. "They can't be very heavy."

"The weight o' the pair, mum," said George, eyeing them with the look of a man who was calculating within half an ounce or so, "would be a trifle under that of Oliver Cromwell."

Nell was very much surprised that the man should be so accurately acquainted with the weight of one whom she had read of in books as having lived considerably before their time, but speedily forgot the subject in the joy of hearing that they were to go forward in the caravan, for which she thanked its lady with unaffected earnestness. She helped with great readiness and alacrity to put away the tea-things and other matters that were lying about, and, the horses being by that time harnessed, mounted into the vehicle, followed by her delighted grandfather. Their patroness then shut the door and sat herself down by her drum at an open window; and, the steps being struck by George and stowed under the carriage, away they went, with a great noise of flapping and creaking and straining, and the bright brass knocker, which nobody ever knocked at, knocking one perpetual double knock of its own accord as they jolted heavily along.

CHAPTER XXVII

WHEN they had travelled slowly forward for some short distance, Nell ventured to steal a look round the caravan and observe it more closely. One half of it-that moiety in which the comfortable proprietess was then seated-was carpeted, and so partitioned off at the further end as to accommodate a sleeping place, constructed after the fashion of a berth on board ship, which was shaded, like the little windows, with fair white curtains, and looked comfortable enough, though by what kind of gymnastic exercise the lady of the caravan ever contrived to get into it, was an unfathomable mystery. The other half served for a kitchen, and was fitted up with a stove whose small chimney passed through the roof. It held also a closet or larder, several chests, a great pitcher of water, and a few cooking-utensils and articles of crockery. These latter necessaries hung upon the walls, which, in that portion of the establishment devoted to the lady of the caravan, were ornamented with such gayer and lighter decorations as a triangle and a couple of well-thumbed tambourines.

The lady of the caravan sat at one window in all the pride and poetry of the musical instruments, and little Nell and her grandfather sat at the other in all the humility of the kettle and saucepans, while the machine jogged on and shifted the darkening prospect very slowly. At first the two travellers spoke little, and only in whispers, but as they grew more familiar with the place they ventured to converse with greater freedom, and talked about the country through which they were passing, and the different objects that presented themselves, until the old man fell asleep; which the lady of the caravan observing, invited Nell to come and sit beside her.

"Well, child," she said, "how do you like this way of travelling?"

Nell replied that she thought it was very pleasant indeed, to which the lady assented in the case of people who had their spirits. For herself, she said, she was troubled with a lowness in that respect which required a constant stimulant; though whether the aforesaid stimulant was derived from the suspicious bottle of which mention has been already made, or from other sources, she did not say.

"That's the happiness of you young people," she continued. "You don't know what it is to be low in your feelings. You always have your appetites too, and what a comfort that is."

Nell thought that she could sometimes dispense with her own appetite very conveniently; and thought, moreover, that there was nothing either in the lady's personal appearance or in her manner of taking tea, to lead to the conclusion that her natural relish for meat and drink had at all failed her. She silently assented, however, as in duty bound, to what the lady had said, and waited until she should speak again.

Instead of speaking, however, she sat looking at the child for a long time in silence, and then getting up, brought out from a corner a large roll of canvas about a yard in width, which she laid upon the floor and spread open with her foot until it nearly reached from one end of the caravan to the other.

"There, child," she said, "read that."

Nell walked down it, and read aloud, in enormous black letters, the inscription, "JARLEY'S WAX-WORK."

"Read it again," said the lady, complacently.

"Jarley's Wax-Work," repeated Nell.

"That's me," said the lady. "I am Mrs. Jarley."

Giving the child an encouraging look, intended to reassure her and let her know, that, although she stood in the presence of the original Jarley, she must not allow herself to be utterly overwhelmed and borne down, the lady of the caravan unfolded another scroll, whereon was the inscription, "One hundred figures the full size of life," and then another scroll, on which was written, "The only stupendous collection of real wax-work in the world," and then several smaller scrolls with such inscriptions as "Now exhibiting within"- The genuine and only Jarley"-"Jarley's unrivalled collection"- "Jarley is the delight of the Nobility and Gentry"-"The Royal Family are the Patrons of Jarley." When she had exhibited these leviathans of public announcement to the astonished child, she brought forth specimens of the lesser fry in the shape of hand-bills, some of which were crouched in the form of parodies on popular melodies, as "Believe me if all Jarley's wax-work so rare"-"I saw thy show in youthful prime"-"Over the water to Jarley;" while, to consult all tastes, others were composed with a view to the lighter and more facetious spirits, as a parody on the favourite air of "If I had a donkey," beginning

> If I know'd a donkey wot wouldn't go
> To see Mrs. JARLEY'S wax-work show,
> Do you think I'd acknowledge him?
> Oh no no!
> Then run to Jarley's-

-besides several compositions in prose, purporting to be dialogues between the Emperor of China and an oyster, or the Archbishop of Canterbury and a Dissenter on the subject of church-rates, but all having the same moral, namely, that the reader must make haste to Jarley's, and that children and servants were admitted at half-price. When she had brought all these testimonials of her important position in society to bear upon her young companion, Mrs. Jarley rolled them up, and having put them carefully away, sat down again, and looked at the child in triumph.

"Never go into the company of a filthy Punch any more," said Mrs. Jarley, "after this."

"I never saw any wax-work, ma'am," said Nell. "Is it funnier than Punch?"

"Funnier!" said Mrs. Jarley in a shrill voice: "It is not funny at all."

"Oh!" said Nell, with all possible humility.

"It isn't funny at all," repeated Mrs. Jarley. "It's calm and-what's that word again-critical?-no-classical, that's it-it's calm and classical. No low beatings and knockings about, no jokings and squeakings like your precious Punches, but always the same, with a constantly unchanging air of coldness and gentility; and so like life, that if wax-work only spoke and walked about, you'd hardly know the difference. I won't go so far as to say, that, as it is, I've seen wax-work quite like life, but I've certainly seen some life that was exactly like wax-work."

"Is it here, ma'am?" asked Nell, whose curiosity was awakened by this description.

"Is what here, child?"

"The wax-work, ma'am?"

"Why, bless you, child, what are you thinking of? How could such a collection be here, where you see everything except the inside of one little cupboard and a few boxes? It's gone on in the other wans to the assembly-rooms, and there it'll be exhibited the day after to-morrow. You are going to the same town, and you'll see it I dare say. It's natural to expect that you'll see it, and I've no doubt you will. I suppose you couldn't stop away if you was to try ever so much."

"I shall not be in the town, I think, ma'am," said the child.

"Not there I" cried Mrs. Jarley. "Then where will you be?"

"I-I-don't quite know. I am not certain."

"You don't mean to say that you're travelling about the country without knowing where you're going to?" said the lady of the caravan. "What curious people you are! What line are you in? You looked to me at the races, child, as if you were quite out of your element, and got there by accident."

"We were there quite by accident," returned Nell, confused by this abrupt questioning. "We are poor people, ma'am, and are only wandering about. We have nothing to do;-I wish we had."

"You amaze me more and more," said Mrs. Jarley, after remaining for some time as mute as one of her own figures. "Why, what do you call yourselves? Not beggars?"

"Indeed, ma'am, I don't know what else we are," returned the child.

"Lord bless me," said the lady of the caravan. "I never heard of such a thing. Who'd have thought it!"

She remained so long silent after this exclamation, that Nell feared she felt her having been induced to bestow her protection and conversation upon one so poor, to be an outrage upon her dignity that nothing could repair. This persuasion was rather confirmed than otherwise by the tone in which she at length broke silence and said,

"And yet you can read. And write too, I shouldn't wonder?"

"Yes, ma'am," said the child, fearful of giving new offence by the confession.

"Well, and what a thing that is," returned Mrs. Jarley. "I can't!"

Nell said "indeed" in a tone which might imply, either that she was reasonably surprised to find the genuine and only Jarley, who was the delight of the Nobility and Gentry and the peculiar pet of the Royal Family, destitute of these familiar arts; or that she presumed so great a lady could scarcely stand in need of such ordinary accomplishments. In whatever way Mrs. Jarley received the response, it did not provoke her to further questioning, or tempt her into any more remarks at the time, for she relapsed into a thoughtful silence, and remained in that state so long that Nell withdrew to the other window and rejoined her grandfather, who was now awake.

At length the lady of the caravan shook off her fit of meditation, and, summoning the driver to come under the window at which she was seated, held a long conversation with him in a low tone of voice, as if she were asking his advice on an important point, and discussing the pros and cons of some very weighty matter. This conference at length concluded, she drew in her head again, and beckoned Nell to approach.

"And the old gentleman too," said Mrs. Jarley; "for I want to have a word with him. Do you want a good situation for your grand-daughter, master? If you do, I can put her in the way of getting one. What do you say?"

"I can't leave her," answered the old man. "We can't separate. What would become of me without her?"

"I should have thought you were old enough to take care of yourself, if you ever will be," retorted Mrs. Jarley sharply.

"But he never will be," said the child in an earnest whisper. "I fear he never will be again. Pray do not speak harshly to him. We are very thankful to you," she added aloud; "but neither of us could part from the other if all the wealth of the world were halved between us."

Mrs. Jarley was a little disconcerted by this reception of her proposal, and looked at the old man, who tenderly took Nell's hand and detained it in his own, as if she could have very well dispensed with his company or even his earthly existence. After an awkward pause, she thrust her head out of the window again, and had another conference with the driver upon a point on which they did not seem to agree quite so readily as on their former topic of discussion; but they concluded at last, and she addressed the grandfather again.

"If you're really disposed to employ yourself," said Mrs. Jarley, "there would be plenty for you to do in the way of helping to dust the figures, and take the checks, and so forth. What I want your grand-daughter for, is to point 'em out to the company; they would be soon learnt, and she has a way with her that people wouldn't think unpleasant, though she does come after me; for I've been always accustomed to go round with visitors myself, which I should keep on doing now, only that my spirits make a little ease absolutely necessary. It's not a common offer, bear in mind," said the lady, rising into the tone and manner in which she was accustomed to address her audiences; "it's Jarley's wax-work, remember. The duty's very light and genteel, the company particular select, the exhibition takes place in assembly rooms, town-halls, large rooms at inns, or auction galleries. There is none of your open-air wagrancy at Jarley's, recollect; there is no tarpaulin and sawdust at Jarley's, remember. Every expectation held out in the handbills is realised to the utmost, and the whole forms an effect of imposing brilliancy hitherto unrivalled in this kingdom. Remember that the price of admission is only sixpence, and that this is an opportunity which may never occur again!"

Descending from the sublime when she had reached this point, to the details of common life, Mrs. Jarley remarked that with reference to salary she could pledge herself to no specific sum until she had sufficiently tested Nell's abilities, and narrowly watched her in the performance of her duties. But board and lodging, both for her and her grandfather, she bound herself to provide, and she furthermore passed her word that the board should always be good in quality, and in quantity plentiful.

Nell and her grandfather consulted together, and while they were so engaged, Mrs. Jarley with her hands behind her walked up and down the caravan, as she had walked after tea on the dull hearth, with uncommon dignity and self-esteem. Nor will this appear so slight a circumstance as to be unworthy of mention, when it is remembered that the caravan was in uneasy motion all the time, and that none but a person of great and natural stateliness and acquired grace could have forborne to stagger.

"Now, child?" cried Mrs. Jarley, coming to a halt as Nell turned towards her.

"We are very much obliged to you, ma'am," said Nell, "and thankfully accept your offer."

"And you'll never be sorry for it," returned Mrs. Jarley. "I'm pretty sure of that. So as that's all settled, let us have a bit of supper."

In the meanwhile, the caravan blundered on as if it too had been drinking strong beer and was drowsy, and came at last upon the paved streets of a town which were clear of passengers, and quiet, for it was by this time near mid- night, and the townspeople were all abed. As it was too late an hour to repair to the exhibition room, they turned aside into a piece of waste ground that lay just within the old town-gate, and drew up there for the night, near to another caravan, which, notwithstanding that it bore on the lawful panel the great name of Jarley, and was employed besides in conveying from place to place the wax-work which was its country's pride, was designated by a grovelling stamp-office as a "Common Stage Waggon," and numbered too-seven thousand odd hundred-as though its precious freight were mere flour or coals!

This ill-used machine being empty (for it had deposited its burden at the place of exhibition, and lingered here until its services were again required) was assigned to the old man as his sleeping-place for the night; and within its wooden walls, Nell made him up the best bed she could, from the materials at hand. For herself, she was to sleep in Mrs. Jarley's own travelling carriage, as a signal mark of that lady's favour and confidence.

She had taken leave of her grandfather and was returning to the other waggon, when she was tempted by the pleasant coolness of the night to linger for a little while in the air. The moon was shining down upon the old gateway of the town, leaving the low archway very black and dark; and with a mingled sensation of curiosity and fear, she slowly approached the gate, and stood still to look up at it, wondering to see how dark, and grim, and old, and cold, it looked.

There was an empty niche from which some old statue had fallen or been carried away hundreds of years ago, and she was thinking what strange people it must have looked down upon when it stood there, and how many hard struggles might have taken place, and how many murders might have been done, upon that silent spot, when there suddenly emerged from the black shade of the arch, a man. The instant he appeared, she recognised him-Who could have failed to recognise, in that instant, the ugly misshapen Quilp!

The street beyond was so narrow, and the shadow of the houses on one side of the way so deep, that he seemed to have risen out of the earth. But there he was. The child withdrew into a dark corner, and saw him pass close to her. He had a stick in his hand, and, when he had got clear of the shadow of the gateway, he leant upon it, looked back -directly, as it seemed, towards where she stood-and beckoned.

To her? oh no, thank God, not to her; for as she stood, in an extremity of. fear, hesitating whether to scream for help, or come from her hiding-place and fly, before he should draw nearer, there issued slowly forth from the arch another figure-that of a boy-who carried on his back a trunk.

"Faster, sirrah!" said Quilp, looking up at the old gateway, and showing in the moonlight like some monstrous image that had come down from its niche and was casting a backward glance at its old house, "faster!"

"It's a dreadful heavy load, sir," the boy pleaded. "I've come on very fast, considering."

"*You* have come fast, considering!" retorted Quilp; "you creep, you dog, you crawl, you measure distance like a worm. There are the chimes now, half-past twelve."

He stopped to listen, and then turning upon the boy with a suddenness and ferocity that made him start, asked at what hour that London coach passed the corner of the road. The boy replied, at one.

"Come on then," said Quilp, "or I shall be too late. Faster-do you hear me? Faster."

The boy made all the speed he could, and Quilp led onward, constantly turning back to threaten him, and urge him to greater haste. Nell did not dare to move until they were out of sight and hearing, and then hurried to where she had left her grandfather, feeling as if the very passing of the dwarf so near him must have filled him with alarm and terror. But he was sleeping soundly, and she softly withdrew.

As she was making her way to her own bed, she determined to say nothing of this adventure, as upon whatever errand the dwarf had come (and she feared it must have been in search of them) it was clear by his inquiry about the London coach that he was on his way homeward, and as he had passed through that place, it was but reasonable to suppose that they were safer from his inquiries there, than they could be elsewhere. These reflections did not remove her own alarm, for she had been too much terrified to be easily composed, and felt as if she were hemmed in by a legion of Quilps, and the very air itself were filled with them.

The delight of the Nobility and Gentry and the patronised of Royalty had, by some process of self-abridgment known only to herself, got into her travelling bed, where she was snoring peacefully, while the large bonnet, carefully disposed upon the drum, was revealing its glories by the light of a dim lamp that swung from the roof. The child's bed was already made upon the floor, and it was a great comfort to her to hear the steps removed as soon as she had entered, and to know that all easy communication between persons outside and the brass knocker was by this means effectually prevented. Certain guttural sounds, too, which from time to time ascended through the floor of the caravan, and a rustling of straw in the same direction, apprised her that the driver was couched upon the ground beneath, and gave her an additional feeling of security.

Notwithstanding these protections, she could get none but broken sleep by fits and starts all night, for fear of Quilp, who throughout her uneasy dreams was somehow connected with the wax-work, or was wax-work himself, or was Mrs. Jarley and wax-work too, or was himself, Mrs. Jarley, wax-work, and a barrel organ all in one, and yet not exactly any of them either. At length, towards break of day, that deep sleep came upon her which succeeds to weariness and over-watching, and which has no consciousness but one of overpowering and irresistible enjoyment.

CHAPTER XXVIII

SLEEP hung upon the eyelids of the child so long, that, when she awoke, Mrs. Jarley was already decorated with her large bonnet, and actively engaged in preparing breakfast. She received Nell's apology for being so late with perfect good humour, and said that she should not have roused her if she had slept on until noon.

"Because it does you good," said the lady of the caravan, "when you're tired, to sleep as long as ever you can, and get the fatigue quite off; and that's another blessing of your time of life-you can sleep so very sound."

"Have you had a bad night, ma'am?" asked Nell.

"I seldom have anything else, child." replied Mrs. Jarley, with the air of a martyr. "I sometimes wonder how I bear it."

Remembering the snores which had proceeded from that cleft in the caravan in which the proprietress of the wax- work passed the night, Nell rather thought she must have been dreaming of lying awake. However, she expressed herself very sorry to hear such a dismal account of her state of health, and shortly afterwards sat down with her grandfather and Mrs. Jarley to breakfast. The meal finished, Nell assisted to wash the cups and saucers, and put them in their proper places, and these household duties performed, Mrs. Jarley arrayed herself in an exceedingly bright shawl for the purpose of making a progress through the streets of the town.

"The wan will come on to bring the boxes," said Mrs. Jarley, "and you had better come in it, child. I am obliged to walk, very much against my will; but the people expect it of me, and public characters can't be their own masters and mistresses in such matters as these. How do I look, child?"

Nell returned a satisfactory reply, and Mrs. Jarley, after sticking a great many pins into various parts of her figure, and making several abortive attempts to obtain a full view of her own back, was at last satisfied with her appearance, and went forth majestically.

The caravan followed at no great distance. As it went jolting through the streets, Nell peeped from the window, curious to see in what kind of place they were, and yet fearful of encountering at every turn the dreaded face of Quilp. It was a pretty large town, with an open square which they were crawling slowly across, and in the middle of which was the Town-Hall, with a clock-tower and a weathercock. There were houses of stone, houses of red brick, houses of yellow brick, houses of lath and plaster; and houses of wood, many of them very old, with withered faces carved upon the beams, and staring down into the street. These had very little winking windows, and low-arched doors, and, in some of the narrower ways, quite overhung the pavement. The streets were very clean, very sunny, very empty, and very dull. A few idle men lounged about the two inns, and the empty market-place, and the tradesmen's doors, and some old people were dozing in chairs outside an almshouse wall; but scarcely any passengers who seemed bent on going anywhere, or to have any object in view, went by; and if perchance some straggler did, his footsteps echoed on the hot bright pavement for minutes afterwards. Nothing seemed to be going on but the clocks, and they had such drowsy faces, such heavy lazy hands, and such cracked voices, that they surely must have been too slow. The very dogs were all asleep, and the flies, drunk with moist sugar in the grocer's shop, forgot their wings and briskness, and baked to death in dusty corners of the window.

Rumbling along with most unwonted noise, the caravan stopped at last at the place of exhibition, where Nell dismounted amidst an admiring group of children, who evidently supposed her to be an important item of the curiosities, and, were fully impressed with the belief that her grandfather was a cunning device in wax. The chests were taken out with all convenient despatch, and taken in to be unlocked by Mrs. Jarley, who, attended by George and another man in velveteen shorts and a drab hat ornamented with turnpike tickets, were waiting to dispose their contents (consisting of red festoons and other ornamental devices in upholstery work) to the best advantage in the decoration of the room.

They all got to work without loss of time, and very busy they were. As the stupendous collection were yet concealed by cloths, lest the envious dust should injure their complexions, Nell bestirred herself to assist in the embellish-ment of the room, in which her grandfather also was of great service. The two men being well used to it, did a great deal in a short time; and Mrs. Jarley served out the tin tacks from a linen pocket like a toll-collector's which she wore for the purpose, and encouraged her assistants to renewed exertion.

While they were thus employed, a tallish gentleman with a hook nose and black hair, dressed in a military surtout very short and tight in the sleeves, and which had once been frogged and braided all over, but was now sadly shorn of its garniture and quite threadbare-dressed too in ancient grey pantaloons fitting tight to the leg, and a pair of pumps in the winter of their existence-looked in at the door, and smiled affably. Mrs. Jarley's back being then towards him, the military gentleman shook his forefinger as a sign that her myrmidons were not to apprise her of his presence, and steal-ing- up close behind her, tapped her on the neck, and cried playfully "Boh!"

"What, Mr. Slum I" cried the lady of the wax-work. "Lor! who'd have thought of seeing you here!"

"Pon my soul and honour," said Mr. Slum, "that's a good remark. 'Pon my soul and honour, that's a wise remark. Who *would* have thought it! George, my faithful feller, how are you?"

George received this advance with a surly indifference, observing that he was well enough for the matter of that, and hammering lustily all the time.

"I came here," said the military gentleman turning to Mrs. Jarley,- "'pon my soul and honour, I hardly know what I came here for. It would puzzle me to tell you, it would by Gad. I wanted a little inspiration, a little freshening up, a little change of ideas, and-'Pon my soul and honour," said the military gentleman, checking himself and looking round the room, "what a devilish classical thing this is! By Gad, it's quite Minervian!"

"It'll look well enough when it comes to be finished," observed Mrs. Jarley.

"Well enough!" said Mr. Slum. "Will you believe me when I say it's the delight of my life to have dabbled in poetry, when I think I've exercised my pen upon this charming theme? By the way-any orders? Is there any little thing I can do for you?"

"It comes so very expensive, sir," replied Mrs. Jarley, "and I really don't think it does much good."

"Hush! No, no!" returned Mr. Slum, elevating his hand. "No fibs. I'll not hear it. Don't say it don't do good. Don't say it. I know better!"

"I don't think it does," said Mrs. Jarley.

"Ha, ha!" cried Mr. Slum, "you're giving way, you're coming down. Ask the perfumers, ask the blacking-makers, ask the hatters, ask the old lot-tery-office-keepers-ask any man among 'em what my poetry has done for him, and mark my words, he blesses the name of Slum. If he's an honest man, he raises his eyes to heaven, and blesses the name of Slum-mark that! You are acquainted with Westminster Abbey, Mrs. Jarley?"

"Yes, surely."

"Then upon my soul and honour, ma'am, you'll find in a certain angle of that dreary pile, called Poets' Corner, a few smaller names than Slum," retorted that gentleman, tapping himself expressively on the forehead to imply that . there was some slight quantity of brains behind it. "I've got a little trifle here, now," said Mr. Slum, taking off his hat which was full of scraps of paper, "a little trifle here, thrown off in the heat of the moment, which I should say was exactly the thing you wanted to set this place on fire with. It's an acrostic-the name at this moment is Warren, but the idea's a convertible one, and a positive inspiration for Jarley. Have the acrostic."

"I suppose it's very dear," said Mrs. Jarley.

"Five shillings," returned Mr. Slum, using his pencil as a tooth-pick. "Cheaper than any prose."

"I couldn't give more than three," said Mrs. Jarley.

"And six," retorted Slum. "Come. Three-and-six."

Mrs. Jarley was not proof against the poet's insinuating manner, and Mr. Slum entered the order in a small note-book as a three-and-sixpenny one. Mr. Slum then withdrew to alter the acrostic, after taking a most affectionate leave of his patroness, and promising to return, as soon as he possibly could, with a fair copy for the printer.

As his presence had not interfered with or interrupted the preparations, they were now far advanced, and were completed shortly after his departure. When the festoons were all put up as tastily as they might be, the stupendous collection was uncovered, and there were displayed, on a raised platform some two feet from the floor, running round the room and parted from the rude public by a crimson rope breast high, divers sprightly effigies of celebrated characters, singly and in groups, clad in glittering dresses of various climes and times, and standing more or less unsteadily upon their legs, with their eyes very wide open, and their nostrils very much inflated, and the muscles of their legs and arms very strongly developed, and all their countenances expressing great surprise. All the gentlemen were very pigeon-breasted and very blue about the beards; and all the ladies were miraculous figures; and all the ladies and all the gentlemen were looking intensely nowhere, and staring with extraordinary earnestness at nothing.

When Nell had exhausted her first raptures at this glorious sight, Mrs. Jarley ordered the room to be cleared of all but herself and the child, and, sitting herself down in an arm-chair in the centre, formally invested her with a willow wand, long used by herself for pointing out the characters, and was at great pains to instruct her in her duty.

"That," said Mrs. Jarley in her exhibition tone, as Nell touched a figure at the beginning of the platform, "is an unfortunate Maid of Honour in the Time of Queen Elizabeth, who died from pricking her finger in consequence of working upon a Sunday. Observe the blood which is trickling from her finger; also the gold-eyed needle of the period, with which she is at work."

All this Nell repeated twice or thrice, pointing to the finger and the needle at the right times, and then passed on to the next.

"That, ladies and gentlemen," said Mrs. Jarley, "is jasper Packlemerton of atrocious memory, who courted and married fourteen wives, and destroyed them all by tickling the soles of their feet when they was sleeping in the consciousness of innocence and virtue. On being brought to the scaffold and asked if he was sorry for what he had done, he replied yes, he was sorry for having let 'em off so easy, and hoped all Christian husbands would pardon him the offence. Let this be a warning to all young ladies to be particular in the character of the gentlemen of their choice. Observe that his fingers is curled as if in the act of tickling, and that his face is represented with a wink, as he appeared when committing his barbarous murders."

When Nell knew all about Mr. Packlemerton, and could say it without faltering, Mrs. Jarley passed on to the fat man, and then to the thin man, the tall man, the short man, the old lady who died of dancing at a hundred and thirty- two, the wild boy of the woods, the woman who poisoned fourteen families with pickled walnuts, and other historical characters and interesting but misguided individuals. And so well did Nell profit by her instructions, and so apt was she to remember them, that by the time they had been shut up together for a couple of hours, she was in full possession of the history of the whole establishment, and perfectly competent to the enlightenment of visitors.

Mrs. Jarley was not slow to express her admiration at this happy result, and carried her young friend and pupil to inspect the remaining arrangements within doors, by virtue of which the passage had been already converted into a grove of green-baize hung with the inscriptions she had already seen (Mr. Slum's productions), and a highly ornamented table placed at the upper end for Mrs. Jarley herself, at which she was to preside and take the money, in company with his Majesty King George the Third, Mr. Grimaldi as clown, Mary Queen of Scots, an anonymous gentleman of the Quaker persuasion, and Mr. Pitt holding in his hand a correct model of the bill for the imposition of the window duty. The preparations without doors had not been neglected either; for a nun of great personal attractions was telling her beads on the little portico over the door; and a brigand with the blackest possible head of hair, and the clearest possible complexion, was at that moment going round the town in a cart, consulting the miniature of a lady.

It now only remained that Mr. Slum's compositions should be judiciously distributed; that the pathetic effusions should find their way to all private houses and tradespeople; and that the parody commencing "If I know'd a donkey," should be confined to the taverns, and circulated only among the lawyers' clerks and choice spirits of the place. When this had been done, and Mrs. Jarley had waited upon the boarding-schools in person, with a handbill composed expressly for them, in which it was distinctly proved that wax-work refined the mind, cultivated the taste, and enlarged the sphere of the human understanding, that indefatigable lady sat down to dinner, and drank out of the suspicious bottle to a flourishing campaign.

CHAPTER XXIX

UNQUESTIONABLY Mrs. Jarley had an inventive genius. In the midst of the various devices for attracting visitors to the exhibition, little Nell was not forgotten. The light cart in which the Brigand usually made his perambulations being gaily dressed with flags and streamers, and the Brigand placed therein, contemplating the miniature of his beloved as usual, Nell was accommodated with a seat beside him, decorated with artificial flowers, and in this state and ceremony rode slowly through the town every morning, dispersing handbills from a basket, to the sound of drum and trumpet. The beauty of the child, coupled with her gentle and timid bearing, produced quite a sensation in the little country place. The Brigand, heretofore a source of exclusive interest in the streets, became a mere secondary consideration, and to be important only as a part of the show of which she was the chief attraction. Grown-up folks began to be interested in the bright-eyed girl, and some score of little boys fell desperately in love, and constantly left inclosures of nuts and apples, directed in small text, at the wax-work door.

This desirable impression was not lost upon Mrs. Jarley, who, lest Nell should become too cheap, soon sent the Brigand out alone again, and kept her in the exhibition room, where she described the figures every half-hour to the great satisfaction of admiring audiences. And these audiences were of a very superior description, including a great many young ladies' boarding-schools, whose favour Mrs. Jarley had been at great pains to conciliate, by altering the face and costume of Mr. Grimaldi as clown to represent Mr. Lindley Murray as he appeared when engaged in the composition of his English Grammar, and turning a murderess of great renown into Mrs. Hannah More-both of which likenesses were admitted by Miss Monflathers, who was at the head of the head Boarding and Day Establishment in the town, and who condescended to take a Private View with eight chosen young ladies, to be quite startling from their extreme correctness. Mr. Pitt in a night-cap and bedgown, and without his boots, represented the poet Cowper with perfect exactness; and Mary Queen of Scots in a dark wig, white shirt-collar, and male attire, was such a complete image of Lord Byron that the young ladies quite screamed when they saw it. Miss Mon-flathers, however, rebuked this enthusiasm, and took occasion to reprove Mrs. Jarley for not keeping her collection more select, observing that His Lordship had held certain free opinions quite incompatible with wax-work honours, and adding something about a Dean and Chapter, which Mrs. Jarley did not understand.

Although her duties were sufficiently laborious, Nell found in the lady of the caravan a very kind and considerate person, who had not only a peculiar relish for being comfortable herself, but for making everybody about her comfortable also; which latter taste, it may be remarked, is, even in persons who live in much finer places than caravans, a far more rare and uncommon one than the first, and is not by any means its necessary consequence.

As her popularity procured her various little fees from the visitors on which her patroness never demanded any toll, and as her grandfather too was well-treated and useful, she had no cause of anxiety in connexion with the wax-work, beyond that which sprang from her recollection of Quilp, and her fears that he might return and one day suddenly encounter them.

Quilp indeed was a perpetual nightmare to the child, who was constantly haunted by a vision of his ugly face and stunted figure. She slept, for their better security, in the room where the wax-work figures were, and she never retired to this place at night but she tortured herself-she could not help it-with imagining a resemblance, in some one or other of their death-like faces, to the dwarf, and this fancy would sometimes so gain upon her that she would almost believe he had removed the figure and stood within the clothes. Then there were so many of them with their great glassy eyes-and, as they stood one behind the other all about her bed, they looked so like living creatures, and yet so unlike in their grim stillness and silence, that she had a kind of terror of them for their own sakes, and would often lie watching their dusky figures until she was obliged to rise and light a candle, or go and sit at the open window and feel a companionship in the bright stars. At these times, she would recall the old house and the window at which she used to sit alone; and then she would think of poor Kit and all his kindness, until the tears came into her eyes, and she would weep and smile together.

Often and anxiously at this silent hour, her thoughts reverted to her grandfather, and she would wonder how much he remembered of their former life, and whether he was ever really mindful of the change in their condition and of their late helplessness and destitution. When they were wandering about, she seldom thought of this, but now she could not help considering what would become of them if he fell sick, or her own strength were to fail her. He was very patient and willing, happy to execute any little task, and glad to be of use; but he was in the same listless state, with no prospect of improvement-a mere child-a poor, thoughtless, vacant creature-a harmless fond old man, susceptible of tender love and regard for her, and of pleasant and painful impressions, but alive to nothing more. It made her very sad to know that this was so-so sad to see it that sometimes when he sat idly by, smiling and nodding- to her when she looked round, or when he caressed some little child and carried it to and fro, as he was fond of doing by the hour together, perplexed by its simple questions, yet patient under his own infirmity, and seeming almost conscious of it too, and humbled even before the mind of an infant-so sad it made her to see him thus, that she would burst into tears, and, withdrawing into some secret place, fall down upon her knees and pray that he might be restored.

But the bitterness of her grief was not in beholding him in this condition, when he was at least content and tranquil, nor in her solitary meditations on his altered state, though these were trials for a young heart. Cause for deeper and heavier sorrow was yet to come.

One evening, a holiday night with them, Nell and her grandfather went out to walk. They had been rather closely confined for some days, and the weather being warm, they strolled a long distance. Clear of the town, they took a footpath which struck through some pleasant fields, judging that it would terminate in the road they quitted and enable them to return that way. It made, however, a much wider circuit than they had supposed, and thus they were tempted onward until sunset, when they reached the track of which they were in search, and stopped to rest.

It had been gradually getting overcast, and now the sky was dark and lowering, save where the glory of the departing sun piled up masses of gold and burning fire, decaying embers of which gleamed here and there through the black veil, and shone redly down upon the earth. The wind began to moan in hollow murmurs, as the sun went down carrying glad day else-where; and a train of dull clouds coming up against it, menaced thunder and lightning. Large drops of rain soon began to fall, and, as the storm clouds came sailing onward, others supplied the void they left behind and spread over all the sky. Then was heard the low rumbling of distant thunder, then the lightning quivered, and then the darkness of an hour seemed to have gathered in an instant.

Fearful of taking shelter beneath a tree or hedge, the old man and the child hurried along the high road, hoping to find some house in which they could seek a refuge from the storm, which had now burst forth in earnest, and every moment increased in violence. Drenched with the pelting rain, confused by the deafening thunder, and bewildered by the glare of the forked lightning, they would have passed a solitary house without being aware of its vicinity, had not a man, who was standing at the door, called lustily to them to enter.

"Your ears ought to be better than other folks' at any rate, if you make so little of the chance of being struck blind," he said, retreating from the door and shading his eyes with his hands as the jagged lightning came again. "What were you going past for, eh?" he added, as he closed the door and led the way along a passage to a room behind.

"We didn't see the house, sir, till we heard you calling," Nell replied.

"No wonder," said the man, "with this lightning in one's eyes, by the bye. You had better stand by the fire here, and dry yourselves a bit. You can call for what you like if you want anything. If you don't want anything, you are not obliged to give an order, don't be afraid of that. This is a public-house, that's all. The Valiant Soldier is pretty well known hereabouts."

"Is this house called the Valiant Soldier, sir?" asked Nell.

"I thought everybody knew that," replied the landlord. "Where have you come from, if you don't know the Valiant Soldier as well as the Church catechism? This is the Valiant Soldier, by Jemes Groves,-Jem Groves- honest Jam Groves, as is a man of unblemished moral character, and has a good dry skittle-ground. If any man has got anything to say again Jem Groves, let him say it to Jem Groves, and Jem Groves can accommodate him with a cus-tomer on any terms from four pound a side to forty."

With these words, the speaker tapped himself on the waistcoat to inti-mate that he was the Jem Groves so highly eulogised; sparred scientifically at a counterfeit Jem Groves, who was sparring at society in general from a black frame over the chimney-piece; and, applying a half-emptied glass of spirits and water to his lips, drank Jem Groves's health.

The night being warm, there was a large screen drawn across the room, for a barrier against the heat of the fire. It seemed as if somebody on the other side of this screen; had been insinuating doubts of Mr. Groves's prowess, and had thereby given rise to these egotistical expressions, for Mr. Groves wound up his defiance by giving a loud knock, upon it with his knuckles and pausing for a reply from the other side.

"There an't many men," said Mr. Groves, no answer being returned, "who would ventur' to cross Jem Groves, under his own roof. There's only one man, I know, that has nerve enough for that, and that man's not a hundred mile from here neither. But he's worth a dozen men, and I let him say of me whatever he likes in consequence,-he knows that."

In return for this complimentary address, a very gruff hoarse voice bade Mr. Groves "hold his noise and light a candle." And the same voice remarked that the same gentleman "needn't waste his breath in brag, for most people knew pretty well what sort of stuff he was made of."

"Nell, they're-they're playing cards," whispered the old man, suddenly interested. "Don't you hear them?"

"Look sharp with that candle," said the voice; "it's as much as I can do to see the pips on the cards as it is; and get this shutter closed as quick as you can, will you? Your beer will be the worse for to-night's thunder I expect.- Game! Seven-and-sixpence to me, old Isaac. Hand over."

"Do you hear, Nell, do you hear them?" whispered the old man again, with increased earnestness, as the money chinked upon the table.

"I haven't seen such a storm as this," said a sharp cracked voice of most disagreeable quality, when a tremendous peal of thunder had died away, "since the night when old Luke Withers won thirteen times running, upon the red. We all said he had the Devil's luck and his own, and as it was the kind of night for the Devil to be out and busy, I suppose he *was* looking over his shoulder, if anybody could have seen him."

"Ah!" returned the gruff voice; "for all old Luke's winning through thick and thin of late years, I remember the time when he was the unluckiest and unfortunatest of men. He never took a dice-box in his hand, or held a card, but he was plucked, pigeoned, and cleaned out completely."

"Do you hear what he says?" whispered the old man. "Do you hear that, Nell?"

The child saw with astonishment and alarm that his whole appearance had undergone a complete change. His face was flushed and eager, his eyes were strained, his teeth set, his breath came short and thick, and the hand he laid upon her arm trembled so violently that she shook beneath its grasp.

"Bear witness," he muttered, looking upward, "that I always said it; that I knew it, dreamed of it, felt it was the truth, and that it must be so! What money have we, Nell? Come! I saw you with money yesterday. What money have we? Give it to me."

"No, no, let me keep it, grandfather," said the frightened child. "Let us go away from here. Do not mind the rain. Pray let us go."

"Give it to me, I say," returned the old man fiercely. "Hush, hush, don't cry, Nell. If I spoke sharply, dear, I didn't mean it. It's for thy good. I have wronged thee, Nell, but I will right thee yet, I will indeed. Where is the money?"

"Do not take it," said the child. "Pray do not take it, dear. For both our sakes let me keep it, or let me throw it away-better let me throw it away, than you take it now. Let us go; do let us go."

"Give me the money," returned the old man, "I must have it. There-there-that's my dear Nell. I'll right thee one day, child, I'll right thee, never fear!"

She took from her pocket a little purse. He seized it with the same rapid impatience which had characterised his speech, and hastily made his way to the other side of the screen. It was impossible to restrain him, and the trembling child followed close behind.

The landlord had placed a light upon the table, and was engaged in drawing the curtain of the window. The speakers whom they had heard were two men, who had a pack of cards and some silver money between them, while upon the screen itself the games they had played were scored in chalk. The man with the rough voice was a burly fellow of middle age, with large black whiskers, broad cheeks, a coarse wide mouth, and bull neck, which was pretty freely displayed as his shirt-collar was only confined by a loose red neckerchief. He wore his hat, which was of a brownish-white, and had beside him a thick knotted stick. The other man, whom his companion had called Isaac, was of a more slender figure-stooping, and high in the shoulders-with a very ill-favoured face, and a most sinister and villainous squint.

"Now, old gentleman," said Isaac, looking round. "Do you know either of us? This side of the screen is private, sir."

"No offence, I hope," returned the old man.

"But by G-, sir, there is offence," said the other, interrupting him, "when you intrude yourself upon a couple of gentlemen who are particularly engaged."

"I had no intention to offend," said the old man, looking anxiously at the cards, "I thought that-"

"But you had no right to think, sir," retorted the other. "What the devil has a man at your time of life to do with thinking?"

"Now, bully boy," said the stout man, raising his eyes from his cards for the first time, "can't you let him speak?"

The landlord, who had apparently resolved to remain neutral until he knew which side of the question the stout man would espouse, chimed in at this place with "Ah, to be sure, can't you let him speak, Isaac List?"

"Can't I let him speak," sneered Isaac in reply, mimicking as nearly as he could, in his shrill voice, the tones of the landlord. "Yes, I can let him speak, Jemmy Groves."

"Well then, do it, will you?" said the landlord.

Mr. List's squint assumed a portentous character, which seemed to threaten a prolongation of this controversy, when his companion, who had been looking sharply at the old man, put a timely stop to it.

"Who knows," said he, with a cunning look, "but the gentleman may have civilly meant to ask if he might have the honour to take a hand with us!"

"I did mean it," cried the old man. "That is what I mean. That is what I want now!"

"I thought so," returned the same man. "Then who knows but the gentleman, anticipating our objection to play for love, civilly desired to play for money?"

The old man replied by shaking the little purse in his eager hand, and then throwing it down upon the table, and gathering up the cards as a miser would clutch at gold.

"Oh! That indeed-" said Isaac; "if that's what the gentleman meant, I beg the gentleman's pardon. Is this the gentleman's little purse? A very pretty little purse. Rather a light purse," added Isaac, throwing it into the air and catching it dexterously, "but enough to amuse a gentleman for half an hour or so."

"We'll make a four-handed game of it, and take in Groves," said the stout man. "Come, Jemmy."

The landlord, who conducted himself like one who was well used to such little parties, approached the table and took his seat. The child, in a perfect agony, drew her grandfather aside, and implored him, even then, to come away.

"Come; and we may be so happy," said the child.

"We will be happy," replied the old man hastily. "Let me go, Nell. The means of happiness are on the cards and in the dice. We must rise from little winnings to great. There's little to be won here; but great will come in time. I shall but win back my own, and it's all for thee, my darling."

"God help us!" cried the child. "Oh! what hard fortune brought us here?"

"Hush!" rejoined the old man laying his hand upon her mouth, "Fortune will not bear chiding. We must not reproach her, or she shuns us; I have found that out."

"Now, mister," said the stout man. "If you're not coming yourself, give us the cards, will you?"

"I am coming," cried the old man. "Sit thee down, Nell, sit thee down and look on. Be of good heart, it's all for thee-all-every penny. I don't tell them, no, no, or else they wouldn't play, dreading the chance that such a cause must give me. Look at them. See what they are and what thou art. Who doubts that we must win!"

"The gentleman has thought better of it, and isn't coming," said Isaac, making as though he would rise from the table. "I'm sorry the gentleman's daunted-nothing venture, nothing have-but the gentleman knows best."

"Why, I am ready. You have all been slow but me," said the old man. "I wonder who's more anxious to begin than I."

As he spoke he drew a chair to the table; and the other three closing round it at the same time, the game commenced.

The child sat by, and watched its progress with a troubled mind. Regardless of the run of luck, and mindful only of the desperate passion which had its hold upon her grandfather, losses and gains were to her alike. Exulting in some brief triumph, or cast down by a defeat, there he sat so wild and restless, so feverishly and intensely anxious, so terribly eager, so ravenous for the paltry stakes, that she could have almost better borne to see him dead. And yet she was the innocent cause of all this torture, and he, gambling with such a savage thirst for gain as the most insatiable gambler never felt, had not one selfish thought!

On the contrary, the other three-knaves and gamesters by their trade-while intent upon their game, were yet as cool and quiet as if every virtue had been centred in their breasts. Sometimes one would look up to smile to another, or to snuff the feeble candle, or to glance at the lightning as it shot through the open window and fluttering curtain, or to listen to some louder peal of thunder than the rest, with a kind of momentary impatience, as if it put him out; but there they sat, with a calm indifference to everything but their cards, perfect philosophers in appearance, and with no greater show of passion or excitement than if they had been made of stone.

The storm had raged for full three hours; the lightning had grown fainter and less frequent; the thunder, from seeming to roll and break above their heads, had gradually died away into a deep hoarse distance; and still the game went on, and still the anxious child was quite forgotten.

CHAPTER XXX

AT length the play came to an end, and Mr. Isaac List rose the only winner. Mat and the landlord bore their losses with professional fortitude. Isaac pocketed his gains with the air of a man who had quite made up his mind to win, all along, and was neither surprised nor pleased.

Nell's little purse was exhausted; but, although it lay empty by his side, and the other players had now risen from the table, the old man sat poring over the cards, dealing them as they had been dealt before, and turning up the different hands to see what each man would have held if they had still been playing. He was quite absorbed in this occupation, when the child drew near and laid her hand upon his shoulder, telling him it was near midnight.

"See the curse of poverty, Nell," he said, pointing to the packs he had spread out upon the table. "If I could have gone on a little longer, only a little longer, the luck would have turned on my side. Yes, it's as plain as the marks upon the cards. See here-and there-and here again."

"Put them away," urged the child. "Try to forget them."

"Try to forget them!" he rejoined, raising his haggard face to hers, and regarding her with an incredulous stare.

"To forget them! How are we ever to grow rich if I forget them?"
The child could only shake her head.

"No, no, Nell," said the old man, patting her cheek; "they must not
be forgotten. We must make amends for this as soon as we can. Patience-
patience, and we'll right thee yet, I promise thee. Lose to-day, win to-morrow. And nothing can be won without anxiety and care-nothing. Come, I
am ready."

"Do you know what the time is?" said Mr. Groves, who was smoking
with his friends. "Past twelve o'clock-"

"And a rainy night," added the stout man.

"The Valiant Soldier, by James Groves. Good beds. Cheap entertainment for man and beast," said Mr. Groves, quoting his sign-board. "Half-
past twelve o'clock."

"It's very late," said the uneasy child. "I wish we had gone before.
What will they think of us! It will be two o'clock by the time we get back.
What would it cost, sir, if we stopped here?"

"Two good beds, one-and-sixpence; supper and beer, one shilling; total, two shillings and sixpence," replied the Valiant Soldier.

Now, Nell had still the piece of gold sewn in her dress; and when she
came to consider the lateness of the hour, and the somnolent habits of Mrs.
Jarley, and to imagine the state of consternation in which they would certainly throw that good lady by knocking her up in the middle of the night-
and when she reflected, on the other hand, that if they remained where they
were, and rose early in the morning, they might get back before she awoke,
and could plead the violence of the storm by which they had been overtak-
en, as a good apology for their absence-she decided, after a great deal of
hesitation, to remain. She therefore took her grandfather aside, and telling
him that she had still enough left to defray the cost of their lodging, proposed that they should stay there for the night.

"If I had had but that money before-If I had only known of it a few
minutes ago!" muttered the old man.

"We will decide to stop here if you please," said Nell, turning hastily to
the landlord.

"I think that's prudent," returned Mr. Groves. "You shall have your
suppers directly."

Accordingly, when Mr. Groves had smoked his pipe out, knocked out
the ashes, and placed it carefully in a corner of the fireplace, with the bowl
downwards, he brought in the bread and cheese, and beer, with many high
encomiums upon their excellence, and bade his guests to fall to and make
themselves at home. Nell and her grandfather ate sparingly, for both were
occupied with their own reflections; the other gentlemen, for whose constitutions beer was too weak and tame a liquid, consoled themselves with spirits and tobacco.

As they would leave the house very early in the morning, the child was
anxious to pay for their entertainment before they retired to bed. But as she
felt the necessity of concealing her little board from her grandfather, and had
to change the piece of gold, she took it secretly from its place of conceal-

ment, and embraced an opportunity of following the landlord when he went out of the room, and tendered it to him in the little bar.

"Will you give me the change here, if you please?" said the child.

Mr. James Groves was evidently surprised, and looked at the money, and rang it, and looked at the child, and at the money again, as though he had a mind to inquire how she came by it. The coin being genuine, however, and changed at his house, he probably felt, like a wise landlord, that it was no business of his. At any rate, he counted out the change, and gave it to her. The child was returning to the room where they had passed the evening, when she fancied she saw a figure just gliding in at the door. There was nothing but a long dark passage between this door and the place where she had changed the money, and, being very certain that no person had passed in or out while she stood there, the thought struck her that she had been watched.

But by whom? When she re-entered the room, she found its inmates exactly as she had left them. The stout fellow lay upon two chairs, resting his head on his hand, and the squinting man reposed in a similar attitude on the opposite side of the table. Between them sat her grandfather, looking intently at the winner with a kind of hungry admiration, and hanging upon his words as if he were some superior being. She was puzzled for a moment, and looked round to see if any one else were there. No. Then she asked her grandfather in a whisper whether anybody had left the room while she was absent. "No," he said, "nobody."

It must have been her fancy then; and yet it was strange, that, without anything in her previous thoughts to lead to it, she should have imagined this figure so very distinctly. She was still wondering and thinking of it, when a girl came to light her to bed.

The old man took leave of the company at the same time, and they went up stairs together. It was a great, rambling house, with dull corridors and wide staircases which the flaring candles seemed to make more gloomy. She left her grandfather in his chamber, and followed her guide to another, which was at the end of a passage, and approached by some half-dozen crazy steps. This was prepared for her. The girl lingered a little while to talk, and tell her grievances. She had not a good place, she said; the wages were low, and the work was hard. She was going to leave it in a fortnight; the child couldn't recommend her to another, she supposed? Indeed she was afraid another would be difficult to get after living there, for the house had a very indifferent character; there was far too much card-playing, and such like. She was very much mistaken if some of the people who came there oftenest were quite as honest as they might be, but she wouldn't have it known that she had said so, for the world. Then there were some rambling allusions to a rejected sweetheart, who had threatened to go a soldiering-a final promise of knocking at the door early in the morning-and "Good night."

The child did not feel comfortable when she was left alone. She could not help thinking of the figure stealing through the passage down stairs; and what the girl had said did not tend to reassure her. The men were very ill-looking. They might get their living by robbing and murdering traveller. Who could tell?

Reasoning herself out of these fears, or losing sight of them for a little while, there came the anxiety to which the adventures of the night gave rise. Here was the old passion awakened again in her grandfather's breast, and to what further distraction it might tempt him Heaven only knew. What fears their absence might have occasioned already! Persons might be seeking for them even then. Would they be forgiven in the morning, or turned adrift again? Oh! why had they stopped in that strange place? It would have been better, under any circumstances, to have gone on!

At last, sleep gradually stole upon her-a broken, fitful sleep, troubled by dreams of falling from high towers, and waking with a start and in great terror. A deeper slumber, followed this-and then- What! That figure in the room!

A figure was there. Yes, she had drawn up the blind to admit the light when it should dawn, and there, between the foot of the bed and the dark casement, it crouched and slunk along, groping its way with noiseless hands, and stealing round the bed. She had no voice to cry for help, no power to move, but lay still watching it.

On it came-on, silently and stealthily, to the bed's head. The breath so near her pillow, that she shrank back into it, lest those wandering hands should light upon her face. Back again it stole to the window-then turned its head towards her.

The dark form was a mere blot upon the lighter darkness of the room, but she saw the turning of the head, and felt and knew how the eyes looked and the ears listened. There it remained, motionless as she. At length, still keeping the face towards her, it busied its hands in something, and she heard the chink of money.

Then, on it came again, silent and stealthy as before, and, replacing the garments it had taken from the bedside, dropped upon its hands and knees, and crawled away. How slowly it seemed to move, now that she could hear but not see it, creeping along the floor! It reached the door at last, and stood upon its feet. The steps creaked beneath its noiseless tread, and it was gone.

The first impulse of the child was to fly from the terror of being by herself in that room-to have somebody by not to be alone-and then her power of speech would be restored. With no consciousness of having moved, she gained the door.

There was the dreadful shadow, pausing at the bottom of the steps.

She could not pass it; she might have done so, perhaps, in the darkness, without being seized, but her blood curdled at the thought. The figure stood quite still, and so did she; not boldly, but of necessity; for going back into the room was hardly less terrible than going on.

The rain beat fast and furiously without, and ran down in plashing streams from the thatched roof. Some summer insect, with no escape into the air, flew blindly to and fro, beating its body against the walls and ceiling, and filling the silent place with his murmurs. The figure moved again. The child involuntarily did the same. Once in her grandfather's room, she would be safe.

It crept along the passage until it came to the very door she longed so ardently to reach. The child, in the agony of being so near, had almost darted forward with the design of bursting into the room and closing it behind her, when the figure stopped again.

The idea flashed suddenly upon her-what if it entered there, and had a design upon the old man's life! She turned faint and sick. It did. It went in. There was a light inside. The figure was now within the chamber, and she, still dumb-quite dumb, and almost senseless-stood looking on.

The door was partly open. Not knowing what she meant to do, but meaning to preserve him or be killed herself, she staggered forward and looked in. What sight was that which met her view!

The bed had not been lain on, but was smooth and empty. And at a table sat the old man himself, the only living creature there, his white face pinched and sharpened by the greediness which made his eyes unnaturally bright, counting the money of which his hands had robbed her.

CHAPTER XXXI

WITH steps more faltering and unsteady than those with which she had approached the room, the child withdrew from the door, and groped her way back to her own chamber. The terror she had lately felt was nothing compared with that which now oppressed her. No strange robber, no treacherous host conniving at the plunder of his guests, or stealing to their beds to kill them in their sleep, no nightly prowler, however terrible and cruel, could have awakened in her bosom half the dread which the recognition of her silent visitor inspired. The grey-headed old man gliding like a ghost into her room and acting the thief while he supposed her fast asleep, then bearing off his prize and hanging over it with the ghastly exultation she had witnessed, was worse-immeasurably worse, and far more dreadful, for the moment, to reflect upon-than anything her wildest fancy could have suggested. If he should return there was no lock or bolt upon the door, and if, distrustful of having left some money yet behind, he should come back to seek for more-a vague awe and horror surrounded the idea of his slinking in again with stealthy tread, and turning his face toward the empty bed, while she shrank down close at his feet to avoid his touch, which was almost insupportable. She sat and listened. Hark! A footstep on the stairs, and now the door was slowly opening. It was but imagination, yet imagination had all the terrors of reality; nay, it was worse, for the reality would have come and gone, and there an end, but in imagination it was always coming, and never went away.

The feeling which beset the child was one of dim uncertain horror. She had no fear of the dear old grandfather, in whose love for her this disease of the brain had been engendered; but the man she had seen that night, wrapt in the game of chance, lurking in her room, and counting the money by the glimmering light, seemed like another creature in his shape, a monstrous distortion of his image, a something to recoil from, and be the more afraid of, because it bore a likeness to him, and kept close about her, as he did. She could scarcely connect her own affectionate companion, save by his loss, with this old man, so like yet so unlike him. She had wept to see him dull and quiet. How much greater cause she had for weeping now!

The child sat watching and thinking of these things, until the phantom in her mind so increased in gloom and terror, that she felt it would be a relief to hear the old man's voice, or, if he were asleep, even to see him, and banish some of the fears that clustered round his image. She stole down the stairs and passage again. The door was still ajar as she had left it, and the candle burning as before.

She had her own candle in her hand, prepared to say, if he were waking, that she was uneasy and could not rest, and had come to see if his were still alight. Looking into the room, she saw him lying calmly on his bed, and so took courage to enter.

Fast asleep-no passion in the face, no avarice, no anxiety, no wild desire; all gentle, tranquil, and at peace. This was not the gambler, or the shadow in her room; this was not even the worn and jaded man whose face had so often met her own in the grey morning light; this was her dear old friend, her harmless fellow-traveller, her good, kind grandfather.

She had no fear as she looked upon his slumbering features, but she had a deep and weighty sorrow, and it found its relief in tears.

"God bless him!" said the child, stooping softly to kiss his placid cheek. "I see too well now, that they would indeed part us if they found us out, and shut him up from the light of the sun and sky. He has only me to help him. God bless us both!"

Lighting her candle, she retreated as silently as she had come, and, gaining her own room once more, sat up during the remainder of that long, long, miserable night.

At last the day turned her waning candle pale, and she fell asleep. She was quickly roused by the girl who had shown her up to bed; and, as soon as she was dressed, prepared to go down to her grandfather. But first she searched her pocket and found that her money was all gone-not a sixpence remained.

The old man was ready, and in a few seconds they were on their road. The child thought he rather avoided her eye, and appeared to expect that she would tell him of her loss. She felt she must do that, or he might suspect the truth.

"Grandfather," she said in a tremulous voice, after they had walked about a mile in silence, "do you think they are honest people at the house yonder?"

"Why?" returned the old man trembling. "I think them honest-yes, they played honestly."

"I'll tell you why I ask," rejoined Nell. "I lost some money last night-out of my bedroom I am sure. Unless it was taken by somebody in jest-only in jest, dear grandfather, which would make me laugh heartily if I could but know it-"

"Who would take money in jest?" returned the old man in a hurried manner. "Those who take money, take it to keep. Don't talk of jest."

"Then it was stolen out of my room, dear," said the child, whose last hope was destroyed by the manner of this reply.

"But is there no more, Nell?" said the old man; "no more anywhere? Was it all taken-every farthing of it was there nothing left?"

"Nothing," replied the child.

"We must get more," said the old man, "we must earn it, Nell, board it up, scrape it together, come by it somehow. Never mind this loss. Tell nobody of it and perhaps we may regain it. Don't ask how;-we may regain it, and a great deal more; -but tell nobody, or trouble may come of it. And so they took it out of thy room, when thou wert asleep!" he added in a compassionate tone, very different from the secret, cunning way in which he had spoken until now. "Poor Nell, poor little Nell!"

The child hung down her head and wept. The sympathising tone in which he spoke, was quite sincere; she was sure of that. It was not the lightest part of her sorrow to know that this was done for her.

"Not a word about it to any one but me," said the old man, "no, not even to me," he added hastily, "for it can do no good. All the losses that ever were, are not worth tears from thy eyes, darling. Why should they be, when we will win them back?"

"Let them go," said the child looking up. "Let them go, once and for ever, and I would never shed another tear if every penny had been a thousand pounds."

"Well, well," returned the old man, checking himself as some impetuous answer rose to his lips, "she knows no better. I ought to be thankful for it."

"But listen to me," said the child earnestly, "will you listen to me?"

"Ay, ay, I'll listen," returned the old man, still without looking at her; "a pretty voice. It has always a sweet sound to me. It always had when it was her mother's, poor child."

"Let me persuade you, then-oh, do let me persuade you," said the child, "to think no more of gains or losses, and to try no fortune but the fortune we pursue together."

"We pursue this aim together," retorted her grandfather, still looking away and seeming to confer with himself. "Whose image sanctifies the game?"

"Have we been worse off," resumed the child, "since you forgot these cares, and we have been travelling on together? Have we not been much better and happier without a home to shelter us, than ever we were in that unhappy house, when they were on your mind?"

"She speaks the truth," murmured the old man in the same tone as before. "It must not turn me, but it is the truth-no doubt it is."

"Only remember what we have been since that bright morning when we turned our backs upon it for the last time," said Nell, "only remember what we have been since we have been free of all those miseries-what peaceful days and quiet nights we have had-what pleasant times we have known-what happiness we have enjoyed. If we have been tired or hungry, we have been soon refreshed, and slept the sounder for it. Think what beautiful things we have seen, and how contented we have felt. And why was this blessed change?"

He stopped her with a motion of his hand, and bade her talk to him no more just then, for he was busy. After a time he kissed her cheek, still motioning her to silence, and walked on, looking far before him, and sometimes stopping and gazing with a puckered brow upon the ground, as if he were painfully trying to collect his disordered thoughts. Once she saw tears in his eyes. When he had gone on thus for some time, he took her hand in his as he was accustomed to do, with nothing of the violence or animation of his late manner; and so, by degrees so fine that the child could not trace them, settled down into his usual quiet way, and suffered her to lead him where she would.

When they presented themselves in the midst of the stupendous collection, they found, as Nell had anticipated, that Mrs. Jarley was not yet out of bed, and that, although she had suffered some uneasiness on their account over night, and had indeed sat up for them until past eleven o'clock, she had retired in the persuasion, that, being over taken by storm at some distance from home, they had sought the nearest shelter, and would not return before morning. Nell immediately applied herself with great assiduity to the decoration and preparation of the room, and had the satisfaction of completing her task, and dressing herself neatly, before the beloved of the Royal Family came down to breakfast.

"We haven't had," said Mrs. Jarley when the meal was over, "more than eight of Miss Monflathers's young ladies all the time we've been here, and there's twenty-six of 'em, as I was told by the cook when I asked her a question or two and put her on the free-list. We must try 'em with a parcel of new bills, and you shall take it, my dear, and see what effect that has upon 'em."

The proposed expedition being one of paramount importance, Mrs. Jarley adjusted Nell's bonnet with her own hands, and declaring that she certainly did look very pretty, and reflected credit on the establishment, dismissed her with many commendations, and certain needful directions as to the turnings on the right which she was to take, and the turnings on the left which she was to avoid. Thus instructed, Nell had no difficulty in finding out Miss Monflathers's Boarding and Day Establishment, which was a large house, with a high wall, and a large garden-gate with a large brass plate, and a small grating through which Miss Monflathers's parlour-maid inspected all visitors before admitting them; for nothing in the shape of a man-no, not even a milkman-was suffered, without special licence, to pass that gate. Even the tax-gatherer, who was stout, and wore spectacles and a broad-brimmed hat, had the taxes handed through the grating. More obdurate than gate of adamant or brass, this gate of Miss Monflathers's frowned on all mankind. The very butcher respected it as a gate of mystery, and left off whistling when he rang the bell.

As Nell approached the awful door, it turned slowly upon its hinges with a creaking noise, and, forth from the solemn grove beyond, came a long file of young ladies, two and two, all with open books in their hands, and some with parasols likewise. And last of the goodly procession came Miss Monflathers, bearing herself a parasol of lilac silk, and supported by two smiling teachers, each mortally envious of the other, and devoted unto Miss Monflathers.

Confused by the looks and whispers of the girls, Nell stood with downcast eyes and suffered the procession to pass on, until Miss Monflathers, bringing up the rear, approached her, when she curtseyed and presented her little packet; on receipt whereof Miss Monflathers commanded that the line should halt.

"You're the wax-work child, are you not?" said Miss Monflathers.

"Yes, ma'am," replied Nell, colouring deeply, for the young ladies had collected about her, and she was the centre on which all eyes were fixed.

"And don't you think you must be a very wicked little child," said Miss Monflathers, who was of rather uncertain temper, and lost no opportunity of impressing moral truths upon the tender minds of the young ladies, "to be a wax- work child at all?"

Poor Nell had never viewed her position in this light, and not knowing what to say, remained silent, blushing more deeply than before.

"Don't *you* know," said Miss Monflathers, "that it's very naughty and unfeminine, and a perversion of the properties wisely and benignantly transmitted to us, with expansive powers to be roused from their dormant state through the medium *of* cultivation?"

The two teachers murmured their respectful approval of this home-thrust, and looked at Nell as though they would have said that there indeed Miss Monflathers had hit her very hard. Then they smiled and glanced at Miss Monflathers, and then, their eyes meeting, they exchanged looks which plainly said that each considered herself smiler in ordinary to Miss Monflathers, and regarded the other as having no right to smile, and that her so doing was an act of presumption and impertinence.

"Don't you feel how naughty it is of you," resumed Miss Monflathers, "to be a wax-work child, when you might have the proud consciousness of assisting, to the extent of your infant powers, the manufactures of your country; of improving your mind by the constant contemplation of the steam-engine; and of earning a comfortable and independent subsistence of from two-and-ninepence to three shillings per week? Don't you know that the harder you are at work, the happier you are?"

"How doth the little-" murmured one of the teachers, in quotation from Doctor Watts.

"Eh?" said Miss Monflathers, turning smartly round. "Who said that?"

Of course the teacher who had not said it, indicated the rival who had, whom Miss Monflathers frowningly requested to hold her peace; by that means throwing the informing teacher into raptures of joy.

"The little busy bee," said Miss Monflathers, drawing herself up, "is applicable only to genteel children.

'In books, or work, or healthful play'
is quite right as far as they are concerned; and the work means painting on velvet, fancy needle-work, or embroidery. In such cases as these," pointing to Nell, with her parasol, "and in the case of all poor people's children, we should read it thus:

'In work, work, work. In work always
Let my first years be past,
That I may give for ev'ry day
Some good account at last.'"

A deep hum of applause rose not only from the two teachers, but from all the pupils, who were equally astonished to hear Miss Monflathers improvising alter this brilliant style; for although she had been long known as a politician, she had never appeared before as an original poet. Just then somebody happened to discover that Nell was crying, and all eyes were again turned towards her.

There were indeed tears in her eyes, and drawing out her handkerchief to brush them away, she happened to let it fall. Before she could stoop to pick it up, one young lady of about fifteen or sixteen, who had been standing a little apart from the others, as though she had no recognised place among them, sprang forward and put it in her hand. She was gliding timidly away again, when she was arrested by the governess.

"It was Miss Edwards who did that, I know," said Miss Monflathers predictively. "Now I am sure that was Miss Edwards."

It was Miss Edwards, and everybody said it was Miss Edwards, and Miss Edwards herself admitted that it was.

"Is it not," said Miss Monflathers, putting down her parasol to take a severer view of the offender, "a most remarkable thing, Miss Edwards, that you have an attachment to the lower classes which always draws you to their sides; or, rather, is it not a most extraordinary thing that all I say and do will not wean you from propensities which your original station in life have unhappily rendered habitual to you, you extremely vulgar-minded girl?"

"I really intended no harm, ma'am," said a sweet voice. "It was a momentary impulse, indeed."

"An impulse!" repeated Miss Monflathers scornfully. "I wonder that you presume to speak of impulses to me" -both the teachers assented- "I am astonished" -both the teachers were astonished- "I suppose it is an impulse which induces you to take the part of every grovelling and debased person that comes in your way" -both the teachers supposed so too.

"But I would have you know, Miss Edwards," resumed the governess in a tone of increased severity, "that you cannot be permitted-if it be only for the sake of preserving a proper example and decorum in this establishment-that you cannot be permitted, and that you shall not be permitted, to fly in the face of your superiors in this exceedingly gross manner. If you have no reason to feel a becoming pride before wax-work children, there are young ladies here who have, and you must either defer to those young ladies or leave the establishment, Miss Edwards."

This young lady, being motherless and poor, was apprenticed at the school-taught for nothing-teaching others what she learnt, for nothing-boarded for nothing-lodged for nothing-and set down and rated as something immeasurably less than nothing, by all the dwellers in the house. The servant-maids felt her inferiority, for they were better treated; free to come and go, and regarded in their stations with much more respect. The teachers were infinitely superior, for they had paid to go to school in their time, and were paid now. The pupils cared little for accompanion who had no grand stories to tell about home; no friends to come with post-horses, and be received in all humility, with cake and wine, by the governess; no deferential servant to attend and bear her home for the holidays; nothing genteel to talk about, and nothing to display. But why was Miss Monflathers always vexed and irritated with the poor apprentice-how did that come to pass?

Why, the gayest feather in Miss Monflathers's cap, and the brightest glory of Miss Monflathers's school, was a baronet's daughter-the real live daughter of a real live baronet-who, by some extraordinary reversal of the Laws of Nature, was not only plain in features but dull in intellect, while the poor apprentice had both a ready wit, and a handsome face and figure. It seems incredible. Here was Miss Edwards, who only paid a small premium which had been spent long ago, every day outshining and excelling the baronet's daughter, who learned all the extras (or was taught them all) and whose half-yearly bill came to double that of any other young lady's in the school, making no account of the honour and reputation of her pupilage. Therefore, and because she was a dependant, Miss Monflathers had a great dislike to Miss Edwards, and was spiteful to her, and aggravated by her, and, when she had compassion on little Nell, verbally fell upon and maltreated her as we have already seen.

"You will not take the air to-day, Miss Edwards," said Miss Monflathers. "Have the goodness to retire to your own room, and not to leave it without permission."

The poor girl was moving hastily away, when she was suddenly, in nautical phrase, "brought to" by a subdued shriek from Miss Monflathers.

"She has passed me without any salute!" cried the governess, raising her eyes to the sky. "She has actually passed me without the slightest acknowledgment of my presence!"

The young lady turned and curtsied. Nell could see that she raised her dark eyes to the face of her superior, and that their expression, and that of her whole attitude for the instant, was one of mute but most touching appeal against this ungenerous usage. Miss Monflathers only tossed her head in reply, and the great gate closed upon a bursting heart.

"As for you, you wicked child," said Miss Monflathers, turning to Nell, "tell your mistress that if she presumes to take the liberty of sending to me any more, I will write to the legislative authorities and have her put in the stocks, or compelled to do penance in a white sheet; and you may depend upon it that you shall certainly experience the treadmill if you dare to come here again. Now ladies, on."

The procession filed off, two and two, with the books and parasols, and Miss Monflathers, calling the Baronet's daughter to walk with her and smooth her ruffled feelings, discarded the two teachers-who by this time had ex- changed their smiles for looks of sympathy-and left them to bring up the rear, and hate each other a little more for being obliged to walk together.

CHAPTER XXXII

MRS. Jarley's wrath on first learning that she had been threatened with the indignity of Stocks and Penance, passed all description. The genuine and only Jarley exposed to public scorn, jeered by children, and flouted by beadles! The delight of the Nobility and Gentry shorn of a bonnet which a Lady Mayoress might have sighed to wear, and arrayed in a white sheet as a spectacle of mortification and humility! And Miss Monflathers, the audacious creature who presumed, even in the dimmest and remotest distance of her imagination, to conjure up the degrading picture, "I am a'most inclined," said Mrs. Jarley, bursting with the fulness of her anger and the weakness of her means of revenge, "to turn atheist when I think of it!"

But instead of adopting this course of retaliation, Mrs. Jarley, on second thoughts, brought out the suspicious bottle, and ordering glasses to be set forth upon her favourite drum, and sinking into a chair behind it, called her satellites about her, and to them several times recounted, word for word, the affronts she had received. This done, she begged them in a kind of deep despair to drink; then laughed, then cried, then took a little sip herself, then laughed and cried again, and took a little more; and so by degrees the worthy lady went on, increasing in smiles and decreasing in tears, until at last she could not laugh enough at Miss Monflathers, who, from being an object of dire vexation, became one of sheer ridicule and absurdity.

"For which of us is best off, I wonder," quoth Mrs. Jarley, "she or me! It's only talking, when all is said and done, and if she talks of me in the stocks, why I can talk of her in the stocks, which is a good deal funnier if we come to that. Lord, what does it matter, after all!"

Having arrived at this comfortable frame of mind (to which she had been greatly assisted by certain short interjectional remarks of the philosophic George), Mrs. Jarley consoled Nell with many kind words, and requested as a personal favour that whenever she thought of Miss Monflathers she would do nothing else but laugh at her, all the days of her life.

So ended Mrs. Jarley's wrath, which subsided long before the going down of the sun. Nell's anxieties, however, were of a deeper kind, and the checks they imposed upon her cheerfulness were not so easily removed,

That evening, as she had dreaded, her grandfather stole away, and did not come back until the night was far spent. Worn out as she was, and fatigued in mind and body, she sat up alone, counting the minutes, until he returned-penniless, broken-spirited, and wretched, but still hotly bent upon his infatuation.

"Get me money," he said wildly, as they parted for the night. "I must have money, Nell. It shall be paid thee back with gallant interest one day, but all the money that comes unto thy hands, must be mine-not for myself, but to use for thee. Remember, Nell, to use for thee!"

What could the child do, with the knowledge she had, but give him every penny that came into her hands, lest he should be tempted on to rob their benefactress? If she told the truth (so thought the child) he would be treated as a madman; if she did not supply him with money, he would supply himself; supplying him, she fed the fire that burnt him up, and put him perhaps beyond recovery. Distracted by these thoughts, borne down by the weight of the sorrow which she dared not tell, tortured by a crowd of apprehensions whenever the old man was absent, and dreading alike his stay and his return, the colour forsook her cheek, her eye grew dim, and her heart was oppressed and heavy. All her old sorrows had come back upon her, augmented by new fears and doubts; by day they were ever present to her mind; by night they hovered round her pillow, and haunted her in dreams.

It was natural that, in the midst of her affliction, she should often revert to that sweet young lady of whom she had only caught a hasty glance, but whose sympathy, expressed in one slight brief action, dwelt in her memory like the kindnesses of years. She would often think, if she had such a friend as that to whom to tell her griefs, how much lighter her heart would be-that if she were but free to hear that voice, she would be happier. Then she would wish that she were something better, that she were not quite so poor and humble, that she dared address her without fearing a repulse; and then feel that there was an immeasurable distance between them, and have no hope that the young lady thought of her any more.

It was now holiday-time at the schools, and the young ladies had gone home, and Miss Monflathers was reported to be flourishing in London and damaging the hearts of middle-aged gentlemen, but nobody said anything about Miss Edwards, whether she had gone home, or whether she had any home to go to, whether she was still at the school, or anything about her. But one evening, as Nell was returning from a lonely walk, she happened to pass the inn where the stage-coaches stopped, just as one drove up, and there was the beautiful girl she so well remembered, pressing forward to embrace a young child whom they were helping down from the roof.

Well, this was her sister, her little sister, much younger than Nell, whom she had not seen (so the story went afterwards) for five years, and to bring home to that place on a short visit, she had been saving her poor means all that time. Nell felt as if her heart would break when she saw them meet. They went a little apart from the knot of people who had congregated about the coach, and fell upon each other's neck, and sobbed, and wept with joy. Their plain and simple dress, the distance which the child had come alone, their agitation and delight, and the tears they shed, would have told their history by themselves.

They became a little more composed in a short time, and went away, not so much hand in hand as clinging to each other. "Are you sure you're happy, sister?" said the child as they passed where Nell was standing. "Quite happy now," she answered. "But always?" said the child. "Ah, sister, why do you turn away your face?"

Nell could not help following at a little distance. They went to the house of an old nurse, where the elder sister had engaged a bedroom for the child. "I shall come to you early every morning," she said, "and we can be together all the day."-"Why not at night-time too? Dear sister, would they be angry with you for that?"

Why were the eyes of little Nell wet, that night, with tears like those of the two sisters? Why did she bear a grateful heart because they had met, and feel it pain to think that they would shortly part? Let us not believe that any selfish reference-unconscious though it might have been-to her own trials awoke this sympathy, but thank God that the innocent joys of others can strongly move us, and that we, even in our fallen nature, have one source of pure emotion which must be prized in Heaven!

By morning's cheerful glow, but oftener still by evening's gentle light, the child, with a respect for the short and happy intercourse of these two sisters which forbade her to approach and say a thankful word, although she yearned to do so, followed them at a distance in their walks and rambles, stopping when they stopped, sitting on the grass when they sat down, rising when they went on, and feeling it a companionship and delight to be so near them. Their evening walk was by the river's side. Here, every night, the child was too, unseen by them, unthought of, unregarded; but feeling as if they were her friends, as if they had confidences and trusts together, as if her load were lightened and less hard to bear; as if they mingled their sorrows, and found mutual consolation. It was a weak fancy, perhaps, the childish fancy of a young and lonely creature; but night after night, and still the sisters loitered in the same place, and still the child followed with a mild and softened heart.

She was much startled, on returning home one night, to find that Mrs. Jarley had commanded an announcement to be prepared, to the effect that the stupendous collection would only remain in its present quarters one day longer; in fulfilment of which threat (for all announcements connected with public amusements are well known to be irrevocable and most exact), the stupendous collection shut up next day.

"Are we going from this place directly, ma'am?" said Nell.

"Look here, child," returned Mrs. Jarley. "That'll inform you." And so saying-. Mrs. Jarley produced another announcement, wherein it was stated, that, in consequence of numerous inquiries at the wax-work door, and in conse- quence of crowds having been disappointed in obtaining admission, the Exhibition would be continued for one week longer, and would re-open next day.

"For now that the schools are gone, and the regular sightseers exhausted," said Mrs. Jarley, "we come to the General Public, and they want stimulating."

Upon the following day at noon, Mrs. Jarley established herself behind the highly-ornamented table, attended by the distinguished effigies before mentioned, and ordered the doors to be thrown open for the re-admission of a discerning and enlightened public. But the first day's operations were by no means of a successful character, inasmuch as the general public, though they manifested a lively interest in Mrs. Jarley personally, and such of her waxen satellites as were to be seen for nothing, were not affected by any impulses moving them to the payment of sixpence a head. Thus, notwithstanding that a great many people continued to stare at the entry and the figures therein displayed; and remained there with great perseverance, by the hour at a time, to hear the barrel organ played and to read the bills; and notwithstanding that they were kind enough to recommend their friends to patronise the exhibition in the like manner, until the doorway was regularly blockaded by half the population of the town, who, when they went off duty, were relieved by the other half; it was not found that the treasury was any the richer, or that the prospects of the establishment were at all encouraging.

In this depressed state of the classical market, Mrs. Jarley made extraordinary efforts to stimulate the popular taste, and whet the popular curiosity. Certain machinery in the body of the nun on the leads over the door was cleaned up and put in motion, so that the figure shook its head paralytically all day long, to the great admiration of a drunken, but very Protestant barber over the way, who looked upon the said paralytic motion as typical of the degrading effect wrought upon the human mind by the ceremonies of the Romish Church, and discoursed upon that theme with great eloquence and morality. The two carters constantly passed in and out of the exhibition-room, under various disguises, protesting aloud that the sight was better worth the money than anything they had beheld in all their lives, and urging the bystanders, with tears in their eyes, not to neglect such a brilliant gratification. Mrs. Jarley sat in the pay-place, chinking silver moneys from noon till night, and solemnly calling upon the crowd to take notice that the price of admission was only six pence, and that the departure of the whole collection, on a short tour among the Crowned Heads of Europe, was positively fixed for that day week.

"So be in time, be in time, be in time," said Mrs. Jarley, at the close of every such address. "Remember that this is Jarley's stupendous collection of upwards of One Hundred Figures, and that it is the only collection in the world; all others being impostors and deceptions. Be in time, be in time, be in time!"

CHAPTER XXXIII

AS the course of this tale requires that we should become acquainted, somewhere hereabouts, with a few particulars connected with the domestic economy of Mr. Sampson Brass, and as a more convenient place than the present is not likely to occur for that purpose, the historian takes the friendly reader by the hand, and springing with him into the air, and cleaving the same at a greater rate than ever Don Cleophas Leandro Perez Zambullo and his familiar travelled through that pleasant region in company, alights with him upon the pavement of Bevis Marks.

The intrepid aeronauts alight before a small dark house, once the residence of Mr. Sampson Brass.

In the parlour window of this little habitation, which is so close upon the footway that the passenger who takes the wall brushes the dim glass with his coat sleeve-much to its improvement, for it is very dirty-in this parlour window in the days of its occupation by Sampson Brass, there hung, all awry and slack, and discoloured by the sun, a curtain of faded green, so threadbare from long service as by no means to intercept the view of the little dark room, but rather to afford a favourable medium through which to observe it accurately. There was not much to look at. A rickety table, with spare bundles of papers, yellow and ragged from long carriage in the pocket, ostentatiously displayed upon its top; a couple of stools set face to face on opposite sides of this crazy piece of furniture; a treacherous old chair by the fireplace, whose withered arms had hugged full many a client and helped to squeeze him dry; a second-hand wig box, used as a depository for blank writs and declarations and other small forms of law, once the sole contents of the head which belonged to the wig which belonged to the box, as they were now of the box itself; two or three common books of practice; a jar of ink, a pounce box; a stunted hearth- broom, a carpet trodden to shreds but still clinging with the tightness of desperation to its tacks-these, with the yellow wainscot of the walls, the smoke-discoloured ceiling, the dust and cobwebs, were among the most prominent decorations of the office of Mr. Sampson Brass.

But this was mere still-life, of no greater importance than the plate, "Brass, Solicitor," upon the door, and the bill, "First floor to let to a single gentleman," which was tied to the knocker. The office commonly held two examples of animated nature, more to the purpose of this history, and in whom it has a stronger interest and more particular concern.

Of these, one was Mr. Brass himself, who has already appeared in these pages. The other was his clerk, assistant, housekeeper, secretary, confidential plotter, adviser, intriguer, and bill of cost increaser, Miss Brass-a kind of amazon at common law, of whom it may be desirable to offer a brief description.

Miss Sally Brass, then, was a lady of thirty-five or thereabouts, of a gaunt and bony figure, and a resolute bearing, which if it repressed the softer emotions of love, and kept admirers at a distance, certainly inspired a feeling akin to awe in the breasts of those male strangers who had the happiness to approach her. In face she bore a striking resemblance to her brother, Sampson-so exact, indeed, was the likeness between them, that had it consorted with Miss Brass's maiden modesty and gentle womanhood to have assumed her brother's clothes in a frolic and sat down beside him, it would have been difficult for the oldest friend of the family to determine which was Sampson and which Sally, especially as the lady carried upon her upper lip certain reddish demonstrations, which, if the imagination had been assisted by her attire, might have been mistaken for a beard. These were, however, in all probability, nothing more than eyelashes in a wrong place, as the eyes of Miss Brass were quite free from any such natural impertinencies. In complexion Miss Brass was sallow- rather a dirty sallow, so to speak-but this hue was agreeably relieved by the healthy glow which mantled in the extreme tip of her laughing nose. Her voice was exceedingly impressive-deep and rich in quality, and, once heard, not easily forgotten. Her usual dress was a green gown, in colour not unlike the curtain of the office window, made tight to the figure, and terminating at the throat, where it was fastened behind by a peculiarly large and massive button. Feeling, no doubt, that simplicity and plainness are the soul of elegance, Miss Brass wore no collar or kerchief except upon her head, which was invariably ornamented with a brown gauze scarf, like the wing of the fabled vampire, and which, twisted into any form that happened to suggest itself, formed an easy and graceful head-dress.

Such was Miss Brass in person. In mind, she was of a strong and vigorous turn, having from her earliest youth devoted herself with uncommon ardour to the study of the law; not wasting her speculation upon its eagle flights, which are rare, but tracing it attentively through all the slippery and eel-like crawlings in which it commonly pursues its way. Nor had she, like many persons of great intellect, confined herself to theory, or stopped short where practical usefulness begins; inasmuch as she could ingross, fair-copy, fill up printed forms with perfect accuracy, and in short transact any ordinary duty of the office down to pouncing a skin of parchment or mending a pen. It is difficult to understand how, possessed of these combined attractions, she should remain Miss Brass; but whether she had steeled her heart against mankind, or whether those who might have wooed and won her, were deterred by fears that, being learned in the law, she might have too near her fingers' ends those particular statutes which regulate what are familiarly termed actions for breach, certain it is that she was still in a state of celibacy, and still in daily occupation of her old stool opposite to that of her brother Sampson. And equally certain it is, by the way, that between these two stools a great many people had come to the ground.

One morning Mr. Sampson Brass sat upon his stool copying some legal process, and viciously digging his pen deep into the paper, as if he were writing upon the very heart of the party against whom it was directed; and Miss Sally Brass sat upon her stool making a new pen preparatory to drawing out a little bill, which was her favourite occupation; and so they sat in silence for a long time, until Miss Brass broke silence.

"Have you nearly done, Sammy?" said Miss Brass; for in her mild and feminine lips, Sampson became Sammy, and all things were softened down.

"No," returned her brother. "It would have been all done though, if you had helped at the right time."

"Oh yes, indeed," cried Miss Sally; "you want my help, don't you-you, too, that are going to keep a clerk!"

"Am I going to keep a clerk for my own pleasure, or because of my own wish, you provoking rascal?" said Mr. Brass, putting his pen in his mouth, and grinning spitefully at his sister. "What do you taunt me about going to keep a clerk for?"

It may be observed in this place, lest the fact of Mr. Brass calling a lady a rascal, should occasion any wonderment or surprise, that he was so habituated to having her near him in a man's capacity, that he had gradually accustomed himself to talk to her as though she were really a man. And this feeling was so perfectly reciprocal, that not only did Mr. Brass often call Miss Brass a rascal, or even put an adjective before the rascal, but Miss Brass looked upon it as quite a matter of course, and was as little moved as any other lady would be by being called an angel.

"What do you taunt me, after three hours' talk last night, with going to keep a clerk for?" repeated Mr. Brass, grinning again with the pen in his mouth, like some nobleman's or gentleman's crest. "Is it my fault?"

"All I know is," said Miss Sally, smiling dryly, for she delighted in nothing so much as irritating her brother, "that if every one of your clients is to force us to keep a clerk, whether we want to or not, you had better leave off business, strike yourself off the roll, and get taken in execution as soon as you can."

"Have we got any other client like him?" said Brass. "Have we got another client like him, now-will you answer me that?"

"Do you mean in the face?" said his sister.

"Do I mean in the face!" sneered Sampson Brass, reaching over to take up the bill-book, and fluttering its leaves rapidly. "Look here-Daniel Quilp, Esquire- Daniel Quilp, Esquire-Daniel Quilp, Esquire-all through. Whether should I take a clerk that he recommends, and says 'this is the man for you,' or lose all this-eh?"

Miss Sally deigned to make no reply, but smiled again, and went on with her work.

"But I know what it is," resumed Brass after a short silence. "You're afraid you won't have as long a finger in the business as you've been used to have. Do you think I don't see through that?"

"The business wouldn't go on very long, I expect, with out me," returned his sister composedly. "Don't you be a fool and provoke me, Sammy, but mind what you're doing, and do it."

Sampson Brass, who was at heart in great fear of his sister, sulkily bent over his writing again, and listened as she said:

"If I determined that the clerk ought not to come, of course he wouldn't be allowed to come. You know that well enough; so don't talk nonsense."

Mr. Brass received this observation with increased meekness, merely remarking, under his breath, that he didn't like that kind of joking, and that Miss Sally would be "a much better fellow" if she forbore to aggravate him. Te this compliment Miss Sally replied that she had a relish for the amusement, and had no intention to forego its gratification. Mr. Brass not caring, as it seemed, to pursue the subject any further, they both plied their pens at a great pace, and there the discussion ended.

While they were thus employed, the window was suddenly darkened, as by some person standing close against it. As Mr. Brass and Miss Sally looked up to ascertain the cause, the top sash was nimbly lowered from without, and Quilp thrust in his head.

"Hallo!" he said, standing on tiptoe on the windowsill, and looking down into the room. "Is there anybody at home? Is there any of the Devil's ware here? Is Brass at a premium, eh?"

"Ha, ha, ha!" laughed the lawyer in an affected ecstasy. "Oh, very good, sir! Oh, very good indeed! Quite eccentric! Dear me, what humour he has!"

"Is that my Sally?" croaked the dwarf, ogling the fair Miss Brass. "Is it Justice with the bandage off her eyes, and without the sword and scales? Is it the Strong Arm of the Law? Is it the Virgin of Bevis?"

"What an amazing flow of spirits!" cried Brass. "Upon my word, it's quite extraordinary!"

"Open the door," said Quilp, "I've got him here. Such a clerk for you, Brass, such a prize, such an ace of trumps. Be quick and open the door, or, if there's another lawyer near and he should happen to look out of window, he'll snap him up before your eyes, he will."

It is probable that the loss of the phoenix of clerks, even to a rival practitioner, would not have broken Mr. Brass's heart; but, pretending great alacrity, he rose from his seat, and going to the door, returned, introducing his client, who led by the hand no less a person than Mr. Richard Swiveller.

"There she is," said Quilp, stopping short at the door, and wrinkling up his eyebrows as he looked towards Miss Sally; "there is the woman I ought to have married- there is the beautiful Sarah-there is the female who has all the charms of her sex and none of their weaknesses. Oh Sally, Sally!"

To this amorous address Miss Brass briefly responded "Bother!"

"Hard-hearted as the metal from which she takes her name," said Quilp. "Why don't she change it-melt down the brass, and take another name?"

"Hold your nonsense, Mr. Quilp, do," returned Miss Sally, with a grim smile. "I wonder you're not ashamed of yourself before a strange young man."

"The strange young man," said Mr. Quilp, handing Dick Swiveller forward, "is too susceptible himself not to understand me well. This is Mr. Swiveller, my intimate friend-a gentleman of good family and great expectations, but who, having rather involved himself by youthful indiscretion, is content for a time to fill the humble station of a clerk-humble, but here most enviable. What a delicious atmosphere!"

If Mr. Quilp spoke figuratively, and meant to imply that the air breathed by Miss Sally Brass was sweetened and rarefied by that dainty creature, he had doubtless good reason for what he said. But if he spoke of the delights of the atmosphere of Mr. Brass's office in a literal sense, he had certainly a peculiar taste, as it was of a close and earthy kind, and, besides being frequently impregnated with strong whiffs of the second-hand wearing apparel exposed for sale in Duke's Place and Houndsditch, had a decided flavour of rats and mice, and a taint of mouldiness. Perhaps some doubts of its pure delight presented themselves to Mr. Swiveller, as he gave vent to one or two short abrupt sniffs, and looked incredulously at the grinning dwarf.

"Mr. Swiveller," said Quilp, "being pretty well accustomed to the agricultural pursuits of sowing wild oats, Miss Sally, prudently considers that half a loaf is better than no bread. To be out of harm's way he prudently thinks is something too, and therefore he accepts your brother's offer. Brass, Mr. Swiveller is yours."

"I am very glad, sir," said Mr. Brass, "very glad indeed. Mr. Swiveller, sir, is fortunate to have your friendship. You may be very proud, sir, to have the friendship of Mr. Quilp."

Dick murmured something about never wanting a friend or a bottle to give him, and also gasped forth his favourite allusion to the wing of friendship and its never moulting a feather; but his faculties appeared to be absorbed in the contemplation of Miss Sally Brass, at whom he stared with blank and rueful looks, which delighted the watchful dwarf beyond measure. As to the divine Miss Sally herself, she rubbed her hands as men of business do, and took a few turns up and down the office with her pen behind her ear.

"I suppose," said the dwarf, turning briskly to his legal friend, "that Mr. Swiveller enters upon his duties at once? It's Monday morning."

"At once, if you please, sir, by all means," returned Brass.

"Miss Sally will teach him law, the delightful study of the law," said Quilp; "she'll be his guide, his friend, his companion, his Blackstone, his Coke upon Littleton, his Young Lawyer's Best Companion."

"He is exceedingly eloquent," said Brass, like a man abstracted, and looking at the roofs of the opposite houses, with his hands in his pockets; "he has an extraordinary flow of language. Beautiful, really."

"With Miss Sally," Quilp went on, "and the beautiful fictions of the law, his days will pass like minutes. Those charming creations of the poet, John Doe and Richard Roe, when they first dawn upon him, will open a new world for the enlargement of his mind and the improvement of his heart."

"Oh, beautiful, beautiful! Beau-ti-ful indeed!" cried Brass. "It's a treat to hear him."

"Where will Mr. Swiveller sit?" said Quilp, looking round.

"Why, we'll buy another stool, sir," returned Brass. "We hadn't any thoughts of having a gentleman with us, sir, until you were kind enough to suggest it, and our accommodation's not extensive. We'll look about for a second-hand stool, sir. In the meantime, if Mr. Swiveller will take my seat, and try his hand at a fair copy of this ejectment, as I shall be out pretty well all the morning-"

"Walk with me," said Quilp. "I have a word or two to say to you on points of business. Can you spare the time?"

"Can I spare the time to walk with you, sir? You're joking, sir, you're joking with me," replied the lawyer, putting on his hat. "I'm ready, sir, quite ready. My time must be fully occupied indeed, sir, not to leave me time to walk with you. It's not everybody, sir, who has an opportunity of improving himself by the conversation of Mr. Quilp."

The dwarf glanced sarcastically at his brazen friend, and, with a short dry cough, turned upon his heel to bid adieu to Miss Sally. After a very gallant parting on his side, and a very cool and gentlemanly sort of one on hers, he nodded to Dick Swiveller, and withdrew with the attorney.

Dick stood at the desk in a state of utter stupefaction, staring with all his might at the beauteous Sally, as if she had been some curious animal whose like had never lived. When the dwarf got into the street, he mounted again upon the window-sill, and looked into the office for a moment with a grinning face, as a man might peep into a cage. Dick glanced upward at him, but without any token of recognition; and long after he had disappeared, still stood gazing upon Miss Sally Brass, seeing or thinking of nothing else, and rooted to the spot.

Miss Brass being by this time deep in the bill of costs, took no notice whatever of Dick, but went scratching on, with a noisy pen, scoring down the figures with evident delight, and working like a steam-engine. There stood Dick, gazing now at the green gown, now at the brown headdress, now at the face, and now at the rapid pen, in a state of stupid perplexity, wondering how he got into the company of that strange monster, and whether it was a dream and he would ever wake. At last he heaved a deep sigh, and began slowly pulling off his coat.

Mr. Swiveller pulled off his coat and folded it up with great elaboration, staring at Miss Sally all the time; then put on a blue jacket with a double row of gilt buttons, which he had originally ordered for aquatic expeditions, but had brought with him that morning for office purposes; and, still keeping his eye upon her, suffered himself to drop down silently upon Mr. Brass's stool. Then he underwent a relapse, and becoming powerless again, rested his chin upon his hand, and opened his eyes so wide, that it appeared quite out of the question that he could ever close them any more.

When he had looked so long that he could see nothing, Dick took his eyes off the fair object of his amazement, turned over the leaves of the draft he was to copy, dipped his pen into the inkstand, and at last, and by slow approaches, began to write. But he had not written half a dozen words when, reaching over to the inkstand to take a fresh dip, he happened to raise his eyes, and there was the intolerable brown head-dress-there was the green gown there, in short, was Miss Sally Brass, arrayed in all her charms, and more tremendous than ever.

This happened so often, that Mr. Swiveller by degrees began to feel strange influences creeping over him-horrible desires to annihilate this Sally Brass-mysterious promptings to knock her head-dress off and try how she looked without it. There was a very large ruler on the table-a large, black, shining ruler. Mr. Swiveller took it up and began to rub his nose with it.

From rubbing his nose with the ruler, to poising it in his hand and giving it an occasional flourish after the tomahawk manner, the transition was easy and natural. In some of these flourishes it went close to Miss Sally's head; the ragged edges of the head-dress fluttered with the wind it raised; advance it but an inch, and that great brown knot was on the ground: yet still the unconscious maiden worked away, and never raised her eyes.

Well, this was a great relief. It was a good thing to write doggedly and obstinately until he was desperate, and then snatch up the ruler and whirl it about the brown head-dress with the consciousness that he could have it off if he liked. It was a good thing to draw it back, and rub his nose very hard with it, if he thought Miss Sally was going to look up, and to recompense himself with more hardy flourishes when he found she was still absorbed. By these means Mr. Swiveller calmed the agitation of his feelings, until his applications to the ruler became less fierce and frequent, and he could even write as many as half a dozen consecutive lines without having recourse to it,- which was a great victory.

CHAPTER XXXIV

IN course of time, that is to say, after a couple of hours , or so, of diligent application, Miss Brass arrived at the conclusion of her task, and recorded the fact by wiping her pen upon the green gown, and taking a pinch of snuff from a little round tin box which she carried in her pocket. Having disposed of this temperate refreshment, she arose from her stool, tied her papers into a formal packet with red tape, and taking them under her arm, marched out of the office.

Mr. Swiveller had scarcely sprung- off his seat and commenced the performance of a maniac hornpipe, when he was interrupted, in the fulness of his joy at being again alone, by the opening of the door, and the reappearance of Miss Sally's head.

"I am going out," said Miss Brass.

"Very good, ma'am," returned Dick. "And don't hurry yourself on my account to come back, ma'am," he added inwardly.

"If anybody comes on office business, take their messages, and say that the gentleman who attends to that matter isn't in at present, will you?" said Miss Brass.

"I will, ma'am," replied Dick.

"I shan't be very long," said Miss Brass, retiring.

"I'm sorry to hear it, ma'am," rejoined Dick when she had shut the door. "I hope you may be unexpectedly detained, ma 'am. If you could manage to be run over, ma'am, but not seriously, so much the better."

Uttering these expressions of good-will with extreme gravity, Mr. Swiveller sat down in the client's chair and pondered; then took a few turns up and down the room and fell into the chair again.

"So I'm Brass's clerk, am I?" said Dick. "Brass's clerk, eh? And the clerk of Brass 's sister-clerk to a female Dragon. Very good, very good! What shall I be next? Shall I be a convict in a felt hat and a grey suit, trotting about a dockyard with my number neatly embroidered on my uniform, and the order of the garter on my leg, restrained from chafing my ankle by a twisted Belcher handkerchief? Shall I be that? Will that do, or is it too genteel? Whatever you please, have it your own way of course."

As he was entirely alone, it may be presumed that, in these remarks, Mr. Swiveller addressed himself to his fate or destiny, whom, as we learn by the precedents, it is the custom of heroes to taunt in a very bitter and ironical manner when they find themselves in situations of an unpleasant nature. This is the more probable from the circumstance of Mr. Swiveller directing his observations to the ceiling, which these bodily personages are usually supposed to inhabit-except in theatrical cases, when they live in the heart of the great chandelier.

"Quilp offers me this place, which he says he can insure me," resumed Dick after a thoughtful silence, and telling off the circumstances of his position, one by one, upon his fingers; "Fred, who, I could have taken my affidavit, would not have heard of such a thing, backs Quilp to my astonishment, and urges me to take it also-staggerer, number one. My aunt in the country stops the supplies, and writes an affectionate note to say that she has made a new will, and left me out of it-staggerer, number two. No money; no credit; no support from Fred, who seems to turn steady all at once; notice to quit the old lodgings-staggerers three, four, five, and six. Under an accumulation of staggerers, no man can be considered a free agent. No man knocks himself down; if his destiny knocks him down, his destiny must pick him up again. Then I'm very glad that mine has brought all this upon itself, and I shall be as careless as I can, and make myself quite at home to spite it. So go on, my buck," said Mr. Swiveller, taking his leave of the ceiling with a significant nod, "and let us see which of us will be tired first!"

Dismissing the subject of his downfall with these reflections, which were no doubt very profound, and are indeed not altogether unknown in certain systems of moral philosophy, Mr. Swiveller shook off his despondency and assumed the cheerful ease of an irresponsible clerk.

As a means towards his composure and self-possession, he entered into a more minute examination of the office than he had yet had time to make; looked into the wig-box, the books, and ink-bottle; untied and inspected all the paper; carved a few devices on the table with the sharp blade of Mr. Brass's penknife; and wrote his name on the inside of the wooden coal-scuttle. Having, as it were, taken formal possession of his clerkship in virtue of these proceedings, he opened the window and leaned negligently out of it until a beer-boy happened to pass, whom he commanded to set down his tray and to serve him with a pint of mild porter, which he drank upon the spot and promptly paid for, with the view of breaking ground for a system of future credit and opening a correspondence tending thereto, without loss of time. Then three or four little boys dropped in, on legal errands from three or four attorneys of the Brass grade: whom Mr. Swiveller received and dismissed with about as professional a manner, and as correct and comprehensive an understanding of their business, as would have been shown by a clown in a pantomime under similar circumstances. These things done and over, he got upon his stool again and tried his hand at drawing caricatures of Miss Brass with a pen and ink, whistling very cheerfully all the time.

He was occupied in this diversion when a coach stopped near the door, and presently afterwards there was a loud double knock. As this was no business of Mr. Swiveller's, the person not ringing the office bell, he pursued his diversions with perfect composure, notwithstanding that he rather thought there was nobody else in the house.

In this, however, he was mistaken; for, after the knock had been repeated with increased impatience, the door was opened, and somebody with a very heavy tread went up the stairs and into the room above. Mr. Swiveller was wondering whether this might be another Miss Brass, twin sister to the Dragon, when there came a rapping of knuckles at the office door.

"Come in!" said Dick. "Don't stand upon ceremony. The business will get rather complicated if I've many more customers. Come in!"

"Oh, please," said a little voice very low down in the doorway, "will you come and show the lodgings?"

Dick leant over the table, and descried a small slipshod girl in a dirty coarse apron and bib, which left nothing of her visible but her face and feet. She might as well have been dressed in a violin-case.

"Why, who are you?" said Dick.

To which the only reply was, "Oh, please will you come and show the lodgings?"

There never was such an old-fashioned child in her looks and manner. She must have been at work from her cradle. She seemed as much afraid of Dick as Dick was amazed at her.

"I hav'n't got anything to do with the lodgings," said Dick. "Tell 'em to call again."

"Oh, but please will you come and show the lodgings," returned the girl; "it's eighteen shillings a week and us finding plate and linen. Boots and clothes is extra, and fires in winter time is eightpence a day."

"Why don't you show 'em yourself? You seem to know all about 'em," said Dick.

"Miss Sally said I wasn't to, because people wouldn't believe the attendance was good if they saw how small I was first."

"Well, but they'll see how small you are afterwards, won't they?" said Dick.

"Ah! But then they'll have taken 'em for a fortnight certain," replied the child with a shrewd look; "and people don't like moving when they're once settled."

"This is a queer sort of thing," muttered Dick, rising. "What do you mean to say you are-the cook?"

"Yes, I do plain cooking," replied the child. "I'm housemaid too; I do all the work of the house."

"I suppose Brass and the Dragon and I, do the dirtiest part of it," thought Dick. And he might have thought much more, being in a doubtful and hesitating mood, but that the girl again urged her request, and certain mysterious bumping sounds on the passage and staircase seemed to give note of the applicant's impatience. Richard Swiveller, therefore, sticking a pen behind each ear, and carrying another in his mouth as a token of his great importance and devotion to business, hurried out to meet and treat with the single gentleman.

He was a little surprised to perceive that the bumping sounds were occasioned by the progress up stairs of the single gentleman's trunk, which, being nearly twice as wide as the staircase, and exceedingly heavy withal, it was no easy matter for the united exertions of the single gentleman and the coachman to convey up the steep ascent. But there they were, crushing each other, and pushing and pulling with all their might, and getting the trunk tight and fast in all kinds of impossible angles, and to pass them was out of the question; for which sufficient reason, Mr. Swiveller followed slowly behind, entering a new protest on every stair against the house of Mr. Sampson Brass being thus taken by storm.

To these remonstrances, the single gentleman answered not a word, but when the trunk was at last got into the bedroom, sat down upon it and wiped his bald head and face with his handkerchief. He was very warm, and well he might be; for, not to mention the exertion of getting the trunk up stairs, he was closely muffled up in winter garments, though the thermometer had stood all day at eighty-one in the shade.

"I believe, sir," said Richard Swiveller, taking his pen out of his mouth, "that you desire to look at these apartments. They are very charming apartments, sir. They command an uninterrupted view of-of over the way, and they are within one minute's walk of-of the corner of the street. There is exceedingly mild porter, sir, in the immediate vicinity, and the contingent advantages are extraordinary."

"What's the rent?" said the single gentleman.

"One pound per week," replied Dick, improving on the terms.

"I'll take 'em."

"The boots and clothes are extras," said Dick; "and the fires in winter time are-"

"Are all agreed to," answered the single gentleman.

"Two weeks certain," said Dick, "are the-"

"Two weeks!" cried the single gentleman gruffly, eyeing him from top to toe. "Two years. I shall live here for two years. Here. Ten pounds down. The bargain's made."

"Why, you see," said Dick, "my name is not Brass, and-"

"Who said it was? My name's not Brass. What then?"

"The name of the master of the house is," said Dick.

"I'm glad of it," returned the single gentleman; "it's a good name for a lawyer. Coachman, you may go. So may you, sir."

Mr. Swiveller was so much confounded by the single gentleman riding rough-shod over him at this rate, that he stood looking at him almost as hard as he had looked at Miss Sally. The single gentleman, however, was not in the slightest degree affected by this circumstance, but proceeded with perfect composure to unwind the shawl which was tied round his neck, and then to pull off his boots. Freed of these encumbrances, he went on to divest himself of his other clothing, which he folded up piece by piece, and ranged in order upon the trunk. Then he pulled down the window-blinds, drew the curtains, wound up his watch, and, quite leisurely and methodically, got into bed.

"Take down the bill," were his parting words, as he looked out from between the curtains; "and let nobody call me till I ring the bell."

With that the curtains closed, and he seemed to snore immediately.

"This is a most remarkable and supernatural sort of house!" said Mr. Swiveller, as he walked into the office with the bill in his hand. "She-dragons in the business, conducting themselves like professional gentlemen; plain cooks of three feet high appearing mysteriously from under ground; strangers walking in and going to bed without leave or licence in the middle of the day! If he should be one of the miraculous fellows that turn up now and then, and has gone to sleep for two years, I shall be in a pleasant situation. It's my destiny, however, and I hope Brass may like it. I shall be sorry if he don't. But it's no business of mine-I have nothing whatever to do with it!"

CHAPTER XXXV

MR. Brass on returning home received the report of his clerk with much complacency and satisfaction, and was particular in inquiring after the ten-pound note, which, proving on examination to be a good and lawful note of the Governor and Company of the Bank of England, increased his good-humour considerably. Indeed he so overflowed with liberality and condescension, that in the fulness of his heart he invited Mr. Swiveller to partake of a bowl of punch with him at that remote and indefinite period which is currently denominated "one of these days," and paid him many handsome compliments on the uncommon aptitude for business which his conduct on the first day of his devotion to it had so plainly evinced.

It was a maxim with Mr. Brass that the habit of paying compliments kept a man's tongue oiled without any expense; and, as that useful member ought never to grow rusty or creak in turning on its hinges in the case of a practitioner of the law, in whom it should be always glib and easy, he lost few opportunities of improving himself by the utterance of handsome speeches and eulogistic expressions. And this had passed into such a habit with him, that, if he could not be correctly said to have his tongue at his fingers' ends, he might certainly be said to have it anywhere but in his face: which being, as we have already seen, of a harsh and repulsive character, was not oiled so easily, but frowned above all the smooth speeches-one of nature's beacons, warning off those who navigated the shoals and breakers of the World, or of that dangerous strait the Law, and admonishing them to seek less treacherous harbours and try their fortune elsewhere.

While Mr. Brass by turns overwhelmed his clerk with compliments and inspected the ten-pound note, Miss Sally showed little emotion and that of no pleasurable kind, for as the tendency of her legal practice had been to fix her thoughts on small gains and gripings, and to whet and sharpen her natural wisdom, she was not a little disappointed that the single gentleman had obtained the lodgings at such an easy rate, arguing that when he was seen to have set his mind upon them, he should have been at the least charged double or treble the usual terms, and that, in exact proportion as he pressed forward, Mr. Swiveller should have hung back. But neither the good opinion of Mr. Brass, nor the dissatisfaction of Miss Sally, wrought any impression upon that young gentleman, who, throwing the responsibility of this and all other acts and deeds there after to be done by him, upon his unlucky destiny, was quite resigned and comfortable: fully prepared for the worst, and philosophically indifferent to the best.

"Good morning, Mr. Richard," said Brass, on the second day of Mr. Swiveller's clerkship. "Sally found you a second-hand stool, sir, yesterday evening in White chapel. She's a rare fellow at a bargain, I can tell you, Mr. Richard. You'll find that a first-rate stool, sir, take my word for it."

"It's rather a crazy one to look at," said Dick.

"You'll find it a most amazing stool to sit down upon, you may depend," returned Mr. Brass. "It was bought in the open street just opposite the hospital, and as it has been standing there a month or two, it has got rather dusty and a little brown from being in the sun, that's all."

"I hope it hasn't got any fevers or anything of that sort in it," said Dick, sitting himself down discontentedly, between Mr. Sampson and the chaste Sally. "One of the legs is longer than the other."

"Then we get a bit of timber in, sir," retorted Brass. "Ha, ha, ha! We get a bit of timber in, sir, and that's another advantage of my sister's going to market for us. Miss Brass, Mr. Richard, is the-"

"Will you keep quiet?" interrupted the fair subject of these remarks, looking up from her papers. "How am I to work if you keep on chattering?"

"What an uncertain chap you are!" returned the lawyer. "Sometimes you're all for a chat. At another time you're all for work. A man never knows what humour he'll find you in."

"I'm in a working humour now," said Miss Sally, "so don't disturb me, if you please. And don't take him," Miss Sally pointed with the feather of her pen to Richard, "off his business. He won't do more than he can help, I dare say."

Mr. Brass had evidently a strong inclination to make an angry reply, but was deterred by prudent or timid considerations, as he only muttered something about aggravation and a vagabond; not associating the terms with any individual, but mentioning them as connected with some abstract ideas which happened to occur to him. They went on writing for a long time in silence after this-in such a dull silence that Mr. Swiveller (who required excitement) had several times fallen asleep, and written divers strange words in an unknown character with his eyes shut, when Miss Sally at length broke in upon the monotony of the office by pulling out the little tin box, taking a noisy pinch of snuff, and then expressing her opinion that Mr. Richard Swiveller had "done it."

"Done what, ma'am?" said Richard.

"Do you know," returned Miss Brass, "that the lodger isn't up yet-that nothing has been seen or heard of him since he went to bed yesterday afternoon?"

"Well, ma'am," said Dick, "I suppose he may sleep his ten pound out, in peace and quietness, if he likes."

"Ah! I begin to think he'll never wake," observed Miss Sally.

"It's a very remarkable circumstance," said Brass, laying down his pen; "really, very remarkable. Mr. Richard, you'll remember, if this gentleman should be found to have hung himself to the bed-post, or any unpleasant accident of that kind should happen-you'll remember, Mr. Richard, that this ten-pound note was given to you in part payment of two years' rent? You'll bear that in mind, Mr. Richard; you had better make a note of it, sir, in case you should ever be called upon to give evidence."

Mr. Swiveller took a large sheet of foolscap, and with a countenance of profound gravity, began to make a very small note in one corner.

"We can never be too cautious," said Mr. Brass. "There is a deal of wickedness going about the world, a deal of wickedness. Did the gentleman happen to say, sir-but never mind that at present, sir; finish that little memorandum first."

Dick did so, and handed it to Mr. Brass, who had dismounted from his stool and was walking up and down the office.

"Oh, this is the memorandum, is it?" said Brass, running his eye over the document. "Very good. Now Mr. Richard, did the gentleman say anything else."

"No."

"Are you sure, Mr. Richard," said Brass, solemnly "that the gentleman said nothing else?"

"Devil a word, sir," replied Dick.

"Think again, sir," said Brass; "it's my duty, sir, in the position in which I stand, and as an honourable member of the legal profession-the first profession in this country, sir, or in any other country, or in any of the planets that shine above us at night and are supposed to be inhabited- it's my duty, sir, as an honourable member of that profession, not to put to you a leading question in a matter of this delicacy and importance. Did the gentleman, sir, who took the first floor of you yesterday afternoon, and who brought with him a box of property-a box of property- say anything more than is set down in this memorandum?"

"Come, don't be a fool," said Miss Sally.

Dick looked at her, and then at Brass, and then at Miss Sally again and still said "No."

"Pooh, pooh! Deuce take it. Mr. Richard, how dull you are!" cried Brass, relaxing into a smile. "Did he say anything about his property?-there!"

"That's the way to put it," said Miss Sally, nodding to her brother.

"Did he say, for instance," added Brass, in a kind of comfortable, cozy tone- "I don't -assert that he did say so, mind; I only ask you, to refresh your memory-did he say, for instance, that be was a stranger in London- that it was not his humour or within his ability to give any references-that he felt we had a right to require them- and that, in case anything- should happen to him, at any time, he particularly desired that whatever property he had upon the premises should be considered mine, as some slight recompense for the trouble and annoyance I should sustain-and were you, in short," added Brass, still more comfortably and cozily than before, "were you induced to accept him on my behalf, as a tenant, upon those conditions?"

"Certainly not," replied Dick.

"Why, then, Mr. Richard," said Brass, darting at him a supercilious and reproachful look, "it's my opinion that you've mistaken your calling, and will never make a lawyer."

"Not if you live a thousand years," added Miss Sally. Whereupon the brother and sister took each a noisy pinch of snuff from the little tin box, and fell into a gloomy thoughtfulness.

Nothing further passed up to Mr. Swiveller's dinner time, which was at three o'clock, and seemed about three weeks in coming. At the first stroke of the hour, the new clerk disappeared. At the last stroke of five, he reappeared, and the office, as if by magic, became fragrant with the smell of gin and water and lemon-peel.

"Mr. Richard," said Brass, "this man's not up yet. Nothing will wake him, sir. What's to be done?"

"I should let him have his sleep out," returned Dick.

"Sleep out! "cried Brass; "why he has been asleep now, six-and-twenty hours. We have been moving chests of drawers over his head, we have knocked double-knocks at the street-door, we have made the servant-girl fall down stairs several times (she's a light weight, and it don't hurt her much), but nothing wakes him."

"Perhaps a ladder," suggested Dick, "and getting in at the first-floor window-"

"But then there's a door between; besides, the neighbourhood would be up in arms," said Brass.

"What do you say to getting on the roof of the house through the trap-door, and dropping down the chimney?" suggested Dick.

"That would be an excellent plan," said Brass, "if anybody would be" and here he looked very hard at Mr. Swiveller- "would be kind, and friendly, and generous enough, to undertake it. I dare say it would not be anything like as disagreeable as one supposes."

Dick had made the suggestion, thinking that the duty might possibly fall within Miss Sally's department. As he said nothing further, and declined taking the hint, Mr. Brass was fain to propose that they should go up stairs together, and make a last effort to awaken the sleeper by some less violent means, which, if they failed on this last trial, must positively be succeeded by stronger measures. Mr. Swiveller, assenting, armed himself with his stool and the large ruler, and repaired with his employer to the scene of action, where Miss Brass was already ringing a hand bell with all her might, and yet without producing the smallest effect upon their mysterious lodger.

"There are his boots, Mr. Richard," said Brass.

"Very obstinate-looking articles they are too," quoth Richard Swiveller. And truly they were as sturdy and bluff a pair of boots as one would wish to see; as firmly planted on the ground as if their owner's legs and feet had been in them, and seeming, with their broad soles and blunt toes, to hold possession of their place by main force.

"I can't see anything but the curtain of the bed," said Brass, applying his eye to the key-hole of the door. "Is he a strong man, Mr. Richard?"

"Very," answered Dick.

"It would be an extremely unpleasant circumstance if he was to bounce out suddenly," said Brass. "Keep the stairs clear. I should be more than a match for him, of course, but I'm the master of the house, and the laws of hospitality must be respected.-Hallo there! Hallo, hallo!"

While Mr. Brass, with his eye curiously twisted into the key-hole, uttered these sounds as a means of attracting the lodger's attention, and while Miss Brass plied the hand-bell, Mr. Swiveller put his stool close against the wall by the side of the door, and mounting on the top and standing bolt upright, so that if the lodger did make a rush, he would most probably pass him in its onward fury, began a violent battery with the ruler upon the upper panels of the door. Captivated with his own ingenuity, and confident in the strength of his position, which he had taken up after the method of those hardy individuals who open the pit and gallery doors of theatres on crowded nights, Mr. Swiveller rained down such a shower of blows that the noise of the bell was drowned; and the small servant, who lingered on the stairs below, ready to fly at a moment's notice, was obliged to hold her ears lest she should be rendered deaf for life.

Suddenly the door was unlocked on the inside and flung violently open. The small servant fled to the coal-cellar; Miss Sally dived into her own bedroom; Mr. Brass, who was not remarkable for personal courage, ran into the next street, and finding that nobody followed him, armed with a poker or other offensive weapon, put his hands in his pockets, walked very slowly all at once, and whistled.

Meanwhile Mr. Swiveller, on the top of the stool, drew himself into as flat a shape as possible against the wall and looked, not unconcernedly, down upon the single gentleman, who appeared at the door growling and cursing in a very awful manner, and, with the boots in his hand, seemed to have an intention of hurling them down stairs on speculation. This idea, however, he abandoned, and he was turning into his room again, still growling vengefully, when his eyes met those of the watchful Richard.

"Have you been making that horrible noise?" said the single gentleman.

"I have been helping, sir," returned Dick, keeping his eye upon him, and waving the ruler gently in his right hand, as an indication of what the single gentleman had to expect if he attempted any violence.

"How dare you then," said the lodger, "Eh?"

To this, Dick made no other reply than by inquiring whether the lodger held it to be consistent with the conduct and character of a gentleman to go to sleep for six-and twenty hours at a stretch, and whether the peace of an amiable and virtuous family was to weigh as nothing in the balance.

"Is my peace nothing, sir?" said the single gentleman.

"Is their peace nothing, sir?" returned Dick. "I don't wish to hold out any threats, sir-indeed the law does not allow of threats, for to threaten is an indictable offence but if ever you do that again, take care you're not sat upon by the coroner and buried in a cross road before you wake. We have been distracted with fears that you were dead, sir," said Dick, gently sliding to the ground, "and the short and the long of it is, that we cannot allow single gentlemen to come into this establishment and sleep like double gentlemen without paying extra for it."

"Indeed!" cried the lodger.

"Yes, sir, indeed," returned Dick, yielding to his destiny and saying whatever came uppermost; "an equal quantity of slumber was never got out of one bed and bedstead, and if you're going to sleep in that way, you must pay for a double-bedded room."

Instead of being thrown into a greater passion by these remarks, the lodger lapsed into a broad grin and looked at Mr. Swiveller, with twinkling eyes. He was a brown faced sun-burnt man, and appeared browner and more sunburnt from having a white night-cap on. As it was clear that he was a choleric fellow in some respects, Mr. Swiveller was relieved to find him in such good humour, and, to encourage him in it, smiled himself.

The lodger, in the testiness of being so rudely roused, had pushed his night-cap very much on one side of his bald head. This gave him a rakish eccentric air which, now that he had leisure to observe it, charmed Mr. Swiveller exceedingly; therefore, by way of propitiation, he expressed his hope that the gentleman was going to get up, and further that he would never do so any more.

"Come here, you impudent rascal!" was the lodger's answer as he re-entered his room.

Mr. Swiveller followed him in, leaving the stool outside but reserving the ruler in case of a surprise. He rather congratulated himself upon his prudence when the single gentleman, without notice or explanation of any kind double-locked the door.

"Can you drink anything?" was his next inquiry.

Mr. Swiveller replied that he had very recently bee assuaging the pangs of thirst, but that he was still open to "a modest quencher," if the materials were at hand. Without another word spoken on either side, the lodge took from his great trunk a kind of temple, shining as of polished silver, and placed it carefully on the table.

Greatly interested in his proceedings, Mr. Swiveller observed him closely. Into one little chamber of this temple he dropped an egg, into another some coffee, into a third, a compact piece of raw steak from a neat tin case, into a fourth he poured some water. Then, with the aid of a phosphorus-box and some matches, he procured a light and applied it to a spirit-lamp which had a place of its own below the temple; then he shut down the lids of all the little chambers; then he opened them; and then, by some wonderful and unseen agency, the steak was done, the egg was boiled, the coffee was accurately prepared, and his breakfast was ready.

"Hot water-" said the lodger, handing it to Mr Swiveller with as much coolness as if he had a kitchen fire before him- "extraordinary rum-sugar-and a travelling glass. Mix for yourself. And make haste."

Dick complied, his eyes wandering all the time from the temple on the table which seemed to do everything, to the great trunk which seemed to hold everything. The lodger took his breakfast like a man who was used to work these miracles, and thought nothing of them.

"The man of the house is a lawyer, is he not?" said the lodger.

Dick nodded. The rum was amazing.

"The woman of the house-what's she?"

"A dragon," said Dick.

The single gentleman, perhaps because he had met with such things in his travels, or perhaps because he was a single gentleman, evinced no surprise, but merely inquired "Wife or sister?" "Sister," said Dick.- "So much the better," said the single gentleman, "he can get rid of her when he likes."

"I want to do as I like, young man," he added after a short silence; "to go to bed when I like, get up when I like, come in when I like, go out when I like,-to be asked no questions and be surrounded by no spies. In this last respect, servants are the devil. There's only one here."

"And a very little one," said Dick.

"And a very little one," repeated the lodger. "Well, the place will suit me, will it?"

"Yes," said Dick.

"Sharks, I suppose?" said the lodger.

Dick nodded his assent, and drained his glass.

"Let them know my humour," said the single gentleman, rising. "If they disturb me, they lose a good tenant. If they know me to be that, they know enough. If they try to know more, it's a notice to quit. It's better to understand these things at once. Good day."

"I beg your pardon," said Dick, halting in his passage to the door, which the lodger prepared to open. "When he who adores thee has left but the name-"

"What do you mean?"

"-But the name," said Dick- "has left but the name -in case of letters or parcels-"

"I never have any," returned the lodger.

"Or in case anybody should call."

"Nobody ever calls on me."

"If any mistake should arise from not having the name, don't say it was my fault, sir," added Dick, still lingering. "Oh blame not the bard-"

"I'll blame nobody," said the lodger, with such irascibility that in a moment Dick found himself on the staircase, and the locked door between them.

Mr. Brass and Miss Sally were lurking hard by, having been, indeed, only routed from the key-hole by Mr. Swiveller's abrupt exit. As their utmost exertions had not enabled them to overhear a word of the interview, however, in consequence of a quarrel for precedence, which, though limited of necessity to pushes and pinches and such quiet pantomime, had lasted the whole time, they hurried him down to the office to hear his account of the conversation.

This Mr. Swiveller gave them-faithfully as regarded the wishes and character of the single gentleman, and poetically as concerned the great trunk, of which he gave a description more remarkable for brilliancy of imagination than a strict adherence to truth; declaring, with many strong asseverations, that it contained a specimen of every kind of rich food and wine known in these times, and in particular that it was of a self-acting kind and served up whatever was required, as he supposed by clockwork. He also gave them to understand that the cooking apparatus roasted a fine piece of sirloin of beef, weighing about six pounds avoirdupois, in two minutes and a quarter, as he had himself witnessed, and proved by his sense of taste; and further that, however the effect was produced, he had distinctly seen water boil and bubble up when the single gentleman winked; from which facts he (Mr. Swiveller) was led to infer that the lodger was some great conjuror or chemist, or both, whose residence under that roof could not fail at some future day to shed a great credit and distinction upon the name of Brass, and add a new interest to the history of Bevis Marks.

There was one point which Mr. Swiveller deemed it unnecessary to enlarge upon, and that was the fact of the modest quencher, which, by reason of its intrinsic strength and its coming close upon the heels of the temperate beverage he had discussed at dinner, awakened a slight degree of fever, and rendered necessary two or three other modest quenchers at the public-house in the course of the evening.

CHAPTER XXXVI

AS the single gentleman, after some weeks' occupation of his lodgings, still declined to correspond by word or gesture either with Mr. Brass or his sister Sally, but invariably chose Richard Swiveller as his channel of communication; and as he proved himself in all respects a highly desirable inmate, paying for everything beforehand, giving very little trouble, making no noise, and keeping early hours; Mr. Richard imperceptibly rose to an important position in the family, as one who had influence over mysterious lodger, and could negotiate with him, for good or evil, when nobody else durst approach his person.

If the truth must be told, even Mr. Swiveller's approaches to the single gentleman were of a very distant kind, and met with small encouragement; but, as he never returned from a monosyllabic conference with the unknown, without quoting such expressions as "Swiveller, I know I can rely upon you,"-"I have no hesitation in saying, Swiveller, that I entertain a re-gard for you,"-"Swiveller, you are my friend, and will stand by me I am sure," with many other short speeches of the same familiar and confiding kind, purporting to have been addressed by the single gentleman to himself, and to form the staple of their ordinary discourse, neither Mr. Brass nor Miss Sally for a moment questioned the extent of his influence, but accorded to him their fullest and most unqualified belief.

But quite apart from and independent of this source of popularity, Mr. Swiveller had another, which promised to be equally enduring, and to light-en his position considerably.

He found favour in the eyes of Miss Sally Brass. Let not the light scorners of female fascination erect their ears to listen to a new tale of love which shall serve them for a jest; for Miss Brass, however accurately formed to be beloved, was not of the loving kind. That amiable virgin, having clung to the skirts of the Law from her earliest youth-having sustained herself by their aid, as it were, in her first running alone, and maintained a firm grasp upon them ever since-had passed her life in a kind of legal childhood. She had been remarkable, when a tender prattler, for an uncommon talent in counterfeiting the walk and manner of a bailiff: in which character she had learned to tap her little playfellows on the shoulder, and to carry them off to imaginary sponging-houses, with a correctness of imitation which was the surprise and delight of all who witnessed her performances, and which was only to be exceeded by her exquisite manner of putting an execution into her doll's house, and taking an exact inventory of the chairs and tables. These artless sports had naturally soothed and cheered the decline of her widowed father: a most exemplary gentleman (called "old Foxey" by his friends from his extreme sagacity), who encouraged them to the utmost, and whose chief regret on finding that he drew near to Houndsditch Churchyard was, that his daughter could not take out an attorney's certificate and hold a place upon the roll. Filled with this affectionate and touching sorrow, he had solemnly confided her to his son Sampson as an invaluable auxiliary; and from the old gentleman's decease to the period of which we treat, Miss Sally Brass had been the prop and pillar of his business.

It is obvious that, having devoted herself from infancy to this one pur-suit and study, Miss Brass could know but little of the world, otherwise than in connexion with the law; and that from a lady gifted with such high tastes, proficiency in those gentler and softer arts in which women usually excel, was scarcely to be looked for. Miss Sally's accomplishments were all of a masculine and strictly legal kind. They began with the practice of an attor-ney and they ended with it. She was in a state of lawful innocence, so to speak. The law had been her nurse, and, as handy legs or such physical de-formities in children are held to be the consequence of bad nursing, so, if in a mind so beautiful any moral twist or bandiness could be found, Miss Sally Brass's nurse was alone to blame.

It was upon this lady, then, that Mr. Swiveller burst in full freshness as something new and hitherto undreamed of, lighting up the office with scraps of song and merriment, conjuring with inkstands and boxes of wafers, catching three oranges in one hand, balancing stools upon his chin and penknives on his nose, and constantly performing a hundred other feats of equal ingenuity; for with such unbendings did Richard, in Mr. Brass's absence, relieve the tedium of his confinement. These social qualities, which Miss Sally first discovered by accident, gradually made such an impression upon her, that she would entreat Mr. Swiveller to relax as though she were not by, which Mr. Swiveller, nothing loth, would readily consent to do. By these means a friendship sprang up between them. Mr. Swiveller gradually came to look upon her as her brother Sampson did, and as he would have looked upon any other clerk. He imparted to her the mystery of going the odd man or plain Newmarket for fruit, ginger-beer, baked potatoes, or even a modest quencher, of which Miss Brass did not scruple to partake. He would often persuade her to undertake his share of writing in addition to her own; nay, he would sometimes reward her with a hearty slap on the back, and protest that she was a devilish good fellow, a jolly dog, and so forth; all of which compliments Miss Sally would receive in entire good part and with perfect satisfaction.

One circumstance troubled Mr. Swiveller's mind very much, and that was that the small servant always remained somewhere in the bowels of the earth under Bevis Marks, and never came to the surface unless the single gentleman rang his bell, when she would answer it and immediately disappear again. She never went out, or came into the office, or had a clean face, or took off the coarse apron, or looked out of any one of the windows, or stood at the street door for a breath of air, or had any rest or enjoyment whatever. Nobody ever came to see her, nobody spoke of her, nobody cared about her. Mr. Brass had said once, that he believed she was a "love-child" (which means anything but a child of love), and that was all the information Richard Swiveller could obtain.

"It's of no use asking the dragon," thought Dick one day, as he sat contemplating the features of Miss Sally Brass. "I suspect if I asked any questions on that head, our alliance would be at an end. I wonder whether she is a dragon by the bye, or something in the mermaid way. She has rather a scaly appearance. But mermaids are fond of looking at themselves in the glass, which she can't be. And they have a habit of combing their hair, which she hasn't. No, she's a dragon."

"Where are you going, old fellow?" said Dick aloud, as Miss Sally wiped her pen as usual on the green dress, and uprose from her seat.

"To dinner," answered the dragon.

"To dinner!" thought Dick, "that's another circumstance. I don't believe that small servant ever has anything to eat."

"Sammy won't be home," said Miss Brass. "Stop till I come back. I shan't be long."

Dick nodded, and followed Miss Brass-with his eyes to the door, and with his ears to a little back parlour, where she and her brother took their meals.

"Now," said Dick, walking up and down with his hands in his pockets, "I'd give something-if I had it- to know how they use that child, and where they keep her. My mother must have been a very inquisitive woman; I have no doubt I'm marked with a note of interrogation somewhere. My feelings I smother, but thou hast been the cause of this anguish, my-upon my word," said Mr. Swiveller, checking himself and falling thoughtfully into the client's chair, "I should like to know how they use her!"

After running on in this way for some time, Mr. Swiveller softly opened the office door, with the intention of darting cross the street for a glass of the mild porter. At that moment he caught a parting glimpse of the brown headress of Miss Brass flitting down the kitchen stairs. "And by Jove!" thought Dick, "she's going to feed the servant. Now or never!"

First peeping over the handrail and allowing the headress to disappear in the darkness below, he groped his way down, and arrived at the door of a back kitchen immediately after Miss Brass had entered the same, bearing in her hand a cold leg of mutton. It was a very dark miserable place, very low and very damp: the walls disfigured by a thousand rents and blotches. The water was trickling out of a leaky butt, and a most wretched cat was lapping up the drops with the sickly eagerness of starvation. The grate, which was a wide one, was wound and screwed up tight, so as to hold no more than a little thin sandwich of fire. Everything was locked up; the coal-cellar, the candle-box, the salt-box, the meat-safe, were all padlocked. There was nothing that a beetle could have lunched upon. The pinched and meagre aspect of the place would have killed a chameleon. He would have known at the first mouthful that the air was not eatable, and must have given up the ghost in despair.-The small servant stood with humility in presence of Miss Sally, and hung her head.

"Are you there?" said Miss Sally.

"Yes, ma'am," was the answer in a weak voice.

"Go further away from the leg of mutton, or you'll be picking it, I know," said Miss Sally.

The girl withdrew into a corner, while Miss Brass took a key from her pocket, and opening the safe, brought from it a dreary waste of cold potatoes, looking as eatable as it Stonehenge. This she placed before the small servant, ordering her to sit down before it, and then, taking up a great carving-knife, made a mighty show of sharpening it upon the carving-fork.

"Do you see this?" said Miss Brass, slicing off about two square inches of cold mutton, after all this preparation, and holding it out on the point of the fork.

The small servant looked hard enough at it with her hungry eyes to see every shred of it, small as it was, and answered, "yes."

"Then don't you ever go and say" retorted Miss Sally, "that you hadn't meat here. There, eat it up."

This was soon done. "Now, do you want any more?" said Miss Sally.

The hungry creature answered with a faint "No." They were evidently going through an established form.

"You've been helped once to meat," said Miss Brass, summing up the facts; "you have had as much as you can eat, you're asked if you want any more, and you answer, 'no!' Then don't you ever go and say you were allowanced, mind that."

With those words, Miss Sally put the meat away and locked the safe, and then drawing near to the small servant, overlooked her while she finished the potatoes.

It was plain that some extraordinary grudge was working in Miss Brass's gentle breast, and that it was this which impelled her, without the smallest present cause, to rap the child with the blade of the knife, now on her hand, now on her head, and now on her back, as if she found it quite impossible to stand so close to her without administering a few slight knocks. But Mr. Swiveller was not a little surprised to see his fellow-clerk, after walking slowly backwards towards the door, as if she were trying to with draw herself from the room but could not accomplish it, dart suddenly forward, and falling on the small servant give her some hard blows with her clenched hand. The victim cried, but in a subdued manner as if she feared to raise her voice, and Miss Sally, comforting herself with a pinch of snuff, ascended the stairs, just as Richard had safely reached the office.

CHAPTER XXXVII

THE single gentleman among his other peculiarities- and he had a very plentiful stock, of which he every day furnished some new specimen-took a most extraordinary and remarkable interest in the exhibition of Punch. If the sound of a Punch's voice, at ever so remote a distance, reached Bevis Marks, the single gentleman, though in bed and asleep, would start up, and, hurrying on his clothes, make for the spot with all speed, and presently return at the head of a long procession of idlers, having in the midst the theatre and its proprietors. Straightway, the stage would be set up in front of Mr. Brass's house; the single gentleman would establish himself at the first-floor window; and the entertainment would proceed with all its exciting accompaniments of fife and drum and shout, to the excessive consternation of all sober votaries of business in that silent thoroughfare. It might have been expected that when the play was done, both players and audience would have dispersed; but the epilogue was as bad as the play, for no sooner was the Devil dead, than the manager of the puppets and his partner were summoned by the single gentleman to his chamber, where they were regaled with strong waters from his private store, and where they held with him long conversations, the purport of which no human being could fathom. But the secret of these discussions was of little importance. It was sufficient to know that while they were proceeding, the concourse without still lingered round the house; that boys beat upon the drum with their fists, and imitated Punch with their tender voices; that the office-window was rendered opaque by flattened noses, and the key-hole of the street-door luminous with eyes; that every time the single gentleman or either of his guests was seen at the upper window, or so much as the end of one of their noses was visible, there was a great shout of execration from the excluded mob, who remained howling and yelling, and refusing consolation, until the exhibitors were delivered up to them to be attended elsewhere. It was sufficient, in short, to know that Bevis Marks was revolutionised by these popular movements, and that peace and quietness fled from its precincts.

Nobody was rendered more indignant by these proceedings than Mr. Sampson Brass, who, as he could by no means afford to lose so profitable an inmate, deemed it prudent to pocket his lodger's affront along with his cash, and to annoy the audiences who clustered round his door by such imperfect means of retaliation as were open to him, and which were confined to the trickling down of foul water on their heads from unseen watering-pots, pelting them with fragments of tile and mortar from the roof of the house, and bribing the drivers of hackney cabriolets to come suddenly round the corner and dash in among them precipitately. It may at first sight be matter of surprise to the thoughtless few that Mr. Brass, being a professional gentleman, should not have legally indicted some party or parties, active in the promotion of the nuisance; but they will be good enough to remember that as Doctors seldom take their own prescriptions, and Divines do not always practise what they preach, so Lawyers are shy of meddling with the Law on their own account, knowing it to be an edged tool of uncertain application, very expensive in the working, and rather remarkable for its properties of close shaving, than for its always shaving the right person.

"Come," said Mr. Brass one afternoon, "this is two days without a Punch. I'm in hopes he has run through 'em all, at last."

"Why are you in hopes?" returned Miss Sally. "What harm do they do?"

"Here's a pretty sort of fellow!" cried Brass, laying down his pen in despair. "Now here's an aggravating animal!"

"Well, what harm do they do?" retorted Sally.

"What harm!" cried Brass. "Is it no harm to have a constant hallooing and hooting under one's very nose, distracting one from business, and making one grind one's teeth with vexation? Is it no harm to be blinded and choked up, and have the King's highway stopped with a set of screamers and roarers whose throats must be made of-of-"

"Brass," suggested Mr. Swiveller.

"Ah! of brass," said the lawyer, glancing at his clerk, to assure himself that he had suggested the word in good faith and without any sinister intention. "Is that no harm?"

The lawyer stopped short in his invective, and listening for a moment, and recognising the well-known voice, rested his head upon his hand, raised his eyes to the ceiling and muttered faintly, "There's another!"

Up went the single gentleman's window directly.

"There's another," repeated Brass; "and if I could get a break and four blood horses to cut into the Marks when the crowd is at its thickest, I'd give eighteen-pence and never grudge it!"

The distant squeak was heard again. The single gentleman's door burst open. He ran violently down the stairs, out into the street, and so past the window, without any hat, towards the quarter whence the sound proceeded-bent, no doubt, upon securing the strangers' services directly.

"I wish I only knew who his friends were," muttered Sampson, filling his pockets with papers; "if they'd just get up a pretty little Commission *de lunatico* át the Gray's Inn Coffee House and give me the job, I'd be content to have the lodgings empty for one while, at all events."

With which words, and knocking his hat over his eyes as if for the purpose of shutting out even a glimpse of the dreadful visitation, Mr. Brass rushed from the house and hurried away.

As Mr. Swiveller was decidedly favourable to these performances upon the ground that looking at a Punch, or indeed looking at anything out of window, was better than working; and as he had been for this reason at some pains to awaken in his fellow-clerk a sense of their beauties and manifold deserts; both he and Miss Sally rose as with one accord and took up their positions at the window: upon the sill whereof, as in a post of honour, sundry young ladies and gentlemen who were employed in the dry nurture of babies, and who made a point of being present, with their young charges, on such occasions, had already established themselves as comfortably as the circumstances would allow.

The glass being dim, Mr. Swiveller, agreeably to a friendly custom which he had established between them, hitched off the brown head-dress from Miss Sally's head, and dusted it carefully therewith. By the time he had handed it back, and its beautiful wearer had put it on again (which she did with perfect composure and indifference), the lodger returned with the show and showmen at his heels, and a strong addition to the body of spectators. The exhibitor disappeared with all speed behind the drapery, and his partner, stationing himself by the side of the Theatre, surveyed the audience with a remarkable expression of melancholy, which became more remarkable still when he breathed a hornpipe tune into that sweet musical instrument which is popularly termed a mouth-organ, without at all changing the mournful expression of the upper part of his face, though his mouth and chin were, of necessity, in lively spasms.

The drama proceeded to its close, and held the spectators enchained in the customary manner. The sensation which kindles in large assemblies, when they are relieved from a state of breathless suspense and are again free to speak and move, was yet rife, when the lodger, as usual, summoned the men up stairs.

"Both of you," he called from the window; for only the actual exhibitor-a little fat man-prepared to obey the summons. "I want to talk to you. Come, both of you."

"Come, Tommy," said the little man.

"I an't a talker," replied the other. "Tell him so. What should I go and talk for?"

"Don't you see the gentleman's got a bottle and glass up there?" returned the little man.

"And couldn't you have said so, at first?" retorted the other with sudden alacrity. "Now, what are you waiting for? Are you going to keep the gentleman expecting us all day? haven't you no manners?"

With this remonstrance, the melancholy man, who was no other than Mr. Thomas Codlin, pushed past his friend and brother in the craft, Mr. Harris, otherwise Short or Trotters, and hurried before him to the single gentleman's apartment.

"Now, my men," said the single gentleman; "you have done very well. What will you take? Tell.that little man behind, to shut the door."

"Shut the door, can't you?" said Mr. Codlin, turning gruffly to his friend. "You might have knowed that the gentleman wanted the door shut, without being told, I think."

Mr. Short obeyed, observing under his breath that his friend seemed unusually "cranky," and expressing a hope that there was no dairy in the neighbourhood, or his temper would certainly spoil its contents.

The gentleman pointed to a couple of chairs, and intimated by an emphatic nod of his head that he expected them to be seated. Messrs. Codlin and Short, after looking at each other with considerable doubt and indecision, at length sat down-each on the extreme edge of the chair pointed out to him-and held their hats very tight, while the single gentleman filled a couple of glasses from a bottle on the table beside him, and presented them in due form.

"You're pretty well browned by the sun, both of you," said their entertainer. "Have you been travelling?"

Mr. Short replied in the affirmative with a nod and a smile. Mr. Codlin added a corroborative nod and a short groan, as if he still felt the weight of the Temple upon his shoulders.

"To fairs, markets, races, and so forth, I suppose?" pursued the single gentleman.

"Yes, sir," returned Short, "pretty nigh all over the West of England."

"I have talked to men of your craft from North, East, and South," returned their host, in rather a hasty manner; "but I never lighted on any from the West before."

"It's our reg'lar summer circuit is the West, master," said Short; "that's where it is. We take the East of London in the spring and winter, and the West of England in the summer time. Many's the hard day's walking in rain and mud, and with never a penny earned, we've had down in the West."

"Let me fill your glass again."

"Much obleeged to you, sir, I think I will," said Mr. Codlin, suddenly thrusting in his own and turning Short's aside. "I'm the sufferer, sir, in all the travelling, and in all the staying at home. In town or country, wet or dry, hot or cold, Tom Codlin suffers. But Tom Codlin isn't to complain for all that. Oh, no! Short may complain, but if Codlin grumbles by so much as a word-oh dear, down with him, down with him directly. It isn't his place to grumble. That's quite out of the question."

"Codlin an't without his usefulness," observed Short with an arch look, "but he don't always keep his eyes open. He falls asleep sometimes, you know. Remember them last races, Tommy."

"Will you never leave off aggravating a man?" said Codlin. "It's very likely I was asleep when five-and-tenpence was collected, in one round, isn't it? I was attending to my business, and couldn't have my eyes in twenty places at once, like a peacock, no more than you could. If I an't a match for an old man and a young child, you an't neither, so don't throw that out against me, for the cap fits your head quite as correct as it fits mine."

"You may as well drop the subject, Tom," said Short. "It isn't particularly agreeable to the gentleman, I dare say."

"Then you shouldn't have brought it up," returned Mr. Codlin; "and I ask the gentleman's pardon on your account, as a giddy chap that likes to hear himself talk, and don't much care what he talks about, so that he does talk."

Their entertainer had sat perfectly quiet in the beginning of this dispute, looking first at one man and then at the other, as if he were lying in wait for an opportunity of putting some further question, or reverting to that from which the discourse had strayed. But, from the point where Mr. Codlin was charged with sleepiness, he had shown an increasing interest in the discussion: which now attained a very high pitch.

"You are the two men I want," he said, "the two men I have been looking for, and searching after. Where are that old man and that child you speak of?"

"Sir?" said Short, hesitating, and looking towards his friend.

"The old man and his grandchild who travelled with you-where are they? It will be worth your while to speak out, I assure you; much better worth your while than you believe. They left you, you say-at those races, as I understand. They have been traced to that place, and there lost sight of. Have you no clue, can you suggest no clue, to their recovery?"

"Did I always say, Thomas," cried Short, turning with a look of amazement to his friend, "that there was sure to be an inquiry after them two travellers?"

"You said!" returned Mr. Codlin. "Did I always say that that 'ere blessed child was the most interesting I ever see? Did I always say I loved her, and doted on her? Pretty creetur, I think I hear her now. 'Codlin's my friend,' she says, with a tear of gratitude a trickling down her little eye; 'Codlin's my friend,' she says- 'not Short. Short's very well,' she says; 'I've no quarrel with Short; he means to be kind, I dare say; but Codlin,' she says, 'has the feelings for my money, though he mayn't look it.'"

Repeating these words with great emotion, Mr. Codlin rubbed the bridge of his nose with his coat-sleeve, and shaking his head mournfully from side to side, left the single gentleman to infer that, from the moment when he lost sight of his dear young charge, his peace of mind and happiness had fled.

"Good God!" said the single gentleman, pacing up and down the room, "have I found these men at last, only to discover that they can give me no information or assistance! It would have been better to have lived on in hope from day to day, and never to have lighted on them, than to have my expectations scattered."

"Stay a minute," said Short. "A man of the name of Jerry-you know Jerry, Thomas?"

"Oh, don't talk to me of Jerrys," replied Mr. Codlin. "How can I care a pinch of snuff for Jerrys, when I think of that 'ere darling child? 'Codlin's my friend,' she says, 'dear, good, kind Codlin, as is always a devising pleasures for me! I don't object to Short,' she says, 'but I cotton to Codlin.' once," said that gentleman reflectively, "she called me Father Codlin. I thought I should have bust!"

"A man of the name of Jerry, sir," said Short, turning from his selfish colleague to their new acquaintance, "wot keeps a company of dancing dogs, told me in a accidental sort of way, that he had seen the old gentleman in con- nexion with a travelling wax-work, unbeknown to him. As they'd given us the slip, and nothing had come of it, and this was down in the country that he'd been seen, I took no measures about it, and asked no questions-But I can, if you like."

"Is this man in town?" said the impatient single gentleman. "Speak faster."

"No he isn't, but he will be to-morrow, for he lodges in our house," replied Mr. Short rapidly.

"Then bring him here," said the single gentleman. "Here's a sovereign a-piece. If I can find these people through your means, it is but a prelude to twenty more. Return to me to-morrow, and keep your own counsel upon this subject-though I need hardly tell you that, for you'll do so for your own sakes. Now, give me your address, and leave me."

The address was given, the two men departed, the crowd went with them, and the single gentleman for two mortal hours walked in uncommon agitation up and down his room, over the wondering heads of Mr. Swiveller and Miss Sally Brass.

CHAPTER XXXVIII

KIT-for it happens at this juncture, not only that we have breathing time to follow his fortunes, but that the necessities of these adventures so adapt themselves to our ease and inclination as to call upon us imperatively to pur- sue the track we most desire to take-Kit, while the matters treated of in the last fifteen chapters were yet in progress, was, as the reader may suppose, gradually familiarising himself more and more with Mr. and Mrs. Garland, Mr. Abel, the pony, and Barbara, and gradually coming to consider them one and all as his particular private friends, and Abel Cottage, Finchley, as his own proper home.

Stay-the words are written, and may go, but if they convey any notion that Kit, in the plentiful board and comfortable lodging of his new abode, began to think slightly of the poor fare and furniture of his old dwelling, they do their office badly and commit injustice. Who so mindful of those he left at home-albeit they were but a mother and two young babies-as Kit? What boastful father in the fulness of his heart ever related such wonders of his infant prodigy, as Kit never wearied of telling Barbara in the evening time, concerning little Jacob? Was there ever such a mother as Kit's mother, on her son's showing; or was there ever such comfort in poverty as in the poverty of Kit's family, if any correct judgment might be arrived at, from his own glowing account!

And let us linger in this place for an instant to remark that if ever household affections and loves are graceful things, they are graceful in the poor. The ties that bind the wealthy and the proud to home may be forged on earth, but those which link the poor man to his humble hearth are of the true metal and bear the stamp of Heaven. The man of high descent may love the halls and lands of his inheritance as a part of himself, as trophies of his birth and power; his associations with them are associations of pride and wealth and triumph; the poor man's attachment to the tenements he holds, which strangers have held before, and may to-morrow occupy again, has a worthier root, struck deep into a purer soil. His household gods are of flesh and blood, with no alloy of silver, gold, or precious stone, he has no property but in the affections of his own heart; and when they endear bare floors and walls, despite of rags and toil and scanty meals, that man has his love of home from God, and his rude hut becomes a solemn place.

Oh! if those who rule the destinies of nations would but remember this-if they would but think how hard it is for the very poor to have engendered in their hearts that love of home from which all domestic virtues spring, when they live in dense and squalid masses where social decency is lost, or rather never found,-if they would but turn aside from the wide thoroughfares and great houses, and strive to improve the wretched dwellings in bye-ways where only Poverty may walk,-many low roofs would point more truly to the sky, than the loftiest steeple that now rears proudly up from the midst of guilt, and crime, and horrible disease, to mock them by its contrast. In hollow voices from Workhouse, Hospital, and Jail, this truth is preached from day to day, and has been proclaimed for years. It is no light matter-no outcry from the working vulgar- no mere question of the people's health and comforts that may be whistled down on Wednesday nights. In love of home, the love of country has its rise; and who are the truer patriots or the best in time of need-those who venerate the land, owning its wood, and stream, and earth, and all that they produce? or those who love their country, boasting not a foot of ground in all its wide domain?

Kit knew nothing about such questions, but he knew that his old home was a very poor place and that his new one was very unlike it, and yet he was constantly looking back with grateful satisfaction and affectionate anxiety, and often indited square-folded letters to his mother, inclosing a shilling or eighteen-pence or such other small remittance, which Mr. Abel's liberality enabled him to make. Sometimes, being in the neighbourhood, he had leisure to call upon her, and then great was the joy and pride of Kit's mother, and extremely noisy the satisfaction of little Jacob and the baby, and cordial the congratulations of the whole court, who listened with admiring ears to the accounts of Abel Cottage, and could never be told too much of its wonders and magnificence.

Although Kit was in the very highest favour with the old lady and gentleman, and Mr. Abel, and Barbara, it is certain that no member of the family evinced such a remarkable partiality for him as the self-willed pony, who, from being the most obstinate and opinioned pony on the face of the earth, was in his hands the meekest and most tractable of animals. It is true that in exact proportion as he became manageable by Kit he became utterly ungovernable by anybody else (as if he had determined to keep him in the family at all risks and hazards), and that, even under the guidance of his favourite, he would sometimes perform *a* great variety of strange freaks and capers, to the extreme discomposure of the old lady's nerves; but as Kit always represented that this was only his fun, or a way he had of showing his attachment to his employers, Mrs. Garland gradually suffered herself to be persuaded into the belief, in which she at last became so strongly confirmed that if in one of these ebullitions he had overturned the chaise, she would have been quite satisfied that he did it with the very best intentions.

Besides becoming in a short time a perfect marvel in all stable matters, Kit soon made himself a very tolerable gardener, a handy fellow within doors, and an indispensable attendant on Mr. Abel, who every day gave him some new proof of his confidence and approbation. Mr. Witherden the notary, too, regarded him with a friendly eye; and even Mr. Chuckster would sometimes condescend to give him a slight nod, or to honour him with that peculiar form of recognition which is called "taking a sight," or to favour him with some other salute combining pleasantry with patronage.

One morning Kit drove Mr. Abel to the Notary's office, as he sometimes did, and having set him down at the house, was about to drive off to a livery stable hard by, when this same Mr. Chuckster emerged from the office door, and cried "Woa-a-a-a-a!"-dwelling upon the note a long time, for the purpose of striking terror into the pony's heart, and asserting the supremacy of man over the inferior animals.

"Pull up, Snobby," cried Mr. Chuckster, addressing "himself to Kit. "You're wanted inside here."

"Has Mr. Abel forgotten anything, I wonder?" said Kit as he dismounted.

"Ask no questions, Snobby," returned Mr. Chuckster, "but go and see. Woa-a-a then, will you? If that pony was mine, I'd break him."

"You must be very gentle with him, if you please," said Kit, "or you'll find him troublesome. You'd better not keep on pulling his ears, please. I know he won't like it."

To this remonstrance Mr. Chuckster deigned no other answer, than addressing Kit with a lofty and distant air as "young- feller," and requesting- him to cut and come again with all speed. The "young feller" complying, Mr. Chuck- ster put his hands in his pockets, and tried to look as if he were not minding the pony, but happened to be lounging there by accident.

Kit scraped his shoes very carefully (for he had not yet lost his reverence for the bundles of papers and the tin boxes), and tapped at the office door, which was quickly opened by the Notary himself.

"Oh! come in, Christopher," said Mr. Witherden.

"Is that the lad?" asked an elderly gentleman, but of a stout, bluff figure-who was in the room.

"That's the lad," said Mr. Witherden. "He fell in with my client, Mr. Garland, sir, at this very door. I have reason to think he is a good lad, sir, and that you may believe what he says. Let me introduce Mr. Abel Garland, sir-his young master; my articled pupil, sir, and most particular friend. My most particular friend, sir," repeated the Notary, drawing out his silk handkerchief and flourishing it about his face.

"Your servant, sir," said the stranger gentleman.

"Yours, sir, I'm sure," replied Mr. Abel mildly. "You were wishing to speak to Christopher, sir?"

"Yes, I was. Have I your permission?"

"By all means."

"My business is no secret; or I should rather say it need be no secret here," said the stranger, observing that Mr. Abel and the Notary were preparing to retire. "It relates to a dealer in curiosities with whom he lived, and in whom I am earnestly and warmly interested. I have been a stranger to this country, gentlemen, for very many years, and if I am deficient in form and ceremony, I hope you will forgive me."

"No forgiveness is necessary, sir;-none whatever," replied the Notary, and so said Mr. Abel.

"I have been making inquiries in the neighbourhood in which his old master lived," said the stranger, "and I learnt that he had been served by this lad. I found out his mother's house, and was directed by her to this place as the nearest in which I should be likely to find him. That's the cause of my presenting myself here this morning."

"I am very glad of any cause, sir," said the Notary, "which procures me the honour of this visit."

"Sir," retorted the stranger, "you speak like a mere man of the world, and I think you something better. Therefore, pray do not sink your real character in paying unmeaning compliments to me."

"Hem!" coughed the Notary. You're a plain speaker, sir."

"And a plain dealer," returned the stranger. "It may be my long absence and inexperience that lead me to the conclusion, but if plain speakers are scarce in this part of the world, I fancy that plain dealers are still scarcer. If my speaking should offend you, sir, my dealing, I hope, will make amends."

Mr. Witherden seemed a little disconcerted by the elderly gentleman's mode of conducting the dialogue; and as for Kit, he looked at him in openmouthed astonishment, wondering what kind of language he would address to him, if he talked in that free and easy way to a Notary. It was with no harshness, however, though with something of constitutional irritability and haste, that he turned to Kit and said:

"If you think, my lad, that I am pursuing these inquiries with any other view than that of serving and reclaiming those I am in search of, you do me a very great wrong, and deceive yourself. Don't be deceived, I beg of you, but rely upon my assurance. The fact is, gentlemen," he added, turning again to the Notary and his pupil, "that I am in a very painful and wholly unexpected position. I came to this city with a darling object at my heart, expecting to find no obstacle or difficulty in the way of its attainment. I find myself suddenly checked and stopped short in the execution of my design, by a mystery which I cannot penetrate. Every effort I have made to penetrate it, has only served to render it darker and more obscure; and I am afraid to stir openly in the matter, lest those whom I anxiously pursue should fly still farther from me. I assure you that if you could give me any assistance, you would not be sorry to do so, if you knew how greatly I stand in need of it, and what a load it would relieve me from."

There was a simplicity in this confidence which occasioned it to find a quick response in the breast of the good-natured Notary, who replied, in the same spirit, that the stranger had not mistaken his desire, and that if he could be of service to him, he would most readily.

Kit was then put under examination and closely questioned by the unknown gentleman touching his old master and the child, their lonely way of life, their retired habits, and strict seclusion. The nightly absence of the old man, the solitary existence of the child at those times, his illness and recovery, Quilp's possession of the house, and their sudden disappearance, were all the subjects of much questioning and answer. Finally, Kit informed the gentleman that the premises were now to let, and that a board upon the door referred all inquirers to Mr. Sampson Brass, Solicitor, of Bevis Marks, from whom he might perhaps learn some further particulars.

"Not by inquiry," said the gentleman shaking his head. "I live there."

"Live at Brass's the attorney's!" cried Mr. Witherden in some surprise, having professional knowledge of the gentleman in question.

"Ay," was the reply. "I entered upon his lodgings t'other day, chiefly because I had seen this very board. It matters little to me where I live, and I had a desperate hope that some intelligence might be cast in my way there, which would not reach me elsewhere. Yes, I live at Brass's -more shame for me, I suppose?"

"That's a mere matter of opinion," said the Notary, shrugging his shoulders. "He is looked upon as rather a doubtful character."

"Doubtful?" echoed the other. "I am glad to hear there's any doubt about it. I supposed that had been thoroughly settled, long ago. But will you let me speak a word or two with you in private?"

Mr. Witherden consenting, they walked into that gentleman's private closet, and remained there in close conversation for some quarter of an hour, when they returned into the outer office. The stranger had left his hat in Mr. Witherden's room, and seemed to have established himself in this short interval on quite a friendly footing.

"I'll not detain you any longer now," he said, putting a crown into Kit's hand, and looking towards the Notary. "You shall hear from me again.

Not a word of this, you know, except to your master and mistress."

"Mother, sir, would be glad to know-" said Kit, faltering.

"Glad to know what?"

"Anything-so that it was no harm-about Miss Nell."

"Would she? Well then, you may tell her if she can keep a secret. But mind, not a word of this to anybody else. Don't forget that. Be particular."

"I'll take care, sir," said Kit. "Thankee, sir, and good morning."

Now, it happened that the gentleman, in his anxiety to impress upon Kit that he was not to tell anybody what had passed between them, followed him out to the door to repeat his caution, and it further happened that at that moment the eyes of Mr. Richard Swiveller were turned in that direction, and beheld his mysterious friend and Kit together.

It was quite an accident, and the way in which it came about was this. Mr. Chuckster, being a gentleman of a cultivated taste and refined spirit, was one of that Lodge of Glorious Apollos whereof Mr. Swiveller was Perpetual Grand. Mr. Swiveller, passing through the street in the execution of some Brazen errand, and beholding one of his Glorious Brotherhood intently gazing on a pony, crossed over to give him that fraternal greeting with which Perpetual Grands are, by the very constitution of their office, bound to cheer and encourage their disciples. He had scarcely bestowed upon him his blessing, and followed it with a general remark touching the present state and prospects of the weather, when lifting up his eyes he beheld the single gentleman of Bevis Marks in earnest conversation with Christopher Nubbles.

"Hallo!" said Dick, "who is that?"

"He called to see my Governor this morning," replied Mr. Chuckster; "and beyond that I don't know him from Adam."

"At least you know his name?" said Dick.

To which Mr. Chuckster replied, with an elevation of speech becoming a Glorious Apollo, that he was "everlastingly blessed" if he did.

"All I know, my dear feller," said Mr. Chuckster, running his fingers through his hair, "is, that he is the cause of my having stood here twenty minutes, for which I hate him with a mortal and undying hatred, and would pursue him to the confines of eternity, if I could afford the time."

While they were thus discoursing, the subject of their conversation (who had not appeared to recognise Mr. Richard Swiveller) re-entered the house, and Kit came down the steps and joined them: to whom Mr. Swiveller again propounded his inquiry with no better success.

"He is a very nice gentleman, sir," said Kit, "and that's all I know about him."

Mr. Chuckster waxed wroth at this answer, and without applying the remark to any particular case, mentioned as a general truth that it was expedient to break the heads of Snobs, and to tweak their noses. Without expressing his concurrence in this sentiment, Mr. Swiveller after a few moments of abstraction inquired which way Kit was driving, and, being informed, declared it was his way, and that he would trespass on him for a lift. Kit would gladly have declined the proffered honour, but as Mr.

Swiveller was already established in the seat beside him, he had no means of doing so otherwise than by a forcible ejectment, and therefore drove briskly off-so briskly indeed as to cut short the leave-taking between Mr. Chuckster and his Grand Master, and to occasion the former gentleman some inconvenience from having his corns squeezed by the impatient pony.

As Whisker was tired of standing, and Mr. Swiveller was kind enough to stimulate him still further by shrill whistles, and various sporting cries, they rattled off at too sharp a pace to admit of much conversation, especially as the pony, incensed by Mr. Swiveller's admonitions, took a particular fancy for the lamp-posts and cart-wheels, and evinced a strong desire to run on the pavement and rasp himself against brick walls. It was not, therefore, until they had arrived at the stable, and the chaise had been extricated from a very small doorway, into which the pony dragged it under the impression that he would take it along with him into his usual stall, that Mr. Swiveller found time to talk.

"It's hard work," said Richard. "What do you say to some beer?"

Kit at first declined, but presently consented, and they adjourned to the neighbouring bar together.

"We'll drink our friend what's-his-name," said Dick, holding up the bright frothy pot; "-that was talking to you this morning, you know-I know him-a good fellow, but eccentric-very-here's what's-his-name!"

Kit pledged him.

"He lives in my house," said Dick; "at least in the house occupied by the firm in which I'm a sort of a-of a managing partner-a difficult fellow to get anything out of, but we like him-we like him."

"I must be going, sir, if you please," said Kit, moving away.

"Don't be in a hurry, Christopher," replied his patron, "we'll drink your mother."

"Thank you, sir."

"An excellent woman, that mother of yours, Christopher," said Mr. Swiveller. "Who ran to catch me when I fell, and kissed the place to make it well? My mother. A charming woman. He's a liberal sort of fellow. We must get him to do something for your mother. Does he know her, Christopher?"

Kit shook his head, and glancing slyly at his questioner, thanked him, and made off before he could say another word.

"Humph!" said Mr. Swiveller pondering, "this is queer. Nothing but mysteries in connexion with Brass's house. I'll keep my own counsel, however. Everybody and anybody has been in my confidence as yet, but now I think I'll set up in business for myself. Queer-very queer!"

After pondering deeply and with a face of exceeding wisdom for some time, Mr. Swiveller drank some more of the beer, and summoning a small boy who had been watching his proceedings, poured forth the few remaining drops as a libation upon the gravel, and bade him carry the empty vessel to the bar with his compliments, and above all things to lead a sober and temperate life, and abstain from all intoxicating and exciting liquors. Having given him this piece of moral advice for his trouble (which, as he wisely observed, was far better than half-pence) the Perpetual Grand Master of the Glorious Apollos thrust his hands into his pockets and sauntered away; still pondering as he went.

CHAPTER XXXIX

ALL that day, though he waited for Mr. Abel until the evening, Kit kept clear of his mother's house, determined not to anticipate by the slightest approach the pleasures of the morrow, but to let them come in their full rush of delight; for to-morrow was the great and long looked-for epoch in his life-to-morrow was the end of his first quarter -the day of receiving for the first time one fourth part of his annual income of Six Pounds in one vast sum of Thirty Shillings-to-morrow was to be a half-holiday devoted to a whirl of entertainments, and little Jacob was to know what oysters meant, and to see a play.

All manner of incidents combined in favour of the occasion: not only had Mr. and Mrs. Garland forewarned him that they intended to make no deduction for his outfit from the great amount, but to pay it him unbroken in all its gigantic grandeur; not only had the unknown gentleman increased the stock by the sum of five shillings, which was a perfect godsend and in itself a fortune; not only had these things come to pass which nobody could have calculated upon, or in their wildest dreams have hoped; but it was Barbara's quarter too-Barbara's quarter, that very day-and Barbara had a half-holiday as well as Kit, and Barbara's mother was going to make one of the party, and to take tea with Kit's mother, and cultivate her acquaintance.

To be sure Kit looked out of his window very early that morning to see which way the clouds were flying, and to be sure Barbara would have been at hers too if she had not sat up so late over-night, starching and ironing small pieces of muslin, and crimping them into frills, and sewing them on to other pieces to form magnificent wholes for next day's wear. But they were both up very early for all that, and had small appetites for breakfast and less for dinner, and were in a state of great excitement when Barbara's mother came in with astonishing accounts of the fineness of the weather out of doors (but with a very large umbrella notwithstanding, for people like Barbara's mother seldom make holiday without one), and when the bell rang for them to go up stairs and receive their quarter's money in gold and silver.

Well, wasn't Mr. Garland kind when he said "Christopher, here's your money, and you have earned it well;" and wasn't Mrs. Garland kind when she said "Barbara, here's yours, and I'm much pleased with you;" and didn't Kit sign his name bold to his receipt, and didn't Barbara sign her name all a trembling to hers; and wasn't it beautiful to see how Mrs. Garland poured out Barbara's mother a glass of wine; and didn't Barbara's mother speak up when she said "Here's blessing you, ma'am, as a good lady, and you, sir, as a good gentleman, and Barbara, my love to you, and here's towards you, Mr. Christopher;" and wasn't she as long drinking it as if it had been a tumbler-ful; and didn't she look genteel standing there with her gloves on; and wasn't there plenty of laughing and talking among them as they reviewed all these matters upon the top of the coach; and didn't they pity the people who had-n't got a holiday!

But Kit's mother, again-wouldn't anybody have supposed she had come of a good stock and been a lady all her life? There she was, quite ready to receive them, with a display of tea-things that might have warmed the heart of a china-shop; and little Jacob and the baby in such a state of perfec-tion that their clothes looked as good as new, though Heaven knows they were old enough! Didn't she say before they had sat down five minutes that Barbara's mother was exactly the sort of lady she expected, and didn't Barbara's mother say that Kit's mother was the very picture of what she had expected, and didn't Kit's mother compliment Barbara's mother on Barbara, and didn't Barbara's mother compliment Kit's mother on Kit, and wasn't Barbara herself quite fascinated with little Jacob, and did ever a child show off when he was wanted, as that child did, or make such friends as he made?

"And we are both widows too!" said Barbara's mother. "We must have been made to know each other."

"I haven't a doubt about it," returned Mrs. Nubbles. "And what a pity it is we didn't know each other sooner."

"But then you know it's such a pleasure," said Barbara's mother, "to have it brought about by one's son and daughter, that it's fully made up for, now, an't it?"

To this, Kit's mother yielded her full assent, and tracing things back from effects to causes, they naturally reverted to their deceased husbands, re-specting whose lives, deaths, and burials, they compared notes, and discov-ered sundry circumstances that tallied with wonderful exactness; such as Barbara's father having been exactly four years and ten months older than Kit's father, and one of them having died on a Wednesday and the other on a Thursday, and both of them having been of a very fine make and remark-ably good-looking, with other extraordinary coincidences. These recollec-tions being of a kind calculated to cast a shadow on the brightness of the hol-iday, Kit diverted the conversation to general topics, and they were soon in great force again, and as merry as before. Among other things, Kit told them about his old place, and the extraordinary beauty of Nell (of whom he had talked to Barbara a thousand times already); but the last-named circum-stance failed to interest his hearers to anything like the extent he had sup-posed, and even his mother said (looking accidentally at Barbara at the same time) that there was no doubt Miss Nell was very pretty, but she was but a child after all, and there were many young women quite as pretty as she; and Barbara mildly observed that she should think so, and that she never could help believing Mr. Christopher must be under a mistake-which Kit won-dered at very much, not being able to conceive what reason she had for doubting him. Barbara's mother too observed that it was very common for young folks to change at about fourteen or fifteen, and whereas they had been pretty before, to grow up quite plain; which truth she illustrated by many forcible examples, especially one of a young man who, being a builder with great prospects, had been particular in his attentions to Barbara, but whom Barbara would have nothing to say to; which (though everything happened for the best) she almost thought was a pity. Kit said he thought so too, and so he did honestly, and he wondered what made Barbara so silent all at once, and why his mother looked at him as if he shouldn't have said it.

However, it was high time now to be thinking of the play; for which great preparation was required in the way of shawls and bonnets, not to mention one handkerchief full of oranges and another of apples, which took some time tying up, in consequence of the fruit having a tendency to roll out at the corners. At length everything was ready, and they went off very fast; Kit's mother carrying the baby, who was dreadfully wide awake, and Kit holding little Jacob in one hand, and escorting Barbara with the other-a state of things which occasioned the two mothers, who walked behind, to declare that they looked quite family folks, and caused Barbara to blush and say, "Now don't, mother!" But Kit said she had no call to mind what they said; and indeed she need not have had, if she had known how very far from Kit's thoughts any love-making was. Poor Barbara!

At last they got to the theatre, which was Astley's: and in some two minutes after they had reached the yet unopened door, little Jacob was squeezed flat, and the baby had received divers concussions, and Barbara's mother's umbrella had been carried several yards off and passed back to her over the shoulders of the people, and Kit had hit a man on the head with the handkerchief of apples for "scrowdging" his parent with unnecessary violence, and there was a great uproar. But when they were once past the pay-place and tearing- away for very life with their checks in their hands; and above all, when they were fairly in the theatre, and seated in such places that they couldn't have had better if they had picked them out and taken them beforehand; all this was looked upon as quite a capital joke, and an essential part of the entertainment.

Dear, dear, what a place it looked, that Astley's! with all the paint, gilding, and looking-glass; the vague smell of horses suggestive of coming wonders; the curtain that hid such gorgeous mysteries; the clean white sawdust down in the circus; the company coming in and taking their places; the fiddlers looking carelessly up at them while they tuned their instruments, as if they didn't want the play to begin, and knew it all beforehand! What a glow was that which burst upon them all, when that long, clear, brilliant row of lights came slowly up; and what the feverish excitement when the little bell rang and the music began in good earnest, with strong parts for the drums, and sweet effects for the triangles! Well might Barbara's mother say to Kit's mother that the gallery was the place to see from, and wonder it wasn't much dearer than the boxes; and well might Barbara feel doubtful whether to laugh or cry, in her flutter of delight.

Then the play itself! the horses which little Jacob believed from the first to be alive, and the ladies and gentlemen of whose reality he could be by no means persuaded, having never seen or heard anything at all like them-the firing, which made Barbara wink-the forlorn lady, who made her cry-the tyrant, who made her tremble-the man who sang the song with the lady's-maid and danced the chorus, who made her laugh-the pony who reared up on his hind legs when he saw the murderer, and wouldn't hear of walking on all fours again until he was taken into custody-the clown who ventured on such familiarities with the military man in boots-the lady who jumped over the nine-and-twenty ribbons and came down safe upon the horse's back-everything was delightful, splendid, and surprising. Little Jacob applauded till his hands were sore; Kit cried "ankor" at the end of everything, the three-act piece included; and Barbara's mother beat her umbrella on the floor, in her ecstasies, until it was nearly worn down to the gingham.

In the midst of all these fascinations, Barbara's thoughts seemed to have been still running upon what Kit had said at tea-time; for when they were coming out of the play, she asked him, with an hysterical simper, if Miss Nell was as handsome as the lady who jumped over the ribbons.

"As handsome as *her?*" said Kit. "Double as handsome."

"Oh Christopher! I'm sure she was the beautifullest creature ever was," said Barbara.

"Nonsense!" returned Kit. "She was well enough, I don't deny that; but think how she was dressed and painted, and what a difference that made. Why *you* are a good deal better-looking than her, Barbara."

"Oh Christopher!" said Barbara, looking down.

"You are, any day," said Kit, - "and so's your mother."

Poor Barbara!

What was all this though-even all this-to the extraordinary dissipation that ensued, when Kit, walking into an oyster-shop as bold as if he lived there, and not so much as looking at the counter or the man behind it, led his party into a box-a private box, fitted up with red curtains, white table-cloth, and cruet-stand complete-and ordered a fierce gentleman with whiskers, who acted as waiter and called him, him, Christopher Nubbles, "sir," to bring three dozen of his largest-sized oysters, and to look sharp about it! Yes, Kit told this gentleman to look sharp, and he not only said he would look sharp, but he actually did, and presently came running back with the newest loaves, and the freshest butter, and the largest oysters, ever seen. Then said Kit to this gentleman, "a pot of beer,"-just so-and the gentleman, instead of replying, "Sir, did you address that language to me?" only said, "Pot o' beer, sir? Yes, sir," and went off and fetched it, and put it on the table in a small decanter-stand, like those which blind men's dogs carry about the streets in their mouths to catch the half-pence in; and both Kit's mother and Barbara's mother declared as he turned away that he was one of the slimmest and grace- fullest young men she had ever looked upon.

Then they fell to work upon the supper in earnest; and there was Barbara, that foolish Barbara, declaring that she couldn't eat more than two, and wanting more pressing than you would believe before she would eat four; though her mother and Kit's mother made up for it pretty well, and ate and laughed and enjoyed themselves so thoroughly that it did Kit good to see them, and made him laugh and eat likewise from strong sympathy. But the greatest miracle of the night was little Jacob, who ate oysters as if he had been born and bred to the business, sprinkled the pepper and the vinegar with a discretion beyond his years, and afterwards built a grotto on the table with the shells. There was the baby too, who had never closed an eye all night, but had sat as good as gold, trying to force a large orange into his mouth, and gazing intently at the lights in the chandelier-there he was, sitting up in his mother's lap, staring at the gas without winking, and making indentations in his soft visage with an oyster-shell, to that degree that a heart of iron must have loved him! In short, there never was a more successful supper; and when Kit ordered in a glass of something hot to finish with, and proposed Mr. and Mrs. Garland before sending it round, there were not six happier people in all the world.

But all happiness has an end-hence the chief pleasure of its next beginning-and as it was now growing late, they agreed it was time to turn their faces homewards. So, after going a little out of their way to see Barbara and Barbara's mother safe to a friend's house where they were to pass the night, Kit and his mother left them at the door, with an early appointment for returning to Finchley next morning, and a great many plans for next quarter's enjoyment. Then Kit took little Jacob on his back, and giving his arm to his mother, and a kiss to the baby, they all trudged merrily home together.

CHAPTER XL

FULL of that vague kind of penitence which holidays awaken next morning, Kit turned out at sunrise, and, with his faith in last night's enjoyments a little shaken by cool daylight and the return to every-day duties and occupations, went to meet Barbara and her mother at the appointed place. And being careful not to awaken any of the little household, who were yet resting from their unusual fatigues, Kit left his money on the chimney-piece, with an inscription in chalk calling his mother's attention to the circumstance, and informing her that it came from her dutiful son; and went his way, with a heart something heavier than his pockets, but free from any very great oppression notwithstanding.

Oh these holidays! why will they leave us so me regret! why cannot we push them back only a week or two in our memories, so as to put them at once at that convenient distance whence they may be regarded either with a calm indifference or a pleasant effort of recollection! why will they hang about us like the flavour of yesterday's wine, suggestive of headaches and lassitude, and those good intentions for the future, which under the earth form the everlasting pavement of a large estate, and upon it usually endure until dinner-time or thereabouts!

Who will wonder that Barbara had a headache, or that Barbara's mother was disposed to be cross, or that she slightly underrated Astley's, and thought the clown was older than they had taken him to be last night? Kit was not surprised to hear her say so-not he. He had already had a misgiving that the inconstant actors in that dazzling vision had been doing the same thing the night before last, and would do it again that night, and the next, and for weeks and months to come, though he would not be there. Such is the difference between yesterday and to-day. We are all going to the play, or coming home from it.

However, the Sun himself is weak when he first rises, and gathers strength and courage as the day gets on. By degrees, they began to recall circumstances more and more pleasant in their nature, until, what between talking, walking, and laughing, they reached Finchley in such good heart, that Barbara's mother declared she never felt less tired or in better spirits, and so said Kit. Barbara had been silent all the way, but she said so too. Poor little Barbara! she was very quiet.

They were at home in such good time that Kit had rubbed down the pony and made him as spruce as a racehorse, before Mr. Garland came down to breakfast; which punctual and industrious conduct the old lady, and the old gentleman, and Mr. Abel, highly extolled. At his usual hour (or rather at his usual minute and second, for he was the soul of punctuality) Mr. Abel walked out, to be overtaken by the London coach, and Kit and the old gentleman went to work in the garden.

This was not the least pleasant of Kit's employments, for on a fine day they were quite a family party; the old lady sitting hard by with her work-basket on a little table; the old gentleman digging, or pruning, or clipping about with a large pair of shears, or helping Kit in some way or other with great assiduity; and Whisker looking on from his paddock in placid contemplation of them all. To-day they were to trim the grape-vine, so Kit mounted half-way up a short ladder, and began to snip and hammer away, while the old gentleman, with a great interest in his proceedings, handed up the nails and shreds of cloth as he wanted them. The old lady and Whisker looked on as usual.

"Well, Christopher," said Mr. Garland, "and so you have made a new friend, eh?"

"I beg your pardon, sir?" returned Kit, looking down from the ladder.

"You have made a new friend, I hear from Mr. Abel," said the old gentleman, "at the office?"

"Oh-yes sir, yes. He behaved very handsome, sir."

"I'm glad to hear it," returned the old gentleman with a smile. "He is disposed to behave more handsomely still though, Christopher."

"Indeed, sir! It's very kind in him, but I don't want him to, I'm sure," said Kit, hammering stoutly at an obdurate nail.

"He is rather anxious," pursued the old gentleman, "to have you in his own service-take care what you're doing, or you will fall down and hurt yourself."

"To have me in his service, sir!" cried Kit, who had stopped short in his work and faced about upon the ladder like some dexterous tumbler. "Why, sir, I don't think he can be in earnest when he says that."

"Oh! But he is indeed," said Mr. Garland. "And he has told Mr. Abel so."

"I never heard of such a thing!" muttered Kit, looking ruefully at his master and mistress. "I wonder at him; that I do."

"You see, Christopher," said Mr. Garland, "this is a point of much importance to you, and you should understand and consider it in that light. This gentleman is able to give you more money than I-not, I hope, to carry through the various relations of master and servant, more kindness and confidence, but certainly, Christopher, to give you more money."

"Well," said Kit, "after that, sir-"

"Wait a moment," interposed Mr. Garland. "That is not all. You were a very faithful servant to your old employers, as I understand, and should this gentleman recover them, as it is his purpose to attempt doing by every means in his power, I have no doubt that you, being in his service, would meet with your reward. Besides," added the old gentleman with stronger emphasis, "besides having the pleasure of being again brought into communication with those to whom you seem to be so very strongly and disinterestedly attached. You must think of all this, Christopher, and not be rash or hasty in your choice."

Kit did suffer one twinge, one momentary pang in keeping the resolution he had already formed, when this last argument passed swiftly into his thoughts, and conjured up the realisation of all his hopes and fancies. But it was gone in a minute, and he sturdily rejoined that the gentleman must look out for somebody else, as he did think he might have done at first.

"He has no right to think that I'd be led away to go to him, sir," said Kit, turning round again after half a minute's hammering. "Does he think I'm a fool?"

"He may, perhaps, Christopher, if you refuse his offer," said Mr. Garland gravely.

"Then let him, sir," retorted Kit; "what do I care, sir, what he thinks? why should I care for his thinking, sir, when I know that I should be a fool, and worse than a fool, sir, to leave the kindest master and mistress that ever was or can be, who took me out of the streets a very poor and hungry lad indeed-poorer and hungrier perhaps than ever you think for, sir-to go to him or anybody? If Miss Nell was to come back, ma'am," added Kit, turning suddenly to his mistress, "why that would be another thing, and perhaps if she wanted me, I might ask you now and then to let me work for her when all was done at home. But when she comes back, I see now that she'll be rich as old master always said she would, and being a rich young lady, what could she want of me? No, no" added Kit, shaking his head sorrowfully, "she'll never want me any more, and bless her, I hope she never may, though I should like to see her too!"

Here Kit drove a nail into the wall, very hard-much harder than was necessary-and having done so, faced about again.

"There's the pony, sir," said Kit- "Whisker, ma'am (and he knows so well I'm talking about him that he begins to neigh directly, sir),-would he let anybody come near him but me, ma'am? Here's the garden, sir, and Mr. Abel, ma'am. Would Mr. Abel part with me, sir, or is there anybody that could be fonder of the garden, ma'am? It would break mother's heart, sir, and even little Jacob would have sense enough to cry his eyes out, ma'am, if he thought Mr. Abel could wish to part with me so soon, after having told me only the other day, that he hoped we might be together for years to come-"

There is no telling how long Kit might have stood upon the ladder, addressing his master and mistress by turns, and generally turning towards the wrong person, if Barbara had not at that moment come running up to say that a messenger from the office had brought a note, which, with an expression of some surprise at Kit's oratorical appearance, she put into her master's hand.

"Oh!" said the old gentleman after reading it, "ask the messenger to walk this way." Barbara tripping off to do as she was bid, he turned to Kit and said that they would not pursue the subject any further, and that Kit could not be more unwilling to part with them, than they would be to part with Kit; a sentiment which the old lady very generously echoed.

"At the same time, Christopher," added Mr. Garland, glancing at the note in his hand, "if the gentleman should want to borrow you now and then for an hour or so, or even a day or so, at a time, we must consent to lend you, and you must consent to be lent.-Oh! here is the young gentleman. How do you do, sir?"

This salutation was addressed to Mr. Chuckster, who, with his hat extremely on one side, and his hair a long way beyond it, came swaggering up the walk.

"Hope I see you well, sir," returned that gentleman. "Hope I see you well, ma'am. Charming box this, sir. Delicious country, to be sure."

"You want to take Kit back with you, I find?" observed Mr. Garland.

"I've got a chariot-cab waiting on purpose," replied the clerk. "A very spanking grey in that cab, sir, if you're a judge of horseflesh."

Declining to inspect the spanking grey, on the plea that he was but poorly acquainted with such matters, and would but imperfectly appreciate his beauties, Mr. Garland invited Mr. Chuckster to partake of a slight repast in the way of lunch, and that gentleman readily consenting, certain cold viands, flanked with ale and wine, were speedily prepared for his refreshment.

At this repast, Mr. Chuckster exerted his utmost abilities to enchant his entertainers, and impress them with a conviction of the mental superiority of those who dwelt in town; with which view he led the discourse to the small scandal of the day, in which he was justly considered by his friends to shine prodigiously. Thus, he was in a condition to relate the exact circumstances of the difference between the Marquis of Mizzler and Lord Bobby, which it appeared originated in a disputed bottle of champagne, and not in a pigeon-pie, as erroneously reported in the newspapers; neither had Lord Bobby said to the Marquis of Mizzler, "Mizzler, one of us two tells a lie, and I'm not the man," as incorrectly stated by the same authorities; but "Mizzler, you know where I'm to be found, and damme, sir, find me if you want me" -which, of course, entirely changed the aspect of this interesting question, and placed it in a very different light. He also acquainted them with the precise amount of the income guaranteed by the Duke of Thigsberry to Violetta Stetta of the Italian Opera, which it appeared was payable quarterly, and not half-yearly, as the public had been given to understand, and which was exclusive, and not inclusive (as had been monstrously stated), of jewellery, perfumery, hair-powder for five footmen, and two daily changes of kid-gloves for a page. Having entreated the old lady and gentleman to set their minds at rest upon these absorbing points, for they might rely on his statement being the correct one, Mr. Chuckster entertained them with theatrical chit-chat and the court circular; and so wound up a brilliant and fascinating conversation which he had maintained alone, and without any assistance whatever, for upwards of three-quarters of an hour.

"And now that the nag has got his wind again," said Mr. Chuckster, rising in a graceful manner, "I'm afraid I must cut my stick."

Neither Mr. nor Mrs. Garland offered any opposition to his tearing himself away (feeling, no doubt, that such a man could ill be spared from his proper sphere of action), and therefore Mr. Chuckster and Kit were shortly afterwards upon their way to town; Kit being perched upon the box of the cabriolet beside the driver, and Mr. Chuckster seated in solitary state inside, with one of his boots sticking out at each of the front windows.

When they reached the Notary's house, Kit followed into the office, and was desired by Mr. Abel to sit down and wait, for the gentleman who wanted him had gone out, and perhaps might not return for some time. This anticipation was strictly verified, for Kit had had his dinner, and his tea, and had read all the light matter in the Law-List, and the Post-Office Directory, and had fallen asleep a great many times, before the gentleman whom he had seen before, came in; which he did at last in a very great hurry.

He was closeted with Mr. Witherden for some little time, and Mr. Abel had been called in to assist at the conference, before Kit, wondering very much what he was wanted for, was summoned to attend them.

"Christopher," said the gentleman, turning to him directly he entered the room, "I have found your old master and young mistress."

"No, sir! Have you though?" returned Kit, his eyes sparkling with delight. "Where are they, sir? How are they, sir? Are they-are they near here?"

"A long way from here," returned the gentleman, shaking his head. "But I am going away to-night to bring them back, and I want you to go with me."

"Me, sir," cried Kit, full of joy and surprise.

"The place," said the strange gentleman, turning thoughtfully to the Notary, "indicated by this man of the dogs, is-how far from here-sixty miles?"

"From sixty to seventy."

"Humph! If we travel post all night, we shall reach there in good time to-morrow morning. Now, the only question is, as they will not know me, and the child, God bless her, would think that any stranger pursuing them had a design upon her grandfather's liberty,-can I do better than take this lad, whom they both know and will readily remember, as an assurance to them of my friendly intentions?"

"Certainly not," replied the Notary. "Take Christopher by all means."

"I beg your pardon, sir," said Kit, who had listened to this discourse with a lengthening countenance, "but if that's the reason, I'm afraid I should do more harm than good-Miss Nell, sir, she knows me, and would trust in me, I am sure; but old master-I don't know why, gentlemen; nobody does-would not bear me in his sight after he had been ill, and Miss Nell herself told me that I must not go near him or let him see me any more. I should spoil all that you were doing if I went, I'm afraid. I'd give the world to go, but you had better not take me, sir."

"Another difficulty!" cried the impetuous gentleman. "Was ever man so beset as I? Is there nobody else that knew them, nobody else in whom they had any confidence? Solitary as their lives were, is there no one person who would serve my purpose?"

"Is there, Christopher?" said the Notary.

"Not one, sir," replied Kit.- "Yes, though-there's my mother."

"Did they know her?" said the single gentleman.

"Know her, sir! why, she was always coming backwards and forwards. They were as kind to her as they were to me. Bless you, sir, she expected they'd come back to her house."

"Then where the devil is the woman?" said the impatient gentleman, catching up his hat. "Why isn't she here? Why is that woman always out of the way when she is most wanted?"

In a word, the single gentleman was bursting out of the office, bent upon laying violent hands on Kit's mother, forcing her into a post-chaise, and carrying her off, when this novel kind of abduction was with some difficulty prevented by the joint efforts of Mr. Abel and the Notary, who restrained him by dint of their remonstrances, and persuaded him to sound Kit upon the probability of her being able and willing to undertake such a journey on so short a notice.

This occasioned some doubts on the part of Kit, and some violent demonstrations on that of the single gentleman, and a great many soothing speeches on that of the Notary and Mr. Abel. The upshot of the business was, that Kit, alter weighing the matter in his mind and considering it carefully, promised, on behalf of his mother, that she should be ready within two hours from that time to undertake the expedition, and engaged to produce her in that place, in all respects equipped and prepared for the journey, before the specified period had expired.

Having given this pledge, which was rather a bold one, and not particularly easy of redemption, Kit lost no time in sallying forth, and taking measures for its immediate fulfilment.

CHAPTER XLI

KIT made his way through the crowded streets, dividing the stream of people, dashing across the busy roadways, diving into lanes and alleys, and stopping or turning aside for nothing, until he came in front of the Old Curiosity Shop, when he came to a stand; partly from habit and partly from being out of breath.

It was a gloomy autumn evening, and he thought the old place had never looked so dismal as in its dreary twilight. The windows broken, the rusty sashes rattling in their frames, the deserted house a dull barrier dividing the glaring lights and bustle of the street into two long lines, and standing in the midst, cold, dark, and empty, presented a cheerless spectacle which mingled harshly with the bright prospects the boy had been building up for its late inmates, and came like a disappointment or misfortune. Kit would have had a good fire roaring up the empty chimneys, lights sparkling and shining through the windows, people moving briskly to and fro, voices in cheerful conversation, something in unison with the new hopes that were astir. He had not expected that the house would wear any different aspect—had known indeed that it could not—but coming upon it in the midst of eager thoughts and expectations, it checked the current in its flow, and darkened it with a mournful shadow.

Kit, however, fortunately for himself, was not learned enough or contemplative enough to be troubled with presages of evil afar off, and, having no mental spectacles to assist his vision in this respect, saw nothing but the dull house, which jarred uncomfortably upon his previous thoughts. So, almost wishing that he had not passed it, though hardly knowing why, he hurried on again, making up by his increased speed for the few moments he had lost.

"Now, if she should be out," thought Kit, as he approached the poor dwelling of his mother, "and I not able to find her, this impatient gentleman would be in a pretty taking. And sure enough there's no light, and the door's fast. Now, God forgive me for saying so, but if this is Little Bethel's doing, I wish Little Bethel was-was farther off," said Kit checking himself, and knocking at the door.

A second knock brought no reply from within the house; but caused a woman over the way to look out and inquire who that was, wanting Mrs. Nubbles.

"Me," said Kit. "She's at-at Little Bethel, I suppose?" -getting out the name of the obnoxious conventicle with some reluctance, and laying a spiteful emphasis upon the words.

The neighbour nodded assent.

"Then pray tell me where it is," said Kit, "for I have come on a pressing matter, and must fetch her out, even if she was in the pulpit."

It was not very easy to procure a direction to the fold in question, as none of the neighbours were of the flock that resorted thither, and few knew anything more of it than the name. At last a gossip of Mrs. Nubbles's, who had accompanied her to chapel on one or two occasions when a comfortable cup of tea had preceded her devotions, furnished the needful information, which Kit had no sooner obtained than he started off again.

Little Bethel might have been nearer, and might have been in a straighter road, though in that case the reverend gentleman who presided over its congregation would have lost his favourite allusion to the crooked ways by which it was approached, and which enabled him to liken it to Paradise itself, in contradistinction to the parish church and the broad thoroughfare leading thereunto. Kit found it at last after some trouble, and pausing at the door to take breath that he might enter with becoming decency, passed into the chapel.

It was not badly named in one respect, being in truth a particularly little Bethel-a Bethel of the smallest dimensions-with a small number of small pews, and a small pulpit, in which a small gentleman (by trade a Shoemaker, and by calling a Divine) was delivering in a by no means small voice, a by no means small sermon, judging of its dimensions by the condition of his audience, which, if their gross amount were but small, comprised a still smaller number of hearers, as the majority were slumbering.

Among these was Kit's mother, who, finding it matter of extreme difficulty to keep her eyes open after the fatigues of last night, and feeling their inclination to close strongly backed and seconded by the arguments of the preacher, had yielded to the drowsiness that overpowered her, and fallen asleep; though not so soundly but that she could from time to time utter a slight and almost inaudible groan, as if in recognition of the orator's doctrines. The baby in her arms was as fast asleep as she; and little Jacob, whose youth prevented him from recognising in this prolonged spiritual nourishment anything half as interesting as oysters, was alternately very fast asleep and very wide awake, as his inclination to slumber, or his terror of being personally alluded to in the discourse, gained the mastery over him.

"And now I'm here," thought Kit, gliding into the nearest empty pew which was opposite his mother's, and on the other side of the little aisle, "how am I ever to get at her, or persuade her to come out! I might as well be twenty miles off. She'll never wake till it's all over, and there goes the clock again! If he would but leave off for a minute, or if they'd only sing!"

But there was little encouragement to believe that either event would happen for a couple of hours to come. The preacher went on telling them what he meant to convince them of before he had done, and it was clear that if he only kept to one-half of his promises and forgot the other, he was good for that time at least.

In his desperation and restlessness Kit cast his eyes about the chapel, and happening to let them fall upon a little seat in front of the clerk's desk, could scarcely believe them when they showed him-Quilp!

He rubbed them twice or thrice, but still they insisted that Quilp was there, and there indeed he was, sitting with his hands upon his knees, and his hat between them on a little wooden bracket, with the accustomed grin upon his dirty face, and his eyes fixed upon the ceiling. He certainly did not glance at Kit or at his mother, and appeared utterly unconscious of their presence;

still Kit could not help feeling directly that the attention of the sly little fiend was fastened upon them, and upon nothing else.

But astounded as he was by the apparition of the dwarf among the Little Bethelites, and not free from a misgiving that it was the forerunner of some trouble or annoyance, he was compelled to subdue his wonder and to take active measures for the withdrawal of his parent, as the evening was now creeping on, and the matter grew serious. Therefore the next time little Jacob woke, Kit set himself to attract his wandering attention, and this not being a very difficult task (one sneeze effected it), he signed to him to rouse his mother.

I'll luck would have it, however, that just then the preacher, in a forcible exposition of one head of his discourse, leaned over upon the pulpit desk so that very little more of him than his legs remained inside; and, while he made vehement gestures with his right hand, and held on with his left, stared, or seemed to stare, straight into little Jacob's eyes, threatening him by his strained look and attitude-so it appeared to the child-that if he so much as moved a muscle, he, the preacher, would be literally, and not figuratively, "down upon him," that instant. In this fearful state of things, distracted by the sudden appearance of Kit, and fascinated by the eyes of the preacher, the miserable Jacob sat bolt upright, wholly incapable of motion, strongly disposed to cry but afraid to do so, and returning his pastor's gaze until his infant eyes seemed starting from their sockets.

"If I must do it openly, I must," thought Kit. With that, he walked softly out of his pew and into his mother's, and as Mr. Swiveller would have observed if he had been present, collared" the baby without speaking a word.

"Hush, mother!" whispered Kit. "Come along with me, I've got something to tell you."

"Where am I?" said Mrs. Nubbles.

"In this blessed Little Bethel," returned her son peevishly.

"Blessed indeed!" cried Mrs. Nubbles, catching at the word. "Oh, Christopher, how have I been edified this night!"

"Yes, yes, I know," said Kit hastily; "but come along, mother, everybody's looking at us. Don't make a noise- bring Jacob-that's right."

"Stay, Satan, stay!" cried the preacher, as Kit was moving off.

"The gentleman says you're to stay, Christopher," whispered his mother.

"Stay, Satan, stay!" roared the preacher again. "Tempt not the woman that doth incline her ear to thee, but hearken to the voice of him that calleth. He hath lamb from the fold!" cried the preacher, raising his voice still higher and pointing to the baby. "He beareth off a lamb, a precious lamb! He goeth about like a wolf in the night season, and inveigleth the tender Iambs!"

Kit was the best-tempered fellow in the world, but considering this strong language, and being somewhat excited by the circumstances in which he was placed, he faced round to the pulpit with the baby in his arms, and replied aloud,   ˙

"No, I don't. He's my brother."

"He's my brother!" cried the preacher.

"He isn't," said Kit indignantly. "How can you say such a thing? -And don't call me names if you please; what harm have I done? I shouldn't have come to take 'em away unless I was obliged, you may depend upon that; and I wanted to do it very quiet, but you wouldn't let me. Now, you have the goodness to abuse Satan and them as much as you like, sir, and to let me alone if you please."

So saying, Kit marched out of the chapel, followed by his mother and little Jacob, and found himself in the open air, with an indistinct recollection of having seen the people wake up and look surprised, and of Quilp having remained throughout the interruption in his old attitude, without moving his eyes from the ceiling, or appearing to take the smallest notice of anything that passed.

"Oh Kit!" said his mother, with her handkerchief to her eyes, "what have you done! I never can go there again-never!"

"I'm glad of it, mother. What was there in the little bit of pleasure you took last night that made it necessary for you to be low-spirited and sorrowful to-night? That's the way you do. If you're happy or merry ever, you come here to say, along with that chap, that you're sorry for it. More shame for you, mother, I was going to say."

"Hush, dear!" said Mrs. Nubbles; "you don't mean what you say, I know, but you're talking sinfulness."

"Don't mean it? But I do mean it!" retorted Kit. "I don't believe, mother, that harmless cheerfulness and good-humour are thought greater sins in Heaven than shirt-collars are, and that those chaps are just about as right and sensible in putting down the one as in leaving off the other-that's my belief. But I won't say anything more about it, if you'll promise not to cry, that's all; and you take the baby that's a lighter weight, and give me little Jacob; and as we go along (which we must do pretty quick) I'll tell you the news I bring, which will surprise you a little, I can tell you. There-that's right. Now you look as if you'd never seen Little Bethel in all your life, as I hope you never will again; and here's the baby; and little Jacob, you get atop of my back and catch hold of me tight round the neck, and whenever a Little Bethel parson calls you a precious lamb or says your brother's one, you tell him it's the truest things he's said for a twelvemonth, and that if he'd got a little more of the lamb himself, and less of the mint-sauce-not being quite so sharp and sour over it-I should like him all the better. That's what you've got to say to him, Jacob."

Talking on in this way, half in jest and half in earnest, and cheering up his mother, the children, and himself, by the one simple process of determining to be in a good humour, Kit led them briskly forward; and on the road home he related what had passed at the Notary's house, and the purpose with which he had intruded on the solemnities of Little Bethel.

His mother was not a little startled on learning what service was required of her, and presently fell into a confusion of ideas, of which the most prominent were that it was a great honour and dignity to ride in a post-chaise, and that it was a moral impossibility to leave the children behind. But this objection, and a great many others, founded upon certain articles of dress being at the wash, and certain other articles having no existence in the wardrobe of Mrs. Nubbles, were overcome by Kit, who opposed to each and every of them, the pleasure of recovering Nell, and the delight it would be to bring her back in triumph.

"There's only ten minutes now, mother" -said Kit when they reached home. "There's a bandbox. Throw in what you want, and we'll be off directly."

To tell how Kit then hustled into the box all sorts of things which could by no remote contingency be wanted, and how he left out everything likely to be of the smallest use; how a neighbour was persuaded to come and stop with the children, and how the children at first cried dismally, and then laughed heartily on being promised all kinds of impossible and unheard-of toys; how Kit's mother wouldn't leave off kissing them, and how Kit couldn't make up his mind to be vexed with her for doing it; would take more time and room than we can spare. So, passing over all such matters, it is sufficient to say that within a few minutes after the two hours had expired, Kit and his mother arrived at the Notary's door, where a post-chaise was already waiting.

"With four horses I declare!" said Kit, quite aghast at the preparations. "Well you are going to do it, mother! Here she is, sir. Here's my mother. She's quite ready, sir."

"That's well"-returned the gentleman. "Now, don't be in a flutter, ma'am; you'll be taken great care of. Where's the box with the new clothing and necessaries for them?"

"Here it is," said the Notary. "In with it, Christopher."

"All right, sir," replied Kit. "Quite ready now, sir."

"Then come along," said the single gentleman. And thereupon he gave his arm to Kit's mother, handed her into the carriage as politely as you please, and took his seat beside her.

Up went the steps, bang went the door, round whirled the wheels, and off they rattled, with Kit's mother hanging out at one window waving a clamp pocket-handkerchief and screaming out a great many messages to little Jacob and the baby, of which nobody heard a word.

Kit stood in the middle of the road, and looked after them with tears in his eyes-not brought there by the departure he witnessed, but by the return to which he looked forward. "They went away," he thought, "on foot with nobody to speak to them or say a kind word at parting, and they'll come back, drawn by four horses, with this rich gentleman for their friend, and all their troubles over! She'll forget that she taught me to write-"

Whatever Kit thought about after this, took some time to think of, for he stood gazing up at the lines of shining lamps, long after the chaise had disappeared, and did not return into the house until the Notary and Mr. Abel, who had themselves lingered outside till the sound of the wheels was no longer distinguishable, had several times wondered what could possibly detain him.

CHAPTER XLII

IT behoves us to leave Kit for a while, thoughtful and expectant, and to follow the fortunes of little Nell; resuming the thread of the narrative at the point where it was left, so me chapters back.

In one of those wanderings in the evening time, when, following the two sisters at a humble distance, she felt, in her sympathy with them and her recognition in their trials of something akin to her own loneliness of spirit, a comfort and consolation which made such moments a time of deep delight, though the softened pleasure they yielded was of that kind which lives and dies in tears-in one of those wanderings at the quiet hour of twilight, when sky, and earth, and air, and rippling water, and sound of distant bells, claimed kindred with the emotions of the solitary child, and inspired her with soothing thoughts, but not of a child's world or its easy joys-in one of those rambles which had now become her only pleasure or relief from care, light had faded into darkness and evening deepened into night, and still the young creature lingered in the gloom; feeling a companionship in Nature so serene and still, when noise of tongues and glare of garish lights would have been solitude indeed.

The sisters had gone home, and she was alone. She raised her eyes to the bright stars, looking down so mildly from the wide worlds of air, and, gazing on them, found new stars burst upon her view, and more beyond, and more beyond again, until the whole great expanse sparkled with shining spheres, rising higher and higher in immeasurable space, eternal in their numbers as in their changeless and incorruptible existence. She bent over the calm river, and saw them shining in the same majestic order as when the dove beheld them gleaming through the swollen waters, upon the mountain tops down far below, and dead mankind, a million fathoms deep.

The child sat silently beneath a tree, hushed in her very breath by the stillness of the night, and all its attendant wonders. The time and place awoke reflection, and she thought with a quiet hopeless hope, perhaps, than resignation-on the past, and present, and what was yet before her. Between the old man and herself there had come a gradual separation, harder to bear than any former sorrow. Every evening, and often in the day-time too, he was absent, alone; and although she well knew where he went, and why-too well from the constant drain upon her scanty purse and from his haggard looks-he evaded all inquiry, ,maintained a strict reserve, and even shunned her presence.

She sat meditating sorrowfully upon this change, and mingling it, as it were, with everything about her, when the distant church-clock bell struck nine. Rising at the sound, she retraced her steps, and turned thoughtfully towards the town.

She had gained a little wooden bridge, which, thrown across the stream, led into a meadow in her way, when she came suddenly upon a ruddy light, and looking forward more attentively, discerned that it proceeded from what appeared to be an encampment of gipsies, who had made a fire in one corner at no great distance from the path, and were sitting or lying round it. As she was too poor to have any fear of them, she did not alter her course (which, indeed, she could not have done without going a long way round), but quickened her pace a little, and kept straight on.

A movement of timid curiosity impelled her, when she approached the spot, to glance towards the fire. There was a form between it and her, the outline strongly developed against the light, which caused her to stop abruptly. Then, as if she had reasoned with herself and were assured that it could not be, or had satisfied herself that it was not that of the person she had supposed, she went on again.

But at that instant the conversation, whatever it was, which had been carrying on near this fire was resumed, and the tones of the voice that spoke-she could not distinguish words-sounded as familiar to her as her own.

She turned, and looked back. The person had been seated before, but was now in a standing posture, and leaning forward upon a stick on which he rested both hands. The attitude was no less familiar to her than the tone of voice had been. It was her grandfather.

Her first impulse was to call to him; her next to wonder who his associates could be, and for what purpose they were together. Some vague apprehension succeeded, and, yielding to the strong inclination it awakened, she drew nearer to the place; not advancing across the open field, however, but creeping towards it by the hedge.

In this way she advanced within a few feet of the fire, and standing among a few young trees, could both see and hear, without much danger of being observed.

There were no women or children, as she had seen in other gipsy camps they had passed in their wayfaring, and but one gipsy-a tall, athletic man, who stood with his arms folded, leaning against a tree at a little distance off, looking now at the fire, and now, under his black eye-lashes, at three other men who were there, with a watchful but half-concealed interest in their conversation. Of these her grandfather was one; the others she recognised as the first card-players at the public-house on the eventful night of the storm-the man whom they had called Isaac List, and his gruff companion. One of the low, arched gipsy- tents, common to that people, was pitched hard by, but it either was, or appeared to be, empty.

"Well, are you going?" said the stout man, looking up from the ground where he was lying at his ease, into her grandfather's face. "You were in a mighty hurry a minute ago. Go, if you like. You're your own master, I hope?"

"Don't vex him," returned Isaac List, who was squatting like a frog on the other side of the fire, and had so screwed himself up that he seemed to be squinting all over; "he didn't mean any offence."

"You keep me poor, and plunder me, and make a sport and jest of me besides," said the old man, turning from one to the other. "Ye'll drive me mad among ye."

The utter irresolution and feebleness of the grey-haired child, contrasted with the keen and cunning looks of those in whose hands he was, smote upon the little listener's heart. But she constrained herself to attend to all that passed, and to note each look and word.

"Confound you, what do you mean?" said the stout man rising a little, and supporting himself upon his elbow. "Keep you poor! You'd keep us poor if you could, wouldn't you? That's the way with you whining, puny, pitiful players. When you lose, you're martyrs; but I don't find that when you win, you look upon the other losers in that light. As to plunder!" cried the fellow, raising his voice- "Damme, what do you mean by such ungentle-manly language as plunder, eh?"

The speaker laid himself down again at full length, and gave one or two short, angry kicks, as if in further expression of his unbounded indignation. It was quite plain that he acted the bully, and his friend the peacemaker, for some particular purpose; or rather, it would have been to any one but the weak old man; for they exchanged glances quite openly, both with each other and with the gipsy, who grinned his approval of the jest until his white teeth shone again.

The old man stood helplessly among them for a little time, and then said, turning to his assailant:

"You yourself were speaking of plunder just now, you know. Don't be so violent with me. You were, were you not?"

"Not of plundering among present company! Honour among-among gentlemen, sir," returned the other, who seemed to have been very near giving an awkward termination to the sentence.

"Don't be hard upon him, Jowl," said Isaac List. "He's very sorry for giving offence. There-go on with what you were saying-go on."

"I'm a jolly old tender-hearted lamb, I am," cried Mr. Jowl, "to be sitting here at my time of life giving advice when I know it won't be taken, and that I shall get nothing but abuse for my pains. But that's the way I've gone through life. Experience has never put a chill upon my warm-heartedness."

"I tell you he's very sorry, don't I?" remonstrated Isaac List, "and that he wishes you'd go on."

"Does he wish it?" said the other.

"Ay," groaned the old man sitting down, and rocking himself to and fro. "Go on, go on. It's in vain to fight with it; I can't do it; go on."

"I go on then," said Jowl, where I left off, when you got up so quick. If you're persuaded that it's time for luck to turn, as it certainly is, and find that you haven't means enough to try it (and that's where it is, for you know yourself that you never have the funds to keep on long enough at a sitting), help yourself to what seems put in your way on purpose. Borrow it, I say, and, when you're able, pay it back again."

"Certainly," Isaac List struck in, "if this good lady as keeps the waxworks has money, and does keep it in a tin box when she goes to bed, and doesn't lock her door for fear of fire, it seems a easy thing; quite a Providence, I should call it-but then I've been religiously brought up."

"You see, Isaac," said his friend, growing more eager, and drawing himself closer to the old man, while he signed to the gipsy not to come between them; "you see, Isaac, strangers are going in and out every hour of the day; nothing would be more likely than for one of these strangers to get under the good lady's bed, or lock himself in the cupboard; suspicion would be very wide, and would fall a long way from the mark, no doubt. I'd give him his revenge to the last farthing he brought, whatever the amount was."

"But could you?" urged Isaac List. "Is your bank strong enough?"

"Strong enough!" answered the other, with assumed disdain. "Here, you sir, give me that box out of the straw!"

This was addressed to the gipsy, who crawled into the low tent on all fours, and after some rummaging and rustling returned with a cash-box, which the man who had spoken opened with a key he wore about his person.

"Do you see this?" he said, gathering up the money in his hand and letting it drop back into the box, between his fingers, like water. "Do you hear it? Do you know the sound of gold? There, put it back-and don't talk about banks again, Isaac, till you've got one of your own."

Isaac List, with great apparent humility, protested that he had never doubted the credit of a gentleman so notorious for his honourable dealing as Mr. Jowl, and that he had hinted at the production of the box, not for the satisfaction of his doubts, for he could have none, but with a view to being regaled with a sight of so much wealth, which, though it might be deemed by some but an unsubstantial and visionary pleasure, was to one in his circumstances a source of extreme delight, only to be surpassed by its safe depository in his own personal pockets. Although Mr. List and Mr. Jowl addressed themselves to each other, it was remarkable that they both looked narrowly at the old man, who, with his eyes fixed upon the fire, sat brooding over it, yet listening eagerly-as it seemed from a certain involuntary motion of the head, or twitching of the face from time to time-to all they said.

"My advice," said Jowl, lying down again with a careless air, "is plain-I have given it, in fact. I act as a friend. Why should I help a man to the means perhaps of winning all I have, unless I considered him my friend? It's foolish, I dare say, to be so thoughtful of the welfare of other people, but that's my constitution, and I can't help it; so don't blame me, Isaac List."

"I blame you!" returned the person addressed; "not for the world, Mr. Jowl. I wish I could afford to be as liberal as you; and, as you say, he might pay it back if he won-and if he lost-"

"You're not to take that into consideration at all," said Jowl. "But suppose he did (and nothing's less likely, from all I know of chances), why, it's better to lose other people's money than one's own, I hope?"

"Ah!" cried Isaac List rapturously, "the pleasures of winning! The delight of picking up the money-the bright, shining yellow-boys-and sweeping 'em into one's pocket! The deliciousness of having a triumph at last, and thinking that one didn't stop short and turn back, but went half-way to meet it! The-but you're not going, old gentleman?"

"I'll do it," said the old man, who had risen and taken two or three hurried steps away, and now returned as hurriedly. "I'll have it, every penny."

"Why, that's brave," cried Isaac, jumping up and slapping him on the shoulder; "and I respect you for having so much young blood left. Ha, ha, ha! Joe Jowl's half sorry he advised you now. We've got the laugh against him. Ha, ha, ha!"

"He gives me my revenge, mind," said the old man, pointing to him eagerly with his shrivelled hand: "mind- he stakes coin against coin, down to the last one in the box, be there many or few. Remember that!"

"I'm witness," returned Isaac. "I'll see fair between you."

"I have passed my word," said Jowl with feigned reluctance, "and I'll keep it. When does this match come off? I wish it was over.-To-night?"

"I must have the money first," said the old man; "and that I'll have to-morrow-"

"Why not to-night?" urged Jowl.

"It's late now, and I should be flushed and flurried," said the old man. "It must be softly done. No, to-morrow night."

"Then to-morrow be it," said Jowl. "A drop of comfort here. Luck to the best man! Fill!"

The gipsy produced three tin cups, and filled them to the brim with brandy. The old man turned aside and muttered to himself before he drank. Her own name struck upon the listener's ear, coupled with some wish so fervent, that he seemed to breathe it in an agony of supplication.

"God be merciful to us!" cried the child within herself, "and help us in this trying hour! What shall I do to save him!"

The remainder of their conversation was tarried on in a lower tone of voice, and was sufficiently concise; relating merely to the execution of the project, and the best precautions for diverting suspicion. The old man then shook hands with his tempters, and withdrew.

They watched his bowed and stooping figure as it retreated slowly, and when he turned his head to look back, which he often did, waved their hands, or shouted some brief encouragement. It was not until they had seen him gradually diminish into a mere speck upon the distant road, that they turned to each other, and ventured to laugh aloud.

"So," said Jowl, warming his hands at the fire, "it's done at last. He wanted more persuading than I expected. It's three weeks ago since we first put this in his head. What'll he bring, do you think?"

"Whatever he brings, it's halved between us," returned Isaac List.

The other man nodded. "We must make quick work of it," he said, "and then cut his acquaintance, or we may be suspected. Sharp's the word."

List and the gipsy acquiesced. When they had all three amused themselves a little with their victim's infatuation, they dismissed the subject as one which had been sufficiently discussed, and began to talk in a jargon which the child did not understand. As their discourse appeared to relate to matters in which they were warmly interested, however, she deemed it the best time for escaping unobserved; and crept away with slow and cautious steps, keeping in the shadow of the hedges, or forcing a path through them or the dry ditches, until she could emerge upon the road at a point beyond their range of vision. Then she fled homewards as quickly as she could, torn and bleeding from the wounds of thorns and briars, but more lacerated in mind, and threw herself upon her bed, distracted.

The first idea that flashed upon her mind was flight, instant flight; dragging him from that place, and rather dying of want upon the roadside, than ever exposing him again to such terrible temptations. Then she remembered that the crime was not to be committed until next night, and there was the intermediate time for thinking, and resolving what to do. Then she was distracted with a horrible fear that he might be committing it at that moment; with a dread of hearing shrieks and cries piercing the silence of the night; with fearful thoughts of what he might be tempted and led on to do, if he were detected in the act, and had but a woman to struggle with. It was impossible to bear such torture. She stole to the room where the money was, opened the door, and looked in. God be praised! He was not there, and she was sleeping soundly.

She went back to her own room, and tried to prepare herself for bed. But who could sleep-sleep! who could lie passively down, distracted by such terrors? They came upon her more and more strongly yet. Half undressed, and with her hair in wild disorder, she flew to the old man's bedside, clasped him by the wrist, and roused him from his sleep;

What's this!" he cried, starting up in bed, and fixing his eyes upon her spectral face.

"I have had a dreadful dream," said the child, with an energy that nothing but such terrors could have inspired. "A dreadful, horrible dream. I have had it once before. It is a dream of grey-haired men like you, in darkened rooms by night, robbing the sleepers of their gold. Up, "up!" The old man shook in every joint, and folded his hands like one who prays.

"Not to me," said the child, "not to me-to Heaven, to save us from such deeds! This dream is too real. I cannot sleep, I cannot stay here, I cannot leave you alone under the roof where such dreams come. Up! We must fly."

He looked at her as if she were a spirit-she might have I been, for all the look of earth she had-and trembled more and more.

"There is no time to lose; I will not lose one minute" said the child. "Up! and away with me!"

"To-night!" murmured the old man.

"Yes, to-night," replied the child. "To-morrow night will be too late. The dream will have come again. Nothing but flight can save us. Up!"

The old man rose from his bed, his forehead bedewed with the cold sweat of fear, and, bending before the child as if she had been an angel messenger sent to lead him where she would, made ready to follow her. She took him by the hand and led him on. As they passed the door of the room he had proposed to rob, she shuddered and looked up into his face. What a white face was that, and with what a look did he meet hers!

She took him to her own chamber, and, still holding him by the hand as if she feared to lose him for an instant, gathered together the little stock she had, and hung her basket on her arm. The old man took his wallet from her hands and strapped it on his shoulders-his staff, too, she had brought away-and then she led him forth.

Through the strait streets, and narrow crooked outskirts, their trembling feet passed quickly. Up the steep hill too, crowned by the old grey castle, they toiled with rapid steps, and had not once looked behind.

But as they drew nearer the ruined walls, the moon rose in all her gentle glory, and, from their venerable age, garlanded with ivy, moss, and waving grass, the child looked back upon the sleeping town, deep in the valley's shade, and on the far-off river with its winding track of light, and on the distant hills; and as she did so, she clasped the hand she held, less firmly, and bursting into tears, fell upon the old man's neck.

CHAPTER XLIII

HER momentary weakness past, the child again summoned the resolution which had until now sustained her, and, endeavouring to keep steadily in her view the one idea that they were flying from disgrace and crime, and that her grandfather's preservation must depend solely upon her firmness, unaided by one word of advice or any helping hand, urged him onward and looked back no more.

While he, subdued and abashed, seemed to crouch before her, and to shrink and cower down as if in the presence of some superior creature, the child herself was sensible of a new feeling within her, which elevated her nature, and inspired her with an energy and confidence she had never known. There was no divided responsibility now; the whole burden of their two lives had fallen upon her, and henceforth she must think and act for both. "I have saved him," she thought. "In all dangers and distresses, I will remember that."

At any other time the recollection of having deserted the friend who had shown them so much homely kindness, without a word of justification-the thought that they were guilty, in appearance, of treachery and ingratitude-even the having parted from the two sisters-would have filled her with sorrow and regret. But now, all other considerations were lost in the new uncertainties and anxieties of their wild and wandering life; and the very desperation of their condition roused and stimulated her.

In the pale moonlight, which lent a wanness of its own, the delicate face where thoughtful care already mingled with the winning grace and loveliness of youth, the too bright eye, the spiritual head, the lips that pressed each other with such high resolve and courage of the heart, the slight figure firm in its bearing and yet so very weak, told their silent tale; but told it only to the wind that rustled by, which, taking up its burden, carried, perhaps to some mother's pillow, faint dreams of childhood fading in its bloom, and resting in the sleep that knows no waking.

The night crept on apace, the moon went down, the stars grew pale and dim, and morning, cold as they, slowly approached. Then, from behind a distant hill, the noble sun rose up, driving the mists in phantom shapes before it, and clearing the earth of their ghostly forms till darkness came again. When it had climbed higher into the sky, and there was warmth in its cheerful beams, they laid them down to sleep, upon a bank, hard by some water.

But Nell retained her grasp upon the old man's arm, and long after he was slumbering soundly, watched him with untiring eyes. Fatigue stole over her at last; her grasp relaxed, tightened, relaxed again, and they slept side by side.

A confused sound of voices, mingled with her dreams, awoke her. A man of very uncouth and rough appearance was standing over them, and two of his companions were looking on from a long heavy boat which had come close to the bank while they were sleeping. The boat had neither oar nor sail, but was towed by a couple of horses, who, with the rope to which they were harnessed slack and dripping in the water, were resting on the path.

"Holloa!" said the man roughly. "What's the matter here, eh?"

"We were only asleep, sir," said Nell. "We have been walking all night."

"A pair of queer travellers to be walking all night," observed the man who had first accosted them. "One of you is a trifle too old for that sort of work, and the other a trifle too young. Where are you going?"

Nell faltered, and pointed at hazard towards the West, upon which the man inquired if she meant a certain town which he named. Nell, to avoid further questioning, said "Yes, that was the place."

"Where have you come from?" was the next question; and this being an easier one to answer, Nell mentioned the name of the village in which their friend the schoolmaster dwelt, as being less likely to be known to the men or to provoke further inquiry.

"I thought somebody had been robbing and ill-using you, might be," said the man. "That's all. Good day."

Returning his salute and feeling greatly relieved by his departure, Nell looked after him as he mounted one of the horses, and the boat went on. It had not gone very far, when it stopped again, and she saw the men beckoning to her.

"Did you call to me?" said Nell, running up to them.

"You may go with us if you like," replied one of those in the boat. "We're going to the same place."

The child hesitated for a moment, and thinking, as she had thought with great trepidation more than once before, that the men whom she had seen with her grandfather might perhaps, in their eagerness for the booty, follow them, and, regaining their influence over him, set hers at nought; and that if they went with these men, all traces of them must surely be lost at that spot; determined to accept the offer. The boat came close to the bank again, and before she had had any time for further consideration, she and her grandfather were on board, and gliding smoothly down the canal.

The sun shone pleasantly upon the bright water, which was sometimes shaded by trees, and sometimes open to a wide extent of country, intersected by running streams, and rich with wooded hills, cultivated land,

and sheltered farms. Now and then a village with its modest spire, thatched roofs, and gable-ends, would peep out from among the trees; and more than once a distant town, with great church towers looming through its smoke, and high factories or workshops rising above the mass of houses, would come in view, and, by the length of time it lingered in the distance, show them how slowly they travelled. Their way lay for the most part through the low grounds, and open plains; and except these distant places, and occasionally some men working in the fields, or lounging on the bridges under which they passed, to see them creep along, nothing encroached on their monotonous and secluded track.

Nell was rather disheartened, when they stopped at a kind of wharf late in the afternoon, to learn from one of the men that they would not reach their place of destination until next day, and that if she had no provision with her she had better buy it there. She had but a few pence, having already bargained with them for some bread, but even of these it was necessary to be very careful, as they were on their way to an utterly strange place, with no resource whatever. A small loaf and a morsel of cheese, therefore, were all she could afford, and with these she took her place in the boat again, and, after half an hour's delay during which the men were drinking at the public-house, proceeded on the journey.

They brought some beer and spirits into the boat with them, and what with drinking freely before, and again now, were soon on a fair way of being quarrelsome and intoxicated. Avoiding the small cabin, therefore, which was very dark and filthy, and to which they often invited both her and her grandfather, Nell sat in the open air with the old man by her side; listening to their boisterous hosts with a palpitating heart, and almost wishing herself safe on shore again though she should have to walk all night.

They were in truth very rugged, noisy fellows, and quite brutal among themselves, though civil enough to their two passengers. Thus, when a quarrel arose between the man who was steering and his friend in the cabin, upon the question who had first suggested the propriety of offering Nell some beer, and when the quarrel led to a scuffle in which they beat each other fearfully, to her inexpressible terror, neither visited his displeasure upon her, but each contented himself with venting it on his adversary, on whom, in addition to blows, he bestowed a variety of compliments, which, happily for the child, were conveyed in terms, to her quite unintelligible. The difference was finally adjusted, by the man who had come out of the cabin knocking the other into it head first, and taking the helm into his own hands, without evincing the least discomposure himself, or causing any in his friend, who, being of a tolerably strong constitution and perfectly inured to such trifles, went to sleep as he was, with his heels upwards, and in a couple of minutes or so was snoring comfortably.

By this time it was night again, and though the child felt cold, being but poorly clad, her anxious thoughts were far removed from her own suffering or uneasiness, and busily engaged in endeavouring to devise some scheme for their joint subsistence. The same spirit which had supported her on the previous night, upheld and sustained her now. Her grandfather lay sleeping safely at her side, and the crime to which his madness urged him, was not committed. That was her comfort.

How every circumstance of her short, eventful life, came thronging into her mind as they travelled on! Slight incidents, never thought of or remembered until now; faces seen once and ever since forgotten; words spoken and scarcely heeded at the time; scenes of a year ago and those of yesterday mixing up and linking themselves together; familiar places shaping themselves out in the darkness from things which, when approached, were of all others the most remote and most unlike them; sometimes a strange confusion in her mind relative to the occasion of her being there, and the place to which she was going, and the people she was with; and imagination suggesting remarks and questions which sounded so plainly in her ears, that she would start, and turn, and be almost tempted to reply;-all the fancies and contradictions common in watching and excitement and restless change of place, beset the child.

She happened, while she was thus engaged, to encounter the face of the man on deck, in whom the sentimental stage of drunkenness had now succeeded to the boisterous, and who, taking from his mouth a short pipe, quilted over with string for its longer preservation, requested that she would oblige him with a song.

"You've got a very pretty voice, a very soft eye, and a very strong memory," said this gentleman; "the voice and eye I've got evidence for, and the memory's an opinion of my own. And I'm never wrong. Let me hear a song this minute."

"I don't think I know one, sir," returned Nell.

"You know forty-seven songs," said the man, with a gravity which admitted of no altercation on the subject. "Forty-seven's your number. Let me hear one of 'em- the best. Give me a song this minute."

Not knowing what might be the consequences of irritating her friend, and trembling with the fear of doing so, poor Nell sang him some little ditty which she had learned in happier times, and which was so agreeable to his ear, that on its conclusion he in the same peremptory manner requested to be favoured with another, to which he was so obliging as to roar a chorus to no particular tune, and with no words at all, but which amply made up in its amazing energy for its deficiency in other respects. The noise of this vocal performance awakened the other man, who, staggering upon deck and shaking his late opponent by the hand, swore that singing was his pride and joy and chief delight, and that he desired no better entertainment. With a third call, more imperative than either of the two former, Nell felt obliged to comply, and this time a chorus was maintained not only by the two men together, but also by the third man on horseback, who, being by his position debarred from a nearer participation in the revels of the night, roared when his companions roared, and rent the very air. In this way, with little cessation, and singing the same songs again and again, the tired and exhausted child kept them in good humour all that night; and many a cottager, who was roused from his soundest sleep by the discordant chorus as it floated away upon the wind, hid his head beneath the bed-clothes, and trembled at the sounds.

At length the morning dawned. It was no sooner light than it began to rain heavily. As the child could not endure the intolerable vapours of the cabin, they covered her, in return for her exertions, with some pieces of sail-cloth and ends of tarpaulin, which sufficed to keep her tolerably dry and to shelter her grandfather besides. As the day advanced the rain increased. At noon it poured down more hopelessly and heavily than ever, without the faintest promise of abatement.

They had for some time been gradually approaching the place for which they were bound. The water had become thicker and dirtier; other barges coming from it passed them frequently; the paths of coal-ash and huts of staring brick, marked the vicinity of some great manufacturing town; while scattered streets and houses, and smoke from distant furnaces, indicated that they were already in the outskirts. Now, the clustered roofs, and piles of buildings trembling with the working of engines, and dimly resounding with their shrieks and throbbings; the tall chimneys vomiting forth a black vapour, which hung in a dense ill-favoured cloud above the housetops and filled the air with gloom; the clank of hammers beating upon iron, the roar of busy streets and noisy crowds, gradually augmenting until all the various sounds blended into one and none was distinguishable for itself, announced the termination of their journey.

The boat floated into the wharf to which it belonged. The men were occupied directly. The child and her grandfather, after waiting in vain to thank them, or ask them whither they should go, passed through a dirty lane into a crowded street, and stood amid its din and tumult, and in the pouring rain, as strange, bewildered, and confused, as if they had lived a thousand years before, and were raised from the dead and placed there by a miracle.

CHAPTER XLIV

THE throng of people hurried by, in two opposite streams, with no symptom of cessation or exhaustion; intent upon their own affairs; and undisturbed in their business speculations, by the roar of carts and waggons laden with clashing wares, the slipping of horses' feet upon the wet and greasy pavement, the rattling of the rain on windows and umbrella-tops, the jostling of the more impatient passengers, and all the noise and tumult of a crowded street in the high tide of its occupation; while the two poor strangers, stunned and bewildered by the hurry they beheld but had no part in, looked mournfully on; feeling amidst the crowd a solitude which has no parallel but in the thirst of the shipwrecked mariner, who, tossed to and fro upon the billows of a mighty ocean, his red eyes blinded by looking on the water which hems him in on every side, has not one drop to cool his burning tongue.

They withdrew into a low archway for shelter from the rain, and watched the faces of those who passed, to find in one among them a ray of encouragement or hope. Some frowned, some smiled, some muttered to themselves, some made slight gestures, as if anticipating the conversation in which they would shortly be engaged, some wore the cunning look of bargaining and plotting, some were anxious and eager, some slow and dull; in some countenances were written gain; in others loss. It was like being in the confidence of all these people to stand quietly there, looking into their faces as they flitted past. In busy places, where each man has an object of his own, and feels assured that every other man has his, his character and purpose are written broadly in his face. In the public walks and lounges of a town, people go to see and to be seen, and there the same expression, with little variety, is repeated a hundred times. The working-day faces come nearer to the truth, and let it out more plainly.

Falling into that kind of abstraction which such a solitude awakens, the child continued to gaze upon the passing crowd with a wondering interest, amounting almost to a temporary forgetfulness of her own condition. But cold, wet, hunger, want of rest, and lack of any place in which to lay her aching head, soon brought her thoughts back to the point whence they had strayed. No one passed who seemed to notice them, or to whom she durst appeal. After some time, they left their place of refuge from the weather, and mingled with the concourse.

Evening came on. They were still wandering up and down, with fewer people about them, but with the same sense of solitude in their own breasts, and the same indifference from all around. The lights in the streets and shops made them feel yet more desolate, for with their help, night and darkness seemed to come on faster. Shivering with the cold and damp, ill in body, and sick to death at heart, the child needed her utmost firmness and resolution even to creep along.

Why had they ever come to this noisy town, when there were peaceful country places, in which, at least, they might have hungered and thirsted, with less suffering than in its squalid strife! They were but an atom, here, in a mountain heap of misery, the very sight of which increased their hopelessness and suffering.

The child had not only to endure the accumulated hardships of their destitute condition, but to bear the reproaches of her grandfather, who began to murmur at having been led away from their late abode, and demand that they should return to it. Being now penniless, and no relief or prospect of relief appearing, they retraced their steps through the deserted streets, and went back to the wharf, hoping to find the boat in which they had come, and to be allowed to sleep on board that night. But here again they were disappointed, for the gate was closed, and some fierce dogs, barking at their approach, obliged them to retreat.

"We must sleep in the open air to-night, dear," said the child in a weak voice, as they turned away from this last repulse; "and to-morrow we will beg our way to some quiet part of the country, and try to earn our bread in very humble work."

"Why did you bring me here?" returned the old man fiercely. "I cannot bear these close eternal streets. We came from a quiet part. Why did you force me to leave it?"

"Because I must have that dream I told you of, no more," said the child, with a momentary firmness that lost itself in tears; "and we must live among poor people, or it will come again. Dear grandfather, you are old and weak, I know; but look at me. I never will complain if you will not, but I have some suffering indeed."

"Ah! poor, houseless, wandering, motherless child!" cried the old man, clasping his hands and gazing as if for the first time upon her anxious face, her travel-stained dress, and bruised and swollen feet; "has all my agony of care brought her to this at last! Was I a happy man once, and have I lost happiness and all I had, for this!"

"If we were in the country now," said the child, with assumed cheerfulness, as they walked on looking about them for a shelter, "we should find some good old tree, stretching out his green arms as if he loved us, and nodding and rustling as if he would have us fall asleep, thinking of him while he watched. Please God, we shall be there soon-to-morrow or next day at the farthest-and in the meantime let us think, dear, that it was a good thing we came here; for we are lost in the crowd and hurry of this place, and if any cruel people should pursue us, they could surely never trace us further. There's comfort in that. And here's a deep old doorway-very dark, but quite dry, and warm too, for the wind don't blow in here- What's that!"

Uttering a half shriek, she recoiled from a black figure which came suddenly out of the dark recess in which they were about to take refuge, and stood still looking at them.

"Speak again," it said; "do I know the voice?"

"No," replied the child timidly; "we are strangers, and having no money for a night's lodging, were going to rest here."

There was a feeble lamp at no great distance; the only one in the place, which was a kind of square yard, but sufficient to show how poor and mean it was. To this, the figure beckoned them; at the same time drawing within its rays, as if to show that it had no desire to conceal itself or take them at an advantage.

The form was that of a man, miserably clad and begrimed with smoke, which, perhaps by its contrast with the natural colour of his skin, made him look paler than he really was. That he was naturally of a very wan and pallid aspect, however, his hollow cheeks, sharp features, and sunken eyes, no less than a certain look of patient endurance, sufficiently testified. His voice was harsh by nature, but not brutal; and though his face, besides possessing the characteristics already mentioned, was overshadowed by a quantity of long dark hair, its expression was neither ferocious nor cruel.

"How came you to think of resting there?" he said. "Or how," he added, looking more attentively at the child, "do you come to want a place of rest at this time of night?"

"Our misfortunes," the grandfather answered, "are the cause."

"Do you know," said the man, looking still more earnestly at Nell, "how wet she is, and that the damp streets are not a place for her?"

"I know it well, God help me," he replied. "What can I do!"

The man looked at Nell again, and gently touched her garments, from which the rain was running off in little streams. "I can give you warmth," he said, after a pause; "nothing else. Such lodging as I have is in that house," pointing to the doorway from which he had emerged, "but she is safer and better there than here. The fire is in a rough place, but you can pass the night beside it safely, if you'll trust yourselves to me. You see that red light yonder?"

They raised their eyes, and saw a lurid glare hanging in the dark sky; the dull reflection of some distant fire.

"It's not far," said the man. "Shall I take you there? You were going to sleep upon cold bricks; I can give you a bed of warm ashes-nothing better."

Without waiting for any further reply than he saw in their looks, he took Nell in his arms, and bade the old man follow.

Carrying her as tenderly, and as easily too, as if she had been an infant, and showing himself both swift and sure of foot, he led the way through what appeared to be the poorest and most wretched quarter of the town; not turning aside to avoid the overflowing kennels or running waterspouts, but holding his course, regardless of such obstructions, and making his way straight through them. They had proceeded thus in silence for some quarter of an hour, and had lost sight of the glare to which he had pointed, in the dark and narrow ways by which they had come, when it suddenly burst upon them again, streaming up from the high chimney of a building close before them.

"This is the place," he said, pausing at a door to put Nell down and take her hand. "Don't be afraid. There's nobody here will harm you."

It needed a strong confidence in this assurance to induce them to enter, and what they saw inside did not diminish their apprehension and alarm. In a large and lofty building, supported by pillars of iron, with great black apertures in the upper walls, open to the external air; echoing to the roof with the beating of hammers and roar of furnaces, mingled with the hissing of red-hot metal plunged in water, and a hundred strange unearthly noises never heard else-where; in this gloomy place, moving like demons among the flame and smoke, dimly and fitfully seen, flushed and tormented by the burning fires, and wielding great weapons, a faulty blow from any one of which must have crushed some workman's skull, a number of men laboured like giants. Others, reposing upon heaps of coals or ashes with their faces turned to the black vault above, slept or rested from their toil. Others again, opening the white-hot furnace-doors, cast fuel on the flames, which came rushing and roaring forth to meet it, and licked it up like oil. Others drew forth, with clashing noise upon the ground, great sheets of glowing steel, emitting an insupportable heat, and a dull deep light like that which reddens in the eyes of savage beasts.

Through these bewildering sights and deafening sounds, their conductor led them to where, in a dark portion of the building, one furnace burnt by night and day-so at least they gathered from the motion of his lips, for as yet they could only see him speak: not hear him. The man who had been watching this fire, and whose task was ended for the present, gladly withdrew, and left them with their friend, who, spreading Nell's little cloak upon a heap of ashes, and showing her where she could hang her outer clothes to dry, signed to her and the old man to lie down and sleep. For himself, he took his station on a rugged mat before the furnace-door, and resting his chin upon his hands, watched the flame as it shone through the iron chinks, and the white ashes as they fell into their bright hot grave below.

The warmth of her bed, hard and humble as it was, combined with the great fatigue she had undergone, soon caused the tumult of the place to fall with a gentler sound upon the child's tired ears, and was not long in lulling her to sleep. The old man was stretched beside her, and with her hand upon his neck she lay and dreamed.

It was yet night when she awoke, nor did she know how long, or for how short a time, she had slept. But she found herself protected, both from any cold air that might find its way into the building, and from the scorching heat, by some of the workmen's clothes; and glancing at their friend saw that he sat in exactly the same attitude, looking with a fixed earnestness of attention towards the fire, and keeping so very still that he did not even seem to breathe. She lay in the state between sleeping and waking, looking so long at his motionless figure that at length she almost feared he had died as he sat there; and, softly rising and drawing close to him, ventured to whisper in his ear.

He moved, and glancing from her to the place she had lately occupied, as if to assure himself that it was really the child so near him, looked inquiringly into her face.

"I feared you were ill," she said. "The other men are all in motion, and you are so very quiet."

"They leave me to myself," he replied. "They know my humour. They laugh at me, but don't harm me in it. See yonder there-that's my friend."

"The fire?" said the child.

"It has been alive as long as I have," the man made answer. "We talk and think together all night long."

The child glanced quickly at him in her surprise, but he had turned his eyes in their former direction, and was musing as before.

"It's like a book to me," he said- "the only book I ever learned to read; and many an old story it tells me. It's music, for I should know its voice among a thousand, and there are other voices in its roar. It has its pictures too. You don't know how many strange faces and different scenes I trace in the red-hot coals. It's my memory, that fire, and shows me all my life."

The child, bending down to listen to his words, could not help remarking with what brightened eyes he continued to speak and muse.

"Yes," he said, with a faint smile, "it was the same when I was quite a baby, and crawled about it, till I fell asleep. My father watched it then."

"Had you no mother?" asked the child.

"No, she was dead. Women work hard in these parts. She worked herself to death they told me, and, as they said so then, the fire has gone on saying the same thing ever since. I suppose it was true. I have always believed it."

"Were you brought up here, then?" said the child.

"Summer and winter," he replied. "Secretly at first, but when they found it out, they let him keep me here. So the fire nursed me-the same fire. It has never gone out."

"You are fond of it?" said the child.

"Of course I am. He died before it. I saw him fall down-just there, where those ashes are burning now-and wondered, I remember, why it didn't help him."

"Have you be en here ever since?" asked the child.

"Ever since I came to watch it; but there was a while between, and a very cold dreary while it was. It burned all the time though, and roared and leaped when I came back, as it used to do in our play days. You may guess from looking at me what kind of child I was, but for all the difference between us I was a child, and when I saw you in the street to-night, you put me in mind of myself as I was after he died, and made me wish to bring you to the old fire. I thought of those old times again when I saw you sleeping by it. You should be sleeping now. Lie down again, poor child, lie down again."

With that he led her to her rude couch, and covering her with the clothes with which she had found herself enveloped when she woke, returned to his seat, whence he moved no more unless to feed the furnace, but remained motionless as a statue. The child continued to watch him for a little time, but soon yielded to the drowsiness that came upon her, and, in the dark strange place and on the heap of ashes, slept as peacefully as if the room had been a palace chamber, and the bed a bed of down.

When she awoke again, broad day was shining through the lofty openings in the walls, and, stealing in slanting rays but midway down, seemed to make the building darker than it had been at night. The clang and tumult were still going on, and the remorseless fires were burning fiercely as before; for few changes of night and day brought rest or quiet there.

Her friend parted his breakfast-a scanty mess of coffee and some coarse bread-with the child and her grandfather, and inquired whither they were going. She told him that they sought some distant country place remote from towns or even other villages, and with a faltering tongue inquired what road they would do best to take.

"I know little of the country," he said, shaking his head, "for such as I, pass all our lives before our furnace doors, and seldom go forth to breathe. But there are such places yonder."

"And far from here?" said Nell.

"Ay surely. How could they be near us, and be green and fresh? The road lies too, through miles and miles, all lighted up by fires like ours-a strange black road, and one that would frighten you by night."

"We are here and must go on," said the child boldly; for she saw that the old man listened with anxious ears to this account.

"Rough people-paths never made for little feet like yours-a dismal, blighted way-is there no turning back, my child?"

"There is none," cried Nell, pressing forward. "If you can direct us, do. If not, pray do not seek to turn us from our purpose. Indeed you do not know the danger that we shun, and how right and true we are in flying from it, or you would not try to stop us, I am sure you would not."

"God forbid, if it is so!" said their uncouth protector, glancing from the eager child to her grandfather, who hung his head and bent his eyes upon the ground. "I'll direct you from the door, the best I can. I wish I could do more."

He showed them, then, by which road they must leave the town, and what course they should hold when they had gained it. He lingered so long on these instructions, that the child, with a fervent blessing, tore herself away, and stayed to hear no more.

But before they had reached the corner of the lane, the man came running after them, and, pressing her hand, left something in it-two old, battered, smoke-encrusted penny pieces. Who knows but they shone as brightly in the eyes of angels as golden gifts that have been chronicled on tombs?

And thus they separated; the child to lead her sacred charge farther from guilt and shame; and the labourer to attach a fresh interest to the spot where his guests had slept, and read new histories in his furnace fire.

CHAPTER XLV

IN all their journeying, they had never longed so ardently, they had never so pined and wearied, for the freedom of pure air and open country, as now. No, not even on that memorable morning, when, deserting their old home, they abandoned themselves to the mercies of a strange world, and left all the dumb and senseless things they had known and loved, behind-not even then, had they so yearned for the fresh solitudes of wood, hillside, and field, as now; when the noise and dirt and vapour of the great manufacturing town, reeking with lean misery and hungry wretchedness, hemmed them in on every side, and seemed to shut out hope, and render escape impossible.

"Two days and nights!" thought the child. "He said two days and nights we should have to spend among such scenes as these. Oh! if we live to reach the country once again, if we get clear of these dreadful places, though it is only to lie down and die, with what a grateful heart I shall thank God for so much mercy!"

With thoughts like this, and with some vague design of travelling to a great distance among streams and mountains, where only very poor and simple people lived, and where they might maintain themselves by very humble helping work in farms, free from such terrors as that from which they fled-the child, with no resource but the poor man's gift, and no encouragement but that which flowed from her own heart, and its sense of the truth and right of what she did, nerved herself to this last journey and boldly pursued her task.

"We shall be very slow to-day, dear," she said, as they toiled painfully through the streets; "my feet are sore, and I have pains in all my limbs from the wet of yesterday. I saw that he looked at us and thought of that, when he said how long we should be upon the road."

"It was a dreary way he told us of," returned her grandfather, piteously. "Is there no other road? Will you not let me go some other way than this?"

"Places lie beyond these," said the child, firmly, "where we may live in peace, and be tempted to do no harm. We will take the road that promises to have that end, and we would not turn out of it, if it were a hundred times worse than our fears lead us to expect. We would not, dear, would we?"

"No," replied the old man, wavering in his voice, no less than in his manner. "No. Let us go on. I am ready. I am quite ready, Nell."

The child walked with more difficulty than she had led her companion to expect, for the pains that racked her joints were of no common severity, and every exertion increased them. But they wrung from her no complaint, or look of suffering; and, though the two travellers proceeded very slowly, they did proceed; and clearing the town in course of time, began to feel that they were fairly on their way.

A long suburb of red brick houses,-some with patches of garden ground, where coal-dust and factory smoke darkened the shrinking leaves, and coarse rank flowers; and where the struggling vegetation sickened and sank under the hot breath of kiln and furnace, making them by its presence seem yet more blighting and unwholesome than in the town itself,-a long, flat, straggling suburb passed, they came by slow degrees upon a cheerless region, where not a blade of grass was seen to grow; where not a bud put forth its promise in the spring; where nothing green could live but on the surface of the stagnant pools, which here and there lay idly sweltering by the black roadside.

Advancing more and more into the shadow of this mournful place, its dark depressing influence stole upon their spirits, and filled them with a dismal gloom. On every side, and as far as the eye could see into the heavy distance, tall chimneys, crowding on each other, and presenting that endless repetition of the same dull, ugly form, which is the horror of oppressive dreams, poured out their plague of smoke, obscured the light, and made foul the melancholy air. On mounds of ashes by the wayside, sheltered only by a few rough boards, or rotten pent-house roofs, strange engines spun and writhed like tortured creatures; clanking their iron chains, shrieking in their rapid whirl from time to time as though in torment unendurable, and making the ground tremble with their agonies. Dismantled houses here and there appeared, tottering to the earth, propped up by fragments of others that had fallen down, unroofed, windowless, blackened, desolate, but yet inhabited. Men, women, children, wan in their looks and ragged in attire, tended the engines, fed their tributary fires, begged upon the road, or scowled half-naked from the doorless houses. Then came more of the wrathful monsters, whose like they almost seemed to be in their wildness and their untamed air, screeching and turning round and round again; and still, before, behind, and to the right and left, was the same interminable perspective of brick towers, never ceasing in their black vomit, blasting all things living or inanimate, shutting out the face of day, and closing in on all these horrors with a dense dark cloud.

But night-time in this dreadful spot!-night, when the smoke was changed to fire; when every chimney spirted up its flame; and places, that had been dark vaults all day, now shone red-hot, with figures moving to and fro within their blazing jaws, and calling to one another with hoarse cries-night, when the noise of every strange machine was aggravated by the darkness; when the people near them looked wilder and more savage; when hands of unemployed labourers paraded in the roads, or clustered by torch-light round their leaders, who told them in stern language of their wrongs, and urged them on to frightful cries and threats; when maddened men, armed with sword and fire- brand, spurning the tears and prayers of women who would restrain them, rushed forth on errands of terror and destruction, to work no ruin half so surely as their own-night, when carts came rumbling by, filled with rude coffins (for contagious disease and death had been busy with the living crops); when orphans cried, and distracted women shrieked and followed in their wake-night, when some called for bread, and some for drink to drown their cares; and some with tears, and some with staggering feet, and some with bloodshot eyes, went brooding home-night, which, un-like the night that Heaven sends on earth, brought with it no peace, nor quiet, nor signs of blessed sleep-who shall tell the terrors of the night to that young wandering child!

And yet she lay down, with nothing between her and the sky; and, with no fear for herself, for she was past it now, put up a prayer for the poor old man. So very weak and spent she felt, so very calm and unresisting, that she had no thought of any wants of her own, but prayed that God would raise up some friend for him. She tried to recall the way they had come, and to look in the direction where the fire by which they had slept last night was burning. She had forgotten to ask the name of the poor man, their friend, and when she had remembered him in her prayers, it seemed ungrate-ful not to turn one look towards the spot where he was watching.

A penny loaf was all they had had that day. It was very little, but even hunger was forgotten in the strange tranquillity that crept over her senses. She lay down very gently, and, with a quiet smile upon her face, fell into a slumber. It was not like sleep-and yet it must have been, or why those pleas-ant dreams of the little scholar all night I long!

Morning came. Much weaker, diminished powers even of sight and hearing, and yet the child made no complaint- perhaps would have made none, even if she had not that, inducement to be silent, travelling by her side. She felt a hopelessness of their ever being extricated together from that for-lorn place, a dull conviction that she was very ill, perhaps dying; but no fear or anxiety.

A loathing of food, that she was not conscious of until they expended their last penny in the purchase of another loaf, prevented her partaking even of this poor repast. Her grandfather ate greedily, which she was glad to see.

Their way lay through the same scenes as yesterday, with no variety or improvement. There was the same thick air, difficult to breathe; the same blighted ground, the same hopeless prospect, the same misery and distress. Objects appeared more dim, the noise less, the path more rugged and uneven, for sometimes she stumbled, and became roused, as it were, in the effort to prevent herself from falling. Poor child! the cause was in her tottering feet.

Towards the afternoon, her grandfather complained bitterly of hunger. She approached one of the wretched hovels by the wayside, and knocked with her hand upon the door.

"What would you have here?" said a gaunt miserable man, opening it.

"Charity. A morsel of bread."

"Do you see that?" returned the man hoarsely, pointing to a kind of bundle on the ground. "That's a dead child. I and five hundred other men were thrown out of work three months ago. That is my third dead child, and last. Do you think I have charity to bestow, or a morsel of bread to spare?"

The child recoiled from the door, and it closed upon her. Impelled by strong necessity, she knocked at another: a neighbouring one, which, yielding to the slight pressure of her hand, flew open.

It seemed that a couple of poor families lived in this hovel, for two women, each among children of her own, occupied different portions of the room. In the centre stood a grave gentleman in black who appeared to have just entered, and who held by the arm a boy.

"Here, woman," he said, "here's your deaf and dumb son. You may thank me for restoring him to you. He was brought before me this morning, charged with theft; and with any other boy it would have gone hard, I assure you. But as I had compassion on his infirmities, and thought he might have learnt no better, I have managed to bring him back to you. Take more care of him for the future."

"And won't you give me back my son!" said the other woman, hastily rising and confronting him. "Won't you give me back my son, sir, who was transported for the same offence!"

"Was he deaf and dumb, woman?" asked the gentleman sternly.

"Was he not, sir?"

"You know he was not."

"He was," cried the woman. "He was deaf, dumb, and blind, to all that was good and right, from his cradle. Her boy may have learnt no better! where did mine learn better? where could he? who was there to teach him better, or where was it to be learnt?"

"Peace, woman," said gentleman, "your boy was in possession of all his senses."

"He was," cried the mother; "and he was the more easy to be led astray because he had them. If you save this boy because he may not know right from wrong, why did you not save mine who was never taught the difference? You gentlemen have as good a right to punish her boy, that God has kept in ignorance of sound and speech, as you have to punish mine, that you kept in ignorance yourselves. How many of the girls and boys-ah, men and women too-that are brought before you and you don't pity, are deaf and dumb in their minds, and go wrong in that state, and are punished in that state, body and soul, while you gentlemen are quarrelling among your-selves whether they ought to learn this or that?-Be a just man, sir, and give me back my son."

"You are desperate," said the gentleman, taking out his snuff-box, "and I am sorry for you."

"I am desperate," returned the woman, "and you have made me *so*. Give me back my son, to work for these helpless children. Be a just man, sir, and for God's sake, as you have had mercy upon this boy, give me back my son!"

The child had seen and heard enough to know that this was not a place at which to ask for alms. She led the old man softly from the door, and they pursued their journey.

With less and less of hope or strength, as they went on, but with an undiminished resolution not to betray by any word or sign her sinking state, *so* long as she had energy to move, the child throughout the remainder of that hard day compelled herself to proceed: not even stopping to rest as frequent-ly as usual, to compensate in some measure for the tardy pace at which she was obliged to walk. Evening was drawing on, but had not closed in, when-still travelling among the same dismal objects-they came to a busy town.

Faint and spiritless as they were, its streets were insupportable. After humbly asking for relief at some few doors and being repulsed, they agreed to make their way out of it as speedily as they could, and try if the inmates of any lone house beyond, would have more pity on their exhausted state.

They were dragging themselves along through the last street, and the child felt that the time was close at hand when her enfeebled powers would bear no more. There appeared before them, at this juncture, going in the same direction as themselves, a traveller on foot, who, with a portmanteau strapped to his back, leant upon a stout stick as he walked, and read from a book which he held in his other hand.

It was not an easy matter to come up with him, and beseech his aid, for he walked fast, and was a little distance in advance. At length he stopped to look more attentively at some passage in his book. Animated with a ray of hope, the child shot on before her grandfather, and, going close to the stranger without rousing him by the sound of her footsteps, began in a few faint words to implore his help.

He turned his head, the child clapped her hands together, uttered a wild shriek, and fell senseless at his feet.

CHAPTER XLVI

IT was the poor schoolmaster. No other than the poor schoolmaster. Scarcely less moved and surprised by the sight of the child than she had been on recognising him, he stood for a moment silent and confounded by this unexpected apparition, without even the presence of mind to raise her from the ground.

But quickly recovering his self-possession he threw down his stick and book, and dropping on one knee beside her, endeavoured by such simple means as occurred to him, to restore her to herself; while her grandfather, standing idly by, wrung his hands, and implored her with many endearing expressions to speak to him, were it only a word.

"She is quite exhausted," said the schoolmaster, glancing upward into his face. "You have taxed her powers too far, friend."

"She is perishing of want," rejoined the old man. "I never thought how weak and ill she was, till now."

Casting a look upon him, half-reproachful and half-compassionate, the schoolmaster took the child in his arms, and, bidding the old man gather up her little basket and follow him directly, bore her away at his utmost speed.

There was a small inn within sight, to which it would seem he had been directing his steps when so unexpectedly overtaken. Towards this place he hurried with his unconscious burden, and rushing into the kitchen, and calling upon the company there assembled to make way for God's sake, deposited it on a chair before the fire.

The company, who rose in confusion upon the schoolmaster's entrance, did as people usually do under such circumstances. Everybody called for his or her favourite remedy, which nobody brought; each cried for more air, at the same time carefully excluding what air there was, by closing round the object of sympathy; and all wondered why somebody else didn't do what it never appeared to occur to them might be done by themselves.

The landlady, however, who possessed more readiness and activity than any of them, and who had withal a quicker perception of the merits of the case, soon came running in, with a little hot brandy and water, followed by her servant-girl, carrying vinegar, hartshorn, smelling-salts, and such other restoratives; which, being duly administered, recovered the child so far as to enable her to thank them in a faint voice, and to extend her hand to the poor schoolmaster, who stood with an anxious face, hard by. Without suffering her to speak another word, or so much as to stir a finger any more, the women straightway carried her off to bed; and having covered her up warm, bathed her cold feet, and wrapped them in flannel, they despatched a messenger for the doctor.

The doctor, who was a red-nosed gentleman with a great bunch of seals dangling below a waistcoat of ribbed black satin, arrived with all speed, and taking his seat by the bedside of poor Nell, drew out his watch, and felt her pulse. Then he looked at her tongue, then he felt her pulse again, and while he did so, he eyed the half-emptied wine-glass as if in profound abstraction.

"I should give her-" said the doctor at length, "a tea- spoonful, every now and then, of hot brandy and water."

"Why, that's exactly what we've done, sir!" said the delighted landlady.

"I should also," observed the doctor, who had passed the foot-bath on the stairs, "I should also," said the doctor, in the voice of an oracle, "put her feet in hot water, and wrap them up in flannel. I should likewise," said the doctor with increased solemnity, "give her something light for supper-the wing of a roasted fowl now-"

"Why, goodness gracious me, sir, it's cooking at the kitchen tire this instant!" cried the landlady. And so indeed it was, for the schoolmaster had ordered it to be put down, and it was getting on so well that the doctor might have smelt it if he had tried-perhaps he did.

"You may then," said the doctor, rising gravely, "give her a glass of hot mulled port wine, if she likes wine-"

"And a toast, sir?" suggested the landlady.

"Ay," said the doctor, in the tone of a man who makes a dignified concession. "And a toast-of bread. But be very particular to make it of bread, if you please, ma'am."

With which parting injunction, slowly and portentously delivered, the doctor departed, leaving the whole house in admiration of that wisdom which tallied so closely with their own. Everybody said he was a very shrewd doctor indeed, and knew perfectly what people's constitutions were; which there appears some reason to suppose he did.

While her supper was preparing, the child fell into a refreshing sleep, from which they were obliged to rouse her when it was ready. As she evinced extraordinary uneasiness on learning that her grandfather was below stairs, and as she was greatly troubled at the thought of their being apart, he took his supper with her. Finding her still very restless on this head, they made him up a bed in an inner room, to which he presently retired. The key of this chamber happened by good fortune to be on that side of the door which was in Nell's room; she turned it on him when the landlady had withdrawn, and crept to bed again with a thankful heart.

The schoolmaster sat for a long time smoking his pipe by the kitchen fire, which was now deserted, thinking, with a very happy face, on the fortunate chance which had brought him so opportunely to the child's assistance, and parrying, as well as in his simple way he could, the inquisitive cross-examination of the landlady, who had a great curiosity to be made acquainted with every particular of Nell's life and history. The poor schoolmaster was so openhearted, and so little versed in the most ordinary cunning or deceit, that she could not have failed to succeed in the first five minutes, but that he happened to be unacquainted with what she wished to know; and so he told her. The landlady, by no means satisfied with this assurance, which she considered an ingenious evasion of the question, rejoined that he had his reasons of course. Heaven forbid that she should wish to pry into the affairs of her customers, which indeed were no business of hers, who had so many of her own. She had merely asked a civil question, and to be sure she knew it would meet with a civil answer. She was quite satisfied-quite. She had rather perhaps that he would have said at once that he didn't choose to be communicative, because that would have been plain and intelligible. However, she had no right to be offended of course. He was the best judge, and had a perfect right to say what he pleased; nobody could dispute that, for a moment. Oh dear, no!

"I assure you, my good lady," said the mild schoolmaster, "that I have told you the plain truth-as I hope to be saved, I have told you the truth."

"Why then, I do believe you are in earnest," rejoined the landlady, with ready good-humour, "and I'm very sorry I have teased you. But curiosity you know is the curse of our sex, and that's the fact."

The landlord scratched his head, as if he thought the curse sometimes involved the other sex likewise; but he was prevented from making any remark to that effect, if he had it in contemplation to do so, by the schoolmaster's rejoinder.

"You should question me for half a dozen hours at a sitting, and welcome, and I would answer you patiently for the kindness of heart you have shown to-night, if I could," he said. "As it is, please to take care of her in the morning, and let me know early how she is; and to understand that I am paymaster for the three."

So, parting with them on most friendly terms, not the less cordial perhaps for this last direction, the schoolmaster went to his bed, and the host and hostess to theirs.

The report in the morning was, that the child was better, but was extremely weak, and would at least require a day's rest, and careful nursing, before she could proceed upon her journey. The schoolmaster received this communication with perfect cheerfulness, observing that he had a day to spare-two days for that matter-and could very well afford to wait. As the patient was to sit up in the evening, he appointed to visit her in her room at a certain hour, and rambling out with his book, did not return until the hour arrived.

Nell could not help weeping when they were left alone; whereat, and at sight of her pale face and wasted figure, the simple schoolmaster shed a few tears himself, at the same time showing in very energetic language how foolish it was to do so, and how very easily it could be avoided, if one tried.

"It makes me unhappy even in the midst of all this kindness," said the child, "to think that we should be a burden upon you. How can I ever thank you? If I had not met you so far from home, I must have died, and he would have been left alone."

"We'll not talk about dying," said the schoolmaster; "and as to burdens, I have made my fortune since you slept at my cottage."

"Indeed!" cried the child joyfully.

"Oh yes," returned her friend. "I have been appointed clerk and schoolmaster to a village a long way from here- and a long way from the old one as you may suppose-at five-and-thirty pounds a year. Five-and-thirty pounds!"

"I am very glad," said the child- "so very, very glad."

"I am on my way there now," resumed the schoolmaster. "They allowed me the stage-coach hire-outside stage-coach hire all the way. Bless you, they grudge me nothing. But as the time at which I am expected there, left me ample leisure, I determined to walk instead. How glad I am, to think I did so!"

"How glad should we be!"

"Yes, yes," said the schoolmaster, moving restlessly in his chair, "certainly, that's very true. But you-where are you going, where are you coming from, what have you been doing since you left me, what had you been doing before? Now, tell me-do tell me. I know very little of the world, and perhaps you are better fitted to advise me in its affairs than I am qualified to give advice to you; but I am very sincere, and I have a reason (you have not forgotten it) for loving you. I have felt since that time as if my love for him who died, had been transferred to you who stood beside his bed. If this," he added, looking upwards, "is the beautiful creation that springs from ashes, let its peace prosper with me, as I deal tenderly and compassionately by this young child!"

The plain, frank kindness of the honest schoolmaster, the affectionate earnestness of his speech and manner, the truth which was stamped upon his every word and look, gave the child a confidence in him, which the utmost arts of treachery and dissimulation could never have awakened in her breast. She told him all-that they had no friend or relative-that she had fled with the old man, to save him from a madhouse and all the mi series he dreaded- that she was flying now, to save him from himself-and that she sought an asylum in some remote and primitive place, where the temptation before which he fell would never enter, and her late sorrows and distresses could have no place.

The schoolmaster heard her with astonishment. "This child!"-he thought- "Has this child heroically persevered under all doubts and dangers, struggled with poverty and suffering, upheld and sustained by strong affection and the consciousness of rectitude alone! And yet the world is full of such heroism. Have I yet to learn that the hardest and best-borne trials are those which are never chronicled in any earthly record, and are suffered every day! And should I be surprised to hear the story of this child!"

What more he thought or said, matters not. It was concluded that Nell and her grandfather should accompany him to the village whither he was bound, and that he should endeavour to find them some humble occupation by which they could subsist. "We shall be sure to succeed," said the schoolmaster, heartily. "The cause is too good a one to fail."

They arranged to proceed upon their journey next evening, as a stage-waggon, which travelled for some distance on the same road as they must take, would stop at the inn to change horses, and the driver for a small gratuity would give Nell a place inside. A bargain was soon struck when the waggon came; and in due time it rolled away; with the child comfortably bestowed among the softer packages, her grandfather and the schoolmaster walking on beside the driver, and the landlady and all the good folks of the inn screaming out their good wishes and farewells.

What a soothing, luxurious, drowsy way of travelling, to lie inside that slowly-moving mountain, listening to the tinkling of the horses' bells, the occasional smacking of the carter's whip, the smooth rolling of the great broad wheels, the rattle of the harness, the cheery good nights of passing travellers jogging past on little short-stepped horses-all made pleasantly indistinct by the thick awning, which seemed made for lazy listening under, till one fell asleep! The very going to sleep, still with an indistinct idea, as the head jogged to and fro upon the pillow, of moving onward with no trouble or fatigue, and hearing all these sounds like dreamy music, lulling to the senses-and the slow waking up, and finding one's self staring out through the breezy curtain half-opened in the front, far up into the cold bright sky with its countless stars, and downward at the driver's lantern dancing on like its namesake Jack of the swamps and marshes, and sideways at the dark grim trees, and forward at the long bare road rising up, up, up, until it stopped abruptly at a sharp high ridge as if there were no more road, and all beyond was sky-and the stopping at the inn to bait, and being helped out, and going into a room with fire and candles, and winking very much, and being agreeably reminded that the night was cold, and anxious for very comfort's sake to think it colder than it was!-What a delicious journey was that journey in the waggon!

Then the going on again-so fresh at first, and shortly afterwards so sleepy. The waking from a sound nap as the mail came dashing past like a highway comet, with gleaming lamps and rattling hoofs, and visions of a guard behind, standing up to keep his feet warm, and of a gentleman in a fur cap opening his eyes and looking wild and stupefied-the stopping at the turnpike where the man was gone to bed, and knocking at the door until he answered with a smothered shout from under the bedclothes in the little room above, where the faint light was burning, and presently came down, night-capped and shivering, to throw the gate wide open, and wish all waggons off the road except by day. The cold sharp interval between night and morning-the distant streak of light widening and spreading, and turning from grey to white, and from white to yellow, and from yellow to burning red-the presence of day, with all its cheerfulness and life-men and horses at the plough-birds in the trees and hedges, and boys in solitary fields, frightening them away with rattles. The coming to a town-people busy in the markets; light carts and chaises round the tavern yard; tradesmen standing at their doors; men running horses up and down the street for sale; pigs plunging and grunting in the dirty distance, getting off with long strings at their legs, running into clean chemists' shops and being dislodged with brooms prentices; the night coach changing horses-the passengers cheerless, cold, ugly, and discontented, with three months' growth of hair in one night-the coachman fresh as from a bandbox, and exquisitely beautiful by contrast:- so much bustle, so many things in motion, such a variety of incidents-when was there a Journey with so many delights as that journey in the waggon!

Sometimes walking for a mile or two while her grandfather rode inside, and sometimes even prevailing upon the schoolmaster to take her place and lie down to rest, Nell travelled on very happily until they came to a large town, where the waggon stopped, and where they spent a night. They passed a large church; and in the streets were a number of old houses, built of a kind of earth or plaster, crossed and re-crossed in a great many directions with black beams, which gave them a remarkable and very ancient look. The doors, too, were arched and low, some with oaken portals and quaint benches, where the former inhabitants had sat on summer evenings. The windows were latticed in little diamond panes, that seemed to wink and blink upon the passengers as if they were dim of sight. They had long since got clear of the smoke and furnaces, except in one or two solitary instances, where a factory planted among fields withered the space about it, like a burning mountain. When they had passed through this town, they entered again upon the country, and began to draw near their place of destination.

It was not so near, however, but that they spent another night upon the road; not that their doing so was quite an act of necessity, but that the schoolmaster, when they approached within a few miles of his village, had a fidgety sense of his dignity as the new clerk, and was unwilling to make his entry in dusty shoes, and travel-disordered dress. It was a fine, clear, autumn morning, when they came upon the scene of his promotion, and stopped to contemplate its beauties.

"See-here's the church!" cried the delighted schoolmaster, in a low voice; "and that old building close beside it, is the school-house, I'll be sworn. Five-and-thirty pounds a year in this beautiful place!"

They admired everything-the old grey porch, the mullioned windows, the venerable gravestones dotting the green churchyard, the ancient tower, the very weathercock; the brown thatched roofs of cottage, barn, and home-stead, peeping from among the trees; the stream that rippled by the distant watermill; the blue Welsh mountains far away. It was for such a spot the child had wearied in the dense, dark, miserable haunts of labour. Upon her bed of ashes, and amidst the squalid horrors through which they had forced their way, visions of such scenes-beautiful indeed, but not more beautiful than this sweet reality-had been always present to her mind. They had seemed to melt into a dim and airy distance, as the prospect of ever behold-ing them again grew fainter; but, as they receded, she had loved and panted for them more.

"I must leave you somewhere for a few minutes," said the schoolmas-ter, at length breaking the silence into which they had fallen in their gladness. "I have a letter to present, and inquiries to make, you know. Where shall I take you? To the little inn yonder?"

"Let us wait here," rejoined Nell. "The gate is open. We will sit in the church porch till you come back."

"A good place too," said the schoolmaster, leading the way towards it, disencumbering himself of his portmanteau, and placing it on the stone seat. "Be sure that I come back with good news, and am not long gone."

So, the happy schoolmaster put on a bran-new pair of gloves which he had carried in a little parcel in his pocket all the way, and hurried off, full of ardour and excitement.

The child watched him from the porch until the intervening foliage bid him from her view, and then stepped softly out into the old churchyard-so solemn and quiet, that every rustle of her dress upon the fallen leaves, which strewed the path and made her footsteps noiseless, seemed an invasion of its silence. It was a very aged, ghostly place; the church had been built many hundreds of years ago, and had once had a convent or monastery attached; for arches in ruins, remains of oriel windows, and fragments of blackened walls, were yet standing; while other portions of the old building, which had crumbled away and fallen down, were mingled with the churchyard earth and overgrown with grass, as if they too claimed a burying- place and sought to mix their ashes with the dust of men. Hard by these gravestones of dead years, and forming a part of the ruin which some pains had been taken to render habitable in modern times, were two small dwellings with sunken windows and oaken doors, fast hastening to decay, empty and desolate.

Upon these tenements, the attention of the child became exclusively riveted. She knew not why. The church, the ruin, the antiquated graves, had equal claims at least upon a stranger's thoughts, but from the moment when her eyes first rested on these two dwellings, she could turn to nothing else. Even when she had made the circuit of the inclosure, and, returning to the porch, sat pensively waiting for their friend, she took her station where she could still look upon them, and felt as if fascinated towards that spot.

CHAPTER XLVII

KIT'S mother and the single gentleman-upon whose track it is expedient to follow with hurried steps, lest this history should be chargeable with inconstancy, and the offence of leaving its characters in situations of uncertainty and doubt-Kit's mother and the single gentleman, speeding onward in the post-chaise-and-four whose departure from the Notary's door we have already witnessed, soon left the town behind them, and struck fire from the flints of the broad highway.

The good woman, being not a little embarrassed by the novelty of her situation, and certain maternal apprehensions that perhaps by this time little Jacob, or the baby, or both, had fallen into the fire, or tumbled down stairs, or had been squeezed behind doors, or had scalded their windpipes in endeavouring to allay their thirst at the spouts of teakettles, preserved an uneasy silence; and meeting from the window the eyes of turnpike-men, omnibus-drivers, and others, felt in the new dignity of her position like a mourner at a funeral, who, not being greatly afflicted by the loss of the departed, recognises his every-day acquaintance from the window of the mourning-coach, but is constrained to preserve a decent solemnity, and the appearance of being indifferent to all external objects.

To have been indifferent to the companionship of the single gentleman would have been tantamount to being gifted with nerves of steel. Never did chaise inclose, or horses draw, such a restless gentleman as he. He never sat in the same position for two minutes together, but was perpetually tossing his arms and legs about, pulling up the sashes and letting them violently down, or thrusting his head out of one window to draw it in again and thrust it out of another. He carried in his pocket, too, a fire-box of mysterious and unknown construction; and as sure as ever Kit's mother closed her eyes, so surely-whisk, rattle, fizz -there was the single gentleman consulting his watch by a flame of fire, and letting the sparks fall down among the straw as if there were no such thing as a possibility of himself and Kit's mother being roasted alive before the boys could stop their horses. Whenever they halted to change, there he was-out of the carriage without letting down the steps, bursting about the inn-yard like a lighted cracker, pulling out his watch by lamplight and forgetting to look at it before he put it up again, and in short committing so many extravagances that Kit's mother was quite afraid of him. Then, when the horses were to, in he came like a harlequin, and before they had gone a mile, out came the watch and the fire-box together, and Kit's mother was wide awake again, with no hope of a wink of sleep for that stage.

"Are you comfortable?" the single gentleman would say after one of these exploits, turning sharply round.

"Quite, sir, thank you."

"Are you sure? An't you cold?"

"It is a little chilly, sir," Kit's mother would reply.

"I knew it!" cried the single gentleman, letting down one of the front glasses. "She wants some brandy and water! Of course she does. How could I forget it? 'Hallo! Stop at the next inn, and call out for a glass of hot brandy and water."

It was in vain for Kit's mother to protest that she stood in need of nothing of the kind. The single gentleman was inexorable; and whenever he had exhausted all other modes and fashions of restlessness, it invariably occurred to him that Kit's mother wanted brandy and water.

In this way they travelled on until near midnight, when they stopped to supper, for which meal the single gentleman ordered everything eatable that the house contained; and because Kit's mother didn't eat everything at once, and eat it all, he took it into his head that she must be ill.

"You're faint," said the single gentleman, who did nothing himself but walk about the room. "I see what's the matter with you, ma'am. You're faint."

"Thank you, sir, I'm not indeed."

"I know you are. I'm sure of it. I drag this poor woman from the bosom of her family at a minute's notice, and she goes on getting fainter and fainter before my eyes. I'm a pretty fellow! How many children have you got, ma'am?"

"Two, sir, besides Kit."

"Boys, ma'am?"

"Yes, sir."

"Are they christened?"

"Only hall baptised, as yet, sir."

"I'm godfather to both of 'em. Remember that, if you please, ma'am. You had better have some mulled wine."

"I couldn't touch a drop indeed, sir."

"You must," said the single gentleman. "I see you want it. I ought to have thought of it before."

Immediately flying to the bell, and calling for mulled wine as impetuously as if it had been wanted for instant use in the recovery of some person apparently drowned, the single gentleman made Kit's mother swallow a bumper of it at such a high temperature that the tears ran down her face, and then hustled her off to the chaise again, where-not impossibly from the effects of this agreeable sedative-she soon became insensible to his restlessness, and fell fast asleep. Nor were the happy effects of this prescription of a transitory nature, as, notwithstanding that the distance was greater, and the journey longer, than the single gentleman had anticipated, she did not awake until it was broad day, and they were clattering over the pavement of a town.

"This is the place!" cried her companion, letting down all the glasses. "Drive to the wax-work!"

The boy on the wheeler touched his hat, and setting spurs to his horse, to the end that they might go in brilliantly, all four broke into a smart canter, and dashed through the streets with a noise that brought the good folks wondering to their doors and windows, and drowned the sober voices of the town-clocks as they chimed out half-past eight. They drove up to a door round which a crowd of persons were collected, and there stopped.

"What's this?" said the single gentleman thrusting out his head. "Is anything the matter here?"

"A wedding, sir, a wedding!" cried several voices. "Hurrah!"

The single gentleman, rather bewildered by finding himself the centre of this noisy throng, alighted with the assistance of one of the postilions, and handed out Kit's mother, at sight of whom the populace cried out, "Here's another wedding!" and roared and leaped for joy.

"The world has gone mad, I think," said the single gentleman, pressing through the concourse with his supposed bride. "Stand back here, will you, and let me knock."

Anything that makes a noise is satisfactory to a crowd. A score of dirty hands were raised directly to knock for him, and seldom has a knocker of equal powers been made to produce more deafening sounds than this particular engine on the occasion in question. Having rendered these voluntary services, the throng modestly retired a little, preferring that the single gentleman should bear their consequences alone.

"Now, sir, what do you want?" said a man with a large white bow at his button-hole, opening the door, and confronting him with a very stoical aspect.

"Who has been married here, my friend?" said the single gentleman.

"I have."

"You! and to whom in the devil's name?"

"What right have you to ask?" returned the bridegroom, eyeing him from top to toe.

"What right!" cried the single gentleman, drawing the arm of Kit's mother more tightly through his own, for that good woman evidently had it in contemplation to run away. "A right you little dream of. Mind, good people, if this fellow has been marrying a minor-tut, tut, that can't be. Where is the child you have here, my good fellow? You call her Nell. Where is she?"

As he propounded this question, which Kit's mother echoed, somebody in a room near at hand uttered a great shriek, and a stout lady in a white dress came running to the door, and supported herself upon the bride-groom's arm.

"Where is she!" cried this lady. "What news have you brought me? What has become of her?"

The single gentleman started back, and gazed upon the face of the late Mrs. Jarley (that morning wedded to the philosophic George, to the eternal wrath and despair of Mr. Slum the poet), with looks of conflicting apprehension, disappointment, and incredulity. At length he stammered out,

"I ask you where she is? What do you mean?"

"Oh sir!" cried the bride, "If you have come here to do her any good, why weren't you here a week ago?"

"She is not-not dead?" said the person to whom she addressed herself, turning very pale.

"No, not so bad as that."

"I thank God!" cried the single gentleman feebly. "Let me come in."

They drew back to admit him, and when he had entered, closed the door.

"You see in me, good people," he said, turning to the newly-married couple, "one to whom life itself is not dearer than the two persons whom I seek. They would not know me. My features are strange to them, but if they or either of them are here, take this good woman with you, and let them see her first, for her they both know. If you deny them from any mistaken regard or fear for them, judge of my intentions by their recognition of this person as their old humble friend."

"I always said it!" cried the bride, "I knew she was not a common child! Alas, sir! we have no power to help you, for all that we could do has been tried in vain."

With that, they related to him, without disguise or concealment, all that they knew of Nell and her grandfather, from their first meeting with them, down to the time of their sudden disappearance; adding (which was quite true) that they had made every possible effort to trace them, but without success; having been at first in great alarm for their safety, as well as on account of the suspicions to which they themselves might one day be exposed in consequence of their abrupt departure. They dwelt upon the old man's imbecility of mind, upon the uneasiness the child had always testified when he was absent, upon the company he had been supposed to keep, and upon the increased depression which had gradually crept over her and changed her both in health and spirits. Whether she had missed the old man in the night, and, knowing or conjecturing whither he had bent his steps, had gone in pursuit, or whether they had left the house together, they had no means of determining. Certain they considered it, that there was but slender prospect left of hearing of them again, and that whether their flight originated with the old man, or with the child, there was now no hope of their return.

To all this, the single gentleman listened with the air of a man quite borne down by grief and disappointment. He shed tears when he spoke of the grandfather, and appeared in deep affliction.

Not to protract this portion of our narrative, and to make short work of a long story, let it be briefly written that before the interview came to a close, the single gentleman deemed he had sufficient evidence of having been told the truth, and that he endeavoured to force upon the bride and bridegroom an acknowledgment of their kindness to the unfriended child, which, however, they steadily declined accepting. In the end, the happy couple jolted away in the caravan to spend their honeymoon in a country excursion; and the single gentleman and Kit's mother stood ruefully before their carriage-door.

"Where shall we drive you, sir?" said the post-boy.

"You may drive me," said the single gentleman, "to the-" He was not going to add "inn," but he added it for the sake of Kit's mother; and to the inn they went.

Rumours had already got abroad that the little girl who used to show the wax-work, was the child of great people who had been stolen from her parents in infancy, and had only just been traced. Opinion was divided whether she was the daughter of a prince, a duke, an earl, a viscount, or a baron, but all agreed upon the main fact, and that the single gentleman was her father; and all bent forward to catch a glimpse, though it were only of the tip of his noble nose, as he rode away, desponding, in his four-horse chaise.

What would he have given to know, and what sorrow would have been saved if he had only known, that at that moment both child and grandfather were seated in the old church porch, patiently awaiting the schoolmaster's return!

CHAPTER XLVIII

POPULAR rumour concerning the single gentleman and his errand, travelling from mouth to mouth, and waxing stronger in the marvellous as it was bandied about-for your popular rumour, unlike the rolling stone of the proverb, is one which gathers a deal of moss in its wanderings up and down,-occasioned his dismounting at the inn-door to be looked upon as an exciting and attractive spectacle, which could scarcely be enough admired; and drew together a large concourse of idlers, who having recently been, as it were, thrown out of employment by the closing of the wax- work and the completion of the nuptial ceremonies, considered his arrival as little else than a special providence, and hailed it with demonstrations of the liveliest joy.

Not at all participating in the general sensation, but wearing the depressed and wearied look of one who sought to meditate on his disappointment in silence and privacy, the single gentleman alighted, and handed out Kit's mother with a gloomy politeness which impressed the lookers-on extremely. That done, he gave her his arm and escorted her into the house, while several active waiters ran on before as a skirmishing party, to clear the way and to show the room which was ready for their reception.

"Any room will do," said the single gentleman. "Let, it, be near at hand, that's all."

"Close here, sir, if you please to walk this way."

"Would the gentleman like this room?" said a voice, as a little out-of-the-way door at the foot of the well-staircase flew briskly open and a head popped out. "He's quite welcome to it. He's as welcome as flowers in May, or coals at Christmas. Would you like this room, sir? Honour me by walking in. Do me the favour, pray."

"Goodness gracious me!" cried Kit's mother, falling back in extreme surprise, "only think of this!"

She had some reason to be astonished, for the person who had proffered the gracious invitation was no other than Daniel Quilp. The little door out of which he had thrust his head was close to the inn larder; and there he stood, bowing with grotesque politeness; as much at his ease as if the door were that of his own house; blighting all the legs of mutton and cold roast fowls by his close companionship, and looking like the evil genius of the cellars come from under ground upon some work of mischief.

"Would you do me the honour?" said Quilp.

"I prefer being alone," replied the single gentleman.

"Oh!" said Quilp. And with that, he darted in again with one jerk and clapped the little door to, like a figure in a Dutch clock when the hour strikes.

"Why it was only last night, sir," whispered Kit's mother, "that I left him in Little Bethel."

"Indeed!" said her fellow-passenger. "When did that person come here, waiter?"

"Come down by the night-coach this morning, sir."

"Humph! And when is he going?"

"Can't say, sir, really. When the chambermaid asked him just now if he should want a bed, sir, he first made faces at her, and then wanted to kiss her."

"Beg him to walk this way," said the single gentleman. "I should be glad to exchange a word with him, tell him. Beg him to come at once, do you hear?"

The man stared on receiving these instructions, for the single gentleman had not only displayed as much astonishment as Kit's mother at sight of the dwarf, but, standing in no fear of him, had been at less pains to conceal his dislike and repugnance. He departed on his errand, however, and immediately returned, ushering in its object.

"Your servant, sir," said the dwarf. "I encountered your messenger half-way. I thought you'd allow me to pay my compliments to you. I hope you're well. I hope you're very well."

There was a short pause, while the dwarf, with half-shut eyes and puckered face, stood waiting for an answer. Receiving none, he turned towards his more familiar acquaintance.

"Christopher's mother!" he cried. "Such a dear lady, such a worthy woman, so blest in her honest son! How is Christopher's mother? Have change of air and scene improved her? Her little family too, and Christopher? Do they thrive? Do they flourish? Are they growing into worthy citizens, eh?"

Making his voice ascend in the scale with every succeeding question, Mr. Quilp finished in a shrill squeak, and subsided into the panting look which was customary with him, and which, whether it were assumed or natural, had equally the effect of banishing all expression from his face, and rendering it, as far as it afforded any index to his mood or meaning, a perfect blank.

"Mr. Quilp," said the single gentleman.

The dwarf put his hand to his great flapped ear, and counterfeited the closest attention.

"We two have met before-"

"Surely," cried Quilp, nodding his bead. "Oh surely, sir. Such an honour and pleasure-it's both, Christopher's mother, it's both-is not to be forgotten so soon. By no means!"

"You may remember that the day I arrived in London, and found the house to which I drove empty and deserted, I was directed by some of the neighbours to you, and waited upon you without stopping for rest or refreshment?"

"How precipitate that was, and yet what an earnest and vigorous measure!" said Quilp, conferring with himself, in imitation of his friend Mr. Sampson Brass.

"I found," said the single gentleman, "you, most unaccountably, in possession of everything that had so recently belonged to another man, and that other man, who up to the time of your entering upon his property had been looked upon as affluent, reduced to sudden beggary, and driven from house and home."

"We had warrant for what we did, my good sir," rejoined Quilp, "we had our warrant. Don't say driven either. He went of his own accord-vanished in the night, sir."

"No matter," said the single gentleman angrily. "He was gone."

"Yes, he was gone," said Quilp, with the same exasperating composure. "No doubt he was gone. The only question was, where. And it's a question still."

"Now, what am I to think," said the single gentleman, sternly regarding him, "of you, who, plainly indisposed to give me any information then-nay, obviously holding back, and sheltering yourself with all kinds of cunning, trickery, and evasion,-are dogging my footsteps now?"

"I dogging!" cried Quilp.

"Why, are you not?" returned his questioner, fretted into a state of the utmost irritation. "Were you not a few hours since, sixty miles off, and in the chapel to which this good woman goes to say her prayers?"

"She was there too, I think?" said Quilp, still perfectly unmoved. "I might say, if I was inclined to be rude, how do I know but you are dogging my footsteps. Yes, I was at chapel. What then? I've read in books that pilgrims were used to go to chapel before they went on journeys, to put up petitions for their safe return. Wise men! journeys are very perilous-especially outside the coach. Wheels come off, horses take fright, coachmen drive too fast, coaches overturn. I always go to chapel before I start on journeys. It's the last thing I do on such occasions, indeed."

That Quilp lied most heartily in this speech, it needed no very great penetration to discover, although for anything that he suffered to appear in his face, voice, or manner, he might have been clinging to the truth with the quiet constancy of a martyr.

"In the name of all that's calculated to drive one crazy, man," said the unfortunate single gentleman, "have you not, for some reason of your own, taken upon yourself my errand? don't you know with what object I have come here, and if you do know, can you throw no light upon it?"

"You think I'm a conjuror, sir," replied Quilp, shrugging up his shoulders. "If I was, I should tell my own fortune-and make it."

"Ah! we have said all we need say, I see," returned the other, throwing himself impatiently upon a sofa. "Pray leave us, if you please."

"Willingly," returned Quilp. "Most willingly. Christopher's mother, my good soul, farewell. A pleasant journey-back, sir. Ahem!"

With these parting words, and with a grin upon his features altogether indescribable, but which seemed to be compounded of every monstrous grimace of which men or monkeys are capable, the dwarf slowly retreated and closed the door behind him.

"Oho!" he said when he had regained his own room, and sat himself down in a chair with his arms akimbo. "Oho! Are you there, my friend? In-deed!"

Chuckling as though in very great glee, and recompensing himself for the restraint he had lately put upon his countenance by twisting it into all imaginable varieties of ugliness, Mr. Quilp, rocking himself to and fro in his chair and nursing his left leg at the same time, fell into certain meditations, of which it may be necessary to relate the substance.

First, he reviewed the circumstances which had led to his repairing to that spot, which were briefly these. Dropping in at Mr. Sampson Brass's office on the previous evening, in the absence of that gentleman and his learned sister, he had lighted upon Mr. Swiveller, who chanced at the moment to be sprinkling a glass of warm gin and water on the dust of the law, and to be moistening his clay, as the phrase goes, rather copiously. But as clay in the abstract, when too much moistened, becomes of a weak and uncertain consistency, breaking down in unexpected places, retaining impressions but faintly, and preserving no strength or steadiness of character, so Mr. Swiveller's clay, having imbibed a considerable quantity of moisture, was in a very loose and slippery state, insomuch that the various ideas impressed upon it were fast losing their distinctive character, and running into each other. It is not uncommon for human clay in this condition to value itself above all things upon its great prudence and sagacity; and Mr. Swiveller, especially prizing himself upon these qualities, took occasion to remark that he had made strange discoveries in connexion with the single gentleman who lodged above, which he had determined to keep within his own bosom, and which neither tortures nor cajolery should ever induce him to reveal. Of this determination Mr. Quilp expressed his high approval, and setting himself in the same breath to goad Mr. Swiveller on to further hints, soon made out that the single gentleman had been seen in communication with Kit, and that this was the secret which was never to be disclosed.

Possessed of this piece of information, Mr. Quilp directly supposed that the single gentleman above stairs must be the same individual who had waited on him, and having assured himself by further inquiries that this surmise was correct, had no difficulty in arriving at the conclusion that the intent and object of his correspondence with Kit was the recovery of his old client and the child. Burning with curiosity to know what proceedings were afoot, he resolved to pounce upon Kit's mother as the person least likely to resist his arts, and consequently the most likely to be entrapped into such revelations as he sought; so taking an abrupt leave of Mr. Swiveller, he hurried to her house. The good woman being from home, he made inquiries of a neighbour, as Kit himself did soon afterwards, and being directed to the chapel betook himself there, in order to waylay her, at the conclusion of the service.

He had not sat in the chapel more than a quarter of an hour, and with his eyes piously fixed upon the ceiling was chuckling inwardly over the joke of his being there at all, when Kit himself appeared. Watchful as a lynx, one glance showed the dwarf that he had come on business. Absorbed in appearance, as we have seen, and feigning a profound abstraction, he noted every circumstance of his behaviour, and when he withdrew with his family, shot out after him. In fine, he traced them to the Notary's house; learnt the destination of the carriage from one of the postilions; and knowing that a fast night-coach started for the same place, at the very hour which was on the point of striking, from a street hard by, darted round to the coach-office without more ado, and took his seat upon the roof. After passing and repassing the carriage on the road, and being passed and repassed by it sundry times in the course of the night according as their stoppages were longer or shorter, or their rate of travelling varied, they reached the town almost together. Quilp kept the chaise in sight, mingled with the crowd, learnt the single gentleman's errand, and its failure, and having possessed himself of all that it was material to know, hurried off, reached the inn before him, had the interview just now detailed, and shut himself up in the little room in which he hastily reviewed all these occurrences.

"You are there, are you, my friend?" he repeated, greedily biting his nails. "I am suspected and thrown aside, and Kit's the confidential agent, is he? I shall have to dispose of him, I fear. If we had come up with them this morning," he continued, after a thoughtful pause, "I was ready to prove a pretty good claim. I could have made my profit. But for these canting hypocrites, the lad and his mother, I could get this fiery gentleman as comfortably into my net as our old friend-our mutual friend, ha! ha!-and chubby, rosy Nell. At the worst, it's a golden opportunity, not to be lost. Let us find them first, and I'll find means of draining you of some of your superfluous cash, sir, while there are prison bars, and bolts, and locks, to keep your friend or kinsman safely. I hate your virtuous people!" said the dwarf, throwing off a bumper of brandy, and smacking his lips, "ah! I hate 'em every one!"

This was not a mere empty vaunt, but a deliberate avowal of his real sentiments; for Mr. Quilp, who loved nobody, had by little and little come to hate everybody nearly or remotely connected with his ruined client:-the old man himself, because he had been able to deceive him and elude his vigilance-the child, because she was the object of Mrs. Quilp's commiseration and constant self-reproach-the single gentleman, because of his unconcealed aversion to himself-Kit and his mother, most mortally, for the reasons already shown. Above and beyond that general feeling of opposition to them, which would have been inseparable from his ravenous desire to enrich himself by these altered circumstances, Daniel Quilp hated them everyone.

In this amiable mood, Mr. Quilp enlivened himself and his hatreds with more brandy, and then, changing his quarters, withdrew to an obscure alehouse, under cover of which seclusion he instituted all possible inquiries that might lead to the discovery of the old man and his grand child. But all was in vain. Not the slightest trace or clue could be obtained. They had left the town by night; no one had seen them go; no one had met them on the road; the driver of no coach, cart, or waggon, had seen any travellers answering their description; nobody had fallen in with them, or heard of them. Convinced at last that for the present all such attempts were hopeless, he appointed two or three scouts, with promises of large rewards in case of their forwarding him any intelligence, and returned to London by next day's coach.

It was some gratification to Mr. Quilp to find, as he took his place upon the roof, that Kit's mother was alone inside; from which circumstance he derived in the course of the journey much cheerfulness of spirit, inasmuch as her solitary condition enabled him to terrify her with many extraordinary annoyances; such as hanging over the side of the coach at the risk of his life, and staring in with his great goggle eyes, which seemed in hers the more horrible from his face being upside down; dodging her in this way from one window to another; getting nimbly down when ever they changed horses and thrusting his head in at the window with a dismal squint: which ingenious tortures had such an effect upon Mrs. Nubbles, that she was quite unable for the time to resist the belief that Mr. Quilp did in his own person represent and embody that Evil Power, who was so vigorously attacked at Little Bethel, and who, by reason of her backslidings in respect of Astley's and oysters, was now frolicsome and rampant.

Kit, having been apprised by letter of his mother's intended return, was waiting for her at the coach-office; and great was his surprise when he saw, leering over the coachman's shoulder like some familiar demon invisible to all eyes but his, the well-known face of Quilp.

"How are you, Christopher?" croaked the dwarf from the coach-top. "All right, Christopher. Mother's inside."

"Why, how did he come here, mother?" whispered Kit.

"I don't know how he came or why, my dear," rejoined Mrs. Nubbles, dismounting with her son's assistance, "but he has been a terrifying of me out of my seven senses all this blessed day."

"He has?" cried Kit.

"You wouldn't believe it, that you wouldn't," replied his mother; "but don't say a word to him, for I really don't believe he's human. Hush! Don't turn round as if I was talking of him, but he's a squinting at me now in the full blaze of the coach-lamp, quite awful!"

In spite of his mother's injunction, Kit turned sharply round to look. Mr. Quilp was serenely gazing at the stars quite absorbed in celestial contemplation.

"Oh, he's the artfullest creetur!" cried Mrs. Nubbles. "But come away. Don't speak to him for the world."

"Yes I will, mother. What nonsense. I say, sir-" Mr. Quilp affected to start, and looked smilingly round. "You let my mother alone, will you?" said Kit. "How dare you tease a poor lone woman like her, making her miserable and melancholy as if she hadn't got enough to make her so, without you. An't you ashamed of yourself, you little monster?"

"Monster!" said Quilp inwardly, with a smile. "Ugliest dwarf that could be seen anywhere for a penny-monster- ah!"

"You show her any of your impudence again," resumed Kit, shouldering the handbox, "and I tell you what, Mr. Quilp, I won't bear with you any more. You have no right to do it; I'm sure we never interfered with you. This isn't the first time; and if ever you worry or frighten her again, you'll oblige me (though I should be very sorry to do it, on account of your size) to beat you."

Quilp said not a word in reply, but walking up so close to Kit as to bring his eyes within two or three inches of his face, looked fixedly at him, retreated a little distance without averting his gaze, approached again, again withdrew, and so on for hall a dozen times, like a head in a phantas-magoria. Kit stood his ground as if in expectation of an immediate assault, but finding that nothing came of these gestures, snapped his fingers and walked away; his mother dragging him off as fast as she could, and, even in the midst of his news of little Jacob and the baby, looking anxiously over her shoulder to see if Quilp were following.

CHAPTER XLIX

KIT'S mother might have spared herself the trouble of looking back so often, for nothing was further from Mr. Quilp's thoughts than any intention of pursuing her and her son, or renewing the quarrel with which they had parted. He went his way, whistling from time to time some fragments of a tune; and with a face quite tranquil and composed, jogged pleasantly towards home; entertaining himself as he went with visions or the fears and terrors of Mrs. Quilp, who, having received no intelligence of him for three whole days and two nights, and having had no previous notice of his ab-

sence, was doubtless by that time in a state of distraction, and constantly
fainting away with anxiety and grief.

This facetious probability was so congenial to the dwarf's humour, and so
exquisitely amusing to him, that he laughed as he went along until the tears ran
down his cheeks; and more than once, when he found himself in a bye-street,
vented his delight in a shrill scream, which greatly terrifying any lonely passenger, who happened to be walking on before him expecting nothing so little, increased his mirth, and made him remarkably cheerful and light-hearted.

In this happy flow of spirits Mr. Quilp reached Tower Hill, when, gazing up at the window of his own sitting-room, he thought he descried more
light than is usual in a house of mourning. Drawing nearer, and listening attentively, he could hear several voices in earnest conversation, among which
he could distinguish, not only those of his wife and mother-in-law, but the
tongues of men.

"Ha!" cried the jealous dwarf. "What's this! Do they entertain such
visitors while I'm away!"

A smothered cough from above, was the reply. He felt in his pockets
for his latch-key, but had forgotten it. There was no resource but to knock at
the door.

"A light in the passage," said Quilp, peeping through the key-hole.
"A very soft knock; and, by your leave, my lady, I may yet steal upon you
unawares. Soho!"

A very low and gentle rap received no answer from within. But after a
second application to the knocker, no louder than the first, the door was
softly opened by the boy from the wharf, whom Quilp instantly gagged
with one hand, and dragged into the street with the other.

"You'll throttle me, master," whispered the boy. "Let go, will you."

"Who's up stairs, you dog?" retorted Quilp in the same tone. "Tell
me. And don't speak above your breath, or I'll choke you in good earnest."

The boy could only point to the window, and reply with a stifled giggle, expressive of such intense enjoyment, that Quilp clutched him by the
throat again and might have carried his threat into execution, or at least
have made very good progress towards that end, but for the boy's nimbly
extricating himself from his grasp, and fortifying himself behind the nearest
post, at which, after some fruitless attempts to catch him by the hair of his
head, his master was obliged to come to a parley.

"Will you answer me?" said Quilp. "What's going on, above?"

"You won't let one speak," replied the boy. "They,-ha ha ha!-they
think you're-you're dead. Ha ha ha!"

"Dead!" cried Quilp, relaxing into a grim laugh himself. "No. Do
they? Do they really, you dog?"

"They think you're-you're drowned," replied the boy, who in his malicious nature had a strong infusion of his master. "You was last seen on the
brink of the wharf, and they think you tumbled over. Ha ha!"

The prospect of playing the spy under such delicious circumstances,
and of disappointing them all by walking in alive, gave more delight to Quilp
than the greatest stroke of good fortune could possibly have inspired him

with. He was no less tickled than his hopeful assistant, and they both stood for some seconds, grinning and gasping, and wagging their heads at each other, on either side of the post, like an unmatchable pair of Chinese idols.

"Not a word," said Quilp, making towards the door on tiptoe. "Not a sound, not so much as a creaking board, or a stumble against a cobweb. Drowned, eh, Mrs. Quilp? Drowned!"

So saying, he blew out the candle, kicked off his shoes, and groped his way up stairs; leaving his delighted young friend in an ecstasy of summersets on the pavement.

The bedroom-door on the staircase being unlocked, Mr. Quilp slipped in, and planted himself behind the door of communication between that chamber and the sitting-room, which standing ajar to render both more airy, and having a very convenient chink (of which he had often availed himself for purposes of espial, and had indeed enlarged with his pocket-knife), enabled him not only to hear, but to see distinctly, what was passing.

Applying his eye to this convenient place, he descried Mr. Brass seated at the table with pen, ink, and paper, and the case-bottle of rum-his own case-bottle, and his own particular Jamaica-convenient to his hand; with hot water, fragrant lemons, white lump sugar, and all things fitting; from which choice materials, Sampson, by no means insensible to their claims upon his attention, had compounded a mighty glass of punch reeking hot; which he was at that very moment stirring up with a teaspoon, and contemplating with looks in which a faint assumption of sentimental regret struggled but weakly with a bland and comfortable joy. At the same table, with both her elbows upon it, was Mrs. Jiniwin; no longer sipping other people's punch feloniously with teaspoons, but taking deep draughts from a jorum of her own; while her daughter- not exactly with ashes on her head, or sackcloth on her back, but preserving a very decent and becoming appearance of sorrow nevertheless-was reclining in an easy chair, and soothing her grief with a smaller allowance of the same glib liquid. There were also present a couple of waterside men, bearing between them certain machines called drags; even these fellows were accommodated with a stiff glass apiece; and as they drank with a great relish, and were naturally of a red-nosed, pimple-faced, convivial look, their presence rather increased than detracted from that decided appearance of comfort, which was the great characteristic of the party.

"If I could poison that dear old lady's rum and water," murmured Quilp, "I'd die happy."

"Ah!" said Mr. Brass, breaking the silence, and raising his eyes to the ceiling with a sigh, "Who knows but he may be looking down upon us now! Who knows but he may be surveying of us from-from somewheres or another, and contemplating us with a watchful eye! Oh Lor!"

Here Mr. Brass stopped to drink hall his punch, and then resumed; looking at the other hall, as he spoke, with a dejected smile.

"I can almost fancy," said the lawyer shaking his head, "that I see his eye glistening down at the very bottom of my liquor. When shall we look upon his like again? Never, never! One minute we are here"-holding his tumbler before his eyes- "the next we are there" -gulping down its contents, and striking himself emphatically a little below the chest- "in the silent tomb. To think that I should be drinking his very rum! It seems like a dream."

With the view, no doubt, of testing the reality of his position, Mr. Brass pushed his tumbler as he spoke towards Mrs. Jiniwin for the purpose of being replenished; and turned towards the attendant mariners.

"The search has been quite unsuccessful then?"

"Quite, master. But I should say that if he turns up anywhere, he'll come ashore somewhere about Grinidge to-morrow, at ebb tide, eh, mate?"

The other gentleman assented, observing that he was expected at the Hospital, and that several pensioners would be ready to receive him whenever he arrived.

"Then we have nothing for it but resignation," said Mr. Brass; "nothing but resignation, and expectation. It would be a comfort to have his body; it would be a dreary comfort."

"Oh, beyond a doubt," assented Mrs. Jiniwin hastily; "if we once had that, we should be quite sure."

"With regard to the descriptive advertisement," said Sampson Brass, taking up his pen. "It is a melancholy pleasure to recall his traits. Respecting his legs now-?"

"Crooked, certainly," said Mrs. Jiniwin.

"Do you think they were crooked?" said Brass, in an insinuating tone. "I think I see them now coming up the street very wide apart, in nankeen pantaloons a little shrunk and without straps. Ah! what a vale of tears we live in. Do we say crooked?"

"I think they were a little so," observed Mrs. Quilp with a sob.

"Legs crooked," said Brass, writing as he spoke. "Large head, short body, legs crooked-"

"Very crooked," suggested Mrs. Jiniwin.

"We'll not say very crooked, ma'am," said Brass piously. "Let us not bear hard upon the weaknesses of the deceased. He is gone, ma'am, to where his legs will never come in question.-We will content ourselves with crooked, Mrs. Jiniwin."

"I thought you wanted the truth," said the old lady. "That's all."

"Bless your eyes, how I love you," muttered Quilp. "There she goes again. Nothing but punch!"

"This is an occupation," said the lawyer, laying down his pen and emptying his glass, "which seems to bring him before my eyes like the Ghost of Hamlet's father, in the very clothes that he wore on work-a-days. His coat, his waistcoat, his shoes and stockings, his trousers, his hat, his wit and humour, his pathos and his umbrella, all come before me like visions of my youth. His linen!" said Mr. Brass smiling fondly at the wall, "his linen which was always of a particular colour, for such was his whim and fancy-how plain I see his linen now I"

"You had better go on, sir," said Mrs, Jiniwin impatiently.

"True, ma'am, true," cried Mr. Brass. "Our faculties must not freeze with grief. I'll trouble you for a little more of that, ma'am. A question now arises, with relation to his nose."

"Flat," said Mrs. Jiniwin.

"Aquiline!" cried Quilp, thrusting in his head, and striking the feature with his fist. "Aquiline, you hag. Do you see it? Do you call this flat? Do you? Eh?"

"Oh capital, capital!" shouted Brass, from the mere force of habit. "Excellent! How very good he is! He's a most remarkable man-so extremely whimsical! Such an amazing power of taking people by surprise!"

Quilp paid no regard whatever to these compliments, nor to the dubious and frightened look into which the lawyer gradually subsided, nor to the shrieks of his wife and mother-in-law, nor to the latter's running from the room, nor to the former's fainting away. Keeping his eye fixed on Sampson Brass, he walked up to the table, and beginning with his glass, drank off the contents, and went regularly round until he had emptied the other two, when he seized the case-bottle, and hugging it under his arm, surveyed him with a most extraordinary leer.

"Not yet, Sampson," said Quilp. "Not just yet!"

"Oh very good indeed!" cried Brass, recovering his spirits a little. "Ha ha ha! Oh exceedingly good! There's not another man alive who could carry it off like that. A most difficult position to carry off. But he has such a flow of good-humour, such an amazing flow!"

"Good night," said the dwarf, nodding expressively.

"Good night, sir, good night," cried the lawyer, retreating backwards towards the door. "This is a joyful occasion indeed, extremely joyful. Ha ha ha! oh very rich, very rich indeed, remarkably so!"

Waiting until Mr. Brass's ejaculations died away in the distance (for he continued to pour them out, all the way down stairs), Quilp advanced towards the two men, who yet lingered in a kind of stupid amazement.

"Have you been dragging the river all day, gentlemen?" said the dwarf, holding the door open with great politeness.

"And yesterday too, master."

"Dear me, you've had a deal of trouble. Pray consider everything yours that you find upon the-upon the body. Good night!"

The men looked at each other, but had evidently no inclination to argue the point just then, and shuffled out of the room. This speedy clearance effected, Quilp locked the doors; and, still embracing the case-bottle with shrugged-up shoulders and folded arms, stood looking at his insensible wife like a dismounted nightmare.

CHAPTER L

MATRIMONIAL differences are usually discussed by their parties concerned in the form of dialogue, in which the lady bears at least her full half share. Those of Mr. and Mrs. Quilp, however, were an exception to the general rule; the remarks which they occasioned being limited to a long soliloquy on the part of the gentleman, with perhaps a few deprecatory observations from the lady, not extending beyond a trembling monosyllable uttered at long intervals, and in a very submissive and humble tone. On the present occasion, Mrs. Quilp did not for a long time venture even upon this gentle defence, but when she had recovered from her fainting-fit sat in a tearful silence, meekly listening to the reproaches of her lord and master.

Of these Mr. Quilp delivered himself with the utmost animation and rapidity, and with so many distortions of limb and feature, that even his wife, although tolerably well accustomed to his proficiency in these respects, was well- nigh beside herself with alarm. But the Jamaica rum, and the joy of having occasioned a heavy disappointment, by degrees cooled Mr. Quilp's wrath; which, from being at savage heat, dropped slowly to the bantering or chuckling point, at which it steadily remained.

"So you thought I was dead and gone, did you?" said Quilp. "You thought you were a widow, eh? Ha, ha, ha, you jade!"

"Indeed, Quilp," returned his wife. "I'm very sorry-"

"Who doubts it!" cried the dwarf. "You very sorry! to be sure you are. Who doubts that you're very sorry!"

"I don't mean sorry that you have come home again alive and well," said his wife, "but sorry that I should have been led into such a belief. I am glad to see you, Quilp; indeed I am."

In truth Mrs. Quilp did seem a great deal more glad to behold her lord than might have been expected, and did evince a degree of interest in his safety which, all things considered, was rather unaccountable. Upon Quilp, however, this circumstance made no impression, further than as it moved him to snap his fingers close to his wife's eyes, with divers grins of triumph and derision.

"How could you go away so long without saying a word to me or letting me hear of you or know anything about you?" asked the poor little woman, sobbing. "How could you be so cruel, Quilp?"

"How could I be so cruel! cruel" cried the dwarf. "Because I was in the humour. I'm in the humour now. I shall be cruel when I like. I'm going away again."

"Not again!"

"Yes again. I'm going away now. I'm off directly. I mean to go and live wherever the fancy seizes me, at the wharf-at the counting-house-and be a jolly bachelor. You were a widow in anticipation. Damme," screamed the dwarf, "I'll be a bachelor in earnest."

"You can't be serious, Quilp," sobbed his wife.

"I tell you," said the dwarf, exulting in his project, "that I'll be a bachelor, a devil-may-care bachelor; and I'll have my bachelor's hall at the counting-house, and at such times come near it if you dare. And mind too that I don't pounce in upon you at unseasonable hours again, for I'll be a spy upon you, and come and go like a mole or a weazel. Tom Scott-where's Tom Scott?"

"Here I am, master," cried the voice of the boy, as Quilp threw up the window.

"Wait there, you dog," returned the dwarf, "to carry a bachelor's portmanteau. Pack it up, Mrs. Quilp. Knock up the dear old lady to help; knock her up. Hallo there! Hallo!"

With these exclamations, Mr. Quilp caught up the poker, and hurrying to the door of the good lady's sleeping-closet beat upon it therewith until she awoke in inexpressible terror, thinking that her amiable son-in-law surely intended to murder her in justification of the legs she had slandered. Impressed with this idea, she was no sooner fairly awake than she screamed violently, and would have quickly precipitated herself out of the window and through a neighbouring skylight, if her daughter had not hastened in to undeceive her, and implore her assistance. Somewhat reassured by her account of the service she was required to render, Mrs. Jiniwin made her appearance in a flannel dressing-gown; and both mother and daughter, trembling with terror and cold-for the night was now far advanced -obeyed Mr. Quilp's directions in submissive silence. Prolonging his preparations as much as possible, for their greater comfort, that eccentric gentleman superintended the packing of his wardrobe, and having added to it with his own hands, a plate, knife and fork, spoon, tea-cup and saucer, and other small household matters of that nature, strapped up the portmanteau, took it on his shoulders, and actually marched off without another word, and with the case-bottle (which he had never once put down) still tightly clasped under his arm. Consigning his heavier burden to the care of Tom Scott when he reached the street, taking a dram from the bottle for his own encouragement, and giving the boy a rap on the head with it as a small taste for himself, Quilp very deliberately led the way to the wharf, and reached it at between three and four o'clock in the morning.

"Snug!" said Quilp, when he had groped his way to the wooden counting-house, and opened the door with a key he carried about with him. "Beautifully snug! Call me at eight, you dog."

With no more formal leave-taking or explanation, he clutched the portmanteau, shut the door upon his attendant, and climbing on the desk, and rolling himself up as round as a hedgehog, in an old boat-cloak, fell fast asleep.

Being roused in the morning at the appointed time, and roused with difficulty, after his late fatigues, Quilp instructed Tom Scott to make a fire in the yard of sundry pieces of old timber, and to prepare some coffee for breakfast; for the better furnishing of which repast he entrusted him with certain small moneys, to be expended in the purchase of hot rolls, butter, sugar, Yarmouth bloaters, and other articles of housekeeping; so that in a few minutes a savoury meal was smoking on the board. With this substantial comfort, the dwarf regaled himself to his heart's content; and being highly satisfied with this free and gipsy mode of life (Which he had often meditated, as offering, whenever he chose to avail himself of it, an agreeable freedom from the restraints of matrimony, and a choice means of keeping Mrs. Quilp and her mother in a state of incessant agitation and suspense), bestirred himself to improve his retreat, and render it more commodious and comfortable.

With this view, he issued forth to a place hard by, where such stores were sold; purchased a second-hand hammock, and had it slung in seaman-like fashion from the ceiling of the counting-house. He also caused to be erected, in the same mouldy cabin, an old ship's stove with a rusty funnel to carry the smoke through the roof; and these arrangements completed, surveyed them with ineffable delight.

"I've got a country-house like Robinson Crusoe-" said the dwarf, ogling the accommodations; "a solitary, sequestered, desolate-island sort of spot, where I can be quite alone when I have business on hand, and be secure from all spies and listeners. Nobody near me here, but rats, and they are fine stealthy secret fellows. I shall be as merry as a grig among these gentry. I'll look out for one like Christopher, and poison him-ha, ha, ha! Business though-business-we must be mindful of business in the midst of pleasure, and the time has flown this morning, I declare."

Enjoining Tom Scott to await his return, and not to stand upon his head, or throw a summerset, or so much as walk upon his hands meanwhile, on pain of lingering torments, the dwarf threw himself into a boat, and crossing to the other side of the river, and then speeding away on foot, reached Mr. Swiveller's usual house of entertainment in Bevis Marks, just as that gentleman sat down alone to dinner in its dusky parlour.

"Dick"-said the dwarf, thrusting his head in at the door, "my pet, my pupil, the apple of my eye, hey, hey!"

"Oh you're there, are you?" returned Mr. Swiveller; "how are you?"

"How's Dick?" retorted Quilp. "How's the cream of clerkship, eh?"

"Why, rather sour, sir," replied Mr. Swiveller. "Beginning to border upon cheesiness, in fact."

"What's the matter?" said the dwarf, advancing. "Has Sally proved unkind? 'Of all the girls that are so smart, there's none like-' eh, Dick!"

"Certainly not," replied Mr. Swiveller, eating his dinner with great gravity, "none like her. She's the sphynx of private life is Sally B."

"You're out of spirits," said Quilp, drawing up a chair. "What's the matter?"

"The law don't agree with me," returned Dick. "It isn't moist enough, and there's too much confinement. I have been thinking of running away."

"Bah!" said the dwarf. "Where would you run to, Dick?"

"I don't know," returned Mr. Swiveller. "Towards Highgate, I suppose. Perhaps the bells might strike up 'Turn again Swiveller, Lord Mayor of London.' Whit tington's name was Dick. I wish cats were scarcer."

Quilp looked at his companion with his eyes screwed up into a comical expression of curiosity, and patiently awaited his further explanation; upon which, however, Mr. Swiveller appeared in no hurry to enter, as he ate a very long dinner in profound silence, and finally pushed away his plate, threw himself back into his chair, folded his arms, and stared ruefully at the fire, in which some ends of cigars were smoking on their own account, and sending up a fragrant odour.

"Perhaps you'd like a bit of cake" -said Dick, at last turning to the dwarf. "You're quite welcome to it. You ought to be, for it's of your making."

"What do you mean?" said Quilp.

Mr. Swiveller replied by taking from his pocket a small and very greasy parcel, slowly unfolding it, and displaying a little slab of plum cake extremely indigestible in appearance, and bordered with a paste of white sugar an inch and a half deep.

"What should you say this was?" demanded Mr. Swiveller.

"It looks like bride-cake," replied the dwarf, grinning.

"And whose should you say it was?" inquired Mr. Swiveller, rubbing the pastry against his nose with a dreadful calmness. "Whose?"

"Not-"

"Yes," said Dick, "the same. You needn't mention her name. There's no such name now. Her name is Cheggs now, Sophy Cheggs. Yet loved I as man never loved that hadn't wooden legs, and my heart, my heart is breaking for the love of Sophy Cheggs."

With this extemporary adaptation of a popular ballad to the distressing circumstances of his own case, Mr. Swiveller folded up the parcel again, beat it very flat between the palms of his hands, thrust it into his breast, buttoned his coat over it, and folded his arms upon the whole.

"Now I hope you're satisfied, sir," said Dick; "and I hope Fred's satisfied. You went partners in the mischief, and I hope you like it. This is the triumph I was to have, is it? It's like the old country-dance of that name, where there are two gentlemen to one lady, and one has her, and the other hasn't, but comes limping up behind to make out the figure. But it's Destiny, and mine's a crusher!"

Disguising his secret joy in Mr. Swiveller's defeat, Daniel Quilp adopted the surest means of soothing him, by ringing the bell, and ordering in a supply of rosy wine (that is to say, of its usual representative), which he put about with great alacrity, calling upon Mr. Swiveller to pledge him in various toasts derisive of Cheggs, and eulogistic of the happiness of single men. Such was their impression on Mr. Swiveller, coupled with the reflection that no man could oppose his destiny, that in a very short space of time his spirits rose surprisingly, and he was enabled to give the dwarf an account of the receipt of the cake, which, it appeared, had been brought to Bevis Marks by the two surviving Miss Wackleses in person, and delivered at the office door with much giggling and joyfulness.

"Ha!" said Quilp. "It will be our turn to giggle soon. And that reminds me-you spoke of young Trent- where is he?"

Mr. Swiveller explained that his respectable friend had recently accepted a responsible situation in a locomotive gaming-house, and was at that time absent on a professional tour among the adventurous spirits of Great Britain.

"That's unfortunate," said the dwarf, "for I came, in fact, to ask you about him. A thought has occurred to me, Dick; your friend over the way-"

"Which friend?"

"In the first floor."

"Yes?"

"Your friend in the first floor, Dick, may know him."

"No, he don't," said Mr. Swiveller, shaking his head.

"Don't! No, because he has never seen him," rejoined Quilp; "but if we were to bring them together, who knows, Dick, but Fred, properly introduced, would serve his turn almost as well as little Nell or her grandfather who knows but it might make the young fellow's fortune, and through him, yours, eh?"

"Why, the fact is, you see," said Mr. Swiveller, "that they have been brought together."

"Have been!" cried the dwarf, looking suspiciously at his companion. "Through whose means?"

"Through mine," said Dick, slightly confused. "Didn't I mention it to you the last time you called over yonder?"

"You know you didn't," returned the dwarf.

"I believe you're right," said Dick. "No. I didn't, I recollect. Oh yes, I brought 'em together that very day. It was Fred's suggestion."

"And what came of it?"

"Why, instead of my friend's bursting into tears when he knew who Fred was, embracing him kindly, and telling him that he was his grandfather, or his grandmother in disguise (which we fully expected), he flew into a tremendous passion; called him all manner of names; said it was in a great measure his fault that little Nell and the old gentleman had ever been brought to poverty; didn't hint at our taking anything to drink; and-and in short rather turned us out of the room than otherwise."

"That's strange," said the dwarf, musing.

"So we remarked to each other at the time," returned Dick coolly, "but quite true."

Quilp was plainly staggered by this intelligence, over which he brooded for some time in moody silence, often raising his eyes to Mr. Swiveller's face, and sharply scanning its expression. As he could read in it, however, no additional information or anything to lead him to believe he had spoken falsely; and as Mr. Swiveller, left to his own meditations, sighed deeply, and was evidently growing maudlin on the subject of Mrs. Cheggs; the dwarf soon broke up the conference and took his departure, leaving the bereaved one to his melancholy ruminations.

"Have been brought together, eh?" said the dwarf as I he walked the streets alone. "My friend has stolen a march upon me. It led him to nothing, and therefore is no great matter, save in the intention. I'm glad he has lost his mistress. Ha ha! The blockhead mustn't leave I the law at present. I'm sure of him where he is, Whenever I want him for my own purposes, and, besides, he's a good unconscious spy on Brass, and tells, in his cups, all that he sees and hears. You're useful to me, Dick, and cost nothing but a little treating now and then. I am not sure that it may not be worth while, before long, to take credit with the stranger, Dick, by discovering your designs upon the child; but for the present, we'll remain the best friends, in the world, with your good leave."

Pursuing these thoughts, and gasping as he went along, after his own peculiar fashion, Mr. Quilp once more crossed the Thames and shut himself up in his Bachelor's Hall, which, by reason of its newly-erected chimney depositing the smoke inside the room and carrying none of it off, was not quite so agreeable as more fastidious people might have desired. Such inconveniences, however, instead of disgusting the dwarf with his new abode, rather suited his humour; so, after dining luxuriously from the public house, he lighted his pipe, and smoked against the chimney until nothing of him was visible through the mist but a pair of red and highly inflamed eyes, with sometimes a dim vision of his head and face, as, in a violent fit of coughing, he slightly stirred the smoke and scattered the heavy wreaths by which they were obscured. In the midst of this atmosphere, which must infallibly have smothered any other man, Mr. Quilp passed the evening with great cheerfulness; solacing himself all the time with the pipe and the case-bottle; and occasionally entertaining himself with a melodious howl, in tended for a song, but bearing not the faintest resemblance to any scrap of any piece of music, vocal or instrumental, ever invented by man. Thus he amused himself until nearly midnight, when he turned into his hammock with the utmost satisfaction.

The first sound that met his ears in the morning-as he half opened his eyes, and, finding himself unusually near the ceiling, entertained a drowsy idea that he must have been transformed into a fly or blue-bottle in the course of the night,-was that of a stifled sobbing and weeping in the room. Peeping cautiously over the side of his hammock he descried Mrs. Quilp, to whom, after contemplating her for some time in silence, he communicated a violent start by suddenly yelling out,

"Halloa!"

"Oh, Quilp!" cried his poor little wife, looking up. "How you frightened me!"

"I meant to, you jade," returned the dwarf. "What do you want here? I'm dead, an't I?"

"Oh, please come home, do come home," said Mrs. Quilp, sobbing; "we'll never do so any more, Quilp, and after all it was only a mistake that grew out of our anxiety."

"Out of your anxiety," grinned the dwarf. "Yes, I know that-out of your anxiety for my death. I shall come home when I please, I tell you. I shall come home when I please, and go when I please. I'll be a Will o' the Wisp, now here, now there, dancing about you always, starting up when you least expect me, and keeping you in a constant state of restlessness and irritation. Will you begone?"

Mrs. Quilp durst only make a gesture of entreaty,

"I tell you no," cried the dwarf. "No. If you dare to come here again unless you're sent for, I'll keep watch-dogs in the yard that'll growl and bite-I'll have man-traps, cunningly altered and improved for catching women-I'll have spring guns, that shall explode when you tread upon the wires, and blow you into little pieces, Will you be gone?"

"Do forgive me. Do come back," said his wife, earnestly.

"No-o-o-o-o!" roared Quilp. "Not till my own good time, and then I'll return again as often as I choose, and be accountable to nobody for my goings or comings. You see the door there. Will you go?"

Mr. Quilp delivered this last command in such a very energetic voice, and moreover accompanied it with such a sudden gesture, indicative of an intention to spring out of his hammock, and, night-capped as he was, bear his wife home again through the public streets, that she sped away like an arrow. Her worthy lord stretched his neck and eyes until she had crossed the yard, and then, not at all sorry to have had this opportunity of carrying his point, and asserting the sanctity of his castle, fell into an immoderate fit of laughter, and laid himself down to sleep again.

CHAPTER LI

THE bland and open-hearted proprietor of Bachelor's. Hall slept on amidst the congenial accompaniments of rain, mud, dirt, clamp, fog, and rats, until late in the day; when, summoning his valet Tom Scott to assist him to rise, and to prepare breakfast, he quitted his couch, and made his toilet. This duty performed, and his repast ended, he again betook himself to Bevis Marks.

This visit was not intended for Mr. Swiveller, but for his friend and employer Mr. Sampson Brass. Both gentlemen however were from home, nor was the life and light of law, Miss Sally, at her post either. The fact of their joint desertion of the office was made known to all comers by a scrap of paper in the handwriting of Mr. Swiveller, which was attached to the bell-handle, and which, giving the reader no clue to the time of day when it was first posted, furnished him with the rather vague and unsatisfactory information that that gentleman would "return in an hour."

"There's a servant, I suppose," said the dwarf, knocking at the house-door. "She'll do."

After a sufficiently long interval, the door was opened, and a small voice immediately accosted him with, "Oh please will you leave a card or message?"

"Eh?" said the dwarf, looking down (it was something quite new to him) upon the small servant.

To this, the child, conducting her conversation as upon the occasion of her first interview with Mr. Swiveller, again replied, "Oh please will you leave a card or message?"

"I'll write a note," said the dwarf, pushing past her into the office; "and mind your master has it directly he comes home." So Mr. Quilp climbed up to the top of a tall stool to write the note, and the small servant, carefully tutored for such emergencies, looked on with her eyes wide open, ready, if he so much as abstracted a wafer, to rush into the street and give the alarm to the police.

As Mr. Quilp folded his note (which was soon written: being a very short one) he encountered the gaze of the small servant. He looked at her long and earnestly.

"How are you?" said the dwarf, moistening a wafer with horrible grimaces.

The small servant, perhaps frightened by his looks, returned no audible reply; but it appeared from the motion of her lips that she was inwardly repeating the same form of expression concerning the note or message.

"Do they use you ill here? is your mistress a Tartar?" said Quilp with a chuckle.

In reply to the last interrogation, the small servant, with a look of infinite cunning mingled with fear, screwed up her mouth very tight and round, and nodded violently.

Whether there was anything in the peculiar slyness of her action which fascinated Mr. Quilp, or anything in the expression of her features at the moment which attracted his attention for some other reason; or whether it merely occurred to him as a pleasant whim to stare the small servant out of countenance; certain it is, that he planted his elbows square, and firmly on the desk, and squeezing up his cheeks with his hands, looked at her fixedly.

"Where do you come from?" he said after a long pause, stroking his chin.

"I don't know."

"What's your name?"

"Nothing."

"Nonsense!" retorted Quilp. "What does your mistress call you when she wants you?"

"A little devil," said the child.

She added in the same breath, as if fearful of any further questioning, "But please will you leave a card or message?"

These unusual answers might naturally have provoked some more inquiries. Quilp, however, without uttering another word, withdrew his eyes from the small servant, stroked his chin more thoughtfully than before, and then, bending over the note as if to direct it with scrupulous and hairbreadth nicety, looked at her, covertly but very narrowly, from under his bushy eyebrows. The result of this secret survey was, that he shaded his face with his hands, and laughed slyly and noiselessly, until every vein in it was swollen almost to bursting. Pulling his hat over his brow to conceal his mirth and its effects, he tossed the letter to the child, and hastily withdrew.

Once in the street, moved by some secret impulse, he laughed, and held his sides, and laughed again, and tried to peer through the dusty area railings as if to catch another glimpse of the child, until he was quite tired out. At last, he travelled back to the Wilderness, which was within rifle-shot of his bachelor retreat, and ordered tea in the wooden summer-house that afternoon for three persons; an invitation to Miss Sally Brass and her brother to partake of that entertainment at that place, having been the object both of his journey and his note.

It was not precisely the kind of weather in which people usually take tea in summer-houses, lay less in summer-houses in an advanced state of decay, and overlooking the slimy banks of a great river at low water. Nevertheless, it was in this choice retreat that Mr. Quilp ordered a cold collation to be prepared, and it was beneath its cracked and leaky roof that he in due course of time received Mr. Sampson and his sister Sally.

"You're fond of the beauties of nature," said Quilp with a grin. "Is this charming, Brass? Is it unusual, unsophisticated, primitive?"

"It's delightful indeed, sir," replied the lawyer.

"Cool?" said Quilp.

"N-not particularly so, I think, sir," rejoined Brass, with his teeth chattering in his head.

"Perhaps a little clamp and agueish?" said Quilp.

"Just damp enough to be cheerful, sir," rejoined Brass. "Nothing more, sir, nothing more."

"And Sally?" said the delighted dwarf. "Does she like it?"

"She'll like it better," returned that strong-minded lady, "when she has tea; so let us have it, and don't bother."

"Sweet Sally?" cried Quilp, extending his arms as if about to embrace her. "Gentle, charming, overwhelming Sally."

"He's a very remarkable man indeed!" soliloquised Mr. Brass. "He's quite a Troubadour, you know; quite a Troubadour!"

These complimentary expressions were uttered in a somewhat absent and distracted manner; for the unfortunate lawyer, besides having a bad cold in his head, had got wet in coming, and would have willingly borne some pecuniary sacrifice if he could have shifted his present raw quarters to a warm room, and have dried himself at a fire. Quilp, however ,-who, beyond the gratification of his demon whims, owed Sampson some acknowledgment of the part he had played in the mourning scene of which he had been a hidden witness, marked these symptoms of uneasiness with a delight past all expression, and derived from them a secret joy which the costliest banquet could never have afforded him.

It is worthy of remark, too, as illustrating a little feature in the character of Miss Sally Brass, that, although on her own account she would have borne the discomforts of the Wilderness with a very ill grace, and would probably, in-deed, have walked off before the tea appeared, she no sooner beheld the latent uneasiness and misery of her brother than she developed a grim satisfaction, and began to enjoy herself after her own manner. Though the wet came stealing through the roof and trickling down upon their heads, Miss Brass uttered no complaint, but presided over the tea equipage with imperturbable composure. While Mr. Quilp, in his uproarious hospitality, seated himself upon an empty beer-barrel, vaunted the place as the most beautiful and comfortable in the three kingdoms, and elevating his glass, drank to their next merry-meeting in that jovial spot; and Mr. Brass, with the rain plashing down into his tea-cup, made a dismal attempt to pluck up his spirits and appear at his ease; and Tom Scott, who was in waiting at the door under an old umbrella, exulted in his agonies and bade fair to split his sides with laughing; while all this was passing, Miss Sally Brass, unmindful of the wet which dripped down upon her own feminine person and fair apparel, sat placidly behind the tea-board, erect and grizzly, contemplating the unhappiness of her brother with a mind at ease, and content, in her amiable disregard of self, to sit there all night, witnessing the torments which his avaricious and grovelling nature compelled him to endure and forbade him to resent. And this, it must be observed, or the illustration would be incomplete, although in a business point of view she had the strongest sympathy with Mr. Sampson, and would have been beyond measure indignant if he had thwarted their client in any one respect.

In the height of his boisterous merriment, Mr. Quilp, having on some pretence dismissed his attendant sprite for the moment, resumed his usual manner all at once, dismounted from his cask, and laid his hand upon the lawyer's sleeve.

"A word," said the dwarf, "before we go further. Sally, hark'ee for a minute."

Miss Sally drew closer, as if accustomed to business conferences with their host which were the better for not having air.

"Business," said the dwarf, glancing from brother to sister. "Very private business. Lay your heads together when you're by yourselves."

"Certainly, sir," returned Brass, taking out his pocket book and pencil. "I'll take down the heads if you please, sir. Remarkable documents," added the lawyer, raising his eyes to the ceiling, "most remarkable documents. He states his points so clearly that it's a treat to have 'em! I don't know any Act of Parliament that's equal to him in clearness."

"I shall deprive you of a treat," said Quilp. "Put up your book. We don't want any documents. So. There's a lad named Kit-"

Miss Sally nodded, implying that she knew of him.

"Kit!" said Mr. Sampson.-" Kit! Ha! I've heard the name before, but I don't exactly call to mind-I don't exactly-"

"You're as slow as a tortoise, and more thick-headed than a rhinoceros," returned his obliging client with an impatient gesture.

"He's extremely pleasant!" cried the obsequious Sampson. "His acquaintance with Natural History too is surprising. Quite a Buffoon, quite!"

There is no doubt that Mr. Brass intended some compliment or other; and it has been argued with show of reason that he would have said Buffon, but made use of a superfluous vowel. Be this as it may, Quilp gave him no time for correction, as he performed that office himself by more than tapping him on the head with the handle of his umbrella.

"Don't let's have any wrangling," said Miss Sally, staying his hand. "I've showed you that I know him, and that's enough."

"She's always foremost!" said the dwarf, patting her on the back and looking contemptuously at Sampson. "I don't like Kit, Sally."

"Nor I," rejoined Miss Brass.

"Nor I," said Sampson.

"Why, that's right!" cried Quilp. "Half our work is done already. This Kit is one of your honest people; one of your fair characters; a. prowling prying hound; a hypocrite; a double-faced, white-livered, sneaking spy; a crouching cur to those that feed and coax him, and a barking yelping dog to all besides."

"Fearfully eloquent!" cried Brass with a sneeze. "Quite appalling!"

"Come to the point," said Miss Sally, "and don't talk so much."

"Right again!" exclaimed Quilp, with another contemptuous look at Sampson, "always foremost! I say, Sally, he is a yelping, insolent dog to all besides, and most of all, to me. In short, I owe him a grudge."

"That's enough, sir," said Sampson.

"No, it's not enough, sir," sneered Quilp; "will you hear me out? Besides that I owe him a grudge on that account, he thwarts me at this minute, and stands between me and an end which might otherwise prove a golden one to us all. Apart from that, I repeat that he crosses my humour, and I hate him. Now, you know the lad, and can guess the rest. Devise your own means of putting him out of my way, and execute them. Shall it be done?"

"It shall, sir," said Sampson.

"Then give me your hand," retorted Quilp. "Sally, girl, yours. I rely as much or more, on you than him. Tom Scott comes back. Lantern, pipes, more grog, and a jolly night of it!"

No other word was spoken, no other look exchanged, which had the slightest reference to this, the real occasion of their meeting. The trio were well accustomed to act together, and were linked to each other by ties of mutual interest and advantage, and nothing more was needed. Resuming his boisterous manner with the same ease with which he had thrown it off, Quilp was in an instant the same uproarious, reckless little savage he had been a few seconds before. It was ten o'clock at night before the amiable Sally supported her beloved and loving brother from the Wilderness, by Which time he needed the utmost support her tender frame could render; his walk being for some unknown reason anything but steady, and his legs constantly doubling up in unexpected places.

Overpowered, notwithstanding his late prolonged slumbers, by the fatigues of the last few days, the dwarf lost no time in creeping to his dainty house, and was soon dreaming in his hammock. Leaving him to visions, in which perhaps the quiet figures we quitted in the old church porch were not without their share, be it our task to rejoin them as they sat and watched.

CHAPTER LII

AFTER a long time, the schoolmaster appeared at the wicket-gate of the churchyard, and hurried towards them, jingling in his hand, as he came along, a bundle of rusty keys. He was quite breathless with pleasure and haste when he reached the porch, and at first could only point towards the old building which the child had been contemplating so earnestly.

"You see those two old houses," he said at last.

"Yes surely," replied Nell. "I have been looking at them nearly all the time you have been away."

"And you would have looked at them more curiously, yet, if you could have guessed what I have to tell you," said the friend. "One of those houses is mine."

Without saying any more, or giving the child time to reply, the schoolmaster took her hand, and, his honest face quite radiant with exultation, led her to the place of which he spoke.

They stopped before its low arched door. After trying several of the keys in vain, the schoolmaster found one to fit the huge lock, which turned back, creaking, and admitted them into the house.

The room into which they entered was a vaulted chamber once nobly ornamented by cunning architects, and still retaining, in its beautiful groined roof and rich stone tracery, choice remnants of its ancient splendour. Foliage carved in the stone, and emulating the mastery of Nature's hand, yet remained to tell how many times the leaves outside had come and gone, while it lived on unchanged. The broken figures supporting the burden of the chimney-piece, though mutilated, were still distinguishable for what they had been-far different from the dust without-and showed sadly by the empty hearth, like creatures who had outlived their kind, and mourned their own too slow decay.

In some old time-for even change was old in that old place-a wooden partition had been constructed in one part of the chamber to form a sleeping closet, into which the light was admitted at the same period by a rude window, or rather niche, cut in the solid wall. This screen, together with two seats in the broad chimney, had at some forgotten date been part of the church or convent; for the oak, hastily appropriated to its present purpose, had been little altered from its former shape, and presented to the eye a pile of fragments of rich carving from old monkish stalls.

An open door leading to a small room or cell, dim with the light that came through leaves of ivy, completed the interior of this portion of the ruin. It was not quite destitute of furniture. A few strange chairs, whose arms and legs looked as though they had dwindled away with age: a table, the very spectre of its race: a great old chest that had once held records in the church, with other quaintly-fashioned domestic necessaries, and store of fire-wood for the winter, were scattered around, and gave evident tokens of its occupation as a dwelling-place at no very distant time.

The child looked around her, with that solemn feeling with which we contemplate the work of ages that have become but drops of water in the great ocean of eternity. The old man had followed them, but they were all three hushed for a space, and drew their breath softly, as if they feared to break the silence even by so slight a sound.

"It is a very beautiful place!" said the child, in a low voice.

"I almost feared you thought otherwise," returned the schoolmaster. "You shivered when we first came in, as if you felt it cold or gloomy."

"It was not that," said Nell, glancing round with a slight shudder. "Indeed I cannot tell you what it was, but when I saw the outside, from the church porch, the same feeling came over me. It is its being so old and grey perhaps."

"A peaceful place to live in, don't you think so?" said her friend.

"Oh yes," rejoined the child, clasping her hands earnestly. "A quiet, happy place-a place to live and learn to die in!" She would have said more, but that the energy of her thoughts caused her voice to falter, and come in trembling whispers from her lips.

"A place to live, and learn to live, and gather health of mind and body in," said the schoolmaster; "for this old house is yours."

"Ours!" cried the child.

"Ay," returned the schoolmaster gaily, "for many a merry year to come, I hope. I shall be a close neighbour -only next door-but this house is yours."

Having now disburdened himself of his great surprise, the schoolmaster sat down, and drawing Nell to his side, told her how he had learnt that that ancient tenement had been occupied for a very long time by an old person, nearly a hundred years of age, who kept the keys of the church, opened and closed it for the services, and showed it to strangers; how she had died not many weeks ago, and nobody had yet been found to fill the office; how, learning all this in an interview with the sexton, who was confined to his bed by rheumatism, he had been bold to make mention of his fellow-traveller, which had been so favourably received by that high authority, that he had taken courage, acting on his advice, to propound the matter to the clergyman. In a word, the result of his exertions was, that Nell and her grandfather were to be carried before the last-named gentleman next day; and, his approval of their conduct and appearance reserved as a matter of form, that they were already appointed to the vacant post.

"There's a small allowance of money," said the schoolmaster. "It is not much, but still enough to live upon in this retired spot, By clubbing our funds together, we shall do bravely; no fear of that."

"Heaven bless and prosper you!" sobbed the child.

"Amen, my dear," returned her friend cheerfully; "and all of us, as it will, and has, in leading us through sorrow and trouble to this tranquil life. But we must look at my house now. Come!"

They repaired to the other tenement; tried the rusty keys as before; at length found the right one; and opened the worm-eaten door. It led into a chamber, vaulted and old, like that from which they had come, but not so spacious, and having only one other little room attached. It was not difficult to divine that the other house was of right the schoolmaster's, and that he had chosen for himself the least commodious, in his care and regard for them. Like the adjoining habitation, it held such old articles of furniture as were absolutely necessary, and had its stack of firewood.

To make these dwellings as habitable and full of comfort as they could, was now their pleasant care. In a short time, each had its cheerful fire glowing and crackling on the hearth, and reddening the pale old wall with a hale and healthy blush. Nell, busily plying her needle, repaired the tattered window-hangings, drew together the rents that time had worn in the threadbare scraps of carpet, and made them whole and decent. The schoolmaster swept and smoothed the ground before the door, trimmed the long grass, trained the ivy and creeping plants which hung their drooping heads in melancholy neglect; and gave to the outer walls a cheery air of home. The old man, sometimes by his side and sometimes with the child, lent his aid to both, went here and there on little patient services, and was happy. Neighbours too, as they came from work, proffered their help; or sent their children with such small presents or loans as the strangers needed most. It was a busy day; and night came on, and found them wondering that there was yet so much to do, and that it should be dark so soon.

They took their supper together, in the house which may be henceforth called the child's; and when they had finished their meal drew round the fire, and almost in whispers-their hearts were too quiet and glad for loud expression-discussed their future plans. Before they separated, the schoolmaster read some prayers aloud; and then, full of gratitude and happiness, they parted for the night.

At that silent hour, when her grandfather was sleeping peacefully in his bed, and every sound was hushed, the child lingered before the dying embers, and thought of her past fortunes as if they had been a dream and she only now awoke. The glare of the sinking flame, reflected in the oaken panels whose carved tops were dimly seen in the gloom of the dusky roof-the aged walls, where strange shadows came and went with every flickering of the fire-the solemn presence, within, of that decay which falls on senseless things the most enduring in their nature: and, without, and round about on every side, of Death-filled her with deep and thoughtful feelings, but with none of terror or alarm. A change had been gradually stealing over her, in the time of her loneliness and sorrow. With failing strength and heightening resolution, there had sprung up a purified and altered mind; there had grown in her bosom blessed thoughts and hopes, which are the portion of few but the weak and drooping. There were none to see the frail, perishable figure, as it glided from the fire and leaned pensively at the open casement; none but the stars, to look into the upturned face and read its history. The old church bell rang out the hour with a mournful sound, as if it had grown sad from so much communing with the dead and unheeded warning to the living; the fallen leaves rustled; the grass stirred upon the graves; all else was still and sleeping.

Some of those dreamless sleepers lay close within the shadow of the church-touching the wall, as if they clung to it for comfort and protection. Others had chosen to lie beneath the changing shade of trees; others by the path, that footsteps might come near them; others among the graves of little children. Some had desired to rest beneath the very ground they had trodden in their daily walks; some where the setting sun might shine upon their beds; some where its light would fall upon them when it rose. Perhaps not one of the imprisoned souls had been able quite to separate itself in living thought from its old companion. If any had, it had still felt for it a love like that which captives have been known to bear towards the cell in which they have been long confined, and even at parting hung upon its narrow bounds affectionately.

It was long before the child closed the window, and approached her bed. Again something of the same sensation as before-an involuntary chill-a momentary feeling akin to fear-but vanishing directly, and leaving no alarm behind. Again too, dreams of the little scholar; of the roof opening, and a column of bright faces, rising far away into the sky, as she had seen in some old Scriptural picture once, and looking down on her, asleep. It was a sweet and happy dream. The quiet spot, outside, seemed to remain the same, saving that there was music in the air, and a sound of angels' wings. After a time the sisters came there hand in hand, and stood among the graves. And then the dream grew dim, and faded.

With the brightness and joy of morning, came the renewal of yesterday's labours, the revival of its pleasant thoughts, the restoration of its energies, cheerfulness, and hope. They worked gaily in ordering and arranging their houses until noon, and then went to visit the clergyman.

He was a simple-hearted old gentleman, of a shrinking, subdued spirit, accustomed to retirement, and very little acquainted with the world, which he had left many years before to come and settle in that place. His wife had died in the house in which he still lived, and he had long since lost sight of any earthly cares or hopes beyond it.

He received them very kindly, and at once showed an interest in Nell; asking her name, and age, her birthplace, the circumstances which had led her there, and so forth. The schoolmaster had already told her story. They had no other friends or home to leave, he said, and had come to share his fortunes. He loved the child as though she were his own.

"Well, well," said the clergyman. "Let it be as you desire. She is very young."

"Old in adversity and trial, sir," replied the schoolmaster.

"God help me! Let her rest, and forget them," said the old gentleman. "But an old church is a dull and gloomy place for one so young as you, my child."

"Oh no, sir," returned Nell. "I have no such thoughts, indeed."

"I would rather see her dancing on the green at nights," said the old gentleman, laying his hand upon her head, and smiling sadly, "than have her sitting in the shadow of our mouldering arches. You must look to this, and see that her heart does not grow heavy among these solemn ruins. Your request is granted, friend."

After more kind words, they withdrew, and repaired to the child's house; where they were yet in conversation on their happy fortune, when another friend appeared.

This was a little old gentleman, who lived in the parsonage-house, and had resided there (so they learnt soon after wards) ever since the death of the clergyman's wife, which had happened fifteen years before. He had been his college friend and always his close companion; in the first shock of his grief had come to console and comfort him; and from that time they had never parted company. The little old gentleman was the active spirit of the place; the adjuster of all differences, the promoter of all merry-makings, the dispenser of his friend's bounty, and of no small charity of his own besides; the universal mediator, comforter, and friend. None of the simple villagers had cared to ask his name, or, when they knew it, to store in in their memory.

Perhaps from some vague rumour of his college honours which had been whispered abroad on his first arrival, perhaps because he was an unmarried, unencumbered gentleman, he had been called the Bachelor. The name pleased him, or suited him as well as any other, and the Bachelor he had ever since remained. And the bachelor it was, it may be added, who with his own hands had laid in the stock of fuel which the wanderers had found in their new habitation.

The bachelor, then-to call him by his usual appellation -lifted the latch, showed his little round mild face for a moment at the door, and stepped into the room like one who was no stranger to it.

"You are Mr. Marton, the new schoolmaster?" he said, greeting Nell's kind friend.

"I am, sir."

"You come well recommended, and I am glad to see you. I should have been in the way yesterday, expecting you, but I rode across the country to carry a message from a sick mother to her daughter in service some miles off, and have but just now returned. This is our young church-keeper? You are not the less welcome, friend, for her sake, or for this old man's; nor the worst teacher for having learnt humanity."

"She has been ill, sir, very lately," said the schoolmaster, in answer to the look with which their visitor regarded Nell when he had kissed her cheek.

"Yes, yes. I know she has," he rejoined. "There have been suffering and heartache here."

"Indeed there have, sir."

The little old gentleman glanced at the grandfather, and back again at the child, whose hand he took tenderly in his, and held.

"You will be happier here," he said; "we will try, at least, to make you so. You have made great improvements here already. Are they the work of your hands?"

"Yes, sir."

"We may make some others-not better in themselves, but with better means perhaps," said the bachelor. "Let us see now, let us see."

Nell accompanied him into the other little rooms, and over both the houses, in which he found various small comforts wanting, which he engaged to supply from a certain collection of odds and ends he had at home, and which must have been a very miscellaneous and extensive one, as it comprehended the most opposite articles imaginable. They all came, however, and came without loss of time; for the little old gentleman, disappearing for some five or ten minutes, presently returned, laden with old shelves, rugs, blankets, and other household gear, and followed by a boy bearing a similar load. These being cast on the floor in a promiscuous heap, yielded a quantity of occupation in arranging, erecting, and putting away; the superintendence of which task evidently afforded the old gentleman extreme delight, and engaged him for some time with great briskness and activity. When nothing more was left to be done, he charged the boy to run off and bring his school-mates to be marshalled before their new master, and solemnly reviewed.

THE OLD CURIOSITY SHOP

"As good a set of fellows, Marton, as you'd wish to see," he said, turning to the schoolmaster when the boy was gone; "but I don't let 'em know I think so. That wouldn't do, at all."

The messenger soon returned at the head of a long row of urchins, great and small, who, being confronted by the bachelor at the house door, fell into various convulsions of politeness; clutching their hats and caps, squeezing them into the smallest possible dimensions, and making all manner of bows and scrapes, which the little old gentleman contemplated with excessive satisfaction, and expressed his approval of by a great many nods and smiles. Indeed, his approbation of the boys was by no means so scrupulously disguised as he had led the schoolmaster to suppose, inasmuch as it broke out in sundry loud whispers and confidential remarks which were perfectly audible to them every one.

"This first boy, schoolmaster," said the bachelor, "is John Owen, a lad of good parts, sir, and frank, honest temper; but too thoughtless, too playful, too light-headed by far. That boy, my good sir, would break his neck with pleasure, and deprive his parents of their chief comfort- and between ourselves, when you come to see him at hare and hounds, taking the fence and ditch by the finger-post, and sliding down the face of the little quarry, you'll never forget it. It's beautiful!"

John Owen having been thus rebuked', and being in perfect possession of the speech aside, the bachelor singled out another boy.

"Now, look at that lad, sir," said the bachelor. "You see that fellow? Richard Evans his name is, sir. An amazing boy to learn, blessed with a good memory, and a ready understanding, and moreover with a good voice and ear for psalm-singing, in which he is the best among us. Yet, sir, that boy will come to a bad end; he'll never die in his bed; he's always falling asleep in church in sermon- time-and to tell you the truth, Mr. Marton, I always did the same at his age, and feel quite certain that it was natural to my constitution and I couldn't help it."

This hopeful pupil edified by the above terrible reproval, the bachelor turned to another.

"But if we talk of examples to be shunned," said he, "if we come to boys that should be a warning and a beacon to all their fellows, here's the one, and I hope you won't spare him. This is the lad, sir; this one with the blue eyes and light hair. This is a swimmer, sir, this fellow-a diver, Lord save us! This is a boy, sir, who had a fancy for plunging into eighteen feet of water, with his clothes on, and bringing up a blind man's dog, who was being drowned by the weight of his chain and collar, while his master stood wringing his hands upon the bank, bewailing the loss of his guide and friend. I sent the boy two guineas anonymously, sir," added the bachelor, in his peculiar whisper, "directly I heard of it; but never mention it on any account, for he hasn't the least idea that it came from me."

Having disposed of this culprit, the bachelor turned to another, and from him to another, and so on through the whole array, laying, for their wholesome restriction within due bounds, the same cutting emphasis on such of their propensities as were dearest to his heart and were unquestionably referable to his own precept and example. Thoroughly persuaded, in the end, that he had made them miserable by his severity, he dismissed them with a small present, and an admonition to walk quietly home, without any leapings, scufflings, or turnings out of the way; which injunction (he informed the schoolmaster in the same audible confidence) he did not think he could have obeyed when he was a boy, had his life depended on it.

Hailing these little tokens of the bachelor's disposition as so many assurances of his own welcome course from that time, the schoolmaster parted from him with a light heart and joyous spirits, and deemed himself one of the happiest men on earth. The windows of the two old houses were ruddy again that night with the reflection of the cheerful fires that burnt within; and the bachelor and his friend, pausing to look upon them as they returned from their evening walk, spoke softly together of the beautiful child, and looked round upon the churchyard with a sigh.

CHAPTER LIII

NELL was stirring early in the morning; and having discharged her household tasks, and put everything in order for the good schoolmaster (though sorely against his will, for he would have spared her the pains), took down, from its nail by the fireside, a little bundle of keys with which the bachelor had formally invested her on the previous day, and went out alone to visit the old church.

The sky was serene and bright, the air clear, perfumed with the fresh scent of newly-fallen leaves, and grateful to every sense. The neighbouring stream sparkled, and rolled onward with a tuneful sound; the dew glistened on the green mounds, like tears shed by Good Spirits over the dead.

Some young children sported among the tombs, and hid from each other, with laughing faces. They had an infant with them, and had laid it down asleep upon a child's grave, in a little bed of leaves. It was a new grave-the resting-place, perhaps, of some little creature, who, meek and patient in its illness, had often sat and watched them; and now seemed to their minds scarcely changed.

She drew near and asked one of them whose grave it was. The child answered that that was not its name; it was a garden-his brother's. It was greener, he said, than all the other gardens, and the birds loved it better because he had been used to feed them. When he had done speaking, he looked at her with a smile, and kneeling down and nestling for a moment with his cheek against the turf, bounded merrily away.

She passed the church, gazing upward at its old tower, went through the wicket-gate, and so into the village. The old sexton, leaning on a crutch, was taking the air at his cottage door, and gave her good morrow.

"You are better?" said the child, stopping to speak with him.

"Ay surely," returned the old man. "I'm thankful to say, much better."

"You will be quite well soon."

"With Heaven's leave, and a little patience. But come in, come in."

The old man limped on before, and warning her of the downward step, which he achieved himself with no small difficulty, led the way into his little cottage.

"It is but one room you see. There is another up above, but the stair has got harder to climb o' late years, and I never use it. I'm thinking of taking to it again next summer though."

The child wondered how a grey-headed man like him- one of his trade too-could talk of time so easily. He saw her eyes wandering to the tools that hung upon the wall, and smiled.

"I warrant now," he said, "that you think all those are used in making graves."

"Indeed, I wondered that you wanted so many."

"And well you might. I am a gardener. I dig the ground, and plant things that are to live and grow. My works don't all moulder away and rot in the earth. You see that spade in the centre?"

"The very old one-so notched and worn? Yes."

"That's the sexton's spade, and it's a well-used one, as you see. We're healthy people here, but it has done a power of work. If it could speak now, that spade, it would tell you of many an unexpected job that it and I have done together; but I forget 'em, for my memory's a poor one. That's nothing new," he added hastily. "It always was."

"There are flowers and shrubs to speak to your other work," said the child.

"Oh yes. And tall trees. But they are not so separated from the sexton's labours as you think."

"No!"

"Not in my mind, and recollection-such as it is," said the old man. "Indeed they often help it. For say that I planted such a tree for such a man. There it stands to remind me that he died. When I look at its broad shadow, and remember what it was in his time, it helps me to the age of my other work, and I can tell you pretty nearly when I made his grave."

"But it may remind you of one who is still alive," said the child.

"Of twenty that are dead, in connexion with that one who lives, then," rejoined the old man; "wife, husband, parents, brothers, sisters, children, friends-a score at least. So it happens that the sexton's spade gets worn and battered. I shall need a new one-next summer."

The child looked quickly towards him, thinking that he jested with his age and infirmity; but the unconscious sexton was quite in earnest.

"Ah!" he said, after a brief silence. "People never learn. They never learn. It's only we who turn up the ground, where nothing grows and everything decays, who think of such things as these-who think of them properly, I mean. You have been into the church?"

"I am going there now," the child replied.

"There's an old well there," said the sexton, "right underneath the belfry; a deep, dark, echoing well. Forty year ago, you had only to let down the bucket till the first knot in the rope was free of the windlass, and you heard it splashing in the cold dull water. By little and little the water fell away, so that in ten year after that, a second knot was made, and you must unwind so much rope, or the bucket swung tight and empty at the end. In ten years' time, the water fell again, and a third knot was made. In ten years more the well dried up; and now, if you lower the bucket till your arms are tired and let out nearly all the cord, you'll hear it of a sudden clanking and rattling on the ground below, with a sound of being so deep and so far down, that your heart leaps into your mouth, and you start away as if you were falling in."

"A dreadful place to come on in the dark!" exclaimed the child, who had followed the old man's looks and words until she seemed to stand upon its brink.

"What is it but a grave!" said the sexton. "What else! And which of our old folks, knowing all this, thought, as the spring subsided, of their own failing strength, and lessening life? Not one!"

"Are you very old yourself?" asked the child, involuntarily.

"I shall be seventy-nine-next summer."

"You still work when you are well?"

"Work! To be sure. You shall see my gardens here about. Look at the window there. I made, and have kept, that plot of ground entirely with my own hands. By this time next year I shall hardly see the sky, the boughs will have grown so thick. I have my winter work at night besides."

He opened, as he spoke, a cupboard close to where he sat, and produced some miniature boxes, carved in a homely manner and made of old wood.

"Some gentlefolks who are fond of ancient days, and what belongs to them," he said, "like to buy these keep sakes from our church and ruins. Sometimes, I make them of scraps of oak, that turn up here and there; sometimes of bits of coffins which the vaults have long preserved. See here-this is a little chest of the last kind, clasped at the edges with fragments of brass plates that had writing on 'em once, though it would be hard to read it now. I haven't many by me at this time of year, but these shelves will be full-next summer."

The child admired and praised his work, and shortly afterwards departed; thinking as she went, how strange it was, that this old man, drawing from his pursuits, and everything around him, one stern moral, never contemplated its application to himself; and, while he dwelt upon the uncertainty of human life, seemed both in word and deed to deem himself immortal. But her musings did not stop here, for she was wise enough to think that by a good and merciful adjustment this must be human nature, and that the old sexton, with his plans for next summer, was but a type of all mankind.

Full of these meditations, she reached the church. It was easy to find the key belonging to the outer door, for each was labelled on a scrap of yellow parchment. Its very turning in the lock awoke a hollow sound, and when she entered with a faltering step, the echoes that it raised in closing made her start.

Everything in our lives, whether of good or evil, affects us most by contrast. If the peace of the simple village had moved the child more strongly, because of the dark and troubled ways that lay beyond and through which she had journeyed with such failing feet, what was the deep impression of finding herself alone in that solemn building; where the very light, coming through sunken windows, seemed old and grey, and the air, redolent of earth and mould, seemed laden with decay, purified by time of all its grosser particles, and sighing through arch and aisle, and clustered pillars, like the breath of ages gone! Here was the broken pavement, worn so long ago by pious feet, that Time, stealing on the pilgrims' steps, had trodden out their track, and left but crumbling stones. Here were the rotten beam, the sinking arch, the sapped and mouldering wall, the lowly trench of earth, the stately tomb on which no epitaph remained,-all,-marble, stone, iron, wood, and dust, one common monument of ruin. The best work and the worst, the plainest and the richest, the stateliest and the least imposing-both of Heaven's work and Man's-all found one common level here, and told one common tale.

Some part of the edifice had been a baronial chapel, and here were effigies of warriors stretched upon their beds of stone with folded hands, cross-legged-those who had fought in the Holy Wars-girded with their swords, and cased in armour as they had lived. Some of these knights had their own weapons, helmets, coats of mail, hanging upon the walls hard by, and dangling from rusty hooks. Broken and dilapidated as they were, they yet retained their ancient form, and something of their ancient aspect. Thus violent deeds live after men upon the earth, and traces of war and bloodshed will survive in mournful shapes, long after those who worked the desolation are but atoms of earth themselves.

The child sat down in this old, silent place, among the stark figures on the tombs-they made it more quiet there, than elsewhere, to her fancy-and gazing round with a feeling of awe, tempered with a calm delight, felt that now she was happy, and at rest. She took a Bible from the shelf, and read; then, laying it down, thought of the summer days and the bright spring-time that would come-of the rays of sun that would fall in aslant upon the sleeping forms-of the leaves that would flutter at the window, and play in glistening shadows on the pavement-of the songs of birds, and growth of buds and blossoms out of doors-of the sweet air, that would steal in and gently wave the tattered banners overhead. What if the spot awakened thoughts of death! Die who would, it would still remain the same; these sights and sounds would still go on as happily as ever. It would be no pain to sleep amidst them.

She left the chapel-very slowly and often turning back to gaze again-and coming to a low door, which plainly led into the tower, opened it, and climbed the winding stair in darkness; save where she looked down through narrow loopholes on the place she had left, or caught a glimmering vision of the dusty bells. At length she gained the end of the ascent and stood upon the turret top.

Oh! the glory of the sudden burst of light; the freshness of the fields and woods, stretching away on every side and meeting the bright blue sky;

the cattle grazing in the pasturage; the smoke, that, coming from among the trees, seemed to rise upward from the green earth; the children yet at their gambols down below-all, everything, so beautiful and happy! It was like passing from death to life; it was drawing nearer Heaven.

The children were gone by the time she emerged into the porch, and locked the door. As she passed the school-house she could hear the busy hum of voices. Her friend had begun his labours only that day. The noise grew louder, and, looking back, she saw the boys come trooping out and disperse themselves with merry shouts and play. "It's a good thing," thought the child, "I am very glad they pass the church." And then she stopped, to fancy how the noise would sound inside, and how gently it would seem to die away upon the ear.

Again that day, yes, twice again, she stole back to the old chapel, and in her former seat read from the same book, for indulged the same quiet train of thought. Even when it had grown dusk, and the shadows of coming night made it more solemn still, the child remained like one rooted to the spot, and had no fear, or thought of stirring.

They found her there at last, and took her home. She looked pale but very happy, until they separated for the night; and then, as the poor schoolmaster stooped down to kiss her cheek, he thought he felt a tear upon his face.

CHAPTER LIV

THE bachelor, among his various occupations, found in the old church a constant source of interest and amusement. Taking that pride in it which men conceive for the wonders of their own little world, he bad made its history his study; and many a summer day within its walls, and many a winter's night beside the parsonage fire, had found the bachelor still poring over and adding to his goodly store of tale and legend.

As he was not one of those rough spirits who would strip fair Truth of every little shadowy vestment to which time and teeming fancies love to array her-and some of which become her pleasantly enough, serving, like the waters of her well, to add new graces to the charms they half conceal and half suggest, and to awaken interest and pursuit rather than languor and indifference-as, unlike this stern and obdurate class, he loved to see the goddess crowned with those garlands of wild flowers which tradition wreathes for her gentle wearing, and which are often freshest in their homeliest shapes,-he trod with a light step and bore with a light hand upon the dust of centuries, unwilling to demolish any of the airy shrines that had been raised above it, if one good feeling or affection of the human heart were hiding therabouts. Thus, in the case of an ancient coffin of rough stone, supposed for many generations to contain the bones of a certain baron, who, after ravaging, with cut, and thrust, and plunder, in foreign lands, came back with a penitent and sorrowing heart to die at home, but which had been lately shown by learned antiquaries to be no such thing, as the baron in question (so they contended) had died hard in battle, gnashing his teeth and cursing with his latest breath,-the bachelor stoutly maintained that the old tale was the true one; that the baron, repenting him of the evil, had done great charities and meekly given up the ghost; and that, if ever baron went to heaven, that baron was then at peace. In like manner, when the aforesaid antiquaries did argue and contend that a certain secret vault was not the tomb of a grey-haired lady who had been hanged and drawn and quartered by glorious Queen Bess for succouring a wretched priest who fainted of thirst and hunger at her door, the bachelor did solemnly maintain against all comers that the church was hallowed by the said poor lady's ashes; that her remains had been collected in the night from four of the city's gates, and thither in secret brought, and there deposited; and the bachelor did further (being highly excited at such times) deny the glory of Queen Bess, and assert the immeasurably greater glory of the meanest woman in her realm who had a merciful and tender heart. As to the assertion that the flat stone near the door was not the grave of the miser who had disowned his only child and left a sum of money to the church to buy a peal of bells, the bachelor did readily admit the same, and that the place had given birth to no such man. In a word, he would have had every stone, and plate of brass, the monument only of deeds whose memory should survive. All others he was willing to forget. They might be buried in consecrated ground, but he would have had them buried deep, and never brought to light again.

It was from the lips of such a tutor, that the child learnt her easy task. Already impressed, beyond all telling, by the silent building and the peaceful beauty of the spot in which it stood-majestic age surrounded by perpetual youth-it seemed to her, when she heard these things, sacred to all goodness and virtue. It was another world, where sin and sorrow never came; a tranquil place of rest, where nothing evil entered.

When the bachelor had given her in connexion with almost every tomb and flat grave-stone some history of its own, he took her down into the old crypt, now a mere dull vault, and showed her how it had been lighted up in the time of the monks, and how, amid lamps depending from the roof, and swinging censers exhaling scented odours, and habits glittering with gold and silver, and pictures, and precious stuffs, and jewels all flashing and glistening through the low arches, the chant of aged voices had been many a time heard there at midnight in old days, while hooded figures knelt and prayed around, and told their rosaries of beads. Thence, he took her above ground again, and showed her, high up in the old walls, small galleries, where the nuns had been wont to glide along- dimly seen in their dark dresses so far off-or to pause like gloomy shadows, listening to the prayers. He showed her too, how the warriors, whose figures rested on the tombs, had worn those rotting scraps of armour up above -how this had been a helmet, and that a shield, and that a gauntlet-and how they had wielded the great two-handed swords, and beaten men down with yonder iron mace. All that he told the child she treasured in her mind; and sometimes, when she woke at night from dreams of those old times, and rising from her bed looked out at the dark church, she almost hoped to see the windows lighted up, and hear the organ's swell, and sound of voices, on the rushing wind.

The old sexton soon got better, and was about again. From him the child learnt many other things, though of a different kind. He was not able to work, but one day there was a grave to be made, and he came to overlook the man who dug it. He was in a talkative mood; and the child, at first standing by his side, and afterwards sitting on the grass at his feet, with her thoughtful face raised towards his, began to converse with him.

Now the man who did the sexton's duty was a little older than he, though much more active. But he was deaf; and when the sexton (who peradventure, on a pinch, might have walked a mile with great difficulty in half a dozen hours) exchanged a remark with him about his work, the child could not help noticing that he did so with an impatient kind of pity for his infirmity, as if he were himself the strongest and heartiest man alive.

"I'm sorry to see there is this to do," said the child, when she approached. "I heard of no one having died."

"She lived in another hamlet, my dear," returned the sexton. "Three mile away."

"Was she young?"

"Ye-yes," said the sexton; "not more than sixty-four, I think. David, was she more than sixty-four?"

David, who was digging hard, heard nothing of the question. The sexton, as he could not reach to touch him with his crutch, and was too infirm to rise without assistance, called his attention by throwing a little mould upon his red night-cap.

"What's the matter now?" said David, looking up.

"How old was Becky Morgan?" asked the sexton.

"Becky Morgan?" repeated David.

"Yes," replied the sexton; adding in a half compassionate, half irritable tone, which the old man couldn't hear, "you're getting very deaf, Davy, very deaf to be sure!"

The old man stopped in his work, and cleansing his spade with a piece of slate he had by him for the purpose-and scraping off, in the process, the essence of Heaven knows how many Becky Morgans-set himself to consider the subject.

"Let me think," quoth he. "I saw last night what they had put upon the coffin-was it seventy-nine?"

"No, no," said the sexton.

"Ah yes, it was though," returned the old man with a sigh. "For I remember thinking she was very near our age. Yes, it was seventy-nine."

"Are you sure you didn't mistake a figure, Davy?" asked the sexton, with signs of some emotion.

"What?" said the old man. "Say that again."

"He's very deaf. He's very deaf indeed," cried the sexton petulantly; "are you sure you're right about the figures?"

"Oh quite," replied the old man. "Why not?"

"He's exceedingly deaf," muttered the sexton to himself. "I think he's getting foolish."

The child rather wondered what had led him to this belief, as to say the truth the old man seemed quite as sharp as he, and was infinitely more robust. As the sexton said nothing more just then, however, she forgot it for the time, and spoke again.

"You were telling me," she said, "about your gardening. Do you ever plant things here?"

"In the churchyard?" returned the sexton. "Not I."

"I have seen some flowers and little shrubs about," the child rejoined; "there are some over there, you see. I thought they were of your rearing, though indeed they grow but poorly."

"They grow as Heaven wills," said the old man; "and it kindly ordains that they shall never flourish here."

"I do not understand you."

"Why, this it is," said the sexton. "They mark the graves of those who had very tender, loving friends."

"I was sure they did!" the child exclaimed. "I am very glad to know they do!"

"Ay," returned the old man, "but stay. Look at them. See how they hang their heads, and droop, and wither. Do you guess the reason?"

"No," the child replied.

"Because the memory of those who lie below, passes away so soon. At first they tend them, morning, noon, and night; they soon begin to come less frequently; from once a day, to once a week; from once a week to once a month; then, at long and uncertain intervals; then, not at all. Such tokens seldom flourish long. I have known the briefest summer flowers outlive them."

"I grieve to hear it," said the child.

"Ah! so say the gentlefolks who come down here to look about them," returned the old man, shaking his head, "but I say otherwise. 'It's a pretty custom you have in this part of the country,' they say to me sometimes, 'to plant the graves, but it's melancholy to see these things all withering or dead.' I crave their pardon and tell them that, as I take it, 'tis a good sign for the happiness of the living. And so it is. It's nature."

"Perhaps the mourners learn to look to the blue sky by day, and to the stars by night, and to think that the dead are there, and not in graves," said the child in an earnest voice.

"Perhaps so," replied the old man doubtfully. "It may be."

"Whether it be as I believe it is, or no," thought the child within herself, "I'll make this place my garden. It will be no harm at least to work here day by day, and pleasant thoughts will come of it, I am sure."

Her glowing cheek and moistened eye passed unnoticed by the sexton, who turned towards old David, and called him by his name. It was plain that Becky Morgan's age still troubled him; though why, the child could scarcely understand.

The second or third repetition of his name attracted the old man's attention. Pausing from his work, he leant upon his spade, and put his hand to his dull ear.

"Did you call?" he said.

"I have been thinking, Davy," replied the sexton, "that she," he pointed to the grave, "must have been a deal older than you or me."

"Seventy-nine," answered the old man with a sorrowful shake of the head, "I tell you that I saw it."

"Saw it?" replied the sexton; "ay, but, Davy, women don't always tell the truth about their age."

"That's true indeed," said the other old man, with a sudden sparkle in his eye. "She might have been older."

"I'm sure she must have been. Why, only think how old she looked. You and I seemed but boys to her."

"She did look old," rejoined David. "You're right. She did look old."

"Call to mind how old she looked for many a long, long year, and say if she could be but seventy-nine at last-only our age," said the sexton.

"Five year older at the very least!" cried the other.

"Five!" retorted the sexton. "Ten. Good eighty-nine. I call to mind the time her daughter died. She was eighty-nine if she was a day, and tries to pass upon us now, for ten year younger. Oh! human vanity!"

The other old man was not behindhand with some moral reflections on this fruitful theme, and both adduced a mass of evidence, of such weight as to render it doubtful-not whether the deceased was of the age suggested, but whether she had not almost reached the patriarchal term of a hundred. When they had settled this question to their mutual satisfaction, the sexton, with his friend's assistance, rose to go.

"It's chilly, sitting here, and I must be careful-till the summer," he said, as he prepared to limp away.

"What?" asked old David.

"He's very deaf, poor fellow!" cried the sexton. "Good-bye."

"Ah!" said old David, looking after him. "He's failing very fast. He ages every day."

And so they parted: each persuaded that the other had less life in him than himself; and both greatly consoled and comforted by the little fiction they had agreed upon, respecting Becky Morgan, whose decease was no longer a precedent of uncomfortable application, and would be no business of theirs for half a score of years to come.

The child remained for some minutes, watching the deaf old man as he threw out the earth with his shovel, and, often stopping to cough and fetch his breath, still muttered to himself, with a kind of sober chuckle, that the sexton was wearing fast. At length she turned away, and walking thoughtfully through the churchyard, came unexpectedly upon the schoolmaster, who was sitting on a green grave in the sun, reading.

"Nell here?" he said cheerfully, as he closed his book. "It does me good to see you in the air and light. I feared you were again in the church, where you so often are."

"Feared!" replied the child, sitting down beside him. "Is it not a good place?"

"Yes, yes," said the schoolmaster. "But you must be gay sometimes-nay, don't shake your head and smile so very sadly."

"Not sadly, if you knew my heart. Do not look at me as if you thought me sorrowful. There is not a happier creature on the earth than I am now."

Full of grateful tenderness, the child took his hand, and folded it between her own. "It's God's will!" she said, when they had been silent for some time.

"What?"

"All this," she rejoined; "all this about us. But which of us is sad now? You see that I am smiling."

"And so am I," said the schoolmaster; "smiling to think how often we shall laugh in this same place. Were you not talking yonder?"

"Yes," the child rejoined.

"Of something that has made you sorrowful?"

There was a long pause.

"What was it?" said the schoolmaster, tenderly. "Come. Tell me what it was."

"I rather grieve-I do rather grieve to think," said the child, bursting into tears, "that those who die about us, are so soon forgotten."

"And do you think," said the schoolmaster, marking the glance she had thrown around, "that an unvisited grave, a withered tree, a faded flower or two, are tokens of forgetfulness or cold neglect? Do you think there are no deeds far away from here, in which these dead may be best remembered? Nell, Nell, there may be people busy in the world at this instant, in whose good actions and good thoughts these very graves-neglected as they look to us- are the chief instruments."

"Tell me no more," said the child quickly. "Tell me no more. I feel, I know it. How could I be unmindful of it, when I thought of you?"

"There is nothing," cried her friend, "no, nothing innocent or good, that dies, and is forgotten. Let us hold to that faith, or none. An infant, a prattling child, dying in its cradle, will live again in the better thoughts of those who loved it, and play its part, through them, in the redeeming actions of the world, though its body be burnt to ashes or drowned in the deepest sea. There is not an angel added to the Host of Heaven but does its blessed work on earth in those that loved it here. Forgotten! oh, if the good deeds of human creatures could be traced to their source, how beautifully would even death appear; for how much charity, mercy, and purified affection, would be seen to have their growth in dusty graves!"

"Yes," said the child, "it is the truth; I know it is. Who should feel its force so much as I, in whom your little scholar lives again! Dear, dear, good friend, if you knew the comfort you have given me!"

The poor schoolmaster made her no answer, but bent over her in silence; for his heart was full.

They were yet seated in the same place, when the grandfather approached. Before they had spoken many words together, the church clock struck the hour of school, and their friend withdrew.

"A good man," said the grandfather, looking after him; "a kind man. Surely he will never harm us, Nell. We are safe here, at last-eh? We will never go away from here."

The child shook her head and smiled.

"She needs rest," said the old man, patting her cheek; "too pale-too pale. She is not like what she was."

"When?" asked the child.

"Ha!" said the old man, "to be sure-when? How many weeks ago? Could I count them on my fingers? Let them rest though; they're better gone."

"Much better, dear," replied the child. "We will forget them; or, if we ever call them to mind, it shall be only as some uneasy dream that has passed away."

"Hush!" said the old man, motioning hastily to her with his hand and looking over his shoulder; "no more talk of the dream, and all the miseries it brought. There are no dreams here. 'Tis a quiet place, and they keep away. Let us never think about them, lest they should pursue us again. Sunken eyes and hollow cheeks-wet, cold, and famine-and horrors before them all, that were even worse-we must forget such things if we would be tranquil here."

"Thank Heaven!" inwardly exclaimed the child, "for this most happy change!"

"I will be patient," said the old man, "humble, very thankful and obedient, if you will let me stay. But do not hide from me; do not steal away alone; let me keep beside you. Indeed, I will be very true and faithful, Nell."

"I steal away alone! why that," replied the child, with assumed gaiety, "would be a pleasant jest indeed. See here, dear grandfather, we'll make this place our garden- why not? It is a very good one-and to-morrow we'll begin, and work together, side by side."

"It is a brave thought!" cried her grandfather. "Mind darling-we begin to-morrow!"

Who so delighted as the old man, hen they next day began their labour! Who so unconscious of all associations connected with the spot, as he! They plucked the long grass and nettles from the tombs, thinned the poor shrubs and roots, made the turf smooth, and cleared it of the leaves and weeds. They were yet in the ardour of their work, hen the child, raising her head from the ground over which she bent, observed that the bachelor was sitting on the stile close by, watching them in silence.

"A kind office," said the little gentleman, nodding to Nell as she curtseyed to him. "Have you done all that, this morning?"

"It is very little, sir," returned the child, with down- cast eyes, "to what we mean to do."

"Good work, good work," said the bachelor. "But do you only labour at the graves of children, and young people?"

"We shall come to the others in good time, sir," replied Nell, turning her head aside, and speaking softly.

It was a slight incident, and might have been design or accident, or the child's unconscious sympathy with youth. But it seemed to strike upon her grandfather, though he had not noticed it before. He looked in a hurried manner at the graves, then anxiously at the child, then pressed her to his side, and bade her stop to rest. Something he had long forgotten appeared to struggle faintly in his mind. It did not pass away, as weightier things had done; but came uppermost again, and yet again, and many times that day, and often afterwards. Once, while they were yet at work, the child, seeing that he often turned and looked uneasily at her, as though he were trying to resolve some painful doubts or collect some scattered thoughts, urged him to tell the reason. But he said it was nothing-nothing -and, laying her head upon his arm, patted her fair check with his hand, and muttered that she grew stronger every day, and would be a woman, soon.

CHAPTER LV

FROM that time, there sprang up in the old man's mind, a solicitude about the child which never slept or left him. There are chords in the human heart-strange, varying strings-which are only struck by accident; which will remain mute and senseless to appeals the most passionate and earnest, and respond at last to the slightest casual touch. In the most insensible or childish minds, there is some train of reflection which art can seldom lead, or skill assist, but which will reveal itself, as great truths have done, by chance, and when the discoverer has the plainest and simplest end in View. From that time, the old man never for a moment forgot the weakness and devotion of the child: from the time of that slight incident, he, who had seen her toiling by his side through so much difficulty and suffering, and had scarcely thought of her otherwise than as the partner of miseries which he felt severely in his own person, and deplored for his own sake at least as much as hers, awoke to a sense of what he owed her, and what those miseries had made her. Never, no, never once, in one unguarded moment from that time to the end, did any care for himself, any thought of his own comfort, any selfish consideration or regard distract his thoughts from the gentle object of his love.

He would follow her up and down, waiting till she should tire and lean upon his arm-he would sit opposite to her in the chimney-corner, content to watch, and look, until she raised her head and smiled upon him as of old- he would discharge, by stealth, those household duties which tasked her powers too heavily-he would rise, in the cold dark nights, to listen to her breathing in her sleep, and sometimes crouch for hours by her bedside only to touch her hand. He Who knows all, can only know what hopes, and fears, and thoughts of deep affection, were in that one disordered brain, and what a change had fallen on the poor old man.

Sometimes-weeks had crept on, then-the child, exhausted, though with little fatigue, would pass whole evenings on a couch beside the fire. At such times, the schoolmaster would bring in books, and read to her aloud; and seldom an evening passed, but the bachelor came in, and took his turn of reading. The old man sat and listened, - with little understanding for the words, but with his eyes fixed upon the child,-and if she smiled or brightened with the story, he would say it was a good one, and conceive a fondness for the very book. When, in their evening talk, the bachelor told some tale that pleased her (as his tales were sure to do), the old man would painfully try to store it in his mind: nay, when the bachelor left them, he would sometimes slip out after him, and humbly beg that he would tell him such a part again, that he might learn to win a smile from Nell.

But these were rare occasions, happily; for the child yearned to be out of doors, and walking in her solemn garden. Parties, too, would come to see the church; and those who came, speaking to others of the child, sent more; so that even at that season of the year they had visitors almost daily. The old man would follow them at a little distance through the building, listening to the voice he loved so well; and when the strangers left, and parted from Nell, he would mingle with them to catch up fragments of their conversation; or he would stand for the same purpose, with his grey head uncovered, at the gate, as they passed through. They always praised the child, her sense and beauty, and he was proud to hear them! But what was that, so often added, which wrung his heart, and made him sob and weep alone, in some dull corner! Alas! even careless strangers-they who had no feeling for her, but the interest of the moment-they who would go away and forget next week that such a being lived-even they saw it-even they pitied her-even they bade him good day compassionately, and whispered as they passed.

The people of the village, too, of whom there was not one but grew to have a fondness for pool Nell; even among them, there was the same feeling; a tenderness towards her-a compassionate regard for her, increasing every day. The very schoolboys, light-hearted and thoughtless as they were, even they cared for her. The roughest among them was sorry if he missed her in the usual place upon his way to school, and would turn out of the path to ask for her at the latticed window. If she were sitting in the church, they perhaps might peep in softly at the open door; but they never spoke to her, unless she rose and went to speak to them. Some feeling was abroad which raised the child above them all.

So, when Sunday came. They were all poor country people in the church, for the castle in which the old family had lived, was an empty ruin, and there were none but humble folks for seven miles around. There, as elsewhere, they had an interest in Nell. They would gather round her in the porch, before and after service; young children would cluster at her skirts; and aged men and women for sake their gossips, to give her kindly greeting. None of them, young or old, thought of passing the child without a friendly word. Many who came from three or four miles distant, brought her little presents; the humblest and rudest had good wishes to bestow.

She had sought out the young children whom she first saw playing in the churchyard. One of these-he who had spoken of his brother-was her little favourite and friend, and often sat by her side in the church, or climbed with her to the tower-top. It was his delight to help her, or to fancy that he did so, and they soon became close companions.

It happened, that, as she was reading in the old spot by herself one day, this child came running in with his eyes full of tears, and after holding her from him and looking at her eagerly for a moment, clasped his little arms passionately about her neck.

"What now?" said Nell, soothing him. "What is the matter?"

"She is not one yet!" cried the boy, embracing her still more closely. "No, no. Not yet!"

She looked at him wonderingly, and putting his hair back from his face, and kissing him, asked what he meant.

"You must not be one, dear Nell," cried the boy. "We can't see them. They never come to play with us, or talk to us. Be what you are. You are better so."

"I do not understand you," said the child. "Tell me what you mean."

"Why, they say," replied the boy, looking up into her face, "that you will be an angel, before the birds sing again. But you won't be, will you? Don't leave us, Nell, though the sky is bright. Do not leave us!"

The child drooped her head, and put her hands before her face.

"She cannot bear the thought!" cried the boy, exulting through his tears. "you will not go. You know how sorry we should be. Dear Nell, tell me that you'll stay amongst us. Oh! Pray, pray, tell me that you will."

The little creature folded his hands, and knelt down at her feet.

"Only look at me, Nell," said the boy, "and tell me that you'll stop, and then I shall know that they are wrong, and will cry no more. Won't you say yes, Nell?"

Still the drooping head and hidden face, and the child quite silent-save for her sobs.

"After a time," pursued the boy, trying to draw away her hand, "the kind angels will be glad to think that you are not among them, and that you stayed here to be with us. Willy went away, to join them; but if he had known how I should miss him in our little bed at night, he never would have left me, I am sure."

Yet the child could make him no answer, and sobbed as though her heart were bursting.

"Why would you go, dear Nell? I know you would not be happy when you heard that we were crying for your loss. They say that Willy is in Heaven now, and that it's always summer there, and yet I'm sure he grieves when I lie down upon his garden bed, and he cannot turn to kiss me. But if you do go, Nell," said the boy, caressing her, and pressing his face to hers, "be fond of him, for my sake. Tell him how I love him still, and how much I loved you; and when I think that you two are together, and are happy, I'll try to bear it, and never give you pain by doing wrong -indeed I never will!"

The child suffered him to move her hands, and put them round his neck. There was a tearful silence, but it was not long before she looked upon him with a smile, and promised him, in a very gentle, quiet voice, that she would stay, and be his friend, as long as Heaven would let her. He clapped his hands for joy, and thanked her many times; and being charged to tell no person what had passed between them, gave her an earnest promise that he never would.

Nor did he, so far as the child could learn; but was her quiet companion in all her walks and musings, and never again adverted to the theme, which he felt had given her pain, although he was unconscious of its cause. Something of distrust lingered about him still; for he would often come, even in the dark evenings, and call in a timid voice outside the door to know if she were safe within; and being answered yes, and bidden to enter, would take his station on a low stool at her feet, and sit there patiently until they came to seek, and take him home. Sure as the morning came, it found him lingering near the house to ask if she were well; and, morning, noon, or night, go where she would, he would forsake his playmates and his sports to bear her company.

"And a good little friend he is, too," said the old sexton, to her once. "When his elder brother died-elder seems a strange word, for he was only seven year old-I remember this one took it sorely to heart."

The child thought of what the schoolmaster had told her and felt how its truth was shadowed out even in this infant.

"It has given him something of a quiet way, I think" said the old man, "though for that he is merry enough at times. I'd wager now that you and he have been listening by the old well."

"Indeed we have not," the child replied. "I have been afraid to go near it; for I am not often down in that part of the church, and do not know the ground."

"Come down with me," said the old man. "I have known it from a boy. Come!"

They descended the narrow steps which led into the crypt, and paused among the gloomy arches, in a dim and murky spot.

"This is the place," said the old man. "Give me your hand while you throw back the cover, lest you should stumble and fall in. I am too old-I mean rheumatic-to stoop, myself."

"A black and dreadful place!" exclaimed the child.

"Look, in," said the old man, pointing downward with his finger.

The child complied, and gazed down into the pit.

"It looks like a grave itself," said the old man.

"It does," replied the child.

"I have often had the fancy," said the sexton, "that it might have been dug at first to make the old place more gloomy, and the old monks more religious. It's to be closed up, and built over."

The child still stood, looking thoughtfully into the vault. "We shall see," said the sexton, "on what gay heads other earth will have closed, when the light is shut out from here. God knows! They'll close it up, next spring."

"The birds sing again in spring," thought the child, as she leant at her casement window, and gazed at the declining sun. "Spring! a beautiful and happy time!"

CHAPTER LVI

A DAY or two after the Quilp tea-party at the Wilderness. Mr. Swiveller walked into Sampson Brass's office at the usual hour, and being alone in that Temple of Probity, placed his hat upon the desk, and taking from his pocket a small parcel of black crape, applied himself to folding and pinning the same upon it, after the manner of a hat-band. Having completed the construction of this append- age, he surveyed his work with great complacency, and put his hat on again-very much over one eye, to increase the mournfulness of the effect. These arrangements perfected to his entire satisfaction, he thrust his hands into his pockets, and walked up and down the office with measured steps.

"It has always been the same with me," said Mr. Swiveller, "always. 'Twas ever thus-from childhood's hour I've seen my fondest hopes decay, I never loved a tree or flower but 'twas the first to fade away. I never nursed a dear Gazelle, to glad me with its soft black eye, but when it came to know me well, and love me, it was sure to marry a market-gardener."

Overpowered by these reflections, Mr. Swiveller stopped short at the clients' chair, and flung himself into its open arms.

"And this," said Mr. Swiveller, with a kind of bantering composure, "is life, I believe. Oh, certainly. Why not! I'm quite satisfied. I shall wear," added Richard, taking off his hat again and looking hard at it, as if he were only deterred by pecuniary considerations from spurning it with his foot, "I shall wear this emblem of woman's perfidy, in remembrance of her with whom I shall never again thread the windings of the mazy; whom I shall never more pledge in the rosy; who, during the short remainder of my existence, will murder the balmy. Ha, ha, ha!"

It may be necessary to observe, lest there should appear any incongruity in the close of this soliloquy, that Mr. Swiveller did not wind up with a cheerful hilarious laugh, which would have been undoubtedly at variance with his solemn reflections, but that, being in a theatrical mood, he merely achieved that performance which is designated in melodramas" laughing like a fiend,"-for it seems that your fiends always laugh in syllables, and always in three syllables, never more or less, which is a remarkable property in such gentry, and one worthy of remembrance.

The baleful sounds had hardly died away, and Mr. Swiveller was still sitting in a very grim state in the clients' chair, when there came a ring-or, if we may adapt the sound to his then humour, a knell-at the office bell. Opening the door with all speed, he beheld the expressive countenance of Mr. Chuckster, between whom and himself a fraternal greeting ensued.

"You're devilish early at this pestiferous old slaughter house," said that gentleman, poising himself on one leg, and shaking the other in an easy manner.

"Rather," returned Dick.

"Rather!" retorted Mr. Chuckster, with that air of graceful trifling which so well became him. "I should think so. Why, my good feller, do you know what o'clock it is-half-past nine a.m. in the morning?"

"Won't you come in?" said Dick. "All alone. Swiveller solus. 'Tis now the witching-'"

"'Hour of night!'"

"'When churchyards yawn,'"

"'And graves give up their dead.'"

At the end of this quotation in dialogue, each gentleman struck an attitude, and immediately subsiding into prose walked into the office. Such morsels of enthusiasm were common among the Glorious Apollos, and were indeed the links that bound them together, and raised them above the cold dull earth.

"Well, and how are you, my buck?" said Mr. Chuckster, taking a stool. "I was forced to come into the City upon some little private matters of my own, and couldn't pass the corner of the street without looking in, but upon my soul I didn't expect to find you. It is so everlastingly early."

Mr. Swiveller expressed his acknowledgments; and it appearing on further conversation that he was in good health, and that Mr. Chuckster was in the like enviable condition, both gentlemen, in compliance with a solemn custom of the ancient Brotherhood to which they belonged, joined in a fragment of the popular duet of "All's Well," with a long shake at the end.

"And what's the news?" said Richard.

"The town's as flat, my dear feller," replied Mr. Chuckster, "as the surface of a Dutch oven. There's no news. By the bye, that lodger of yours is a most extraordinary person. He quite eludes the most vigorous comprehension, you know. Never was such a feller!"

"What has he been doing now?" said Dick.

"By Jove, sir," returned Mr. Chuckster, taking out an oblong snuffbox, the lid whereof was ornamented with a fox's head curiously carved in brass, "that man is an unfathomable. Sir, that man has made friends with our articled clerk. There's no harm in him, but he is so amazingly slow and soft. Now, if he wanted a friend, why couldn't he have one that knew a thing or two, and could do him some good by his manners and conversation. I have my faults, sir," said Mr. Chuckster.-

"No, no," interposed Mr. Swiveller.

"Oh yes I have, I have my faults, no man knows his faults better than I know mine. But," said Mr. Chuckster, "I'm not meek. My worst enemies-every man has his enemies, sir, and I have mine-never accused me of being meek. And I tell you what, sir, if I hadn't more of these qualities that commonly endear man to man, than our articled clerk has, I'd steal a Cheshire cheese, tie it round my neck, and drown myself. I'd die degraded, as I had lived. I would upon my honour."

Mr. Chuckster paused, rapped the fox's head exactly on the nose with the knuckle of the forefinger, took a pinch of snuff, and looked steadily at Mr. Swiveller, as much as to say that if he thought he was going to sneeze, he would find himself mistaken.

"Not contented, sir," said Mr. Chuckster, "with making friends with Abel, he has cultivated the acquaintance of his father and mother. Since he came home from that wild-goose chase, he has been there-actually been there. He patronises young Snobby besides; you'll find, sir, that he'll be constantly coming backwards and forwards to this place: yet I don't suppose that beyond the common forms of civility, he has ever exchanged half a dozen words with me. Now, upon my soul, you know," said Mr. Chuckster, shaking his head gravely, as men are wont to do when they consider things are going a little too far, "this is altogether such a low-minded affair, that if I didn't feel for the governor, and know that he could never get on without me, I should be obliged to cut the connexion. I should have no alternative."

Mr. Swiveller, who sat on another stool opposite to his friend, stirred the fire in an excess of sympathy, but said nothing.

"As to young Snob, sir," pursued Mr. Chuckster with a prophetic look, "you'll find he'll turn out bad. In our profession we know something of human nature, and take my word for it, that the feller that came back to work out that shilling, will show himself one of these days in his true colours. He's a low thief, sir. He must be."

Mr. Chuckster being roused, would probably have pursued this subject further, and in more emphatic language, but for a tap at the door, which seeming to announce the arrival of somebody on business, caused him to assume a greater appearance of meekness than was perhaps quite consistent with his late declaration. Mr. Swiveller, hearing the same sound, caused his stool to revolve rapidly on one leg until it brought him to his desk, into which, having forgotten in the sudden flurry of his spirits to part with the poker, he thrust it as he cried "Come in!"

Who should present himself but that very Kit who had been the theme of Mr. Chuckster's wrath! Never did man pluck up his courage so quickly, or look so fierce, as Mr. Chuckster when he found it was he. Mr. Swiveller stared at him for a moment, and then leaping from his stool, and drawing out the poker from its place of concealment, performed the broad-sword exercise with all the cuts and guards complete, in a species of frenzy.

"Is the gentleman at borne?" said Kit, rather astonished by this uncommon reception.

Before Mr. Swiveller could make any reply, Mr. Chuckster took occasion to enter his indignant protest against this form of inquiry; which he held to be of a disrespectful and snobbish tendency, inasmuch as the inquirer, seeing two gentlemen then and there present, should have spoken of the other gentleman; or rather (for it was not impossible that the object of his search might be of inferior quality) should have mentioned his name, leaving it to his hearers to determine his degree as they thought proper. Mr. Chuckster further remarked, that he had some reason to believe this form of address was personal to himself, and that he was not a man to be trifled with, as certain snobs (whom he did not more particularly mention or describe) might find, to their cost.

"I mean the gentleman up stairs," said Kit, turning to Richard Swiveller. "Is he at home?"

"Why?" rejoined Dick.

"Because if he is, I have a letter for him."

"From whom?" said Dick.

"From Mr. Garland."

"Oh!" said Dick, with extreme politeness. "Then you may hand it over, sir. And if you're to wait for an answer, sir, you may wait in the passage, sir, which is an airy and well-ventilated apartment, sir."

"Thank you," returned Kit. "But I am to give it to himself, if you please."

The excessive audacity of this retort so overpowered Mr. Chuckster, and so moved his tender regard for his friend's honour, that he declared, if he were not restrained by official considerations, he must certainly have annihilated Kit upon the spot; a resentment of the affront which he did consider, under the extraordinary circumstances of aggravation attending it, could but have met with the proper sanction and approval of a jury of Englishmen, who, he had no doubt, would have returned a verdict of Justifiable Homicide, coupled with a high testimony to the morals and character of the Avenger. Mr. Swiveller, without being quite so hot upon the matter, was rather shamed by his friend's excitement, and not a little puzzled how to act (Kit being quite cool and good-humoured), when the single gentleman was heard to call violently down the stairs.

"Didn't I see somebody for me, come in?" cried the lodger.

"Yes, sir," replied Dick. "Certainly, sir."

"Then where is he!" roared the single gentleman.

"He's here, sir," rejoined Mr. Swiveller. "Now young man, don't you hear you're to go up stairs? Are you deaf?"

Kit did not appear to think it worth his while to enter into any further altercation, but hurried off and left the Glorious Apollos gazing at each other in silence.

"Didn't I tell you so?" said Mr. Chuckster. "What do you think of that?"

Mr. Swiveller being in the main a good-natured fellow, and not perceiving in the conduct of Kit any villany of enormous magnitude, scarcely knew what answer to return. He was relieved from his perplexity, however, by the entrance of Mr. Sampson and his sister, Sally, at sight of whom Mr. Chuckster precipitately retired.

Mr. Brass and his lovely companion appeared to have been holding a consultation over their temperate breakfast, upon some matter of great interest and importance. On the occasion of such conferences, they generally appeared in the office some half an hour after their usual time, and in a very smiling state, as though their late plots and designs had tranquillised their minds and shed a light upon their toilsome way. In the present instance, they seemed particularly gay; Miss Sally's aspect being of a most oily kind, and Mr. Brass rubbing his hands in an exceedingly jocose and light-hearted manner.

"Well, Mr. Richard," said Brass. "How are we this morning? Are we pretty fresh and cheerful, sir-eh, Mr. Richard?"

"Pretty well, sir," replied Dick.

"That's well," said Brass. "Ha ha! We should be gay as larks, Mr. Richard-why not? It's a pleasant world we live in, sir, a very pleasant world.

There are bad people in it, Mr. Richard, but if there were no bad people, there would be no good lawyers. Ha ha! Any letters by the post this morning, Mr. Richard?"

Mr. Swiveller answered in the negative.

"Ha!" said Brass, "no matter. If there's little business to-day, there'll be more to-morrow. A contented spirit, Mr. Richard, is the sweetness of existence. Anybody been here, sir?"

"Only my friend" -replied Dick. " 'May we ne'er want a-' "

" 'Friend,' " Brass chimed in quickly, " 'or a bottle to give him.' Ha ha! That's the way the song runs, isn't it? A very good song, Mr. Richard, very good. I like the sentiment of it. Ha ha! Your friend's the young man from Witherden's office, I think -yes- 'May we ne'er want a-.' Nobody else at all, been, Mr. Richard?"

"Only somebody to the lodger," replied Mr. Swiveller.

"Oh indeed!" cried Brass. "Somebody to the lodger, eh? Ha ha! 'May we ne'er want a friend, or a-' "Somebody to the lodger, eh Mr. Richard?"

"Yes," said Dick, a little disconcerted by the excessive buoyancy of spirits which his employer displayed. "With him now."

"With him now!" cried Brass; "Ha ha! There let 'em be, merry and free, toor rul lol le, Eh, Mr. Richard? Ha ha!"

"Oh certainly," replied Dick.

"And who," said Brass, shuffling among his papers, "who is the lodger's visitor -not a lady visitor, I hope, eh Mr. Richard? The morals of the Marks you know, sir -'when lovely woman stoops to folly'-and all that -eh, Mr. Richard?"

"Another young man, who belongs to Witherden's too, or half belongs there," returned Richard. "Kit, they call him."

"Kit, eh!" said Brass, "Strange name-name of a dancing-master's fiddle, eh, Mr, Richard? Ha ha! Kit's there, is he? Oh!"

Dick looked at Miss Sally, wondering that she didn't check this uncommon exuberance on the part of Mr. Sampson; but as she made no attempt to do so, and rather appeared to exhibit a tacit acquiescence in it, he concluded that they had just been cheating somebody, and receiving the bill.

"Will you have the goodness, Mr. Richard," said Brass, taking a letter from his desk, "just to step over to Peckham Rye with that? There's no answer, but it's rather particular and should go by hand. Charge the office with your coach-hire back, you know; don't spare the office; get as much out of it as you can-clerk's motto-Eh, Mr. Richard? Ha ha!"

Mr. Swiveller solemnly doffed the aquatic jacket, put on his coat, took down his hat from its peg, pocketed the letter, and departed. Directly he was gone, up rose Miss Sally Brass, and smiling sweetly at her brother (who nodded and smote his nose in return) withdrew also.

Sampson Brass was no sooner left alone, than he set the office-door wide open, and establishing himself at his desk directly opposite, so that he could not fail to see anybody who came down stairs and passed out at the street-door, began to write with extreme cheerfulness and assiduity; humming as he did so, in a voice that was anything but musical, certain vocal snatches which appeared to have reference to the union between Church and State, inasmuch as they were compounded of the Evening Hymn and God save the King.

Thus, the attorney of Bevis Marks sat, and wrote, and hummed, for a long time, except when he stopped to listen with a very cunning face, and hearing nothing, went on humming louder, and writing slower than ever. At length, in one of these pauses, he heard his lodger's door opened and shut, and footsteps coming down the stairs. Then Mr. Brass left off writing entirely, and with his pen in his hand hummed his very loudest; shaking his head meanwhile from side to side like a man whose whole soul was in the music, and smiling in a manner quite seraphic.

It was towards this moving spectacle that the staircase and the sweet sounds guided Kit, on whose arrival before his door, Mr. Brass stopped his singing, but not his smiling, and nodded affably, at the same time beckoning to him with his pen.

"Kit," said Mr. Brass, in the pleasantest way imaginable, "how do you do?"

Kit, being rather shy of his friend, made a suitable reply, and had his hand upon the lock of the street-door when Mr. Brass called him softly back.

"You are not to go, if you please, Kit," said the attorney in a mysterious and yet business-like way. "You are to step in here, if you please. Dear me, dear me! When I look at you," said the lawyer, quitting his stool, and standing before the fire with his back towards it, "I am reminded of the sweetest little face that ever my eyes beheld. I remember your coming there twice or thrice when we were in possession. Ah Kit, my dear fellow, gentlemen in my profession have such painful duties to perform sometimes, that you needn't envy us-you needn't indeed."

"I don't, sir," said Kit, "though it isn't for the like of me to judge."

"Our only consolation, Kit," pursued the lawyer, looking at him in a sort of pensive abstraction, "is, that although we cannot turn away the wind, we can soften it; we can temper it, if I may say so, to the shorn lambs."

"Shorn indeed!" thought Kit. "Pretty close!" But he didn't say so.

"On that occasion, Kit," said Mr. Brass, "on that occasion that I have just alluded to, I had a hard battle with Mr. Quilp (for Mr. Quilp is a very hard man) to obtain them the indulgence they had. It might have cost me a client. But suffering virtue inspired me, and I prevailed."

"He's not so bad after all," thought honest Kit, as the attorney pursed up his lips and looked like a man who was struggling with his better feelings.

"I respect you, Kit," said Brass with emotion. "I saw enough of your conduct at that time to respect you, though your station is humble, and your fortune lowly. It isn't the waistcoat that I look at. It is the heart. The checks in the waistcoat are but the wires of the cage. But the heart is the bird. Ah! How many sich birds are perpetually moulting, and putting their beaks through the wires to peck at all mankind!"

This poetic figure, which Kit took to be in special allusion to his own checked waistcoat, quite overcame him; Mr. Brass's voice and manner added not a little to its effect, for he discoursed with all the mild austerity of a hermit, and wanted but a cord round the waist of his rusty surtout, and a skull on the chimney-piece, to be completely set up in that line of business.

"Well, well," said Sampson, smiling as good men smile when they compassionate their own weakness or that of their fellow-creatures, "this is wide of the bull's-eye. You're to take that, if you please." As he spoke, he pointed to a couple of half-crowns upon the desk.

Kit looked at the coins, and then at Sampson, and hesitated.

"For yourself," said Brass.

"From-"

"No matter about the person they came from," replied the lawyer. "Say me, if you like. We have eccentric friends overhead, Kit, and we mustn't ask questions or talk too much-you understand. You're to take them, that's all; and between you and me, I don't think they'll be the last you'll have to take from the same place. I hope not. Good-bye, Kit. Good-bye!"

With many thanks, and many more self-reproaches for having on such slight grounds suspected one who in their very first conversation turned out such a different man from what he had supposed, Kit took the money and made the best of his way home. Mr. Brass remained airing himself at the tire, and resumed his vocal exercise, and his seraphic smile, simultaneously.

"May I come in?" said Miss Sally, peeping.

"Oh yes, you may come in," returned her brother.

"Ahem?" coughed Miss Brass interrogatively.

"Yes," returned Sampson, "I should say as good as done."

CHAPTER LVII

MR. Chuckster's indignant apprehensions were not without foundation. Certainly the friendship between the single gentleman and Mr. Garland was not suffered to cool, but had a rapid growth and flourished exceedingly. They were soon in habits of constant intercourse and communication; and the single gentleman labouring at this time under a slight attack of illness -the consequence most probably of his late excited feelings and subsequent disappointment- furnished a reason for their holding yet more frequent correspondence; so that some one of the inmates of Abel Cottage, Finchley, came backwards and forwards between that place and Bevis Marks, almost every day.

As the pony had now thrown off all disguise, and without any mincing of the matter or beating about the bush, sturdily refused to be driven by anybody but Kit, it generally happened that whether old Mr. Garland came, or Mr. Abel, Kit was of the party. Of all messages and inquiries, Kit was in right of his position the bearer; thus it came about that, while the single gentleman remained indisposed, Kit turned into Bevis Marks every morning with near-ly as much regularity as the General Postman.

Mr. Sampson Brass, who no doubt had his reasons for looking sharply about him, soon learnt to distinguish the pony's trot and the clatter of the lit-tle chaise at the corner of the street. Whenever this sound reached his ears, he would immediately lay down his pen and fall to rubbing his hands and ex-hibiting the greatest glee.

"Ha ha!" he would cry. "Here's the pony again. Most remarkable pony, extremely docile, eh Mr. Richard, eh sir?"

Dick would return some matter-of-course reply, and Mr. Brass, stand-ing on the bottom rail of his stool, so as to get a view of the street over the top of the window-blind, would take an observation of the visitors.

"The old gentleman again!" he would exclaim, "a very prepossessing old gentleman, Mr. Richard- charming countenance, sir -extremely calm-benevolence in every feature, sir. He quite realises my idea of King Lear, as he appeared when in possession of his kingdom, Mr. Richard- the same good humour, the same white hair and partial baldness, the same liability to be im-posed upon. Ah! A sweet subject for contemplation, sir, very sweet!"

Then, Mr. Garland having alighted and gone up stairs, Sampson would nod and smile to Kit from the window, and presently walk out into the street to greet him, when some such conversation as the following would ensue.

"Admirably groomed, Kit" -Mr. Brass is patting the pony- "does you great credit- amazingly sleek and bright to be sure He literally looks as if he had been varnished all over."

Kit touches his hat, smiles, pats the pony himself, and expresses his conviction, "that Mr. Brass will not find many like him."

"A beautiful animal indeed!" cries Brass. "Sagacious too!"

"Bless you!" replies Kit, "he knows what you say to him as well as a Christian does."

"Does he indeed!" cries Brass, who has heard the same thing in the same place from the same person in the same words a dozen times, but is paralysed with astonishment notwithstanding. "Dear me!"

"I little thought the first time I saw him, sir," says Kit, pleased with the attorney's strong interest in his favourite, "that I should come to be as in-timate with him as I am now."

"Ah!" rejoins Mr. Brass, brim-full of moral precepts and love of virtue. "A charming subject of reflection for you, very charming. A subject of prop-er pride and congratulation, Christopher. Honesty is the best policy. -I al-ways find it so myself. I lost forty-seven pound ten by being honest this morning. But it's all gain, it's gain!"

Mr. Brass slyly tickles his nose with his pen, and looks at Kit with the water standing in his eyes. Kit thinks that if ever there was a good man who belied his appearance, that man is Sampson Brass.

"A man," says Sampson, "who loses forty-seven pound ten in one morning by his honesty, is a man to be envied. If it had been eighty pound, the luxuriousness of feeling would have been increased. Every pound lost, would have been a hundredweight of happiness gained. The still, small voice,

Christopher," cries Brass smiling, and tapping himself on the bosom, "is a singing comic songs within me, and all is happiness and joy!"

Kit is so improved by the conversation, and finds it go so completely home to his feelings, that he is considering what he shall say, when Mr. Garland appears. The old gentleman is helped into the chaise with great obsequiousness by Mr. Sampson Brass; and the pony, after shaking his head several times, and standing for three or four minutes with all his four legs planted firmly on the ground as if he had made up his mind never to stir from that spot, but there to live and die, suddenly darts off without the smallest notice, at the rate of twelve English miles an hour. Then Mr. Brass and his sister (who has joined him at the door) exchange an odd kind of smile-not at all a pleasant one in its expression- and return to the society of Mr. Richard Swiveller, who during their absence has been regaling himself with various feats of pantomime, and is discovered at his desk, in a very flushed and heated condition, violently scratching out nothing with half a penknife.

Whenever Kit came alone, and without the chaise, it always happened that Sampson Brass was reminded of some mission, calling Mr. Swiveller, if not to Peckham Rye again, at all events to some pretty distant place from which he could not be expected to return for two or three hours, or in all probability a much longer period, as that gentleman was not, to say the truth, renowned for using great expedition on such occasions, but rather for protracting and spinning out the time to the very utmost limit of possibility. Mr. Swiveller out of sight, Miss Sally immediately withdrew. Mr. Brass would then set the office- door wide open, hum his old tune with great gaiety of heart, and smile seraphically as before. Kit coming down stairs would be called in; entertained with some moral and agreeable conversation; perhaps entreated to mind the office for an instant while Mr. Brass stepped over the way; and afterwards presented with one or two halfcrowns as the case might be. This occurred so often, that Kit, nothing doubting but that they came from the single gentleman, who had already rewarded his mother with great liberality, could not enough admire his generosity; and bought so many cheap presents for her, and for little Jacob, and for the baby, and for Barbara to boot, that one or other of them was having some new trifle every day of their lives.

While these acts and deeds were in progress in and out of the office of Sampson Brass, Richard Swiveller, being often left alone therein, began to find the time hang heavy on his hands. For the better preservation of his cheerfulness therefore, and to prevent his faculties from rusting, he provided himself with a cribbage-board and pack of cards, and accustomed himself to play at cribbage with a dummy, for twenty, thirty, or sometimes even fifty thousand pounds a side, besides many hazardous bets to a considerable amount.

As these games were very silently conducted, notwithstanding the magnitude of the interests involved, Mr. Swiveller began to think that on those evenings when Mr. and Miss Brass were out (and they often went out now) he heard a kind of snorting or hard-breathing sound in the direction of the door, which it occurred to him, after some reflection, must proceed from the small servant, who always had a cold from damp living. Looking intently that way one night, he plainly distinguished an eye gleaming and glistening at the key-hole; and having now no doubt that his suspicions were correct, he stole softly to the door, and pounced upon her before she was aware of his approach.

"Oh! I didn't mean any harm indeed. Upon my word I didn't," cried the small servant, struggling like a much larger one. "It's so very dull, down stairs. Please don't you tell upon me; please don't."

"Tell upon you!" said Dick. "Do you mean to say you were looking through the key-hole for company?"

"Yes, upon my word I was," replied the small servant.

"How long have you been cooling your eye there?" said Dick.

"Oh ever since you first began to play them cards, and long before."

Vague recollections of several fantastic exercises with which he had refreshed himself after the fatigues of business, and to all of which, no doubt, the small servant was a party, rather disconcerted Mr. Swiveller; but he was not very sensitive on such points, and recovered himself speedily.

"Well, - come in" -he said, after a little consideration. "Here-sit down, and I'll teach you how to play."

"Oh! I durstn't do it," rejoined the small servant; "Miss Sally'ud kill me, if she know'd I came up here."

"Have you got a tire down stairs?" said Dick.

"A very little one," replied the small servant.

"Miss Sally couldn't kill me if she know'd I went down there, so I'll come," said Richard, putting the cards into his pocket. "Why, how thin you are! What do you mean by it?"

"It an't my fault."

"Could you eat any bread and meat?" said Dick, taking down his hat. "Yes? Ah! I thought so. Did you ever taste beer?"

"I had a sip of it once," said the small servant.

"Here's a state of things!" cried Mr. Swiveller, raising his eyes to the ceiling. "She *never* tasted it -it can't be tasted in a sip! Why, how old are you?"

"I don't know."

Mr. Swiveller opened his eyes very wide, and appeared thoughtful for a moment; then, bidding the child mind the door until he came back, vanished straightway.

Presently he returned, followed by the boy from the public-house, who bore in one hand a plate of bread and beef, and in the other a great pot, filled with some very fragrant compound, which sent forth a grateful steam, and was indeed choice purl, made after a particular recipe which Mr. Swiveller had imparted to the landlord at a period when he was deep in his books and desirous to conciliate his friendship. Relieving the boy of his burden at the door, and charging his little companion to fasten it to prevent surprise, Mr. Swiveller followed her into the kitchen.

"There!" said Richard, putting the plate before her. "First of all, clear that off, and then you'll see what's next."

The small servant needed no second bidding, and the plate was soon empty.

"Next," said Dick, handing the purl, "take a pull at that; but moderate your transports, you know, for you're not used to it. Well, is it good?"

"Oh! isn't it?" said the small servant.

Mr. Swiveller appeared gratified beyond all expression by this reply, and took a long draught himself, steadfastly regarding his companion while he did so. These preliminaries disposed of, he applied himself to teaching her the game, which she soon learnt tolerably well, being both sharp-witted and cunning.

"Now," said Mr. Swiveller, putting two sixpences into a saucer, and trimming the wretched candle, when the cards had been cut and dealt, "those are the stakes. If you win, you get 'em all. If I win, I get 'em. To make it seem more real and pleasant, I shall call you the Marchioness, do you hear?"

The small servant nodded.

"Then, Marchioness," said Mr. Swiveller, "fire away!" The Marchioness, holding her cards very tight in both hands, considered which to play, and Mr. Swiveller, assuming the gay and fashionable air which such society required, took another pull at the tankard, and waited for her lead.

CHAPTER LVIII

MR. Swiveller and his partner played several rubbers with varying success, until the loss of three sixpences, the gradual sinking of the purl, and the striking of ten o'clock, combined to render that gentleman mindful of the flight of Time, and the expediency of withdrawing before Mr. Sampson and Miss Sally Brass returned.

"With which object in view, Marchioness," said Mr. Swiveller gravely, "I shall ask your ladyship's permission to put the board in my pocket, and to retire from the presence when I have finished this tankard; merely observing, Marchioness, that since life like a river is flowing, I care not how fast it rolls on, ma'am, on, while such purl on the bank still is growing, and such eyes light the waves as they run. Marchioness, your health. You will excuse my wearing my hat, but the palace is damp, and the marble floor is -if I may be allowed the expression- sloppy."

As a precaution against this latter inconvenience, Mr. Swiveller had been sitting for some time with his feet on the hob, in which attitude he now gave utterance to these apologetic observations, and slowly sipped the last choice drops of nectar.

"The Baron Sampsono Brasso and his fair sister are (you tell me) at the Play?" said Mr. Swiveller, leaning his left arm heavily upon the table, and raising his voice and his right leg after the manner of a theatrical bandit.

The Marchioness nodded.

"Ha!" said Mr. Swiveller, with a portentous frown. "Tis well. Marchioness! - but no matter. Some wine there. Ho!" He illustrated these melodramatic morsels by handing the tankard to himself with great humility, receiving it haughtily, drinking from it thirstily, and smacking his lips fiercely.

The small servant, who was not so well acquainted with theatrical conventionalities as Mr. Swiveller (having indeed never seen a play, or heard one spoken of, except by chance through chinks of doors and in other forbidden places), was rather alarmed by demonstrations so novel in their nature, and showed her concern so plainly in her looks, that Mr. Swiveller felt it necessary to discharge his brigand manner for one more suitable to private life, as he asked,

"Do they often go where glory waits 'em, and leave you here?"

"Oh, yes; I believe you they do," returned the small servant. "Miss Sally's such a one-er for that, she is."

"Such a what?" said Dick.

"Such a one-er," returned the Marchioness.

After a moment's reflection, Mr. Swiveller determined to forego his responsible duty of setting her right, and to suffer her to talk on; as it was evident that her tongue was loosened by the purl, and her opportunities for conversation were not so frequent as to render a momentary check of little consequence.

"They sometimes go to see Mr. Quilp," said the small servant with a shrewd look; "they go to a many places, bless you."

"Is Mr. Brass a wunner?" said Dick.

"Not half what Miss Sally is, he isn't," replied the small servant, shaking her head. "Bless you, he'd never do anything without her."

"Oh! He wouldn't, wouldn't he?" said Dick.

"Miss Sally keeps him in such order," said the small servant; "he always asks her advice, he does; and he catches it sometimes. Bless you, you wouldn't believe how much he catches it."

"I suppose," said Dick, "that they consult together a good deal, and talk about a great many people -about me for instance, sometimes, eh, Marchioness?"

The Marchioness nodded amazingly.

"Complimentary?" said Mr. Swiveller.

The Marchioness changed the motion of her head, which had not yet left off nodding, and suddenly began to shake it from side to side with a vehemence which threatened to dislocate her neck.

"Humph!" Dick muttered. "Would it be any breach of confidence, Marchioness, to relate what they say of the humble individual who has now the honour to -?"

"Miss Sally says you're a funny chap," replied his friend.

"Well, Marchioness," said Mr. Swiveller, "that's not uncomplimentary. Merriment, Marchioness, is not a bad or degrading quality. Old King Cole was himself a merry old soul, if we may put any faith in the pages of history."

"But she says," pursued his companion, "that you an't to be trusted."

"Why, really, Marchioness," said Mr. Swiveller, thoughtfully; "several ladies and gentlemen -not exactly professional persons, but tradespeople, ma'am, tradespeople -have made the same remark. The obscure citizen who keeps the hotel over the way, inclined strongly to that opinion to-night when I ordered him to prepare the banquet. It's a popular prejudice, Marchioness; and yet I am sure I don't know why, for I have been trusted in my time to a considerable amount, and I can safely say that I never forsook my trust until it deserted me –never. Mr. Brass is of the same opinion, I suppose?"

His friend nodded again, with a cunning look which seemed to hint that Mr. Brass held stronger opinions on the subject than his sister; and seeming to recollect herself, added imploringly, "But don't you ever tell upon me, or I shall be beat to death."

"Marchioness," said Mr. Swiveller, rising, "the word of a gentleman is as good as his bond -sometimes better; as in the present case, where his bond might prove but a doubtful sort of security. I am your friend, and I hope we shall play many more rubbers together in this same saloon. But, Marchioness," added Richard, stopping in his way to the door, and wheeling slowly round upon the small servant, who was following with the candle; "it occurs to me that you must be in the constant habit of airing your eye at key-holes, to know all this."

"I only wanted," replied the trembling Marchioness, "to know where the key of the safe was hid; that was all; and I wouldn't have taken much, if I had found it- only enough to squench my hunger."

"You didn't find it then?" said Dick. "But of course you didn't or you'd be plumper. Good night, Marchioness. Fare thee well, and if for ever, then for ever fare thee well -and put up the chain, Marchioness, in case of accidents."

With this parting injunction, Mr. Swiveller emerged from the house; and feeling that he had by this time taken quite as much to drink as promised to be good for his constitution (purl being a rather strong and heady compound), wisely resolved to betake himself to his lodgings, and to bed at once. Homeward he went therefore; and his apartments (for he still retained the plural fiction) being at no great distance from the office, he was soon seated in his own bedchamber, where, having pulled off one boot and forgotten the other, he fell into deep cogitation.

"This Marchioness," said Mr. Swiveller, folding his arms, "is a very extraordinary person -surrounded by mysteries, ignorant of the taste of beer, unacquainted with her own name (which is less remarkable), and taking a limited view of society through the key-holes of doors- can these things be her destiny, or has some unknown person started an opposition to the decrees of fate? It is a most inscrutable and unmitigated staggerer!"

When his meditations had attained this satisfactory point, he became aware of his remaining boot, of which, with unimpaired solemnity, he proceeded to divest himself; shaking his head with exceeding gravity all the time, and sighing deeply.

"These rubbers," said Mr. Swiveller, putting on his night-cap in exactly the same style as he wore his hat, "remind me of the matrimonial fireside. Cheggs's wife plays cribbage; all-fours likewise. She rings the changes on'em now. From sport to sport they hurry her, to banish her regrets, and when they win a smile from her, they think that she forgets -but she don't. By this time, I should say," added Richard, getting his left cheek into profile, and looking complacently at the reflection of a very little scrap of whisker in the looking-glass; "by this time, I should say, the iron has entered into her soul. It serves her right!"

Melting from this stern and obdurate, into the tender and pathetic mood, Mr. Swiveller groaned a little, walked wildly up and down, and even made a show of tearing his hair, which however he thought better of, and wrenched the tassel from his night-cap instead. At last, undressing himself with a gloomy resolution, he got into bed.

Some men in his blighted position would have taken to drinking; but as Mr. Swiveller had taken to that before, he only took, on receiving the news that Sophy Wackles was lost to him for ever, to playing the flute; thinking after mature consideration that it was a good, sound, dismal occupation, not only in unison with his own sad thoughts, but calculated to awaken a fellow-feeling in the bosoms of his neighbours. In pursuance of this resolution, he now drew a little table to his bedside, and arranging the light and a small oblong music-book to the best advantage, took his flute from its box, and began to play most mournfully.

The air was "Away with melancholy"-a composition which, when it is played very slowly on the flute in bed, with the further disadvantage of being performed by a gentleman but imperfectly acquainted with the instrument, who repeats one note a great many times before he can find the next, has not a lively effect. Yet for half the night, or more, Mr. Swiveller, lying sometimes on his back with his eyes upon the ceiling, and sometimes half out of bed to correct himself by the book, played this unhappy tune over and over again; never leaving off, save for a minute or two at a time to take breath and soliloquise about the Marchioness, and then beginning again with renewed vigour. It was not until he had quite exhausted his several subjects of meditation, and had breathed into the flute the whole sentiment of the purl down to its very dregs, and had nearly maddened the people of the house, and at both the next doors, and over the way, -that he shut up the music-book, extinguished the candle, and finding himself greatly lightened and relieved in his mind, turned round and fell asleep.

He awoke in the morning, much refreshed; and having taken half an hour's exercise at the flute, and graciously received a notice to quit from his landlady, who had been in waiting on the stairs for that purpose since the dawn of day, repaired to Bevis Marks; where the beautiful Sally was already at her post, bearing in her looks a radiance, mild as that which beameth from the virgin moon.

Mr. Swiveller acknowledged her presence by a nod, and exchanged his coat for the aquatic jacket; which usually took some time fitting on, for in consequence of a tightness in the sleeves, it was only to be got into by a series of struggles. This difficulty overcome, he took his seat at the desk.

"I say" -quoth Miss Brass, abruptly breaking the silence, "you haven't seen a silver pencil-case this morning, have you?"

"I didn't meet many in the street," rejoined Mr. Swiveller. "I saw one - a stout pencil-case of respectable appearance- but as he was in company with an elderly penknife and a young toothpick, with whom he was in earnest conversation, I felt a delicacy in speaking to him."

"No, but have you?" returned Miss Brass. "Seriously, you know."

"What a dull dog you must be to ask me such a question seriously," said Mr. Swiveller, "Haven't I this moment come?"

"Well, all I know is," replied Miss Sally, "that it's not to be found, and that it disappeared one day this week, when I left it on the desk."

"Halloa!" thought Richard, "I hope the Marchioness hasn't been at work here."

"There was a knife too," said Miss Sally, "of the same pattern. They were given to me by my father, years ago, and are both gone. You haven't missed anything yourself, have you?"

Mr. Swiveller involuntarily clapped his hands to the jacket to be quite sure that it *was* a jacket and not a skirted coat; and having satisfied himself of the safety of this, his only moveable in Bevis Marks, made answer in the negative.

"It's a very unpleasant thing, Dick-" said Miss Brass, pulling out the tin box and refreshing herself with a pinch of snuff; "but between you and me –between friends you know, for if Sammy knew it, I should never hear the last of it- some of the office money, too, that has been left about, has gone in the same way. In particular, I have missed three half-crowns at three different times."

"You don't mean that?" cried Dick. "Be careful what you say, old boy, for this is a serious matter. Are you quite sure? Is there no mistake?"

"It is so, and there can't be any mistake at all," rejoined Miss Brass emphatically.

"Then, by Jove," thought Richard, laying down his pen, "I'm afraid the Marchioness is done for!"

The more he discussed the subject in his thoughts, the more probable it appeared to Dick that the miserable little servant was the culprit. When he considered on what a spare allowance of food she lived, how neglected and untaught she was, and how her natural cunning had been sharpened by necessity and privation, he scarcely doubted it. And yet he pitied her so much, and felt so unwilling to have a matter of such gravity disturbing the oddity of their acquaintance, that he thought, and thought truly, that rather than receive fifty pounds down, he would have the Marchioness proved innocent.

While he was plunged in very profound and serious meditation upon this theme, Miss Sally sat shaking her head with an air of great mystery and doubt; when the voice of her brother Sampson, carolling a cheerful strain, was heard in the passage, and that gentleman himself, beaming with virtuous smiles, appeared.

"Mr. Richard, sir, good morning! Here we are again, sir, entering upon another day, with our bodies strengthened by slumber and breakfast, and our spirits fresh and flowing. Here we are, Mr. Richard, rising with the sun to run our little course -our course of duty, sir- and, like him, get through our day's work with credit to ourselves and advantage to our fellow-creatures. A charming reflection, sir, very charming!"

While he addressed his clerk in these words, Mr. Brass was somewhat ostentatiously engaged in minutely examining and holding up against the light a five-pound bank note, which he had brought in, in his hand.

Mr. Richard not receiving his remarks with anything like enthusiasm, his employer turned his eyes to his face, and observed that it wore a troubled expression.

"You're out of spirits, sir," said Brass. "Mr. Richard, sir, we should fall to work cheerfully, and not in a despondent state. It becomes us, Mr. Richard, sir, to-"

Here the chaste Sarah heaved a loud sigh.

"Dear me!" said Mr. Sampson, "you too! Is anything the matter? Mr. Richard, sir-"

Dick, glancing at Miss Sally, saw that she was making signals to him, to acquaint her brother with the subject of their recent conversation. As his own position was not a very pleasant one until the matter was set at rest one way or other, he did so; and Miss Brass, plying her snuff-box at a most wasteful rate, corroborated his account.

The countenance of Sampson fell, and anxiety overspread his features. Instead of passionately bewailing the loss of his money, as Miss Sally had expected, he walked on tiptoe to the door, opened it, looked outside, shut it softly, returned on tiptoe, and said in a whisper,

"This is a most extraordinary and painful circumstance -Mr. Richard, sir, a most painful circumstance. The fact is, that I myself have missed several small sums from the desk of late, and have refrained from mentioning it, hoping that accident would discover the offender; but it has not done so -it has not done so. Sally- Mr. Richard, sir- this is a particularly distressing affair!"

As Sampson spoke, he laid the bank-note upon the desk among some papers, in an absent manner, and thrust his hands into his pockets. Richard Swiveller pointed to it, and admonished him to take it up.

"No, Mr. Richard, sir," rejoined Brass with emotion. "I will not take it up. I will let it lie there, sir. To take it up, Mr. Richard, sir, would imply a doubt of you; and in you, sir, I have unlimited confidence. We will let it lie there, sir, if you please, and we will not take it up by any means." With that, Mr. Brass patted him twice or thrice upon the shoulder, in a most friendly manner, and entreated him to believe that he had as much faith in his honesty as he had in his own.

Although at another time Mr. Swiveller might have looked upon this as a doubtful compliment, he felt it, under the then-existing circumstances, a great relief to be assured that he was not wrongfully suspected. When he had made a suitable reply, Mr. Brass wrung him by the hand, and fell into a brown study, as did Miss Sally likewise. Richard too remained in a thoughtful state; fearing every moment to hear the Marchioness impeached, and unable to resist the conviction that she must be guilty.

When they had severally remained in this condition for some minutes, Miss Sally all at once gave a loud rap upon the desk with her clenched fist, and cried, "I've hit it!" -as indeed she had, and chipped a piece out of it too; but that was not her meaning.

"Well!" cried Brass anxiously. "Go on, will you?"

"Why," replied his sister with an air of triumph, "hasn't there been somebody always coming in and out of this office for the last three or four weeks; hasn't that somebody been left alone in it sometimes -thanks to you; and do you mean to tell me that that somebody isn't the thief!"

"What somebody?" blustered Brass.

"Why, what do you call him -Kit?"

"Mr. Garland's young man?"

"To be sure."

"Never!" cried Brass. "Never. I'll not hear of it. Don't tell me-" said Sampson, shaking his head and working with both his hands as if he were clearing away ten thousand cobwebs. "I'll never believe it of him. Never!"

"I say," repeated Miss Brass, taking another pinch of snuff, "that he's the thief."

"I say," returned Sampson violently, "that he is *not*. What do you mean? How dare you? Are characters to be whispered away like this? Do you know that he's the honestest and faithfullest fellow that ever lived, and that he has an irreproachable good name? Come in, come in!"

These last words were not addressed to Miss Sally, though they partook of the tone in which the indignant remonstrances that preceded them had been uttered. They were addressed to some person who had knocked at the office door; and they had hardly passed the lips of Mr. Brass, when this very Kit himself looked in.

"Is the gentleman up stairs, sir, if you please?"

"Yes, Kit," said Brass, still fired with an honest indignation, and frowning with knotted brows upon his sister; "Yes, Kit, he is. I am glad to see you, Kit, I am rejoiced to see you. Look in again, as you come down stairs, Kit. *That* lad a robber!" cried Brass when he had withdrawn, "with that frank and open countenance! I'd trust him with untold gold. Mr. Richard, sir, have the goodness to step directly to Wrasp and Co.'s in Broad Street, and inquire if they have had instructions to appear in Carkem and Painter. *That* lad a robber," sneered Sampson, flushed and heated with his wrath. "Am I blind, deaf, silly; do I know nothing of human nature when I see it before me? Kit a robber! Bah!"

Flinging this final interjection at Miss Sally with immeasurable scorn and contempt, Sampson Brass thrust his head into his desk as if to shut the base world from his view, and breathed defiance from under its half-closed lid.

CHAPTER LIX

WHEN Kit, having discharged his errand, came down stairs from the single gentleman's apartment after the lapse of a quarter of an hour or so, Mr. Sampson Brass was alone in the office. He was not singing as usual, nor was he seated at his desk. The open door showed him standing before the fire with his back towards it, and looking so very strange that Kit supposed he must have been suddenly taken ill.

"Is anything the matter, sir?" said Kit.

"Matter!" cried Brass. "No. Why anything the matter?"

"You are so very pale," said Kit, "that I should hardly have known you."

"Pooh pooh! mere fancy," cried Brass, stooping to throw up the cinders.

"Never better, Kit, never better in all my life. Merry too. Ha ha! How's our friend above-stairs, eh?"

"A great deal better," said Kit.

"I'm glad to hear it," rejoined Brass; "thankful, I may say. An excellent gentleman-worthy, liberal, generous, gives very little trouble-an admirable lodger. Ha ha! Mr. Garland-he's well, I hope, Kit-and the pony-my friend, my particular friend, you know. Ha ha!"

Kit gave a satisfactory account of all the little household at Abel Cottage. Mr. Brass, who seemed remarkably inattentive and impatient, mounted on his stool, and beckoning him to come nearer, took him by the button-hole.

"I have been thinking, Kit," said the lawyer, "that I could throw some little emoluments into your mother's way-You have a mother, I think? If I recollect right, you told me-"

"Oh yes, sir, yes certainly."

"A widow, I think? an industrious widow?"

"A harder-working woman or a better mother never lived, sir."

"Ah!" cried Brass. "That's affecting, truly affecting. A poor widow struggling to maintain her orphans in decency and comfort, is a delicious picture of human goodness.-Put down your hat, Kit."

"Thank you, sir, I must be going directly."

"Put it down while you stay, at any rate," said Brass, taking it from him and making some confusion among the papers, in finding a place for it on the desk. "I was thinking, Kit, that we have often houses to let for people we are concerned for, and matters of that sort. Now you know we're obliged to put people into those houses to take care of 'em-very often undeserving people that we can't depend upon. What's to prevent our having a person that we can depend upon, and enjoying the delight of doing a good action at the same time? I say, what's to prevent our employing this worthy woman, your mother? What with one job and another, there's lodging-and good lodging too-pretty well all the year round, rent free, and a weekly allowance besides, Kit, that would provide them with a great many comforts they don't at present enjoy. Now what do you think of that? Do you see any objection? My only desire is to serve you, Kit; therefore if you do, say so freely."

As Brass spoke, he moved the hat twice or .thrice, and shuffled among the papers again, as if in search of something.

"How can I see any objection to such a kind offer, sir?" replied Kit with his whole heart. "I don't know how to thank you, sir, I don't indeed."

"Why then," said Brass, suddenly turning upon him and thrusting his face close to Kit's with such a repulsive smile that the latter, even in the very height of his gratitude, drew back quite startled. "Why then, it's *done*."

Kit looked at him in some confusion.

"Done, I say-" added Sampson, rubbing his hands and veiling himself again in his usual oily manner. "Ha ha! and so you shall find, Kit, so you shall find. But dear me," said Brass, "what a time Mr. Richard is gone! A sad loiterer to be sure! Will you mind the office one minute, while I run up stairs? Only one minute. I'll not detain you an instant longer, on any account, Kit."

Talking as he went, Mr. Brass bustled out of the office, and in a very short time returned. Mr. Swiveller came back almost at the same instant; and as Kit was leaving the room hastily to make up for lost time, Miss Brass herself encountered him in the doorway.

"Oh!" sneered Sally, looking after him as she entered. "There goes your pet, Sammy, eh?"

"Ah! There he goes," replied Brass. "My pet, if you please. An honest fellow, Mr. Richard, sir-a worthy fellow indeed!"

"Hem!" coughed Miss Brass.

"I tell you, you aggravating vagabond," said the angry Sampson, "that I'd stake my life upon his honesty. Am I never to hear the last of this? Am I always to be baited, and beset, by your mean suspicions? Have you no regard for true merit, you malignant fellow? If you come to that, I'd sooner suspect your honesty than his."

Miss Sally pulled out the tin snuff-box, and took a long, slow pinch: regarding her brother with a steady gaze all the time.

"She drives me wild, Mr. Richard, sir," said Brass, "she exasperates me beyond all bearing. I am heated and excited, sir, I know I am. These are not business manners, sir, nor business looks, but she carries me out of myself."

"Why don't you leave him alone?" said Dick.

"Because she can't, sir," retorted Brass; "because to chafe and vex me is a part of her nature, sir, and she will and must do it, or I don't believe she'd have her health. But never mind," said Brass, "never mind. I've carried my point. I've shown my confidence in the lad. He has minded the office again. Ha ha! Ugh, you viper!"

The beautiful virgin took another pinch, and put the snuff-box in her pocket; still looking at her brother with perfect composure.

"He has minded the office again," said Brass triumphantly; "he has had my confidence, and he shall continue to have it; he-why, where's the-"

"What have you lost?" inquired Mr. Swiveller.

"Dear me!" said Brass, slapping all his pockets one after another, and looking into his desk, and under it, and upon it, and wildly tossing the papers about, "the note, Mr. Richard, sir, the five-pound note-what can have become of it? I laid it down here-God bless me!"

"What!" cried Miss Sally, starting up, clapping her hands, and scattering the papers on the floor. "Gone! Now, who's right? Now, who's got it? Never mind five pounds-what's five pounds? He's honest you know, quite honest. It would be mean to suspect him. Don't run after him. No, no, not for the world!"

"Is it really gone though?" said Dick, looking at Brass with a face as pale as his own.

"Upon my word, Mr. Richard, sir," replied the lawyer, feeling in all his pockets with looks of the greatest agitation, "I fear this is a black business. It's certainly gone, sir. What's to be done?"

"Don't run after him," said Miss Sally, taking more snuff. "Don't run after him on any account. Give him time to get rid of it, you know. It would be cruel to find him out!"

Mr. Swiveller and Sampson Brass looked from Miss Sally to each other in a state of utter bewilderment, and then, as by one impulse, caught up their hats and rushed out into the street-darting along in the middle of the road, and dashing aside all obstructions as though they were running for their lives.

It happened that Kit had been running too, though not so fast, and having the start of them by some few minutes, was a good distance ahead. As they were pretty certain of the road he must have taken, however, and kept on at a great pace, they came up with him, at the very moment when he had taken breath, and was breaking into a run again.

"Stop!" cried Sampson, laying his hand on one shoulder, while Mr. Swiveller pounced upon the other. "Not so fast, sir. You're in a hurry?"

"Yes, I am," said Kit, looking from one to the other in great surprise.

"I-I-can hardly believe it," panted Sampson, "but something of value is missing from the office. I hope you don't know what."

"Know what! good Heaven, Mr. Brass!" cried Kit, trembling from head to foot; "you don't suppose-"

"No, no," rejoined Brass quickly, "I don't suppose anything. Don't say I said you did. You'll come back quietly, I hope?"

"Of course I will," returned Kit. Why not?"

"To be sure!" said Brass. "Why not? I hope there may turn out to be no why not. If you knew the trouble I've been in this morning through taking your part, Christopher, you'd be sorry for it."

"And I am sure you'll be sorry for having suspected me, sir," replied Kit. "Come. Let us make haste back."

"Certainly!" cried Brass, "the quicker, the better. Mr. Richard-have the goodness, sir, to take that arm. I'll take this one. It's not easy walking three abreast, but under these circumstances it must be done, sir; there's no help for it."

Kit did turn from white to red, and from red to white again, when they secured him thus, and for a moment seemed disposed to resist. But quickly recollecting himself, and remembering that if he made any struggle, he would perhaps be dragged by the collar through the public streets, he only repeated, with great earnestness and with tears standing in his eyes, that he would be sorry for this-and suffered them to lead him off. While they were on the way back, Mr. Swiveller, upon whom his present functions sat very irksomely, took an opportunity of whispering in his ear that if he would confess his guilt, even by so much as a nod, and promise not to do so any more, he would connive at his kicking Sampson Brass on the shins and es-caping up a court; but Kit indignantly rejecting this proposal, Mr. Richard had nothing for it, but to hold him tight until they reached Bevis Marks, and ushered him into the presence of the charming Sarah, who immediately took the precaution of locking the door.

"Now, you know," said Brass, "if this is a case of innocence, it is a case of that description, Christopher, where the fullest disclosure is the best satisfaction for everybody. Therefore if you'll consent to an examination," he demonstrated what kind of examination he meant by turning back the cuffs of his coat, "it will be a comfortable , and pleasant thing for all parties."

"Search me," said Kit, proudly, holding up his arms. "But mind, sir-I know you'll be sorry for this, to the last day of your life."

"It is certainly a very painful occurrence," said Brass with a sigh, as he dived into one of Kit's pockets, and fished up a miscellaneous collection of small articles; "very painful. Nothing here, Mr. Richard, sir, all perfectly satisfactory. Not here, sir. Nor in the waistcoat, Mr. Richard, nor in the coat tails. So far, I am rejoiced, I am sure."

Richard Swiveller, holding Kit's hat in his hand, was watching the pro-ceedings with great interest, and bore upon his face the slightest possible in-dication of a smile, as Brass, shutting one of his eyes, looked with the other up the inside of one of the poor fellow's sleeves as if it were a telescope, when Sampson turning hastily to him, bade him search the hat.

"Here's a handkerchief," said Dick.

"No harm in that, sir," rejoined Brass, applying his eye to the other sleeve, and speaking in the voice of one who was contemplating an immense extent of prospect. "No harm in a handkerchief, sir, whatever. The faculty don't consider it a healthy custom, I believe, Mr. Richard, to carry one's handkerchief in one's hat-I have heard that it keeps the head too warm-but in every other point of view, its being there, is extremely satisfactory-ex-tremely so."

An exclamation, at once from Richard Swiveller, Miss Sally, and Kit himself, cut the lawyer short. He turned his head, and saw Dick standing with the bank-note in his hand.

"In the hat?" cried Brass, in a sort of shriek.

"Under the handkerchief, and tucked beneath the lining," said Dick, aghast at the discovery.

Mr. Brass looked at him, at his sister, at the walls, at the ceiling, at the floor-everywhere but at Kit, who stood quite stupefied and motionless.

"And this," cried Sampson, clasping his hands, "is the world that turns upon its own axis, and has Lunar influences, and revolutions round Heavenly Bodies, and various games of that sort! This is human natur, is it! Oh natur, natur! This is the miscreant that I was going to benefit with all my little arts, and that even now I feel so much for, as to wish to let him go! But," added Mr. Brass with great fortitude, "I am myself a lawyer, and bound to set an example in carrying the laws of my happy country into effect. Sally my dear, forgive me, and catch hold of him on the other side. Mr. Richard, sir, have the goodness to run and fetch a constable. The weakness is past and over, sir, and moral strength returns. A constable, sir, if you please!"

CHAPTER LX

KIT stood as one entranced, with his eyes opened wide and fixed upon the ground, regardless alike of the tremulous hold which Mr. Brass maintained on one side of his cravat, and of the firmer grasp of Miss Sally upon the other; although this latter detention was in itself no small inconvenience, as that fascinating woman, besides screwing her knuckles rather inconveniently into his throat from time to time, had fastened upon him in the first instance with so tight a grip that even in the disorder and distraction of his thoughts he could not divest himself of an uneasy sense of choking. Between the brother and sister he remained in this posture, quite unresisting and passive, until Mr. Swiveller returned with a police constable at his heels.

This functionary, being of course well used to such scenes, looking upon all kinds of robbery from petty larceny up to house-breaking or ventures on the highway as matters in the regular course of business, and regarding the perpetrators in the light of so many customers coming to be served at the wholesale and retail shop of criminal law where he stood behind the counter, received Mr. Brass's statement of facts with about as much interest and surprise, as an undertaker might evince if required to listen to a circumstantial account of the last illness of a person whom he was called in to wait upon professionally; and took Kit into custody with a decent indifference.

"We had better," said this subordinate minister of justice, "get to the office while there's a magistrate sitting. I shall want you to come along with us, Mr. Brass, and the-" he looked at Miss Sally as if in some doubt whether she might not be a griffin or other fabulous monster.

"The lady, eh?" said Sampson.

"Ah!" replied the constable. "Yes-the lady. Likewise the young man that found the property."

"Mr. Richard, sir," said Brass in a mournful voice. "A sad necessity. But the altar of our country, sir-"

"You'll have a hackney-coach, I suppose?" interrupted the constable, holding Kit (whom his other captors had released) carelessly by the arm, a little above the elbow. "Be so good as send for one, will you?"

"But hear me speak a word," cried Kit, raising his eyes and looking imploringly about him. "Hear me speak a word. I am no more guilty than any one of you. Upon my soul I am not. I a thief! Oh, Mr. Brass, you know me better. I am sure you know me better. This is not right of you, indeed."

"I give you my word, constable-" said Brass. But here the constable interposed with the constitutional principle "words be blowed;" observing that words were but spoonmeat for babes and sucklings, and that oaths were the food for strong men.

"Quite true, constable," assented Brass in the same mournful tone. "Strictly correct. I give you my oath, constable, that down to a few minutes ago, when this fatal discovery was made, I had such confidence in that lad, that I'd have trusted him with-a hackney-coach, Mr. Richard, sir; you're very slow, sir."

"Who is there that knows me," cried Kit, "that would not trust me-that does not? ask anybody whether they have ever doubted me; whether I have ever wronged them of a farthing. Was I ever once dishonest when I was poor and hungry, and is it likely I would begin now! Oh consider what you do. How can I meet the kindest friends that ever human creature had, with this dreadful charge upon me!"

Mr. Brass rejoined that it would have been well for the prisoner if he had thought of that before, and was about to make some other gloomy observations, when the voice of the single gentleman was heard demanding from above- stairs what was the matter, and what was the cause of all that noise and hurry. Kit made an involuntary start towards the door in his anxiety to answer for himself, but being speedily detained by the constable, had the agony of seeing Sampson Brass run out alone to tell the story in his own way.

"And he can hardly believe it either," said Sampson, when he returned, "nor nobody will. I wish I could doubt the evidence of my senses, but their depositions are unimpeachable. It's of no use cross-examining my eyes," cried Sampson, winking and rubbing them, "they stick to their first account, and will. Now, Sarah, I hear the coach in the Marks; get on your bonnet, and we'll be off. A sad errand! a moral funeral, quite!"

"Mr. Brass," said Kit, "do me one favour. Take me to Mr. Witherden's first."

Sampson shook his head irresolutely.

"Do," said Kit. "My master's there. For Heaven's sake, take me there first."

"Well, I don't know," stammered Brass, who perhaps had his reasons for wishing to show as fair as possible in the eyes of the notary. "How do we stand in point of time, constable, eh?"

The constable, who had been chewing a straw all this while with great philosophy, replied that if they went away at once they would have time enough, but that if they stood shilly-shallying there any longer they must go straight to the Mansion House; and finally expressed his opinion that that was where it was, and that was all about it.

Mr. Richard Swiveller having arrived inside the coach, and still remaining immoveable in the most commodious corner with his face to the horses, Mr. Brass instructed the officer to remove his prisoner, and declared himself quite ready. Therefore the constable, still holding Kit in the same manner, and pushing him on a little before him, so as to keep him at about three-quarters of an arm's length in advance (which is the professional mode), thrust him into the vehicle and followed himself. Miss Sally entered next; and there being now four inside, Sampson Brass got upon the box, and made the coachman drive on.

Still completely stunned by the sudden and terrible change which had taken place in his affairs, Kit sat gazing out of the coach window, almost hoping to see some monstrous phenomenon in the streets which might give him reason to believe he was in a dream. Alas! Everything was too real and familiar: the same succession of turnings, the same houses, the same streams of people running side by side in different directions upon the pavement, the same bustle of carts and carriages in the road, the same well-remembered objects in the shop windows: a regularity in the very noise and hurry which no dream ever mirrored. Dreamlike as the story was, it was true. He stood charged with robbery; the note had been found upon him, though he was innocent in thought and deed; and they were carrying him back, a prisoner.

Absorbed in these painful ruminations, thinking with a drooping heart of his mother and little Jacob, feeling as though even the consciousness of innocence would be insufficient to support him in the presence of his friends if they believed him guilty, and sinking in hope and courage more and more as they drew nearer to the notary's, poor Kit was looking earnestly out of the window, observant of nothing,-when all at once, as though it had been conjured up by magic, he became aware of the face of Quilp.

And what a leer there was upon the face! It was from the open window of a tavern that it looked out; and the dwarf had so spread himself over it, with his elbows on the window-sill and his head resting on both his hands, that what between this attitude and his being swoln with suppressed laughter, he looked puffed and bloated into twice his usual breadth. Mr. Brass on recognising him immediately stopped the coach. As it came to a halt directly opposite to where he stood, the dwarf pulled off his hat, and saluted the party with a hideous and grotesque politeness.

"Aha!" he cried. "Where now, Brass? where now? Sally with you too? Sweet Sally! And Dick? Pleasant Dick! And Kit? Honest Kit!"

"He's extremely cheerful!" said Brass to the coachman. "Very much so! Ah, sir-a sad business! Never believe in honesty any more, sir."

"Why not?" returned the dwarf. "Why not, you rogue of a lawyer, why not?"

"Bank-note lost in our office, sir," said Brass, shaking his head. "Found in his hat, sir-he previously left alone there-no mistake at all, sir-chain of evidence complete-not a link wanting."

"What!" cried the dwarf, leaning half his body out of window. "Kit a thief! Kit a thief! Ha ha ha! Why, he's an uglier-looking thief than can be seen any- where for a penny. Eh, Kit-eh? Ha ha ha! Have you taken Kit into custody before he had time and opportunity to beat me! Eh, Kit-eh?" And with that, he burst into a yell of laughter, manifestly to the great terror of the coachman, and pointed to a dyer's pole hard by, where a dangling suit of clothes bore some resemblance to a man upon a gibbet.

"Is it coming to that, Kit!" cried the dwarf, rubbing his hands violently. "Ha ha ha ha! What a disappointment for little Jacob, and for his darling mother! Let him have the Bethel minister to comfort and console him, Brass. Eh, Kit-eh? Drive on, coachey, drive on. Bye bye, Kit; all good go with you; keep up your spirits; my love to the Garlands-the dear old lady and gentleman. Say I inquired after 'em, will you? Blessings on 'em, on you, and on everybody, Kit. Blessings on all the world!"

With such good wishes and farewells, poured out in a rapid torrent until they were out of hearing, Quilp suffered them to depart; and when he could see the coach no longer, drew in his head, and rolled upon the ground in an ecstasy of enjoyment.

When they reached the notary's, which they were not long in doing, for they had encountered the dwarf in a bye-street at a very little distance from the house, Mr. Brass dismounted; and opening the coach-door with a melancholy visage, requested his sister to accompany him into the office, with a view of preparing the good people within for the mournful intelligence that awaited them. Miss Sally complying, he desired Mr. Swiveller to accompany them. So, into the office they went; Mr. Sampson and his sister arm in arm; and Mr. Swiveller following, alone.

The notary was standing before the fire in the outer office, talking to Mr. Abel and the elder Mr. Garland, while Mr. Chuckster sat writing at the desk, picking up such crumbs of their conversation as happened to fall in his way. This posture of affairs Mr. Brass observed through the glass-door as he was turning the handle, and seeing that the notary recognised him, he began to shake his head and sigh deeply while that partition yet divided them.

"Sir," said Sampson, taking off his hat, and kissing the two forefingers of his right-hand beaver glove, "my name is Brass-Brass of Bevis Marks, sir. I have had the honour and pleasure, sir, of being concerned against you in some little testamentary matters. How do you do, sir?"

"My clerk will attend to any business you may have come upon, Mr. Brass," said the notary, turning away.

"Thank you, sir," said Brass, "thank you, I am sure. Allow me, sir, to introduce my sister-quite one of us, sir, although of the weaker sex-of great use in my business, sir, I assure you. Mr. Richard, sir, have the goodness to come forward if you please-No really," said Brass, stepping between the notary and his private office (towards which he had begun to retreat), and speaking in the tone of an injured man, "really, sir, I must, under favour, request a word or two with you, indeed."

"Mr. Brass," said the other, in a decided tone, "I am engaged. You see that I am occupied with these gentlemen. If you will communicate your business to Mr. Chuckster yonder, you will receive every attention."

"Gentlemen," said Brass, laying his right hand on his waistcoat, and looking towards the father and son with a smooth smile-" Gentlemen, I appeal to you-really, gentlemen-consider, I beg of you. I am of the law. I am styled 'gentleman' by Act of Parliament. I maintain the title by the annual payment of twelve pound sterling for a certificate. I am not one of your players of music, stage actors, writers of books, or painters of pictures, who assume a station that the laws of their country don't recognise. I am none of your strollers or vagabonds. If any man brings his action against me, he must describe me as a gentleman, or his action is null and void. I appeal to you-is this quite respectful? Really, gentlemen-"

"Well, will you have the goodness to state your business then, Mr. Brass?" said the notary.

"Sir," rejoined Brass, "I will. Ah, Mr. Witherden! you little know the-but I will not be tempted to travel from the point, sir. I believe the name of one of these gentlemen is Garland."

"Of both," said the notary.

"In-deed!" rejoined Brass, cringing excessively. "But I might have known that, from the uncommon likeness. Extremely happy, I am sure, to have the honour of an introduction to two such gentlemen, although the occasion is a most painful one. One of you gentlemen has a servant called Kit?"

"Both," replied the notary.

"Two Kits?" said Brass smiling. "Dear me!"

"One Kit, sir," returned Mr. Witherden angrily, "who is employed by both gentlemen. What of him?"

"This of him, sir," rejoined Brass, dropping his voice impressively. "That young man, sir, that I have felt unbounded and unlimited confidence in, and always behaved to as if he was my equal-that young man has this morning committed a robbery in my office, and been taken almost in the fact."

"This must be some falsehood!" cried the notary.

"It is not possible," said Mr. Abel.

"I'll not believe one word of it," exclaimed the old gentleman.

Mr. Brass looked mildly round upon them, and rejoined, "Mr. Witherden, sir, your words are actionable, and if I was a man of low and mean standing, who couldn't afford to be slandered, I should proceed for damages. Hows'ever, sir, being what I am, I merely scorn such expressions. The honest warmth of the other gentleman I respect, and I'm truly sorry to be the messenger of such unpleasant news. I shouldn't have put myself in this painful position, I assure you, but that the lad himself desired to be brought here in the first instance, and I yielded to his prayers. Mr. Chuckster, sir, will you have the goodness to tap at the window for the constable that's waiting in the coach?"

The three gentlemen looked at each other with blank faces when these words were uttered, and Mr. Chuckster, doing as he was desired, and leaping off his stool with something of the excitement of an inspired prophet whose foretellings had in the fulness of time been realised, held the door open for the entrance of the wretched captive.

Such a scene as there was, when Kit came in, and bursting into the rude eloquence with which Truth at length inspired him, called Heaven to witness that he was innocent, and that how the property came to be found upon him he knew not! Such a confusion of tongues, before the circumstances were related, and the proofs disclosed! Such a dead silence when all was told, and his three friends exchanged looks of doubt and amazement!

"Is it not possible," said Mr. Witherden, after a long pause, "that this note may have found its way into the hat by some accident,-such as the removal of papers on the desk, for instance?"

But this was clearly shown to be quite impossible. Mr. Swiveller, though an unwilling witness, could not help proving to demonstration, from the position in which it was found, that it must have been designedly secreted.

"It's very distressing," said Brass, "immensely distressing, I am sure. When he comes to be tried, I shall be very happy to recommend him to mercy on account of his previous good character. I did lose money before, certainly, but it doesn't quite follow that he took it. The presumption's against him-strongly against him-but we're Christians, I hope?"

"I suppose," said the constable, looking round, "that no gentleman here can give evidence as to whether he's been flush of money of late. Do you happen to know, sir?"

"He has had money from time to time, certainly," returned Mr. Garland, to whom the man had put the question. "But that, as he always told me, was given him by Mr. Brass himself."

"Yes to be sure," said Kit eagerly. "You can bear me out in that, sir?"

"Eh?" cried Brass, looking from face to face with an expression of stupid amazement.

"The money you know, the half-crowns, that you gave me-from the lodger," said Kit.

"Oh dear me!" cried Brass, shaking his head and frowning heavily. "This is a bad case, I find; a very bad case indeed."

"What! Did you give him no money on account of anybody, sir?" asked Mr. Garland, with great anxiety.

"I give him money, sir!" returned Sampson. "Oh, come you know, this is too barefaced. Constable, my good fellow, we had better be going."

"What!" shrieked Kit. "Does he deny that he did? ask him, somebody, pray. Ask him to tell you whether he did or not!"

"Did you, sir?" asked the notary.

"I tell you what, gentlemen," replied Brass, in a very grave manner, "he'll not serve his case this way, and really, if you feel any interest in him, you had better advise him to go upon some other tack. Did I, sir? Of course I never did."

"Gentlemen," cried Kit, on whom a light broke suddenly, "Master, Mr. Abel, Mr. Witherden, every one of you-he did it! What I have done to offend him I don't know, but this is a plot to ruin me. Mind, gentlemen, it's a plot, and whatever comes of it, I will say with my dying breath that he put that note in my hat himself! Look at him, gentlemen! see how he changes colour. Which of us looks the guilty person-he, or I?"

"You hear him, gentlemen?" said Brass, smiling, "you hear him. Now, does this case strike you as assuming rather a black complexion, or does it not? Is it at all a treacherous case, do you think, or is it one of mere ordinary guilt? Perhaps, gentlemen, if he had not said this in your presence and I had reported it, you'd have held this to be impossible likewise, eh?"

With such pacific and bantering remarks did Mr. Brass refute the foul aspersion on his character; but the virtuous Sarah, moved by stronger feelings, and having at heart, perhaps, a more jealous regard for the honour of her family, flew from her brother's side, without any previous intimation of her design, and darted at the prisoner with the utmost fury. It would undoubtedly have gone hard with Kit's face, but that the wary constable, foreseeing her design, drew him aside at the critical moment, and thus placed Mr. Chuckster in circumstances of some jeopardy; for that gentleman happening to be next the object of Miss Brass's wrath; and rage being, like Love and Fortune, blind; was pounced upon by the fair enslaver, and had a false collar plucked up by the roots, and his hair very much dishevelled, before the exertions of the company could make her sensible of her mistake.

The constable, taking warning by this desperate attack, and thinking perhaps that it would be more satisfactory to the ends of justice if the prisoner was taken before a magistrate, whole, rather than in small pieces, led him back to the hackney-coach without more ado, and further insisted on Miss Brass becoming an outside passenger; to which proposal the charming creature, after a little angry discussion, yielded her consent; and so took her brother Sampson's place upon the box: Mr. Brass with some reluctance agreeing to occupy her seat inside. These arrangements perfected, they drove to the justice-room with all speed, followed by the notary and his two friends in another coach. Mr. Chuckster alone was left behind-greatly to his indignation; for he held the evidence he could have given, relative to Kit's returning to work out the shilling, to be so very material as bearing upon his hypocritical and designing character, that he considered its suppression little better than a compromise of felony.

At the justice-room, they found the single gentleman, who had gone straight there, and was expecting them with desperate impatience. But not fifty single gentlemen rolled into one could have helped poor Kit, who in half an hour afterwards was committed for trial, and was assured by a friendly officer on his way to prison that there was no occasion to be cast down, for the sessions would soon be on, and he would in all likelihood get his little affair disposed of, and be comfortably transported, in less than a fortnight.

CHAPTER LXI

LET moralists and philosophers say what they may, it is very questionable whether a guilty man would have felt half as much misery that night, as Kit did, being innocent. The world, being in the constant commission of vast quantities of injustice, is a little too apt to comfort itself with the idea that if the victim of its falsehood and malice have a clear conscience, he cannot fail to be sustained under his trials, and somehow or other to come right at last; "in which case," say they who have hunted him down, "-though we certainly don't expect it-nobody will be better pleased than we." Whereas, the world would do well to reflect, that injustice is in itself, to every generous and properly constituted mind, an injury, of all others the most insufferable, the most torturing, and the most hard to bear; and that many clear consciences have gone to their account elsewhere, and many sound hearts have broken, because of this very reason; the knowledge of their own deserts only aggravating their sufferings, and rendering them the less endurable.

The world, however, was not in fault in Kit's case. But Kit was innocent; and knowing this, and feeling that his best friends deemed him guilty-that Mr. and Mrs. Garland would look upon him as a monster of ingratitude-that Barbara would associate him with all that was bad and criminal-that the pony would consider himself forsaken-and that even his own mother might perhaps yield to the strong appearances against him, and believe him to be the wretch he seemed-knowing and feeling all this, he experienced at first an agony of mind which no words can describe, and walked up and down the little cell in which he was locked up for the night, almost beside himself with grief.

Even when the violence of these emotions had in some degree subsided, and he was beginning to grow more calm, there came into his mind a new thought, the anguish of which was scarcely less. The child-the bright star of the simple fellow's life-she, who always came back upon him like a beautiful dream, -who had made the poorest part of his existence, the happiest and best-who had ever been so gentle, and considerate, and good-if she were; ever to hear of this, what would she think! As this idea occurred to him, the walls of the prison seemed to melt away, and the old place to reveal itself in their stead, as it was wont to be on winter nights-the fireside, the little supper-table, the old man's hat and coat, and stick-the half-opened door, leading to her little room-they were all there. And Nell herself was there, and he-both laughing heartily as they had often done-and when he had got as far as this, Kit could go no farther, but flung himself upon his poor bedstead and wept.

It was a long night, which seemed as though it would have no end; but he slept too, and dreamed-always of being at liberty, and roving about, now with one person and now with another, but ever with a vague dread of being recalled to prison; not that prison, but one which was in itself a dim idea, not of a place, but of a care and sorrow: of something oppressive and always present, and yet impossible to define. At last the morning dawned, and there was the jail itself-cold, black, and dreary, and very real indeed.

He was left to himself, however, and there was comfort in that. He had liberty to walk in a small paved yard at a certain hour, and learnt from the turnkey, who came to unlock his cell and show him where to wash, that there was a regular time for visiting, every day, and that if any of his friends came to see him, he would be fetched down to the grate. When he had given him this information, and a tin porringer containing his breakfast, the man locked him up again; and went clattering along the stone passage, opening and shutting a great many other doors, and raising numberless loud echoes which resounded through the building for a long time, as if they were in prison too, and unable to get out.

This turnkey had given him to understand that he was lodged, like some few others in the jail, apart from the mass of prisoners; because he was not supposed to be utterly depraved and irreclaimable, and had never occupied apartments in that mansion before. Kit was thankful for this indulgence, and sat reading the Church Catechism very attentively (though he had known it by heart from a little child), until he heard the key in the lock, and the man entered again.

"Now then," he said, "come on!"

"Where to, sir?" asked Kit.

The man contented himself by briefly replying , Wisitors; "and taking him by the arm in exactly the same manner as the constable had done the day before, led him through several winding ways and strong gates into a passage, where he placed him at a grating, and turned upon his heel. Beyond this grating, at the distance of about four or five feet, was another exactly like it. In the space between, sat a turnkey reading a newspaper; and outside the further railing, Kit saw, with a palpitating heart, his mother with the baby in her arms; Barbara's mother with her never-failing umbrella; and poor little Jacob, staring in with all his might, as though he were looking for the bird, or the wild beast, and thought the men were mere accidents with whom the bars could have no possible concern.

But directly little Jacob saw his brother, and thrusting his arms between the rails to hug him, found that he came no nearer, but still stood afar off with his head resting on the arm by which he held to one of the bars, he began to cry most piteously; whereupon, Kit's mother and Barbara's mother, who had restrained themselves as much as possible, burst out sobbing and weeping afresh. Poor Kit could not help joining them, and not one of them could speak a word.

During this melancholy pause, the turnkey read his newspaper with a waggish look (he had evidently got among the facetious paragraphs), until, happening to take his eyes off it for an instant, as if to get by dint of contemplation at the very marrow of some joke of a deeper sort than the rest, it appeared to occur to him for the first time that somebody was crying.

"Now, ladies, ladies," he said, looking round with surprise, "I'd advise you not to waste time like this. It's allowanced here, you know. You mustn't let that child make that noise either. It's against all rules."

"I'm his poor mother, sir," sobbed Mrs. Nubbles, curtseying humbly, "and this is his brother, sir. Oh dear me, dear me!"

"Well!" replied the turnkey, folding his paper on his knee, so as to get with greater convenience at the top of the next column. "It can't be helped, you know. He an't the only one in the same fix. You mustn't make a noise about it!"

With that, he went on reading. The man was not unnaturally cruel or hard-hearted. He had come to look upon felony as a kind of disorder, like the scarlet fever or erysipelas: some people had it-some hadn't-just as it might be.

"Oh! my darling Kit-" said his mother, whom Barbara's mother had charitably relieved of the baby- "that I should see my poor hoy here!"

"You don't believe that I did what they accuse me of, mother dear?" cried Kit, in a choking voice.

"I believe it!" exclaimed the poor woman, "I that never knew you tell a lie, or do a bad action from your cradle-that have never had a moment's sorrow on your account, except it was for the poor meals that you have taken with such good-humour and content, that I forgot how little there was when I thought how kind and thought- full you were, though you were but a child!-I believe it of the son that's been a comfort to me from the hour of his birth to this time, and that I never laid down one night in anger with! I believe it of you, Kit!-"

"Why then, thank God!" said Kit, clutching the bars with an earnestness that shook them, "and I can bear it, mother. Come what may, I shall always have one drop of happiness in my heart when I think that you said that."

At this the poor woman fell a-crying again, and Barbara's mother too. And little Jacob, whose disjointed thoughts had by this time resolved themselves into a pretty distinct impression that Kit couldn't go out for a walk if he wanted, and that there were no birds, lions, tigers, or other natural curiosities behind those bars-nothing indeed, but a caged brother-added his tears to theirs with as little noise as possible.

Kit's mother, drying her eyes (and moistening them, poor soul, more than she dried them), now took from the ground a small basket, and submissively addressed herself to the turnkey, saying, would he please to listen to her for a minute? The turnkey, being in the very crisis and passion of a joke, motioned to her with his hand to keep silent one minute longer, for her life. Nor did he remove his hand into its former posture, but kept it in the same warning attitude until he had finished the paragraph, when he paused for a few seconds, with a smile upon his face, as who should say "this editor is a comical blade-a funny dog," and then asked her what she wanted.

"I have brought him a little something to eat," said the good woman. "If you please, sir, might he have it?"

"Yes,-he may have it. There's no rule against that. Give it to me when you go, and I'll take care he has it."

"No, but if you please, sir-don't be angry with me, sir-I am his mother, and you had a mother once-if I might only see him eat a little bit, I should go away so much more satisfied that he was all comfortable."

And again the tears of Kit's mother burst forth, and of Barbara's mother, and of little Jacob. As to the baby, it was crowing and laughing with all its might-under the idea, apparently, that the whole scene had been invented and got up for its particular satisfaction.

The turnkey looked as if he thought the request a strange one and rather out of the common way, but nevertheless he laid down his paper, and coming round to where Kit's mother stood, took the basket from her, and after inspecting its contents, handed it to Kit, and went back to his place. It may be easily conceived that the prisoner had no great appetite, but he sat down upon the ground, and ate as hard as he could, while, at every morsel he put into his mouth, his mother sobbed and wept afresh, though with a softened grief that bespoke the satisfaction the sight afforded her.

While he was thus engaged, Kit made some anxious inquiries about his employers, and whether they had expressed any opinion about him; but all he could learn was that Mr. Abel had himself broken the intelligence to his mother with great kindness and delicacy late on the previous night, but had himself expressed no opinion of his innocence or guilt. Kit was on the point of mustering courage to ask Barbara's mother about Barbara, when the turnkey who had conducted him reappeared, a second turnkey appeared behind his visitors, and the third turnkey with the newspaper cried "Time's up!"-adding in the same breath "Now for the next party!" and then plunging deep into his newspaper again. Kit was taken off in an instant, with a blessing from his mother, and a scream from little Jacob, ringing in his ears. As he was crossing the next yard with the basket in his hand, under the guidance of his former conductor, another officer called to them to stop, and came up with a pint-pot of porter in his band.

"This is Christopher Nubbles, isn't it, that come in last night for felony?" said the man.

His comrade replied that this was the chicken in question.

"Then here's your beer," said the other man to Christopher. "What are you looking at? There an't a discharge in it."

"I beg your pardon," said Kit. "Who sent it me?"

"Why, your friend," replied the man. "You're to have it every day, he says. And so you will, if he pays for it."

"My friend!" repeated Kit.

"You're all abroad, seemingly," returned the other man. "There's his letter. Take hold!"

Kit took it, and when he was locked up again, read as follows.

"Drink of this cup. You'll find there's a spell in its every drop 'gainst the ills of mortality. Talk of the cordial that sparkled for Helen! Her cup was a fiction, but this is reality (Barclay & Co.'s). If they ever send it in a flat state, complain to the Governor. Yours, R. S."

"R. S.!" said Kit, after some consideration. "It must be Mr. Richard Swiveller. Well, it's very kind of him, and I thank him heartily."

CHAPTER LXII

A FAINT light, twinkling from the window of the counting house on Quilp's wharf, and looking inflamed and red through the night-fog, as though it suffered from it like an eye, forewarned Mr. Sampson Brass, as he approached the wooden cabin with a cautious step, that the excellent proprietor, his esteemed client, was inside, and probably waiting with his accustomed patience and sweetness of temper the fulfilment of the appointment which now brought Mr. Brass within his fair domain.

"A treacherous place to pick one's steps in of a dark night," muttered Sampson, as he stumbled for the twentieth time over some stray lumber, and limped in pain. "I believe that boy strews the ground differently every day, on purpose to bruise and maim one; unless his master does it with his own hands, which is more than likely. I hate to come to this place without Sally. She's more protection than a dozen men."

As he paid this compliment to the merit of the absent charmer, Mr. Brass came to a halt; looking doubtfully towards the light, and over his shoulder.

"What's he about, I wonder?" murmured the lawyer, standing on tiptoe and endeavouring to obtain a glimpse of what was passing inside, which at that distance was impossible- "drinking, I suppose,-making himself more fiery and furious, and heating his malice and mischievousness till they boil. I'm always afraid to come here by myself, when his account's a pretty large one. I don't believe he'd mind throttling me, and dropping me softly into the river when the tide was at its strongest, any more than he'd mind killing a rat-indeed I don't know whether he wouldn't consider it a pleasant joke. Hark! Now he's singing!"

Mr. Quilp was certainly entertaining himself with vocal exercise, but it was rather a kind of chant than a song; being a monotonous repetition of one sentence in a very rapid manner, with a long stress upon the last word, which he swelled into a dismal roar. Nor did the burden of this performance bear any reference to love, or war, or wine, or loyalty, or any other, the standard topics of song, but to a subject not often set to music or generally known in ballads; the words being these:- "The worthy magistrate, after remarking that the prisoner would find some difficulty in persuading a jury to believe his tale, committed him to take his trial at the approaching sessions; and directed the customary recognisances to be entered into for the pros-e-cu-tion."

Every time he came to this concluding word, and had exhausted all possible stress upon it, Quilp burst into a shriek of laughter, and began again.

"He's dreadfully imprudent," muttered Brass, after he had listened to two or three repetitions of the chant. "Horribly imprudent. I wish he was dumb. I wish he was deaf. I wish he was blind. Hang him," cried Brass, as the chant began again, "I wish he was dead!"

Giving utterance to these friendly aspirations in behalf of his client, Mr. Sampson composed his face into its usual state of smoothness, and waiting until the shriek came again and was dying away, went up to the wooden house, and knocked at the door.

"Come in!" cried the dwarf.

"How do you do to-night, sir?" said Sampson, peeping in. "Ha ha ha!

How do you do, sir? Oh dear me, how very whimsical! Amazingly whimsical to be sure!"

"Come in, you fool!" returned the dwarf, "and don't stand there shaking your head and showing your teeth. Come in, you false witness, you perjurer, you suborner of evidence, come in!"

"He has the richest humour!" cried Brass, shutting the door behind him; "the most amazing vein of comicality! But isn't it rather injudicious, sir-?"

"What?" demanded Quilp, "What, Judas?"

"Judas!" cried Brass. "He has such extraordinary spirits! His humour is so extremely playful! Judas! Oh yes-dear me, how, very good! Ha ha ha!"

All this time, Sampson was rubbing his hands, and staring, with ludicrous surprise and dismay, at a great, goggle-eyed, blunt-nosed figure-head of some old ship, which was reared up against the wall in a corner near the stove, looking like a goblin or hideous idol whom the dwarf worshipped. A mass of timber on its head, carved into the dim and distant semblance of a cocked hat, together with a representation of a star on the left breast and epaulettes on the shoulders, denoted that it was intended for the effigy of some famous admiral; but, without those helps, any observer might have supposed it the authentic portrait of a distinguished merman, or great sea-monster. Being originally much too large for the apartment which it was now employed to decorate, it had been sawn short off at the waist. Even in this state it reached from floor to ceiling; and thrusting itself forward with that excessively wide-awake aspect, and air of somewhat obtrusive politeness, by which figure-heads are usually characterised, seemed to reduce everything else to mere pigmy proportions.

"Do you know it?" said the dwarf, watching Sampson's eyes. "Do you see the likeness?"

"Eh?" said Brass, holding his head on one side, and throwing it a little back, as connoisseurs do. "Now I look at it again, I fancy I see a-yes, there certainly is something in the smile that reminds me of-and yet upon my word I-"

Now, the fact was, that Sampson, having never seen anything in the smallest degree resembling this substantial phantom, was much perplexed; being uncertain whether Mr. Quilp considered it like himself, and had therefore bought it for a family portrait; or whether he was pleased to consider it as the likeness of some enemy. He was not very long in doubt; for, while he was surveying it with that knowing look which people assume when they are contemplating for the first time portraits which they ought to recognise but don't, the dwarf threw down the newspaper from which he had been chanting the words already quoted, and seizing a rusty iron bar, which he used in lieu of poker, dealt the figure such a stroke on the nose that it rocked again.

"Is it like Kit-is it his picture, his image, his very self?" cried the dwarf, aiming a shower of blows at the insensible countenance, and covering it with deep dimples. "Is it the exact model and counterpart of the dog-is it-is it-is it?"

And with every repetition of the question, he battered the great image until the perspiration streamed down his face with the violence of the exercise.

Although this might have been a very comical thing to look at from a secure gallery, as a bull-fight is found to be a comfortable spectacle by those who are not in the arena and a house on fire is better than a play to people who don't live near it, there was something in the earnestness of Mr. Quilp's manner which made his legal adviser feel that the counting-house was a little too small, and a great deal too lonely, for the due enjoyment of these humours. Therefore he stood as far off as he could while the dwarf was thus engaged; whimpering out but feeble applause; and when he left off and sat down again from pure exhaustion, approached with more obsequiousness than ever.

"Excellent indeed!" cried Brass. "He he! Oh, very good, sir. You know," said Sampson, looking round as if in appeal to the bruised admiral, "he's quite a remarkable man-quite!"

"Sit down," said the dwarf. "I bought the dog yesterday. I've been screwing gimlets into him, and sticking forks in his eyes, and cutting my name on him. I mean to burn him at last."

"Ha ha!" cried Brass. "Extremely entertaining, indeed!"

"Come here!" said Quilp, beckoning him to draw near. "What's injudicious, hey?"

"Nothing, sir-nothing. Scarcely worth mentioning, sir; but I thought that song-admirably humorous in itself you know-was perhaps rather-"

"Yes," said Quilp, "rather what?"

"Just bordering, or as one may say remotely verging upon the confines of injudiciousness perhaps, sir," returned Brass, looking timidly at the dwarf's cunning eyes, which were turned towards the fire and reflected its red light.

"Why?" inquired Quilp, without looking up.

"Why, you know, sir," returned Brass, venturing to be more familiar: "-the fact is, sir, that any allusion to these little combinings together of friends for objects in themselves extremely laudable, but which the law terms conspiracies, are-you take me, sir?-best kept snug and among friends, you know."

"Eh!" said Quilp, looking up with a perfectly vacant countenance. "What do you mean?"

"Cautious, exceedingly cautious, very right and proper!" cried Brass, nodding his head. "Mum, sir, even here-my meaning, sir, exactly."

"Your meaning exactly, you brazen scarecrow,-what's your meaning?" retorted Quilp. "Why do you talk to me of combining together? Do I combine? Do I know anything about your combinings?"

"No no, sir-certainly not; not by any means," returned Brass.

"If you so wink and nod at me," said the dwarf, looking about him as if for his poker, "I'll spoil the expression of your monkey's face, I will."

"Don't put yourself out of the way I beg, sir," rejoined Brass, checking himself with great alacrity. "You're quite right, sir, quite right. I shouldn't have mentioned the subject, sir. It's much better not to. You're quite right, sir. Let us change it, if you please. You were asking, sir, Sally told me, about our lodger. He has not returned, sir."

"No?" said Quilp, heating some rum in a little sauce- pan, and watching it to prevent its boiling over. "Why not?"

"Why, sir," returned Brass, "he-dear me, Mr. Quilp, sir"-

"What's the matter?" said the dwarf, stopping his hand in the act of carrying the saucepan to his mouth.

"You have forgotten the water, sir," said Brass. "And -excuse me, sir- but it's burning hot."

Deigning no other than a practical answer to this remonstrance, Mr. Quilp raised the hot saucepan to his lips, and deliberately drank off all the spirit it contained, which might have been in quantity about half a pint, and had been but a moment before, when he took it off the fire, bubbling and hissing fiercely. Having swallowed this gentle stimulant, and shaken his fist at the admiral, he bade Mr. Brass proceed.

"But first," said Quilp, with his accustomed grin, "have a drop yourself-a nice drop-a good, warm, fiery drop."

"Why, sir," replied Brass, "if there was such a thing as a mouthful of water that could be got without trouble-"

"There's no such thing to be had here," cried the dwarf. "Water for lawyers! Melted lead and brimstone, you mean, nice hot blistering pitch and tar-that's the thing for them-eh, Brass, eh?"

"Ha ha ha!" laughed Mr. Brass. "Oh very biting! and yet it's like being tickled-there's a pleasure in it too, Sir!"

"Drink that," said the dwarf, who had by this time heated some more. "Toss it off, don't leave any heeltap, scorch your throat and be happy."

The wretched Sampson took a few short sips of the liquor, which immediately distilled itself into burning tears, and in that form came rolling down his cheeks into the pipkin again, turning the colour of his face and eyelids to a deep red, and giving rise to a violent fit of coughing, in the midst of which he was still heard to declare, with the constancy of a martyr, that it was "beautiful indeed!" While he was yet in unspeakable agonies the dwarf renewed their conversation.

"The lodger," said Quilp,- "what about him?"

"He is still, sir," returned Brass, with intervals of coughing, "stopping with the Garland family. He has only been home once, sir, since the day of the examination of that culprit. He informed Mr. Richard, sir, that he couldn't bear the house after what had taken place; that he was wretched in it; and that he looked upon himself as being in a certain kind of way the cause of the occurrence. -A very excellent lodger, sir. I hope we may not lose him."

"Yah!" cried the dwarf. "Never thinking of anybody but yourself-why don't you retrench then-scrape up, hoard, economise, eh?"

"Why, sir," replied Brass, "upon my word I think Sarah's as good an economiser as any going. I do indeed, Mr. Quilp."

"Moisten your clay, wet the other eye, drink, man!" cried the dwarf. "You took a clerk to oblige me."

"Delighted, sir, I am sure, at any time," replied Sampson. "Yes, sir, I did."

"Then, now you may discharge him," said Quilp. "There's a means of retrenchment for you at once."

"Discharge Mr. Richard, sir?" cried Brass.

"Have you more than one clerk, you parrot, that you ask the question? Yes."

"Upon my word, sir," said Brass, "I wasn't prepared for this-"

"How could you be?" sneered the dwarf, "when I wasn't! How often am I to tell you that I brought him to you that I might always have my eye on him and know where he was-and that I had a plot, a scheme, a little quiet piece of enjoyment afoot, of which the very cream and essence was, that this old man and grandchild (who have sunk underground I think) should be, while he and his precious friend believed them rich, in reality as poor as frozen rats?"

"I quite understood that, sir," rejoined Brass. "Thoroughly."

"Well, sir," retorted Quilp, "and do you understand now, that they're not poor-that they can't be, if they have such men as your lodger searching for them and scouring the country far and wide?"

"Of course I do, sir," said Sampson.

"Of course you do," retorted the dwarf, viciously snapping at his words. "Of course do you understand then, that it's no matter what comes of this fellow? of course do you understand that for any other purpose he's no man for me, nor for you?"

"I have frequently said to Sarah, sir," returned Brass, "that he was of no use at all in the business. You can't put any confidence in him, sir. If you'll believe me I've found that fellow, in the commonest little matters of the office that have been trusted to him, blurting out the truth, though expressly cautioned. The aggravation of that chap, sir, has exceeded anything you can imagine, it has indeed. Nothing but the respect and obligation I owe to you, sir-"

As it was plain that Sampson was bent on a complimentary harangue, unless he received a timely interruption, Mr. Quilp politely tapped him on the crown of his head with the little saucepan, and requested that he would be so obliging as to hold his peace.

"Practical, sir, practical," said Brass, rubbing the place and smiling; "but still extremely pleasant-immensely so!"

"Hearken to me, will you?" returned Quilp, "or I'll be a little more pleasant, presently. There's no chance of his comrade and friend returning. The scamp has been obliged to fly, as I learn, for some knavery, and has found his way abroad. Let him rot there."

"Certainly, sir. Quite proper.-Forcible!" cried Brass, glancing at the admiral again, as if he made a third in company. "Extremely forcible!"

"I hate him," said Quilp between his teeth, "and have always hated him, for family reasons. Besides, he was an intractable ruffian; otherwise he would have been of use. This fellow is pigeon-hearted, and light-headed. I don't want him any longer. Let him hang or drown-starve- go to the devil."

"By all means, sir," returned Brass. "When would you wish him, sir, to-ha, ha!-to make that little excursion?"

"When this trial's over," said Quilp. "As soon as that's ended, send him about his business."

"It shall be done, sir," returned Brass; "by all means. It will be rather a blow to Sarah, sir, but she has all her feelings under control. Ah, Mr. Quilp, I often think, sir, if it had only pleased Providence to bring you and Sarah together in earlier life, what blessed results would have flowed from such a union! You never saw our dear father, sir?-A charming gentleman. Sarah was his pride and joy, sir. He would have closed his eyes in bliss, would Foxey, Mr. Quilp, if he could have found her such a partner. You esteem her, sir?"

"I love her," croaked the dwarf.

"You're very good, sir," returned Brass, "I am sure. Is there any other order, sir, that I can take a note of, besides this little matter of Mr. Richard?"

"None," replied the dwarf, seizing the saucepan. "Let us drink the lovely Sarah."

"If we could do it in something, sir, that wasn't quite boiling," suggested Brass humbly, "perhaps it would be better. I think it will be more agreeable to her feelings, when she comes to hear from me of the honour you have done her, if she learns it was in liquor rather cooler than the last, sir."

But to these remonstrances Mr. Quilp turned a deaf ear. Sampson Brass, who was by this time anything but sober, being compelled to take further draughts of the same strong bowl, found that, instead of at all contributing to his recovery, they had the novel effect of making the counting-house spin round and round with extreme velocity, and causing the floor and ceiling to heave in a very distressing manner. After a brief stupor, he awoke to a consciousness of being partly under the table and partly under the grate. This position not being the most comfortable one he could have chosen for himself, he managed to stagger to his feet, and, holding on by the admiral, looked round for his host.

Mr. Brass's first impression was, that his host was gone and had left him there alone-perhaps locked him in for the night. A strong smell of tobacco, however, suggested a new train of ideas, he looked upwards, and saw that the dwarf was smoking in his hammock.

"Good-bye, sir," cried Brass faintly. "Good-bye, sir."

"Won't you stop all night?" said the dwarf, peeping out. "Do stop all night."

"I couldn't indeed, sir," replied Brass, who was almost dead from nausea and the closeness of the room. "If you'd have the goodness to show me a light, so that I may see my way across the yard, sir-"

Quilp was out in an instant; not with his legs first, or his head first, or his arms first, but bodily-altogether.

"To be sure," he said, taking up a lantern, which was now the only light in the place. "Be careful how you go, my dear friend. Be sure to pick your way among the timber, for all the rusty nails are upwards. There's a dog in the lane. He bit a man last night, and a woman the night before, and last Tuesday he killed a child-but that was in play. Don't go too near him."

"Which side of the road is he, sir?" asked Brass, in great dismay.

"He lives on the right hand," said Quilp, "but sometimes he hides on the left, ready for a spring. He's uncertain in that respect. Mind you take care of yourself. I'll never forgive you if you don't. There's the light out- never mind-you know the way-straight on!"

Quilp had slily shaded the light by holding it against his breast, and now stood chuckling and shaking from head to foot in a rapture of delight, as he heard the lawyer stumbling up the yard, and now and then falling heavily down. At length, however, he got quit of the place, and was out of hearing.

The dwarf shut himself up again, and sprang once more into his hammock.

CHAPTER LXIII

THE professional gentleman who had given Kit that consolatory piece of information relative to the settlement of his trifle of business at the Old Bailey, and the probability of its being very soon disposed of, turned out to be quite correct in his prognostications. In eight days' time, the sessions commenced. In one day afterwards, the Grand Jury found a True Bill against Christopher Nubbles for felony; and in two days from that finding, the aforesaid Christopher Nubbles was called upon to plead Guilty or Not Guilty to an Indictment for that he the said Christopher did feloniously abstract and steal from the dwelling-house and office of one Sampson Brass, gentleman, one Bank Note for Five Pounds issued by the Governor and Company of the Bank of England; in contravention of the Statutes in that case made and provided, and against the peace of our Sovereign Lord the King, his crown, and dignity.

To this indictment, Christopher Nubbles, in a low and trembling voice, pleaded Not Guilty: and here let those who are in the habit of forming hasty judgments from appearances, and who would have had Christopher, if innocent, speak out very strong and loud, observe, that confinement and anxiety will subdue the stoutest hearts; and that to one who has been close shut up, though it be only for ten or eleven days, seeing but stone walls and a very few stony faces, the sudden entrance into a great hall filled with life is a rather disconcerting and startling circumstance. To this it must be added, that life in a wig is to a large class of people much more terrifying and impressive than life with its own head of hair; and if, in addition to these considerations, there be further taken into account Kit's natural emotion on seeing the two Mr. Garlands and the little Notary looking on with pale and anxious faces, it will perhaps seem matter of no very great wonder that he should have been rather out of sorts, and unable to make himself exactly at home.

Although he had never seen either of the Mr. Garlands, or Mr. Witherden, since the time of his arrest, he had been given to understand

that they had employed counsel for him. Therefore, when one of the gentlemen in wigs got up and said "I am for the prisoner, my Lord," Kit made
him a bow; and when another gentleman in a wig got up and said "And I'm
against him, my Lord," Kit trembled very much, and bowed to him too.
And didn't he hope in his own heart that his gentleman was a match for the
other gentleman, and would make him ashamed of himself in no time!

The gentleman who was against him had to speak first, and being in
dreadfully good spirits (for he had, in the last trial, very nearly procured the
acquittal of a young gentleman who had had the misfortune to murder his
father) he spoke up you may be sure; telling the Jury that if they acquitted
this prisoner they must expect to suffer no less pangs and agonies than he
had told the other Jury they would certainly undergo if they convicted that
prisoner. And when he had told them all about the case, and that he had never known a worse case, he stopped a little while, like a man who had something terrible to tell them, and then said that he understood an attempt
would be made by his learned friend (and here he looked sideways at Kit's
gentleman) to impeach the testimony of those immaculate witnesses whom
he should call before them; but he did hope and trust that his learned friend
would have a greater respect and veneration for the character of the prosecutor, than whom, as he well knew, there did not exist, and never had existed,
a more honourable member of that most honourable profession to which
he was attached. And then he said, did the Jury know Bevis Marks? And if
they did know Bevis Marks (as he trusted, for their own characters, they did)
did they know the historical and elevating associations connected with that
most remarkable spot? Did they believe that a man like Brass could reside
in a place like Bevis Marks, and not be a virtuous and most upright character? And when he had said a great deal to them on this point, he remembered
that it was an insult to their understandings to make any remarks on what
they must have felt so strongly without him, and therefore called Sampson
Brass into the witness-box, straighway.

Then up comes Mr. Brass, very brisk and fresh; and, having bowed to
the judge, like a man who has had the pleasure of seeing him before and who
hopes he has been pretty well since their last meeting, folds his arms, and
looks at his gentleman as much as to say "Here I am-full of evidence-Tap
me!" And the gentleman does tap him presently, and with great discretion
too; drawing off the evidence by little and little, and making it run quite clear
and bright in the eyes of all present. Then Kit's gentleman takes him in hand,
but can make nothing of him; and after a great many very long questions and
very short answers, Mr. Sampson Brass goes down in glory.

To him succeeds Sarah, who in like manner is easy to be managed by
Mr. Brass's gentleman, but very obdurate to Kit's. In short, Kit's gentleman
can get nothing out of her but a repetition of what she has said before (only
a little stronger this time, as against his client), and therefore lets her go, in
some confusion. Then Mr. Brass's gentleman calls Richard Swiveller, and
Richard Swiveller appears accordingly.

Now, Mr. Brass's gentleman has it whispered in his ear that this witness
is disposed to be friendly to the prisoner -which, to say the truth, he is rather

glad to hear, as his strength is considered to lie in what is familiarly termed badgering. Wherefore, he begins by requesting the officer to be quite sure that this witness kisses the book, and then goes to work at him, tooth and nail.

"Mr. Swiveller," says this gentleman to Dick, when he has told his tale with evident reluctance and a desire to make the best of it: "Pray, sir, where did you dine yesterday?"-"Where did I dine yesterday?"-"Ay, sir, where did you dine yesterday-was it near here, sir?"-"Oh to be sure-yes-just over the way."-"To be sure. Yes. Just over the way," repeats Mr. Brass's gentleman, with a glance at the Court- "Alone, sir?"- "I beg your pardon," says Mr. Swiveller, who has not caught the question- "Alone, sir?" repeats Mr. Brass's gentleman in a voice of thunder, "did you dine alone? Did you treat any-body, sir? Come I"-"Oh yes, to be sure-yes, I did," says Mr. Swiveller with a smile. "Have the goodness to banish a levity, sir, which is very ill-suite to the place in which you stand (though perhaps you have reason to be thank-ful that it's only that place)," says Mr. Brass's gentleman, with a nod of the head insinuating that the dock is Mr. Swiveller's legitimate sphere of action; "and attend to me. You were waiting about here yesterday in expectation that this trial was coming on. You dined over the way. You treated some-body. Now, was that somebody brother to the prisoner at the bar?"-Mr. Swiveller is proceeding to explain- "Yes or No, sir," cries Mr. Brass's gentle-man- "But will you allow me-"- "Yes or No, sir"- "Yes it was, but-"- "Yes it was," cries the gentleman, taking him up short- "And a very pretty witness you are!"

Down sits Mr. Brass's gentleman. Kit's gentleman, not knowing how the matter really stands, is afraid to pursue the subject. Richard Swiveller re-tires abashed. Judge, jury, and spectators have visions of his lounging about with an ill-looking, large-whiskered, dissolute young fellow of six feet high. The reality is, little Jacob, with the calves of his legs exposed to the open air, and himself tied up in a shawl. Nobody knows the truth, everybody believes a falsehood-and all because of the ingenuity of Mr. Brass's gentleman!

Then came the witnesses to character, and here Mr. Brass's gentleman shines again. It turns out that Mr. Garland has had no character with Kit, no recommendation of him but from his own mother, and that he was sud-denly dismissed by his former master for unknown reasons. "Really, Mr. Garland," says Mr. Brass's gentleman, "for a person who has arrived at your time of life, you are, to say the least of it, singularly indiscreet, I think." The Jury think so too, and find Kit guilty. He is taken off, humbly protesting his innocence. The spectators settle themselves in their places with renewed attention, for there are several female witnesses to be examined in the next case, and it has been rumoured that Mr. Brass's gentleman will make great fun in cross-examining them for the prisoner.

Kit's mother, poor woman, is waiting at the grate below stairs, accom-panied by Barbara's mother (who, honest soul! never does anything but cry, and hold the baby), and a sad interview ensues. The newspaper-reading turnkey has told them all. He don't think it will be transportation for life, because there's time to prove the good character yet, and that is sure to

serve him. He wonders what he did it for. "He never did it!" cries Kit's
mother. "Well," says the turnkey, "I won't contradict you. It's all one now,
whether he did or not."

Kit's mother can reach his hand through the bars, and clasps it-God,
and those to whom he has given such tenderness, only know in how much
agony. Kit bids her keep a good heart, and, under pretence of having the children lifted up to kiss him, prays Barbara's mother in a whisper to take her
home.

"Some friend will rise up for us, mother," cries Kit, "I am sure. If not
now, before long. My innocence will come out, mother, and I shall be
brought back again; I feel confidence in that. You must teach little Jacob
and the baby how all this was, for if they thought I had ever been dishonest,
when they grow old enough to understand, it would break my heart to
know it, if I was thousands of miles away.-Oh! is there no good gentleman
here, who will take care of her!"

The hand slips out of his, for the poor creature sinks down upon the
earth, insensible. Richard Swiveller comes hastily up, elbows the bystanders
out of the way, takes her (after some trouble) in one arm after the manner of
theatrical ravishers, and nodding to Kit, and commanding Barbara's mother
to follow, for he has a coach waiting, bears her swiftly off.

Well; Richard took her home. And what astonishing absurdities in the
way of quotation from song and poem he perpetrated on the road, no man
knows. He took her home, and stayed till she was recovered; and, having
no money to pay the coach, went back in state to Bevis Marks, bidding the
driver (for it was Saturday night) wait at the door while he went in for
"change."

"Mr. Richard, sir," said Brass cheerfully, "Good evening."

Monstrous as Kit's tale had appeared at first, Mr. Richard did, that
night, half suspect his affable employer of some deep villany. Perhaps it was
but the misery he had just witnessed which gave his careless nature this impulse; but, be that as it may, it was very strong upon him, and he said in as
few words as possible, what he wanted.

"Money!" cried Brass, taking out his purse. "Ha ha! To be sure, Mr.
Richard, to be sure, sir. All men must live. You haven't change for a five-
pound note, have you, sir?"

"No," returned Dick, shortly.

"Oh!" said Brass, "here's the very sum. That saves trouble. You're very
welcome I'm sure.-Mr. Richard, sir-"

Dick, who had by this time reached the door, turned round.

"You needn't," said Brass, "trouble yourself to come back any more,
sir."

"Eh?"

"You see, Mr. Richard," said Brass, thrusting his hands in his pockets
and rocking himself to and fro upon his stool, "the fact is, that a man of your
abilities is lost, sir, quite lost, in our dry and mouldy line. It's terrible drudg-
ery- shocking. I should say now that the stage, or the-or the army, Mr.
Richard-or something very superior in the licensed victualling way-was the

kind of thing that would call out the genius of such a man as you. I hope you'll look in to see us now and then. Sally, sir, will be delighted I'm sure. She's extremely sorry to lose you, Mr. Richard, but a sense of her duty to society reconciles her.-An amazing creature that, sir! You'll find the money quite correct, I think. There's a cracked window, sir, but I've not made any deduction on that account. Whenever we part with friends, Mr. Richard, let us part liberally. A delightful sentiment, sir!"

To all these rambling observations, Mr. Swiveller answered not one word, but, returning for the aquatic jacket, rolled it into a tight round ball, looking steadily at Brass meanwhile as if he had some intention of bowling him down with it. He only took it under his arm, however, and marched out of the office in profound silence. Directly he had closed the door, he opened it, stared in again for a few moments with the same portentous gravity; and nodding his head once, in a slow and ghost-like manner, vanished.

He paid the coachman and turned his back on Bevis Marks, big with great designs for the comforting of Kit's mother and the aid of Kit himself.

But the lives of gentlemen devoted to such pleasures as Richard Swiveller, are extremely precarious. The spiritual excitement of the last fortnight, working upon a system affected in no slight degree by the spirituous excitement of some years, proved a little too much for him. That very night, Mr. Richard was seized with an alarming illness, and in twenty-four hours was stricken with a raging fever.

CHAPTER LXIV

TOSSING to and fro upon his hot, uneasy bed; tormented by a fierce thirst which nothing could appease; unable to find, in any change of posture, a moment's peace or ease; and rambling ever through deserts of thought where there was no resting-place, no sight or sound suggestive of refreshment or repose, nothing but a dull eternal weariness, with no change but the restless shiftings of his miserable body, and the weary wanderings of his mind, constant still to one ever-present anxiety-to a sense of something left undone, of some fearful obstacle to be surmounted, of some carking care that would not be driven away. and haunted the distempered brain, now in this form, now in that- always shadowy and dim, but recognisable for the same phantom in every shape it took, darkening every vision like an evil conscience, and making slumber horrible; in these slow tortures of his dread disease, the unfortunate Richard lay wasting and consuming inch by inch, until at last when he seemed to fight and struggle to rise up, and to be held down by devils, he sank into a deep sleep, and dreamed no more.

He awoke; and, with a sensation of most blissful rest, better than sleep itself, began gradually to remember something of these sufferings, and to think what a long night it had been, and whether he had not been delirious twice or thrice. Happening in the midst of these cogitations to raise his hand, he was astonished to find how heavy it seemed, and yet how thin and light it really was. Still he felt indifferent and happy; and having no curiosity to pursue the subject, remained in the same waking slumber until his attention was attracted by a cough. This made him doubt whether he had locked his door last night, and feel a little surprised at having a companion in the room. Still, he lacked energy to follow up this train of thought; and unconsciously fell, in a luxury of repose, to staring at some green stripes upon the bed-furniture, and associating them strangely with patches of fresh turf, while the yellow ground between made gravel-walks, and so helped out a long perspective of trim gardens.

He was rambling in imagination upon these terraces, and had quite lost himself among them indeed, when he heard the cough once more. The walks shrank into stripes again at the sound; and raising himself a little in the bed, and holding the curtain open with one hand, he looked out.

The same room certainly, and still by candle-light; but with what unbounded astonishment did he see all those bottles, and basins, and articles of linen airing by the fire, and such-like furniture of a sick chamber-all very clean and neat, but all quite different from anything he had left there, when he went to bed! The atmosphere, too, filled with a cool smell of herbs and vinegar; the floor newly sprinkled; the-the what? The Marchioness? Yes; playing cribbage with herself at the table. There she sat, intent upon her game, coughing now and then in a subdued manner as if she feared to disturb him-shuffling the cards, cutting, dealing, playing, counting, pegging-going through all the mysteries of cribbage as though she had been in full practice from her cradle!

Mr. Swiveller contemplated these things for a short time, and suffering the curtain to fall into its former position, laid his head upon the pillow again.

"I'm dreaming," thought Richard, "that's clear. When I went to bed, my hands were not made of egg-shells; and now I can almost see through 'em. If this is not a dream, I have woke up by mistake in an Arabian Night, instead of a London one. But I have no doubt I'm asleep. Not the least."

Here the small servant had another cough.

"Very remarkable!" thought Mr. Swiveller. "I never dreamt such a real cough as that before. I don't know, indeed, that I ever dreamt either a cough or a sneeze. Perhaps it's part of the philosophy of dreams that one never does. There's another-and another-I say,-I'm dreaming rather fast!"

For the purpose of testing his real condition, Mr. Swiveller, after some reflection, pinched himself in the arm.

"Queerer still!" he thought. "I came to bed rather plump than otherwise, and now there's nothing to lay hold of. I'll take another survey."

The result of this further inspection was, to convince Mr. Swiveller that the objects by which he was surrounded were real, and that he saw them, beyond all question, with his waking eyes.

"It's an Arabian Night, that's what it is," said Richard. "I'm in Damascus or Grand Cairo. The Marchioness is a Genie, and having had a wager with another Genie about who is the handsomest young man alive, and the worthiest to be the husband of the Princess of China, has brought me away, room and all, to compare us together. Perhaps," said Mr. Swiveller, turning languidly round upon his pillow, and looking on that side of his bed which was next the wall, "the Princess may be still-No, she's gone."

Not feeling quite satisfied with this explanation, as, even taking it to be the correct one, it still involved a little mystery and doubt, Mr. Swiveller raised the curtain again, determined to take the first favourable opportunity of addressing his companion. An occasion soon presented itself. The Marchioness dealt, turned up a knave, and omitted to take the usual advantage; upon which Mr. Swiveller called out as loud as he could- "Two for his heels!"

The Marchioness jumped up quickly, and clapped her hands. "Arabian Night, certainly," thought Mr. Swiveller; "they always clap their hands instead of ringing the bell. Now for the two thousand black slaves, with jars of jewels on their heads!"

It appeared, however, that she had only clapped her hands in joy; for directly afterwards she began to laugh, and then to cry; declaring, not in choice Arabic but in familiar English, that she was "so glad, she didn't know what to do."

"Marchioness," said Mr. Swiveller, thoughtfully, "be pleased to draw nearer. First of all, will you have the goodness to inform me where I shall find my voice; and secondly, what has become of my flesh?"

The Marchioness only shook her head mournfully, and cried again; whereupon Mr. Swiveller (being very weak) felt his own eyes affected likewise.

"I begin to infer, from your manner and these appearances, Marchioness,"-said' Richard after a pause, and smiling with a trembling lip, "that I have been ill."

"You just have!" replied the small servant, wiping her eyes. "And haven't you been a talking nonsense!"

"Oh!" said Dick. "Very ill, Marchioness, have I been?"

"Dead, all but," replied the small servant. "I never thought you'd get better. Thank Heaven you have!"

Mr. Swiveller was silent for a long while. By-and-by, he began to talk again-inquiring how long he had been there.

"Three weeks to-morrow," replied the small servant.

"Three what?" said Dick.

"Weeks," returned the Marchioness emphatically; "three long, slow weeks."

The bare thought of having been in such extremity caused Richard to fall into another silence, and to lie flat down again at his full length. The Marchioness, having arranged the bed-clothes more comfortably, and felt that his hands and forehead were quite cool-a discovery that filled her with delight-cried a little more, and then applied herself to getting tea ready, and making some thin dry toast.

While she was thus engaged, Mr. Swiveller looked on with a grateful heart, very much astonished to see how thoroughly at home she made herself, and attributing this attention, in its origin, to Sally Brass, whom, in his own mind, he could not thank enough. When the Marchioness had finished her toasting, she spread a clean cloth on a tray, and brought him some crisp slices and a great basin of weak tea, with which (she said) the doctor had left word he might refresh himself when he awoke. She propped him up with pillows, if not as skilfully as if she had been a professional nurse all her life, at least as tenderly; and looked on with unutterable satisfaction while the patient stopping every now and then to shake her by the hand took his poor meal with an appetite and relish, which the greatest dainties of the earth, under any other circumstances, would have failed to provoke. Having cleared away, and disposed everything comfortably about him again, she sat down at the table to take her own tea.

"Marchioness," said Mr. Swiveller, "how's Sally?"

The small servant screwed her face into an expression of the very uttermost entanglement of slyness, and shook her head.

"What, haven't you seen her lately?" said Dick.

"Seen her!" cried the small servant. "Bless you, I've run away!"

Mr. Swiveller immediately laid himself down again quite flat, and so remained for about five minutes. By slow degrees he resumed his sitting posture after that lapse of time, and inquired:

"And where do you live, Marchioness?"

"Live!" cried the small servant. "Here!"

"Oh!" said Mr. Swiveller.

And with that he fell down flat again, as suddenly as if he had been shot. Thus he remained, motionless and bereft of speech, until she had finished her meal, put everything in its place, and swept the hearth; when he motioned her to bring a chair to the bedside, and, being propped up again, open a farther conversation.

"And so," said Dick, "you have run away?"

"Yes," said the Marchioness, "and they've been a tizing of me."

"Been-I beg your pardon," said Dick- "what have they been doing?"

"Been a tizing of me-tizing you know-in the newspapers," rejoined the Marchioness.

"Ay, ay," said Dick, "advertising?"

The small servant nodded, and winked. Her eyes were so red with waking and crying, that the Tragic Muse might have winked with greater consistency. And so Dick felt.

"Tell me," said he, "how it was that you thought of coming here."

"Why, you see," returned the Marchioness, "when you was gone, I hadn't any friend at all, because the lodger he never come back, and I didn't know where either him or you was to be found, you know. But one morning, when I was-"

"Was near a key-hole?" suggested Mr. Swiveller, observing that she faltered.

"Well then," said the small servant, nodding; "when I was near the office key-hole-as you see me through, you know-I heard somebody saying that she lived here, and was the lady whose house you lodged at, and that you was took very bad, and wouldn't nobody come and take care of you. Mr. Brass, he says, 'It's no business of mine;' and Miss Sally, she says, 'He's a funny chap, but it's no business of mine;' and the lady went away, and slammed the door to, when she went out, I can tell you. So I run away that night, and come here, and told 'em you was my brother, and they believed me, and I've been here ever since."

"This poor little Marchioness has been wearing herself to death!" cried Dick.

"No I haven't," she returned, "not a bit of it. Don't you mind about me. I like sitting up, and I've often had a sleep, bless you, in one of them chairs. But if you could have seen how you tried to jump out o' winder, and if you could have heard how you used to keep on singing and making speeches, you wouldn't have believed it-I'm so glad you're better, Mr. Liverer."

"Liverer indeed!" said Dick thoughtfully. "It's well I am a liverer. I strongly suspect I should have died, Marchioness, but for you."

At this point, Mr. Swiveller took the small servant's hand in his again, and being, as we have seen, but poorly, might in struggling to express his thanks have made his eyes as red as hers, but that she quickly changed the theme by making him lie down, and urging him to keep very quiet.

"The doctor," she told him, "said you was to be kept quite still, and there was to be no noise nor nothing. Now, take a rest, and then we'll talk again. I'll sit by you, you know. If you shut your eyes, perhaps you'll go to sleep. You'll be all the better for it, if you do."

The Marchioness, in saying these words, brought a little table to the bedside, took her seat at it, and began to work away at the concoction of some cooling drink, with the address of a score of chemists. Richard Swiveller, being indeed fatigued, fell into a deep slumber, and waking in about half an hour, inquired what time it was.

"Just gone half after six," replied his small friend, helping him to sit up again.

"Marchioness," said Richard, passing his hand over his forehead and turning suddenly round, as though the subject but that moment flashed upon him, "what has become of Kit?"

He had been sentenced to transportation for a great many years, she said.

"Has he gone?" asked Dick-" his mother-how is she,-what has become of her?"

His nurse shook her head, and answered that she knew nothing about them.

"But, if I thought," said she, very slowly, "that you'd keep quiet, and not put yourself into another fever, I could tell you-but I won't now."

"Yes, do," said Dick. "It will amuse me."

"Oh! would it though!" rejoined the small servant, with a horrified look. "I know better than that. Wait till you're better and then I'll tell you."

Dick looked very earnestly at his little friend: and his eyes, being large and hollow from illness, assisted the expression so much, that she was quite frightened, and besought him not to think any more about it. What had already fallen from her, however, had not only piqued his curiosity, but seriously alarmed him, wherefore he urged her to tell him the worst at once.

"Oh! there's no worst in it," said the small servant. "It hasn't anything to do with you."

"Has it anything to do with-is it anything you heard through chinks or key-holes-and that you were not intended to hear?" asked Dick, in a breathless state.

"Yes," replied the small servant.

"In-in Bevis Marks?" pursued Dick hastily. "Conversations between Brass and Sally?"

"Yes," cried the small servant again.

Richard Swiveller thrust his lank arm out of bed, and, gripping her by the wrist and drawing her close to him, bade her out with it, and freely too, or he would not answer for the consequences; being wholly unable to endure that state of excitement and expectation. She, seeing that he was greatly agitated, and that the effects of postponing her revelation might be much more injurious than any that were likely to ensue from its being made at once, promised compliance, on condition that the patient kept himself perfectly quiet, and abstained from starting up or tossing about.

"But if you begin to do that," said the small servant, "I'll leave off. And so I tell you."

"You can't leave off till you have gone on," said Dick. "And do go on, there's a darling. Speak, sister, speak. Pretty Polly say-Oh tell me when, and tell me where, pray Marchioness, I beseech you!"

Unable to resist these fervent adjurations, which Richard Swiveller poured out as passionately as if they had been of the most solemn and tremendous nature, his companion spoke thus:

"Well! Before I run away, I used to sleep in the kitchen-where we played cards, you know. Miss Sally used to keep the key of the kitchen door in her pocket, and she always come down at night to take away the candle and rake out the fire. When she had done that, she left me to go to bed in the dark, locked the door on the outside, put the key in her pocket again, and kept me locked up till she come down in the morning-very early I can tell you-and let me out. I was terrible afraid of being kept like this, because if there was a fire, I thought they might forget me and only take care of themselves you know. So whenever I see an old rusty key anywhere, I picked it up and tried if it would fit the door, and at last I found in the dust cellar a key that did fit it."

Here Mr. Swiveller made a violent demonstration with his legs. But the small servant immediately pausing in her talk, he subsided again, and, pleading a momentary forgetfulness of their compact, entreated her to proceed.

"They kept me very short," said the small servant. "Oh! you can't think how short they kept me! So I used to come out at night after they'd gone to bed, and feel about in the dark for bits of biscuit, or sandwitches that you'd left in the office, or even pieces of orange peel to put into cold water and make believe it was wine. Did you ever taste orange peel and water?"

Mr. Swiveller replied that he had never tasted that ardent liquor; and once more urged his friend to resume the thread of her narrative.

"If you make believe very much, it's quite nice," said the small servant; "but if you don't, you know, it seems as if it would bear a little more seasoning, certainly. Well, sometimes I used to come out after they'd gone to bed, and sometimes before, you know; and one or two nights before there was all that precious noise in the office -when the young man was took, I mean-I come up stairs while Mr. Brass and Miss Sally was a sittin' at the office fire; and I'll tell you the truth, that I come to listen again about the key of the safe."

Mr. Swiveller gathered up his knees so as to make a great cone of the bed-clothes, and conveyed into his countenance an expression of the utmost concern. But the small servant pausing, and holding up her finger, the cone gently disappeared, though the look of concern did not.

"There was him and her," said the small servant, "a sittin' by the fire, and talking softly together. Mr. Brass says to Miss Sally, 'Upon my word,' he says, 'it's a dangerous thing, and it might get us into a world of trouble, and I don't half like it.' She says-you know her way- she says, 'You're the chickenest-hearted, feeblest, faintest man I ever see, and I think,' she says, 'that I ought to have been the brother, and you the sister. Isn't Quilp,' she says, 'our principal support?' 'He certainly is,' says Mr. Brass. 'And an't we,' she says, 'constantly ruining somebody or other in the way of business?' 'We certainly are,' says Mr. Brass. 'Then does it signify,' she says, 'about ruining this Kit when Quilp desires it?' 'It certainly does not signify,' says Brass. Then, they whispered and laughed for a long time about there being no danger if it was well done, and then Mr. Brass pulls out his pocket-book, and says, 'Well,' he says, 'here it is-Quilp's own five-pound note. We'll agree that way, then,' he says. 'Kit's coming to-morrow morning, I know. While he's up stairs, you'll get out of the way, and I'll clear off Mr. Richard. Having Kit alone, I'll hold him in conversation, and put this property in his hat. I'll manage so, besides,' he says, 'that Mr. Richard shall find it there, and be the evidence. And if that don't get Christopher out of Mr. Quilp's way, and satisfy Mr. Quilp's grudges,' he says, 'the Devil's in it.' Miss Sally laughed, and said that was the plan, and as they seemed to be moving away, and I was afraid to stop any longer, I went down stairs again. -There!"

The small servant had gradually worked herself into as much agitation as Mr. Swiveller, and therefore made no effort to restrain him when he sat up in bed and hastily demanded whether this story had been told to anybody.

"How could it be?" replied his nurse. "I was almost afraid to think about it, and hoped the young man would be let off. When I heard 'em say they had found him guilty of what he didn't do, you was gone, and so was the lodger-though I think I should have been frightened to tell him, even if he'd been there. Ever since I come here, you've been out of your senses, and what would have been the good of telling you then?"

"Marchioness," said Mr. Swiveller, plucking off his night-cap and flinging it to the other end of the room; "if you'll do me the favour to retire for a few minutes and see what sort, of a night it is, I'll get up."

"You mustn't think of such a thing," cried his nurse.

"I must indeed," said the patient, looking round the room. "Whereabouts are my clothes?"

"Oh, I'm so glad-you haven't got any," replied the Marchioness.

"Ma'am!" said Mr. Swiveller, in great astonishment.

"I've been obliged to sell them, every one, to get the things that was ordered for you. But don't take on about that," urged the Marchioness, as Dick fell back upon his pillow. "You're too weak to stand, indeed."

"I am afraid," said Richard dolefully, "that you're right! What ought I to do! what is to be done!"

It naturally occurred to him on very little reflection, that the first step to take would be to communicate with one of the Mr. Garlands instantly. It was very possible that Mr. Abel had not yet left the office. In as little time as it takes to tell it, the small servant had the address in pencil on a piece of paper; a verbal description of father and son, which would enable her to recognise either without difficulty; and a special caution to be shy of Mr. Chuckster, in consequence of that gentleman's known antipathy to Kit. Armed with these slender powers, she hurried away, commissioned to bring either old Mr. Garland or Mr. Abel, bodily, to that apartment.

"I suppose," said Dick, as she closed the door slowly, and peeped into the room again to make sure that he was comfortable, "I suppose there's nothing left-not so much as a waistcoat even?"

"No, nothing."

"It's embarrassing," said Mr. Swiveller, "in case of fire-even an umbrella would be something-but you did quite right, dear Marchioness. I should have died without you!"

CHAPTER LXV

IT was well for the small servant that she was of a sharp, quick nature, or the consequence of sending her out alone, from the very neighbourhood in which it was most dangerous for her to appear, would probably have been the restoration of Miss Sally Brass to the supreme authority over her person. Not unmindful of the risk she ran, however, the Marchioness no sooner left the house than she dived into the first dark by-way that presented itself, and, without any present reference to the point to which her journey tended, made it her first business to put two good miles of brick and mortar between herself and Bevis Marks.

When she had accomplished this object, she began to shape her course for the notary's office, to which-shrewdly inquiring of apple-women and oyster-sellers at street-corners, rather than in lighted shops or of well-dressed people, at the hazard of attracting notice-she easily procured a direction. As carrier-pigeons, on being first let loose in a strange place beat the air at random for a short time, before darting off towards the spot for which they are designed, so did the Marchioness flutter round and round until she believed herself in safety, and then bear swiftly down upon the port for which she was bound.

She had no bonnet-nothing on her head but a great cap which in some old time had been worn by Sally Brass, whose taste in head-dresses was, as we have seen, peculiar and her speed was rather retarded than assisted by her shoes, which, being extremely large and slipshod, flew off every now and then, and were difficult to find again, among the crowd of passengers. Indeed, the poor little creature experienced so much trouble and delay from having to grope for these articles of dress in mud and kennel, and suffered in these researches so much jostling, pushing, squeezing, and bandying from hand to hand, that by the time she reached the street in which the notary lived, she was fairly worn out and exhausted, and could not refrain from tears.

But to have got there at last was a great comfort, especially as there were lights still burning in the office window, and therefore some hope that she was not too late. So, the Marchioness dried her eyes with the backs of her hands, and, stealing softly up the steps, peeped in through the glass door.

Mr. Chuckster was standing behind the lid of his desk, making such preparations towards finishing off for the night as pulling down his wristbands and pulling up his shirt-collar, settling his neck more gracefully in his stock, and secretly arranging his whiskers by the aid of a little triangular bit of looking-glass. Before the ashes of the fire stood two gentlemen, one of whom she rightly judged to be the notary, and the other (who was buttoning his great coat, and was evidently about to depart immediately) Mr. Abel Garland.

Having made these observations, the small spy took counsel with herself, and resolved to wait in the street until Mr. Abel came out, as there would be then no fear of having to speak before Mr. Chuckster, and less difficulty in delivering her message. With this purpose she slipped out again, and crossing the road, sat down upon a door-step just opposite.

She had hardly taken this position, when there came dancing up the street, with his legs all wrong, and his head everywhere by turns, a pony. This pony had a little phaeton behind him, and a man in it; but neither man nor phaeton seemed to embarrass him in the least, as he reared up on his hind legs, or stopped, or went on, or stood still again, or backed, or went sideways, without the smallest reference to them,-just as the fancy seized him, and as if he were the freest animal in creation. When they came to the notary's door, the man called out in a very respectful manner, "Woa then,"-intimating that if he might venture to express a wish, it would be that they stopped there. The pony made a moment's pause; but as if it occurred to him that to stop when he was required might be to establish an inconvenient and dangerous precedent, he immediately started off again, rattled at a fast trot to the street-corner, wheeled round, came back, and then stopped of his own accord.

"Oh! you're a precious creatur!" said the man-who didn't venture by the bye to come out in his true colours until he was safe on the pavement. "I wish I had the rewarding of you,-I do."

"What has he been doing?" said Mr. Abel, tying a shawl round his neck as he came down the steps.

"He's enough to fret a man's heart out," replied the hostler. "He is the most wicious rascal-Woa then, will you?"

"He'll never stand still, if you call him names," said Mr. Abel, getting in, and taking the reins. "He's a very good fellow if you know how to manage him. This is the first time he has been out, this long while, for he has lost his old driver and wouldn't stir for anybody else, till this morning. The lamps are right, are they? That's well. Be here to take him to-morrow, if you please. Good night!"

And after one or two strange plunges, quite of his own invention, the pony yielded to Mr. Abel's mildness, and trotted gently off.

All this time Mr. Chuckster had been standing at the door, and the small servant had been afraid to approach. She had nothing for it now, therefore, but to run after the chaise, and to call to Mr. Abel to stop. Being out of breath when she came up with it, she was unable to make him hear. The case was desperate; for the pony was quickening his pace. The Marchioness hung on behind for a few moments, and, feeling that she could go no farther, and must soon yield, clambered by a vigorous effort into the hinder seat, and in so doing lost one of the shoes for ever.

Mr. Abel being in a thoughtful frame of mind, and having quite enough to do to keep the pony going, went jogging on without looking round: little dreaming of the strange figure that was close behind him, until the Marchioness, having in some degree recovered her breath, and the loss of her shoe, and the novelty of her position, uttered close into his ear, the words-

"I say, sir"-

He turned his head quickly enough then, and stopping the pony, cried, with some trepidation, "God bless me, what is this!"

"Don't be frightened, sir," replied the still panting messenger. "Oh, I've run such a way after you!"

"What do you want with me?" said Mr. Abel. "How did you come here?"

"I got in behind," replied the Marchioness. "Oh please drive on, sir-don't stop-and go towards the City, will you? And oh do please make haste, because it's of consequence. There's somebody wants to see you there. He sent me to say would you come directly, and that he knowed all about Kit, and could save him yet, and prove his innocence."

"What do you tell me, child?"

"The truth, upon my word and honour I do. But please to drive on-quick, please! I've been such a time gone, he'll think I'm lost."

Mr. Abel involuntarily urged the pony forward. The pony, impelled by some secret sympathy or some new caprice, burst into a great pace, and neither slackened it, nor indulged in any eccentric performances, until they arrived at the door of Mr. Swiveller's lodging, where, marvellous to relate, he consented to stop when Mr. Abel checked him.

"See! It's that room up there," said the Marchioness, pointing to one where there was a faint light. "Come!"

Mr. Abel, who was one of the simplest and most retiring creatures in existence, and naturally timid withal, hesitated; for he had heard of people being decoyed into strange places to be robbed and murdered, under circumstances very like the present, and, for anything he knew to the contrary, by guides very like the Marchioness. His regard for Kit, however, overcame every other consideration. So, entrusting Whisker to the charge of a man who was lingering hard by in expectation of the job, he suffered his companion to take his hand, and to lead him up the dark and narrow stairs.

He was not a little surprised to find himself conducted into a dimly-lighted sick chamber, where a man was sleeping tranquilly in bed.

"An't it nice to see him lying there so quiet?" said his guide, in an earnest whisper. "Oh I you'd say it was, if you had only seen him two or three days ago."

Mr. Abel made no answer, and, to say the truth, kept a long way from the bed and very near the door. His guide, who appeared to understand his reluctance, trimmed the candle, and taking it in her hand, approached the bed. As she did so, the sleeper started up, and he recognised in the wasted face the features of Richard Swiveller.

"Why, how is this?" said Mr. Abel kindly, as he hurried towards him. "You have been ill?"

"Very," replied Dick. "Nearly dead. You might have chanced to hear of your Richard on his bier, but for the friend I sent to fetch you. Another shake of the hand, Marchioness, if you please. Sit down, sir."

Mr. Abel seemed rather astonished to hear of the quality of his guide, and took a chair by the bedside.

"I have sent for you, sir," said Dick- "but she told you on what account?"

"She did. I am quite bewildered by all this. I really don't know what to say or think," replied Mr. Abel.

"You'll say that presently," retorted Dick. "Marchioness, take a seat on the bed, will you? Now, tell this gentleman all that you told me; and be particular. Don't you speak another word, sir."

The story was repeated; it was, in effect, exactly the same as before, without any deviation or omission. Richard Swiveller kept his eyes fixed on his visitor during its narration, and directly it was concluded, took the word again.

"You have heard it all, and you'll not forget it. I'm too giddy and too queer to suggest anything; but you and your friends will know what to do. After this long delay, every minute is an age. If ever you went home fast in your life, go home fast to-night. Don't stop to say one word to me, but go. She will be found here, whenever she's wanted; and as to me, you're pretty sure to find me at home, for a week or two. There are more reasons than one for that. Marchioness, a light! If you lose another minute in looking at me, sir, I'll never forgive you!"

Mr. Abel needed no more remonstrance or persuasion. He was gone in an instant; and the Marchioness, returning from lighting him down stairs, reported that the pony, without any preliminary objection whatever, had dashed away at full gallop.

"That's right," said Dick; "and hearty of him; and I honour him from this time. But get some supper and a mug of beer, for I am sure you must be tired. Do have a mug of beer. It will do me as much good to see you take it as if I might drink it myself."

Nothing but this assurance could have prevailed upon the small nurse to indulge in such a luxury. Having eaten and drunk to Mr. Swiveller's extreme contentment, given him his drink, and put everything in neat order, she wrapped herself in an old coverlet and lay down upon the rug before the fire.

Mr. Swiveller was by that time murmuring in his sleep, "Strew then, oh strew, a bed of rushes. Here will we stay, till morning blushes. Good night, Marchioness!"

CHAPTER LXVI

ON awaking in the morning, Richard Swiveller became conscious by slow degrees of whispering voices in his room. Looking out between the curtains, he espied Mr. Garland, Mr. Abel, the Notary, and the single gentleman, gathered round the Marchioness, and talking to her with great earnestness but in very subdued tones-fearing, no doubt, to disturb him. He lost no time in letting them know that this precaution was unnecessary, and all tour gentlemen directly approached his bedside. Old Mr. Garland was the first to stretch out his hand, and inquire how he felt.

Dick was about to answer that he felt much better, though still as weak as need be, when his little nurse, pushing the visitors aside and pressing up to his pillow as if in jealousy of their interference, set his breakfast before him, and insisted on his taking it before he underwent the fatigue of speaking or of being spoken to. Mr. Swiveller, who was perfectly ravenous, and had had, all night, amazingly distinct and consistent dreams of mutton chops, double stout, and similar delicacies, felt even the weak tea and dry toast such irresistible temptations, that he consented to eat and drink upon one condition.

"And that is," said Dick, returning the pressure of Mr. Garland's hand, "that you answer me this question truly, before I take a bit or drop. Is it too late?"

"For completing the work you began so well last night?" returned the old gentleman. "No. Set your mind at rest upon that point. It is not, I assure you."

Comforted by this intelligence, the patient applied himself to his food with a keen appetite, though evidently not with a greater zest in the eating than his nurse appeared to have in seeing him eat. The manner of his meal was this:-Mr. Swiveller, holding the slice of toast or cup of tea in his left hand, and taking a bite or drink as the case might be, constantly kept, in his right, one palm of the Marchioness tight locked; and to shake, or even to kiss this imprisoned hand, he would stop every now and then, in the very act of swallowing, with perfect seriousness of intention, and the utmost gravity. As often as he put anything into his mouth, whether for eating or drinking, the face of the Marchioness lighted up beyond all description; but whenever he gave her one or other of these tokens of recognition, her countenance became over-shadowed, and she began to sob. Now, whether she was in her laughing joy, or in her crying one, the Marchioness could not help turning to the visitors with an appealing look, which seemed to say, "You see this fellow-can I help this?"-and they being thus made, as it were, parties to the scene, as regularly answered by another look, "No. Certainly not." This dumb-show taking place during the whole time of the invalid's breakfast, and the invalid himself, pale and emaciated, performing no small part in the same, it may be fairly questioned whether at any meal, where no word, good or bad, was spoken from beginning to end, so much was expressed by gestures in themselves so slight and unimportant.

At length-and to say the truth before very long-Mr. Swiveller had despatched as much toast and tea as in that stage of his recovery it was discreet to let him have. But the cares of the Marchioness did not stop here; for, disappearing for an instant and presently returning with a basin of fair water, she laved his face and hands, brushed his hair, and in short made him as spruce and smart as anybody under such circumstances could be made; and all this in as brisk and business-like a manner, as if he were a very little boy, and she his grown-up nurse. To these various attentions, Mr. Swiveller submitted in a kind of grateful astonishment beyond the reach of language. When they were at last brought to an end, and the Marchioness had withdrawn into a distant corner to take her own poor breakfast (cold enough by that time), he turned his face away for some few moments, and shook hands heartily with the air.

"Gentlemen," said Dick, rousing himself from this pause, and turning round again, "you'll excuse me. Men who have been brought so low as I have been, are easily fatigued. I am fresh again now, and fit for talking. We're short of chairs here, among other trifles, but if you'll do me the favour to sit upon the bed-"

"What can we do for you?" said Mr. Garland, kindly.

"If you could make the Marchioness yonder, a Marchioness in real, sober earnest," returned Dick, "I'd thank you to get it done off-hand. But as you can't, and as the question is not what you will do for me, but what you will do for somebody else who has a better claim upon you, pray, sir, let me know what you intend doing."

"It's chiefly on that account that we have come just now," said the single gentleman, "for you will have another visitor presently. We feared you would be anxious unless you knew from ourselves what steps we intended to take, and therefore came to you before we stirred in the matter."

"Gentlemen," returned Dick, "I thank you. Anybody in the helpless state that you see me in, is naturally anxious. Don't let me interrupt you, sir."

"Then, you see, my good fellow," said the single gentleman, "that while we have no doubt whatever of the truth of this disclosure, which has so providentially come to light-"

"Meaning hers?" said Dick, pointing towards the Marchioness.

"-Meaning hers, of course. While we have no doubt of that, or that a proper use of it would procure the poor lad's immediate pardon and liberation, we have a great doubt whether it would, by itself, enable us to reach Quilp, the chief agent in this villany. I should tell you that this doubt has been confirmed into something very nearly approaching certainty by the best opinions we have been enabled, in this short space of time, to take upon the subject. You'll agree with us, that to give him even the most distant chance of escape, if we could help it, would be monstrous. You say with us, no doubt, if somebody must escape, let it be any one but he."

"Yes," returned Dick, "certainly. That is if somebody must-but upon my word, I'm unwilling that anybody should. Since laws were made for every degree, to curb vice in others as well as in me-and so forth you know-doesn't it strike you in that light?"

The single gentleman smiled as if the light in which Mr. Swiveller had put the question were not the clearest in the world, and proceeded to explain that they contemplated proceeding by stratagem in the first instance; and that their design was to endeavour to extort a confession from the gentle Sarah.

"When she finds how much we know, and how we know it," he said, "and that she is clearly compromised already, we are not without strong hopes that we may be enabled through her means to punish the other two effectually. If we could do that, she might go scot-free for aught I cared."

Dick received this project in anything but a gracious manner, representing with as much warmth as he was then capable of showing, that they would find the old buck (meaning Sarah) more difficult to manage than Quilp himself-that for any tampering, terrifying, or cajolery, she was a very unpromising and unyielding subject-that she was of a kind of brass not easily melted or moulded into shape-in short, that they were no match for her, and would be signally defeated. But, it was in vain to urge them to adopt some other course. The single gentleman has been described as explaining their joint intentions, but it should have been written that they all spoke together; that if any one of them by chance held his peace for a moment, he stood gasping and panting for an opportunity to strike in again: in a word, that they had reached that pitch of impatience and anxiety where men can neither be persuaded nor reasoned with; and that it would have been easier to turn the most impetuous wind that ever blew, than to prevail on them to reconsider their determination. So, after telling Mr. Swiveller how they had not lost sight of Kit's mother and the children; how they had never once even lost sight of Kit himself, but had been unremitting in their endeavours to procure a mitigation of his sentence; how they had been perfectly distracted between the strong proofs of his guilt, and their own fading hopes of his innocence; and how he, Richard Swiveller, might keep his mind at rest, for everything should be happily adjusted between that time and night;-after telling him all this, and adding a great many kind and cordial expressions, personal to himself, which it is unnecessary to recite, Mr. Garland, the Notary, and the single gentleman, took their leaves at a very critical time, or Richard Swiveller must assuredly have been driven into another fever, whereof the results might have been fatal.

Mr. Abel remained behind, very often looking at his watch and at the room-door, until Mr. Swiveller was roused from a short nap, by the setting-down on the landing-place outside, as from the shoulders of a porter, of some giant load, which seemed to shake the house, and made the little physic bottles on the mantel-shelf ring again. Directly this sound reached his ears, Mr. Abel started up, and hobbled to the door, and opened it; and behold! there stood a strong man, with a mighty hamper, which, being hauled into the room and presently unpacked, disgorged such treasures of tea, and coffee, and wine, and rusks, and oranges, and grapes, and fowls ready trussed for boiling, and calves'-foot jelly, and arrow-root, and sago, and other delicate restoratives, that the small servant, who had never thought it possible that such things could be, except in shops, stood rooted to the spot in her one shoe, with her mouth and eyes watering in unison, and her power of speech quite gone. But not so Mr. Abel; or the strong man who emptied the hamper, big as it was, in a twinkling; and not so the nice old lady, who appeared so suddenly that she might have come out of the hamper too (it was quite large enough), and who, bustling about on tiptoe and with- out noise-now here, now there, now everywhere at once- began to fill out the jelly in tea-cups, and to make chicken broth in small saucepans, and to peel oranges for the sick man and to cut them up in little pieces, and to ply the small servant with glasses of wine and choice bits of everything until more substantial meat could be prepared for her refreshment. The whole of which appearances were so unexpected and bewildering, that Mr. Swiveller, when he had taken two oranges and a little jelly, and had seen the strong man walk off with the empty basket, plainly leaving all that abundance for his use and benefit, was fain to lie down and fall asleep again, from sheer inability to entertain such wonders in his mind.

Meanwhile the single gentleman, the Notary, and Mr. Garland, repaired to a certain coffee-house, and from that place indited and sent a letter to Miss Sally Brass, requesting her, in terms mysterious and brief, to favour an unknown friend who wished to consult her, with her company there, as speedily as possible. The communication performed its errand so well, that within ten minutes of the messenger's return and report of its delivery, Miss Brass herself was announced.

"Pray, ma'am," said the single gentleman, whom she found alone in the room, "take a chair."

Miss Brass sat herself down in a very stiff and frigid state, and seemed-as indeed she was-not a little astonished to find that the lodger and her mysterious correspondent were one and the same person.

"You did not expect to see me?" said the single gentleman.

"I didn't think much about it," returned the beauty. "I supposed it was business of some kind or other. If it's about the apartments, of course you'll give my brother regular notice, you know-or money. That s very easily set-tled. You're a responsible party, and in such a case lawful money and lawful notice are pretty much the same."

"I am obliged to you for your good opinion," retorted the single gen-tleman, "and quite concur in those sentiments. But that is not the subject on which I wish to speak with you."

"Oh!" said Sally. "Then just state the particulars, will you? I suppose it's professional business?"

"Why, it is connected with the law, certainly."

"Very well," returned Miss Brass. "My brother and I are just the same. I can take any instructions, or give you any advice."

"As there are other parties interested besides myself," said the single gentleman, rising and opening the door of an inner room, "we had better confer together. Miss Brass is here, gentlemen!"

Mr. Garland and the Notary walked in, looking very grave; and draw-ing up two chairs, one on each side of the single gentleman, formed a kind of fence round the gentle Sarah, and penned her into a corner. Her brother Sampson under such circumstances would certainly have evinced some con-fusion or anxiety, but she-all composure -pulled out the tin box and calmly took a pinch of snuff.

"Miss Brass," said the Notary, taking the word at this crisis, "we pro-fessional people understand each other, and, when we choose, can say what we have to say, in very few words. You advertised a runaway servant, the other day?"

"Well," returned Miss Sally, with a sudden flush over spreading her features, "what of that?"

"She is found, ma'am," said the Notary, pulling out his pocket-hand-kerchief with a flourish. "She is found."

"Who found her?" demanded Sarah hastily.

"We did, ma'am-we three. Only last night, or you would have heard from us before."

"And now I have heard from you," said Miss Brass, folding her arms resolutely, as though she were about to deny something to the death, "what have you got to say? Something you have got into your heads about her, of course. Prove it, will you-that's all. Prove it. You have found her, you say. I can tell you (if you don't know it) that you have found the most artful, lying, pilfering, and devilish little minx that was ever born.-Have you got her here?" she added, looking sharply round.

"No, she is not here at present," returned the Notary. "But she is quite safe."

"Ha!" cried Sally, twitching a pinch of snuff out of her box, as spiteful-ly as if she were in the very act of wrenching off the small servant's nose; "she shall be safe enough from this time, I warrant you."

"I hope so," replied the Notary.- "Did it occur to you for the first time when you found she had run away, that there were two keys to your kitchen door?"

Miss Sally took another pinch, and putting her head on one side, looked at her questioner with a curious kind of spasm about her mouth, but with a cunning aspect of immense expression.

"Two keys," repeated the Notary; "one of which gave her the opportunities of roaming through the house at nights when you supposed her fast locked up, and of over hearing confidential consultations-among others, that particular conference to be described to-day before a justice, which you will have an opportunity of hearing her relate; that conference which you and Mr. Brass held together on the night before that most unfortunate and innocent young man was accused of robbery, by a horrible device of which I will only say that it may be characterised by the epithets you have applied to this wretched little witness, and by a few stronger ones besides."

Sally took another pinch. Although her face was wonderfully composed, it was apparent that she was wholly taken by surprise, and that what she had expected to be taxed with, in connexion with her small servant, was something very different from this.

"Come, come, Miss Brass," said the Notary, "you have great command of feature, but you feel, I see, that by a chance which never entered your imagination, this base design is revealed, and two of its plotters must be brought to justice. Now, you know the pains and penalties you are liable to, and so I need not dilate upon them, but I have a proposal to make to you. You have the honour of being sister to one of the greatest scoundrels unhung; and, if I may venture to say so to a lady, you are in every respect quite worthy of him. But, connected with you two is a third party, a villain of the name of Quilp, the prime mover of the whole diabolical device, who I believe to be worse than either. For his sake, Miss Brass, do us the favour to reveal the whole history of this affair. Let me remind you that your doing so at our instance will place you in a safe and comfortable position-your present one is not desirable-and cannot injure your brother, for against him and you we have quite sufficient evidence (as you hear) already. I will not say to you that we suggest this course in mercy (for, to tell you the truth, we do not entertain any regard for you), but it is a necessity to which we are reduced, and I recommend it to you as a matter of the very best policy. Time," said Mr. Witherden, pulling out his watch, "in a business like this, is exceedingly precious. Favour us with your decision as speedily as possible, ma'am."

With a smile upon her face, and looking at each of the three by turns, Miss Brass took two or three more pinches of snuff, and having by this time very little left, travelled round and round the box with her forefinger and thumb, scraping up another. Having disposed of this likewise and put the box carefully in her pocket, she said,-

"I am to accept or reject at once, am I?"

"Yes," said Mr. Witherden.

The charming creature was opening her lips to speak in reply, when the door was hastily opened too, and the head of Sampson Brass was thrust into the room.

"Excuse me," said that gentleman hastily. "Wait a bit!"

So saying, and quite indifferent to the astonishment his presence occasioned, he crept in, shut the door, kissed his greasy glove as servilely as if it were the dust, and made a most abject bow.

"Sarah," said Brass, "hold your tongue if you please, and let me speak. Gentlemen, if I could express the pleasure it gives me to see three such men in a happy unity of feeling and concord of sentiment, I think you would hardly believe me. But though I am unfortunate-nay, gentlemen, criminal, if we are to use harsh expressions in a company like this-still I have my feelings like other men. I have heard of a poet, who remarked that feelings were the common lot of all. If he could have been a pig, gentlemen, and have uttered that sentiment, he would still have been immortal."

"If you're not an idiot," said Miss Brass harshly, "hold your peace."

"Sarah, my dear," returned her brother, "thank you. But I know what I am about, my love, and will take the liberty of expressing myself accordingly. Mr. Witherden, sir, your handkerchief is hanging out of your pocket-would you allow me to-"

As Mr. Brass advanced to remedy this accident, the Notary shrank from him with an air of great disgust. Brass, who over and above his usual prepossessing qualities, had a scratched face, a green shade over one eye, and a hat grievously crushed, stopped short, and looked round with a pitiful smile.

"He shuns me," said Sampson, "even when I would, as I may say, heap coals of fire upon his head. Well! Ah! But I am a falling house, and the rats (if I may be allowed the expression in reference to a gentleman that I respect and love beyond everything) fly from me! Gentlemen- regarding your conversation just now, I happened to see my sister on her way here, and, wondering where she could be going to, and being-may I venture to say?-naturally of a suspicious turn, followed her. Since then, I have been listening."

"If you're not mad," interposed Miss Sally, "stop there, and say no more."

"Sarah, my dear," rejoined Brass with undiminished politeness, "I thank you kindly, but will still proceed. Mr. Witherden, sir, as we have the honour to be members of the same profession-to say nothing of that other gentleman having been my lodger, and having partaken, as one may say, of the hospitality of my roof-I think you might have given me the refusal of this offer in the first instance. I do indeed. Now, my dear sir," cried Brass, seeing that the Notary was about to interrupt him, "suffer me to speak, I beg."

Mr. Witherden was silent, and Brass went on.

"If you will do me the favour," he said, holding up the green shade, and revealing an eye most horribly discoloured, "to look at this, you will naturally inquire in your own minds how did I get it. If you look from that, to my face, you will wonder what could have been the cause of all these scratches. And if from them to my hat, how it came into the state in which you see it. Gentlemen," said Brass, striking the hat fiercely with his clenched hand, "to all these questions I answer-Quilp!"

The three gentlemen looked at each other, but said nothing. "I say," pursued Brass, glancing aside at his sister, as though he were talking for her information, and speaking with a snarling malignity, in violent contrast to his usual smoothness, "that I answer to all these questions,-Quilp -Quilp, who deludes me into his infernal den, and takes a delight in looking on and chuckling while I scorch, and burn, and bruise, and maim myself-Quilp, who never once, no never once, in all our communications together, has treated me otherwise than as a dog-Quilp, whom I have always hated with my whole heart, but never so much as lately. He gives me the cold shoulder on this very matter as if he had had nothing to do with it, instead of being the first to propose it. I can't trust him. In one of his howling, raving, blazing humours, I believe he'd let it out if it was murder, and never think of himself so long as he could terrify me. Now," sad Brass, picking up his hat again, replacing the shade over his eye, and actually crouching down, in the excess of his servility, "What does all this lead me to?-what should you say it led me to, gentlemen? -could you guess at all near the mark?"

Nobody spoke. Brass stood smirking for a little while as if he had propounded some choice conundrum; and then said:

"To be short with you, then, it leads me to this. If the truth has come out, as it plainly has in a manner that there's no standing up against-and a very sublime and grand thing is Truth, gentlemen, in its way, though like other sublime and grand things, such as thunder-storms and that, we're not always over and above glad to see it- I had better turn upon this man than let this man turn upon me. It's clear to me that I am done for. Therefore, if anybody is to split, I had better be the person and have the advantage of it. Sarah, my dear, comparatively speaking you're safe. I relate these circumstances for my own profit."

With that, Mr. Brass, in a great hurry, revealed the whole story; bearing as heavily as possible on his amiable employer, and making himself out to be rather a saint-like and holy character, though subject-he acknowledged-to human weaknesses. He concluded thus:

"Now gentlemen, I am not a man who does things by halves. Being in for a penny, I am ready, as the saying is, to be in for a pound. You must do with me what you please and take me where you please. If you wish to have this in writing, we'll reduce it into manuscript immediately. You will be tender with me, I am sure. I am quite confident you will be tender with me. You are men of honour, and have feeling hearts. I yielded from necessity to Quilp, for though necessity has no law, she has her lawyers. I yield to you from necessity too; from policy besides; and because of feelings that have been a pretty long time working within me. Punish Quilp, gentlemen. Weigh heavily upon him. Grind him down. Tread him under foot. He has done as much by me, for many and many a day."

Having now arrived at the conclusion of his discourse, Sampson checked the current of his wrath, kissed his glove again, and smiled as only parasites and cowards can.

"And this," said Miss Brass, raising her head, with which she had hitherto sat resting on her hands, and surveying him from head to foot with a bitter sneer, "this is my brother, is it! This is my brother, that I have worked and toiled for, and believed to have had something of the man in him!"

"Sarah, my dear," returned Sampson, rubbing his hands feebly; "you disturb our friends. Besides you-you're disappointed, Sarah, and, not knowing what you say, expose yourself."

"Yes, you pitiful dastard," retorted the lovely damsel, "I understand you. You feared that I should be before hand with you. But do you think that I would have been enticed to say a word! I'd have scorned it, if they had tried and tempted me for twenty years."

"He he!" simpered Brass, who in his deep debasement really seemed to have changed sexes with his sister, and to have made over to her any spark of manliness he might have possessed. "You think so, Sarah, you think so perhaps; but you would have acted quite different, my good fellow. You will not have forgotten that it was a maxim with Foxey-our revered father, gentlemen- 'Always suspect everybody.' That's the maxim to go through life with! If you were not actually about to purchase your own safety when I showed myself, I suspect you'd have done it by this time. And therefore I've done it myself, and spared you the trouble as well as the shame. The shame, gentlemen," added Brass, allowing himself to be slightly overcome, "if there is any, is mine. It's better that a female should be spared it."

With deference to the better opinion of Mr. Brass, and more particularly to the authority of his Great Ancestor, it may be doubted with humility whether the elevating principle laid down by the latter gentleman, and acted upon by his descendant, is always prudent one, or attended in practice with the desired results. This is beyond question a bold and presumptuous doubt, inasmuch as many distinguished characters, called men of the world, long-headed customers, knowing dogs, shrewd fellows, capital hands at business, and the like, have made, and do daily make, this axiom their polar star and compass. Still the doubt may be gently insinuated. And in illustration it may be observed, that if Mr. Brass, not being over-suspicious, had, without prying and listening, left his sister to manage the conference on their joint behalf, or prying and listening, had not been in such a mighty hurry to anticipate her (which he would not have been, but for his distrust and jealousy), he would probably have found himself much better off in the end. Thus it will always happen that these men of the world, who go through it in armour, defend themselves from quite as much good as evil; to say nothing of the inconvenience and absurdity of mounting guard with a microscope at all times, and of wearing a coat of mail on the most innocent occasions.

The three gentlemen spoke together apart for a few moments. At the end of their consultation, which was very brief, the Notary pointed to the writing-materials on the table, and informed Mr. Brass that if he wished to make any statement in writing, he had the opportunity of doing so. At the same time he felt bound to tell him that they would require his attendance presently before a Justice of the Peace, and that in what he did or said, he was guided entirely by his own discretion.

"Gentlemen," said Brass, drawing off his gloves, and crawling in spirit upon the ground before them, "I will justify the tenderness with which I know I shall be treated; and as, without tenderness, I should, now that this discovery has been made, stand in the worst position of the three, you may depend upon it I will make a clean breast. Mr. Witherden, sir, a kind of faint-ness is upon my spirits -if you would do me the favour to ring the bell and order up a glass of something warm and spicy, I shall, notwithstanding what has passed, have a melancholy pleasure in drinking your good health. I had hoped," said Brass, looking round with a mournful smile, "to have seen you three gentlemen one day or another with your legs under the mahogany in my humble parlour in the Marks. But hopes are fleeting. Dear me!"

Mr. Brass found himself so exceedingly affected at this point that he could say or do nothing more until some refreshment arrived. Having par-taken of it, pretty freely for one in his agitated state, he sat down to write.

The lovely Sarah, now with her arms folded, and now with her hands clasped behind her, paced the room with manly strides while her brother was thus employed, and sometimes stopped to pull out her snuff-box and bite the lid. She continued to pace up and down until she was quite tired, and then fell asleep on a chair near the door.

It has been since supposed with some reason that this slumber was a sham or feint, as she contrived to slip away unobserved in the dusk of the af-ternoon. Whether this was an intentional and waking departure, or a som-nambulistic leave-taking and walking in her sleep, may remain a subject of contention; but on one point (and indeed the main one) all parties are agreed. In whatever state she walked away, she certainly did not walk back again.

Mention having been made of the dusk of the afternoon, it will be in-ferred that Mr. Brass's task occupied some time in the completion. It was not finished until evening; but being done at last, that worthy person and the three friends adjourned in a hackney-coach to the private office of a Justice, who, giving Mr. Brass a warm reception and detaining him in a secure place that he might insure to himself the pleasure of seeing him on the morrow, dismissed the others with the cheering assurance that a warrant could not fail to be granted next day for the apprehension of Mr. Quilp, and that a proper application and statement of all the circumstances to the Secretary of State (who was fortunately in town), would no doubt procure Kit's free pardon and liberation without delay.

And now indeed it seemed that Quilp's malignant career was drawing to a close, and that retribution, which often travels slowly-especially when heaviest, had tracked his footsteps with a sure and certain scent and was gaining on him fast. Unmindful of her stealthy tread, her victim holds his course in fancied triumph. Still at his heels she comes, and once afoot, is nev-er turned aside.

Their business ended, the three gentlemen hastened back to the lodg-ings of Mr. Swiveller, whom they found progressing so favourably in his re-covery as to have been able to sit up for half an hour, and to have conversed with cheerfulness. Mrs. Garland had gone home some time since, but Mr. Abel was still sitting with him. After telling him all they had done, the two Mr. Garlands and the single gentleman, as if by some previous understand-ing, took their leaves for the night, leaving the invalid alone with the Notary and the small servant.

"As you are so much better," said Mr. Witherden, sitting down at the bedside, "I may venture to communicate to you a piece of news which has come to me professionally."

The idea of any professional intelligence from a gentleman connected with legal matters appeared to afford Richard anything but a pleasing antic-ipation. Perhaps he connected it in his own mind with one or two outstand-ing accounts, in reference to which he had already received divers threaten-ing letters. His countenance fell as he replied.

"Certainly, sir. I hope it's not anything of a very disagreeable nature, though?"

"If I thought it so, I should choose some better time for communicat-ing it," replied the Notary. "Let me tell you, first, that my friends who have been here to-day, know nothing of it, and that their kindness to you has been quite spontaneous, and with no hope of return. It may do a thoughtless, careless man good to know that."

Dick thanked him, and said he hoped it would.

"I have been making some inquiries about you," said Mr. Witherden, "little thinking that I should find you under such circumstances as those which have brought us together. You are the nephew of Rebecca Swiveller, spinster, deceased, of Cheselbourne in Dorsetshire."

"Deceased!" cried Dick.

"Deceased. If you had been another sort of nephew, you would have come into possession (so says the will, and I see no reason to doubt it) of five-and-twenty thousand pounds. As it is, you have fallen into an annuity of one hundred and fifty pounds a year; but I think I may congratulate you even upon that."

"Sir," said Dick, sobbing and laughing together, "you may. For, please God, we'll make a scholar of the poor Marchioness yet! And she shall walk in silk attire, and siller have to spare, or may I never rise from this bed again!"

CHAPTER LXVII

UNCONSCIOUS of the proceedings faithfully narrated in the last chapter, and little dreaming of the mine which had been sprung beneath him (for, to the end that he should have no warning of the business afoot, the profoundest secrecy was observed in the whole transaction), Mr. Quilp re-mained shut up in his hermitage, undisturbed by any suspicion, and ex-tremely well satisfied with the result of his machinations. Being engaged in the adjustment of some accounts-an occupation to which the silence and solitude of his retreat were very favourable-he had not strayed from his den for two whole days. The third day of his devotion to this pursuit found him still hard at work, and little disposed to stir abroad.

It was the day next after Mr. Brass's confession, and consequently that which threatened the restriction of Mr. Quilp's liberty, and the abrupt communication to him of some very unpleasant and unwelcome facts. Having no intuitive perception of the cloud which lowered upon his house, the dwarf was in his ordinary state of cheerfulness; and, when he found he was becoming too much engrossed by business with a due regard to his health and spirits, he varied its monotonous routine with a little screeching, or howling, or some other innocent relaxation of that nature.

He was attended, as usual, by Tom Scott, who sat crouching over the fire after the manner of a toad, and from time to time, when his master's back was turned, imitated his grimaces with a fearful exactness. The figure head had not yet disappeared, but remained in its old place. The face, horribly seared by the frequent application of the red-hot poker, and further ornamented by the insertion in the tip of the nose of a tenpenny nail, yet smiled blandly in its less lacerated parts, and seemed, like a sturdy martyr, to provoke its tormentor to the commission of new outrages and insults.

The day, in the highest and brightest quarters of the town, was damp, dark, cold, and gloomy. In that low and marshy spot, the fog filled every nook and corner with a thick dense cloud. Every object was obscure at one or two yards' distance. The warning lights and fires upon the river were powerless beneath this pall, and, but for a raw and piercing chillness in the air, and now and then the cry of some bewildered boatman as he rested on his oars and tried to make out where he was, the river itself might have been miles away.

The mist, though sluggish and slow to move, was of a keenly searching kind. No muffling up in furs and broad-cloth kept it out. It seemed to penetrate into the very bones of the shrinking wayfarers, and to rack them with cold and pains. Everything was wet, and clammy to the touch. The warm blaze alone defied it, and leaped and sparkled merrily. It was a day to be at home, crowding about the fire, telling stories of travellers who had lost their way in such weather on heaths and moors; and to love a warm hearth more than ever.

The dwarf's humour, as we know, was to have a fireside to himself; and when he was disposed to be convivial, to enjoy himself alone. By no means insensible to the comfort of being within doors, he ordered Tom Scott to pile the little stove with coals, and, dismissing his work for that day, determined to be jovial.

To this end, he lighted up fresh candles and heaped more fuel on the fire; and having dined off a beefsteak, which he cooked himself in somewhat of a savage and cannibal-like manner, brewed a great bowl of hot punch, lighted his pipe, and sat down to spend the evening.

At this moment, a low knocking at the cabin door arrested his attention. When it had been twice or thrice repeated, he softly opened the little window, and thrusting his head out, demanded who was there.

"Only me, Quilp," replied a woman's voice.

"Only you!" cried the dwarf, stretching his neck to obtain a better view of his visitor. "And what brings you here, you jade? How dare you approach the ogre's castle, eh?"

"I have come with some news," rejoined his spouse. "Don't be angry with me."

"Is it good news, pleasant news, news to make a man skip and snap his fingers?" said the dwarf. "Is the dear old lady dead?"

"I don't know what news it is, or whether it's good or bad," rejoined his wife.

"Then she's alive," said Quilp, "and there's nothing the matter with her. Go home again, you bird of evil note, go home!"

"I have brought a letter-" cried the meek little woman.

"Toss it in at the window here, and go your ways," said Quilp, interrupting her, "or I'll come out and scratch you."

"No, but please, Quilp-do hear me speak," urged his submissive wife, in tears. "Please do!"

"Speak then," growled the dwarf, with a malicious grin. "Be quick and short about it. Speak, will you?"

"It was left at our house this afternoon," said Mrs. Quilp, trembling, "by a boy who said he didn't know from whom it came, but that it was given to him to leave, and that he was told to say it must be brought on to you directly, for it was of the very greatest consequence.-But please," she added, as her husband stretched out his hand for it, "please let me in. You don't know how wet and cold I am, or how many times I have lost my way in coming here through this thick fog. Let me dry myself at the fire for five minutes. I'll go away directly you tell me to, Quilp. Upon my word I will."

Her amiable husband hesitated for a few moments; but bethinking himself that the letter might require some answer, of which she could be the bearer, closed the window, opened the door, and bade her enter. Mrs. Quilp obeyed right willingly, and, kneeling down before the fire to warm her hands, delivered into his a little packet.

"I'm glad you're wet," said Quilp, snatching it, and squinting at her. "I'm glad you're cold. I'm glad you've lost your way. I'm glad your eyes are red with crying. It does my heart good to see your little nose so pinched and frosty."

"Oh Quilp!" sobbed his wife. "How cruel it is of you!"

"Did she think I was dead!" said Quilp, wrinkling his face into a most extraordinary series of grimaces. "Did she think she was going to have all the money, and to marry somebody she liked! Ha ha ha! Did she!"

These taunts elicited no reply from the poor little woman, who remained on her knees, warming her hands, and sobbing, to Mr. Quilp's great delight. But as he was contemplating her, and chuckling excessively, he happened to observe that Tom Scott was delighted too; wherefore, that he might have no presumptuous partner in his glee, the dwarf instantly collared him, dragged him to the door, and after a short scuffle, kicked him into the yard. In return for this mark of attention, Tom immediately walked upon his hands to the window, and-if the expression be allowable-looked in with his shoes: besides rattling his feet upon the glass like a Banshee upside down. As a matter of course, Mr. Quilp lost no time in resorting to the infallible poker, with which, after some dodging and lying in am-bush, he paid his young friend one or two such unequivocal compliments that he vanished precipitately, and left him in quiet possession of the field.

"Sot That little job being disposed of," said the dwarf, coolly, "I'll read my letter. Humph!" he muttered, looking at the direction. "I ought to know this writing. Beautiful Sally!"

Opening it, he read, in a fair, round, legal hand, as follows:

"Sammy has been practised upon, and has broken confidence. It has all come out. You had better not be in the way, for strangers are going to call upon you. They have been very quiet as yet, because they mean to surprise you. Don't lose time. I didn't. I am not to be found anywhere. If I was you, I wouldn't be, either. S. B., late of B. M."

To describe the changes that passed over Quilp's face as he read this letter half a dozen times, would require some new language; such, for power of expression, as was never written, read, or spoken. For a long time he did not utter one word; but after a considerable interval, during which Mrs. Quilp was almost paralysed with the alarm his looks engendered, he contrived to gasp out,

"-If I had him here. If I only had him here-"

"Oh Quilp!" said his wife, "what's the matter? Who are you angry with?"

"-I should drown him," said the dwarf, not heeding her. "Too easy a death, too short, too quick-but the river runs close at hand. Oh! if I had him here! Just to take him to the brink, coaxingly and pleasantly,-holding him by the buttonhole-joking with him,-and, with a sudden push, to send him splashing down! Drowning men come to the surface three times, they say. Ah! To see him those three times, and mock him as his face came bobbing up,-oh, what a rich treat that would be!"

"Quilp!" stammered his wife, venturing at the same time to touch him on the shoulder: "what has gone wrong?"

She was so terrified by the relish with which he pictured this pleasure to himself, that she could scarcely make herself intelligible.

"Such a bloodless cur!" said Quilp, rubbing his hands very slowly, and pressing them tight together. "I thought his cowardice and servility were the best guarantee for his keeping silence. Oh Brass, Brass-my dear, good, affectionate, faithful, complimentary, charming friend-if I only had you here!"

His wife, who had retreated lest she should seem to listen to these mutterings, ventured to approach him again, and was about to speak, when he hurried to the door and called Tom Scott, who, remembering his late gentle admonition, deemed it prudent to appear immediately.

"There!" said the dwarf, pulling him in. "Take her home. Don't come here to-morrow, for this place will be shut up. Come back no more till you hear from me or see me. Do you mind?"

Tom nodded sulkily, and beckoned Mrs. Quilp to lead the way.

"As for you," said the dwarf, addressing himself to her, "ask no questions about me, make no search for me, say nothing concerning me. I shall not be dead, mistress, and that'll comfort you. He'll take care of you."

"But, Quilp? What is the matter? Where are you going? Do say something more."

"I'll say that," said the dwarf, seizing her by the arm, "and do that too, which undone and unsaid would be best for you unless you go directly."

"Has anything happened?" cried his wife. "Oh! Do tell me that."

"Yes," snarled the dwarf. "No. What matter which? I have told you what to do. Woe betide you if you fail to do it, or disobey me by a hair's breadth. Will you go!"

"I am going, I'll go directly; but," faltered his wife, "answer me one question first. Has this letter any connexion with dear little Nell? I must ask you that-I must indeed, Quilp. You cannot think what days and nights of sorrow I have had through having once deceived that child. I don't know what harm I may have brought about, but, great or little, I did it for you, Quilp. My conscience misgave me when I did it. Do answer me this question, if you please."

The exasperated dwarf returned no answer, but turned round and caught up his usual weapon with such vehemence, that Tom Scott dragged his charge away by main force, and as swiftly as he could. It was well he did so, for Quilp, who was nearly mad with rage, pursued them to the neighbouring lane, and might have prolonged the chase but for the dense mist which obscured them from his view, and appeared to thicken every moment.

"It will be a good night for travelling anonymously," he said, as he returned slowly, being pretty well breathed with his run. "Stay. We may look better here. This is too hospitable and free."

By a great exertion of strength, he closed the two old gates which were deeply sunken in the mud, and barred them with a heavy beam. That done, he shook his matted hair from about his eyes, and tried them.-Strong and fast.

"The fence between this wharf and the next is easily climbed," said the dwarf, when he had taken these precautions. "There's a back lane too from there. That shall be my way out. A man need know his road well, to find it in this lovely place to-night. I need fear no unwelcome visitors while this lasts, I think."

Almost reduced to the necessity of groping his way with his hands (it had grown so dark and the fog had so much increased), he returned to his lair; and, after musing for some time over the fire, busied himself in preparations for a speedy departure.

While he was collecting a few necessaries and cramming them into his pockets, he never once ceased communing with himself in a low voice, or unclenched his teeth, which he had ground together on finishing Miss Brass's note.

"Oh Sampson!" he muttered, "good, worthy creature -if I could but hug you! If I could only fold you in my arms, and squeeze your ribs, as I could squeeze them if I once had you tight, what a meeting there would be between us! If we ever do cross each other again, Sampson, we'll have a greeting not easily to be forgotten, trust me. This time, Sampson, this moment when all had gone on so well, was so nicely chosen! It was so thoughtful of you, so penitent, so good. Oh, if we were face to face in this room again, my white-livered man of law, how well contented one of us would be!"

There he stopped; and raising the bowl of punch to his lips, drank a long deep draught, as if it were fair water and cooling to his parched mouth. Setting it down abruptly, and resuming his preparations, he went on with his soliloquy.

"There's Sally," he said with flashing eyes; "the woman has spirit, determination, purpose-was she asleep, or petrified? She could have stabbed him-poisoned him safely. She might have seen this coming on. Why does she give me notice when it's too late? When he sat there,-yonder there, over there,-with his white face, and red head, and sickly smile, why didn't I know what was passing in his heart? It should have stopped beating that night, if I had been in his secret; or there are no drugs to lull a man to sleep, and no fire to burn him!"

Another draught from the bowl; and, cowering over the fire with a ferocious aspect, he muttered to himself again.

"And this, like every other trouble and anxiety I have had of late times, springs from that old dotard and his darling child-two wretched feeble wanderers! I'll be their evil genius yet. And you, sweet Kit, honest Kit, virtuous, innocent Kit, look to yourself. Where I hate, I bite. I hate you, my darling fellow, with good cause, and proud as you are to-night, I'll have my turn.-What's that!"

A knocking at the gate he had closed. A loud and violent knocking. Then a pause; as if those who knocked had stopped to listen. Then the noise again, more clamorous and importunate than before.

"So soon!" said the dwarf. "And so eager! I am afraid I shall disappoint you. It's well I'm quite prepared. Sally, I thank you!"

As he spoke, he extinguished the candle. In his impetuous attempts to subdue the brightness of the fire, he overset the stove, which came tumbling forward, and fell with a crash upon the burning embers it had shot forth in its descent, leaving the room in pitchy darkness. The noise at the gate still continuing, he felt his way to the door, and stepped into the open air.

At that moment the knocking ceased. It was about eight o'clock; but the dead of the darkest night would have been as noon-day, in comparison with the thick cloud which then rested upon the earth, and shrouded everything from view. He darted forward for a few paces, as if into the mouth of some dim, yawning cavern; then, thinking he had gone wrong, changed the direction of his steps; then stood still, not knowing where to turn.

"If they would knock again," said Quilp, trying to peer into the gloom by which he was surrounded, "the sound might guide me. Come. Batter the gate once more!"

He stood listening intently, but the noise was not renewed. Nothing was to be heard in that deserted place, but at intervals the distant barking of dogs. The sound was far away-now in one quarter, now answered in another-nor was it any guide, for it often came from ship- board, as he knew.

"If I could find a wall or fence," said the dwarf, stretching out his arms, and walking slowly on, "I should know which way to turn. A good black, devil's night this, to have my dear friend here! If I had but that wish, it might, for anything I cared, never be day again."

As the word passed his lips, he staggered and fell; and next moment was fighting with the cold dark water.

For all its bubbling up and rushing in his ears, he could hear the knocking at the gate again-could hear a shout that followed it-could recognise the voice. For all his struggling and plashing, he could understand that they had lost their way, and had wandered back to the point from which they started; that they were all but looking on while he was drowned; that they were close at hand, but could not make an effort to save him; that he himself had shut and barred them out. He answered the shout-with a yell, which seemed to make the hundred fires that danced before his eyes tremble and flicker as if a gust of wind had stirred them. It was of no avail. The strong tide filled his throat, and bore him on, upon its rapid current.

Another mortal struggle, and he was up again, beating the water with his hands, and looking out with wild and glaring eyes that showed him some black object he was drifting close upon. The hull of a ship! He could touch its smooth and slippery surface with his hand. One loud cry now-but the resistless water bore him down before he could give it utterance, and, driving him under it, carried away a corpse.

It toyed and sported with its ghastly freight, now bruising it against the slimy piles, now hiding it in mud or long rank grass, now dragging it heavily over rough stones and gravel, now feigning to yield it to its own element, and in the same action luring it away, until, tired of the ugly plaything, it flung it on a swamp-a dismal place where pirates had swung in chains, through many a wintry night-and left it there to bleach.

And there it lay, alone. The sky was red with flame, and the water that bore it there had been tinged with the sullen light as it flowed along. The place the deserted carcase had left so recently, a living man, was now a blazing ruin. There was something of the glare upon its face. The hair, stirred by the damp breeze, played in a kind of mockery of death-such a mockery as the dead man himself would have revelled in when alive-about its head, and its dress fluttered idly in the night wind.

CHAPTER LXVIII

LIGHTED rooms, bright fires, cheerful faces, the music of glad voices, words of love and welcome, warm hearts, and tears of happiness-what a change is this! But it is to such delights that Kit is hastening. They are awaiting him, he knows. He fears he will die of joy before he gets among them.

They have prepared him for this, all day. He is not to be carried off tomorrow with the rest, they tell him first. By degrees they let him know that doubts have arisen, that inquiries are to be made, and perhaps he may be pardoned after all. At last, the evening being come, they bring him to a room where some gentlemen are assembled. Foremost among them is his good old master, who comes and takes him by the hand. He hears that his innocence is established, and that he is pardoned. He cannot see the speaker, but he turns towards the voice, and in trying to answer, falls down insensible.

They recover him again, and tell him he must be composed, and bear this like a man. Somebody says he must think of his poor mother. It is because he does think of her so much, that the happy news has overpowered him. They crowd about him, and tell him that the truth has gone abroad, and that all the town and country ring with sympathy for his misfortunes. He has no ears for this. His thoughts as yet have no wider range than home. Does she know it? what did she say? who told her? He can speak of nothing else.

They make him drink a little wine, and talk kindly to him for a while, until he is more collected, and can listen, and thank them. He is free to go. Mr. Garland thinks, if he feels better, it is time they went away. The gentlemen cluster round him, and shake hands with him. He feels very grateful to them for the interest they have in him, and for the kind promises they make; but the power of speech is gone again, and he has much ado to keep his feet, even though leaning on his master's arm.

As they pass through the dismal passages, some officers of the jail who are in waiting there, congratulate him in their rough way on his release. The newsmonger is of the number, but his manner it not quite hearty-there is something of surliness in his compliments. He looks upon Kit as an intruder, as one who has obtained admission to that place on false pretences, who has enjoyed a privilege without being duly qualified. He may be a very good sort of young man, he thinks, but he has no business there, and the sooner he is gone, the better.

The last door shuts behind them. They have passed the outer wall, and stand in the open air-in the street he has so often pictured to himself when hemmed in by those gloomy stones, and which has been in all his dreams. It seems wider and more busy than it used to be. The night is bad, and yet how cheerful and gay in his eyes! One of the gentlemen, in taking leave of him, pressed some money into his hand. He has not counted it; but when they have gone a few paces beyond the box for poor Prisoners, he hastily returns and drops it in.

Mr. Garland has a coach waiting in a neighbouring street, and, taking Kit inside with him, bids the man drive home. At first they can only travel at a foot pace, and then with torches going on before, because of the heavy fog. But as they get farther from the river, and leave the closer portions of the town behind, they are able to dispense with this precaution and to proceed at a brisker rate. On the road, hard galloping would be too slow for Kit; but when they are drawing near their journey's end, he begs they may go more slowly, and when the house appears in sight, that they may stop-only for a minute or two, to give him time to breathe.

But there is no stopping then, for the old gentleman speaks stoutly to him, the horses mend their pace, and they are already at the garden-gate.

Next minute they are at the door. There is a noise of tongues, and tread of feet, inside. It opens. Kit rushes in, and finds his mother clinging round his neck.

And there, too, is the ever faithful Barbara's mother, still holding the baby as if she had never put it down since that sad day when they little hoped to have such joy as this-there she is, Heaven bless her, crying her eyes out, and sobbing as never woman sobbed before; and there is little Barbara-poor little Barbara, so much thinner and so much paler, and yet so very pretty-trembling like a leaf and supporting herself against the wall; and there is Mrs. Garland, neater and nicer than ever, fainting away stone dead with nobody to help her; and there is Mr. Abel, violently blowing his nose, and wanting to embrace every- body; and there is the single gentleman hovering round them all, and constant to nothing for an instant; and there is that good, dear, thoughtful little Jacob, sitting all alone by himself on the bottom stair, with his hands on his knees like an old man, roaring fearfully without giving any trouble to anybody; and each and all of them are for the time clean out of their wits, and do jointly and severally commit all manner of follies.

And even when the rest have in some measure come to themselves again, and can find words and smiles, Barbara -that soft-hearted, gentle, foolish little Barbara-is suddenly missed, and found to be in a swoon by herself in the back parlour, from which swoon she falls into hysterics, and from which hysterics into a swoon again, and is, indeed, so bad, that despite a mortal quantity of vinegar and cold water she is hardly a bit better at last than she was at first. Then Kit's mother comes in and says, will he come and speak to her; and Kit says "Yes," and goes; and he says in a kind voice "Barbara!" and Barbara' s mother tells her that "it's only Kit;" and Barbara says (with her eyes closed all the time) "Oh! but is it him indeed?" and Barbara's mother says "To be sure it is, my dear; there's nothing the matter now." And in further assurance that he's safe and sound, Kit speaks to her again; and then Barbara goes off into another fit of laughter, and then into another fit of crying; and then Barbara's mother and Kit's mother nod to each other and pretend to scold her-but only to bring her to herself the faster, bless you-and being experienced matrons, and acute at perceiving the first dawning symptoms of recovery, they comfort Kit with the assurance that "she'll do now," and so dismiss him to the place from whence he came.

Well! In that place (which is the next room) there are decanters of wine, and all that sort of thing, set out as grand as if Kit and his friends were first-rate company; and there is little Jacob, walking, as the popular phrase is, into a home-made plum-cake at a most surprising pace, and keeping his eye on the figs and oranges which are to follow, and making the best use of his time, you may believe. Kit no sooner comes in, than that single gentleman (never was such a busy gentleman) charges all the glasses-bumpers -and drinks his health, and tells him he shall never want a friend while he lives; and so does Mr. Garland, and so does Mrs. Garland, and so does Mr. Abel. But even this honour and distinction is not all, for the single gentleman forthwith pulls out of his pocket a massive silver watch- going- hard, and right to half a second-and upon the back of this watch is engraved Kit's name, with flourishes all over; and in short it is Kit's watch, bought expressly for him, and presented to him on the spot. You may rest assured that Mr. and Mrs. Garland can't help hinting about their present in store, and that Mr. Abel tells outright that he has his; and that Kit is the happiest of the happy.

There is one friend he has not seen yet, and as he cannot be conveniently introduced into the family circle, by reason of his being an iron-shod quadruped, Kit takes the first opportunity of slipping away and hurrying to the stable. The moment he lays his hand upon the latch, the pony neighs the loudest pony's greeting; before he has crossed the threshold, the pony is capering about his loose box (for he brooks not the indignity of a halter), mad to give him welcome; and when Kit goes up to caress and pat him, the pony rubs his nose against his coat, and fondles him more lovingly than ever pony fondled man. It is the crowning circumstance of his earnest, heartfelt reception; and Kit fairly puts his arm round Whisker's neck and hugs him.

But how comes Barbara to trip in there? and how smart she is again! she has been at her glass since she recovered. How comes Barbara in the stable, of all places in the world? Why, since Kit has been away, the pony would take his food from nobody but her, and Barbara, you see, not dreaming Christopher was there, and just looking in to see that everything was right, has come upon him unawares. Blushing little Barbara!

It may be that Kit has caressed the pony enough; it may be that there are even better things to caress than ponies. He leaves him for Barbara at any rate, and hopes she is better. Yes. Barbara is a great deal better. She is afraid-and here Barbara looks down and blushes more- that he must have thought her very foolish. "Not at all," says Kit. Barbara is glad of that, and coughs-Hem!- just the slightest cough possible-not more than that.

What a discreet pony, when he chooses! He is as quiet now, as if he were of marble. He has a very knowing look but that he always has. "We have hardly had time to shake hands, Barbara," says Kit. Barbara gives him hers. Why, she is trembling now! Foolish, fluttering Barbara!

Arm's length! The length of an arm is not much. Barbara's was not a long arm by any means, and besides, she didn't hold it out straight, but bent a little. Kit was so near her when they shook hands, that he could see a small tiny tear, yet trembling on an eyelash. It was natural that he should look at it, unknown to Barbara. It was natural that Barbara should raise her eyes unconsciously, and find him out. Was it natural that at that instant, without any previous impulse or design, Kit should kiss Barbara? He did it, whether or no. Barbara said "for shame," but let him do it too-twice. He might have done it thrice, but the pony kicked up his heels and shook his head, as if he were suddenly taken with convulsions of delight, and Barbara being frightened, ran away-not straight to where her mother and Kit's mother were, though, lest they should see how red her cheeks were, and should ask her why. Sly little Barbara!

When the first transports of the whole party had subsided, and Kit and his mother, and Barbara and her mother, with little Jacob and the baby to boot, had had their suppers together-which there was no hurrying over, for they were going to stop there all night-Mr. Garland called Kit to him, and taking him into a room where they could be alone, told him that he had something yet to say, which would surprise him greatly. Kit looked so anxious and turned so pale on hearing this, that the old gentleman hastened to add, he would be agreeably surprised; and asked him if he would be ready next morning for a journey.

"For a journey, sir!" cried Kit.

"In company with me and my friend in the next room. Can you guess its purpose?"

Kit turned paler yet, and shook his head.

"Oh yes. I think you do already," said his master. "Try."

Kit murmured something rather rambling and unintelligible, but he plainly pronounced the words "Miss Nell," three or four times-shaking his head while he did so, as if he would add there was no hope of that.

But Mr. Garland, instead of saying "Try again," as Kit had made sure he would, told him very seriously that he had guessed right.

"The place of their retreat is indeed discovered," he said, "at last. And that is our journey's end."

Kit faltered out such questions as, where was it, and how had it been found, and how long since, and was she well, and happy.

"Happy she is, beyond all doubt," said Mr. Garland. "And well, I-I trust she will be soon. She has been weak and ailing, as I learn, but she was better when I heard this morning, and they were full of hope. Sit you down, and you shall hear the rest."

Scarcely venturing to draw his breath, Kit did as he was told. Mr. Garland then related to him, how he had a brother (of whom he would remember to have heard him speak, and whose picture, taken when he was a young man, hung in the best room), and how this brother lived a long way off in a country-place, with an old clergyman who had been his early friend. How, although they loved each other as brothers should, they had not met for many years, but had communicated by letter from time to time, always looking forward to some period when they would take each other by the hand once more, and still letting the Present time steal on, as it was the habit of men to do, and suffering the Future to melt into the Past. How this brother, whose temper was very mild and quiet and retiring-such as Mr. Abel's-was greatly beloved by the simple people among whom he dwelt, who quite revered the Bachelor (for so they called him), and had every one experienced his charity and benevolence. How even those slight circumstances had come to his knowledge, very slowly and in course of years. for the Bachelor was one of those whose goodness shuns the light, and who have more pleasure in discovering and extolling the good deeds of others, than in trumpeting their own, be they never so commendable. How, for that reason, he seldom told them of his village friends; but how, for all that, his mind had become so full of two among them-a child and an old man, to whom he had been very kind- that, in a letter received a few days before, he had dwelt upon them from first to last, and had told there such a tale of their wanderings, and mutual love, that few could read it without being moved to tears. How he, the recipient of that letter, was directly led to the belief that these must be the very wanderers for whom so much search had been made, and whom Heaven had directed to his brother's care. How he had written for such further information as would put the fact beyond all doubt; how it had that morning arrived; had confirmed his first impression into a certainty; and was the immediate cause of that journey being planned, which they were to take to-morrow.

"In the meantime," said the old gentleman rising, and laying his hand on Kit's shoulder, "you have great need of rest, for such a day as this would wear out the strongest man. Good night, and Heaven send our journey may have a prosperous ending!"

CHAPTER LXIX

KIT was no sluggard next morning, but, springing from his bed some time before day, began to prepare for his welcome expedition. The hurry of spirits consequent upon the events of yesterday, and the unexpected intelligence he had heard at night, had troubled his sleep through the long dark hours, and summoned such uneasy dreams about his pillow that it was rest to rise.

But had it been the beginning of some great labour with the same end in view-had it been the commencement of a long journey, to be performed on foot in that inclement season of the year; to be pursued under every privation and difficulty; and to be achieved only with great distress, fatigue, and suffering-had it been the dawn of some painful enterprise, certain to task his utmost powers of resolution and endurance, and to need his utmost fortitude, but only likely to end, if happily achieved, in good fortune and delight to Nell Kit's cheerful zeal would have been as highly roused, Kit's ardour and impatience would have been at least the same.

Nor was he alone excited and eager. Before he had been up a quarter of an hour the whole house were astir and busy. Everybody hurried to do something towards facilitating the preparations. The single gentleman, it is true, could do nothing himself, but he overlooked everybody else and was more locomotive than anybody. The work of packing and making ready went briskly on, and by day-break every preparation for the journey was completed. Then Kit began to wish they had not been quite so nimble; for the travelling-carriage which had been hired for the occasion was not to arrive until nine o'clock, and there was nothing but breakfast to fill up the intervening blank of one hour and a half.

Yes there was, though. There was Barbara. Barbara was busy, to be sure, but so much the better-Kit could help her, and that would pass away the time better than any means that could be devised. Barbara had no objection to this arrangement, and Kit, tracking out the idea which had come upon him so suddenly overnight, began to think that surely Barbara was fond of him, and surely he was fond of Barbara.

Now, Barbara, if the truth must be told-as it must and ought to be-Barbara seemed, of all the little household, to take least pleasure in the bustle of the occasion; and when Kit, in the openness of his heart, told her how glad and overjoyed it made him, Barbara became more downcast still, and seemed to have even less pleasure in it than before!

"You have not been borne so long, Christopher," said Barbara-and it is impossible to tell how carelessly she said it- "You have not been home so long, that you need be glad to go away again, I should think."

"But for such a purpose," returned Kit. "To bring back Miss Nell! To see her again! Only think of that! I am so pleased too to think that you will see her, Barbara, at last."

Barbara did not absolutely say that she felt no great gratification on this point, but she expressed the sentiment so plainly by one little toss of her head, that Kit was quite disconcerted, and wondered in his simplicity why she was so cool about it.

"You'll say she has the sweetest and beautifullest face you ever saw, I know," said Kit, rubbing his hands.

"I'm sure you'll say that!"

Barbara tossed her head again.

"What's the matter, Barbara?" said Kit.

"Nothing," cried Barbara. And Barbara pouted-not sulkily, or in an ugly manner, but just enough to make her look more cherry-lipped than ever.

There is no school in which a pupil gets on so fast, as that in which Kit became a scholar when he gave Barbara the kiss. He saw what Barbara meant now-he had his lesson by heart all at once-she was the book-there it was before him as plain as print.

"Barbara," said Kit, "you're not cross with me?"

Oh dear no! Why should Barbara be cross? And what right had she to be cross? And what did it matter whether she was cross or no? Who minded her!

"Why, I do," said Kit. "Of course I do."

Barbara didn't see why it was of course, at all.

Kit was sure she must. Would she think again?

Certainly, Barbara would think again. No, she didn't see why it was of course. She didn't understand what Christopher meant. And besides she was sure they wanted her up stairs by this time, and she must go, indeed-

"No, but Barbara," said Kit, detaining her gently, "let us part friends. I was always thinking of you, in my troubles. I should have been a great deal more miserable than I was, if it hadn't been for you."

Goodness gracious, how pretty Barbara was when she coloured-and when she trembled, like a little shrinking bird!

"I am telling you the truth, Barbara, upon my word, but not half so strong as I could wish," said Kit, earnestly. "When I want you to be pleased to see Miss Nell, it's only because I like you to be pleased with what pleases me-that's all. As to her, Barbara, I think I could almost die to do her service, but you would think so too if you knew her as I do. I am sure you would."

Barbara was touched, and sorry to have appeared indifferent.

"I have been used, you see," said Kit, "to talk and think of her, almost as if she was an angel. When I look forward to meeting her again, I think of her smiling as she used to do, and being glad to see me, and putting out her hand and saying, 'It's my own old Kit' or some such words as those-like what she used to say. I think of seeing her happy, and with friends about her, and brought up as she deserves, and as she ought to be. When I think of myself, it's as her old servant, and one that loved her dearly, as his kind, good, gentle mistress; and who would have gone-yes, and still would go-through any harm to serve her. Once I couldn't help being afraid that if she came back with friends about her she might forget, or be ashamed of having known, a humble lad like me, and so speak coldly, which would have cut me, Barbara, deeper than I can tell. But when I came to think again, I felt sure that I was doing her wrong in this; and so I went on as I did at first, hoping to see her once more, just as she used to be. Hoping this, and remembering what she was, has made me feel as if I would always try to please her, and always be what I should like to seem to her if I was still her servant. If I'm the better for that-and I don't think I'm the worse-I am grateful to her for it, and love and honour her the more. That's the plain honest truth, dear Barbara, upon my word it is!"

Little Barbara was not of a wayward or capricious nature, and, being full of remorse, melted into tears. To what further conversation this might have led, we need not stop to inquire; for the wheels of the carriage were heard at that moment, and, being followed by a smart ring at the garden-gate, caused the bustle in the house, which had lain dormant for a short time, to burst again into tenfold life and vigour.

Simultaneously with the travelling equipage, arrived Mr. Chuckster in a hackney-cab, with certain papers and supplies of money for the single gentleman, into whose hands he delivered them. This duty discharged, he subsided into the bosom of the family; and entertaining himself with a strolling or peripatetic breakfast, watched with a genteel indifference the process of loading the carriage.

"Snobby's in this I see, sir?" he said to Mr. Abel Garland. "I thought he wasn't in the last trip because it was expected that his presence wouldn't be very acceptable to the ancient buffalo."

"To whom, sir?" demanded Mr. Abel.

"To the old gentleman," returned Mr. Chuckster, slightly abashed.

"Our client prefers to take him now," said Mr. Abel dryly. "There is no longer any need for that precaution, as my father's relationship to a gentleman in whom the objects of his search have full confidence, will be a sufficient guarantee for the friendly nature of their errand."

"Ah!" thought Mr. Chuckster, looking out of window, "anybody but me! Snobby before me, of course. He didn't happen to take that particular five-pound note, but I have not the smallest doubt that he's always up to something of that sort. I always said it, long before this came out. Devilish pretty girl that! 'Pon my soul, an amazing little creature!"

Barbara was the subject of Mr. Chuckster's commendations; and as she was lingering near the carriage (all being now ready for its departure), that gentleman was suddenly seized with a strong interest in the proceedings, which impelled him to swagger down the garden, and take up his position at a convenient ogling distance. Having had great experience of the sex, and being perfectly acquainted with all those little artifices which find the readiest road to their hearts, Mr. Chuckster, on taking his ground, planted one hand on his hip, and with the other adjusted his flowing hair. This is a favourite attitude in the polite circles, and accompanied with a graceful whistling has been known to do immense execution.

Such, however, is the difference between town and country, that nobody took the smallest notice of this insinuating figure; the wretches being wholly engaged in bidding the travellers farewell, in kissing hands to each other, waving handkerchiefs, and the like tame and vulgar practices. For now the single gentleman and Mr. Garland were in the carriage, and the postboy was in the saddle, and Kit, well wrapped and muffled up, was in the rumble behind; and Mrs. Garland was there, and Mr. Abel was there, and Kit's mother was there, and little Jacob was there, and Barbara's mother was visible in remote perspective, nursing the ever-wakeful baby; and all were nodding, beckoning, curtseying, or crying out "Good-bye!" with all the energy they could express. In another minute, the carriage was out of sight; and Mr. Chuckster remained alone upon the spot where it had lately been, with a vision of Kit standing up in the rumble waving his hand to Barbara, and of Barbara in the full light and lustre of his eyes-his eyes-Chuckster's-Chuckster the successful-on whom ladies of quality had looked with favour from phaetons in the parks on Sundays-waving hers to Kit!

How Mr. Chuckster, entranced by this monstrous fact, stood for some time rooted to the earth, protesting within himself that Kit was the Prince of felonious characters, and very Emperor or Great Mogul of Snobs, and how he clearly traced this revolting circumstance back to that old villany of the shilling, are matters foreign to our purpose; which is to track the rolling wheels, and bear the travellers company on their cold, bleak journey.

It was a bitter day. A keen wind was blowing, and rushed against them fiercely: bleaching the hard ground, shaking the white frost from the trees and hedges, and whirling it away like dust. But little cared Kit for weather. There was a freedom and freshness in the wind, as it came howling by, which, let it cut never so sharp, was welcome. As it swept on with its cloud of frost, bearing down the dry twigs and boughs and withered leaves, and carrying them away pell-mell, it seemed as though some general sympathy had got abroad, and everything was in a hurry like themselves. The harder the gusts, the better progress they appeared to make. It was a good thing to go struggling and fighting forward, vanquishing them one by one; to watch them driving up, gathering strength and fury as they came along; to bend for a moment, as they whistled past; and then to look back and see them speed away, their hoarse noise dying in the distance, and the stout trees cowering down before them.

All day long it blew without cessation. The night was clear and starlight, but the wind had not fallen, and the cold was piercing. Sometimes-towards the end of a long stage-Kit could not help wishing it were a little warmer; but when they stopped to change horses, and he had had a good run; and what with that, and the bustle of paying the old postilion, and rousing the new one, and running to and fro again until the horses were put to, he was so warm that the blood tingled and smarted in his fingers' ends; then he felt as if to have it one degree less cold would be to lose half the delight and glory of the journey: and up he jumped again right cheerily, singing to the merry music of the wheels as they rolled away, and, leaving the towns-people in their warm beds, pursued their course along the lonely road.

Meantime the two gentlemen inside, who were little disposed to sleep, beguiled the time with conversation. As both were anxious and expectant, it naturally turned upon the subject of their expedition, on the manner in which it had been brought about, and on the hopes and fears they entertained respecting it. Of the former they had many, of the latter few-none perhaps beyond that indefinable uneasiness which is inseparable from suddenly awakened hope, and protracted expectation.

In one of the pauses of their discourse, and when half the night had worn away, the single gentleman, who had gradually become more and more silent and thoughtful, turned to his companion and said abruptly:

"Are you a good listener?"

"Like most other men, I suppose," returned Mr. Garland, smiling. "I can be, if I am interested; and if not interested I should still try to appear so. Why do you ask?"

"I have a short narrative on my lips," rejoined his friend, "and will try you with it. It is very brief."

Pausing for no reply, he laid his hand on the old gentleman's sleeve, and proceeded thus:

"There were once two brothers, who loved each other dearly. There was a disparity in their ages-some twelve years. I am not sure but they may insensibly have loved each other the better for that reason. Wide as the interval between them was, however, they became rivals too soon. The deepest and strongest affection of both their hearts settled upon one object.

"The youngest-there were reasons for his being sensitive and watchful-was the first to find this out. I will not tell you what misery he underwent, what agony of soul he knew, how great his mental struggle was. He had been a sickly child. His brother, patient and considerate in the midst of his own high health and strength, had many and many a day denied himself the sports he loved, to sit beside his couch, telling him old stories till his pale face lighted up with an unwonted glow; to carry him in his arms to some green spot, where he could tend the poor pensive boy as he looked upon the bright summer day, and saw all nature healthy but himself; to be in any way his fond and faithful nurse. I may not dwell on all he did, to make the poor, weak creature love him, or my tale would have no end. But when the time of trial came, the younger brother's heart was full of those old days. Heaven strengthened it to repay the sacrifices of inconsiderate youth by one of thoughtful manhood. He left his brother to be happy. The truth never passed his lips, and he quitted the country, hoping to die abroad.

"The elder brother married her. She was in Heaven before long, and left him with an infant daughter.

"If you have seen the picture-gallery of any one old family, you will remember how the same face and figure -often the fairest and slightest of them all-come upon you in different generations; and how you trace the same sweet girl through a long line of portraits-never growing old or changing-the Good Angel of the race-abiding by them in all reverses-redeeming all their sins-

"In this daughter the mother lived again. You may judge with what devotion he who lost that mother almost in the winning, clung to this girl, her breathing image. She grew to womanhood, and gave her heart to one who could not know its worth. Well! Her fond father could not see her pine and droop. He might be more deserving than he thought him. He surely might become so with a wife like her. He joined their hands, and they were married.

"Through all the misery which followed this union; through all the cold neglect and undeserved reproach; through all the poverty he brought upon her; through all the struggles of their daily life, too mean and pitiful to tell, but dreadful to endure; she toiled on, in the deep devotion of her spirit, and in her better nature, as only women can. Her means and substance wasted; her father nearly beggared by her husband's hand, and the hourly witness (for they lived now under one roof) of her ill-usage and unhappiness,-she never, but for him, bewailed her fate. Patient, and upheld by strong affection to the last, she died a widow of some three weeks' date, leaving to her father's care two orphans; one a son of ten or twelve years old; the other a girl-such another infant child- the same in helplessness, in age, in form, in feature-as she had been herself when her young mother died.

"The elder brother, grandfather to these two children, was now a broken man; crushed and borne down, less by the weight of years than by the heavy hand of sorrow. With the wreck of his possessions he began to trade-in pictures first, and then in curious ancient things. He had entertained a fondness for such matters from a boy, and the tastes he had cultivated were now to yield him an anxious and precarious subsistence.

"The boy grew like his father in mind and person; the girl so like her mother, that when the old man had her on his knee, and looked into her mild blue eyes, he felt as if awakening from a wretched dream, and his daughter were a little child again. The wayward boy soon spurned the shelter of his roof, and sought associates more congenial to his taste. The old man and the child dwelt alone together.

"It was then, when the love of two dead people who had been nearest and dearest to his heart, was all transferred to this slight creature; when her face, constantly before him, reminded him from hour to hour of the too early change he had seen in such another-of all the suffering he had watched and known, and all his child had undergone; when the young man's profligate and hardened course drained him of money as his father's had, and even sometimes occasioned them temporary privation and distress; it was then that there began to beset him, and to be ever in his mind, a gloomy dread of poverty and want. He had no thought for himself in this. His fear was for the child. It was a spectre in his house, and haunted him night and day.

"The younger brother had been a traveller in many countries, and had made his pilgrimage through life alone. His voluntary banishment had been misconstrued, and he had borne (not without pain) reproach and slight for doing that which had wrung his heart, and cast a mournful shadow on his path. Apart from this, communication between him and the elder was difficult, and uncertain, and often failed; still it was not so wholly broken off but that he learnt-with long blanks and gaps between each interval of information-all that, I have told you now.

"Then, dreams of their young, happy life-happy to him though laden with pain and early care-visited his pillow yet oftener than before; and every night, a boy again he was at his brother's side. With the utmost speed he could exert, he settled his affairs; converted into money all the goods he had; and, with honourable wealth enough for both, with open heart and hand, with limbs that trembled as they bore him on, with emotion such as men can hardly bear and live, arrived one evening at his brother's door!"

The narrator, whose voice had faltered lately, stopped. "The rest," said Mr. Garland, pressing his hand, "I know."

"Yes," rejoined his friend after a pause, "we may spare ourselves the sequel. You know the poor result of all my search. Even when, by dint of such inquiries as the utmost vigilance and sagacity could set on foot, we found they had been seen with two poor travelling showmen; and in time discovered the men themselves-and in time, the actual place of their retreat; even then, we were too late. Pray God we are not too late again!"

"We cannot be," said Mr. Garland. "This time we must succeed."

"I have believed and hoped so," returned the other. "I try to believe and hope so still. But a heavy weight has fallen on my spirits, my good friend, and the sadness that gathers over me, will yield to neither hope nor reason."

"That does not surprise me," said Mr. Garland; "it is a natural consequence of the events you have recalled; of this dreary time and place; and above all, of this wild and dismal night. A dismal night, indeed! Hark! how the wind is howling!"

CHAPTER LXX

DAY broke, and found them still upon their way. Since leaving home, they had halted here and there for necessary refreshment, and had frequently been delayed, especially in the night time, by waiting for fresh horses. They had made no other stoppages, but the weather continued rough, and the roads were often steep and heavy. It would be night again before they reached their place of destination.

Kit, all bluff and hardened with the cold, went on manfully; and having enough to do to keep his blood circulating, to picture to himself the happy end of this adventurous journey, and to look about him and be amazed at everything, had little spare time for thinking of discomforts. Though his impatience, and that of his fellow-travellers, rapidly increased as the day waned, the hours did not stand still. The short daylight of winter soon faded away, and it was dark again when they had yet many miles to travel.

As it grew dusk, the wind fell; its distant moanings were more low and mournful; and as it came creeping up the road, and rattling covertly among the dry brambles on either hand, it seemed like some great phantom for whom the way was narrow, whose garments rustled as it stalked along. By degrees it lulled and died away; and then it came on to snow.

The flakes fell fast and thick, soon covering the ground some inches deep, and spreading abroad a solemn stillness. The rolling wheels were noiseless; and the sharp ring and clatter of the horses' hoofs, became a dull, muffled tramp. The life of their progress seemed to be slowly hushed, and something death-like to usurp its place.

Shading his eyes from the falling snow, which froze upon their lashes and obscured his sight, Kit often tried to catch the earliest glimpse of twinkling lights denoting their approach to some not distant town. He could descry objects enough at such times, but none correctly. Now a tall church-spire appeared in view, which presently became a tree, a barn, a shadow on the ground, thrown on it by their own bright lamps. Now there were horsemen, foot-passengers, carriages, going on before, or meeting them in narrow ways; which, when they were close upon them, turned to shadows too. A wall, a ruin, a sturdy gable-end, would rise up in the road; and when they were plunging headlong at it, would be the road itself. Strange turnings too, bridges, and sheets of water, appeared to start up here and there, making the way doubtful and uncertain; and yet they were on the same bare road, and these things, like the others, as they were passed, turned into dim illusions.

He descended slowly from his seat-for his limbs were numbed-when they arrived at a lone posting-house, and inquired how far they had to go to reach their journey's end. It was a late hour in such by-places, and the people were abed; but a voice answered from an upper window, Ten miles. The ten minutes that ensued appeared an hour; but at the end of that time, a shivering figure led out the horses they required, and after another brief delay they were again in motion.

It was a cross-country road, full, after the first three or tour miles, of holes and cart-ruts, which, being covered by the snow, were so many pitfalls to the trembling horses, and obliged them to keep a footpace. As it was next to impossible for men so much agitated as they were by this time, to sit still and move so slowly, all three got out and plodded on behind the carriage. The distance seemed interminable, and the walk was most laborious. As each was thinking within himself that the driver must have lost his way, a church bell, close at hand, struck the hour of midnight, and the carriage stopped. It had moved softly enough, but when it ceased to crunch the snow, the silence was as startling as if some great noise had been replaced by perfect stillness.

"This is the place, gentlemen," said the driver, dismounting from his horse, and knocking at the door of a little inn. "Halloa! Past twelve o'clock is the dead of night here."

The knocking was loud and long, but it failed to rouse the drowsy inmates. All continued dark and silent as before. They fell back a little, and looked up at the windows, which were mere black patches in the whitened house front. No light appeared. The house might have been deserted, or the sleepers dead, for any air of life it had about it.

They spoke together, with a strange inconsistency, in whispers; unwilling to disturb again the dreary echoes they had just now raised.

"Let us go on," said the younger brother, "and leave this good fellow to wake them, if he can. I cannot rest until I know that we are not too late. Let us go on, in the name of Heaven!"

They did so, leaving the postilion to order such accommodation as the house afforded, and to renew his knocking. Kit accompanied them with a little bundle, which he had hung in the carriage when they left home, and had not forgotten since-the bird in his old cage-just as she had left him. She would be glad to see her bird, he knew.

The road wound gently downward. As they proceeded, they lost sight of the church whose clock they had heard, and of the small village clustering round it. The knocking, which was now renewed, and which in that stillness they could plainly hear, troubled them. They wished the man would forbear, or that they had told him not to break the silence until they returned.

The old church-tower, clad in a ghostly garb of pure cold white, again rose up before them, and a few moments brought them close beside it. A venerable building-grey, even in the midst of the hoary landscape. An ancient sundial on the belfry wall was nearly hidden by the snow-drift, and scarcely to be known for what it was. Time itself seemed to have grown dull and old, as if no day were ever to displace the melancholy night.

A wicket-gate was close at hand, but there was more than one path across the churchyard to which it led, and, uncertain which to take, they came to a stand again.

The village street-if street that could be called which was an irregular cluster of poor cottages of many heights and ages, some with their fronts, some with their backs, and some with gable-ends towards the road, with here and there a sign-post, or a shed encroaching on the path-was close at hand. There was a faint light in a chamber window not lay off, and Kit ran towards that house to ask their way.

His first shout was answered by an old man within, who presently appeared at the casement, wrapping some garment round his throat as a protection from the cold, and demanded who was abroad at that unseasonable hour, wanting him.

"'Tis hard weather this," he grumbled, "and not a night to call me up in. My trade is not of that kind that I need be roused from bed. The business

ness on which folks want me, will keep cold, especially at this season. What do you want?

"I would not have roused you, if I had known you were old and ill," said Kit.

"Old!" repeated the other peevishly. "How do you know I am old? Not so old as you think, friend, perhaps. As to being ill, you will find many young people in worse case than I am. More's the pity that it should be so-not that I should be strong and hearty for my years, I mean, but that they should be weak and tender. I ask your pardon though," said the old man, "if I spoke rather rough at first. My eyes are not good at night-that's neither age nor illness; they never were-and I didn't see you were a stranger."

"I am sorry to call you from your bed," said Kit, "but those gentlemen you may see by the churchyard gate, are strangers too, who have just arrived from a long journey, and seek the parsonage-house. You can direct us?"

"I should be able to," answered the old man, in a trembling voice, "for come next summer I have been sexton here good fifty years. The right-hand path, friend, is the road. -There is no ill news for our good gentleman, I hope?"

Kit thanked him, and made him a hasty answer in the negative; he was turning back, when his attention was caught by the voice of a child. Looking up, he saw a very little creature at a neighbouring window.

"What is that?" cried the child, earnestly. "Has my dream come true? Pray speak to me, whoever that is, awake and up."

"Poor boy!" said the sexton, before Kit could answer, "how goes it, darling?"

"Has my dream come true?" exclaimed the child again, in a voice so fervent that it might have thrilled to the heart of any listener. "But no, that can never be. How could it be-Oh! how could it!"

"I guess his meaning," said the sexton. "To thy bed again, dear boy!"

"Ay!" cried the child, in a burst of despair, "I knew it could never be, I felt too sure of that, before I asked. But, all to-night and last night too, it was the same. I never fall asleep, but that cruel dream comes back."

"Try to sleep again," said the old man, soothingly. "It will go, in time."

"No no, I would rather that it staid-cruel as it is, I would rather that it staid," rejoined the child. "I am not afraid to have it in my sleep, but I am so sad-so very, very sad."

The old man blessed him, the child in tears replied Good night, and Kit was again alone.

He hurried back, moved by what he had heard, though more by the child's manner than by anything he had said, as his meaning was hidden from him. They took the path indicated by the sexton, and soon arrived before the parsonage wall. Turning round to look about them when they had got thus far, they saw, among some ruined buildings at a distance, one single solitary light.

It shone from what appeared to be an old oriel window, and being surrounded by the deep shadows of overhanging walls, sparkled like a star. Bright and glimmering as the stars above their heads, lonely and motionless as they, it seemed to claim some kindred with the eternal lamps of Heaven, and to burn in fellowship with them.

"What light is that!" exclaimed the younger brother.

"It is surely," said Mr. Garland, "in the ruin where they live. I see no other ruin hereabouts."

"They cannot," returned the brother hastily, "be waking at this late hour-"

Kit interposed directly, and begged that, while they rang and waited at the gate, they would let him make his way to where this light was shining and try to ascertain if any people were about. Obtaining the permission he desired, he darted off with breathless eagerness, and, still carrying the bird-cage in his hand, made straight towards the spot.

It was not easy to hold that pace among the graves, and at another time he might have gone more slowly, or round by the path. Unmindful of all ob-stacles, however, he pressed forward without slackening his speed, and soon arrived within a few yards of the window.

He approached as softly as he could, and advancing so near the wall as to brush the whitened ivy with his dress, listened. There was no sound inside. The church itself was not more quiet. Touching the glass with his check, he lis-tened again. No. And yet there was such a silence all around, that he felt sure he could have heard even the breathing of a sleeper, if there had been one there.

A strange circumstance, a light in such a place at that time of night, with no one near it.

A curtain was drawn across the lower portion of the window, and he could not see into the room. But there was no shadow thrown upon it from within. To have gained a footing on the wall and tried to look in from above, would have been attended with some danger-certainly with some noise, and the chance of terrifying the child, if that really were her habitation. Again and again he listened; again and again the same wearisome blank.

Leaving the spot with slow and cautious steps, and skirting the ruin for a few paces, he came at length to a door. He knocked. No answer. But there was a curious noise inside. It was difficult to determine what it was. It bore a resemblance to the low moaning of one in pain, but it was not that, being far too regular and constant. Now it seemed a kind of song, now a wail-seemed, that is, to his changing fancy, for the sound itself was never changed or checked. It was unlike anything he had ever heard, and in its tone there was something fearful, chilling, and unearthly.

The listener's blood ran colder now than ever it had done in frost and snow, but he knocked again. There was no answer, and the sound went on without any interruption. He laid his hand softly upon the latch, and put his knee against the door. It was not secured on the inside, but yielded to the pressure, and turned upon its hinges. He saw the glimmering of a fire upon the old walls, and entered.

CHAPTER LXXI

THE dull, red glow of a wood fire-for no lamp or candle burnt within the room-showed him a figure, seated on the hearth with its back towards him, bending over the fitful light. The attitude was that of one who sought the beat. It was, and yet was not. The stooping posture and the cowering form were there, but no hands were stretched out to meet the grateful warmth, no shrug or shiver compared its luxury with the piercing cold outside. With limbs huddled together, head bowed down, arms crossed upon the breast, and fingers tightly clenched, it rocked to and fro upon its seat without a moment's pause, accompanying the action with the mournful sound he had heard.

The heavy door had closed behind him on his entrance, with a crash that made him start. The figure neither spoke nor turned to look, nor gave in any other way the faintest sign of having heard the noise. The form was that of an old man, his white head akin in colour to the mouldering embers upon which he gazed. He, and the failing light and dying fire, the time-worn room, the solitude, the wasted life, and gloom, were all in fellowship. Ashes, and dust, and ruin!

Kit tried to speak, and did pronounce some words, though what they were he scarcely knew. Still the same terrible low cry went on-still the same rocking in the chair-the same stricken figure was there, unchanged and heedless of his presence.

He had his hand upon the latch, when something in the form-distinctly seen as one log broke and fell, and, as it fell, blazed up-arrested it. He returned to where he had stood before-advanced a pace-another-another still. Another, and he saw the face. Yes! Changed as it was, he knew it well.

"Master!" he cried, stooping on one knee and catching at his hand. "Dear master. Speak to me!"

The old man turned slowly towards him; and muttered, in a hollow voice,

"This is another!-How many of these spirits there have been to-night!"

"No spirit, master. No one but your old servant. You know me now, I am sure? Miss Nell-where is she- where is she?"

"They all say that!" cried the old man. "They all ask the same question. A spirit!"

"Where is she?" demanded Kit. "Oh tell me but that -but that, dear master!"

"She is asleep-yonder-in there."

"Thank God!"

"Ay! Thank God!" returned the old man. "I have prayed to Him, many, and many, and many a livelong night, when she has been asleep, He knows. Hark! Did she call?"

"I heard no voice."

"You did. You hear her now. Do you tell me that you don't hear that?"

He started up, and listened again.

"Nor that?" he cried, with a triumphant smile. "Can anybody know that voice so well as I! Hush! hush!"

Motioning to him to be silent, he stole away into another chamber. After a short absence (during which he could be heard to speak in a softened soothing tone) he returned, bearing in his hand a lamp.

"She is still asleep," he whispered. "You were right. She did not call-unless she did so in her slumber. She has called to me in her sleep before now, sir; as I sat by, watching, I have seen her lips move, and have known, though no sound came from them, that she spoke of me. I feared the light might dazzle her eyes and wake her, so I brought it here."

He spoke rather to himself than to the visitor, but when he had put the lamp upon the table, he took it up, as if impelled by some momentary recollection or curiosity, and held it near his face. Then, as if forgetting his motive in the very action, he turned away and put it down again.

"She is sleeping soundly," he said; "but no wonder. Angel hands have strewn the ground deep with snow, that the lightest footstep may be lighter yet; and the very birds are dead, that they may not wake her. She used to feed them, sir. Though never so cold and hungry, the timid things would fly from us. They never flew from her!"

Again he stopped to listen, and scarcely drawing breath, listened for a long, long time. That fancy past, he opened an old chest, took out some clothes as fondly as if they had been living things, and began to smooth and brush them with his hand.

"Why dost thou lie so idle there, dear Nell," he murmured, "when there are bright red berries out of doors waiting for thee to pluck them! Why dost thou lie so idle there, when thy little friends come creeping to the door, crying 'where is Nell-sweet Nell?'-and sob, and weep, because they do not see thee. She was always gentle with children. The wildest would do her bidding-she had a tender way with them, indeed she had!"

Kit had no power to speak. His eyes were filled with tears.

"Her little homely dress, -her favourite!" cried the old man, pressing it to his breast, and patting it with his shrivelled hand. "She will miss it when she wakes. They have hid it here in sport, but she shall have it-she shall have it. I would not vex my darling, for the wide world's riches. See here-these shoes-how worn they are-she kept them to remind her of our last long journey. You see where the little feet were bare upon the ground. They told me, afterwards, that the stones had cut and bruised them. She never told me that. No, no, God bless her! and, I have remembered since, she walked behind me, sir, that I might not see how lame she was-but yet she had my hand in hers, and seemed to lead me still."

He pressed them to his lips, and having carefully put them back again, went on communing with himself-looking wistfully from time to time towards the chamber he had lately visited.

"She was not wont to be a lie-abed; but she was well then. We must have patience. When she is well again, she will rise early, as she used to do, and ramble abroad in the healthy morning time. I often tried to track the way she had gone, but her small fairy footstep left no print upon the dewy ground, to guide me. Who is that? Shut the door. Quick!-Have we not enough to do to drive away that marble cold, and keep her warm!"

The door was indeed opened, for the entrance of Mr. Garland and his friend, accompanied by two other persons. These were the schoolmaster, and the bachelor. The former held a light in his hand. He had, it seemed, but gone to his own cottage to replenish the exhausted lamp, at the moment when Kit came up and found the old man alone.

He softened again at sight of these two friends, and, laying aside the angry manner-if to anything so feeble and so sad the term can be applied-in which he had spoken when the door opened, resumed his former seat, and subsided, by little and little, into the old action, and the old, dult, wandering sound.

Of the strangers he took no heed whatever. He had seen them, but appeared quite incapable of interest or curiosity. The younger brother stood apart. The bachelor drew a chair towards the old man, and sat down close beside him. After a long silence, he ventured to speak.

"Another night, and not in bed!" he said softly; "I hoped you would be more mindful of your promise to me. Why do you not take some rest?"

"Sleep has left me," returned the old man. "It is all with her!"

"It would pain her very much to know that you were watching thus," said the bachelor. "You would not give her pain?"

"I am not so sure of that, if it would only rouse her. She has slept so very long. And yet I am rash to say so. It is a good and happy sleep-eh?"

"Indeed it is," returned the bachelor. "Indeed, indeed, it is!"

"That's well!-and the waking,"-faltered the old man.

"Happy too. Happier than tongue can tell, or heart of man conceive."

They watched him as he rose and stole on tiptoe to the other chamber where the lamp had been replaced. They listened as he spoke again within its silent walls. They looked into the faces of each other, and no man's cheek was free from tears. He came back, whispering that she was still asleep, but that he thought she had moved. It was her hand, he said-a little-a very, very little-but he was pretty sure she had moved it-perhaps in seeking his. He had known her do that before now, though in the deepest sleep the while. And when he had said this, he dropped into his chair again, and clasping his hands above his head, uttered a cry never to be forgotten.

The poor schoolmaster motioned to the bachelor that he would come upon the other side, and speak to him. They gently unlocked his fingers, which he had twisted in his grey hair, and pressed them in their own.

"He will hear me," said the schoolmaster, "I am sure. He will hear either me or you if we beseech him. She would, at all times."

"I will hear any voice she liked to hear," cried the old man. "I love all she loved!"

"I know you do," returned the schoolmaster. "I am certain of it. Think of her; think of all the sorrows and afflictions you have shared together; of all the trials, and all the peaceful pleasures, you have jointly known."

"I do. I do. I think of nothing else."

"I would have you think of nothing else to-night-of nothing but those things which will soften your heart, dear friend, and open it to old affections and old times. It is so that she would speak to you herself, and in her name it is that I speak now."

"You do well to speak softly," said the old man. "We will not wake her. I should be glad to see her eyes again, and to see her smile. There is a smile upon her young face now, but it is fixed and changeless. I would have it come and go. That shall be in Heaven's good time. We will not wake her."

"Let us not talk of her in her sleep, but as she used to be when you were journeying together, far away-as she was at home, in the old house from which you fled together-as she was in the old cheerful time," said the schoolmaster.

"She was always cheerful-very cheerful," cried the old man, looking steadfastly at him. "There was ever something mild and quiet about her, I remember, from the first; but she was of a happy nature."

"We have heard you say," pursued the schoolmaster, "that in this, and in all goodness, she was like her mother. You can think of, and remember her?"

He maintained his steadfast look, but gave no answer.

"Or even one before her," said the bachelor. "It is many years ago, and affliction makes the time longer, but you have not forgotten her whose death contributed to make this child so dear to you, even before you knew her worth or could read her heart? Say, that you could carry back your thoughts to very distant days-to the time of your early life-when, unlike this fair flower, you did not pass your youth alone. Say, that you could remember, long ago, another child who loved you dearly, you being but a child yourself. Say, that you had a brother, long forgotten, long unseen, long separated from you, who now, at last, in your utmost need came back to comfort and console you"-

"To be to you what you were once to him," cried the younger, falling on his knee before him; "to repay your old affection, brother dear, by constant care, solicitude, and love; to be, at your right hand, what he never ceased to be when oceans rolled between us; to call to witness his unchanging truth and mindfulness of bygone days, whole years of desolation. Give me but one word of recognition, brother-and never-no never, in the brightest moment of our youngest days, when, poor silly boys, we thought to pass our lives together-have we been half as dear and precious to each other as we shall be from this time hence!"

The old man looked from face to face, and his lips moved; but no sound came from them in reply.

"If we were knit together then," pursued the younger brother, "what will be the bond between us now! Our love and fellowship began in child-hood, when life was all before us, and will be resumed when we have proved it, and are but children at the last. As many restless spirits, who have hunted fortune, fame, or pleasure through the world, retire in their decline to where they first drew breath, vainly seeking to be children once again before they die, so we, less fortunate than they in early life, but hap-pier in its closing scenes, will set up our rest again among our boyish haunts; and going home with no hope realised, that had its growth in manhood-carrying back nothing that we brought away, but our old yearnings to each other-saving no fragment from the wreck of life, but that which first endeared it-may be indeed but children as at first. And even," he added in an altered voice, "even if what I dread to name has come to pass-even if that be so, or is to be (which Heaven forbid and spare us!)-still, dear brother, we are not apart, and have that comfort in our great affliction."

By little and little, the old man had drawn back towards the inner chamber, while these words were spoken. He pointed there, as he replied, with trembling lips,

"You plot among you to wean my heart from her. You never will do that-never while I have life. I have no relative or friend but her-I never had-I never will have. She is all in all to me. It is too late to part us now."

Waving them off with his hand, and calling softly to her as he went, he stole into the room. They who were left behind, drew close together, and after a few whispered words-not unbroken by emotion, or easily ut-tered-followed him. They moved so gently, that their footsteps made no noise; but there were sobs from among the group, and sounds of grief and mourning.

For she was dead. There, upon her little bed, she lay at rest. The solemn stillness was no marvel now.

She was dead. No sleep so beautiful and calm, so free from trace of pain, so fair to look upon. She seemed a creature fresh from the hand of God, and waiting for the breath of life; not one who had lived and suf-fered death.

Her couch was dressed with here and there some winter berries and green leaves, gathered in a spot she had been used to favour. "When I die, put near me something that has loved the light, and had the sky above it always." Those were her words.

She was dead. Dear, gentle, patient, noble Nell was dead. Her little bird-a poor slight thing the pressure of a finger would have crushed-was stirring nimbly in its cage; and the strong heart of its child-mistress was mute and motionless for ever.

Where were the traces of her early cares, her sufferings, and fatigues? All gone. Sorrow was dead indeed in her, but peace and perfect happiness were born; imaged in her tranquil beauty and profound repose.

And still her former self lay there, unaltered in this change. Yes. The old fireside had smiled upon that same sweet face; it had passed like a dream through haunts of misery and care; at the door of the poor schoolmaster on the summer evening, before the furnace fire upon the cold wet night, at the still bedside of the dying boy, there had been the same mild lovely look. So shall we know the angels in their majesty, after death.

The old man held one languid arm in his, and had the small hand tight folded to his breast, for warmth. It was the hand she had stretched out to him with her last smile-the hand that had led him on through all their wanderings. Ever and anon he pressed it to his lips; then hugged it to his breast again, murmuring that it was warmer now; and as he said it he looked, in agony, to those who stood around, as if imploring them to help her.

She was dead, and past all help, or need of it. The ancient rooms she had seemed to fill with life, even while her own was waning fast-the garden she had tended-the eyes she had gladdened-the noiseless haunts of many a thoughtful hour-the paths she had trodden as it were but yesterday-could know her no more.

"It is not," said the schoolmaster, as he bent down to kiss her on the cheek, and gave his tears free vent, "it is not on earth that Heaven's justice ends. Think what it is, compared with the World to which her young spirit has winged its early flight, and say, if one deliberate wish expressed in solemn terms above this bed could call her back to life, which of us would utter it!"

CHAPTER LXXII

WHEN morning came, and they could speak more calmly on the subject of their grief, they heard how her life had closed.

She had been dead two days. They were all about her at the time, knowing that the end was drawing on. She died soon after daybreak. They had read and talked to her in the earlier portion of the night, but as the hours crept on, she sank to sleep. They could tell, by what she faintly uttered in her dreams, that they were of her journeyings with the old man; they were of no painful scenes, but of those who had helped and used them kindly, for she often said "God bless you!" with great fervour. Waking, she never wandered in her mind but once, and that was of beautiful music which she said was in the air. God knows. It may have been.

Opening her eyes at last, from a very quiet sleep, she begged that they would kiss her once again. That done, she turned to the old man with a lovely smile upon her face-such, they said, as they had never seen, and never could forget-and clung with both her arms about his neck. They did not know that she was dead, at first.

She had spoken very often of the two sisters, who, she said, were like dear friends to her. She wished they could be told how much she thought about them, and how she had watched them as they walked together, by the river side at night. She would like to see poor Kit, she had often said of late. She wished there was somebody to take her love to Kit. And even then, she never thought or spoke about him, but with something of her old, clear, merry laugh.

For the rest, she had never murmured or complained; but, with a quiet mind, and manner quite unaltered-save that she every day became more earnest and more grateful to them-faded like the light upon a summer's evening.

The child who had been her little friend came there almost as soon as it was day, with an offering of dried flowers which he begged them to lay upon her breast. It was he who had come to the window overnight and spoken to the sexton, and they saw in the snow traces of small feet, where he had been lingering near the room in which she lay before he went to bed. He had a fancy, it seemed, that they had left her there alone; and could not bear the thought.

He told them of his dream again, and that it was of her being restored to them, just as she used to be. He begged hard to see her, saying that he would be very quiet, and that they need not fear his being alarmed, for he had sat alone by his young brother all day long, when he was dead, and had felt glad to be so near him. They let him have his wish; and indeed he kept his word, and was in his; childish way a lesson to them all.

Up to that time, the old man had not spoken once-except to her-or stirred from the bedside. But when he saw her little favourite, he was moved as they had not seen him yet, and made as though he would have him come nearer. Then pointing to the bed, he burst into tears for the first time, and they who stood by, knowing that the sight of this child had done him good, left them alone altogether.

Soothing him with his artless talk of her, the child persuaded him to take some rest, to walk abroad, to do almost as he desired him. And when the day came on, which must remove her in her earthly shape from earthly eyes for ever, he led him away, that he might not know when she was taken from him.

They were to gather fresh leaves and berries for her bed. It was Sunday-a bright, clear, wintry afternoon-and as they traversed the village street, those who were walking in their path drew back to make way for them, and gave them a softened greeting. Some shook the old man kindly by the hand, some stood uncovered while he tottered by, and many cried, "God help him!" as he passed along.

"Neighbour!" said the old man, stopping at the cottage where his young guide's mother dwelt, "how is it that the folks are nearly all in black to-day? I have seen a mourning ribbon or a piece of crape on almost every one."

She could not tell, the woman said.

"Why, you yourself-you wear the colour too!" he cried. "Windows are closed that never used to be by day. What does this mean?"

Again the woman said she could not tell.

"We must go back," said the old man, hurriedly. "We must see what this is."

"No, no," cried the child, detaining him. "Remember what you promised. Our way is to the old green lane, where she and I so often were, and where you found us more than once making those garlands for her garden. Do not turn back!"

"Where is she now?" said the old man. "Tell me that."

"Do you not know?" returned the child. "Did we not leave her, but just now?"

"True. True. It was her we left-was it!"

He pressed his hand upon his brow, looked vacantly round, and as if impelled by a sudden thought, crossed the road, and entered the sexton's house. He and his deaf assistant were sitting before the fire. Both rose up, on seeing who it was.

The child made a hasty sign to them with his hand. It was the action of an instant, but that, and the old man's look, were quite enough.

"Do you-do you bury any one to-day?" he said, eagerly.

"No, no! Who should we bury, sir?" returned the sexton.

"Ay, who indeed! I say with you, who indeed?"

"It is a holiday with us, good sir," returned the sexton mildly. "We have no work to do to-day."

"Why then, I'll go where you will," said the old man, turning to the child. "You're sure of what you tell me? You would not deceive me? I am changed even in the little time since you last saw me."

"Go thy ways with him, sir," cried the sexton, "and Heaven be with ye
both!"

"I am quite ready," said the old man, meekly. "Come, boy, come-" and so submitted to be led away.

And now the bell-the bell she had so often heard by night and day, and listened to with solemn pleasure almost as a living voice-rang its remorseless toll for her, so young, so beautiful, so good. Decrepit age, and vigorous life, and blooming youth, and helpless infancy, poured forth-on crutches, in the pride of strength and health, in the full blush of promise, in the mere dawn of life-to gather round her tomb. Old men were there, whose eyes were dim and senses failing-grandmothers, who might have died ten years ago, and still been old-the deaf, the blind, the lame, the palsied, the living dead in many shapes and forms, to see the closing of that early grave. What was the death it would shut in, to that which still could crawl and creep above it!

Along the crowded path they bore her now; pure as the newly-fallen snow that covered it; whose day on earth had been as fleeting. Under that porch, where she had sat when Heaven in its mercy brought her to that peaceful spot, she passed again, and the old church received her in its quiet shade.

They carried her to one old nook, where she had many and many a time sat musing, and laid their burden softly on the pavement. The light streamed on it through the coloured window-a window, where the boughs of trees were ever rustling in the summer, and where the birds sang sweetly all day long. With every breath of air that stirred among those branches in the sunshine, some trembling, changing light would fall upon her grave.

Earth to earth, ashes to ashes, dust to dust. Many a young hand dropped in its little wreath, many a stifled sob was heard. Some-and they were not a few-knelt down. All were sincere and truthful in their sorrow.

The service done, the mourners stood apart, and the villagers closed round to look into the grave before the pavement-stone should be re-placed. One called to mind how he had seen her sitting on that very spot, and how her book had fallen on her lap, and she was gazing with a pen-sive face upon the sky. Another told how he had wondered much that one so delicate as she, should be so bold; how she had never feared to enter the church alone at night, but had loved to linger there when all was quiet, and even to climb the tower stair, with no more light than that of the moon rays stealing through the loopholes in the thick old wall. A whisper went about among the oldest there, that she had seen and talked with angels; and when they called to mind how she had looked, and spo-ken, and her early death, some thought it might be so, indeed. Thus, coming to the grave in little knots, and glancing down, and giving place to others, and falling off in whispering groups of three or four, the church was cleared in time of all but the sexton and the mourning friends.

They saw the vault covered and the stone fixed down. Then, when the dusk of evening had come on, and not a sound disturbed the sacred stillness of the place-when the bright moon poured in her light on tomb and monument, on pillar, wall, and arch, and most of all (it seemed to them) upon her quiet grave-in that calm time, when all outward things and inward thoughts teem with assurances of immortality, and worldly hopes and fears are humbled in the dust before them-then, with tranquil and submissive hearts they turned away, and left the child with God.

Oh! it is hard to take to heart the lesson that such deaths will teach, but let no man reject it, for it is one that all must learn, and is a mighty, universal Truth. When Death strikes down the innocent and young, for every fragile form from which he lets the panting spirit free, a hundred virtues rise, in shapes of mercy, charity, and love, to walk the world, and bless it. Of every tear that sorrowing mortals shed on such green graves, some good is born, some gentler nature comes. In the Destroyer's steps there spring up bright creations that defy his power, and his dark path becomes a way of light to Heaven.

It was late when the old man came home. The boy had led him to his own dwelling, under some pretence, on their way back; and, rendered drowsy by his long ramble and late want of rest, he had sunk into a deep sleep by the fireside. He was perfectly exhausted, and they were careful not to rouse him. The slumber held him a long time, and when he at length awoke the moon was shining.

The younger brother, uneasy at his protracted absence, was watch-ing at the door for his coming, when he appeared in the pathway with his little guide. He advanced to meet them, and tenderly obliging the old man to lean upon his arm, conducted him with slow and trembling steps towards the house.

He repaired to her chamber, straight. Not finding what, he had left there, he returned with distracted looks to the room in which they were assembled. From that, he rushed into the schoolmaster's cottage, calling her name. They followed close upon him, and when he had vainly searched it, brought him home.

With such persuasive words as pity and affection could suggest, they prevailed upon him to sit among them and hear what they should tell him. Then, endeavouring by every little artifice to prepare his mind for what must come, and dwelling with many fervent words upon the happy lot to which she had been removed, they told him, at last, the truth. The moment it had passed their lips, he fell down among them like a murdered man.

For many hours, they had little hope of his surviving; but grief is strong, and he recovered.

If there be any who have never known the blank that, follows death-the weary void-the sense of desolation that will come upon the strongest minds, when something familiar and beloved is missed at every turn-the connexion; between inanimate and senseless things, and the object of recollection, when every household god becomes a monument and every room a grave-if there be any who have not known this, and proved it by their own experience, they can never faintly guess how, for many days, the old man pined and moped away the time, and wandered here and there as seeking something, and had no comfort.

Whatever power of thought or memory he retained, was all bound up in her. He never understood, or seemed to care to understand, about his brother. To every endearment and attention he continued listless. If they spoke to him on this, or any other theme-save one-he would hear them patiently for awhile, then turn away, and go on seeking as before.

On that one theme, which was in his and all their minds, it was impossible to touch. Dead! He could not hear or bear the word. The slightest hint of it would throw him into a paroxysm, like that he had had when it was first spoken. In what hope he lived, no man could tell; but that he had some hope of finding her again-some faint and shadowy hope, deferred from day to day, and making him from day to day more sick and sore at heart-was plain to all.

They bethought them of a removal from the scene of this last sorrow; of trying whether change of place would rouse or cheer him. His brother sought the advice of those who were accounted skilful in such matters, and they came and saw him. Some of the number staid upon the spot, conversed with him when he would converse, and watched him as he wandered up and down, alone and silent. Move him where they might, they said, he would ever seek to get back there. His mind would run upon that spot. If they confined him closely, and kept a strict guard upon him, they might hold him prisoner, but if he could by any means escape, he would surely wander back to that place, or die upon the road.

The boy, to whom he had submitted at first, had no longer any influence with him. At times he would suffer the child to walk by his side, or would even take such notice of his presence as giving him his hand, or would stop to kiss his cheek, or pat him on the head. At other times, he would entreat him-not unkindly-to be gone, and would not brook him near. But whether alone; or with this pliant friend; or with those who would have given him, at any cost or sacrifice, some consolation or some peace of mind, if happily the means could have been devised; he was at all times the same-with no love or care for anything in life-a broken-hearted man.

At length they found one day that he had risen early, and, with his knapsack on his back, his staff in hand, her own straw hat, and little basket full of such things as she had been used to carry, was gone. As they were making ready to pursue him far and wide, a frightened schoolboy came who had seen him, but a moment before, sitting in the church-upon her grave, he said.

They hastened there, and going softly to the door, espied him in the attitude of one who waited patiently. They did not disturb him then, but kept a watch upon him all that day. When it grew quite dark, he rose and returned home, and went to bed, murmuring to himself, "She will come to-morrow!"

Upon the morrow he was there again from sunrise until night; and still at night he laid him down to rest, and muttered, "She will come to-morrow!"

And thenceforth, every day, and all day long, he waited at her grave for her. How many pictures of new journeys over pleasant country, of resting-places under the free broad sky, of rambles in the fields and woods, and paths not often trodden-how many tones of that one well-remembered voice-how many glimpses of the form, the fluttering dress, the hair that waved so gaily in the wind-how many visions of what had been, and what he hoped was yet to be-rose up before him, in the old, dull, silent church! He never told them what he thought, or where he went. He would sit with them at night, pondering with a secret satisfaction, they could see, upon the flight that he and she would take before night came again; and still they would hear him whisper in his prayers, "Oh! Let her come tomorrow!"

The last time was on a genial day in spring. He did not return at the usual hour, and they went to seek him. He was lying dead upon the stone.

They laid him by the side of her whom he had loved so well; and, in the church where they had often prayed, and mused, and lingered hand in hand, the child and the old man slept together.

CHAPTER THE LAST

THE magic reel, which, rolling on before, has led the chronicler thus far, now slackens in its pace, and stops. It lies before the goal; the pursuit is at an end.

It remains but to dismiss the leaders of the little crowd who have borne us company upon the road, and so to close the journey.

Foremost among them, smooth Sampson Brass and Sally, arm in arm, claim our polite attention.

Mr. Sampson, then, being detained, as already has been shown, by the Justice upon whom he called, and being so strongly pressed to protract his stay that he could by no means refuse, remained under his protection for a considerable time, during which the great attention of his entertainer kept him so extremely close, that he was quite lost to society, and never even went abroad for exercise saving into a small paved yard. So well, indeed, was his modest and retiring temper understood by those with whom he had to deal, and so jealous were they of his absence, that they required a kind of friendly bond to be entered into by two substantial housekeepers, in the sum of fifteen hundred pounds a-piece, before they would suffer him to quit their hospitable roof-doubting, it appeared, that he would return, if once let loose, on any other terms. Mr. Brass, struck with the humour of this jest, and carrying out its spirit to the utmost, sought from his wide connexion a pair of friends whose joint possessions fell some halfpence short of fifteen pence, and proffered them as bail-for that was the merry word agreed upon on both sides. These gentlemen being rejected after twenty-four hours' pleasantry, Mr. Brass consented to remain, and did remain, until a club of choice spirits called a Grand Jury (who were in the joke) summoned him to a trial before twelve other wags for perjury and fraud, who in their turn found him guilty with a most facetious joy,-nay, the very populace entered into the whim, and when Mr. Brass was moving in a hackney-coach towards the building where these wags assembled, saluted him with rotten eggs and carcases of kittens, and feigned to wish to tear him into shreds, which greatly increased the comicality of the thing, and made him relish it the more, no doubt.

To work this sportive vein still further, Mr. Brass, by his counsel, moved in arrest of judgment that he had been led to criminate himself, by assurances of safety and promises of pardon, and claimed the leniency which the law extends to such confiding natures as are thus deluded. After solemn argument, this point (with others of a technical nature, whose humorous extravagance it would be difficult to exaggerate) was referred to the judges for their decision, Sampson being meantime removed to his former quarters. Finally, some of the points were given in Sampson's favour, and some against him; and the upshot was that, instead of being desired to travel for a time in foreign parts, he was permitted to grace the mother country under certain insignificant restrictions.

These were that he should, for a term of years, reside in a spacious mansion where several other gentlemen were lodged and boarded at the public charge, who went clad in a sober uniform of grey turned up with yellow, had their hair cut extremely short, and chiefly lived on gruel and light soup. It was also required of him that he should partake their exercise of constantly ascending an endless flight of stairs; and lest his legs, unused to such exertion, should be weakened by it, that he should wear upon one ankle an amulet or charm of iron. These conditions being arranged, he was removed one evening to his new abode, and enjoyed, in common with nine other gentlemen and two ladies, the privilege of being taken to his place of retirement in one of Royalty's own carriages.

Over and above these trifling penalties, his name was erased and blotted out from the roll of attorneys; which erasure has been always held in these latter times to be a great degradation and reproach, and to imply the commission of some amazing villany-as indeed would seem to be the case, when so many worthless names remain among its better records, unmolested.

Of Sally Brass, conflicting rumours went abroad. Some said with confidence that she had gone down to the docks in male attire, and had become a female sailor; others darkly whispered that she had enlisted as a private in the second regiment of Foot Guards, and had been seen in uniform and on duty, to wit, leaning on her musket and looking out of a sentry-box in St. James's Park, one evening. There were many such whispers as these in circulation; but the truth appears to be that, after a lapse of some five years (during which there is no direct evidence of her having been seen at all), two wretched people were more than once observed to crawl at dusk from the inmost recesses of St. Giles's, and to take their way along the streets, with shuffling steps and cowering shivering forms, looking into the roads and kennels as they went in search of refuse food or disregarded offal. These forms were never beheld but in those nights of cold and gloom, when the terrible spectres, who lie at all other times in the obscene hiding-places of London, in archways, dark vaults and cellars, venture to creep into the streets; the embodied spirits of Disease, and Vice, and Famine. It was whispered by those who should have known, that these were Sampson and his sister Sally; and to this day, it is said, they sometimes pass, on bad nights, in the same loathsome guise, close at the elbow of the shrinking passenger.

The body of Quilp being found-though not until some days had elapsed-an inquest was held on it near the spot where it had been washed ashore. The general supposition was that he had committed suicide, and, this appearing to be favoured by all the circumstances of his death, the verdict was to that effect. He was left to be buried with a stake through his heart in the centre of four lonely roads.

It was rumoured afterwards that this horrible and barbarous ceremony had been dispensed with, and that the remains had been secretly given up to Tom Scott. But even here, opinion was divided; for some said Tom had dug them up at midnight, and carried them to a place indicated to him by the widow. It is probable that both these stories may have had their origin in the simple fact of Tom's shedding tears upon the inquest—which he certainly di, extraordinary as it may appear. He manifested, besides, a strong desire to assault the jury; and being restrained and conducted out of court, darkened its only window by standing on his head upon the sill, until he was dexterously tilted upon his feet again by a cautious beadle.

Being cast upon the world by his master's death he determined to go through it upon his head and hands, and accordingly began to tumble for his bread. Finding, however, his English birth an insurmountable obstacle to his advancement in this pursuit (notwithstanding that his art was in high repute and favour), he assumed the name of an Italian image lad, with whom he had become acquainted; and afterwards tumbled with extraordinary success, and to overflowing audiences.

Little Mrs. Quilp never quite forgave herself the one deceit that lay so heavy on her conscience, and never spoke or thought of it but with bitter tears. Her husband had no relations, and she was rich. He had made no will, or she would probably have been poor. Having married the first time at her mother's instigation, she consulted in her second choice nobody but herself. It fell upon a smart young fellow enough; and as he made it a preliminary condition that Mrs. Jiniwin should be thence-forth an out-pensioner, they lived together after marriage with no more than the average amount of quarrelling, and led a merry life upon the dead dwarf's money.

Mr. and Mrs. Garland, and Mr. Abel, went on as usual (except that there was a change in their household, as will be seen presently), and in due time the latter went into partnership with his friend the Notary, on which occasion there was a dinner, and a ball, and great extent of dissipation. Unto this ball there happened to be invited the most bashful young lady that was ever seen, with whom Mr. Abel happened to fall in love. How it happened, or how they found it out, or which of them first communicated the discovery to the other, nobody knows. But certain it is that in course of time they were married; and equally certain it is that they were the happiest of the happy; and no less certain it is that they deserved to be so. And it is pleasant to write down that they reared a family; because any propagation of goodness and benevolence is no small addition to the aristocracy of nature, and no small subject of rejoicing for mankind at large.

The pony preserved his character for independence and principle down to the last moment of his life; which was an unusually long one, and caused him to be looked upon, indeed, as the very Old Parr of ponies. He often went to and fro with the little phaeton between Mr. Garland's and his son's, and, as the old people and the young were frequently together, had a stable of his own at the new establishment, into which he would walk of himself with surprising dignity. He condescended to play with the children, as they grew old enough to cultivate his friendship, and would run up and down the little paddock with them like a dog; but though he relaxed so far, and allowed them such small freedoms as caresses, or even to look at his shoes or hang on by his tail, he never permitted any one among them to mount his back or drive him; thus showing that even their familiarity must have its limits, and that there were points between them far too serious for trifling.

He was not unsusceptible of warm attachments in his later life, for when the good bachelor came to live with Mr. Garland upon the clergyman's decease, he conceived a great friendship for him, and amiably submitted to be driven by his hands without the least resistance. He did no work for two or three years before he died, but lived in clover; and his last act (like a choleric old gentleman) was to kick his doctor.

Mr. Swiveller, recovering very slowly from his illness, and entering into the receipt of his annuity, bought for the Marchioness a handsome stock of clothes, and put her to school forthwith, in redemption of the vow he had made upon his fevered bed. After casting about for some time for a name which should be worthy of her, he decided in favour of Sophronia Sphynx, as being euphonious and genteel, and furthermore indicative of mystery. Under this title the Marchioness repaired, in tears, to the school of his selection, from which, as she soon distanced all competitors, she was removed before the lapse of many quarters to one of a higher grade. It is but bare justice to Mr. Swiveller to say, that, although the expenses of her education kept him in straitened circumstances for half- a-dozen years, he never slackened in his zeal, and always held himself sufficiently repaid by the accounts he heard (with great gravity) of her advancement, on his monthly visits to the governess, who looked upon him as a literary gentleman of eccentric habits, and of a most prodigious talent in quotation.

In a word, Mr. Swiveller kept the Marchioness at this establishment until she was, at a moderate guess, full nineteen years of age-good-looking, clever, and good humoured; when he began to consider seriously what was to be done next. On one of his periodical visits, while he was revolving this question in his mind, the Marchioness came down to him, alone, looking more smiling and more fresh than ever. Then it occurred to him, but not for the first time, that if she would marry him, how comfortable they might be! So Richard asked her; whatever she said, it wasn't No; and they were married in good earnest that day week, which gave Mr. Swiveller frequent occasion to remark at divers subsequent periods that there had been a young lady saving up for him after all.

A little cottage at Hampstead being to let, which had in its garden a smoking-box, the envy of the civilised world, they agreed to become its tenants; and when the honey-moon was over, entered upon its occupation. To this retreat Mr. Chuckster repaired regularly every Sunday to spend the day-usually beginning with breakfast; and here he was the great purveyor of general news and fashionable intelligence. For some years he continued a deadly foe to Kit, protesting that he had a better opinion of him when he was supposed to have stolen the five-pound note, than when he was shown to be perfectly free of the crime; inasmuch as his guilt would have had in it something daring and bold, whereas his innocence was but another proof of a sneaking and crafty disposition. By slow degrees, however, he was reconciled to him in the end; and even went so far as to honour him with his patronage, as one who had in some measure reformed, and was therefore to be forgiven. But he never forgot or pardoned that circumstance of the shilling; holding that if he had come back to get another he would have done well enough, but that his returning to work out the former gift was a stain upon his moral character which no penitence or contrition could ever wash away.

Mr. Swiveller, having always been in some measure of a philosophic and reflective turn, grew immensely contemplative, at times, in the smoking-box, and was accustomed at such periods to debate in his own mind the mysterious question of Sophronia's parentage. Sophronia herself supposed she was an orphan; but Mr. Swiveller, putting various slight circumstances together, often thought Miss Brass must know better than that; and, having heard from his wife of her strange interview with Quilp, entertained sundry misgivings whether that person, in his life-time, might not also have been able to solve the riddle, had he chosen. These speculations, however, gave him no uneasiness; for Sophronia was ever a most cheerful, affectionate, and provident wife to him; and Dick (excepting for an occasional outbreak with Mr. Chuckster, which she had the good sense rather to encourage than oppose) was to her an attached and domesticated husband. And they played many hundred thousand games of cribbage together. And let it be added, to Dick's honour, that, though we have called her Sophronia, he called her the Marchioness from first to last; and that upon every anniversary of the day on which he found her in his sick room Mr. Chuckster came to dinner, and there was great glorification.

The gamblers, Isaac List and Jowl, with their trust y confederate Mr. James Groves of unimpeachable memory, pursued their course with varying success, until the failure of a spirited enterprise in the way of their profession, dispersed them in various directions, and caused their career to receive a sudden check from the long and strong arm of the law. This defeat had its origin in the untoward detection of a new associate-young Frederick Trent- who thus became the unconscious instrument of their punishment and his own.

For the young man himself, he rioted abroad for a brief term, living by his wits-which means by the abuse of every faculty that worthily employed raises man above the beasts, and so degraded, sinks him far below them. It was not long before his body was recognised by a stranger, who chanced to visit that hospital in Paris where the drowned are laid out to be owned; despite the bruises and disfigurements which were said to have been occasioned by some previous scuffle. But the stranger kept his own counsel until he returned home, and it was never claimed or cared for.

The younger brother, or the single gentleman, for that designation is more familiar, would have drawn the poor schoolmaster from his lone retreat, and made him his companion and friend. But the humble village-teacher was timid of venturing into the noisy world, and had become fond of his dwelling in the old churchyard. Calmly happy in his school, and in the spot, and in the attachment of Her little mourner, he pursued his quiet course in peace; and was, through the righteous gratitude of his friend-let this brief mention suffice for that-a poor schoolmaster no more.

That friend-single gentleman, or younger brother, which you will-had at his heart a heavy sorrow; but it bred in him no misanthropy or monastic gloom. He went forth into the world, a lover of his kind. For a long, long time, it was his chief delight to travel in the steps of the old man and the child (so far as he could trace them from her last narrative), to halt where they had halted, sympathise where they had suffered, and rejoice where they had been made glad. Those who had been kind to them, did not escape his search. The sisters at the school-they who were her friends, because themselves so friendless- Mrs. Jarley of the wax-work, Codlin, Short-he found them all; and trust me, that the man who fed the furnace fire was not forgotten.

Kit's story having got abroad, raised him up a host of friends, and many offers of provision for his future life. He had no idea at first of ever quitting Mr. Garland's service; but, after serious remonstrance and advice from that gentleman, began to contemplate the possibility of such a change being brought about in time. A good post was procured for him, with a rapidity which took away his breath, by some of the gentlemen who had believed him guilty of the offence laid to his charge, and who had acted upon that belief. Through the same kind agency, his mother was secured from want, and made quite happy. Thus, as Kit often said, his great misfortune turned out to be the source of all his subsequent prosperity.

Did Kit live a single man all his days, or did he marry? Of course he married, and who should be his wife but Barbara? And the best of it was, he married so soon that little Jacob was an uncle, before the calves of his legs, already mentioned in this history, had ever been encased in broadcloth pantaloons,-though that was not quite the best either, for of necessity the baby was an uncle too. The delight of Kit's mother and of Barbara's mother upon the great occasion is past all telling; finding they agreed so well on that, and on all other subjects, they took up their abode together, and were a most harmonious pair of friends from that time forth. And hadn't Astley's cause to bless itself for their all going together once a quarter-to the pit-and didn't Kit's mother always say, when they painted the outside, that Kit's last treat had helped to that, and wonder what the manager would feel if he but knew it as they passed his house!

When Kit had children six and seven years old, there was a Barbara among them, and a pretty Barbara she was. Nor was there wanting an exact facsimile and copy of little Jacob as he appeared in those remote times when they taught him what oysters meant. Of course there was an Abel, own godson to the Mr. Garland of that name; and there was a Dick, whom Mr. Swiveller did especially favour. The little group would often gather round him of a night and beg him to tell again that story of good Miss Nell who died. This Kit would do; and when they cried to hear it, wishing it longer too, he would teach them how she had gone to Heaven, as all good people did; and how, if they were good like her, they might hope to be there too one day, and to see and know her as he had done when he was quite a boy. Then he would relate to them how needy he used to be, and how she had taught him what he was otherwise too poor to learn, and how the old man had been used to say "she always laughs at Kit;" at which they would brush away their tears, and laugh themselves to think that she had done so, and be again quite merry.

He sometimes took them to the street where she had lived; but new improvements had altered it so much, it was not like the same. The old house had been long ago pulled down, and a fine broad road was in its place. At first he would draw with his stick a square upon the ground to show them where it used to stand. But he soon became uncertain of the spot, and could only say it was thereabouts, he thought, and that these alterations were confusing.

Such are the changes which a few years bring about, and so do things pass away, like a tale that is told!

THE END

A TALE OF
TWO CITIES

PREFACE TO THE FIRST EDITION

When I was acting, with my children and friends, in Mr. Wilkie Collins's drama of The Frozen Deep, I first conceived the main idea of this story. A strong desire was upon me then to embody it in my own person; and I traced out in my fancy the state of mind of which it would necessitate the presentation to an observant spectator, with particular care and interest.

As the idea became familiar to me, it gradually shaped itself into its present form. Throughout its execution, it has had complete possession of me; I have so far verified what is done and suffered it all myself.

Whenever any reference (however slight) is made here to the condition of the French people before or during the Revolution, it is truly made, on the faith of trustworthy witnesses. It has been one of my hopes to add something to the popular and picturesque means of understanding that terrible time, though no one can hope to add anything to the philosophy of Mr. Carlyle's wonderful book.

Tavistock House, London
November, 1859

BOOK THE FIRST. RECALLED TO LIFE

CHAPTER I

THE PERIOD

IT was the best of times, it was the worst of times, it was the age of wisdom, it was the age of foolishness, it was the epoch of belief, it was the epoch of incredulity, it was the season of Light, it was the season of Darkness, it was the spring of hope, it was the winter of despair, we had everything before us, we had nothing before us, we were all going direct to Heaven, we were all going direct the other way—in short, the period was so far like the present period, that some of its noisiest authorities insisted on its being received, for good or for evil, in the superlative degree of comparison only.

There were a king with a large jaw and a queen with a plain face, on the throne of England; there were a king with a large jaw and a queen with a fair face, on the throne of France. In both countries it was clearer than crystal to the lords of the State preserves of loaves and fishes, that things in general were settled for ever.

It was the year of Our Lord one thousand seven hundred and seventy-five. Spiritual revelations were conceded to England at that favoured period, as at this. Mrs. Southcott had recently attained her five-and-twentieth blessed birthday, of whom a prophetic private in the Life Guards had heralded the sublime appearance by announcing that arrangements were made for the swallowing up of London and Westminster. Even the Cock-lane ghost had been laid only a round dozen of years, after rapping out its messages, as the spirits of this very year last past (supernaturally deficient in originality) rapped out theirs. Mere messages in the earthly order of events had lately come to the English Crown and People, from a congress of British subjects in America: which, strange to relate, have proved more important to the human race than any communications yet received through any of the chickens of the Cock-lane brood.

France, less favoured on the whole as to matters spiritual than her sister of the shield and trident, rolled with exceeding smoothness down hill, making paper money and spending it. Under the guidance of her Christian pastors, she entertained herself, besides, with such humane achievements as sentencing a youth to have his hands cut off, his tongue torn out with pincers, and his body burned alive, because he had not kneeled down in the rain to do honour to a dirty procession of monks which passed within his view, at a distance of some fifty or sixty yards. It is likely enough that, rooted in the woods of France and Norway, there were growing trees, when that sufferer was put to death, already marked by the Woodman, Fate, to come down and be sawn into boards, to make a certain movable framework with a sack and a knife in it, terrible in history. It is likely enough that in the rough outhouses of some tillers of the heavy lands adjacent to Paris, there were sheltered from the weather that very day, rude carts bespattered with rustic mire, snuffed about by pigs, and roosted in by poultry, which the Farmer, Death, had already set apart to be his tumbrels of the Revolution. But that Woodman and that Farmer, though they work unceasingly, work silently, and no one heard them as they went about with muffled tread: the rather, forasmuch as to entertain any suspicion that they were awake, was to be atheistical and traitorous.

In England, there was scarcely an amount of order and protection to justify much national boasting. Daring burglaries by armed men, and highway robberies, took place in the capital itself every night; families were publicly cautioned not to go out of town without removing their furniture to upholsterers' warehouses for security; the highwayman in the dark was a City tradesman in the light, and, being recognized and challenged by his fellow-tradesman whom he stopped in his character of 'the Captain,' gallantly shot him through the head and rode away; the mail was waylaid by seven robbers and the guard shot three dead, and then got shot dead himself by the other four, 'in consequence of the failure of his ammunition: after which the mail was robbed in peace; that magnificent potentate, the Lord Mayor of London, was made to stand and deliver on Turnham Green, by one highwayman, who despoiled the illustrious creature in sight of all his retinue; prisoners in London jails fought battles with their turnkeys, and the majesty of the law fired blunderbusses in among them, loaded with rounds of shot and ball; thieves snipped off diamond crosses from the necks of noble lords at Court drawing-rooms; musketeers went into St.Gile's, to search for contraband goods, and the mob fired on the musketeers, and the musketeers fired on the mob, and nobody thought any of these occurrences much out of the common way. In the midst of them, the hangman, every busy and ever worse than useless, was in constant requisition; now, stringing up long rows of miscellaneous criminals; now, hanging a houses-breaker on Saturday who had been taken on Tuesday; now, burning people in the hand at Newgate by the dozen, and now burning pamphlets at the door of Westminster Hall; to-day, taking the life of an atrocious murderer, and to-morrow of the wretched pilferer who had robbed a farmer's boy of sixpence.

All these things, and a thousand like them, came to pass in and close upon the dear old year one thousand seven hundred and seventy-five. Environed by them, while the Woodman and the Farmer worked unheeded, those two of the large jaws, and those other two of the plain and the fair faces, trod with stir enough, and carried their divine rights with a high hand. Thus did the year one thousand seven hundred and seventy-five conduct their Greatnesses, and myriads of small creatures–the creatures of this chronicle among the rest–along the roads that lay before them.

CHAPTER II

THE MAIL

IT was the Dover road that lay, on a Friday night, late in November, before the first of the persons with whom this history has business. The Dover road lay, as to him, beyond the Dover mail, as it lumbered up Shooter's Hill. He walked uphill in the mire by the side of the mail, as the rest of the passengers did; not because they had the least relish for walking exercise, under the circumstances, but because the hill, and the harness, and the mud, and the mail, were all so heavy, that the horses had three times already come to a stop, besides once drawing the coach across the road, with the mutinous intent of taking it back to Blackheath. Reins and whip and coachman and guard, however, in combination, had read that article of war which forbade a purpose otherwise strongly in favour of the argument, that some brute animals are endued with Reason; and the team had capitulated and returned to their duty.

With drooping heads and tremulous tails, they mashed their way through the thick mud, floundering and stumbling between whiles, as if they were falling to pieces at the larger joints. As often as the driver rested them and brought them to a stand, with a wary 'Wo-ho! so-ho then!' the near leader violently shook his head and everything upon it–like an unusually emphatic horse, denying that the coach could be got up the hill. Whenever the leader made this rattle, the passenger started, as a nervous passenger might, and was disturbed in mind.

There was a steaming mist in all the hollows, and it had roamed in its forlornness up the hill, like an evil spirit, seeking rest and finding none. A clammy and intensely cold mist, it made its slow way through the air in ripples that visibly followed and overspread one another, as the waves of an unwholesome sea might do. It was dense enough to shut out everything from the light of the coach-lamps but these it own workings, and a few yards of road; and the reek of the labouring horses steamed into it, as if they had made it all.

Two other passengers, besides the one, were plodding up the hill by the side of the mail. All three were wrapped to the cheekbones and over the ears, and wore jack-boots. Not one of the three could have said, from anything he saw, what either of the other two was like; and each was hidden under almost as many wrappers from the eyes of the mind, as from the eyes of the body, of his two companions. In those days, travellers were very shy of being confidential on a short notice, for anybody on the road might be a robber or in league with robbers. As to the latter, when every posting-house and ale-house could produce somebody in 'the Captain's' pay, ranging from the landlord to the lowest stable nondescript, it was the likeliest thing upon the cards. So the guard of the Dover mail thought to himself, that Friday night in November, one thousand seven hundred and seventy-five, lumbering up Shooter's Hill, as he stood on his own particular perch behind the mail, beating his feet, and keeping an eye and a hand on the arm-chest before him, where a loaded blunderbuss lay at the top of six or eight loaded horse-pistols, deposited on a substratum of cutlass.

The Dover mail was in its usual genial position that the guard suspected the passengers, the passengers suspected one another and the guard, they all suspected everybody else, and the coachman was sure of nothing but the horses; as to which cattle he could with a clear conscience have taken his oath on the two Testaments that they were not fit for the journey.

'Who-ho!' said the coachman. 'So, then! One more pull and you're at the top and be damned to you, for I have had trouble enough to get you to it!–Joe!'

'Halloa!' the guard replied.

'What o'clock do you make it, Joe?'

'Ten minutes, good past eleven.'

'My blood!' ejaculated the vexed coachman, 'and not atop of Shooter's yet! Tst! Yah! Get on with you!'

The emphatic horse, cut short by the whip in a most decided negative, made a decided scramble for it, and the three other horses followed suit. Once more, the Dover mail struggled on, with the jack-boots of its passengers squashing along by its side. They had stopped when the coach stopped, and they kept close company with it. If any one of the three had had the hardihood to propose to another to walk on a little ahead into the mist and darkness, he would have put himself in a fair way of getting shot instantly as a highwayman.

The last burst carried the mail to the summit of the hill. The horses stopped to breathe again, and the guard got down to skid the wheel for the descent, and open the coach door to let the passengers in.

'Tst! Joe!' cried the coachman in a warning voice, looking down from his box.

'What do you say, Tom?'

They both listened.

'I say a horse at a canter coming up, Joe.'

'*I* say a horse at a gallop, Tom,' returned the guard, leaving his hold of the door, and mounting nimbly to his place. 'Gentlemen! In the king's name, all of you!'

With this hurried adjuration, he cocked his blunderbuss, and stood on the offensive.

The passenger booked by this history, was on the coach-step, getting in; the other two passengers were close behind him, and about to follow. He remained on the step, half in the coach and half out of; they remained in the road below him. They all looked from the coachman to the guard, and from the guard to the coachman, and listened. The coachman looked back and the guard looked back, and even the emphatic leader pricked up his ears and looked back, without contradicting.

The stillness consequent on the cessation of the rumbling and labouring of the coach, added to the stillness of the night, made it very quiet indeed. The panting of the horses communicated a tremulous motion to the coach, as if it were in a state of agitation. The hearts of the passengers beat loud enough perhaps to be heard; but at any rate, the quiet pause was audibly expressive of people out of breath, and holding the breath, and having the pulses quickened by expectation.

The sound of a horse at a gallop came fast and furiously up the hill.

'So-ho!' the guard sang out, as loud as he could roar. 'Yo there! Stand! I shall fire!'

The pace was suddenly checked, and, with much splashing and floundering, a man's voice called from the mist, 'Is that the Dover mail?'

'Never you mind what it is,' the guard retorted. 'What are you?'

'*Is* that the Dover mail?'

'Why do you want to know?'

'I want a passenger, if it is.'

'What passenger?'

'Mr. Jarvis Lorry.'

Our booked passenger showed in a moment that it was his name. The guard, the coachman, and the two other passengers eyed him distrustfully.

'Keep where you are,' the guard called to the voice in the mist, 'because, if I should make a mistake, it could never be set light in your lifetime. Gentleman of the mane of Lorry answer straight.'

'What is the matter?' asked the passenger, then, with mildly quavering speech. 'Who wants me? Is it Jerry?'

('I don't like Jerry's voice, if it is Jerry,' growled the guard to himself. 'He's hoarser than suits me, is Jerry.')

'Yes, Mr. Lorry.'

'What is the matter?'

'A dispatch sent after you from over yonder. T. and Co.'

'I know this messenger, guard,' said Mr. Lorry, getting down into the road—assisted from behind more swiftly than politely by the other two passengers, who immediately scrambled into the coach, shut the door, and pulled up the window. 'He may come close; there's nothing wrong.'

'I hope there ain't, but can't make so 'Nation sure of that,' said the guard, in gruff soliloquy. 'Hallo you!'

'Well! And hallo you!' said Jerry, more hoarsely than before.

'Come on at a footpace! d'ye mind me? And if you've got holsters to that saddle o' yourn, don't let me see your hand go nigh 'em. For I'm a devil at a quick mistake, and when I make one it takes the form of Lead. So now let's look at you.'

The figures of a horse and rider came slowly through the eddying mist, and came to the side of the mail, where the passenger stood. The rider stooped, and, casting up his eyes at the guard, handed the passenger a small folded paper. The rider's horse was blown, and both horse and rider were covered with mud, from the hoofs of the horse to the hat of the man.

'Guard!' said the passenger, in a tone of quiet business confidence.

The watchful guard, with his right hand at the stock of his raised blunderbuss, his left at the barrel, and his eye on the horseman, answered curtly, 'Sir.'

'There is nothing to apprehend. I belong to Tellson's Bank. You must know Tellson's Bank in London. I am going to Paris on business. A crown to drink. I may read this?'

'If so be as you're quick, sir.'

He opened it in the light of the coach lamp on that side, and read–first to himself and then aloud: "Wait at Dover for Mam'selle." It's not long, you see, guard. Jerry, say that my answer was, RECALLED TO LIFE.'

Jerry started in his saddle. 'That's a Blazing strange answer, too,' said he, at his hoarsest.

'Take that message back, and they will know that I received this, as well as if I wrote. Make the best of your way. Good night.'

With these words the passenger opened the coach door and got in; not at all assisted by his fellow-passengers, who had expeditiously secreted their watches and purses in their boots, and were now making a general pretence of being asleep. With no more definite purpose than to escape the hazard of originating any other kind of action.

The coach lumbered on again, with heavy wreaths of mist closing round it as it began the descent. The guard soon replaced his blunderbuss in his arm-chest, and, having looked to the rest of its contents, and having looked to the supplementary pistols that he wore in his belt, looked to a smaller chest beneath his seat, in which there were a few smith's tools, a couple of torches, and a tinder-box. For he was furnished with that completeness that if the coach lamps had been blown and stormed out, which did occasionally happen, he had only to shut himself up inside, keep the flint and steel sparks well off the straw, and get a light with tolerable safety and ease (if he were lucky) in five minutes.

'Tom!' softly over the coach roof.

'Hallo, Joe.'

'Did you hear the message?'

'I did, Joe.'

'What did you make of it, Tom?'

'Nothing at all, Joe.'

'That's a coincidence, too,' the guard mused, 'for I made the same of it myself.'

Jerry left alone in the mist and darkness, dismounted meanwhile, not only to ease his spent horse, but to wipe the mud from his face, and shake the wet out of his hat brim, which might be capable of holding about half a gallon. After standing with the bridle over his heavily splashed arm, until the wheels of the mail were no longer within hearing and the night was quite still again, he turned to walk down the hill.

'After that there gallop from Temple Bar, old lady, I won't trust your forelegs till I get you on the level,' said this hoarse messenger, glancing at his mare. "Recalled to life." That's a Blazing strange message. Much of that wouldn't do for you, Jerry! I say, Jerry! You'd be in a Blazing bad way, if recalling to life was to come into fashion, Jerry!'

CHAPTER III

THE NIGHT SHADOWS

A WONDERFUL fact to reflect upon, that every human creature is constituted to be that profound secret and mystery to every other. A solemn consideration, when I enter a great city by night, that every one of those darkly clustered houses encloses its own secret; that every beating heart in the hundreds of thousands of breasts there, is in some of its imaginings, a secret to the heart nearest it! Something of the awfulness, even of Death itself, is referable to this. No more can I turn the leaves of this dear book that I loved, and vainly hope in time to read it all. No more can I look into the depths of this unfathomable water, wherein, as momentary lights glanced into it, I have had glimpses of buried treasure and other things submerged. It was appointed that the book should shut with a spring, for ever and for ever, when I had read but a page. It was appointed that the water should be locked in an eternal frost, when the light was playing on its surface, and I stood in ignorance on the shore. My friend is dead, my neighbour is dead, my love, the darling of my soul, is dead; it is the inexorable consolation and perpetuation of the secret that was always in that individuality, and which I shall carry in mine to my life's end. In any of the burial-places of this city through which I pass, is there a sleeper more inscrutable than its busy inhabitants are, in their innermost personality, to me, or than I am to them?

As to this, his natural and not to be alienated inheritance, the messenger on horseback had exactly the same possessions as the King, the first Minister of State, or the richest merchant in London. So with the three passengers shut up in the narrow compass of one lumbering old mail-coach; they were mysteries to one another, as complete as if each had been in his own coach and six, or his own coach and sixty, with the breadth of a county between him and the next.

The messenger rode back at an easy trot, stopping pretty often at alehouses by the way to drink, but evincing a tendency to keep his own counsel, and to keep his hat cocked over his eyes. He had eyes that assorted very well with that decoration, being of a surface black, with no depth in the colour or form, and much too near together–as if they were afraid of being found out in something, singly, if they kept too far apart. They had a sinister expression, under an old cocked hat like a three-cornered spitton, and over a great muffler for the chin and throat, which descended mearly to the wearer's knees. When he stopped for drink, he moved this muffler with his left hand, only while he poured his liquor in with his right; as soon as that was done, he muffled again.

'No, Jerry, no!' said the messenger, harping on one theme as he rode. 'It wouldn't do for you, Jerry. Jerry, you honest tradesman, it wouldn't suit *your* line of business! Recalled–! Bust me if I don't think he'd been a drinking!'

His message perplexed his mind to that degree that he was fain, several times, to take off his hat to scratch his head. Except on the crown, which was raggedly bald, he had stiff, black hair, standing jaggedly all over it, and so like smith's work, so much more like the top of a strongly spiked wall than a head of hair, that the best of players at leap-frog might have declined him, as the most dangerous man in the world to go over.

While he trotted back with the message he was to deliver to the night-watchman in his box at the door of Tellson's Bank, by Temple Bar, who was to deliver it to greater authorities within, the shadows of the night took such shapes to the mare as arose out of *her* private topics of uneasiness. They seemed to be numerous, for she shied at every shadow on the road.

What time, the mail-coach lumbered, jolted, rattled, and bumped upon its tedious way, with its three fellow-inscrutables inside. To whom, likewise, the shadows of the night revealed themselves, in the forms their dozing eyes and wandering thoughts suggested.

Tellson's Bank had a run upon it in the mail. As the bank passenger–with an arm drawn through the leathern strap, which did what lay in it to keep him from pounding against the next passenger, and driving him into his corner whenever the coach got a special jolt–nodded in his place, with half-shut eyes, the little coach windows, and the coach lamp dimly gleaming through them, and the bulky bundle of opposite passenger, became the bank, and did a great stroke of business. The rattle of the harness was the chink of money, and more drafts were honoured in five minutes than even Tellson's, with all its foreign and home connection, ever paid in thrice the time. Then the strong-rooms underground, at Tellson's, with such of their valuable stores and secrets as were known to the passenger (and it was not a little that he knew about them), opened before him, and he went in among them with the great keys and the feebly burning candle, and found them safe, and strong, and sound, and still, just as he had last seen them.

But, though the bank was almost always with him, and though the coach (in a confused way, like the presence of pain under an opiate) was always with him, there was another current of impression that never ceased to run, all through the night. He was on his way to dig someone out of a grave.

Now, which of the multitude of faces that showed themselves before him was the true face of the buried person, the shadows of the night did not indicate; but they were all the faces of a man of five-and-forty by years, and they differed principally in the passions they expressed, and in the ghastliness of their worn and wasted state. Pride, contempt, defiance, stubbornness, submission, lamentation, succeeded one another; so did varieties of sunken cheek, cadaverous colour, emaciated hands and figures. But the face was in the main one face, and every head was prematurely white. A hundred times the dozing passenger inquired of this spectre:

'Buried how long?'

The answer was always the same: 'Almost eighteen years.'

'You had abandoned all hope of being dug out?'

'Long ago.'

'You know that you are recalled to life?'

'They tell me so.'

'I hope you care to live?'

'I can't say.'

'Shall I show her to you? Will you come and see her?'

The answers to this question were various and contradictory. Sometimes the broken reply was, 'Wait! It would kill me if I saw her too soon.' Sometimes, it was given in a tender rain of tears, and then it was, 'Take me to her.' Sometimes it was staring and bewildered, and then it was, 'I don't know her. I don't understand.'

After such imaginary discourse, the passenger in his fancy would dig, and dig, dig–now, with a spade, now with a great key, now with his hands–to dig this wretched creature out. Got out at last, with earth hanging about his grace and hair, he would suddenly fall away to dust. The passenger would then start to himself, and lower the window, to get the reality of mist and rain on his cheek.

Yet even when his eyes were opened on the mist and rain, on the moving patch of light from the lamps, and the hedge at the roadside retreating by jerks, the night shadows outside the coach would fall into the train of the night shadows within. The real banking-house by Temple Bar, the real business of the past day, the real strong-rooms, the real express sent after him, and the real message returned, would all be there. Out of the midst of them, the ghostly face would rise, and he would accost it again.

'Buried how long?'

'Almost eighteen years.'

'I hope you care to live?'

'I can't say.'

Dig–dig–dig–dig–until an impatient movement from one of the two passengers would admonish him to pull up the window, draw his arm securely through the leathern strap, and speculate upon the two slumbering forms, until his mind lost its hold of them, and they again slid away into the bank and the grave.

'Buried how long?'

'Almost eighteen years.'

'You had abandoned all hope of being dug out?'

'Long ago.'

The words were still in his hearing as just spoken–distinctly in his hearing as ever spoken words had been in his life–when the weary passenger started to the consciousness of daylight, and found that the shadows of the night were gone.

He lowered the window, and looked out at the rising sun. There was a ridge of ploughed land, with a plough upon it where it had been left last night when the horses were unyoked; beyond, a quiet coppice-wood, in which many leaves of burning red and golden yellow still remained upon the trees. Though the earth was cold and wet, the sky was clear, and the sun rose bright, placid, and beautiful.

'Eighteen years!' said the passenger, looking at the sun. 'Gracious Creator of day! To be buried alive for eighteen years!'

CHAPTER IV

THE PREPARATION

WHEN the mail got successfully to Dover, in the course of the forenoon, the head drawer at the Royal George Hotel opened the coach door as his custom was. He did it with some flourish of ceremony, for a mail journey from London in winter was an achievement to congratulate an adventurous traveller upon.

By that time, there was only one adventurous traveller left to be congratulated; for the two others had been set down at their respective roadside destinations. The mildewy inside of the coach, with its damp and dirty straw, its disagreeable smell, and its obscurity, was rather like a larger dog kennel. Mr. Lorry, the passenger, shaking himself out of it in chains of straw, a tangle of shaggy wrapper, flapping hat, and muddy legs, was rather like a larger sort of dog.

'There will be a packet to Calais, to-morrow, drawer?'

'Yes, sir, if the weather holds and the wind sets tolerable fair. The tide will serve pretty nicely at about two in the afternoon, sir. Bed, sir?'

'I shall not go to bed till night; but I want a bedroom, and a barber.'

'And then breakfast, sir? Yes, sir. That way, sir, if you please. Show Concord! Gentleman's valise and hot water to Concord. Pull off gentleman's boots in Concord. (You will find a fine sea-coal fire, sir.) Fetch barber to Concord. Stir about there, now, for Concord!'

The Concord bed-chamber being always assigned to a passenger by the mail, and passengers by the mail being always heavily wrapped up from head to foot, the room had the odd interest for the establishment of the 'Royal George,' that although but one kind of man was seen to go into it, all kinds and varieties of men came out of it. Consequently, another drawer, and two porters, and several maids and the landlady, were all loitering by accident at various points of the road between the Concord and the coffee-room, when a gentleman of sixty, formally dressed in a brown suit of clothes, pretty well worn, but very well kept, with large square cuffs and large flaps to the pockets, passed along on his way to his breakfast.

The coffee-room had no other occupant, that forenoon, than the gentleman in brown. His breakfast-table was drawn before the fire, and as he sat, with its light shining on him, waiting for the meal, he sat so still, that he might have been sitting for his portrait.

Very orderly and methodical he looked, with a hand on each knee, and a loud watch ticking a sonorous sermon under his flapped waistcoat, as though it pitted its gravity and longevity against the levity and evanescence of the brisk fire. He had a good leg, and was a little vain of it, for his brown stockings fitted sleek and close, and were of a fine texture; his shoes and buckles, too, though plain, were trim. He wore an odd little sleek crisp flaxen wig, setting very close to his head: which wig, it is to be presumed, was made of hair, but which looked far more as though it were spun from filaments of silk or glass. His linen, though not of a fineness in accordance with his stockings, was as white as the tops of the waves that broke upon the neighboring beach, or the specks of sail that glinted in the sunlight far at sea. A face habitually suppressed and quieted, was still lighted up under the quaint wig by a pair of moist bright eyes that it must have cost their owner, in years gone by, some pains to drill to the composed and reserved expression of Tellson's Bank. He had a healthy colour in his cheeks, and his face, though lined, bore few traces of anxiety. But, perhaps the confidential bachelor clerks in Tellson's Bank were principally occupied with the cares of other people; and perhaps second-hand cares, like second-hand clothes, come easily off and on.

Completing his resemblance to a man who was sitting for his portrait, Mr. Lorry dropped off to sleep. The arrival of his breakfast roused him, and he said to the drawer, as he moved his chair to it:

'I wish accommodation prepared for a young lady who may come here at any time to-day. She may ask for Mr. Jarvis Lorry, or she may only ask for a gentleman from Tellson's Bank. Please to let me know.'

'Yes, sir. Tellson's Bank in London, sir?'

'Yes.'

'Yes, sir. We have oftentimes the honour to entertain your gentlemen in their travelling backwards and forwards betwixt London and Paris, sir. A vast deal of travelling, sir, in Tellson and Company's House.'

'Yes. We are quite a French House, as well as an English one.'

'Yes, sir. Not much in the habit of such travelling yourself, I think, sir?'

'Not of late years. It is fifteen years since we—since I—came last from France.'

'Indeed, sir? That was before my time here, sir. Before our people's time here, sir. The "George" was in other hands at that time, sir.'

'I believe so.'

'But I would hold a pretty wager, sir, that a House like Tellson and Company was flourishing, a matter of fifty, not to speak of fifteen years ago?'

'You might treble that, and say a hundred and fifty, yet not be far from the truth.'

'Indeed, sir!'

Rounding his mouth and both his eyes, as he stepped backward from the table, the waiter shifted his napkin from his right arm to his left, dropped into a comfortable attitude, and stood surveying the guest while he ate and drank, as from an observatory or watch-tower. According to the immemorial usage of waiters in all ages.

When Mr. Lorry had finished his breakfast, he went out for a stroll on the beach. The little narrow, crooked town of Dover hid itself away from the beach, and ran its head into the chalk cliffs, like a marine ostrich. The beach was a desert of heaps of sea and stones tumbling wildly about, and the sea did what it liked, and what it liked was destruction. It thundered at the town, and thundered at the cliffs and brought the coast down, madly. The air among the houses was of so strong a piscatory flavour that one might have supposed sick fish went up to be dipped in it, as sick people went down to be dipped in the sea. A little fishing was done in the port, and a quantity of strolling about by night, and looking seaward: particularly at those times when the tide made, and was near flood. Small tradesmen, who did no business whatever, sometimes unaccountably realized large fortunes, and it was remarkable that nobody in the neighbourhood could endure a lamplighter.

As the day declined into the afternoon, and the air, which had been at intervals clear enough to allow the French coast to be seen, became again charged with mist and vapour, Mr. Lorry's thoughts seemed to cloud too. When it was dark, and he sat before the coffee-room fire, awaiting his dinner as he had awaited his breakfast, his mind was busily digging, digging, digging, in the live red coals.

A bottle of good claret after dinner does a digger in the red coals no harm, otherwise than as it has a tendency to throw him out of work. Mr. Lorry had been idle a long time, and had just poured out his last glassful of wine with found in an elderly gentleman of a fresh complexion who has got to the end of a bottle, when a rattling of wheels came up the narrow street, and rumbled into the inn yard.

He set down his glass untouched. 'This is Mam'selle!' said he.

In a very few minutes the waiter came in to announce that Miss Manette had arrived from London, and would be happy to see the gentleman from Tellson's.

'So soon?'

Miss Manette had taken some refreshment on the road, and required none then, and was extremely anxious to see the gentleman from Tellson's immediately, if it suited his pleasure and convenience.

The gentleman from Tellson's had nothing left for it but to empty his glass with an air of stolid desperation, settle his odd little flaxen wig at the ears, and follow the waiter to Miss Manette's apartment. It was a large, dark room, furnished in a funeral manner with black horsehair, and loaded with heavy dark tables. These had been oiled and oiled, until the two tall candles on the table in the middle of the room were gloomily reflected on every leaf; as if *they* were buried, in deep graves of black mahogany, and no light to speak of could be expected from them until they were dug out.

The obscurity was so difficult to penetrate that Mr. Lorry, picking his way over the well-worn Turkey carpet, supposed Miss Manette to be, for the moment, in some adjacent room, until, having got past the two tall candles, he saw standing to receive him by the table between them and the fire, a young lady of not more than seventeen, in a riding-cloak, and still holding her straw travelling-hat by its ribbon in her hand. As his eyes rested on a short, slight, pretty figure, a quantity of golden hair, a pair of blue eyes that met his own with an inquiring look, and a forehead with a singular capacity (remembering how young and smooth it was), of lifting and knitting itself into an expression that was not quite one of perplexity, or wonder, or alarm, or merely of a bright fixed attention, though it included all the four expressions—as his eyes rested on these things, a sudden vivid likeness passed before him, of a child whom he had held in his arms on the passage across that very Channel, one cold time, when the hail drifted heavily and the sea ran high. The likeness passed away, like a breath along the surface of the gaunt pier-glass behind her, on the frame of which, a hospital procession of negro cupids, several headless and all cripples, were offering black baskets of Dead Sea fruit to black divinities of the feminine gender—and he made his formal bow to Miss Manette.

'Pray take a seat, sir.' In a very clear and pleasant young voice; a little foreign in its accent, but a very little indeed.

'I kiss your hand, miss,' said Mr. Lorry, with the manners of an earlier date, as he made his formal bow again, and took his seat.

'I received a letter from the Bank, sir, yesterday, informing me that some intelligence—or discovery—'

'The word is not material, miss; either word will do.'

'—respecting the small property of my poor father, whom I never saw—so long dead—'

Mr. Lorry moved in his chair, and cast a troubled look towards the hospital procession of negro cupids. As if *they* had any help for anybody in their absurd baskets!

'—rendered it necessary that I should go to Paris, there to communicate with a gentleman of the Bank, so good as to be dispatched to Paris for the purpose.'

'Myself.'

'As I was prepared to hear, sir.'

She curtseyed to him (young ladies made curtseys in those days), with a pretty desire to convey to him that she felt how much older and wiser he was than she. He made her another bow.

'I replied to the Bank, sir, that as it was considered necessary, by those who know, and who are so kind as to advise me, that I should go to France, and that as I am an orphan and have no friend who could go with me, I should esteem it highly if I might be permitted to place myself, during the journey, under that worthy gentleman's protection. The gentleman had left London, but I think a messenger was sent after him to beg the favour of his waiting for me here.'

'I was happy,' said Mr. Lorry, 'to be entrusted with the charge. I shall be more happy to execute it.'

'Sir, I thank you indeed. I thank you very gratefully. It was told me by the Bank that the gentleman would explain to me the details of the business, and that I must prepare myself to find them of a surprising nature. I have done my best to prepare myself, and I naturally have a strong and eager interest to know what they are.'

'Naturally,' said Mr. Lorry. 'Yes–I—'

After a pause, he added, again settling the crisp flaxen wig at the ears.

'It is very difficult to begin.'

He did not begin, but, in his indecision, met her glance. The young forehead lifted itself into that singular expression–but it was pretty and characteristic, besides being singular–and she raised her hand, as if with an involuntary action she caught at, or stayed some passing shadow.

'Are you quite a stranger to me, sir?'

'Am I not?' Mr. Lorry opened his hands, and extended them outwards with an argumentative smile.

Between the eyebrows and just over the little feminine nose, the line of which was as delicate and fine as it was possible to be, the expression deepened itself as she took her seat thoughtfully in the chair by which she had hitherto remained standing. He watched her as she mused, and the moment she raised her eyes again, went on:

'In your adopted country, I presume, I cannot do better than address you as a young English lady, Miss Manette?'

'If you please, sir.'

'Miss Manette, I am a man of business. I have a business charge to acquit myself of. In your reception of it, don't heed me any more than if I was a speaking machine–truly, I am not much else. I will, with your leave, relate to you, miss, the story of one of our customers.'

'Story!'

He seemed willfully to mistake the word she had repeated, when he added, in a hurry, 'yes, customers; in the banking business we usually call our connection our customers. He was a French gentleman; a scientific gentleman, a man of great acquirements–a Doctor.'

'Not a Beauvais?'

'Why, yes, of Beauvais. Like Monsieur Manette, your father, the gentleman was of Beauvais. Like Monsieur Manette, your father, the gentleman was of repute in Paris. I had the honour of knowing him there. Our relations were business relations, but confidential. I was at that time in our French House, and had been–oh! twenty years.'

'At that time–I may ask, at what time, sir?'

'I speak, miss, of twenty years ago. He married–an English lady–and I was one of the trustees. His affairs, like the affairs of many other French gentlemen and French families, were entirely in Tellson's hands. In a similar way I am, or I have been, trustee of one kind or other for scores of our customers. These are mere business relations, miss; there is no friendship in them, no particular interest, nothing like sentiment. I have passed from one to another, in the course of my business life, just as I pass from one of our customers to another in the course of my business day; in short, I have no feelings; I am a mere machine. To go on—'

'But this is my father's story, sir; and I begin to think'–the curiously roughened forehead was very intent upon him–'that when I was left an orphan through my mother's surviving my father only two years, it was you who brought me to England. I am almost sure it was you.'

Mr. Lorry took the hesitating little hand that confidingly advanced to take his, and he put it with some ceremony to his lips. He then conducted the young lady straightway to her chair again, and, holding the chair-back with his left hand, and using his right by turns to rub his chin, pull his wig at the ears, or point what he said, stood looking down into her face while she sat looking up into his.

'Miss Manette, it *was* I. And you will see how truly I spoke of myself just now, in saying I had no feelings, and that all relations I hold with my fellow-creatures are mere business relations, when you reflect that I have never seen you since. No; you have been the ward of Tellson's House since, and I have been busy with the other business of Tellson's House since. Feelings! I have no time for them, no chance of them. I pass my whole life, miss, in turning an immense pecuniary Mangle.'

After this odd description of his daily routine of employment, Mr. Lorry flattened his flaxen wig upon his head with both hands (which was most unnecessary, for nothing could be flatter than its shining surface was before), and resumed his former attitude.

'So far, miss (as you have remarked), this is the story of your regretted father. Now comes the difference. If your father had not died when he did— Don't be frightened! How you start!'

She did, indeed, start. And she caught his wrist with both her hands.

'Pray,' said Mr. Lorry, in a shooting tone, bringing his left hand from the back of the chair to lay it on the supplicatory fingers that clasped him in so violent a tremble: 'pray control your agitation–a matter of business. As I was saying—'

Her look so discomposed him that he stopped, wandered, and began anew:

'As I was saying, if Monsieur Manette had not died; if he had suddenly and silently disappeared; if he had been spirited away; if it had not been difficult to guess to what dreadful place, though no art could trace him; if he had an enemy in some compatriot who could exercise a privilege that I in my own time have known the boldest people afraid to speak of in a whisper, across the water there; for instance, the privilege of filling up blank forms for the consignment of any one to the oblivion of a prison for any length of time; if his wife had implored the king, the queen the court, the clergy, for any tidings of him, and all quite in vain;–then the history of your father would have been the history of this unfortunate gentleman, the Doctor of Beauvais.'

'I entreat you to tell me more, sir.'

'I will, I am going to. You can bear it?'

'I can bear anything but the uncertainty you leave me in at this moment.'

'You speak collectedly, and you–*are* collected. That's good!' (Though his manner was less satisfied than his words.) 'A matter of business. Regard it as a matter of wife, though a lady of great courage and spirit, had suffered so intensely from this cause before her little child was born—'

'The little child was a daughter, sir.'

'A daughter. A–a–matter of business–don't be distressed. Miss, if the poor lady had suffered so intensely before her little child was born, that she came to the determination of sparing the poor child the inheritance of any part of the agony she had known the pains of, by rearing her in the belief that her father was dead—No, don't kneel! In Heaven's name why should you kneel to me!'

'For the truth. O dear, good, compassionate sir, for the truth!'

'A–a matter of business. You confuse me, and how can I transact business if I am confused? Let us be clear-headed. If you could kindly mention now, for instance, what nine times ninepence are, or how many shillings in twenty guineas, it would be so encouraging. I should be so much more at my ease about your state of mind.'

Without directly answering to this appeal, she sat so still when he had very gently raised her, and the hands that had not ceased to clasp his wrists were so much more steady than they had been, that she communicated some reassurance to Mr. Jarvis Lorry.

'That's right, that's right. Courage! Business! You have business before you, useful business. Miss Manette, your mother took this course with you. And when she died–I believe broken-hearted–having never slackened her unveiling search for your father, she left you, at two years old, to grow to be blooming, beautiful, and happy, without the dark cloud upon you of living in uncertainty whether your father soon wore his heart out in prison, or wasted there through many lingering years.'

As he said the words he looked down, with an admiring pity, on the flowing golden hair; as if he pictured to himself that it might have been already tinged with grey.

'You know that your parents had no great possession, and that what they had was secured to your mother and to you. There has been no new discovery, of money, or of any other property; but—'

He felt his wrist held closer, and he stopped. The expression in the forehead, which had so particularly attracted his notice, and which was now immovable, had deepened into one of pain and horror.

'But he has been–been found. He is alive. Greatly changed, it is too probable; almost a wreck, it is possible; though we will hope the best. Still, alive. Your father has been taken to the house of an old servant in Paris, and we are going there: I, to identify him if I can: you, to restore him to life, love, duty, rest, comfort.'

A shiver ran through her frame, and from it through his. She said, in a low, distinct, awe-stricken voice, as if she were saying it in a dream.

'I am going to see his Ghost! It will be his Ghost–not him!'

Mr. Lorry quietly chafed the hands that held his arm. 'There, there, there! See now, see now! The best and the worst are known to you, now.

You are well on your way to the poor wronged gentleman, and, with a fair sea voyage, and a fair land journey, you will soon be at his dear side.'

She repeated in the same tone, sunk to a whisper, 'I have been free, I have been happy, yet his Ghost has never haunted me!'

'Only one thing more,' said Mr. Lorry, laying stress upon it as a wholesome means of enforcing her attention: 'he has been found under another name; his own, long forgotten or long concealed. It would be worse than useless now to inquire which; worse than useless to seek to know whether he has been for years overlooked, or always designedly held prisoner. It would be worse than useless now to make any inquiries because it would be dangerous. Better not to mention the subject, anywhere or in any way, and to remove him–for a while at all events–out of France. Even I, safe as an Englishman, and even Tellson's, important as they are to French credit, avoid all naming of the matter. I carry about me, not a scrap of writing openly referring to it. This is a secret service altogether. My credentials, entries, and memoranda, are all comprehended in the one line, "Recalled to Life"; which may mean anything. But what is the matter! She doesn't notice a word! Miss Manette!'

Perfectly still and silent, and not even fallen back in her chair, she sat under his hand, utterly insensible; with her eyes open and fixed upon him, and with that last expression looking as if it were carved or branded into her forehead. So close was her hold upon his arm, that he feared to detach himself lest he should hurt her; therefore he called out loudly for assistance without moving.

A wild-looking woman, whom even in his agitation, Mr. Lorry observed to be all of red colour, and to have red hair, and to be dressed in some extraordinary tight-fitting fashion, and to have on her head a most wonderful bonnet like a Grenadier wooden measure, and good measure, too, or a great Stilton cheese, came running into the room in advance of the inn servants, and soon settled the question of his detachment from the poor young lady, by laying a brawny hand upon his chest, and sending him flying back against the nearest wall.

('I really think this must be a man!' was Mr. Lorry's breathless reflection, simultaneously with his coming against the wall.)

'Why, look at you all!' bawled this figure, addressing the inn servants. 'Why don't you go and fetch things, instead of standing there staring at me? I am not so much to look at, am I? Why don't you go and fetch things? I'll let you know, if you don't bring smelling-salts, cold water, and vinegar, quick, I will.'

There was an immediate dispersal for these restoratives, and she softly laid the patient on a sofa, and a tended her with great skill and gentleness: calling her 'My precious!' and 'My bird! and spreading her golden hair aside over her shoulders with great pride and care.

'And you in brown!' she said, indignantly turning to Mr. Lorry; 'couldn't you tell her what you had to tell her, without frightening her to death? Look at her, with her pale face and her cold hands. Do you call *that* being a Banker?'

Mr. Lorry was so exceedingly disconcerted by a question so hard to answer, that he could only look on, at a distance, with much feebler sympathy and humility, while the strong woman, having banished the inn servants under the mysterious penalty of 'letting them know' something not mentioned if they stayed there, staring, recovered her charge by a regular series of gradations, and coaxed her to lay her drooping head upon her shoulder.

'I hope she will do well now,' said Mr. Lorry.

'No thanks to you in brown, if she does. My darling pretty!'

'I hope,' said Mr. Lorry, after another pause of feeble sympathy and humility, 'that you accompany Miss Manette to France?'

'A likely thing, too!' replied the strong woman. 'If it was ever intended that I should go across salt water, do you suppose Providence would have cast my lot in an island?'

This being another question hard to answer, Mr. Jarvis Lorry withdrew to consider it.

CHAPTER V

THE WINE SHOP

A LARGE cask of wine had been dropped and broken, in the street. The accident had happened in getting it out of a cart; the cask had tumbled out with a run, the hoops had burst, and it lay on the stones just outside the door of the wine shop, shattered like a walnut-shell.

All the people within reach had suspended their business, or their idleness, to run to the spot and drink the wine. The rough, irregular stones of the street, pointing every way and designed, one might have thought, expressly to lame all living creatures that approached them, had dammed it into little pools; these were surrounded, each by its own jostling group or crowd, according to its size. Some men kneeled down, made scoops of their two hands joined, and sipped, or tried to help women, who bent over their shoulders, to sip, before the wine had all run out between their fingers. Others, men and women, dipped in the puddles with little mugs of mutilated earthenware, or even with handkerchiefs from women's heads, which were squeezed dry into infants' mouths; others made small mud embankments, to stem the wine as it ran; others, directed by lookers-on put up at high windows, darted here and there, to cut off little streams of wine that started away in new directions; others devoted themselves to the sodden and lee-dyed pieces of the cask, licking, and even champing the moister wine-rotted fragments with eager relish. There was no drainage to carry off the wine, and not only did it all get taken up, but so much mud got taken up along with it that there might have been a scavenger in the street, if anybody acquainted with it could have believed in such a miraculous presence.

A shrill sound of laughter and of amused voices—voices of men, women, and children—resounded in the street while this wine game lasted. There was little roughness in the sport, and much playfulness. There was a special companionship in it, an observable inclination on the part of every one to join some other one, which led, especially among the luckier or lighter-hearted, to frolicsome embraces, drinking of healths, shaking of hands, and even joining of hands and dancing, a dozen together. When the wine was gone, and the places where it had been most abundant were raked into a gridiron-pattern by fingers, these demonstrations ceased, as suddenly as they had broken out. The man who had left his saw sticking in the fire-wood he was cutting, set it in motion again; the woman who had left on a door-step the little pot of hot ashes, at which she had been trying to soften the pain in her own starved fingers and toes, or in those of her child, returned to it; men with bare arms, matted locks, and cadaverous faces, who had emerged into the winter light from cellers, moved away, to descend again; and a gloom gathered on the scene that appeared more natural to it than sunshine.

The wine was red wine, and had stained the ground of the narrow street in the suburb of Saint Antoine, in Paris, where it was spilled. It had stained many hands, too, and many faces, and many naked feet, and many wooden shoes. The hands of the man who sawed the wood, left red marks on the billets; and the forehead of the woman who nursed her baby, was stained with the stain of the old rag she wound about her head again. Those who had been greedy with the staves of the cask, had acquired a tigerish smear about the mouth; and one tall joker so besmirched, his head more out of a long squalid bag of a night-cap than in it, scrawled upon the wall with his finger dipped in muddy wine-less—BLOOD.

The time was to come, when that wine too would be spilled on the street stones, and when the stain of it would be red upon many there.

And now that the cloud settled on Saint Antoine, which a momentary gleam had driven from his sacred countenance, the darkness of it was heavy—cold, dirt, sickness, ignorance, and want, were the lords in waiting on the saintly presence—nobles of great power all of them; but, most especially the last. Samples of a people that had undergone a terrible grinding and regrinding in the mill, and certainly not in the fabulous mill which ground old people young, shivered at every corner, passed in and out at every doorway, looked from every window, fluttered in every vestige of a garment that the wind shook. The mill which had worked them down, was the mill that grinds young people old; the children had ancient faces and grave voices; and upon them, and upon the grown faces, and ploughed into every furrow of age and coming up afresh, was the sign, Hunger. It was prevalent everywhere. Hunger was pushed out of the tall houses, in the wretched clothing that hung upon poles and lines; Hunger was patched into them with straw and rag and wood and paper; Hunger was repeated in every fragment of the small modicum of firewood that the man sawed off; Hunger stared down from the smokeless chimneys, and started up from the filthy street that had no offal, among its refuse, of anything to eat. Hunger was the inscription on the baker's shelves, written in every small loaf of his scanty stock of bad bread; at the sausage shop, in every dead-dog preparation that was offered for sale. Hunger rattled its dry bones among the roasting chestnuts in the turned cylinder; Hunger was shred into atomies in every farthing porringer of husky chips of potato, fried with some reluctant drops of oil.

Its abiding place was in all things fitted to it. A narrow winding street, full of offence and stench, with other narrow winding streets diverging, all peopled by rags and night-caps, and all smelling of rags and night-caps, and all visible things with a brooding look upon them that looked ill. In the hunted air of the people there was yet some wild-beast thought of the possibility of turning at bay. Depressed and slinking though they were, eyes of fire were not wanting among them; nor compressed lips, white with what they suppressed; nor foreheads knitted into the likeness of the gallows rope they mused about enduring, or inflicting. The trade signs (and they were almost as many as the shops) were, all, grim illustrations of Want. The butcher and the porkman painted up, only the leanest scrags of meat; the baker, the coarsest of meagre loaves. The people rudely pictured as drinking in the wine shops, croaked over their scanty measures of thin wine and beer, and were gloweringly confidential together. Nothing was represented in a flourishing condition, save tools and weapons; but, the cutler's knives and axes were sharp and bright, the smith's hammers were heavy, and the gunmaker's stock was murderous. The crippling stones of the pavement, with their many little reservoirs of mud and water, had no footways, but broke off abruptly at the doors. The kennel, to make amends, ran down the middle of the street–when it ran at all: which was only after heavy rains, and then it ran, by many eccentric fits, into the houses. Across the streets, at wide intervals, one clumsy lamp was slung by a rope and pulley; at night, when the lamplighter had let these down, and lighted, and hoisted them again, a feeble grove of dim wicks swung in a sickly manner overhead, as if they were at sea. Indeed they were at sea, and the ship and crew were in peril of tempest.

For, the time was to come, when the gaunt scarecrows of that region should have watched the lamplighter, in their idleness and hunger, so long, as to conceive the idea of improving on his method, and hauling up men by those ropes and pulleys, to flare upon the darkness of their condition. But, the time was not come yet; and every wind that blew over France shook the rags of the scarecrows in vain, for the birds, fine of song and feather, took no warning.

The wine shop was a corner shop, better than most others in its appearance and degree, and the master of the wine shop had stood outside it, in a yellow waistcoats and green breeches, looking on at the struggle for the lost wine. 'It's not my affair,' said he, with a final shrug of the shoulders. 'The people from the market did it. Let them bring another.'

There, his eyes happening to catch the tall joker writing up his joke, he called to him across the way:

'Say, them, my Gaspard, what do you do there?'

The fellow pointed to his joke with immense significance, as is often the way with his tribe. It missed its mark, and completely failed, as is often the way with his tribe too.

'What now? Are you a subject for the mad hospital?' said the wine-shop keeper, crossing the road, and obliterating the jest with a handful of mud, picked up for the purpose, and smeared over it. 'Why do you write in the public streets? Is there—tell me thou—is there no other place to write such words in?'

In his expostulation he dropped his cleaner hand (perhaps accidentally, perhaps not) upon the joker's heart. The joker rapped it with his own, took a nimble spring upward, and came down in a fantastic dancing attitude, with one of his stained shoes jerked off his foot into his hand, and held out. A joker of an extremely, not to say wolfishly practical character, he looked, under those circumstances.

'Put it on, put it on,' said the other. 'Call wine, wine; and finish there.' With that advice, he wiped his soiled hand upon the joker's dress, such as it was—quite deliberately, as having dirtied his hand on his account; and then re-crossed the road and entered the wine shop.

This wine-shop keeper was a bull-necked, martial-looking man of thirty, and he should have been of a hot temperament, for, although it was a bitter day, he wore no coat, but carried one slung over his shoulder. His shirt-sleeves were rolled up, too, and his brown arms were bare to the elbows. Neither did he wear anything more on his head than his own crisply curling short dark hair. He was a dark man altogether, with good eyes and good bold breadth between them. Good-humoured looking on the whole, but implacable-looking, too; evidently a man of a strong resolution and a set purpose; a man not desirable to be met, rushing down a narrow pass with a gulf on either side, for nothing would turn the man.

Madame Defarge, his wife, sat in the shop behind the counter as he came in. Madame Defarge was a stout woman of about his own age, with a watchful eye that seldom seemed to look at anything, a large hand heavily ringed, a steady face, strong features, and great composure of manner. There was a character about Madame Defarge from which one might have predicted that she did not often make mistakes against herself in any of the reckonings over which she presided. Madame Defarge being sensitive to cold, was wrapped in fur, and had a quantity of bright shawl twined about her head, though not to the concealment of her large earrings. Her knitting was before her, but she had laid it down to pick her teeth with a toothpick. Thus engaged, with her right elbow supported by her left hand, Madame Defarge said nothing when her lord came in, but coughed just one grain of cough. This, in combination with the lifting of her darkly defined eyebrows over her toothpick by the breadth of a line, suggested to her husband that he would do well to look round the shop among the customers, for any new customer who had dropped in while he stepped over the way.

The wine-shop keeper accordingly rolled his eyed about, until they rested upon an elderly gentleman and a young lady, who were seated in a corner. Other company were there; two playing cards, two playing dominoes, three standing by the counter lengthening out a short supply of wine. As he passed behind the counter, he took notice that the elderly gentleman said in a look to the young lady, 'This is our man.'

'What the devil do *you* do in that gallery there?' said Monsieur Defarge to himself; 'I don't know you.'

But, he feigned not to notice the two strangers, and fell into discourse with the triumvirate of customers who were drinking at the counter.

'How goes it, Jacques?' said one of these three to Monsieur Defarge. 'Is all the spilt wine swallowed?'

'Every drop, Jacques,' answered Monsieur Defarge.

When this interchange of christian name was effected, Madame Defarge, picking her teeth with her toothpick, coughed another grain of cough, and raised her eyebrows by the breadth of another line.

'It is not often,' said the second of the three, addressing Monsieur Defarge, 'that many of these miserable beasts know the taste of wine, or of anything but black bread and death. Is it not so, Jacques?'

'It is so, Jacques,' Monsieur Defarge returned.

At this second interchange of the christian name, Madame Defarge, still using her toothpick with profound composure, coughed another grain of cough, and raised her eyebrows by the breadth of another line.

The last of the three now said his say, as he put down his empty drinking vessel and smacked his lips.

'Ah! So much the worse! A bitter taste it is that such poor cattle always have in their mouths, and hard lives they live, Jacques. Am I right, Jacques?'

'You are right, Jacques,' was the response of Monsieur Defarge.

This third interchange of the christian name was completed at the moment when Madame Defarge put her tooth-pick by, kept her eyebrows up, and slightly rustled in her seat.

'Hold then! True!' muttered her husband. 'Gentlemen—my wife!'

The three customers pulled off their hats to Madam Defarge, with three flourishes. She acknowledged their homage by bending her head, and giving them a quick look. Then she glanced in a casual manner round the wine shop, took up her knitting with great apparent calmness and repose of spirit, and became absorbed in it.

'Gentlemen,' said her husband, who had kept his bright eye observantly upon her, 'good day. The chamber, furnished bachelor fashion, that you wished to seem and were inquiring for when I stepped out, is on the fifth floor. The doorway of the staircase gives on the little courtyard close to the left here,' pointing with his hand, 'near to the window of my establishment. But, now that I remember one of you has already been there, and can show the way. Gentlemen, adieu!'

They paid for their wine, and left the place. The eyes of Monsieur Defarge were studying his wife at her knitting when the elderly gentleman advanced from his corner, and begged the favour of a word.

'Willingly, sir,' said Monsieur Defarge, and quietly stepped with him to the door.

Their conference was very short, but very decided. Almost at the first word, Monsieur Defarge started and became deeply attentive. It had not lasted a minute, when he nodded and went out. The gentleman then beckoned to the young lady, and they, too, went out. Madame Defarge knitted with nimble fingers and steady eyebrows, and saw nothing.

Mr. Jarvis Lorry and Miss Manette, emerging from the wine shop thus, joined Monsieur Defarge in the doorway to which he had directed his other company just before. It opened from a stinking little black courtyard, and was the general public entrance to a great pile of houses, inhabited by a great number of people. In the gloomy tile-paved entry to the gloomy tile-paved staircase, Monsieur Defarge bent down on one knee to the child of his old master, and put her hand to his lips. It was a gentle action, but not at all gently done; a very remarkable transformation had come over him in a few seconds. He had no good-humour in his face, nor any openness of aspect left, but had become a secret, angry, dangerous man.

'It is very high; it is a little difficult. Better to begin slowly.' Thus, Monsieur Defarge, in a stern voice, to Mr. Lorry, as they began ascending the stairs.

'Is he alone?' the latter whispered.

'Alone! God help him, who should be with him!' said the other, in the same low voice.

'Is he always alone, then?'

'Yes.'

'Of his own desire?'

'Of his own necessity. As he was, when I first saw him after they found me and demanded to know if I would take him, and, at my peril be discreet—as he was then, so he is now.'

'He is greatly changed?'

'Changed!'

The keeper of the wine shop stopped to strike the wall with his hand, and mutter a tremendous curse. No direct answer could have been half so forcible. Mr. Lorry's spirits grew heavier and heavier, as he and his two companions ascended higher and higher.

Such a staircase, with its accessories, in the older and more crowded parts of Paris, would be bad enough now; but, at that time, it was vile indeed to unaccustomed and unhardened senses. Every little habitation within the great foul nest of one high building—that is to say, the room or rooms within every door that opened on the general staircase—left its own heap of refuse on its own landing, besides flinging other refuse from its own windows. The uncontrollable have polluted the air, even if poverty and deprivation had not loaded it with their intangible impurities; the two bad sources combined made it almost insupportable. Through such an atmosphere, by a steep dark shaft of dirt and poison, the way lay. Yielding to his own disturbance of mind, and to his young companion's agitation, which became greater every instant, Mr. Jarvis Lorry twice stopped to rest. Each of these stoppages was made at a doleful grating, by which any languishing good airs that were left uncorrupted seemed to escape, and all spoilt and sickly vapours seemed to crawl in. Through the rusted bars, tastes, rather than glimpses, were caught of the jumbled neighbourhood; and nothing within range, nearer or lower

than the summits of the two great towers of Notre-Dame, had any promise
on it of healthy life or wholesome aspirations.

At last, the top of the staircase was gained, and they stopped for the
third time. There was yet an upper staircase, of a steeper inclination and of
contracted dimensions, to be ascended, before the garret storey was reached.
The keeper of the wine shop, always going a little in advance, and always going on the side which Mr. Lorry took, as though he dreaded to be asked any
question by the young lady, turned himself about here, and, carefully feeling
in the pockets of the coat he carried over his shoulder, took out a key.

'The door is locked then, my friend?' said Mr. Lorry, surprised.

'Ay. Yes,' was the grim reply of Monsieur Defarge.

'You think it necessary to keep the unfortunate gentleman so retired?'

'I think it necessary to turn the key.' Monsieur Defarge whispered it
closer in his ear, and frowned heavily.

'Why?'

'Why! Because he has lived so long, locked up, that he would be frightened–rave, tear himself to pieces–die–come to I know not what harm–if his
door was left open.'

'Is it possible?' exclaimed Mr. Lorry.

'Is it possible!' repeated Defarge, bitterly. 'Yes. And a beautiful world
we live in, when it *is* possible, and when many other such things are possible,
and not only possible but done–done, see you!–under that sky there, every
day. Long live the Devil. Let us go on.'

This dialogue had been held in so very low a whisper, that not a word of
it had reached the young lady's ears. But, by this time she trembled under
such strong emotion, her face expressed such deep anxiety, and, above all,
such dread and terror, that Mr. Lorry felt it incumbent on him to speak a
word or two of reassurance.

'Courage, dear miss! Courage! Business! The worst will be over in a
moment; it is but passing the room door, and the worst is over. Then, all the
good you bring to him, all the relief, all the happiness you bring to him, begin. Let our good friend here, assist you on that side. That's well, friend
Defarge. Come, now. Business, business!'

They went up slowly and softly. The staircase was short, and they were
soon at the top. There, as it had an abrupt turn in it, they came all at once in
sight of three men, whose heads were bent down close together at the side of
a door, and who were intently looking into the room to which the door belonged, through some clinks or holes in the wall. On hearing footsteps close
at hand, these three turned, and rose, and showed themselves to be the three
of one name who had been drinking in the wine shop.

'I forgot them in the surprise of your visit,' explained Monsieur
Defarge. 'Leave us, good boys; we have business here.'

The three glided by, and went silently down.

There appearing to be no other door on that floor, and the keeper of the
wine shop going straight to this one when they were left alone, Mr. Lorry
asked him in a whisper, with a little anger:

'Do you make a show of Monsieur Manette?'

'I show him, in the way you have seen, to a chosen few.'

'Is that well?'

'*I* think it is well.'

'Who are the few? How do you choose them?'

'I choose them as real men, of my name–Jacques is my name–to whom the sight is likely to do good. Enough; you are English; that is another thing. Stay there, if you please, a little moment.'

With an admonitory gesture to keep them back, he stooped, and looked in through the crevice in the wall. Soon raising his head again, he struck twice or thrice upon the door–evidently with no other object than to make a noise there. With the same intention, he drew the key across it, three or four times, before he put it clumsily into the lock, and turned if as heavily as he could.

The door slowly opened inward under his hand, and he looked into the room and said something. A faint voice answered something. Little more than a single syllable could have been spoken on either side.

He looked back over his shoulder, and beckoned them to enter. Mr. Lorry got his arm securely round the daughter's waist, and held her; for he felt that she was sinking.

'A–a–a–a–business, business!' he urged with a moisture that was not of business shining on his cheek. 'Come in, come in!'

'I am afraid of it,' she answered, shuddering.

'Of it? What?'

'I mean of him. Of my father.'

Rendered in a manner desperate, by her state and by the beckoning of their conductor, he drew over his neck the arm that shook upon his shoulder, lifted her a little, and hurried her into the room. He set her down just within the door, and held her, clinging to him.

Defarge drew out the key, closed the door, locked it on the inside, took out the key again, and held it in his hand. All this he did, methodically, and with as loud and harsh an accompaniment of noise as he could make. Finally, he walked across the room with a measured tread to where the window was. He stopped there and faced round.

The garret, built to be a depository for firewood and the like, was dim and dark: for, the window of dormer shape, was in truth a door in the roof, with a little crane over it for the hoisting up of stores from the street: unglazed, and closing up the middle in two pieces, like any other door of French construction. To exclude the cold, one half of this door was fast closed, and the other was opened but a very little way. Such a scanty portion of light was admitted through these means, that it was difficult, on first coming in, to see anything, and long habit alone could have slowly formed in any one, the ability to do any work requiring nicety in such obscurity. Yet, work if that kind was being done in the garret; for, with his back towards the door, and his face towards the window where the keeper of the wine shop stood looking at him, a white-haired man sat on a low bench, stooping forward and very busy, making shoes.

CHAPTER VI

THE SHOEMAKER

'GOOD day!' said Monsieur Defarge, looking down at the white head that bent low over the shoemaking.

It was raised for a moment, and a very faint voice responded to the salutation, as if it were at a distance:

'Good day!'

'You are still hard at work, I see?'

After a long silence, the head was lifted for another moment, and the voice replied, 'Yes–I am working.' This time, a pair of haggard eyes had looked at the questioner, before the face had dropped again.

The faintness of the voice was pitiable and dreadful. It was not the faintness of physical weakness, though confinement and hard fare no doubt had their part in it. Its deplorable peculiarity was, that it was the faintness of solitude and disuse. It was like the last feeble echo of a sound made long and long ago. So entirely had it lost the life and resonance of the human voice, that it affected the senses like a once beautiful colour faded away into a poor weak stain. So sunken and suppressed it was, that it was like a voice underground. So expressive it was, of a hopeless and lost creature, that a famished traveller, wearied out by lonely wandering in a wilderness, would have remembered home and friends in such a tone before lying down to die.

Some minutes of silent had passed: and the haggard eyes had looked up again: not with any interest or curiosity, but with a dull mechanical perception, beforehand, that the spot where the only visitor they were aware of had stood, was not yet empty.

'I want,' said Defarge, who had not removed his gaze from the shoemaker, 'to let in a little more light here. You can bear a little more?'

The shoemaker stopped his work; looked with a vacant air of listening, at the floor on one side of him; then similarly, at the floor on the other side of him; then, upward at the speaker.

'What did you say?'

'You can bear a little more light?'

'I must bear it, if you let it in.' (Laying the palest shadow of a stress upon the second word.)

The opened half-door was opened a little further, and secured at that angle for the time. A broad ray of light fell into the garret, and showed the workman with an unfinished shoe upon his lap, pausing in his labour. His few common tools and various scraps of leather were at his feet and on his bench. He had a white beard, raggedly cut, but not very long, a hollow face, and exceedingly bright eyes. The hollowness and thinness of his face would have caused them to look large, under his yet dark eyebrows and his confused white hair, though they had been really otherwise; but, they were naturally large, and looked unnaturally so. His yellow rags of shirt lay open at the throat, and showed his body to be withered and worn. He, and his old canvas frock, and his loose stockings, and all his poor tatters of clothes, had, in a long seclusion from direct light and air, faded down to such a dull uniformity of parchment yellow, that it would have been hard to say which was which.

He had put up a hand between his eyes and the light, and the very bones of it seemed transparent. So he sat, with a steadfastly vacant gaze, pausing in his work. He never looked at the figure before him, without first looking down on this side of himself, then on that, as if he had lost the habit of associating place with sound, he never spoke, without first wandering in this manner, and forgetting to speak.

'Are you going to finish that pair of shoes to-day?' asked Defarge, motioning to Mr. Lorry to come forward.

'What did you say?'

'Do you mean to finish that pair of shoes to-day?'

'I can't say that I mean to. I suppose so. I don't know.'

But the question reminded him of his work, and he bent over it again.

Mr. Lorry same silently forward, leaving the daughter by the door. When he had stood, for a minute or two, by the side of Defarge, the shoemaker looked up. He showed no surprise at seeing another figure, but the unsteady fingers of one of his hands strayed to his lips as he looked at it (his lips and his nails were of the same pale lead-colour), and then the hand dropped to his work, and he once more bent over the shoe. The look and the action had occupied but an instant.

'You have a visitor, you see,' said Monsieur Defarge.

'What did you say?'

'Here is a visitor.'

The shoemaker looked up as before, but without removing a hand from his work.

'Come!' said Defarge. 'Here is monsieur, who knows a well-made shoe when he sees one. Show him that shoe you are working at. Take it, monsieur.'

Mr. Lorry took it in his hand.

'Tell monsieur what kind of shoe it is, and the maker's name.'

There was a longer pause than usual, before the shoemaker replied:

'I forget what it was you asked me. What did you say?'

'I said, couldn't you describe the kind of shoe, for monsieur's information?'

'It is a lady's shoe. It is a young lady's walking-shoe. It is in the present mode. I never saw the mode. I have had a pattern in my hand.' He glanced at the shoe with some little passing touch of pride.

'And the maker's name,' said Defarge.

Now that he had no work to hold, he laid the knuckles of his right hand in the hollow of the left, and then the knuckles of his left hand in the hollow of his right, and then passed a hand across his bearded chin, and so on in regular changes, without a moment's intermission. The task of recalling him from the vacancy into which he always sank when he had spoken, was like recalling some very weak person from a swoon, or endeavouring, in the hope of some disclosure, to stay the spirit of a fast-dying man.

'Did you ask me for my name?'

'Assuredly I did.'

'One Hundred and Five, North Tower.'

'Is that all?'

'One Hundred and Five, North Tower.'

With a weary sound that was not a sigh, nor a groan, he bent to work again, until the silence was again broken.

'You are not a shoemaker by trade' said Mr. Lorry, looking steadfastly at him.

His haggard eyes turned to Defarge as if he would have transferred the question to him: but as no help came from that quarter, they turned back on the questioner when they had sought the ground.

'I am not a shoemaker by trade? No, I was not a shoemaker by trade. I–I learnt it here. I taught myself. I asked to leave to—'

He lapsed away, even for minutes, ringing those measured changes on his hands the whole time. His eyes came slowly back, at last, to the face from which they had wandered; when they rested on it, he started, and resumed, in the manner of a sleeper that moment awake, reverting to a subject of last night.

'I asked leave to teach myself, and I got it with much difficulty after a long while, and I have made shoes ever since.'

As he held out his hand for the shoe that had been taken from him, Mr. Lorry said, still looking steadfastly in his face:

'Monsieur Manette, do you remember nothing of me?'

The shoe dropped to the ground, and he sat looking fixedly at the questioner.

'Monsieur Manette'–Mr. Lorry laid his hand upon Defarge's arm–'do you remember nothing of this man? Look at him. Look at me. Is there no old banker, no old business, no old servant, no old time, rising in your mind, Monsieur Manette?'

As the captive of many years sat looking fixedly, by turns, at Mr. Lorry and at Defarge, some long obliterated marks of an actively intent intelligence in the middle of the forehead, gradually forced themselves through the black mist that had fallen on him. They were overclouded again, they were fainter, they were gone; but they had been there. And so exactly was the expression repeated on the fair young face of her who had crept along the wall to a point where she could see him, and where she now stood looking at him, with hands which at first had been only raised in frightened compassion, if not even to keep him off and shut out the sight of him, but which were now extending towards him trembling with eagerness to lay the spectral face upon her warm young breast, and love it back to life and hope–so exactly was the expression repeated (though in stronger characters) on her fair young face, that it looked as though it had passed like a moving light, from him to her.

Darkness had fallen on him in its place. He looked at the two, less and less attentively, and his eyes in gloomy abstraction sought the ground and looked about him in the old way. Finally, with a deep long sigh, he took the shoe up, and resumed his work.

'Have you recognised him, monsieur?' asked Defarge in a whisper.

'Yes; for a moment. At first I thought it quite hopeless, but I have unquestionably seen, for a single moment, the face that I once knew so well. Hush! Let us draw further back. Hush!'

She had moved from the wall of the garret, very near to the bench on which he sat. There was something awful in his unconsciousness of the figure that could have put out its hand and touched him as he stooped over his labour.

Not a word was spoken, not a sound was made. She stood, like a spirit, beside him, and he bent over his work.

It happened, at length, that he had occasion to change the instrument in his hand, for his shoemaker's knife. It lay on that side of him which was not the side on which she stood. He had taken it up, and was stooping to work again, when his eyes caught the skirt of her dress. He raised them, and saw her face. The two spectators started forward, but she stayed them with a motion of her hand. She had no fear of his striking at her with the knife, though they had.

He started at her with a fearful look, and after a while his lips began to form some words, though no sound proceeded from them. By degrees, in the pauses of his quick and laboured breathing, he was heard to say:

'What is this?'

With the tears streaming down her face, she put her two hands to her lips, and kissed them to him; then clasped them on her breast, as if she laid his ruined head there.

'You are not the jailer's daughter?'

She sighed 'No.'

'Who are you?'

Not yet trusting the tones of her voice, she sat down on the bench beside him. He recoiled, but she laid her hand upon his arm. A strange thrill struck him when she did so, and visibly passed over his frame; he laid the knife down softly, and he sat staring at her.

Her golden hair, which she wore in long curls, had been hurriedly pushed aside, and fell down over her neck. Advancing his hand by little and little, he took it up and looked at it. In the midst of the action he went astray, and, with another deep sigh, fell to work at his shoemaking.

But not for long. Releasing his arm, she laid her hand upon his shoulder. After looking doubtfully at it, two or three times, as if to be sure that it was really there, he laid down his work, put his hand to his neck, and took off a blackened string with a scrap of folded rag attached to it. He opened this, carefully, on his knee, and it contained a very little quantity of hair: not more than one or two long golden hairs, which he had, in some old day, wound off upon his finger.

He took her hair into his hand again, and looked closely at it. 'It is the same. How can it be! When was it! How was it!'

As the concentrating expression returned to his forehead he seemed to become conscious that it was in hers too. He turned her full to the light, and looked at her.

'She had laid her head upon my shoulder, that night when I was summoned out–she had a fear of my going, though I had none–and when I was brought to the North Tower they found these upon my sleeve. "You will leave me them? They can never help me to escape in the body, though they may in the spirit." Those were the words I said. I remember them very well.'

He formed this speech with his lips many times before he could utter it. But when he did find spoken words for it, they came to him coherently, though slowly.

'How was this?–*Was it you?*'

Once more, the two spectators started, as he turned upon her with a frightful suddenness. But she sat perfectly still in his grasp, and only said, in a low voice, 'I entreat you, good gentlemen, do not come near us, do not speak, do not move!'

'Hark!' he exclaimed. 'Whose voice was that?'

His hands released her as he uttered this cry, and went out to his white hair, which they tore in a frenzy. It died out, as everything but his shoemaking did die out of him, and he refolded his little packet and tried to secure it in his breast; but he still looked at her, and gloomily shook his head.

'No, no, no; you are too young, too blooming. It can't be. See what the prisoner is. These are not the hands she knew, this is not the face she knew, this is not the voice she ever heard. No, no. She was–and He was–before the slow years of the North Tower–ages ago. What is your name, my gentle angel?'

Hailing his softened tone and manner, his daughter fell upon her knees before him, with her appealing hands upon his breast.

'Oh, sir, at another time you shall know my name, and who my mother was, and who my father, and how I never knew their hard, hard history. But I cannot tell you at this time, and I cannot tell you here. All that I may tell you, here and now, is, that I pray to you to touch me and to bless me. Kiss me, kiss me! Oh, my dear, my dear!'

His cold white head mingled with her radiant hair, which warmed and lighted it as thought it were the light of Freedom shining on him.

'If you hear in my voice–I don't know that it is so, but I hope it is–if you hear in my voice any resemblance to a voice that once was sweet music in your ears, weep for it, weep for it! If you touch, in touching my hair, anything that recalls a beloved head that lay on your breast when you were young and free, weep for it, weep for it! If, when I hint to you of a Home that is before us, where I will be true to you with all my duty and with all my faithful service, I bring back the remembrance of a Home long desolate, while your poor heart pined away, weep for it, weep for it!'

She held him closer round the neck, and rocked him on her breast like a child.

'If, when I tell you, dearest dear, that your agony is over, and that I have come here to take you from it, and that we go to England to be at peace and at rest, I cause you to think of yourself life laid waste, and of our native France so wicked to you, weep for it, weep for it! And if, when I shall tell you of my name, and of my father who is living, and of my mother who is dead, you learn that I have to kneel to my honoured father, and implore his pardon for having never for his sake striven all day and lain awake and wept all night, because the love of my poor mother hid his torture from me, weep for it, weep for it! Weep for her, then, and for me! Good gentlemen, thank God! I feel his sacred tears upon my face, and his sobs strike against my heart. Oh, see! Thank God for us, thank God!'

He had sunk in her arms, and his face dropped on her breast: a sight so touching, yet so terrible in the tremendous wrong and suffering which had gone before it, that the two beholders covered their faces.

When the quiet of the garret had been long undisturbed and his heaving breast and shaken form had long yielded to the calm that must follow all storms–emblem to humanity, of the rest and silence into which the storm called Life must hush at last–they came forward to raise the father and daughter from the ground. He had gradually dropped to the floor, and lay there in a lethargy, worn out. She had nestled down with him, that his head might lie upon her arm; and her hair drooping over him curtained him from the light.

'If, without disturbing him,' she said, raising her hand to Mr. Lorry as he stooped over them, after repeated blowings of his nose, 'all could be arranged for our leaving Paris at once, so that, from the very door, he could be taken away—'

'But, consider. Is he fit for the journey?' asked Mr. Lorry.

'More fit for that, I think, than to remain in this city, so dreadful to him.'

'It is true,' said Defarge, who was kneeling to look on and hear. 'More than that; Monsieur Manette is, for all reasons, best out of France. Say, shall I hire a carriage and post-horses?'

'That's business,' said Mr. Lorry, resuming on the shortest notice his methodical manners; 'and if business is to be done, I had better do it.'

'Then be so kind,' urged Miss Manette, 'as to leave us here. You see how composed he has become, and you cannot be afraid to leave him with me now. Why should you be? If you will lock the door to secure us from interruption, I do not doubt that you will find him, when you come back, as quiet as you leave him. In any case, I will take care of him until you return, and then we will remove him straight.'

Both Mr. Lorry and Defarge were rather disinclined to this course, and in favour of one of them remaining. But, as there were not only carriages and horses to be seen to, but travelling papers; and as time passed, for the day was drawing to an end, it came at last to their hastily dividing the business that was necessary to be done, and hurrying away to do it.

Then, as the darkness closed in, the daughter laid her head down on the hard ground close at the father's side, and watched him. The darkness deepened and deepened, and they both lay quiet, until a light gleamed through the chinks in the wall.

Mr. Lorry and Monsieur Defarge had made all ready for the journey, and had brought with them, besides travelling cloaks and wrappers, bread and meat, wine, and hot coffee. Monsieur Defarge put this provender, and the lamp he carried, on the shoemaker's bench (there was nothing else in the garret but a pallet bed), and he and Mr. Lorry roused the captive, and assisted him to his feet.

No human intelligence could have read the mysteries of his mind, in the scared blank wonder of his face. Whether he knew what had happened, whether he recollected what they had said to him, whether he knew that he was free, were questions which no sagacity could have solved. They tried speaking to him; but, he was so confused, and so very slow to answer, that they took fright at his bewilderment, and agreed for the time to tamper with him no more. He had a wild, lost manner of occasionally clasping his head in his hands, that had not been seen in him before; yet, he had some pleasure in the mere sound of his daughter's voice, and invariably turned to it when she spoke.

In the submissive way of one long accustomed to obey under coercion, he ate and drank what they gave him to eat and drink, and put on the cloak and other wrappings, that they gave him to wear. He readily responded to his daughter's drawing her arm through his, and took–and kept–her hand in both his own.

They began to descend; Monsieur Defarge going first with the lamp, Mr. Lorry closing the little procession. They had not traversed many steps of the long main staircase when he stopped, and started at the roof and round at the walls.

'You remember the place, my father? You remember coming up here?'
'What did you say?'

But, before she could repeat the question, he murmured an answer as if she had repeated it.

'Remember? No, I don't remember. It was so very long ago.'

That he had no recollection whatever of his having been brought from his prison to that house, was apparent to them. They heard him mutter, 'One Hundred and Five, North Tower'; and when he looked about him, it evidently was for the strong fortress walls which had long encompassed him. On their reaching the courtyard he instinctively altered his tread, as being in expectation of a drawbridge; and when there was no drawbridge, and he saw the carriage waiting in the open street, he dropped his daughter's hand and clasped his head again.

No crowd was about the door; no people were discernible at any of the many windows; not even a chance passer-by was in the street. An unnatural silence and desertion reigned there. Only one soul was to be seen, and that was Madame Defarge–who leaned against the door post, knitting, and saw nothing.

The prisoner had got into a coach, and his daughter had followed him, when Mr. Lorry's feet were arrested on the step by his asking, miserably, for his shoemaking tools and the unfinished shoes. Madame Defarge immediately called to her husband that she would get them, and went, knitting out of the lamplight, through the courtyard. She quickly brought them down and handed them in;—and immediately afterwards leaned against the door post, knitting, and saw nothing.

Defarge got upon the box, and gave the word 'To the Barrier!' The postilion cracked his whip, and they clattered away under the feeble over-swinging lamps.

Under the over-swinging lamps–swinging ever brighter in the better streets, and ever dimmer in the worse–and by lighted shops, gay crowds, illuminated coffee-houses, and theatre doors, to one of the city gates. Soldiers with lanterns, at the guard-house there. 'Your papers, travellers!' 'See here then, Monsieur the Officer,' said Defarge, getting down, and taking him gravely apart, 'these are the papers of monsieur inside, with the white head. They were consigned to me, with him, at the —' He dropped his voice, there was a flutter among the military lanterns, and one of them being handed into the coach by an arm in uniform, the eyes connected with the arm looked, not an every day or an every night look, at monsieur with the white head. 'It is well. Forward!' from the uniform. 'Adieu!' from Defarge. And so, under a short grove of feebler and feebler over-swinging lamps, out under the great grove of stars.

Beneath that arch of unmoved and eternal lights; some, so remote from this little earth that the learned tell us it is doubtful whether their rays had even yet discovered it, as a point in space where anything is suffered or done: the shadows of the night were broad and black. All through the cold and restless interval, until dawn, they once more whispered in the ears of Mr. Jarvis Lorry–sitting opposite the buried man who had been dug out, and wondering what subtle powers were for ever lost to him, and what were capable of restoration–the old inquiry:

'I hope you care to be recalled to life?'

And the old answer:

'I can't say.'

THE END OF THE FIRST BOOK

BOOK THE SECOND. THE GOLDEN THREAD

CHAPTER I

FIVE YEARS LATER

TELLSON'S Bank by Temple Bar was an old-fashioned place, even in the year one thousand seven hundred and eighty. It was very small, very dark, very ugly, very incommodious. It was an old-fashioned place, moreover, in the moral attribute that the partners in the House were proud of its smallness, proud of its darkness, proud of its ugliness, proud of its incommodiousness. They were even boastful of its eminence in those particulars, and were fired by an express conviction that, if it were less objectionable, it would be less respectable. This was no passive belief, but an active weapon which they flashed at more convenient places of business. Tellson's (they said) wanted no elbow room, Tellson's wanted no light, Tellson's wanted no embellishment. Noakes and Co.'s might, or Snooks Brothers' might; but Tellson's, thank Heaven!—

Any one of these partners would have disinherited his son on the question of rebuilding Tellson's. In this respect the House was much on a par with the Country; which did very often disinherit its sons for suggesting improvements in laws and customs that had long been highly objectionable, but were only the more respectable.

Thus it had come to pass, that Tellson's was the triumphant perfection of inconvenience. After bursting open a door of idiotic obstinacy with a weak rattle in its throat you fell into Tellson's down two steps, and came to your senses in a miserable little shop, with two little counters, where the oldest of men made your cheque shake as if the wind rustled it, while they examined the signature by the dingiest of windows, which were always under a shower-bath of mud from Fleet Street, and which were made the dingier by their own iron bars proper, and the heavy shadow of Temple Bar. If your business necessitated your seeing 'the House,' you were put into a species of Condemned Hold at the back, where you meditated on a misspent life, until the House came with its hands in its pockets, and you could hardly blink at it in the dismal twilight. Your money came out of, or went into, wormy old wooden drawers, particles of which flew up your nose and down your throat when they were opened and shut. Your banknotes had a musty odour, as if they were fast decomposing into rags again. Your plate was stowed away among the neighbouring cesspools, and evil communications corrupted its good polish in a day or two. Your deeds got into extemporised strong-rooms made of kitchens and sculleries, and fretted all the fat out of their parchments into the banking-house air. Your lighter boxes of family papers went upstairs into a Barmecide room, that always had a great dining-table in it and never had a dinner, and where, even in the year one thousand seven hundred and eighty, the first letters written to you by your old love, or by your little children, were but newly released from the horror of being ogled through the windows, by the heads exposed on Temple Bar with an insensate brutality and ferocity worthy of Abyssinia or Ashantee.

But indeed, at that time, putting to death was a recipe much in vogue with all trades and professions, and not least of all with Tellson's Death is Nature's remedy for all things, and why not Legislation's? Accordingly, the forger was put to Death; the utterer of a bad note was put to Death; the unlawful opener of a letter was put to Death; the purloiner of forty shillings and sixpence was put to Death; the holder of a horse at Tellson's door, who made off with it, put to Death; the coiner of a bad shilling put to Death; the sounders of three-fourths of the notes in the whole gamut of Crime, were put to Death. Not that it did the least good in the way of prevention–it might almost have been worth remarking that the fact was exactly the reverse–but, it cleared off (as to this world) the trouble of each particular case, and lest nothing else connected with it to be looked after. Thus, Tellson's, in its day, like greater places of business, its contemporaries, had taken so many lives, that, if the heads laid low before it had been ranged on Temple Bar instead of being privately disposed of, they would probably have excluded what little light the ground floor had, in a rather significant manner.

Cramped in all kinds of dim cupboards and hutches at Tellson's, the oldest of men carried on the business gravely. When they took a young man into Tellson's London house, they hid him somewhere till he was old. They kept him in a dark place, like a cheese, until he had the full Tellson flavour and blue-mould upon him. Then only was he permitted to be seen, spectacularly poring over large books, and casting his breeches and gaiters into general weight of the establishment.

Outside Tellson's–never by any means in it, unless called in–was an odd-job man, an occasional porter and messenger, who served as the live sign of the house. He was never absent during business hours, unless upon an errand, ad then he was represented by his son: a grisly urching of twelve, who was his express image. People understood that Tellson's, in a stately way, tolerated the odd-job man. The house had always tolerated some person that capacity, and time and tide had drifted this person to the post. His surname was Cruncher, and on the youthful occasion of his renouncing by proxy the works of darkness in the easterly parish church of Hounsditch, he had received the added appellation of Jerry.

The scene was Mr. Cruncher's private lodging in Hanging-sword-alley, Whitefriars: the time, half-past seven of the clock on a windy March morning, Anno Domini seventeen hundred and eighty. (Mr. Cruncher himself always spoke of the year of our Lord as Anna Dominoes: apparently under the impression that the Christian era dated from the invention of a popular game, by a lady who had bestowed her name upon it.)

Mr. Crunchers's apartments were not in a savoury neighbourhood, and were but two in number, even if a closet with a single pane of glass in it might be counted as one. But they were very decently kept. Early as it was, on the windy March morning, the room in which he lay a-bed was already scrubbed throughout; and between the cups and saucers arranged for break-fast, and the lumbering deal table, a very clean white cloth was spread.

Mr. Cruncher reposed under a patchwork counterpane, like a Harlequin at home. At first, he slept heavily, but, by degrees, began to roll and surge in bed, until he rose above the surface, with his spiky hair looking as if it must tear the sheets to ribbons. At which juncture, he exclaimed, in a voice of dire exasperation:

'Bust me, if she ain't at it again!'

A woman of orderly and industrious appearance rose from her knees in a corner, with sufficient haste and trepidation to show that she was the person referred to.

'What!' said Mr. Cruncher, looking out of bed for a boot. 'You are at it agin, are you?'

After hailing the morn with this second salutation, he threw a boot at the woman as a third. It was a very muddy boot, and may introduce the old circumstance connected with Mr. Cruncher's domestic economy, that, whereas he often came home after banking hours with clean boots, he often got up next morning to find the same boots covered with clay.

'What,' said Mr. Cruncher, varying his apostrophe after missing his mark–'what are you up to, Aggerawayter?'

'I was only saying my prayers.'

'Saying your prayers! You're a nice woman! What do you mean by flooping yourself down and praying agin me?'

'I was not praying against you; I was praying for you.'

'You weren't. And if you were, I won't be took the liberty with. Here! Your mother's a nice woman, young Jerry, going a praying agin your father's prosperity. You've got a dutiful mother, you have, my son. You've got a reli-gious mother, you have, my boy: going and flooping herself down, and praying that the bread-and-butter may be snatched out of the mouth of her only child.'

Master Cruncher (who was in his shirt) took his very ill, and, turning to his mother, strongly deprecated any praying away of his personal board.

'And what do you suppose, you conceited female,' said Mr. Cruncher, with unconscious inconsistency, 'that the worth of *your* prayers may be? Name the price that you put *your* prayers at!'

'Then only come from the heart, Jerry. They are worth no more than that.'

'Worth no more than that,' repeated Mr. Cruncher. 'They ain't worth much, then. Whether or no, I won't be prayed agin, I tell you. I can't afford it. I'm not a going to be made unlucky by *your* sneaking. If you must go flopping yourself down, flop in favour of your husband and child, and not in opposition to 'em. If I had had any but a unnat'ral wife, and this poor boy had had any but a unnat'ral mother, I might have made some money last week instead of being counterprayed and countermined and religiously circumvented into the worst of luck. B-u-u-ust me!' said Mr. Cruncher, who all this time had been putting on his clothes, 'if I ain't, what with piety and one bowed thing an another, been choused this last week into as bad luck as ever a poor devil of a honest tradesman met with! Young Jerry, dress yourself, my boy, and while I clean my boots keep a eye upon your mother now and then, and if you see any signs of more flopping, give me a call. For, I tell you'—here he addressed his wife once more—'I won't be gone again, in this matter. I am as rickety as a hackney-coach, I'm as sleepy as laudanum, my lines is strained to that degree that I shouldn't know, if it wasn't for the pain in 'em, which was me and which somebody else, yet I'm none the better for it in pocket; and it's my suspicion that you've been at it from morning to night to prevent me from being the better for it in pocket, and I won't put up with it, Aggerawayter, and what do you say now!'

Growling, in addition, such phrases as 'Ah! yes! You're religious, too. You wouldn't put yourself in opposition to the interests of your husband and child, would you? Not you!' and throwing off other sarcastic sparks from the whirling grindstone of his indignation, Mr. Cruncher betook himself to his boot-cleaning and his general preparation for business. In the meantime, his son, whose head was garnished with tenderer spikes, and whose young eyes stood close by one another, as his father's did, kept the required watch upon his mother. He greatly disturbed that poor woman at intervals, by darting out of his sleeping closet, where he made his toilet, with a suppressed cry of 'You are going to flop, mother.—Halloa, father!' and, after raising this fictious alarm, darting in again with an undutiful grin.

Mr. Cruncher's temper was not at all improved when he came to his breakfast. He resented Mr. Cruncher's saying grace with particular animosity.

'Now, Aggerawayter! What are you up to? At it agin?'

His wife explained that she had merely asked a blessing.'

'Don't do it!' said Mr. Cruncher, looking about, as if hr rather expected to see the loaf disappear under the efficacy of his wife's petitions. 'I ain't a going to be blest out of house and home. I won't have my wittles blest off my table. Keep still!'

Exceedingly red-eyed and grim, as if he had been up all night at a party which had taken anything but a convivial turn, Jerry Cruncher worried his breakfast rather than ate it, growling over it like any four-footed inmate of a menagerie. Towards nine o'clock he smoothed his ruffled aspect, and, presenting as respectable and business-like an exterior as he could overlay his natural self with, issued forth to the occupation of the day.

It could scarcely be called a trade, in spite of his favourite description of himself as 'a honest tradesman.' His stock consisted of a wooden stool, made out of a broken-backed chair cut down, which stool, young Jerry, walking at his father's side, carried every morning to beneath the banking-house window that was nearest Temple Bar: where, with the addition of the first handful of straw that could be gleaned from any passing vehicle to keep the cold and wet from the odd-job man's feet, it formed the encampment for the day. On this post of his, Mr. Cruncher was as well known to Fleet Street and the Temple, as the Bar itself–and was almost as ill-looking.

Encamped at a quarter before nine, in good time to touch his three-cornered hat to the oldest of the men as they passed in to Tellson's, Jerry took up his station on this windy March morning, with young Jerry standing by him, when not engaged in making forays through the Bar, to inflict bodily and mental injuries of an acute description on passing boys who were small enough for his amiable purpose. Father and son, extremely like each other, looked silently on at the morning traffic in Fleet Street, with their two heads as near to one another as the two eyes of each were, bore a considerable resemblance to a pair of monkeys. The resemblance was not lessened by the accidental circumstance, that the mature Jerry bit and spat out straw, while the twinkling eyes of the youthful Jerry were as restlessly watchful of him as of everything else in Fleet Street.

The head of one of the regular indoor messengers attached to Tellson's establishment was pun throught the door, and the work was given:

'Porter wanted!'

'Hooray, Father! Here's an early job to behin with!'

Having thus given his parent God speed, young Jerry seated himself on the stool, entered on his reversionary interest in the straw his father had been chewing, and cogitated.

'Al-ways rusty! His fingers is always rusty!' muttered young Jerry. 'Were does my father get all that iron rust from? He don't get no iron rust here!'

CHAPTER II

A SIGHT

'YOU know the Old Bailey well, no doubt?' said one of the oldest of clerks to Jerry the messenger.

'Yes, sir,' returned Jerry, in something of a dogged manner. 'I *do* know the Bailey.'

'Just so. And you know Mr. Lorry.'

'I know Mr. Lorry, sir, much better than I know the Bailey. Much better,' said Jerry, not unlike a reluctant witness an the establishment in question, 'than I, as a honest tradesman, wish to know the Bailey'.

'Very will. Find the door where the witnesses go in, and show the doorkeeper this note for Mr. Lorry. He will then let you in.'

'Into the court, sir?'

'Into the court.'

Mr. Cruncher's eyes seemed to get a little closer to one another, and to interchnge the inquiry, 'What do you think of this?'

'Am I to wait in the court, sir?' he asked, as the result of that conference.

'I am going to tell you. The doorkeeper will pass the note to Mr. Lorry, and do you make any gesture thant will attract Mr. Lorry's attention, and show hi where you stand. Then what you have to do, is, to remain there untilhe wants you.'

'Is that all, sir?'

'Thant's all. He wishes to have a messenger at hand. This is to tell him you are there.'

As the ancient clerk deliberately folded and superscribed the note, Mr. Cruncher, after surveying him in silence until he came to the blotting-paper stage, remarked:

'I suppose they'll be trying Forgeries this monging?'

'Treason!'

'Trat's quartering,' said Jerry. 'Barbarous!'

'It is the law,' remarked the ancient clerk, turning his surprised spectacles upon him. 'It is the law.'

'It's hard in the law to spile a man, I think. It's hard enought to kill him, but it´s wery hard to spile him, sir.'

'No at all,' returned the ancient clerk. 'Speak well of the law. Take care of your chest and voice, my good friend, and leave the law to take care of itself. I give you that advice'

'It´s the damp, sir, what settles on my chest and voice,' said Jerry. 'I leave you to judge what a damp way of earning a living mine is.'

'Well, well,' said the old clerk; 'we all have our various ways of gaining a livelihood. Some of us have damp ways, and some of us have dry ways. here is the letter. Go along.'

Jerry took the letter, and, remarking to himself with less internal deference than he made an outward show of, 'You are a lean old one, too,' made his bow, informed his son in passing, of his destination, and went his way.

They hanged al Tyburn, in those days, so the street outside Newgate had not obtained one infamous notoriety that has since attached to it. But, the gaol was a vile place in which most kinds of debauchery and villainy were practised, and where dire diseases were bred, that came into court with the prisoners, and sometimes rushed straight from the dock at my Lord Chief Justice himself, and pulled him off the bench. It had more than once happened, that the Judge in the black cap pronounced his own doom as certainly as the prisoner's, and even died before him. For the rest, the Old Bailey was famous as a kind of deadly inn yard, from which pale travellers set out continually, in carts and coaches, on a violent passage into the other world; traversing some two miles and a half of public street and road, and shaming few good citizens, if any. So powerful is use, and so desirable to be good use in the beginning. It was famous, too, for the pillory, a wise old institution, that inflicted a punishment of which no one could foresee the extent, also, for the whipping-post, another dear old institution, very humanising and softening to behold in action; also, for extensive transactions in blood-money, another fragment of ancestral wisdom, systematically leading to the most frightful mercenary crimes that could be committed under Heaven. Altogether, the Old Bailey, at that date, was a choice illustration of the precept that 'Whatever is, is right'; an aphorism that would be as final as it is lazy, did it not include the troublesome consequence, that nothing that ever was, was wrong.

Making his way through the tainted crowd, dispersed up and down this hideous scene of action, with the skill of a man accustomed to make his way quietly, the messenger found out the door he sought, and handed in his letter through a trap in it. For, people then paid to see the play in Bedlam–only the former entertainment was much the dearer. Therefore, all the Old Bailey doors were well guarded–except, indeed, the social doors by which the criminals got there, and those were always left wide open.

After some delay and demur, the door grudgingly turned on its hinges a very little way, and allowed Mr. Jerry Cruncher to squeeze himself into court.

'What's on?' he asked, in a whisper, of the man he found himself next to.

'Nothing yet.'

'What's coming on?'

'The Treason case.'

'The quartering one, eh?'

'Ah!' returned the man, with a relish; 'he'll be drawn on a hurdle to be half hanged, and then he'll be taken down and sliced before his own face, and then his inside will be taken out and burnt while he looks on, and then his head will be chopped off, and he'll be cut into quarters. That's the sentence.'

'If he's found Guilty, you mean to say?' Jerry added, by way of proviso.

'Oh! they'll find him guilty,' said the other. 'Don't you be afraid of that.'

Mr. Cruncher's attention was here diverted to the door-keeper, whom he saw making his way to Mr. Lorry, with the note in his hand. Mr. Lorry sat at the table, among the gentlemen in wigs: not far from a wigged gentleman, the prisoner's counsel, who had a great bundle of papers before him: and nearly opposite another wigged gentleman with his hands in his pockets, whose whole attention, when Mr. Cruncher looked at him then or afterwards, seemed to be concentrated on the ceiling of the court. After some gruff coughing and rubbing of his chin and signing with his hand, Jerry attracted the notice of Mr. Lorry, who had stood up to look for him, and who quietly nodded and sat down again.

'What's he got to do with the case?' asked the man he had spoken with.

'Blest if I know,' said Jerry.

'What have you got to do with it, then, if a person may inquire.'

'Blest if I know that either,' said Jerry.

The entrance of the Judge, and a consequent great stir and settling down in the court, stopped the dialogue. Presently, the dock became the central point of interest. Two jailers, who had been standing there, went out, and the prisoners were brought in, and put to the bar.

Everybody present, except the one wigged gentleman who looked at the ceiling, stared at him. All the human breath in the place, rolled at him, like a sea, or a wind, or a fire. Eager faces strained round pillars and corners, to get a sight of him; spectators in back rows stood up, not to miss a hair of him; people on the floor of the court, laid their hands on the shoulders of the people before them, to help themselves, at anybody's cost, to a view of him—stood a-tiptoe, got upon ledges, stood upon next to nothing, to see every inch of him. Conspicuous among these latter, like an animated bit of the spiked wall of Newgate, Jerry stood: aiming at the prisoner the beery breath of a whet he had taken as he came along, and discharging it to mingle with the waves of the other beer, and gin, and tea, and coffee, and what not, that flowed at him, and already broke upon the great windows behind him in an impure mist and rain.

The object of all this staring and blaring, was a young man of about five-and-twenty, well grown and well-looking, with a sunburnt cheek and a dark eye. His condition was that of a young gentleman. He was plainly dressed in black, or very dark grey, and his hair, which was long and dark, was gathered in a ribbon at the back of his neck; more to be out of his way than for ornament. As an emotion of the mind will express itself through any covering of the body, so the paleness which his situation engendered came through the brown upon his cheek, showing the soul to be stronger than the sun. He was otherwise quite self-possessed, bowed to the Judge, and stood quiet.

The sort of interest with which this man was stared and breathed at, was not a sort that elevated humanity. Had he stood in peril of a less horrible sentence—had there been a chance of any one of its savage details being spared—by just so much would he have lost in his fascination. The form that was to be doomed to be so shamefully mangled, was the sight, the immortal creature that was to be so butchered and torn asunder, yielded the sensation. Whatever gloss the various spectators put upon the interest, interest was, at the root of it, Ogreish.

Silence in the court! Charles Darnay had yesterday pleaded Not Guilty to an indictment denouncing him (with infinite jingle and jangle) for that he was a false traitor to our serene, illustrious, excellent, and so forth, prince, our Lord the King, by reason of his having, on divers occasions, and by divers means and ways, assisted Lewis, the French King, in his wars against the said serene, illustrious, excellent, and so forth, that was to say, by coming and going, between the dominious of our said serene, illustrious, excellent, and so forth, and those of the said French Lewis, and wickedly, falsely, traitorously, and otherwise eviladverbiously, revealing to the said French Lewis what forces our said serene, illustrious, excellent, and so forth, had in preparation to send to Canada and North America. This much, Jerry, with his head becoming more and more spiky as the law terms bristled it, made out with huge satisfaction, and so arrived circuitously at the understanding that the aforesaid, and over and over again aforesaid, Charles Darnay, stood there before him upon his trial, that the jury were swearing in, and that Mr. Attorney-General was making ready to speak.

The accused, who was (and who knew he was) being mentally hanged, beheaded, and quartered, by everybody there, neither flinched from the situation, nor assumed any theatrical air in it. He was quiet and attentive; watched the opening proceedings with a grave interest; and stood with his hands resting on the slab of wood before him, so composedly, that they had not displaced a leaf of the herbs with which it was strewn. The court was all bestrewn with herbs and sprinkled with vinegar, as a precaution against jail air and jail fever.

Over the prisoners head there was a mirror, to throw the light down upon him. Crowds of the wicked and the wretched had been reflected in it, and had passed from its surface and this earth's together. Hunted in a most ghastly manner that abominable place would have been, if the glass could ever have rendered back its reflections, as the ocean is one day to give up its dead. Some passing thought of the infamy and disgrace for which it had been reserved, may have struck the prisoner's mind. But that as it may, a change in his position making him conscious of a bar of light across his face, he looked up; and when he saw the glass his face flushed, and his right hand pushed the herbs away.

It happened that the action turned his face to that side of the court which was on his left. About on a level with his eyes, there sat, in that corner of the Judge's bench, two persons upon whom his look immediately rested; so immediately, and so much to the changing of his aspect, that all the eyes that were turned upon him, turned to them.

The spectators saw in the two figures, a young lady of little more than twenty, and a gentleman who was evidently her father; a man of a very remarkable appearance in respect of the absolute whiteness of his hair, and a certain indescribable intensity of his face: not of an active kind, but pondering and self-communing. When this expression was upon him, he looked as if he were old; but when it was stirred and broken up–as it was now, in a moment, on his speaking to his daughter–he became a handsome man, not past the prime of life. His daughter had one of her hands drawn through his arm, as she sat by him, and the other pressed upon it. She had drawn close to him, in her dread of the scene, and in her pity for the prisoner. Her forehead had been strikingly expressive of an engrossing terror and compassion that saw nothing but the peril of the accused. This had been so very noticeable, so very powerfully and naturally shown, that starters who had had no pity for him were touched by her; and the whisper went about, 'Who are they?'

Jerry, the messenger, who had made his own observations, in his own manner, and who had been sucking the rust off his fingers in his absorption, stretched his neck to hear who they were. The crowd about him had pressed and passed the inquiry on to the nearest attendant, and from him it had been more slowly pressed and passed back; at last it got to Jerry:

'Witnesses.'

'For which side?'

'Against.'

'Against what side?'

'The prisoner's.'

The Judge, whose eyes had gone in the general direction, recalled them, leaned back in his seat, and looked steadily at the man whose life was in his hand, as Mr. Attorney-General rose to spin the rope, grind the age, and hammer the nails into the scaffold.

CHAPTER III

A DISAPPOINTMENT

MR. Attorney-general had to inform the jury, that the prisoner before them, though young in years, was old in the treasonable practices which claimed the forfeit of his life. That this correspondence with the public enemy was not a correspondence of to-day, or of yesterday, or even of last year, or of the year before. That, it was certain the prisoner had, for longer than that, been in the habit of passing and repassing between France and England, on secret business of which he could give no honest account. That, if it were in the nature of traitorous ways to thrive (which happily it never was), the real wickedness and guilt of his business might have remained undiscovered. That Providence, however, had put it into the heart of a person who was beyond fear and beyond reproach, to ferret out the nature of the prisoner's schemes, and, struck with horror, to disclose them to His Majesty's Chief Secretary of State and most honourable Privy Council. That, this patriot would be produced before them. That, his position and attitude were, on the whole, sublime. That, he had been the prisoner's friend, but, at once in an auspicious and an evil hour detecting his infamy, had resolved to immolate the traitor he could no longer cherish in his bosom, on the sacred altar of his country. That, if statues were decreed in Britain as in ancient Greece and Rome, to public benefactors, this shining citizen would assuredly have had one. That, as they were not so decreed, he probably would not have one. That, Virtue, as had been observed by the poets (in many passages which he well knew the jury would have, word for word, at the tips of their tongues; whereat the jury's countenances displayed a guilty consciousness that they knew nothing about the passages), was in a manner contagious; more especially the bright virtue known as patriotism, or love of country. That, the lofty example of this immaculate and unimpeachable witness for the Crown, to refer to whom however unworthily was an honour, had communicated itself to the prisoner's servant, and had engendered in him a holy determination to examine his master's table drawers and pockets, and secrete his papers. That, he (Mr. Attorney-General) was prepared to hear some disparagement attempted of this admirable servant; but that, in a general way, he preferred him to his (Mr. Attorney-General's) brothers and sisters, and honoured him more than his (Mr. Attorney-General's) father and mother. That, he called with confidence on the jury to come and do likewise. That, the evidence of these two witnesses, coupled with the documents of their discovering that would be produced, would show the prisoner to have been furnished with lists of His Majesty's forces, and of their disposition and preparation, both by sea and land, and would leave no doubt that he had habitually conveyed such information to a hostile power. That, these lists could not be proved to be in the prisoner's handwriting; but that it was all the same; that, indeed, it was rather the better for the prosecution, as showing the prisoner to be artful in his precautions. That, the proof would go back five years, and would show the prisoner already engaged in these pernicious missions within a few weeks before the date of the very first action fought between the British troops and the Americans. That, for these reasons, the jury, being a loyal jury (as he knew they were), and being a responsible jury (as *they* knew they were), must positively find the prisoner Guilty, and make an end of him, whether they liked it or not. That, they never could lay their heads upon their pillows; that, they never could tolerate the idea of their wives laying their heads upon their pillows; that, they never could endure the notion of their children laying their heads upon their pillows; in short, that there never more could be, for them of theirs, any laying of heads upon pillows at all, unless the prisoner's head was taken off. That head Mr. Attorney-General concluded by demanding of them, in the name of everything he could think of with a round turn in it, and on the faith of his solemn asseveration that he already considered the prisoner as good as dead and gone.

When the Attorney-General ceased, a buzz arose in the court as if a cloud of great blue-flies were swarming about the prisoner, in anticipation of what he was soon to become. When toned down again, the unimpeachable patriot appeared in the witness-box.

Mr. Solicitor-General then, following his leader's lead, examined the patriot: John Barsad, gentleman, by name. The story of his pure soul was exactly what Mr. Attorney-General had described it to be—perhaps, if it had a fault, a little too exactly Having released his noble bosom of its burden, he would have modestly withdrawn himself, but that the wigged gentleman with the papers before him, sitting not far from Mr. Lorry, begged to ask him a few questions. The wigged gentleman sitting opposite, still looking at the ceiling of the court.

Had he ever been a spy himself? No, he scorned the base insinuation. What did he live upon? His property. Where was his property? He didn't precisely remember where it was. What was it? No business of anybody's. Had he inherited it? Yes, he had. From whom? Distant relation. Very distant? Rather. Ever been in prison? Certainly not. Never in a debtor's prison? Didn't see what that had to do with it. Never in a debtor's prison?—Come, once again. Never? Yes. How many times? Two or three times. Not five or six? Perhaps. Of what profession? Gentleman. Ever been kicked? Might have been. Frequently? No. Ever kicked downstairs? Decidedly not; once received a kick on the top of the staircase and fell downstairs of his own accord. Kicked on that occasion for cheating at dice? Something to that effect was said by the intoxicated liar who committed the assault, but it was not true. Swear it was not true? Positively. Ever live by cheating at play? Never. Ever live by play? Not more than other gentleman do. Ever borrow money of the prisoner? Yes. Ever pay him? No. Was not this intimacy with the prisoner, in reality a very slight one, forced upon the prisoner in coaches, inns, and packets? No. Sure he saw the prisoner with these lists? Certain. Knew no more about the lists? No. Had not procured them himself, for instance? No. Expect to get anything by this evidence? No. Not in regular government pay and employment, to lay traps? Oh dear no. Or to do anything? Oh dear no. Swear that? Over and over again. No motives but motives of sheer patriotism? None whatever.

The virtuous servant, Roger Clay, swore his way through the case at a great rate. He had taken service with the prisoner, in good faith and simplicity, four years ago. He had asked the prisoner, aboard the Calais packet, if he wanted a handy fellow, and the prisoner had engaged him. He had not asked the prisoner to take the handy fellow as an act of charity—never thought of such a thing. He began to have suspicions of the prisoner, and to keep an eye upon him, soon afterwards. In arranging his clothes, while travelling, he had seen similar lists to these in the prisoner's pockets, over and over again. He had taken these lists from the drawer of the prisoner's desk. He had not put them there first. He had seen the prisoner show these identical lists to French gentlemen, both at Calais, and similar lists to French gentlemen, both at Calais and Boulogne. He loved his country, and couldn't bear it, and had given information. He had never been suspected of stealing a silver teapot; he had been maligned respecting a mustard-pot, but it turned out to be only a plated one. He had known the last witness seven or eight years, that was merely a coincidence. He didn't call it a particularly curious coincidence; most coincidences were curious. Neither did he call it a curious coincidence that true patriotism was *his* only motive too. He was a true Briton, and hoped there were many like him.

The blue-flies buzzed again, and Mr. Attorney-General called Mr. Jarvis Lorry.

'Mr. Jarvis Lorry, are you a clerk in Tellson's Bank?'

'I am.'

'On a certain Friday night in November one thousand seven hundred and seventy-five, did business occasion you to travel between London and Dover by the mail?'

'It did.'

'Where there any other passengers in the mail?'

'Two.'

'Did they alight on the road in the course of the night?'

'They did.'

'Mr. Lorry, look upon the prisoner. Was he one of those two passengers?'

'I cannot undertake to say that he was.'

'Does he resemble either of those two passengers?'

'Both were so wrapped up, and the night was so dark, and we were all so reserved, that I cannot undertake to say even that.'

'Mr. Lorry, look again upon the prisoner. Supposing him wrapped up as those two passengers were, is there anything in his bulk and stature to render it unlikely that he was one of them?'

'No.'

'You will not swear, Mr. Lorry, that he was not one of them?'

'No.'

'So at least you say he may have been one of them?'

'Yes. Except that I remember them both to have been–like myself–timorous of highwaymen, and the prisoner has not a timorous air.'

'Did you ever see a counterfeit of timidity, Mr. Lorry?'

'I certainly have seen that.'

'Mr. Lorry, look once more upon the prisoner. Have you seen him, to your certain knowledge, before?'

'I have.'

'When?'

'I was returning from France a few days afterwards, and, at Calais, the prisoner came on board the packet-ship in which I returned, and made the voyage with me.'

'At what hour did he come on board?'

'At a little after midnight.'

'In the dead of the night. Was he only passenger who came on board at that untimely hour?'

'He happened to be the only one.'

'Never mind about "happening," Mr. Lorry. He was the only passenger who came on board in the dead of the night?'

'He was.'

'Were you travelling alone, Mr. Lorry, or with any companion?'

'With two companions. A gentleman and lady. They are here.'

'They are here. Had you any conversation with the prisoner?'

'Hardly any. The weather was stormy, and the passage long and rough, and I lay on a sofa, almost from shore to shore.'

'Miss Manette!'

The young lady, to whom all eyes had been turned before, and were now turned again, stood up where she had sat. Her father rose with her, and kept her hand drawn through his arm.

'Miss Manette, look upon the prisoner.'

To be confronted with such pity, and such earnest youth and beauty, was far more trying to the accused than to be confronted with all the crowd. Standing, as it were, apart with her on the edge of his grave, not all the staring curiosity that looked on, could, for the moment, nerve him to remain quite still. His hurried right hand parcelled out the herbs before him into imaginary beds of flowers in a garden; and his efforts to control and steady his breathing shook the lips from which the colour rushed to his heart. The buzz of the great flies was loud again.

'Miss Manette, have you seen the prisoner before?'

'Yes, sir.'

'Where?'

'On board of the packet-ship just now referred, to, sir, and on the same occasion.'

'You are the young lady just now referred to?'

'Oh! most unhappily, I am!'

The plaintive tone of her compassion merged into the less musical voice of the Judge, as he said something fiercely: 'Answer the question put to you, and make no remark upon them.'

'Miss Manette had you any conversation with the prisoner on that passage across the Channel?'

'Yes, sir.'

'Recall it.'

In the midst of a profound stillness, she faintly began:

'When the gentleman came on board—'

'Do you mean the prisoner?' inquired the Judge, knitting his brows.

'Yes, my Lord.'

'Then say the prisoner.'

'When the prisoner came on board, he noticed that my father'—turning her eyes lovingly to him as he stood beside her—'was much fatigued and in a very weak state of health. My father was so reduced that I was afraid to take him out of the air, and I had made a bed for him on the eck near the cabin steps, and I sat on the deck at his side to take care of him. There was no other passengers that night, but we four. The prisoner was so good as to beg permission to advise me how I could shelter my father from the wind and weather, better than I had done. I had not known how to do it well, not understanding how the wind would set when we were out of the harbour. He did it for me. He expressed great gentleness and kindness for my father's state, and I am sure he felt it. That was the manner of our beginning to speak together.'

'Let me interrupt you for a moment. He had come on board alone?'

'No.'

'How many were with him?'

'Two French gentlemen.'

'Had they conferred together?'

'They had conferred together until the last moment, when it was necessary for the French gentlemen to be landed in their boat.'

'Had any papers been handed about among them, similar to these lists?'

'Some papers had been handed about among them, but I don't know what papers.'

'Like these in shape and size?'

'Possibly, but indeed I don't know, although they stood whispering very near to me: because they stood at the top of the cabin steps to have the light of the lamp that was hanging there; it was a dull lamp, and they spoke very low, and I did not hear what they said, and saw only that they looked at papers.'

'Now to the prisoner's conversation, Miss Manette.'

'The prisoner was as open in his confidence with me–which arose out of my helpless situation–as he was kind, and good, and useful to my father. I hope'–bursting into tears–'I may not repay him by doing him harm to-day.'

Buzzing from the blue-flies.

'Miss Manette, if the prisoner does not perfectly understand that you give the evidence which it is your duty to give–which you must give–and which you cannot escape from giving–with great unwillingness, he is the only person, present in that condition. Please to go on.'

'He told me that he was travelling on business of a delicate and difficult nature, which might get people into trouble, and that he was therefore travelling under an assumed name. He said that his business had, within a few days, taken him to France, and might, at intervals, take him backwards and forwards between France and England for a long time to come.'

'Did he say anything about America, Miss Manette? Be particular.'

'He tried to explain to me how that quarrel had arisen, and he said that, so far as he could judge, it was a wrong and foolish one on England's part. He added, in a jesting way, that perhaps George Washington might gain almost as great a name in history as George the Third. But there was no harm in his way of saying this: it was said laughingly, and to beguile the time.'

And strongly arked expression of face on the part of a chief actor in a scene of great interest to whom many eyes are directed, will be unconsciously imitated by the spectators. Her forehead was painfully anxious and intent as she gave this evidence, and, in the pauses when she stopped for the Judge to write it down, watched its effect upon the counsel for and against. Among the lookers-on there was the same expression in all quarters of the court; insomuch, that a great majority of the foreheads there, might have been mirrors reflecting the witness, when the Judge looked up from his notes to glare at that tremendous heresy about George Washington.

Mr. Attorney-General now signified to my Lord, that he deemed it necessary, as a matter of precaution and form, to call the young lady's father, Doctor Manette. Who was called accordingly.

'Doctor Manette, look upon the prisoner. Have you ever seen him before'

'Once. When he called at my lodgings in London. Some three years, or three years and a half ago.'

'Can you identify him as your fellow-passenger on board the packet, or speak to his conversation with your daughter?'

'Sir, I can do neither.'

'Is there any particular and special reason for your being unable to do either?'

He answered, in a low voice, 'There is.'

'Has it been your misfortune to undergo a long imprisonment, without trial, or even accusation, in your native country, Doctor Manette?'

He answered, in a tone that went to every heart, 'A long imprisonment.'

'Were you newly released on the occasion in question?'

'They tell me so.'

'Have you no remembrance of the occasion?'

'None. My mind is a blank, from some time–I cannot even say what time–when I employed myself, in my captivity, in making shoes, to the time when I found myself living in London with my dear daughter here. She had become familiar to me, when a gracious God restored my faculties; but, I am quite unable even to say how she had become familiar. I have no remembrance of the process.'

Mr. Attorney-General sat down, and the father and daughter sat down together.

A singular circumstance then arose in the case. The object in hand being to show that the prisoner went down, with some fellow-plotter untracked, in the Dover mail on that Friday night in November five years ago, and got out of the mail in the night, as a blind, at a place where he did not remain, but from which he travelled back some dozen miles or more, to a garrison and dockyard, and there collected information; a witness was called to identify him as having been at the precise time required, in the coffee-room of an hotel in that garrison and dockyard town, waiting for another person. The prisoner's counsel was cross-examining this witness with no result, except that he had never seen the prisoner on any other occasion, when the wigged gentleman who had all this time been looking at the ceiling of the court, wrote a word or two on a little piece of paper, screwed it up, and tossed it to him. Opening this piece of paper in the next pause, the counsel looked with great attention and curiosity at the prisoner.

'You say again you are quite sure that it *was* the prisoner?'

The witness was quite sure.

'Did you ever see anybody very like the prisoner?'

Not so like (the witness said) as that he could be mistaken.

'Look well upon that gentleman, my learned friend there,' pointing to him who had tossed the paper over, 'and then look well upon the prisoner. How say you? Are they very like each other?'

Allowing for my learned friend's appearance being careless and slovenly if not debauched, they were sufficiently like each other to surprise, not only the witness, but everybody present, when they were thus brought into comparison. My Lord being prayed to bid my learned friend lay aside his wig, and giving no very gracious consent, the likeness became much more remarkable. My Lord inquired of Mr. Stryver (the prisoner's counsel) whether they were next to try Mr. Carton (name of my learned friend) for treason? But, Mr. Stryver replied to My Lord, no; but he would ask the witness to tell him whether what happened once, might happen twice; whether he would have been so confident if he had seen the illustration of his rashness sooner, whether he would be so confident, having seen it; and more. The upshot of which, was, to smash this witness like a crockery vessel, and shiver his part of the case to useless lumber.

Mr. Cruncher had by this time taken quite a lunch of rust off his fingers in his following of the evidence. He had now to attend while Mr.

Stryver fitted the prisoner's case on the jury, like a compact suit of clothes; showing then how the patriot, Barsad, was a hired spy and traitor, an unblushing trafficker in blood, and one of the greatest scoundrels upon earth since accursed Judas–which he certainly did look rather like. How the virtuous servant, Cly, was his friend and partner, and was worthy to be; how the watchful eyes of these forgers and false swearers had rested on the prisoner as a victim, because some family affairs in France, he being of French extraction, did require him making those passages across the Channel–though what those affairs were, a consideration for others who were near and dear to him, forbade him, even for his life, to disclose. How the evidence that had been warped and wrested from the young lady, whose anguish in giving it they had witnessed, came to nothing, involving the mere little innocent gallantries and politeness like to pass between any young gentleman and young lady so thrown together;–with the exception of that reference to George Washington, which was altogether too extravagant and impossible to be regarded in any other light than as a monstrous joke. How it would be a weakness in the government to break down in his attempt to practise for popularity on the lowest national antipathies and fears, and therefore Mr. Attorney-General had made the most of it; how, nevertheless, it rested upon nothing, save that vile and infamous character of evidence too often disfiguring such cases, and of which the State Trials of his country were full. But, there my Lord interposed (with as grave a face as if it had not been true), saying that he could not sit upon that Bench and suffer those allusions.

Mr. Stryver then called his few witnesses, and Mr. Cruncher had next to attend while Mr. Attorney-General turned the whole suit of clothes Mr. Stryver had fitted on the jury, inside out: showing how Barsad and Cly were even a hundred times better than he had thought them, and the prisoner a hundred times worse. Lastly, came my Lord himself, turning the suit of clothes, now inside out, now outside in, but on the whole decidedly trimming and shaping them into grave-clothes for the prisoner.

And now, the jury turned to consider, and the great flies swarmed again.

Mr. Carton, who had so long sat looking at the ceiling of the court, changed neither his place nor his attitude, even in this excitement. While his learned friend, Mr. Stryver, massing his papers before him, whispered with those who sat near, and from time to time glanced anxiously at the jury; while all the spectators moved more or less, and grouped themselves anew; while even my Lord himself arose from his seat, and slowly paced up and down his platform, not unattended by a suspicion in the minds of the audience that his state was feverish; this one man sat leaning back, with his torn grown half off him, his untidy wig put on just as it had happened to light on his head after its removal, his hands in his pockets, and his eyes on the ceiling as they had been all day. Something especially reckless in his demeanour, not only gave him a disreputable look, but so disminished the strong resemblance he undoubtedly bore to the prisoner (which his momentary earnestness, when they were compared together, had strengthened), that many of the lookers-on, taking note of him now, said to one another they would hardly have thought the two were so alike. Mr. Cruncher made the observation to his next neighbour, and added, 'I'd hold half a guinea that *he* don't get no law-work to do. Don't look like the sort of one to get any, do he?'

Yet, this Mr. Carton took in more of the details of the scene than he appeared to take in; for now, when Miss Manette's head dropped upon her father's breast, he was the first to see it, and to say audibly: 'Officer! look to that young lady. Help the gentleman to take her out. Don't you see she will fall!'

There was much commiseration for her as she was removed, and much sympathy with her father. It had evidently been a great distress to him, to have the days of his imprisonment recalled. He had shown strong internal agitation when he was questioned, and that pondering or brooding look which made him old, had been upon him, like a heavy cloud, ever since. As he passed out, the jury, who had turned back and paused a moment, spoke, through their foreman.

They were not agreed, and wished to retire. My Lord (perhaps with George Washington on his mind) showed some surprise that they were not agreed, but signified his pleasure that they should retire under watch and ward, and retired himself. The trial had lasted all day, and the lamps in the court were now being lighted. It began to be rumoured that the jury would be out a long while. The spectators dropped off to get refreshment, and the prisoner withdrew to the back of the dock, and sat down.

Mr. Lorry, who had gone out when the young lady and her father went out, now reappeared, and beckoned to Jerry: who, in the slackened interest, could easily get near him.

'Jerry, if you wish to take something to eat, you can. But, keep in the way. You will be sure to hear when the jury come in. Don't be a moment behind them, for I want you to take the verdict back to the bank. You are the quickest messenger I know, and will get to Temple Bar long before I can.'

Jerry had just enough forehead to knuckle, and he knuckled it in acknowledgment of his communication and a shilling. Mr. Carton came up at the moment, and touched Mr. Lorry on the arm.

'How is the young lady?'

'She is greatly distressed; but her father is comforting her, and she feels the better for being out of court.'

'I'll tell the prisoner so. It won't do for a respectable bank gentleman like you, to be seen speaking to him publicly, you know.'

Mr. Lorry reddened as if he were conscious of having debated the point in his mind, and Mr. Carton made his way to the outside of the bar. The way out of court lay in that direction, and Jerry followed him, all eyes, ears, and spikes.

'Mr. Darnay!'

The prisoner came forward directly.

'You will naturally be anxious to hear of the witness, Miss Manette. She will do very well. You have seen the worst of her agitation.'

'I am deeply sorry to have been the cause of it. Could you tell her so for me, with my fervent acknowledgments?'

'Yes, I could. I will if you ask it.'

Mr. Carton's manner was so careless as to be almost insolent. He stood, half turned from the prisoner, lounging with his elbow against the bar.

'I do ask it. Accept my cordial thanks.'

'What,' said Carton, still only half turned towards him, 'do you expect, Mr. Darnay?'

'The worst.'

'It's the wisest thing to expect, and the likeliest. But I think their withdrawing is in your favour.'

Loitering on the way out of court not being allowed, Jerry heard no more: but left them–so like each other in feature, so unlike each other in manner–standing side by side, both reflected in the glass above them.

An hour and a half limped heavily away in the thief-andrascal crowded passages below, even though assisted off with mutton pies and ale. The hoarse messenger, uncomfortably seated on a form after taking that reflection, had dropped into a doze, when a loud murmur and a rapid tide of people setting up the stairs that led to the court, carried him along with them.

'Jerry! Jerry!' Mr. Lorry was already calling at the door when he got there.

'Here, sir! It's a fight to get back again. Here I am, sir!'

Mr. Lorry handed him a paper through the throng. 'Quick! Have you got it'

'Yes, sir!'

Hastily written on the paper was the word 'ACCQUITTED.'

'If you had sent the message, "Recalled to Life," again,' muttered Jerry, as he turned, 'I should have known what you meant, this time.'

He had no opportunity of saying, or so much as thinking anything else, until he was clear of the Old Bailey; for, the crowd came pouring out with a vehemence that nearly took him off his legs, and a loud buzz swept into the street as if the baffled blue-flies were dispersing in search of other carrion.

CHAPTER IV

CONGRATULATORY

FROM the dimly lighted passages of the court, the last sediment of the human stew that had been boiling there all day, was straining off, when Doctor Manette, Lucie Manette, his daughter, Mr. Lorry, the solicitor for the defence, and its counsel, Mr. Stryver, stood gathered round Mr. Charles Darnay-just released–congratulating him on his escape from death.

It would have been difficult by a far brighter light, to recognize in Doctor Manette, intellectual of face and upright of bearing, the shoemaker of the garret in Paris. Yet, no one could have looked at him twice, without looking again: even though the opportunity of observation had not extended to the mournful cadence of his low grave voice, and to the abstraction that overclouded him fitfully, without any apparent reason. While one external cause, and that a reference to his long lingering agony, would always–as on the trial–evoke this condition from the depths of his soul, it was also in its nature to arise of itself, and to draw a gloom over him, as incomprehensible to those unacquainted with his story as if they had seen the shadow of the actual Bastille thrown upon him by a summer sun, when the substance was three hundred miles away.

Only his daughter had the power of charming this black brooding from his mind. She was the golden thread that united him to a Past beyond his misery, and to a Present beyond his misery: and the sound of her voice, the light of her face, the touch of her hand, had a strong beneficial influence with him almost always. Not absolutely always, for she could recall some occasions on which her power had failed; but they were few and slight, and she believed them over.

Mr. Darnay had kissed her hand fervently and gratefully, and had turned to Mr. Stryver, whom he warmly thanked. Mr. Stryver, a man of little more than thirty, but looking twenty years older than he was, stout, loud, red, bluff, and free from any drawback of delicacy, had a pushing way of shouldering himself (morally and physically) into companies and conversations, that argued well for his shouldering his way up in life.

He still had his wig and grown on, and he said, squaring himself at his late client to that degree that he squeezed the innocent Mr. Lorry clean out of the group: 'I am glad to have brought you off with honour, Mr. Darnay. It was an infamous prosecution, grossly infamous; but not the less likely to succeed on that account.'

'You have laid me under an obligation to you for life–in two senses,' said his late client, taking his hand.

'I have done my best for you, Mr. Darnay; and my best is as good as another man's, I believe.'

It clearly being incumbent on someone to say, 'Much better,' Mr. Lorry said it; perhaps not quite disinterestedly, but with the interested object of squeezing himself back again.

'You think so' said Mr. Stryver. 'Well! You have been presently all day, and you ought to know. You are a man of business, too.'

'And as such,' quoth Mr. Lorry, whom the counsel learned in the law had now shouldered back into the group, just as he had previously shouldered him out of it–'as such I will appeal to Doctor Manette, to break up this conference and order us all to our homes. Miss Lucie looks ill, Mr. Darnay has had a terrible day, we are worn out.'

'Speak for yourself, Mr. Lorry,' said Stryver; 'I have a night's work to do yet. Speak for yourself.'

'I speak for myself,' answered Mr. Lorry, 'and for Mr. Darnay, and for Miss Lucie, and— Miss Lucie, do you not think I may speak for us all?' He asked her the question pointedly, and with a glance at her father.

His face had become frozen, as it were, in a very curious look at Darnay: an intent look, deepening into a frown of dislike and distrust, not even unmixed with fear. With this strange expression on him his thoughts had wandered away.

'My father,' said Lucie, softly laying her hand on his.

He slowly shook the shadow off, and turned to her.

'Shall we go home, my father?'

With a long breath, he answered 'Yes.'

The friends of the acquitted prisoner had dispersed, under the impression—which he himself had originated—that he would not be released that night. The lights were nearly all extinguished in the passages, the iron gates were being closed with a jar and a rattle, and the dismal place was deserted until to-morrow morning's interest of gallows, pillory, whipping-post, and branding-iron, should repeople it. Walking between her father and Mr. Darnay, Lucie Manette passed into the open air. A hackney-coach was called, and the father and daughter departed in it.

Mr. Stryver had left them in the passages, to shoulder his way back to the robbing-room. Another person, who had not joined the group, or interchanged a word with any one of them, but who had been leaning against the wall where its shadow was darkest, had silently strolled out after the rest, and had looked on until the coach drove away. He now stepped up to where Mr. Lorry and Mr. Darnay stood upon the pavement.

'So, Mr. Lorry! Men of business may speak to Mr. Darnay now?'

Nobody had made any acknowledgment of Mr. Carton's part in the day's proceedings; nobody had known of it. He was unrobed, and was none the better for it in appearance.

'If you knew what a conflict goes on in the business mind, when the business mind is divided between good-natured impulse and business appearances, you would be assumed, Mr. Darnay.'

Mr. Lorry reddened, and said, warmly, 'You have mentioned that before, sir. We men of business, whose serve a House, are not our own masters. We have to think of the House more than ourselves.'

'*I* know, *I* know,' rejoined Mr. Carton, carelessly. 'Don't be nettled, Mr. Lorry. You are as good as another, I have no doubt: better, I dare say.'

'And indeed, sir,' pursued Mr. Lorry, not minding him, 'I really don't know what you have to do with the matter. If you'll excuse me, as very much of elder, for saying so, I really don't know that it is your business.'

'Business! Bless you, *I* have no business,' said Mr. Carton. '

'It is a pity you have not, sir.'

'I think so, too.'

'If you had,' pursued Mr. Lorry, 'perhaps you would attend to it.'

'Lord love you, no!—I shouldn't,' said Mr. Carton.

'Well, sir!' cried Mr. Lorry, thoroughly heated by his indifference, 'business is a very good thing, and a very respectable thing. And, sir, if business imposes its restraints and its silences and impediments, Mr. Darnay as a young gentleman of generosity knows how to make allowance for that circumstance. Mr. Darnay, good night, God bless you, sir! I hope you have been this day preserved for a prosperous and happy life.–Chair there!'

Perhaps a little angry with myself, as well as with the barrister, Mr. Lorry bustled into the chair, and was carried off to Tellson's. Carton, who smelt of port wine, and did not appear to be quite sober, laughed then, and turned to Darnay:

'This is a strange chance that throws you and me together. This must be a strange night to you, standing alone here with your counterpart on these street stones?'

'I hardly seem yet,' returned Charles Darnay, 'to belong to this world again.'

'I don't wonder at it; it's not so long since you were pretty are advanced on your way to another. You speak faintly.'

'I begin to think I *am* faint.'

'Then why the devil don't you dine? I dined, myself, while those numskulls were deliberating which world you should belong to–this, or some other. Let me show you nearest tavern to dine well at.'

Drawing his arm through his own, he took him down Ludgate Hill to Fleet Street, and so, up a covered way, into a tavern. Here, they were shown into a little room, where Charles Darnay was soon recruiting his strength with a good plain dinner and good wine: while Carton sat opposite to him at the same table, with his separate bottle of port before him, and his fully half-insolent manner upon him.

'Do you feel, yet, that you belong to this terrestrial scheme again, Mr. Darnay?'

'I am frightfully confused regarding time and place; but I am so far mended as to feel that.'

'It must be an immense satisfaction!'

He said it bitterly, and filled up his glass again: which was a large one.

'As to me, the greatest desire I have, is to forget that I belong to it. It has no good in it for me–except wine like this–nor I for it. So we are not much alike in that particular. Indeed, I begin to think we are not much alike in any particular, you and I.'

Confused by the emotion of the day, and feeling his being there with this Double of coarse deportment, to be like a dream, Charles Darnay was at a loss how to answer; finally, answered not at all.

'Now your dinner is done,' Carton presently said, 'why don't you call a health, Mr. Darnay; why don't you give your toast?'

'What health? What toast?'

'Why, it's on the tip of your tongue. It ought to be, it must be, I'll swear it's there.'

'Miss Manette, then!'

'Miss Manette, then!'

Looking his companion full in the face while he drank the toast, Carton flung his glass over his shoulder against the wall, where it shivered to pieces; then, rang the bell, and ordered in another.

'That's a fair young lady to hand to a coach in the dark, Mr. Darnay!'

he said, filling his new goblet.

A slight frown and a laconic 'Yes,' were the answer.

'That's a fair young lady to be pitied by and wept for by! How does it feel? Is it worth being tried for one's life, to be object of such sympathy and compassion, Mr. Darnay?'

Again Darnay answered not a word.

'She was mightily pleased to have your message, when I gave it to her. Not that she showed she was pleased, but I suppose she was.'

The allusion served as a timely reminder to Darnay that this disagreeable companion had, of his own free will, assisted him in the strait of the day. He turned the dialogue to that point, and thanked him for it.

'I neither want any thanks, nor merit any,' was the careless rejoinder. 'It was nothing to do, in the first place; and I don't know why I did it, in the second. Mr. Darnay, let me ask you a question.'

'Willingly, and a small return for your good offices.'

'Do you think I particularly like you?'

'Really, Mr. Carton,' returned the other, oddly disconcerted, 'I have not asked myself the question.'

'But ask yourself the question now.'

'You have acted as if you do; but I don't think you do.'

'*I* don't think I do,' said Carton. 'I begin to have a very good opinion of your understanding.'

'Nevertheless,' pursued Darnay, rising to ring the bell, 'there is nothing in that, I hope, to prevent my calling the reckoning, and our parting without ill-blood on either side.'

Carton rejoining, 'Nothing in life!' Darnay rang. 'Do you call the whole reckoning?' said Carton. On his answering in the affirmative, 'Then bring me another pint of this same wine, drawer, and come and wake me at ten.'

The bill being paid, Charles Darnay rose and wished him good night. Without returning the wish, Carton rose too, with something of a threat of defiance in his manner, and said, 'A last word, Mr. Darnay: you think I am drunk?'

'I think you have been drinking, Mr. Carton.'

'Think? You know I have been drinking.'

'Since I must say so, I know it.'

'Then you shall likewise know why. I am a disappointed drudge, sir. I care for no man on earth, and no man on earth cares for me.'

'Much to be regretted. You might have used your talents better.'

'Maybe so, Mr. Darnay; maybe not. Don't let your sober face elate you, however; you don't know what it may come to. Good night!'

When he was left alone, this strange being took up a candle, went to a glass that hung against the wall, and surveyed himself minutely in it.

'Do you particularly like the man?' he muttered, at his own image; 'why should you particularly like a man who resembles you? There is nothing in you to like; you know that. Ah, confound you! What a change you have made in yourself! A good reason for taking to a man, that he shows you what you have fallen away from, and what you might have been! Change places with him, and would you have been looked at by those blue eyes as he was, and commiserated by that agitated face as he was? Come on, and have it out in plain words! You hate the fellow?'

He resorted to his pint of wine for consolation, drank it all in a few minutes, and fell asleep on his arms, with his hair straggling over the table, and a long winding-sheet in the candle dripping down upon him.

CHAPTER V

THE JACKAL

THOSE were drinking days, and most men drank hard. So very great is the improvement Time has brought about in such habits, that a moderate statement of the quantity of wine and punch which one man would swallow in the course of a night, without any detriment to his reputation as a perfect gentleman, would seem, in those days, a ridiculous exaggeration. The learned profession of the law was certainly not behind any other learned profession in its Bacchanalian propensities; neither was Mr. Stryver, already fast shouldering his way to a large and lucrative practice, behind his compeers in this particular, any more than in the drier parts of the legal race.

A favourite at the Old Bailey, and eke at the Sessions, Mr. Stryver had begun cautiously to hew away the lower staves of the ladder on which he mounted. Sessions and Old Bailey had now to summon their favourite, specially, to their longing arms; and shouldering itself towards the visage of the Lord Chiefs Justice in the Court of King's Bench, the florid countenance of Mr. Stryver might be daily seen, bursting out of the bed of wigs, like a great sunflower pushing its way at the sun from among a rank gardenful of flaring companions.

It had once been noted at the Bar, that while Mr. Stryver was a glib man, and an unscrupulous, and a ready, and a bold, he had not that faculty of extracting the essence from a heap of statements, which is among the most striking and necessary of advocate's accomplishments. But, a remarkable improvement came upon him as to this. The more business he got, the greater his power seemed to grow of getting at its pith and marrow; and however late at night he sat carousing with Sydney Carton, he always had his points at his finger's ends in the morning.

Sydney Carton, idlest and most unpromising of men, was Stryver's great ally. What the two drank together, between Hilary term and Michaelmas, might have floated a king's ship. Stryver never had a case in hand, anywhere, but Carton was there, with his hands in his pockets, staring at the ceiling of the court; they went the same Circuit, and even there they prolonged their usual orgies late into the night, and Carton was rumoured to be seen at broad day, going home stealthily and unsteadily to his lodgings, like a dissipated cat. At last, it began to get about, among such as were interested in the matter, that although Sydney Carton would never be a lion, he was an amazingly good jackal, and that he rendered suit and service to Stryver in that humble capacity.

'Ten o'clock, sir,' said the man at the tavern, whom he had charged to wake him–'ten o'clock, sir.'

'*What's* the matter?'

'Ten o'clock, sir.'

'What do you mean? Ten o'clock at night?'

'Yes, sir. Your honour told me to call you.'

'Oh! I remember. Very well, very well.'

After a few dull efforts to get to sleep again, which the man dexterously combated by stirring the fire continuously for five minutes, he got up, tossed his hat on, and walked out. He turned into the Temple, and, having revived himself by twice pacing the pavements of King's Bench Walk and Paper-buildings, turned into the Stryver chambers.

The Stryver clerk, who never assisted at these conferences, had gone home, and the Stryver principal opened the door. He had his slippers on, and a loose bed-gown, and his throat was bare for his greater ease. He had that rather wild, strange, seared marking about the eyes which may be observed in all free livers of his class, from the portrait of Jeffries downward, and which can be traced, under various disguises of Art, through the portraits of every Drinking Age.

'You are a little late, Memory,' said Stryver.

'About the usual time; it may be a quarter of an hour later.'

They went into a diggy room lined with books and littered with papers, where there was a blazing fire. A kettle steamed upon the hob, and in the midst of the wreck of papers a table shone, with plenty of wine upon it, and brandy, and rum, and sugar, and lemons.

'You have had your bottle, I perceive, Sydney.'

'Two to-night. I think. I have been dining with the day's client; or seeing him dine–it's all one!'

'That was a rare point, Sydney, that you brought to bear upon the identification. How did you come by it? When did it strike you?'

'I thought he was rather a handsome fellow, and I thought I should have been much the same sort of fellow, if I had had any luck.'

Mr. Stryver laughed till he shook his precocious paunch.

'You and your luck, Sydney! Get to work, get to work.'

Sullenly enough, the jackal loosened his dress, went into an adjoining room, and came back with a large jug of cold water, a basin, and a towel or two. Steeping the towels in the water, and partially wringing them out, he folded them on his head in a manner hideous to behold, sat down at the table, and said, 'Now I am ready!'

'Not much boiling down to be done to-night, Memory,' said Mr. Stryver, gaily, as he looked among his papers.

'How much?'

'Only two sets of them.'

'Give me the worst first.'

'There they are, Sydney. Fire away!'

The lion then composed himself on his back on a sofa on one side of the drinking table, while the jackal sat at his own paper-bestrewn table proper, on the other side of it, with the bottles and glasses ready to his hand. Both resorted to the drinking table without snit, but each in a different way; the lion for the most part reclining with his hands on his waistband, looking at the fire, or occasionally flirting with some lighter document; the jackal, with knitted brows and intent face, so deep in his task, that his eyes did not even follow the hand he stretched out for his glass—which often groped about, for a minute or more, before it found the glass for his lips. Two or three times, the matter in hand became so knotty, that the jackal found it imperative on him to get up, and steed his towels anew. From these pilgrimages to the jug and basin, he returned with such eccentricities of damp head-gear as no words can describe; which were made the more ludicrous by his anxious gravity.

At length the jackal had got together a compact repast for the lion, and proceeded to offer it to him. The lion took it with care and caution, made his selections from it, and his remarks upon it, and the jackal assisted both. When the repast was fully discussed, the lion put his hands in his waistband again, and lay down to meditate. The jackal then invigorated himself with a bumper for his throttle, and a fresh application to his head, and applied himself to the collection of a second meal; this was administered to the lion in the same manner, and was not disposed of until the clocks struck three in the morning.

'And now we have done, Sydney, fill a bumper of punch.' Said Mr. Stryver.

The jackal removed the towels from his head, which had been steaming again, shook himself, yawned, shivered, and complied.

'You were very sound, Sydney, in the matter of those crown witnesses to-day. Every question told.'

'I always am sound; am I not?'

'I don't gainsay it. What has roughened your temper? Put some punch to it and smooth it again.'

With a deprecatory grunt, the jackal again complied.

'The old Sydney Carton of old Shrewsbury School,' said Stryver, nodding his head over him as he revived him in the present and the past, 'the old seesaw Sydney. Up one minute and down the next; now in spirits and now in despondency!'

'Ah!' returned the other, sighing: 'yes! The same Sydney, with the same luck. Even then, I did exercises for other, and seldom did my own.'

'And why not?'

'God knows. It was my way, I suppose.'

He sat, with his hands in his pockets and his legs stretched out before him, looking at the fire.

'Carton,' said his friend, squaring himself at him with a bullying air, as if the fire-grate had been the furnace in which sustained endeavour was forged, and the one delicate thing to be done for the old Sydney Carton of old Shrewsbury School was to shoulder him into it, 'your way is, and always was, a lame way. You summon no energy and purpose. Look at me.'

'Oh, botheration!' returned Sydney, with a lighter and more good-humoured laugh, 'don't *you* be moral!'

'How have I done what I have done?' said Stryver; 'how do I do what I do?'

'Partly through paying me to help you, I suppose. But it's not worth your while to apostrophize me, or the air, about it; what you want to do, you do. You were always in the front rank, and I was always behind.'

'I had to get into the front rank; I was not born there, was I?

'I was not present at the ceremony; but my opinions you were,' said Carton. At this, he laughed again, and they both laughed.

'Before Shrewsbury, and at Shrewsbury, and ever since Shrewsbury,' pursued Carton, 'you have fallen into your rank, and I have fallen into mine. Even when we were fellow-students in the Student-Quarter of Paris, picking up French, and French law, and other French crumbs that we didn't get much good of, you were always somewhere, and I was always–nowhere.'

'And whose fault was that?'

'Upon my soul, I am not sure that it was not yours. You were always driving and riving and shouldering and pressing to that restless degree that I had no chance for my life but in rust and repose. It's a gloomy thing, however, to talk about one's own past, with the day breaking. Turn me in some other direction before I go.'

'Well then! Pledge me to the pretty witness,' said Stryver, holding up his glass. 'Are you turned in a pleasant direction?'

Apparently not, for he became gloomy again.

'Pretty witness,' he muttered, looking down into his glass. 'I have had enough of witnesses to-day and to-night, who's your pretty witness?'

'The picturesque doctor's daughter, Miss Manette.'

'*She* pretty?'

'Is she not?'

'No.'

'Why, man alive, she was the admiration of the whole court!'

'Rot the admiration of the whole court! Who made the Old Bailey a judge of beauty? She was a golden-haired doll!'

'Do you know, Sydney,' said Mr. Stryver, looking at him with sharp eyes, and slowly drawing a hand across his florid face; 'do you know, I rather thought, at the time, that you sympathized with the golden-haired doll?'

'Quick to see what happened! If a girl, doll or no doll, swoons within a yard or two of a man's nose, he can see it without a perspective-glass. I pledge you, but I deny the beauty. And now I'll have no more drink; I'll get to bed.'

When his host followed him out on the staircase with a candle, to light him down the stairs, the day was coldly looking in through its grimy windows. When he got out of the house, the air was cold and sad, the dull sky overcast, the river dark and dim, the whole scene like a lifeless desert. And wreaths of dust were spinning round and round before the morning blast, as if the desert sand had risen far away, and the fine spray of it in its advance had begun to overwhelm the city.

Waste forces within him, and a desert all around, this man stood still on his way across a silent terrace, and saw for a moment, lying in the wilderness before him, a mirage of honourable ambition, self-denial, and perseverance. In the fair city of this vision, there were airy galleries from which the loves and graces looked upon him, gardens in which the fruits of life hung ripening, waters of Hope that sparkled in his sight. A moment, and it was gone. Climbing to a high chamber in a well of houses, he threw himself down in his clothes on a neglected bed, and its pillow was wet with wasted tears.

Sadly, sadly, the sun rose; it rose upon no sadder sight than the man of good abilities and good emotions, incapable of their directed exercise, incapable of his own help and his own happiness, sensible of the blight on him, and resigning himself to let it eat him away.

CHAPTER VI

HUNDREDS OF PEOPLE

THE quiet lodgings of Doctor Manette were in a street corner not far from Soho Square. On the afternoon of a certain fine Sunday when the waves of four months had rolled over the trial for treason, and carried it, as to the public interest and memory, far out to sea, Mr. Jarvis Lorry walked along the sunny street from Clerkenwell where he lived, on his way to dine with the Doctor. After several relapses into business absorption, Mr. Lorry had become the Doctor's friend, and the quiet street corner was the sunny part of his life.

On this certain fine Sunday, Mr. Lorry walked towards Soho, early in the afternoon, for three reasons of habit. Firstly, because, on fine Sundays, he often walked out, before dinner, with the Doctor and Lucie, secondly, because, on unfavourable Sundays, he was accustomed to be with them as the family friend, talking, reading, looking out of window, and generally getting through the day; thirdly, because he happened to have his own little shrewd doubts to solve, and knew how the ways of the Doctor's household pointed to that time as a likely time for solving them.

A quainter corner than the corner where the Doctor lived, was not to be found in London. There was no way through it, and the front windows of the Doctor's lodgings commanded a pleasant little vista of street that had a congenial air of retirement on it. There were few buildings then, north of the Oxford Road, and forest trees flourished, and wild flowers grew, and the hawthorn blossomed, in the now vanished fields. As a consequence, country airs circulated in Soho with vigorous freedom, instead of languishing into the parish like stray paupers without a settlement; and there was many a good south wall, not far off, on which the peaches ripened in their season.

The summer light struck into the corner brilliantly in the earlier part of the day; but, when the streets grew hot, the corner was in shadow, though not in shadow so remote but that you could see beyond it into a glare of brightness. It was a cool spot, staid but cheerful, a wonderful place for echoes, and a very harbour from the raging streets.

There ought to have been a tranquil bark in such an anchorage, and there was. The Doctor occupied two floors of a large still house, where several callings purported to be pursued by day, but whereof little was audible any day, and which was shunned by all of them at night. In a building at the back, attainable by a courtyard where a plane-tree rustled its greens leaves, church organs claimed to be made, and silver to be chased, and likewise gold to be beaten by some mysterious giant who had a golden arm starting out of the wall of the front hall—as if he had beaten himself precious, and menaced a similar conversion of all visitors. Very little of these traders, or of a lonely lodger rumoured to live upstairs, or of a dim coach-trimming maker asserted to have a counting-house below, was ever heard or seen. Occasionally, a stray workman putting his coat on, traversed the hall, or a stranger peered about there, or a distant clink was heard across the courtyard, or a thump from the golden giant. These, however, were only the exceptions required to prove the rule that the sparrows in the plane-tree behind the house, and the echoes in the corner before it, had their own way from Sunday morning unto Saturday night.

Doctor Manette received such patients here as his old reputation, and its revival in the floating whispers of his story, brought him. His scientific knowledge, and his vigilance and skill in conducting ingenious experiments, brought him otherwise into moderate request, and he earned as much as he wanted.

These things were within Mr. Jarvis Lorry's knowledge, thoughts, and notice, when he rang the door bell of the tranquil house in the corner, on the fine Sunday afternoon.

'Doctor Manette at home?'

Expected home.

'Miss Lucie at home?'

Expected home.

'Miss Pross at home'

Possibly at home, but of certainty impossible for handmaid to anticipate intentions of Miss Pross, as to admission or denial of the fact.

'As I am at home myself,' said Mr. Lorry, 'I'll go upstairs.'

Although the Doctor's daughter had known nothing of the country of her birth, she appeared to have innately derived from it that ability to make much of little means, which is one of its most useful and most agreeable characteristics. Simple as the furniture was, it was set off by so many little adornments, of no value but for their taste and fancy, that its effect was delightful. The disposition of everything in the rooms, from the largest object to the least; the arrangement of colours, the elegant variety and contrast obtained by thrift in trifles, by delicate hands, clear eyes, and good sense; were at once so pleasant in themselves, and so expressive of their originator, that as Mr. Lorry stood looking about him, the very chairs and tables seemed to ask him, with something of that peculiar expression which he knew so well by this time, whether he approved?

There were three rooms on a floor, and, the doors by which they communicated being put open that the air might pass freely through them all, Mr. Lorry smilingly observant of that fanciful resemblance which he detected all around him, walked from one to another. The first was the best room, and in it were Lucie's birds, and flowers, and books, and desk, and work-table, and box of water-colours; the second was the Doctor's consulting-room, used also as the dining-room; the third, changingly speckled by the rustle of the plane-tree in the yard, was the Doctor's bedroom, and there, in a corner, stood the disused shoemaker's bench and tray of tools, much as it had stood on the fifth floor of the dismal house by the wine shop, in the suburb of Saint Antoine in Paris.

'I wonder,' said Mr. Lorry, pausing in his looking about, 'that he keeps that reminder of his sufferings about him!'

'And why wonder at that?' was the abrupt inquiry that made him start.

It proceeded from Miss Pross, the wild red woman, strong of hand, whose acquaintance he had first made at the Royal George Hotel at Dover, and had since improved.

'I should have thought—' Mr. Lorry began.

'Pooh! You'd have thought!' said Miss Pross; and Mr. Lorry left off.

'How do you do?' inquired the lady then–sharply, and yet as if to express that she bore him no malice.

'I am pretty well, I thank you,' answered Mr. Lorry, with meekness; 'how are you?'

'Nothing to boast of,' said Miss Pross.

'Indeed?'

'Ah! indeed!' said Miss Pross. 'I am very much put out about my Ladybird.'

'Indeed?'

'For gracious sake say something else besides "indeed," or you'll fidget me to death,' said Miss Pross. Whose character (dissociated from stature) was shortness.

'Really, then?' said Mr. Lorry, as an amendment.

'Really, is bad enough,' returned Miss Pross, 'but better. Yes, I am very much put out.'

'May I ask the cause?'

'I don't want dozens of people who are not at all worthy of Ladybird, to come here looking after her,' said Miss Pross.

'*Do* dozens come for that purpose?'

'Hundreds,' said Miss Pross.

It was characteristic of this lady (as of some other people before her time and since) that whenever her original proposition was questioned, she exaggerated it.

'Dear me!' said Mr. Lorry, as the safest remark he could think of.

'I have lived with the darling–or the darling has lived with me, and paid me for it; which she certainly should never have done, you may take your affidavit, if I could have afforded to keep either myself of her for nothing–since she was ten years old. And it's really very hard,' said Miss Pross.

Not seeing with precision what was very hard, Mr. Lorry shook his head; using that important part if himself as a sort of fairy cloak that would fit anything.

'All sorts of people who are not in the least degree worthy of the pet, are always turning up,' said Miss Pross.

'When you began it—'

'*I* began it, Miss Pross?'

'Didn't you? Who brought her father to life?'

'Oh! If that was beginning it—' said Mr. Lorry.

'It wasn't ending it, I suppose? I say, when you began it, it was hard enough; not that I have any fault to find with Doctor Manette, except that he is not worthy of such a daughter, which is no imputation on him, for it was not to be expected that anybody should be, under any circumstances. But it really is doubly and trebly hard to have crowds and multitudes of people turning up after him (I could have forgiven him), to take Ladybird's affections away from me.'

Mr. Lorry knew Miss Pross to be very jealous, but he also knew her by this time to be, beneath the surface of her eccentricity, one of those unselfish creatures–found only among women–who will, for pure love and admiration, bind themselves willing slaves, to youth when they have lost it, to beauty that they never had, to accomplishments that they were never fortunate enough to gain, to bright hopes that never shone upon their own sombre lives. He knew enough of the world to know that there is nothing in it better than the faithful service of the heart; so rendered and so free from any mercenary taint, he had such an exalted respect for it, that in the retributive arrangements made by his own mind–we all make such arrangements, more or less–he stationed Miss Pross much nearer to the lower Angels than many ladies immeasurably better got up both by Nature and Art, who had balances at Tellson's.

'There never was, nor will be, but one man worthy of Ladybird,' said Miss Pross; 'and that was my brother Solomon, if he hadn't made a mistake in life.'

Here again: Mr. Lorry's inquiries into Miss Pross's personal history had established the fact that her brother Solomon was a heartless scoundrel who had stripped her of everything she possessed, as a stake to speculate with, and had abandoned her in her poverty for ever more, with no touch of compunction. Miss Pross's fidelity of belief in Solomon (deducting a mere trifle for this slight mistake) was quite a serious matter with Mr. Lorry, and had its weight in his good opinion of her.

'As we happen to be alone for the moment, and are both people of business,' he said, when they had got back to the drawing-room and had sat down there in friendly relations, let me ask you–does the Doctor, in talking with Lucie, never refer to the shoemaking time, yet?'

'Never.'

'And yet keeps that bench and those tools beside him?'

'Ah!' returned Miss Pross, shaking her head. 'But I don't say he don't refer to it within himself.'

'Do you believe that he thinks of it much?'

'I do,' said Miss Pross.

'Do you imagine—' Mr. Lorry had begun, when Miss Pross took him up short with:

'Never imagine anything. Have no imagination at all.'

'I stand corrected; do you suppose–you go so far as to suppose, sometimes?'

'Now and then,' said Miss Pross.

'Do you suppose,' Mr. Lorry went on, with a laughing twinkle in his bright eye, as it looked kindly at her, 'that Doctor Manette has any theory of his own, preserved through all those years, relative to the cause of his being so oppressed; perhaps, even to the name of his oppressor?'

'I don't suppose anything about it but what Ladybird tells me.'

'And that is—?'

'That she thinks he has.'

'Now don't be angry at my asking all these questions; because I am a mere dull man of business, and you are a woman of business.'

'Dull?' Miss Pross inquired, with placidity.

Rather wishing his modest adjective away, Mr. Lorry replied, 'no, no, no. Surely not. To return to business. Is it not remarkable that Doctor Manette, unquestionably innocent of any crime as we are all well assured he is, should never touch upon that question? I will not say with me, though he had business relations with me many years ago, and we are now intimate; I will say with the fair daughter to whom he is so devotedly attached, and who is so devotedly attached to him? Believe me, Miss Pross, I don't approach the topic with you, out of curiosity, but out of zealous interest.'

'Well! To the best of my understanding, and bad's the best, you'll tell me,' said Miss Pross, softened by the tone of the apology, 'he is afraid of the whole subject.'

'Afraid?'

'It's plain enough, I should think, why he may be. It's a dreadful remembrance. Besides that, his loss of himself grew out of it. Not knowing how he lost himself, or how he recovered himself, he may never feel certain of not losing himself again. That alone wouldn't make the subject pleasant, I should think.'

It was a profounder remark than Mr. Lorry had looked for. 'True,' said he, 'and fearful to reflect upon. Yet, a doubt lurks in my mind, Miss Pross, whether it is good for Doctor Manette to have that suppression always shut up within him. Indeed, it is this doubt and the uneasiness it sometimes causes me that has led me to our present confidence.'

'Can't be helped,' said Miss Pross, shaking hr head. 'Touch that string, and he instantly changes for the worse. Better leave it alone. In short, must leave it alone, like or no like. Sometimes, he gets up in the dead of the night, and will be heard, by us overhead there, walking up and down, walking up and down, in his old prison. She hurries to him, and they go on together, walking up and down, walking up and down, until he is composed. But he never says a word of that true reason of his restlessness, to her, and she finds it best not to hint at it to him. In silence they go walking up and down together, walking up and down together, till her love and company have brought him to himself.'

Notwithstanding Miss Pross's denial of her own imagination, there was a perception of the pain of being monotonously haunted by one sad idea, in her repetition of the phrase, walking up and down, which testified to her possessing such a thing.

The corner had been mentioned as a wonderful corner for echoes; it had begun to echo so resoundingly to the tread of coming feet, that it seemed as though the very mention of that weary pacing to and fro had set it going.

'Here they are!' said Miss Pross, rising to break up the conference; 'and now we shall have hundreds of people pretty soon!'

It was such a curious corner in its acoustical properties, such a peculiar Ear of a place, that as Mr. Lorry stood at the open window, looking for the father and daughter whose steps he heard, he fancied they would never approach. Not only would the echoes die away, as though the steps had gone; but, echoes of other steps that never came would be heard in their stead, and would die away for good when they seemed close at hand. However, father and daughter did at last appear, and Miss Pross was ready at the street door to receive them.

Miss Pross was a pleasant sight, albeit wild, and red, and grim, taking off her darling's bonnet when she came upstairs, and touched it up with the ends of her handkerchief, and blowing the dust off it, and folding her mantle ready for laying by, and smoothing her rich hair with as much pride as she could possibly have taken in her own hair if she had been the vainest and handsomest of women. Her darling was a pleasant sight too, embracing her and thanking her, and protesting against her taking so much trouble for her—which last she only dared to do playfully, or Miss Pross, sorely hurt, would have retired to her own chamber and cried. The Doctor was a pleasant sight too, looking on at them, and telling Miss Pross how she spoilt Lucie, in accents and with eyes that had as much spoiling in them as Miss Pross had, and would have had more if it were possible. Mr. Lorry was a pleasant sight too, beaming at all this in his little wig, and thanking his bachelor stars for having lighted him in his declining years to a Home. But, no Hundreds of people came to see the sights, and Mr. Lorry looked in vain for the fulfillment of Miss Pross's prediction.

Dinner-time, and still no Hundreds of people. In the arrangements of the little household, Miss Pross took charge of the lower regions, and always acquitted herself marvelously. Her dinners, of a very modest quality, were so well cooked and so well served, and so neat in their contrivances, half English and half French, that nothing could be better. Miss Pross's friendship being of the thoroughly practical kind, she had ravaged Soho and the adjacents provinces, in search of improvised French, who, tempted by shillings and half-crowns, would impart culinary mysteries to her. From these decayed sons and daughters of Gaul, she had acquired such wonderful arts, that the woman and girl who formed the staff of domestics regarded her as quiet a Sorceress, or Cinderella's Godmother: who would send out for a fowl, a rabbit, a vegetable or two from the garden, and change them into anything she pleased.

On Sundays, Miss Pross dined at the Doctor's table, but on the other days persisted in taking her meals at unknown periods, either in the lower regions, or in her own room on the second floor—a blue chamber, to which no one but her Ladybird ever gained admittance. On this occasion, Miss Pross, responding to Ladybird's pleasant face and pleasant efforts to please her, unbent exceedingly; so the dinner was very pleasant, too.

It was an oppressive day, and, after dinner, Lucie proposed that the wine should be carried out under the plane-tree, and they should sit there in the air. As everything turned upon her, and revolved about her, they went out under the plane-tree, and she carried the wine down for the special benefit of Mr. Lorry. She had installed herself, some time before, as Mr. Lorry's cup-bearer; and while they sat under the plane-tree, talking, she kept his glass replenished. Mysterious backs and ends of houses peeped at them as they talked, and the plane-tree whispered to them in its own way above their heads.

Still, the Hundreds of people did not present themselves. Mr. Darnay presented himself while they were sitting under the plane-tree, but he was only One.

Doctor Manette received him kindly, and so did Lucie. But, Miss Pross suddenly became afflicted with a twitching in the head and body, and retired into the house. She was not unfrequently the victim of this disorder, and she called it, in familiar conversation, 'a fit of the jerks.'

The Doctor was in his best condition, and looked specially young. The resemblance between him and Lucie was very strong at such times, and as they sat side by side, she leaning on his shoulder, and he resting his arm on the back of her chair, it was very agreeable to trace the likeness.

He had been talking all day, on many subjects, and with unusual vivacity. 'Pray, Doctor Manette,' said Mr. Darnay, as they sat under the plane-tree—and he said it in the natural pursuit of the topic in hand, which happened to be the old buildings of London—'have you seen much of the Tower?'

'Lucie and I have been there; but only casually. We have seen enough of it, to know that it teems with interest; little more.'

'*I* have been there, as you remember,' said Darnay, with a smile, though reddening a little angrily, 'in another character, and not in a character that gives facilities for seeing much of it. They told me a curious thing when I was there.'

'What was that?' Lucie asked.

'In making some alterations, the workmen came upon an old dungeon, which had been, for many years, built up and forgotten. Every stone of its inner wall was covered by inscriptions which had been carved by prisoners—dates, names, complaints, and prayers. Upon a corner stone in an angle of the wall, one prisoner, who seemed to have gone to execution, had cut as his last work, three letter. They were done with some very poor instrument, and hurriedly, with an unsteady hand. At first, they were read as D.I.C.; but, on being more carefully examined, the last letter was found to be G. There was no record or legend of any prisoner with those initials, and many fruitless guesses were made what the name could have been. At length, it was suggested that the letters were not initials, but the complete word, DIG. The floor was examined very carefully under the inscription, and, in the earth beneath a stone, or tile, or some fragment of paving, were found the ashes of a paper, mingled with the ashes of a small leathern case or bag. What the unknown prisoner had written will never be read, but he had written something, and hidden it away to keep it from the jailer.'

'My father,' exclaimed Lucie, 'you are ill!'

He had suddenly started up, with his hand to his head. His manner and his look quite terrified them all.

'No, my dear, not ill. There are large drops of rain falling, and they made me start. We had better go in.'

He recovered himself almost instantly. Rain was really falling in large drops, and he showed the back of his hand with rain-drops on it. But, he said not a single word in reference to the discovery that had been told of, and, as they went into the house, the business eye of Mr. Lorry either detected, or fancied it detected, on his face, as it turned towards Charles Darnay, the same singular look that had been upon it when it turned towards him in the passages of the Court House.

He recovered himself so quickly, however, that Mr. Lorry had doubts of his business eye. The arm of the golden giant in the hall was not more steady than he was, when he stopped under it to remark to them that he was not yet proof against slight surprises (if he ever would be), and that the rain had startled him.

Tea-time, and Miss Pross making tea, with another fit of the jerks upon her, and yet no Hundreds of people. Mr. Carton had lounged in, but he made only Two.

The night was so very sultry, that although they sat with doors and windows open, the overpowered by heat.

When the tea-table was done with, they all moved to one of the windows, and looked out into the heavy twilight. Lucie sat by her father; Darnay sat beside her; Carton leaned against a window. The curtains were long and white, and some of the thunder-gusts that whirled into the corner, caught them up to the ceiling, and waved them like spectral wings.

'The rain-drops are still falling, large, heavy, and few,' said Doctor Manette. 'It comes slowly.'

'It comes surely,' said Carton.

They spoke low, as people watching and waiting mostly do; as people in a dark room, watching and waiting for Lightning, always do.

There was a great hurry in the streets, of people speeding away to get shelter before the storm broke; the wonderful corner for echoes resounded with the echoes of footsteps coming and going, yet not a footstep was there.

'A multitude of people, and yet a solitude!' said Darnay, when they had listened for a while.

'Is it not impressive, Mr. Darnay?' asked Lucie. 'Sometimes, I have sat here of an evening, until I have fancied—but even the shade of a foolish fancy makes me shudder to-night, when all is so black and solemn—'

'Let us shudder too. We may know what it is.'

'It will seem nothing to you. Such whims are only impressive as we originate them, I think; they are not to be communicated. I have sometimes sat alone here of an evening, listening, until I have made the echoes out to be the echoes of all the footsteps that are coming by and by into our lives.'

There is a great crowd coming one day into our lives, if that be so,' Sydney Carton struck in, in his moody way.

The footsteps were incessant, and the hurry of them became more and more rapid. The corner echoed and re-echoed with the tread of feet; some, as it seemed, under the windows; some, as it seemed, in the room; some coming, some going, some breaking off, some stopping altogether; all in the distant streets, and not one within sight.

'Are all these footsteps destined to come to all of us, Miss Manette, or are we to divide them among us?'

'I don't know, Mr. Darnay; I told you it was a foolish fancy, but you asked for it. When I have yielded myself to it, I have been alone, and then I have imagined them the footsteps of the people who are to come into my life, and my father's.'

'I take them into mine!' said Carton. '*I* ask no questions and make no stipulations. There is a great crowd bearing down upon us, Miss Manette, and I see them—by the Lightning.' He added the last words, after there had been a vivid flash which had shown him lounging in the window.

'And I hear them!' he added again, after a peal of thunder. 'Here they come, fast, fierce, and furious!'

It was the rush and roar of rain that he typified, and it stopped him, for no voice could be heard in it. A memorable storm of thunder and lightning broke with that sweep of water, and there was not a moment's interval in crash, and fire, and rain, until after the moon rose at midnight.

The great bell of Saint Paul's was striking One in the cleared air, when Mr. Lorry, escorted by Jerry, high-booted and bearing a lantern, set forth on his return passage to Clerkenwell. There were solitary patches of road on the way between Soho and Clerkenwell, and Mr. Lorry, mindful of footpads, always retained Jerry for this service: though it was usually performed a good two hours earlier.

'What a night it has been! Almost a night, Jerry,' said Mr. Lorry, 'to bring the dead out of their graves.'

'I never see the night, Mr. Carton,' said the man of business. 'Good night, Mr. Darnay. Shall we ever see such a night again, together!'

Perhaps. Perhaps, see the great crowd of people with its rush and roar, bearing down upon them, too.

CHAPTER VII

MONSIEUR THE MARQUIS IN TOWN

MONSEIGNEUR, one of the great lords in power at the Court, held his fortnightly reception in his grand hotel in Paris. Monseigneur was in his inner room, his sanctuary of sanctuaries, the Holiest of Holiest to the crowd of worshippers in the suite of rooms without. Monseigneur was about to take his chocolate. Monseigneur could swallow a great many things with ease, and was by some few sullen minds supposed to be rather rapidly swallowing France; but, his morning's chocolate could not so much as get into the throat of Monseigneur, without the aid of four strong men besides the Cook.

Yes, it took four men, all four ablaze with gorgeous decoration, and the Chief of them unable to exist with fewer than two gold watches in his pocket, emulative of the noble and chaste fashion set by Monseigneur, to conduct the happy chocolate to Monseigneur's lips. One lackey carried the chocolate-pot into the sacred presence; a second, milled and frothed the chocolate with the little instrument he bore for that function; a third, presented the favoured napkin; a fourth (he of the two gold watches), poured the chocolate out. It was impossible for Monseigneur to dispense with one of these attendants on the chocolate and hold his high place under the admiring Heavens. Deep would have been the blot upon his escutcheon if his chocolate had been ignobly waited on by only three men; he must have died of two.

Monseigneur had been out at a little supper last night, where the Comedy and the Grand Opera were charmingly represented. Monseigneur was out at a little supper most nights, with fascinating company. So polite and so impressible was Monseigneur, that the Comedy and the Grand Opera had far more influence with him in the tiresome articles of state affairs and state secrets, than the needs of all France. A happy circumstance for France, as the like always is for all countries similarly favoured!–always was for

England (by way of example), in the regretted days of the mery Stuart who sold it.

Monseigneur had one truly noble idea of general public business, which was, to let everything go on in its own way; of particular public business, Monseigneur had the other truly noble idea that it must all go his way–tend to his own power and pocket. Of his pleasures, general and particular, Monseigneur had the other truly noble idea, that the world was made for them. The text of his order (altered from the original by only a pronoun, which is not much) ran: 'The earth and the fullness thereof are mine, smith Monseigneur.'

Yet, Monseigneur had slowly found that vulgar embarrassments crept into his affairs, both private and public; and he had, as to both classes of affairs, allied himself perforce with a Farmer-General. As to finances public, because Monseigneur could not make anything at all of them, and must consequently let them out to somebody who could; as to finances private, because Farmer-Generals were rich, and Monseigneur, after generations of great luxury and expense, was growing poor. Hence Monseigneur had taken his sister from a convent, while there was yet time to ward off the impending veil, the cheapest garment she could wear, and had bestowed her as a prize upon a very rich Farmer-General, poor in family. Which Farmer-General, carrying an appropriate cane with a golden apple on the top of it, was now among the company in the outer rooms, much prostrated before by mankind–always expecting superior mankind of the blood of Monseigneur, who, his own wife included, looked down upon him with the loftiest contempt.

A sumptuous man was the Farmer-General. Thirty horses stood in his stables, twenty-four male domestics sat in his halls, six body-women waited on his wife. As one who pretended to do nothing but plunder and forage where he could, the Farmer-General–howsoever his matrimonial relations conduced to social morality–was at least the greatest reality among the personages who attended at the hotel of Monseigneur that day.

For, the rooms, though a beautiful scene to look at, and adorned with every device of decoration that the taste and skill of the time could achieve, were, in truth, not a sound business; considered with any reference to the scarecrows in the rags and night-caps elsewhere (and not so far off, either, but that the watching towers of Notre Dame, almost equidistant, from the two extremes, could see them both), they would have been an exceedingly uncomfortable business–if that could have been anybody's business, at the house of Monseigneur. Military officers destitute of military knowledge; naval officers with no idea of a ship; civil officers without a notion of affairs; brazen ecclesiastics, of the worst world worldly, with sensual eyes, loose, tongues, and looser lives; all totally unfit for their several callings, all lying horribly in pretending to belong to them, but all nearly or remotely of the order of Monseigneur, and therefore foisted on all public employments from which anything was to be got, these were to be told off by the score and the score. People not immediately connected with Monseigneur of the State, yet equally unconnected with anything that was real, or by lives passed in travelling by any straight road to any true earthly end, were no less abundant. Doctors who made great fortunes out of dainty remedies for imaginary disorders that never existed, smiled upon their courtly patients in the ante-chambers of Monseigneur. Projectors who had discovered every kind of remedy for the little evils with which the state was touched, except the remedy of setting to work in earnest to root out a single sin, poured their distracting babble into any years they could lay hold of, at the reception of Monseigneur. Unbelieving Philosophers who were remodelling the world with words, and making card-towers of Babel to scale the skies with, talked with Unbelieving Chemists who had an eye on the transmutation of metals, at this wonderful gathering accumulated by Monseigneur. Exquisite gentlemen of the finest breeding–which was at that remarkable time–and had been since–to be known by its fruits of indifference to every natural subject of human interest, were in the most exemplary state of exhaustion, at the hotel of Monseigneur. Such homes had these various notabilities left behind them in the fine world of Paris, that the spies among the assembled devotees of Monseigneur–forming a goodly half of the polite company–would have found it hard to discover among the angels of that sphere one solitary wife, who, in her manners and appearance, owned to being a Mother. Indeed, except for the mere act of bringing a troublesome creature into this world–which does not go far towards the realization of the name of mother–there was no such thing known to the fashion. Peasant women kept the unfashionable babies close, and brought them up, and charming grandmammas of sixty dressed and supped as at twenty.

The leprosy of unreality disfigured every human creature in attendance upon Monseigneur. In the outermost room were half a dozen exceptional people who had had, for a few years, some vague misgiving in them that things in general were going rather wrong. As a promising way of setting them right, half of the half-dozen had become members of a fantastic sect of Convulsionists, and were even then considering within themselves whether they should foam, rage, roar, and turn cataleptic on the spot–thereby setting up a highly intelligible finger-post to the Future, for Monseigneur's guidance. Besides these Devishes, were other three who had rushed into another sect, which mended matters with a jargon about 'the Centre of Truth': holding that Man had got out of the Centre of Truth–which did not need much demonstration–but had not got out of the Circumference, and that he was to be kept from flying out of the Circumference, and was even to be shoved back into the Centre, by fasting and seeing of spirits. Among these, accordingly, much discourising with spirits went on–and it did a world of good which never became manifest.

But, the comfort was, that all the company at the grand hotel of Monseigneur were perfectly dressed. If the Day of Judgment had only been ascertained to be a dress day, everybody there would have been eternally correct. Such frizzling and powdering and sticking up of hair, such delicate complexions artificially preserved and mended, such gallant swords to look at, and such delicate honour to the sense of smell, would surely keep any-thing going, for ever and ever. The exquisite gentlemen of the finest breeding wore little pendant trinkets that chinked as they languidly moved; these golden fetters rang like precious little bells; and what with that ringing, and with the rustle of silk and brocade and fine linen, there was a flutter in the air that fanned Saint Antoine and his devouring hunger far away.

Dress was the one unfailing talisman and charm used for keeping all things in their places. Everybody was dressed for a Fancy Ball that was never to leave off. From the Palace of the Tuileries, through Monseigneur and the whole Court, through the Chambers, the Tribunals of Justice, and all society (except the scarecrows), the Fancy Ball descended to the Common Executioner: who, in pursuance of the charm, was required to officiate 'frizzled, powdered, in a gold-laced coat, pumps, and white silk stockings.' At the gallows and the wheel—the axe was a rarity—Monsieur Paris, as it was the episcopal mode among his brother Professors of the provinces, Monsieur Orleans, and the rest, to call him, presided in this dainty dress. And who among the company at Monseigneur's reception in that seventeen hundred and eightieth year of our Lord, could possibly doubt, that a system rooted in a frizzled hangman, powdered, gold-laced, pumped, and white-silk stockinged, would see the very stars out!

Monseigneur having eased his four men of their burdens and taken his chocolate, caused the doors of the Holiest of Holiests to be thrown open, and issued forth. Then, what submission, what cringing and fawn-ing, what servility, what abject humiliation! As to bowing down in body and spirit, nothing in that way was left for Heaven—which may have been one among other reasons why the worshippers of Monseigneur never troubled it.

Bestowing a word of promise here and a smile there, a whisper on one happy slave and wave of the hand on another, Monseigneur affably passed through his rooms to the remote region of the Circumference of Truth. There, Monseigneur turned, and came back again, and so in due course of time got himself shut up in his sanctuary by the chocolate sprites, and was seen no more.

The show being over, the flutter in the air became quite a little storm, and the precious little bells went ringing downstairs. There was soon but one person left of all the crowd, and he, with his hat under his arm and his snuff-box in his and, slowly passed among the mirrors on his way out.

'I devote you,' said this person, stopping at the last door on his way, turning in the direction of the sanctuary, 'to the Devil!'

With that, he shook he snuff from his fingers as if he had shaken the dust from his feet, and quietly walked downstairs.

He was a man of about sixty, handsomely dressed, haughty in man-ner, and with a face like a fine mask. A face of a transparent paleness; every feature in it clearly defined; one set expression on it. The nose, beautifully formed otherwise, was very slightly pinched at the top of each nostril. In those two compressions, or dints, the only little change that the face ever showed, resided. They persisted in changing colour sometimes, and they would be occasionally dilated and contracted by something like a faint pulsation: then, they gave a look of treachery, and cruelty, to the whole countenance. Examined with attention, its capacity of helping such a look was to be found in the line of the mouth, and the lines of the orbits of the eyes, being much too horizontal and thin; still, in the effect the face made, it was a handsome face, and a remarkable one.

Its owner went downstairs into the courtyard, got into his carriage, and drove away. Not many people had talked with him at the reception; he had stood in a little space apart, and Monseigneur might have been warmer in his manner. It appeared under the circumstances, rather agreeable to him to see the common people dispersed before his horses, and often barely escaping from being run down. His man drove as if he were charging an enemy, and the furious recklessness of the man brought no check into the face, or to the lips, of the master. The complaint had sometimes made itself audible, even in that deaf city and dumb age, that, in the narrow streets without footways, the fierce patrician custom of hard driving endangered and maimed the mere vulgar in a barbarous manner. But few cared enough for that to think of it a second time, and, in this matter, as in all others, the common wretches were left to get out of their difficulties as they could.

With a wild rattle and clatter, and an inhuman abandonment of consideration not easy to be understood in these days, the carriage dashed through streets and swept round corners, with women screaming before it, and men clutching each other and clutching children out of its way. At last, swooping at a street corner by a fountain, one of its wheels came to a sickening little jolt, and there was a loud cry from a number of voice, and the horses reared and plunged.

But for the latter inconvenience, the carriage probably would not have stopped; carriages were often known to drive on, and leave their wounded behind, and why not? But he frightened valet had got down in a hurry, and there were twenty hands at the horses' bridles.

'What has gone wrong?' said Monsieur, calmly looking out.

A tall man in a night-cap had caught up a bundle from among the feet of the horses, and had laid it on the basement of the fountain, and was down in the mud and wet, howling over it like a wild animal.

'Pardon, Monsieur the Marquis!' said a ragged and submissive man, 'it is a child.'

'Why does he make that abominable noise? Is it his child?'

'Excuse me, Monsieur the Marquis—it is a pity—yes.'

The fountain was a little removed; for the street opened, where it was, into a space some ten or twelve yards square. As the tall man suddenly got up from the ground, and came running at the carriage, Monsieur the Marquis clapped his hand for an instant on his sword-hilt.

'Killed!' shrieked the man in wild desperation extending both arms at their length above his head, and staring at him. 'Dead!'

The people closed round, and looked at Monsieur the Marquis. There was nothing revealed by the many eyes that looked at him but watchfulness and eagerness; there was no visible menacing or anger. Neither did the people say anything; after the first cry, they had been silent, and had spoken, was flat and tame in its extreme submission. Monsieur the Marquis ran his eyes over them all, as if they had been mere rats come out of their holes.

He took out his purse.

'It is extraordinary to me,' said he, 'that you people cannot take care of yourselves and your children. One or the other of you is for ever in the way. How do I know what injury you have done my horses. See! Give him that.'

He threw out a gold coin for the valet to pick up, and all the heads craned forward that all the eyes might look down at it as it fell. The tall man called out again with a most unearthly cry, 'Dead!'

He was arrested by the quick arrival of another man, for whom the rest made way. On seeing him, the miserable creature fell upon his shoulder, sobbing and crying, and pointing to the fountain, where some women were stooping over the motionless bundle, and moving gently about it. They were as silent, however, as the men.

'I know all, I know all,' said the last comer. 'Be a brave man, my Gaspard! It is better for the poor little plaything to die so, than to live. It has died in a moment without pain. Could it have lived an hour as happily?'

'You are a philosopher, you there,' said the Marquis, smiling. 'How do they call you?'

'They call me Defarge.'

'Of what trade?'

'Monsieur de Marquis, vendor of wine.'

'Pick up that, philosopher and vendor of wine,' said the Marquis, throwing him another gold coin, 'and spent it as you will. The horses there; are they right?'

Without deigning to look at the assemblage a second time, Monsieur de Marquis leaned back in his seat, and was just being driven away with the air of a gentleman who had accidentally broken some common thing, and had paid for it, and could afford to pay for it; when his ease was suddenly disturbed by a coin flying into his carriage, and ringing on its floor.

'Hold!' said Monsieur de Marquis. 'Hold the horses! Who threw that?'

He looked to the spot where Defarge the vendor of wine had stood, a moment before; but the wretched father was grovelling on his face on the pavement in that spot, and the figure that stood beside him was the figure of a dark stout woman, knitting.

'You dogs,' said the Marquis, but smoothy, and with an unchanged front, except as to the spots on his nose: 'I would ride over any of you're very willingly, and exterminate you from the earth. If I knew which rascal threw at the carriage, and if that brigand were sufficiently near it, he should be crushed under the wheels.'

So cowed was their condition, and so long and hard their experience of what such a man could do them, within the law and beyond it, that not a voice, or a hand, or even an eye was raised. Among the men, not one. But the woman who stood knitting looked up steadily, and looked the Marquis in the face. It was not for his dignity to notice it; his contemptuous eyes passed over her, and over all the other rats; and he leaned back in his seat again, and gave the word, 'Go on!'

He was driven on, and the carriages came whirling by in quick succession; the Minister, the State-Projector, the Farmer-General, the Doctor, the Lawyer, the Ecclesiastic, the Grand Opera, the Comedy, the whole Fancy Ball in a bright continuous flow, came whirling by. The rats had crept out of their holes to look on, and they remained looking on four hours; soldiers and police often passing between them and the spectacle, and making a barrier behind which they slunk, and through which they peeped. The father had long ago taken up his bundle and hidden himself away with it, when the women who had tended the bundle while it lay on the base of the fountain, sat there watching the running of the water and the rolling of the Fancy Ball–when the one woman who had stood conspicuous, knitting, still knitted on with the steadfastness of Fate. The water of the fountain ran, the swift river ran, the day ran into evening, so much life in the city ran into death according to rule, time and tide waited for no man, the rats were sleeping close together in their dark holes again, the Fancy Ball was lighted up at supper, all things ran their course.

CHAPTER VIII

MONSIEUR THE MARQUIS IN THE COUNTRY

A BEAUTIFUL landscape, with the corn bright in it, but not abundant. Patches of poor rye where corn should have been, patches of poor peas and beans, patches of most coarse vegetable substitutes for wheat. On inanimate nature, as on the men and women who cultivated it, a prevalent tendency towards an appearance of vegetating unwillingly–a dejected disposition to give up, and wither away.

Monsieur de Marquis in his travelling carriage (which might have been lighter), conducted by four post-horses and two postilions, fagged up a steep hill. A blush on the countenance of Monsieur de Marquis was no impeachment of his high breeding; it was not from within; it was occasioned by an external circumstance beyond his control–the setting sun.

The sunset struck so brilliantly into the travelling carriage when it gained the hilltop, that its occupant was steeped in crimson. 'It will die out,' said Monsieur de Marquis, glancing at his hands, 'directly.'

In effect, the sun was so low that it dipped at the moment. When the heavy drag had been adjusted to the wheel, and the carriage slid downhill, with a cinderous smell, in a cloud of dust, the red glow departed quickly; the sun and the Marquis going down together, there was no glow left when the drag was taken off.

But, there remained a broken country, bold and open, a little village at the bottom of the hill, a broad sweep and rise beyond it, a church tower, a windmill, a forest for the chase, and a crag with a fortress on it used as a prison. Round upon all these darkening objects as the night drew on, the Marquis looked, with the air of one who was coming near home.

The village had its own poor street, with its poor brewery, poor tannery, poor tavern, poor stable yard for relays of post-horses, poor fountain, all usual poor appointments. It had its poor people too. All its people were poor, and many of them were sitting at their doors, shredding spare onions and the like for supper, while many were at the fountain, washing leaves, and grasses, and any such small yieldings of the earth that could be eaten. Expressive signs of what made them poor, were not wanting; the tax for the state, the tax for the church, the tax for the lord, tax local and tax general, were to be paid here and to be paid there, according to solemn inscription in the little village, until the wonder was, that there was any village left unswallowed.

Few children were to be seen, and no dogs. As to the men and women, their choice on earth was stated in the prospect–Life on the lowest terms that could sustain it, down in the little village under the mill; or captivity and Death in the dominant prison on the crag.

Heralded by a courier in advance, and by the cracking of his postilion's whips, which twined snake-like about their heads in the evening air, as if he came attended by the Furies, Monsieur de Marquis drew up in his travelling carriage at the posting-house gate. It was hard by the fountain, and the peasants suspended their operations to look at him. He looked at them, and saw in them, without knowing it, the slow sure filing down of misery-worn faces and figure, that was to make the meagerness of Frenchmen and English superstition which should survive the truth through the best part of a hundred years.

Monsieur de Marquis cast his eyes over the submissive faces that drooped before him, as the like of himself had drooped before Monseigneur of the Court–only the difference was, that these faces drooped merely to suffer and not to propitiate–when a grizzled member of the roads joined the group.

'Bring me hither that fellow!' said the Marquis to the courier.

The fellow was brought, cap in hand, and the other fellows closed round to look and listen, in the manner of the people at the Paris fountain.

'I passed you on the road?'

'Monseigneur, it is true. I had the honour of being passed on the road.'

'Coming up the hill, and at the top of the hill, both?'

'Monseigneur, it is true.'

'What did you look at so fixedly?'

'Monseigneur, I looked at the man.'

He stooped a little, and with his tattered blue cap pointed under the carriage. All his fellows stooped to look under the carriage.

'What man, pig? And why look there?'

'Pardon, Monseigneur; he swung by the chain of the shoe–the drag.'

'Who?' demanded the traveller.

'Monseigneur, the man.'

'May the Devil carry away these idiots! How do you call the man? You know all the men of this part of the country. Who was he?'

'Your clemency, Monseigneur! He was not of this part of the country. Of all the days of my life, I never saw him.'

'Swinging by the chain? To be suffocated?'

'With your gracious permission, that was the wonder of it, Monseigneur. His head hanging over–like this!'

He turned himself sideways to the carriage, and leaned back, with his face thrown up to the sky, and his head hanging down; the recovered himself, fumbled with his cap, and made a bow.

'What was he like?'

'Monseigneur, he was whiter than the miller. All covered with dust, white as a spectre, tall as a spectre!'

The picture produced an immense sensation notes with other eyes, looked at Monsieur de Marquis. Perhaps, to observe whether he had any spectre on his conscience.

'Truly, you did well,' said the Marquis, felicitously sensible that such vermin were not to ruffle him, 'to see a thief accompanying my carriage, and not open that great mouth of yours. Bah! Put him aside, Monsieur Gabelle!'

Monsieur Gabelle was the Postmaster, and some other taxing functionary united; he had come out with great obsequiousness to assist at this examination, and had held the examined by the drapery of his arm in an official manner.

'Bah! Go aside!' said Monsieur Gabelle.

'Lay hands on this stranger if he seeks to lodge in your village to-night, and be sure that his business is honest, Gabelle.'

'Monseigneur, I am flattered to devote myself to your orders.'

'Did he run away, fellow?–Where is that Accursed?'

The accursed was already under the carriage with some half-dozen particular friends, pointing out the chain with his blue cap. Some half-dozen other particular friends promptly hauled him out, and presented him breathless to Monsieur de Marquis.

'Did the man run away, Dolt, when we stopped fort he drag?'

'Monseigneur, he precipitated himself over the hillside, head first, as a person plunges into the river.'

'See to it, Gabelle. Go on!'

The half-dozen who were peering at the chain were still among the wheels, like the sheep; the wheels turned so suddenly that they were lucky to save their skins and bones; they had very little else to save, or they might not have been so fortunate.

The burst with which the carriage started out of the village and up the rise beyond, was soon checked by the steepness of the hill. Gradually, it subsided to a foot pace, swinging and lumbering upward among the many sweet scents of a summer night. The postilions, with a thousand gossamer gnats circling about them in lieu of the Furies, quietly mended the points to the lashes of their whips; the valet walked by the horses; the courier was audible, trotting on ahead into the dim distance.

At the steepest point of the hill there was a little burial-ground, with a Cross and a new large figure of Our Saviour on it; it was a poor figure in wood, done by some inexperienced rustic carver, but he had studied the figure from the life–his own life, maybe–for it was dreadfully spare and thin.

To this distressful emblem of a great distress that had long been growing worse, and was not at its worst, a woman was kneeling. She turned her head as the carriage came up to her, rose quickly, and presented herself at the carriage door.

'It is you, Monseigneur! Monseigneur, a petition.'

With an exclamation of impatience, but with his unchangeable face, Monseigneur looked out.

'How, then! What is it? Always petitions!'

'Monseigneur. For the love of the great God! My husband, the forester.'

'What of your husband, the forester? Always the same with you people. He cannot pay something?'

'He has paid all, Monseigneur. He is dead.'

'Well! He is quiet. Can I restore him to you?'

'Alas, no, Monseigneur! But he lies yonder, under a little heap of poor grass.'

'Again, well?'

She looked an old woman, but was young. Her manner was one of passionate grief; by turns she clasped her veinous and knotted hands together with wild energy, and laid one of them on the carriage door–tenderly, caressingly, as if it had been a human breast, and could be expected to feel the appealing touch.

'Monseigneur, hear me! Monseigneur, hear my petition! My husband died of want; so many die of want; so many more will die of want.'

'Again, well? Can I feed them?'

'Monseigneur, the good God knows; but I don't ask it. My petition is, that a morsel of stone or wood, with my husband's name, may be placed over him to show where he lies. Otherwise, the place will be quickly forgotten, it will never be found when I am dead of the same malady, I shall be laid under some other heap of poor grass. Monseigneur, there are so many, they increase so fast, there is so much want. Monseigneur! Monseigneur!'

The valet had put her away from the door, the carriage had broken into a brisk trot, the postilions had quickened the pace, she was left far behind, and Monseigneur, again escorted by the Furies, was rapidly diminishing the league or two of distance that remained between him and his château.

The sweet scents of the summer night rose all around him, and rose, as the rain falls, impartially, on the dusty ragged, and toil-worn group at the fountain not far away; to whom the mender of roads, with the aid of the blue cap without which he was nothing, still enlarged upon his man like a spectre, as long as they could bear it. By degrees, as they could bear no more, they dropped off one by one, and lights twinkled in little casements; which lights, as the casements darkened, and more stars came out, seemed to have shot up into the sky instead of having been extinguished.

The shadow of a large high-roofed house, and of many overhanging trees, was upon Monsieur the Marquis by that time; and the shadow was exchanged for the light of a flambeau, as his carriage stopped, and the great door of his château was opened to him.

'Monsieur Charles, whom I expect; is he arrived from England?'

'Monseigneur, not yet.'

CHAPTER IX

THE GORGON'S HEAD

IT was a heavy mass of building, that château of Monsieur the Marquis, with a large stone courtyard before it, and two stone sweeps of staircase meeting in a stone terrace before the principal door. A stony business altogether, with heavy stone balustrades, and stone urns, and stone flowers, and stone face of men, and stone heads of lions, in all directions. As if the Gorgon's head had surveyed it, when it was finished, two centuries ago.

Up the broad flight of shallow steps, Monsieur the Marquis, flambeau preceded, went from his carriage, sufficiently disturbing the darkness to elicit loud remonstrance from an owl in the roof of the great pile of stable building away among the trees. All else was so quiet, that the flambeau carried up the steps, and the other flambeau held at the great door, burnt as if they were in a close room of state, instead of being in the open night air. Other sound than the owl's voice there was none, save the falling of the fountain into its stone basin; for, it was one of those dark nights that hold their breath by the hour together, and then heave a long low sigh, and hold their breath again.

The great door clanged behind him, and Monsieur the Marquis crossed a hall grim with certain old boar-spears, swords, and knives of the chase; grimmer with certain heavy riding-rods and riding-whips, of which many a peasant gone to his benefactor Death, had left the weight when his lord was angry.

Avoiding the larger rooms, which were dark and made fast for the night, Monsieur the Marquis, with his flambeau-bearer going on before, went up the staircase to a door in a corridor. This thrown open, admitted him to his own private apartment of three rooms: his bed-chamber and two others. High vaulted rooms with cool uncarpeted floors, great dogs upon the hearths for the burning of wood in winter-time, and all luxuries befitting the state of a marquis in a luxurious age and country. The fashion of the last

Louis but one, of the line that was never to break—the fourteenth Louis—was conspicuous in their rich furniture; but, it was diversified by many objects that were illustrations of old pages in the history of France.

A supper-table was laid for two, in the third of the rooms; a round room, in one of the château's four extinguisher-topped towers. A small lofty room, with its window wide open, and the wooden jalousie–blinds closed, so that the dark night only showed in slight horizontal lines of black, alternating with their broad lines of stone colour.

'My nephew,' said the Marquis, glancing at the supper preparation; 'they said he was not arrived.'

Nor was he; but, he had been expected with Monseigneur.

'Ah! It is not probable he will arrive to-night; nevertheless, leave the table as it is. I shall be ready in a quarter of an hour.'

In a quarter of an hour Monseigneur was ready, and sat down alone to his sumptuous and choice supper. His chair was opposite to the window, and he had taken his soup, and was raising his glass of Bordeaux to his lips, when he put it down.

'What is that?' he calmly asked, looking with attention at the horizontal lines of black and shone colour.

'Monseigneur! That?'

'Outside the blinds. Open the blinds.'

It was done.

'Well.'

'Monseigneur, it is nothing. The trees and the night are all that are here.'

The servant who spoke, had thrown the blinds wide, had looked out into the vacant darkness, and stood, with that blank behind him, looking round for instructions.

'Good,' said the imperturbable master. 'Close them again.'

That was done too, and the Marquis went on with his supper. He was half-way through it, when he again stopped with his glass in his hand, hearing the sound of wheels. It came on briskly, and came up to the front of the château.

'Ask who is arrived.'

It was the nephew of Monseigneur. He had been some few leagues behind Monseigneur, early in the afternoon. He had disminished the distance rapidly, but no so rapidly as to come up with Monseigneur on the road. He had heard of Monseigneur, at the posting-houses, as being before him.

He was to be told (said Monseigneur) that supper awaited him then and there, and that he was prayed to come to it. In a little while he came. He had been known in England as Charles Darnay.

Monseigneur received him in a courtly manner, but they did not shake hands.

'You left Paris yesterday, sir?' he said to Monseigneur, as he took his seat at table.

'Yesterday. And you?'

'I come direct.'

'From London?'

'Yes.'

'You have been a long time coming,' said the Marquis, with a smile.

'On the contrary; I come direct.'

'Pardon me! I mean, not a long time on the journey; a long time intending the journey.'

'I have been detained by'–the nephew stopped a moment in his answer–'various business.'

'Without doubt,' said the polished uncle.

So long as a servant was present, no other words passed between them. When coffee had been served and they were alone together, the nephew, looking at the uncle and meeting the eyes of the face that was like a fine mask, opened a conversation.

'I have come back, sir, as you anticipate, pursuing the object that took me away. It carried me into great and unexpected peril; but it is a sacred object, and if it had carried me to death I hope it would have sustained me.'

'Not to death,' said the uncle; 'it is not necessary to say, to death.'

'I doubt, sir,' returned the nephew, 'whether, if it had carried me to the utmost brink of death, you would have cared to stop me there.'

The deepened marks in the nose, and the lengthening of the fine straight lines in the cruel face, looked ominous as to that; the uncle made a graceful gesture of protest, which was so clearly a slight form of good breeding that it was not reassuring.'

'Indeed, sir,' pursued the nephew, 'for anything I know, you may have expressly worked to give a more suspicious appearance to the suspicious circumstances that surrounded me.'

'No, no, no,' said the uncle, pleasantly.

'But, however that may be,' resumed the nephew, glancing at him with deep distrust, 'I know that your diplomacy would stop me by any means, and would know no scruples as to means.'

'My friend, I told you so,' said the uncle, with a fine pulsation in the two marks. 'Do me the favour to recall that I told you so, long ago.'

'I recall it.'

'Thank you,' said the Marquis–very sweetly indeed.

His tone lingered in the air, almost like the tone of a musical instrument.

'In effect, sir,' pursued the nephew, 'I believe it to be at once your bad fortune, and my good fortune, that had kept me out of prison in France here.'

'I do not quite understand,' returned the uncle, sipping his coffee. 'Dare I ask you to explain?'

'I believe that if you were not in disgrace with the court, and had not been overshadowed by that cloud for years past, a letter *de cachet* would have sent me to some fortress indefinitely.'

'It is possible,' said the uncle, with great calmness. 'For the honour of the family, I could even resolve to incommode you to that extent. Pray excuse me!'

'I perceive that, happily for me, the Reception of the day before yesterday was, as usual, a cold one,' observed the nephew.

'I would not say happily, my friend,' returned the uncle, with refined politeness; 'I would not be sure of that. A good opportunity for consideration, surrounded by the advantages of solitude, might influence your destiny to far greater advantage than you influence it for yourself. But it is useless to discuss the question. I am, as you say, at a disadvantage. These little instruments of correction, these gentle aids to the power and honour of families, these slight favours that might so incommode you, are only to be obtained now by interest and importunity. They are sought by so many, and they are granted (comparatively) to so few! It used not to be so, but France in all such things is changed for the worse. Our not remote ancestors held the right of life and death over the surrounding vulgar. From this room, many such dogs have been taken out to be hanged; in the next room (my bedroom), one fellow, to our knowledge, was poniarded on the spot for professing some insolent delicacy respecting his daughter–*his* daughter? We have lost many privileges; a new philosophy has become the mode; and the assertion of our station, in these days, might (I do not go so far as to say would, but might) cause us real inconvenience. All very bad, very bad!'

The Marquis took a gentle little pinch of snuff, and shook his head; as elegantly despondent as he could becomingly regeneration.

'We have so asserted our station, both in the old time and in the modern time also,' said the nephew, gloomily, name in France.'

'Let us hope so,' said the uncle. 'Detestation of the high is the involuntary homage of the low.'

'There is not,' pursued the nephew, in his former tone, 'a face I can look at, in all this country round about us, which looks at me with any deference on it but the dark deference of fear and slavery.'

'A compliment,' said the Marquis, 'to the grandeur of the family, merited by the manner in which the family has sustained its grandeur. Hah!' And he took another gentle little pinch of snuff, and lightly crossed his legs.

But, when his nephew, leaning an elbow on the table, covered his eyes thoughtfully and dejectedly with his hand, the fine mask looked at him sideways with a stronger concentration of keenness, closeness, and dislike, than was comfortable with its wearer's assumption of indifference.

'Repression is the only lasting philosophy. The dark deference of fear and slavery, my friend,' observed the Marquis, 'will keep the dogs obedient to the whip, as long as this roof'–looking up to it–'shuts out the sky.'

That might not be so long as the Marquis supposed. If a picture of the château as it was to be a very few years hence, could have been shown to him that night, he might have been at a loss to claim his own from the ghastly, fire-charred, plunder-wrecked ruins. As for the roof he vaunted, he might have found *that* shutting out the sky in a new way–to wit, for ever, from the eyes of the bosies into which its lead was fired, out of the barrels of a hundred thousand muskets.

'Meanwhile,' said the Marquis, 'I will preserve the honour and repose of the family, if you will not. But you must be fatigued. Shall we terminate our conference for the night?'

'A moment more.'

'An hour, if you please.'

'Sir,' said the nephew, 'we have done wrong, and are reaping the fruits of wrong.'

'*We* have done wrong? repeated the Marquis, with an inquiring smile, and delicately pointing, first to his nephew, then to himself.

'Our family; our honourable family, whose honour is of so much account to both of us, in such different ways. Even in my father's time, we did a world of wrong, injuring every human creature who came between us and our pleasure, whatever it was. Why need I speak of my father's time, when it is equally yours? Can I separate my father's twin-brother, joint inheritor, and next successor, from himself?'

'Death has done that!' said the Marquis.

'And has left me,' answered the nephew, 'bound to a system that is frightful to me, responsible for it, but powerless in it; seeking to execute the last request of my dear mother's lips, and obey the last look of my dear mother's eyes, which implored me to have mercy and to redress; and tortured by seeking assistance and power in vain.'

'Seeking them from me, my nephew,' said the Marquis, touching him on the breast with his forefinger–they were now standing by the hearth–'you will for ever seek them in vain, be assured.'

Every fine straight line in the clear whiteness of his face, was cruelly, craftily, and closely compressed, while he stood looking quietly at his nephew, with his snuff-box in his hand. Once again he touched him on the breast, as though his finger were the fine point of a small sword, with which, in delicate finesse, he ran him through the body, and said, in delicate finesse, he ran him through the body, and said,

'My friend, I will die, perpetuating the system under which I have lived.'

When he had said it, he took a culminating pinch of snuff, and put his box in his pocket.

'Better to be a rational creature,' he added then, after ringing a small bell on the table, 'and accept your natural destiny. But you are lost, Monsieur Charles, I see.'

'This property and France are lost to me,' said the nephew, sadly; 'I renounce them.'

'Are they both yours to renounce? France may be, but is the property? It is scarcely worth mentioning; but, is it yet?'

'I had no intention, in the words I used, to claim it yet. If it passed to me from you, to-morrow—'

'Which I have the vanity to hope is not probable.'

'–or twenty years hence—'

'You do me too much honour,' said the Marquis; 'still I prefer that supposition.'

'–I would abandon it, and live otherwise and elsewhere. It is little to relinquish. What is it but a wilderness of misery and ruin!'

'Hah!' said the Marquis, glancing round the luxurious room.

'To the eye it is fair enough, here; but seen in its integrity, under the sky, and by the daylight, it is crumbling tower of waste, mismanagement, extortion, debt, mortgage, oppression, hunger, nakedness, and sufferings.'

'Hah!' said the Marquis again, in a well-satisfied manner.

'If it ever becomes mine, it shall be put into some hands better qualified to free it slowly (if such a thing is possible) from the weight that drags it down, so that the miserable people who cannot leave it and who have been long wrung to the last point of endurance, may, in another generation, suffer less; but it is not for me. There is a curse on it, and on all this land.'

'And you?' said the uncle. 'Forgive my curiosity; do you, under your new philosophy, graciously intend to live?'

'I must do, to live, what others of my countrymen, even with nobility at their backs, may have to do some day–work.'

'In England, for example?'

'Yes. The family honour, sir, is safe from me in this country. The family name can suffer from me in no other, for I bear it in no other.'

The ringing of the bell had caused the adjoining bedchamber to be lighted. It now shone brightly, through the door of communication. The Marquis looked that way, and listened for the retreating step of his valet.

'England is very attractive to you, seeing how indifferently you have prospered there,' he observed then, turning his calm face to his nephew with a smile.

'I have already said, that for my prospering there, I am sensible I may be indebted to you, sir. For the rest, it is my refuge.'

'They say, those boastful English, that it is the refuge of many. You know a compatriot who has found a refuge there? A Doctor?'

'Yes.'

'With a daughter?'

'Yes.'

'Yes,' said the Marquis. 'You are fatigued. Good night!'

As he bent his head in his most courtly manner, there was secrecy in his smiling face, and he conveyed an air of mystery to those words, which struck the eyes and ears of his nephew forcibly. At the same time, the thin straight lines of the setting of the eyes, and the thin straight lips, and the markings in the nose, curved with a sarcasm that looked handsomely diabolic.

'Yes,' repeated the Marquis. 'A doctor with a daughter. Yes. So commences the new philosophy! You are fatigued. Good night!'

It would have been of as much avail to interrogate any stone face outside the château as to interrogate that face of his. The nephew looked at him, in vain, in passing on to the door.

'Good night!' said the uncle. 'I look to the pleasure of seeing you again in the morning. Good repose! Light Monsieur my nephew to his chamber there!–And burn Monsieur my nephew in his bed, if you will,' he added to himself, before he rang his little bell again, and summoned his valet to his own bedroom.

The valet come and gone Monsieur the Marquis walked to and fro in his loose chamber-robe, to prepare himself gently for sleep, that hot still night. Rustling about the room, his softly slippered feet making no noise on the floor, he moved like a refined tiger: looked like some enchanted marquis of the impenitently wicked sort, in story, whose periodical change into tiger form was either just going off, or just coming on.

He moved from end to end of his voluptuous bedroom, looking again at the scraps of the day's journey that came unbidden into his mind; the slow toil up the hill at sunset, the setting sun, the descent, the mill, the prison on the crag, the little village in the hollow, the peasants at the fountain, and the mender of roads with his blue cap pointing out the chain under the carriage. That fountain suggested the Paris fountain, the little bundle lying on the step, the women bending over it, and the tall man with his arms up, crying, 'Dead!'

'I am cool now,' said Monsieur the Marquis, 'and may go to bed.'

So, leaving only light burning on the large hearth, he let his thin gauze curtains fall around him, and heard the night break its silence with a long sigh as he composed himself to sleep.

The stone faces on the outer walls stared blindly at the black night for three heavy hours; for three heavy hours, the horses in the stables rattled at their racks, the dogs barked, and the owl made a noise with very little resemblance in it o the noise conventionally assigned to the owl by men poets. But it is the obstinate custom of such creatures hardly ever to say what is set down for them.

For three heavy hours, the stone faces of the château, lion and human, stared blindly at the night. Dead darkness lay on all the landscape, dead darkness added its own hush to the hushing dust on all the roads. The burial-place had got to the pass that its little heaps of poor grass were undistinguishable from one another; the figure on the Cross-might have come down, for anything that could be seen of it. In the village: taxers and taxed were fast asleep. Dreaming, perhaps, of banquets, as the starved usually do; and of ease and rest, as the driven slave and the yoked ox may, its lean inhabitants slept soundly, and were fed and freed.

The fountain in the village flowed unseen and unheard, and the fountain at the château dropped unseen and unheard–both melting away, like the minutes that were falling from the spring of Time–through three dark hours. Then, the grey water of both began to be ghostly in the light, and the eyes of the stone faces of the château were opened.

Lighter and lighter, until at last the sun touched the tops of the still trees, and poured its radiance over the hill. In the glow, the water of the château fountain seemed to turn to blood, and the stone faces crimsoned. The carol of the birds was loud and high, and, on the weather-beaten sill of the great window of the bed-chamber of Monsieur the Marquis, one little bird sang its sweetest song with all its might. At this, the nearest stone face seemed to stare amazed, and, with open mouth and dropped under-jaw, looked awe-stricken.

Now, the sun was full up, and movement began in the village. Casement windows opened, crazy doors were unbarred, and people came forth shivering–chilled, as yet, by the new sweet air. Then began the rarely lightened toil of the day among the village population. Some, to the fountain; some, to the fields; men and women here, to dig and delve; men and women there, to see to the poor live-stock, and lead the bony cows out, to such pasture as could be found by the roadside. In the church and at the Cross, a kneeling figure or two; attendant on the latter prayers, the led cow, trying for a breakfast among the weeds at its foot.

The château awoke later, as became its quality, but awoke gradually and surely. First, the lonely boar-spears and knives of the chase had been reddened as of old; then had gleamed trenchant in the morning sunshine; now, doors and windows were thrown open, horses in their stables looked round over their shoulders at the light and freshness pouring in at doorways, leaves sparkled and rustled at iron-grated windows, dogs pulled hard at their chains, and reared impatient to be loosed.

All these trivial incidents belonged to the routine of life, and the return of morning. Surely, not so the ringing of the great bell of the château, nor the running up and down the stairs; nor the hurried figures on the terrace, nor the booting and tramping here and there and everywhere, nor the quick saddling of hoarses and riding away?

What winds conveyed this hurry to the grizzled mender of roads, already at work on the hilltop beyond the village, with his day's dinner (not much to carry) lying in a bundle that it was worth no crow's while to peck at, on a heap of stones? Had the birds, carrying some grains of it to a distance, dropped one over him as they sow chance seeds? Whether or no, the mender of roads ran, on the sultry morning, as if for his life, down the hill, knee-high in dust, and never stopped till he got to the fountain.

All the people of the village were at the fountain, standing about in their depressed manner, and whispering low, but showing no other emotions than grim curiosity and surprise. The led cows, hastily brought in and tethered to anything that would hold them, were looking stupidly on, or lying down chewing the cud of nothing particularly repaying their trouble, which they had picked up in their interrupted saunter. Some of the people of the château, and some of those of the posting-house, and all the taxing authorities, were armed more or less, and were crowded on the other side of the little street in a purposeless way, that was highly fraught with nothing. Already, the mender of roads had penetrated into the midst of a group of fifty particular friends, and was smiting himself in the breast with his blue cap. What did all this portend, and what portended the swift hoisting-up of Monsieur Gabelle behind a servant on horseback, and the conveying away of the said Gabelle (double-laden though the horse was), at a gallop, like a new version of the German ballad of Leonora?

It portended that there was one stone face too many, up at the château.

The Gorgon had surveyed the building again in the night, and had added the one stone face wanting; the stone face for which it had waited through about two hundred years.

It lay back on the pillow of Monsieur the Marquis. It was like a fine mask, suddenly startled, made angry, and petrified. Driven home into the heart of the stone figure attached to it, was a knife. Round its hilt was a frill of paper, on which was scrawled:

'Drive him fast to his tomb. This, from JACQUES.'

CHAPTER X

TWO PROMISES

MORE months, to the number of twelve, had come and gone, and Mr. Charles Darnay was established in England as a higher teacher of the French language who was conversant with French literature. In this age, he would have been a Professor; in that age he was a Tutor. He read with young men who could find any leisure and interest for the study of a living tongue spoken all over the world, and he cultivated a taste for its stories of knowledge and fancy. He could write of them, besides, in sound English, and render them into sound English. Such masters were not at that time easily found; Princes that had been, and Kings that were to be, were not yet of the Teacher class, and no ruined nobility had dropped out of Tellson's ledgers, to turn cooks and carpenters. As a tutor, whose attainments made the student's way unusually pleasant and profitable, and as an elegant translator who brought something to his work besides mere dictionary knowledge, young Mr. Darnay soon became known and encouraged. He was well acquainted, moreover, with the circumstances of his country, and those were of ever-growing interest. So, with great perseverance and untiring industry, he prospered.

In London, he had expected neither to walk on pavements of gold, nor to lie on beds of roses; if he had had any such exalted expectation, he would not have prospered. He had expected labour, and he found it, and did it, and made the best of it. In this, his prosperity consisted.

A certain portion of his time was passed at Cambridge, where he read with undergraduates as a sort of tolerated smuggler who drove a contraband trade in European languages, instead of conveying Greek and Latin through the Custom-house. The rest of his time passed in London.

Now, from the days when it was always summer in Eden, to these days when it is mostly winter in fallen latitudes, the world of a man has invariably gone one way–Charles Darnay's way–the way of the love of a woman.

He had loved Lucie Manette from the hour of his danger. He had never heard a sound so sweet and dear as the sound of her compassionate voice; he had never seen a face so tenderly beautiful, as hers when it was confronted with his own on the edge of the grave that had been dug for him. But, he had not yet spoken to her on the subject; the assassination at the deserted château far away beyond the heaving water, and the long, long, dusty roads–the solid stone château which had itself, and he had never yet, by so much as a single spoken word, disclosed to her the state of his heart.

That he had his reasons for this, he knew full well. It was again a summer day when, lately arrived in London from his college occupation, he turned into the quiet corner in Soho, bent on seeking an opportunity of opening his mind to Doctor Manette. It was the close of the summer day, and he knew Lucie to be out with Miss Pross.

He found the Doctor reading in his arm-chair at a window. The energy, which had at once supported him under his old sufferings and aggravated their sharpness, had been gradually restored to him. He was now a very energetic man indeed, with great firmness of purpose, strength of resolution, and vigour of action. In his recovered energy he was sometimes a little fitful and sudden, as he had at first been in the exercise of his other recovered faculties; but, this had never been frequently observable, and had grown more and more rare.

He studied much, slept little, sustained a great deal of fatigue with ease, and was equably cheerful. To him, now entered Charles Darnay, at sigh of whom he laid aside his book and held out his hand.

'Charles Darnay! I rejoice to see you. We have been counting on your return these three or four days past. Mr. Stryver and Sydney Carton were both here yesterday, and both made you out to be more than due.'

'I am obliged to them for their interest in the matter,' he answered, a little coldly as to them, though very warmly as to the Doctor. 'Miss Manette—'

'Is well,' said the Doctor, as he stopped short, 'and your return wild delight us all. She has gone out on some household matters, but will soon be home.'

'Doctor Manette, I knew she was from home. I took the opportunity of her being from home, to beg to speak to you.'

There was a blank silence.

'Yes?' said the Doctor, with evident constraint. 'Bring your chair here, and speak on.'

He complied as to the chair, bur appeared to find the speaking on less easy.

'I have had the happiness, Doctor Manette, of being so intimate here,' so he at length began, 'for some year and a half, that I hope the topic on which I am about to touch may not—'

He was stayed by the Doctor's putting out his hand to stop him. When he kept it so a little while, he said, drawing it back:

'Is Lucie the topic?'

'She is.'

'It is hard for me to speak of her at any time. It is very hard for me to hear her spoken of in that tone of yours, Charles Darnay.'

'It is a tone of fervent admiration, true homage, and deep love, Doctor Manette,' he said deferentially.

There was another blank silence before her father rejoined:

'I believe it. I do you justice; I believe it.'

His constraint was so manifest, and it was so manifest, too, that it originated in an unwillingness to approach the subject, that Charles Darnay hesitated.

'Shall I go on, sir?'

Another blank.

'Yes, go on.'

'You anticipate what I would say, though you cannot know how earnestly I say it, how earnestly I feel it, without knowing my secret heart, and the hopes and fears and anxieties with which it has long been laden. Dear Doctor Manette, I love your daughter fondly, dearly, disinterestedly, devotedly. If ever there were love in the world, I love her. You have loved yourself; let your old love speak for me!'

The Doctor sat with his face turned away, and his eyes bent on the ground. At the last words, he stretched out his hand again, hurriedly, and cried:

'Not that, sir! Let that be! I adjure you, do not recall that!'

His cry was so like a cry of actual pain, that it rang in Charles Darnay's ears long after he had ceased. He motioned with the hand he had extended, and it seemed to be an appeal to Darnay to pause. The latter so received it, and remained silent.

'I ask your pardon,' said the Doctor, in a subdued tone, after some moments. 'I do not doubt your loving Lucie; you may be satisfied of it.'

He turned towards him in his chair, but did not look at him, or raise his eyes. His chin dropped upon his hand, and his white hair overshadowed his face:

'Have you spoken to Lucie?'

'No.'

'Nor written?'

'Never.'

'It would be ungenerous to affect not to know that your self-denial is to be referred to your consideration for her father. Her father thanks you.'

He offered his hand; but his eyes did not go with it.

'I know,' said Darnay, respectfully, 'how can I fail to know, Doctor Manette, I who have seen you together from day to day, that between you and Miss Manette there is an affection so unusual, so touching, so belonging to the circumstances in which it has been nurtured, that it can have few parallels, even in the tenderness between a father and child. I know Dr. Manette–how can I fail to know–that, mingled with the affection and duty of a daughter who has become a woman, there is, in her heart, towards you, all the love and reliance of infancy itself. I know that, as in her childhood she had no parent, so she is now devoted to you with all the constancy and fer-

vour of her present years and character, united to the trustfulness and attachment of the early days in which you were lost to her. I know perfectly well
that if you had been restored to her from the world beyond this life, you
could hardly be invested, in her sight, with a more sacred character than
that in which you are always with her. I know that when she is clinging to
you, the hands of baby, girl, and woman, all in one, are round your neck. I
know that in loving you she sees and loves her mother at her own age, sees
and loves you at my age, loves her mother broken-hearted, loves you
through your dreadful trial and in your blessed restoration. I have known
this, night and day since I have known you in your home.'

Her father sat silent, with his face bent down. His breathing was a little quickened; but he repressed all other signs of agitation.

'Dear Doctor Manette, always knowing this, always seeing her and
you with this hallowed light about you, I have forborne, and forborne, as
long as it was in the nature of man to do it. I have felt, and do even now feel,
that to bring my love–even mine–between you, is to touch your history with
something not quite so good as itself. But I love her. Heaven is my witness
that I love her!'

'I believe it,' answered her father, mournfully. 'I have thought so before
now. I believe it.'

'But, do not believe,' said Darnay, upon whose ear the mournful voice
struck with a reproachful sound, 'that if my fortune were so cast as that, being one day so happy as to make her my wife, I must at any time put any
separation between her and you, I could or would breathe a word of what I
now say. Besides that I should know it to be hopeless, I should know it to be
a baseness. If I had any such possibility, even at a remote distance of years,
harboured in my thoughts, and hidden in my heart–if it ever had been
there–if it ever could be there–I could not now touch this honoured hand.'

He laid his own upon it as he spoke.

'No, dear Doctor Manette. Like you, a voluntary exile from France;
like you, driven from it by its distractions, oppressions, and miseries; like
you, striving to live away from it by my own exertions, and trusting in a
happier future; I look only to sharing your fortunes, sharing your life and
home, and being faithful to you to the death. Not to divide with Lucie her
privilege as your child, companion, and friend; but to come in aid of it, and
bind her closer to you, if such a thing can be.'

His touch still lingered on her father's hand. Answering the touch for a
moment, but not coldly, her father rested his hands upon the arms of his
chair, and looked up for the first time since the beginning of the conference.
A struggle was evidently in his face; a struggle with that occasional look
which had a tendency in it to dark doubt and dread.

'You speak so feelingly and so manfully, Charles Darnay, that I thank
you with all my heart, and will open all my heart–or nearly so. Have you
any reason to believe that Lucie loves you?'

'None. As yet none.'

'Is it the immediate object of this confidence, that you may at once ascertain that, with my knowledge?'

'Not even so. I might not have the hopefulness to do it for weeks; I might (mistaken or not mistaken) have that hopefulness to-morrow.'

'Do you seek any guidance from me?'

'I ask none, sir. But I have thought it possible that you might have it in your power, if you should deem it right, to give me some.'

'Do you seek any promise for me!'

'I do seek that.'

'What is it?'

'I well understand that, without you, I could have no hope. I well understand that, even if Miss Manette held me at this moment in her innocent heart—do not think I have the presumption to assume so much—I could retain no place in it against her love for her father.'

'If that be so, do you see what, on the other hand, is involved in it?'

'I understand equally well, that a word from her father in any suitor's favour, would outweigh herself and all the world. For which reason, Doctor Manette,' said Darnay, modestly but firmly, 'I would not ask that word, to save my life.'

'I am sure of it. Charles Darnay, mysteries arise out of close love, as well as out of close division; in the former case, they are subtle and delicate, and difficult to penetrate. My daughter Lucie is, in this one respect, such a mystery to me; I can make no guess at the state of her heart.'

'May I ask, sir, if you think she is—' As he hesitated, her father supplied the rest.

'Is sought by any other suitor?'

'It is what I meant to say.'

Her father considered a little before he answered:

'You have seen Mr. Carton here, yourself. Mr. Stryver is here too, occasionally. If it be at all, it can only be by one of these.'

'Or both,' said Darnay.

'I had not thought of both; I should not think either, likely. You want a promise from me. Tell me what it is.'

'It is, that if Miss Manette should bring to you at any time, on her own part, such a confidence as I have ventured to lay before you, you will bear testimony to what I have said, and to your belief in it. I hope you may be able to think so well of me, as to urge no influence against me. I say nothing more of my stake in this; this is what I ask. The condition on which I ask it, and which you have an undoubted right to require, I will observe immediately.'

'I give the promise,' said the Doctor, 'without any condition. I believe your object to be, purely and truthfully, as you have stated it. I believe your intention is to perpetuate, and not to weaken, the ties between me and my other and far dearer self. If she should ever tell me that you are essential to her perfect happiness, I will give her to you. If there were—Charles Darnay—if there were—'

The young man had taken his hand gratefully; their hands were joined as the Doctor spoke:

'—any fancies, any reasons, any apprehensions, anything whatsoever,

new or old, against the man she really loved–the direct responsibility thereof not lying on his head–they should all be obliterated for her sake. She is
everything to me; more to me than suffering, more to me that wrong, more
to me— Well! This is idle talk.'

So strange was the way in which he faded into silence, and so strange
his fixed look when he had ceased to speak, that Darnay felt his own hand
turn cold in the hand that slowly released and dropped it.

'You said something to me,' said Doctor Manette, breaking into a
smile. 'What was it you said to me?'

He was at a loss how to answer, until he remembered having spoken of
a condition. Relieved as his mind reverted to that, he answered:

'Your confidence in me ought to be returned with full confidence on
my part. My present name, thought but slightly changed from my mother's, is not, as you will remember, my own. I wish to tell you what it is, and
why I am in England.'

'Stop!' said the Doctor of Beauvais.

'I wish it, that I may the better deserve your confidence, and have no
secret from you.'

'Stop!'

For an instant, the Doctor even had his two hands at his ears; for another instant, even had his two hands laid on Darnay's lips.

'Tell me when I ask you, not now. If your suit should prosper, if Lucie
should love you, you should tell me on your marriage morning. Do you
promise?'

'Willingly.'

'Give me your hand. She will be home directly, and it is better she
should not see us together to-night. Go! God bless you!'

It was dark when Charles Darnay left him, and it was an hour later and
darker when Lucie came home; she hurried into the room alone–for Miss
Pross had gone straight upstairs–and was surprised to find his reading-chair
empty.

'My father!' she called to him. 'Father, dear!'

Nothing was said in answer, but she heard a low hammering sound in
the bedroom. Passing lightly across the intermediate room, she looked in at
his door and came running back frightened, crying to herself, with her blood
all chilled, 'What shall I do! What shall I do!'

Her uncertainty lasted but a moment; she hurried back, and tapped at
his door, and softly called to him. The noise ceased at the sound of her voice,
and he presently came out to her, and they walked up and down together for
a long time.

She came down from her bed, to look at him in his sleep that night.
He slept heavily, and his tray of shoemaking tools, and his old unfinished
work, were all as usual.

CHAPTER XI

A COMPANION PICTURE

'SYDNEY,' said Mr. Stryver, on that selfsame night, or morning, to his jackal; 'mix another bowl of punch; I have something to say to you.'

Sydney had been working double tides that night, and the night before, and the night before that, and a good many nights in succession, making a grand clearance among Mr. Stryver's papers before the setting in of the long vacation. The clearance was affected at last; the Stryver arrears were handsomely fetched up; everything was got rid of until November should come with its fogs atmospheric and fogs legal, and bring grist to the mill again.

Sydney was none the livelier and none the soberer for so much application. It had taken a deal of extra wet-toweling to pull him through the night; a correspondingly extra quantity of wine had preceded the toweling; and he was in a very damaged condition, as he now pulled his turban off and threw it into the basin in which he had steeped it at intervals for the last six hours.

'Are you mixing that other bowl of punch?' said Stryver the portly, with his hands in his waistband, glancing round from the sofa where he lay on his back.

'I am.'

'Now, look here! I am going to tell you something that will rather surprise you, and that perhaps will make you think me not quite as shrewd as you usually do think me. I intend to marry.'

'*Do* you?'

'Yes. And not for money. What do you say now?'

'I don't feel disposed to say much. Who is she?'

'Guess.'

'Do I know her?'

'Guess.'

'I am not going to guess, at five o'clock in the morning, with my brains frying and spluttering in my head. If you want me to guess, you must ask me to dinner.'

'Well then, I'll tell you,' said Stryver, coming slowly into a sitting posture. 'Sydney, I rather despair of making myself intelligible to you, because you are such an insensible dog.'

'And you,' returned Sydney, busy concocting the punch, 'are such a sensitive and poetical spirit.'

'Come,' rejoined Stryver, laughing boastfully, 'though I don't prefer any claim to being the soul of Romance (for I hope I know better), still I am a tenderer sort of fellow than *you*.'

'You are a luckier, if you mean that.'

'I don't mean that. I mean I am a man of more—more—'

'Say gallantry, while you are about it,' suggested Carton.

'Well! I'll say gallantry. My meaning is that I am a man' said Stryver, inflating himself at his friend as he made the punch, 'who cares to be more agreeable, who takes more pains to be agreeable who knows better how to be agreeable, in a woman's society, than you do.'

'Go on,' said Sydney Carton.

'No; but before I go on,' said Stryver, shaking his head in his bullying way, 'I'll have this out with you. You've been at Doctor Manette's house as much as I have, or more than I have. Why, I have been ashamed of your moroseness there! Your manners have been of that silent and sullen and hang-dog kind, that, upon my life and soul, I have been ashamed of you, Sydney!'

'It should be very beneficial to a man in your practice at the bar, to be ashamed of anything,' returned Sydney; 'you ought to be much obliged to me.'

'You shall not get off in that way,' rejoined Stryver, shouldering the rejoinder at him; 'no, Sydney, it's my duty to tell you—and I tell you to your face to do you good—that you are a devilish ill-conditioned fellow in that sort of society. You are a disagreeable fellow.'

Sydney drank a bumper of the punch he had made, and laughed.

'Look at me,' said Stryver, squaring himself; 'I have less need to make myself agreeable than you have, being more independent in circumstances. Why do I do it?'

'I never saw you do it yet,' muttered Carton.

'I do it because it is politic; I do it on principle. And look at me! I get on.'

'You don't get on with your account of your matrimonial intentions,' answered Carton, with a careless air; 'I wish you would keep to that. As to me—will you never understand that I am incorrigible?'

He asked the question with some appearance of scorn.

'You have no business to be, at all, that I know of,' said Sydney Carton. 'Who is the lady?'

'Now, don't let my announcement of the name make your uncomfortable, Sydney,' said Mr. Stryver, preparing him with ostentatious friendliness for the disclosure he was about to make, 'because I know you don't mean half you say; and if you mean it all, it would be of no importance. I make this little preface, because you once mentioned the young lady to me in slighting terms.'

'I did?'

'Certainly; and in these chambers.'

Sydney Carton looked at his punch and looked at his complacent friend, drank his punch and looked at his complacent friend.

'You made mention of the young lady as a golden-haired doll. The young lady is Miss Manette. If you had been a fellow of any sensitiveness or delicacy of feeling in that kind of way, Sydney, I might have been a little resentful of your employing such a designation; but you are not. You want that sense altogether; therefore I am no more annoyed when I think of the expression, than I should be annoyed by a man's opinion of a picture of mine, who had no eye for pictures: or of a piece of music of mine, who had no ear for music.'

Sydney Carton drank the punch at a great rate; drank it by bumpers, looking at his friend.

'Now you know all about it, Syd,' said Mr. Stryver. 'I don't care about fortune: she is a charming creature, and I have made up my mind to please myself: on the whole, I think I can afford to please myself. She will have in me a man already pretty well off, and a rapidly rising man, and a man of some distinction: it is a piece of good fortune for her, but she is worthy of good fortune. Are you astonished?'

Carton, still drinking the punch, rejoined, 'Why should I be astonished?'

'You approve?'

Carton, still drinking the punch, rejoined, 'Why should I not approve?'

'Well!' said his friend Stryver, 'you take it more easily than I fancied you would, and are less mercenary on my behalf than I thought you would be; though, to be sure, you know well enough by this time that your ancient chum is a man of a pretty strong will. Yes, Sydney, I have had enough of this style of life, with no other as a change from it; I feel that it is a pleasant thing for a man to have a home when he feels inclined to go to it (when he doesn't, he can stay away), and I feel that Miss Manette will tell well in any station, and will always do me credit. So I have made up my mind. And now, Sydney, old boy, I want to say a word to *you* about *your* prospects. You are in a bad way, you know; you really are in a bad way. You don't know the value of money, you live hard, you'll knock up one of these days, and be ill and poor; you really ought to think about a nurse.'

The prosperous patronage with which he said it, made him look twice as big as he was, and four times as offensive.

'Now, let me recommend you,' pursued Stryver, 'to look it in the face. I have looked it in the face, in my different way; look it in the face, you, in your different way. Marry. Provide somebody to take care of you. Never mind your having no enjoyment of women's society, nor understanding of it, nor tact for it. Find out somebody. Find out some respectable woman with a little property–somebody in the landlady way, or lodging–letting way–and marry her, against a rainy day. That's the kind of thing for *you*. Now think of it, Sydney.'

'I'll think of it, said Sydney.

CHAPTER XII

THE FELLOW OF DELICACY

MR. Stryver having made up his mind to that magnanimous bestowal of good fortune on the Doctor's daughter, resolved to make her happiness known to her before he left town for the Long Vacation. After some mental debating of the point, he came to the conclusion that it would be as well to get all the preliminaries down with, and they could then arrange at their leisure whether he should give her his hand a week or two before Michaelmas Term, or in the little Christmas vacation between it and Hilary.

As to the strength of his case, he had not a doubt about it, but clearly saw his way to the verdict. Argued with the jury on substantial worldly grounds—the only grounds ever worth taking into account—it was a plain case, and had not a weak spot in it. He called himself for the plaintiff, there was no getting over his evidence, the counsel for the defendant threw up his brief, and the jury did not even turn to consider. After trying it, Stryver, C.J., was satisfied that no plainer case could be.

Accordingly, Mr. Stryver inaugurated the Long Vacation with a formal proposal to take Miss Manette to Vauxhall Gardens; that failing, to Renelagh; that unaccountably failing too, it behooved him to present himself in Soho, and there declare his noble mind.

Towards Soho, therefore, Mr. Stryver shouldered his way from the Temple, while the bloom of the Long Vacation's infancy was still upon it. Anybody who had seen him projecting himself into Soho while he was yet on St. Dunstan's side of Temple Bar, bursting into his full-blown way along the pavement, to the jostlement of all weaker people, might have seen how safe and strong he was.

His way taking him past Tellson's, and he both banking at Tellson's and knowing Mr. Lorry as the intimate friend of the Manettes, it entered Mr. Stryver's mind to enter the bank, and reveal to Mr. Lorry the brightness of the Soho horizon. So, he pushed open the door with a weak rattle in its throat, stumbled down the two steps, got past the two ancient cashiers, and shouldered himself into the musty bank closet where Mr. Lorry sat at great books ruled for figures, with perpendicular iron bars to his window as if what was ruled for figures too, and everything under the clouds were a sum.

'Halloa!' said Mr. Stryver's grand peculiarity that he always seemed too big for any place, or space. He was so much too big for Tellson's, that old clerks in distant corners looked up with looks of remonstrance, as though he squeezed them against the wall. The House itself, magnificently reading the paper quite in thee far-off perspective, lowered displeased, as if the Stryver head had been butted into its respectable waistcoat.

The discreet Mr. Lorry said, in a sample tone of the voice he would recommend under the circumstances, 'How do you do, Mr. Stryver? How do you do, sir?' and shook hands. There was a peculiarity in his manner of shaking hands, always to be seen in any clerk at Tellson's who shook hands with a customer when the House pervaded the air. He shook in a self-abnegating way, as one who shook for Tellson & Co.

'Can I do anything for you, Mr. Stryver?' asked Mr. Lorry; in his business character.

'Why, no, thank you; this is a private visit to yourself, Mr. Lorry; I have come for a private word.'

'Oh, indeed!' said Mr. Lorry, bending down his ear, while his eye strayed to the House afar off.'

'I am going,' said Mr. Stryver, leaning his arms confidentially on the desk: whereupon, although it was a large double one, there appeared to be not half desk enough for him: 'I am going to make an offer of myself in marriage to your agreeable little friend, Miss Manette, Mr. Lorry.'

'Oh dear me!' cried Mr. Lorry, rubbing his chin, and looking at his visitor dubiously.

'Oh dear me, sir? repeated Stryver, drawing back. 'Oh dear you, sir? What may your meaning be, Mr. Lorry?'

'My meaning,' answered the man of business, 'is, of course, friendly and appreciative, and that it does you the greatest credit, and–in short, my meaning is everything you could desire. But–really you know, Mr. Stryver—' Mr. Lorry paused, and shook his head at him in the oddest manner, as if he were compelled against his will to add, internally, 'You know there really is so much too much of you!'

'Well!' said Stryver, slapping the desk with his contentious hand, opening his eyes wider, and taking a long breath 'if I understand you, Mr. Lorry, I'll be hanged!'

Mr. Lorry adjusted his little wig at both ears as a means towards that end, and bit the feather of a pen.

'D–n it all, sir!' said Stryver, staring at him, 'am I not eligible?'

'Oh dear yes! Yes. Oh yes, you're eligible!' said Mr. Lorry. 'If you say eligible, you are eligible.'

'Am I not prosperous?' asked Stryver.

'Oh! if you come too prosperous, you are prosperous,' said Mr. Lorry.

'And advancing?'

'If you come to advancing, you know,' said Mr. Lorry, delighted to be able to made another admission, 'nobody can doubt that.'

'Then what on earth is your meaning, Mr. Lorry?' demanded Stryver, perceptibly crestfallen.

'Well! I— Were you going there now?' asked Mr. Lorry.

'Straight!' said Stryver, with a plump of his fist on the desk.

'Then I think I wouldn't, if I was you.'

'Why?' said Stryver. 'Now, I'll put you in a corner,' forensically shaking s forefinger at him. 'You are a man of business and bound to have a reason. State your reason. Why wouldn't you go?'

'Because,' said Mr. Lorry, 'I wouldn't go on such an object without having some cause to believe that I should succeed.'

'D–ne ME!' cried Stryver, 'but this beats everything.'

Mr. Lorry glanced at the distant House, and glanced at the angry Stryver.

'Here's a man of business–a man of years–a man of experience–*in* a bank,' said Stryver; 'and having summed up three leading reasons for complete success, he says there's no reason at all! Says it with his head on!' Mr. Stryver remarked upon the peculiarity as if it would have been infinitely less remarkable if he had said it with his head off.

'When I speak of success, I speak of success with the young lady; and when I speak of causes and reasons to make success probable, I speak of causes and reasons that will tell as such with the young lady. The young lady, my good sir,' said Mr. Lorry, mildly tapping the Stryver arm, 'the young lady. The young lady goes before all.'

'Then you mean to tell me, Mr. Lorry,' said Stryver, squaring his elbows, 'that it is your deliberate opinion that the young lady at present in question is a mincing Fool?'

'Not exactly so. I mean to tell you, Mr. Stryver,' said Mr. Lorry, reddening, 'that I will hear no disrespectful word of that young lady from any lips; and that if I knew any man—which I hope I do not—whose taste was so coarse, and whose temper was so overbearing, that he could not restrain himself from speaking disrespectfully of that young lady at this desk, not even Tellson's should prevent my giving him a piece of my mind.'

The necessity of being angry in a suppressed tone had put Mr. Stryver's blood-vessels into a dangerous state when it was his turn to be angry; Mr. Lorry's veins, methodical as their courses could usually be, were in no better state now it was his turn.

'That is what I mean to tell you, sir,' said Mr. Lorry. 'Pray let there be no mistake about it.'

Mr. Stryver sucked the end of a ruler for a little while, and then stood hitting a tune out of his teeth with it, which probably gave him the toothache. He broke the awkward silence by saying:

'This is something new to me, Mr. Lorry. You deliberately advice me not to go up to Soho and offer myself—*myself*, Stryver of the King's Bench bar?'

'Do you ask me for my advice, Mr. Stryver?'

'Yes, I do.'

'Very good. Then I give it, and you have repeated it correctly.'

'And all I can say of it is, 'laughed Stryver with a vexed laugh, 'that this—ha, ha!—beats everything past, present, and to come.'

'Now understand me,' pursued Mr. Lorry. 'As a man of business, I am not justified is saying anything about this matter, for, as a man of business, I know nothing of it. But, as an old fellow, who has carried Miss Manette in his arms, who is the trusted friend of Miss Manette and of her father too, and who has a great affection for them, I have spoken. The confidence is not of my seeking, recollect. Now, you think I may not be right?'

'Not I!' said Stryver, whistling. 'I can't undertake to find third parties in common sense; I can only find it for myself. I suppose sense in certain quarters; you suppose mincing bread-and-butter nonsense. It's a new to me, but you are right, I dare say.'

'What I suppose, Mr. Stryver, I claim to characterize for myself. And understand me, sir,' said Mr. Lorry, quickly flushing again, 'I will not—not even at Tellson's—have it characterized for me by any gentleman breathing.'

'There! I beg your pardon!' said Stryver.

'Granted. Thank you. Well, Mr. Stryver, I was about to say—it might be painful to you to find yourself mistaken, it might be painful to Doctor Manette to have the task of being explicit with you, it might be very painful to Miss Manette to have the task of being explicit with you. You know the terms upon which I have the honour and happiness to stand with the family. If you please, committing you in no way, representing you in no way, I will undertake to correct my advice by the exercise of a little new observation and judgment expressly brought to bear upon it. If you should then be dissatisfied with it, you can but test its soundness for yourself; if, on the other hand, you should be satisfied with it, and it should be what it now is, it may spare all sides what is best spared. What do you say?'

'How long would you keep me in town?'

'Oh! It is only a question of a few hours. I could go down to Soho in the evening, and come to your chambers afterwards.'

'Then I say yes,' said Stryver: 'I won't go up there now, I am not so hot upon it as that comes to; I say yes, and I shall expect you to look in to-night. Good morning.'

Then Mr. Stryver turned and burst out of the bank, causing such a concussion of air on his passage through, that to stand up against it bowing the two counters, required the utmost remaining strength of the two ancient clerks. Those venerable and feeble persons were always seen by the public in the act of bowing, and were popularly believed, when they had bowed a customer out, still to keep on bowing in the empty office until they bowed another customer in.

The barrister was keen enough to divine that the banker would not have gone so far in his expression of opinion on any less solid ground than moral certainty. Unprepared as he was for the large pill he had to swallow, he got it down. 'And now,' said Mr. Stryver, shaking his forensic forefinger at the Temple in general, when it was down, 'my way out of this, is, to put you all in the wrong.'

It was a bit of the art of an Old Bailey tactician, in which he found great relief. 'You shall not put me in the wrong, young lady,' said Mr. Stryver; 'I'll do that for you.'

Accordingly, when Mr. Lorry called that night as late as ten o'clock, Mr. Stryver, among a quantity of books and papers littered out for the purpose, seemed to have nothing less on his mind than the subject of the morning. He even showed surprise when he saw Mr. Lorry, and was altogether in an absent and preoccupied state.

'Well!' said that good-natured emissary, after a full half-hour of bootless attempts to bring him round to the question. 'I have been to Soho.'

'To Soho?' repeated Mr. Stryver, coldly. 'Oh, to be sure! What am I thinking of!'

'And I have no doubt,' said Mr. Lorry, 'that I was right in the conversation we had. My opinion is confirmed and I reiterate my advice.'

'I assure you,' returned Mr. Stryver, in the friendliest way, 'that I am sorry for it on your account, and sorry for it on the poor father's account. I know this must always be a sore subject with the family; let us say no more about it.'

'I don't understand you,' said Mr. Lorry.

'I dare say not,' rejoined Stryver, nodding his head in a smoothing and final way; 'no matter, no matter.'

'But it does matter,' Mr. Lorry urged.

'No it doesn't; I assure you it doesn't. Having supposed that there was sense where there is no sense, and a laudable ambition where there is not a laudable ambition, I am well out of my mistake, and no harm is done. Young women have committed similar follies often before, and have repented them in poverty and obscurity often before. In an unselfish aspect, I am sorry that the thing is dropped, because it would have been a bad thing for me in a worldly point of view–it is hardly necessary to say I could have gained nothing by it. There is no harm at all done. I have not proposed to the young lady, and, between ourselves, I am by no means certain, on reflection, that I ever should have committed myself to that extent. Mr. Lorry, you cannot control the mincing vanities and giddinesses of empty-headed girls; you must not expect to do it, or you will always be disappointed. Now, pray say no more about it. I tell you, I regret it on account of others, but I am satisfied on my own account. And I am really very much obliged to you for allowing me to sound you, and for giving me your advice; you know the young lady better than I do; you were right, it never would have done.'

Mr. Lorry was so taken aback, that he looked quite stupidly at Mr. Stryver shouldering him towards the door, with an appearance of showering generosity, forbearance, and goodwill, on his erring head. 'Make the best of it, my dear sir,' said Stryver; 'say no more about it; thank you again for allowing me to sound you; good night!'

Mr. Lorry was out into the night, before he knew where he was. Mr. Stryver was lying back on his sofa, winking at his ceiling.

CHAPTER XIII

THE FELLOW OF NO DELICACY

IF Sydney Carton ever shone anywhere, he certainly never shone in the house of Doctor Manette. He had been there often, during the whole year, and had always been the same moody and morose lounger there. When he cared to talk, he talked well; but, the cloud of caring for nothing, which overshadowed him with such a fatal darkness, was very rarely pierced by the light within him.

And yet he did care something for the streets that environed that house, and for the senseless stones that made their pavements. Many a night he vaguely and unhappily wandered there, when wine had brought no transitory gladness to him; many a dreary daybreak revealed his solitary figure lingering there, and still lingering there when the first beams of the sun brought into strong relief, removed beauties in architecture in spires of churches and lofty buildings, as perhaps the quiet time brought some sense of better things, else forgotten and unattainable, into his mind. Of late, the neglected bed in the Temple Court had known him more scantily than ever; and often when he had thrown himself upon it no longer than a few minutes, he had got up again, and haunted that neighbourhood.

On a day in August, when Mr. Stryver (after notifying to his jackal that 'he had thought better of that marrying matter') had carried his delicacy into Devonshire, and when the sight and scent of flowers in the City streets had some waifs of goodness in them for the worst, of health for the sickliest, and of youth for the oldest, Sydney's feet still trod those stones. From being irresolute and purposeless, his feet being animated by an intention, and, in the working out of that intention, they took him to the Doctor's door.

He was shown upstairs, and found Lucie at her work, alone. She had never been quite at her ease with him, and received him with some little embarrassment as he seated himself near her table. But, looking up at his face in the interchange of the first few commonplaces, she observed a change in it.

'I fear you are not well, Mr. Carton!'

'No. But the life I lead, Miss Manette, is not conducive to health. What is to be expected of, or by, such profligates?'

'Is it not—forgive me; I have begun the question on my lips—a pity to live no better life?'

'God knows it is a shame!'

'Then why not change it?'

Looking gently at him again, she was surprised and saddened to see that there were tears in his eyes. There were tears in his voice too, as he answered:

'It is too late for that. I shall never be better than I am. I shall sink lower, and be worse.'

He leaned an elbow on her table, and covered his eyes with his hand. The table trembled in the silence that followed.

She had never seen him softened, and was much distressed. He knew her to be so, without looking at her, and said:

'Pray forgive me, Miss Manette. I break down before the knowledge of what I want to say to you. Will you hear me?'

'If it will do you any good, Mr. Carton, if it would make you happier, it would make me very glad!'

'God bless you for your sweet compassion!'

He unshaded his face after a little while, and spoke steadily.

'Don't be afraid to hear me. Don't shrink from anything I say. I am like one who died young. All my life might have been.'

'No, Mr. Carton. I am sure that the best part of it might still be; I am sure that you might be much, much worthier of yourself.'

'Say of you, Miss Manette, and although I know better–although in the mystery of my own wretched heart I know better–I shall never forget it!'

She was pale and trembling. He came to her relief with a fixed despair of himself which made the interview unlike any other that could have been holden.

'If it had been possible, Miss Manette, that you could have returned the love of the man you see before you–self-flung away, wasted, drunken, poor creature of misuse as you know him to be–he would have been conscious this day and hour, in spite of his happiness, that he would bring you to misery, bring you to sorrow and repentance, blight you, disgrace you, pull you down with him. I know very well that you can have no tenderness for me; I ask for none; I am even thankful that it cannot be.'

'Without it, can I not save you, Mr. Carton? Can I not recall you–forgive me again!–to a better course? Can I in no way repay your confidence? I know this is a confidence,' she modestly said, after a little hesitation, and in earnest tears, 'I know you would say this to no one else. Can I turn it to no good account for yourself, Mr. Carton?'

He shook his head.

'To none. No, Miss Manette, to none. If you will hear me through a very little more, all you can ever do for me is done. I wish you to know that you have been the last dream of my soul. In my degradation I have not been so degraded but that the sight of you with your father, and of this home made such a home by you, has stirred old shadows that I thought had died out of me. Since I knew you, I have been troubled by a remorse that I thought would never reproach me again, and have heard whispers from old voices impelling me upward, that I thought were silent for ever. I have had unformed ideas of striving afresh, beginning anew, shaking off sloth and sensuality, and fighting out the abandoned fight. A dream, all a dream, that ends in nothing, and leaves the sleeper where he lay down, but I wish you to know that you inspired it.'

'Will nothing of it remain? O Mr. Carton, think again! Try again!'

'No, Miss Manette; all through it, I have known myself to be quite undeserving. And yet I have had the weakness, and have still the weakness, to wish you to know with what a sudden mastery you kindled me, heap of ashes that I am, into fire–a fire, however, inseparable in its nature from myself, quickening nothing, lighting nothing, doing no service, idly burning away.'

'Since it is my misfortune, Mr. Carton, to have made you more unhappy than you were before you knew me—'

'Don't say that, Miss Manette, for you would have reclaimed me, if anything could. You will not be the cause of my becoming worse.'

'Since the state of your mind that you describe, is, at all events, attributable to some influence of mine–this is what I mean, if I can make it plain–can I use no influence to serve you? Have I no power for good, with you, at all?'

'The utmost good that I am capable of now, Miss Manette, I have come here to realize. Let me carry through the rest of my misdirected life, the remembrance that I opened my heart to you, last of all the world; and that there was something left in me at this time which you could deplore and pity.'

'Which I entreated you to believe, again and again, most fervently, with all my heart, was capable of better things, Mr. Carton!'

'Entreat me to believe it no more, Miss Manette. I have proved myself, and I know better. I distress you; I draw fast to an end. Will you let me believe, when I recall this day, that the last confidence of my life was reposed in your pure and innocent breast, and that it lies there alone, and will be shared by no one?'

'If that will be a consolation to you, yes.'

'Not even by the dearest one ever to be known to you?'

'Mr. Carton,' she answered, after an agitated pause, 'the secret is yours, not mine; and I promise to respect it.'

'Thank you. And again, God bless you.'

He put her hands to his lips, and moved towards the door.

'Be under no apprehension, Miss Manette, of my ever resuming this conversation by so much as a passing word. I will never refer to it again. If I were dead, that could not be surer than it is henceforth. In the hour of my death, I shall hold sacred the one good remembrance—and shall thank and bless you for it—that my last avowal of myself was made to you, and that my name, my faults, and miseries were gently carried in your heart. May it otherwise be light and happy!'

He was so unlike what he had ever shown himself to be, and it was so sad to think how much he had thrown away, and how much he every day kept down and perverted, that Lucie Manette wept mournfully for him as he stood looking back at her.

'Be comforted!' he said. 'I am not worth such feeling, Miss Manette. An hour or two hence, and the low companions and low habits that I scorn but yield to, will render me less worth such tears as those, than any wretch who creeps along the streets. Be comforted! But, within myself, I shall always be, towards you, what I am now, through outwardly I shall be what you have heretofore seen me. The last supplication but one I make to you, is, that you will believe this of me.'

'I will, Mr. Carton.'

'My last supplication of all, is this; and with it, I will relieve you of a visitor with whom I know well you have nothing in unison, and between whom and you there is an impassable space. It is useless to say it, I know, but it rises out of my soul. For you, and for any dear to you, I would do anything. If my career were of that better kind that there was any opportunity or capacity of sacrifice in it, I would embrace any sacrifice for you and for those dear to you. Try to hold me in your mind, at some quiet times, as ardent and sincere in this one thing. The time will come, the time will not be long in coming, when new ties will be formed about you—ties that will blind you yet more tenderly and strongly to the home you so adorn—the dearest ties that will ever grace and gladden you. O Miss

Manette, when the little picture of a happy father's face looks up in yours, when you see your own bright beauty springing up anew at your feet, think now and then that there is a man who would give his life, to keep a life you love beside you!'

He said, 'Farewell!' said a last 'God bless you!' and left her.

CHAPTER XIV

THE HONEST TRADESMAN

TO the yes of Mr. Jeremiah Cruncher, sitting on his stool in Fleet Street with his grisly urchin beside him, a vast number and variety of objects in movements were every day presented. Who could sit upon anything in Fleet Street during the busy hours of the day, and not be dazed and deafened by two immense processions, one ever tending westward with the sun, the other ever tending eastward from the sun, both ever tending to the plains beyond the range of red and purple where the sun goes down!

With his straw in his mouth, Mr. Cruncher sat watching the two streams, like the heathen rustic who for several centuries been on duty watching one stream—saving that Jerry had no expectation of their ever running dry. Nor would it have been an expectation of a hopeful kind, since a small part of his income was derived from the pilotage of timid women (mostly of a full habit and past the middle term of life) from Tellson's side of the tides to the opposite shore. Brief as such companionship was in every separate instance, Mr. Cruncher never failed to become so interested in the lady as to express a strong desire to have the honour of drinking her very good health. And it was from the gifts bestowed upon him towards the execution of this benevolent purpose, that he recruited his finances, as just now observed.

Time was, when a poet sat upon a stool in a public place, and mused in the sight of men. Mr. Cruncher, sitting on a stool in a public place, but not being a poet, mused as little as possible, and looked about him.

It fell out that he was thus engaged in a season when crowds were few, and belated women few, and when his affairs in general were so unprosperous as to awaken a strong suspicion in his breast that Mr. Cruncher must have been 'flopping' in some pointed manner, when an unusual concourse pouring down Fleet Street westward, attracted his attention. Looking that way, Mr. Cruncher made out that some kind of funeral was coming along, and that there was popular objection to this funeral, which engendered uproar.

'Young Jerry,' said Mr. Cruncher, turning to his offspring, 'it's a burying.'

'Hooroar, father!' cried Young Jerry.

The young gentleman uttered his exultant sound with mysterious significance. The elder gentleman took the cry so ill, that he watched his opportunity, and smote the young gentleman on the ear.

'What d'ye mean? What are you hooroaring at? What do you want to convey to your own father, you young rip! This boy is getting too many for *me*! said Mr. Cruncher, surveying him. 'Him and his hooroars! Don't let me hear no more of you, or you shall feel some more of me. D'ye hear?'

'I warn't doing no harm,' young Jerry protested, rubbing his cheek.

'Drop it then,' said Mr. Cruncher; 'I won't have none of *your* no harms. Get a top of that there seat, and look at the crowd.'

His son obeyed, and the crowd approached; they were bawling and hissing round a dingy hearse and dingy mourning coach, in which mourning coach there was only one mourner, dressed in the dignity trappings that were considered essential to the dignity of the position. The position appeared by no means to please him, however, with an increasing rabble surrounding the coach, deriding him making grimaces at him, and incessantly groaning and calling out: 'Yah! Spies! Tst! Yaha! Spies!' with many compliments too numerous and forcible to repeat.

Funeral had at all times a remarkable attraction for Mr. Cruncher; he always picked up his senses, and became excited, when a funeral passed Tellson's. Naturally, therefore, a funeral with this uncommon attendance excited him greatly, and he asked of the first man who ran against him.

'What is it, brother? What's it about?'

'*I* don't know,' said the man. 'Spies! Yaha! Tst! Spies!'

He asked another man. 'Who is it?'

'*I* don't know,' returned the man, clapping his hands to his mouth nevertheless, and vociferating in a surprising heat and with the greatest ardour, 'Spies! Yaha! tst! Spi-ies!'

At length, a person better informed on the merits of the case, tumbled against him, and from this person he learned that the funeral was the funeral of one Roger Cly.

'Was he a spy?' asked Mr. Cruncher.

'Old Bailey spy,' returned his informant. 'Yaha! Tst! Yah! Old Bailey Spi-i-ies!'

'Why, to be sure!' exclaimed Jerry, recalling the trial at which he had assisted. 'I've seen him. Dead, is he?'

'Dead as mutton,' returned the other, 'and can't be too dead. Have 'em out, there! Spies! Pull'em out, there! Spies!'

The idea was so acceptable in the prevalent absence of any idea, that the crowd caught it up with eagerness, and loudly repeating the suggestion to have 'em out, and to pull 'em out, mobbed the two vehicles so closely that they came to a stop. On the crowd's opening the coach doors, the one mourner scuffled out of himself and was in their hands for a moment; but he was so alert, and made such good use of his time, that in another moment he was scouring away up a by-street, after shedding his cloak, hat, long hatband, white pocket handkerchief, and other symbolical tears.

These, the people tore to pieces and scattered far and wide with great enjoyment, while the tradesman hurriedly shut up their shops; for a crowd in those times stopped at nothing, and was a monster much dreaded. They had already got the length of opening the hearse to take the coffin out, when some brighter genius proposed instead, its being escorted to its destination amidst general rejoicing. Practical suggestions being much needed, this suggestion, too, was received with acclamation, and the coach was immediately filled with eight inside and a dozen out, while as many people got on the roof of the hearse as could by any exercise of ingenuity stick upon it. Among the first of these volunteers was Jerry Cruncher himself, who modestly concealed his spiky head from the observation of Tellson's, in the further corner of the mourning coach.

The officiating undertakers made some protest against these changes in the ceremonies; but, the river being alarmingly near, and several voices remarking on the efficacy of cold immersion in bringing refractory members of the profession to reason, the protest was faint and brief. The remodelled processions started, with a chimney-sweep driving the hearse–advised by the regular driver, who was perched beside him, under close inspection, for the purpose–and with a pieman, also attended by his cabinet minister, driving the mourning coach. A bear leader, a popular street character of the time, was impressed as an additional ornament, before the cavalcade had gone far down the Strand; and his bear, who was black and very mangy, gave quite an Undertaking air to that part of the procession in which he walked.

Thus, with beer-drinking, pipe-smoking, song-roaring, and infinite caricaturing of woe, the disorderly procession went its way, recruiting at every step, and all the shops shutting up before it. Its destination was the old church of Saint Pancras, far off in the fields. It got there in course of time; insisted on pouring into the burial-ground; finally, accomplished the interment of the deceased Roger Cly in its own way, and highly to its own satisfaction.

The dead man disposed of, and the crowd being under the necessity of providing some other entertainment for itself, another brighter genius (or perhaps the same) conceived the humour of impeaching casual passers-by, as Old Bailey spies, and wreaking vengeance on them. Chase was given to some scores of inoffensive persons who had never been near the Old Bailey in their lives, in the realization of this fancy, and they were roughly hustled and maltreated. The transition to the sport of window-breaking, and thence to the plundering of public-houses, was easy and natural. At last, after several hours, when sundry summer-houses had been pulled down, and some area railings had been torn up, to arm the more belligerent spirits, a rumour got about that the Guards were coming. Before the rumour, the crowd gradually melted away, and perhaps the Guards came, and perhaps they never came, and this was the usual progress of a mob.

Mr. Cruncher did not assist at the closing sports, but had remained behind in the churchyard, to confer and condole with the undertakers. The place had a soothing influence on him. He procured a pipe from a neighbouring public-house, and smoked it, looking in at the railings and maturely considering the spot.

'Jerry,' said Mr. Cruncher, apostrophizing himself in his usual way, 'you see that there Cly that day, and you see with your own eyes that he was a young 'un and a straight made 'un.'

Having smoked his pipe out, and ruminated a little longer, he turned himself about, that he might appear before the hour of closing, on his station at Tellson's. Whether his meditations or mortality had touched his liver, or whether his general health had been previously at all amiss, or whether he desired to show a little attention to an eminent man, is not so much to the purpose, as that he made a short call upon his medical adviser—a distinguished surgeon—on his way back.

Young Jerry relieved his father with dutiful interest, and reported no job in his absence. The bank closed, the ancient clerks came out, the usual watch was set, and Mr. Cruncher and his son went home to tea.

'Now, I tell you where it is!' said Mr. Cruncher to his wife, on entering. 'If, as a honest tradesman, my wenturs goes wrong to-night, I shall make sure that you've been praying again me, and I shall work you for it just the same as if I seen you do it.'

The dejected Mr. Cruncher shook her head.

'Why, you're at it afore my face!' said Mr. Cruncher, with signs of angry apprehension.

'I am saying nothing.'

'Well, then; don't meditate nothing. You might as well flop as meditate. You may as well go again me one way as another. Drop it altogether.'

'Yes, Jerry.'

'Yes, Jerry,' repeated Mr. Cruncher, sitting down to tea. 'Ah! It is yes, Jerry. That's about it. You may say yes, Jerry.'

Mr. Cruncher had no particular meaning in these sulky corroborations, but made use of them, as people not unfrequently do, to express general ironical dissatisfaction.

'You and your yes, Jerry,' said Mr. Cruncher, taking a bite out of his bread and butter, and seeming to help it down with a large invisible oyster out of his saucer. 'Ah! I think so. I believe you.'

'You are going out to-night?' asked his decent wife, when he took another bite.

'Yes, I am.'

'May I go with you, father?' asked his son, briskly.

'No, you mayn't. I'm going—as your mother knows—a fishing. That's where I'm going to. Going a fishing.'

'Your fishing-rod gets rayther rusty; don't it, father?'

'Never you mind.'

'Shall you bring any fish home, father?'

'If I don't, you'll have short commons, to-morrow,' returned that gentleman, shaking his head; 'that's questions enough for you; I ain't a going out, till you've been long a-bed.'

He devoted himself during the remainder of the evening to keeping a most vigilant watch on Mrs. Cruncher, and sullenly holding her in conversation that she might be prevented from meditating any petitions to his disadvantage. With this view, he urged his son to hold her in conversation also, and led the unfortunate woman a hard life by dwelling on any causes of complaint he could bring against her, rather than he would leave her for a moment to her own reflections. The devoutest person could have rendered no greater homage to the efficacy of an honest prayer than he did in this distrust of his wife. It was as if a professed unbeliever in ghosts should be frightened by a ghost story.

'And mind you!' said Mr. Cruncher. 'No games tomorrow! If I, as a honest tradesman, succeed in providing a jinte of meat or two, none of your not touching of it, and sticking to bread. If I, as a honest tradesman, am able to provide a little beer, none of your declaring on water. When you go to Rome, do as Rome does. Rome will be a ugly customer to you, if you don't. *I*'m your Rome, you know.'

Then he began grumbling again:

'With you flying into the face of your own wittles and drink! I don't know how scarce you mayn't make the wittles and drink here, by your flopping tricks and your unfeeling conduct. Look at your boy: he *is* your'n, ain't he? He's as thin as a lath. Do you call yourself a mother, and not know that a mother's first duty is to blow her boy out?'

This touched young Jerry on a tender place; who adjured his mother to perform her first duty, and, whatever else she did or neglected, above all things to lay especial stress on the discharge of that maternal function so affectingly and delicately indicated by his other parent.

Thus the evening wore away with the Cruncher family, until young Jerry was ordered to bed, and his mother, laid under similar injunctions, obeyed them. Mr. Cruncher beguiled the earlier watched of the night with solitary pipes, and did not start upon his excursion until one o'clock. Towards that small and ghostly hour, he rose up from his chair, took a key out of his pocket, opened a locked cupboard, and brought forth a sack, a crowbar of convenient size, a rope and chain, and other fishing tackle of that nature. Disposing these articles about him in skilful manner, he bestowed a parting defiance on Mrs. Cruncher, extinguished the light, and went out.

Young Jerry, who had only made a feint of undressing when he went to bed, was not long after his father. Under cover of the darkness he followed out of the room, followed down the stairs, followed down the court, followed out into the streets. He was in no uneasiness concerning his getting into the house again, for it was full of lodgers, and the door stood ajar all night.

Impelled by a laudable ambition to study the art and mystery of his father's honest calling, young Jerry, keeping as close to house fronts, walls, and doorways, as his eyes were close to one another, held his honoured parent in view. The honoured parent steering northward, had not gone far, when he was joined by another disciple of Izaak Walton, and the two trudged on together.

Within half an hour from the first starting, they were beyond the winking lamps, and the more than winking watchmen, and were out upon a lonely road. Another fisherman was picked up here—and that so silently, that if young Jerry had been superstitious, he might have supposed the second follower of the gentle craft to have, all of a sudden, split himself into two.

The three went on, and young Jerry went on, until the three stopped under a bank overhanging the road. Upon the top of the bank was a low brick wall, surmounted by an iron railing. In the shadow of bank and wall the three turned out of the road, and up a blind lane, of which the wall–there, risen to some eight or ten feet high–formed one side. Crouching down in a corner, peeping up the lane, the next object that young Jerry saw, was the form of his honoured parent, pretty well defined against a watery and clouded moon, nimbly scaling an iron gate. He was soon over, and then the second fisherman got over, and then the third. They all dropped softly on the ground within the gate, and lay there a little–listening perhaps. Then they moved away on their hands and knees.

It was now young Jerry's turn to approach the gate: which he did, holding his breath. Crouching down again in a corner there, and looking in, he made out the three fishermen creeping through some rank grass! and all the gravestones in the churchyard–it was a large churchyard that they were in–looking on like ghosts in white, while the church tower itself looked on like ghost of a monstrous giant. They did not creep far, before they stopped and stood upright. And then they began to fish.

They fished with a spade, at first. Presently the honoured parent appeared to be adjusting some instrument like a great corkscrew. Whatever tools they worked with, they worked hard, until the awful striking of the church clock so terrified young Jerry, that he made off, with his hair stiff as his father's.

But, his long-cherished desire to know more about these matters, not only stopped him in his running away, but lured him back again. They were still fishing perseveringly, when he peeped in at the gate for the second time; but, now they seemed to have got a bite. There was a screwing and complaining sound down below, and their bent figures were strained, as if by a weight. By slow degrees the weight broke away the earth upon it, and came to the surface. Young Jerry very well knew what it would be; but, when he saw it, and saw his honoured parent about to wrench it open, he was so frightened, being new to the sight, that he made off again, and never stopped until he had run a mile or more.

He would not have stopped then, for anything less necessary than breath, it being a spectral sort of race that he ran, and one highly desirable to get to the end of. He had a strong idea that the coffin he had seen was running after him; and, pictured as hopping on behind him, bolt upright, upon its narrow end, always on the point of overtaking him and hopping on at his side–perhaps taking his arm–it was a purser to shun. It was an inconsistent and ubiquitous fiend too, for while it was making the whole night behind him dreadful, he darted out into the roadway to avoid dark alleys, fearful of its coming hopping out of them like a dropsical boy's kite without tail and wings. It hid in doorways too, rubbing its horrible shoulders against doors, and drawing them up to its ears, as if it were laughing. It got into shadows on the road, and lay cunningly on its back to trip him up. All this time it was incessantly hopping on behind and gaining on him, so that when the boy got to his own door he had reason for being half dead. And even then it would not leave him, but followed him upstairs with a bump on every stair, scrambled into bed with him, and bumped down, dead and heavy, on his breast when he fell asleep.

From his oppressed slumber, young Jerry in his closet was awakened after daybreak and before sunrise, by the presence of his father in the family room. Something had gone wrong with him; at least, so young Jerry inferred, from the circumstance of his holding Mrs. Cruncher by the ears, and knocking the back of her head against the head-board of the bed.

'I told you I would,' said Mr. Cruncher, 'and I did.'

'Jerry, Jerry, Jerry!' his wife implored.

'You oppose yourself to the profit of the business,' said Jerry, 'and me and my partners suffer. You was to honour and obey; why the devil don't you?'

'I try to be a good wife,' the poor woman protested, with tears.

'Is it being a good wife to oppose your husband's business? Is it honouring your husband to dishonour his business? Is it obeying your husband to disobey him on the wital subject of his business?'

'You hadn't taken to the dreadful business then, Jerry.'

'It's enough for you,' retorted Mr. Cruncher, 'to be the wife of a honest tradesman, and not to occupy your female mind with calculations when he took to his trade or when he didn't. A honouring and obeying wife would let his trade alone altogether. Call yourself a religious woman? If you're a religious woman, give me a irreligious one! You have no more nat'ral sense of duty than the bed of this here Thames river has of a pile, and similarly it must be knocked into you.'

The altercation was conducted in a low tone of voice, and terminated in the honest tradesman's kicking off his clay-soiled boots, and lying down at his length on the floor. After taking a timid peep at him lying on his back, with his rusty hands under his head for a pillow, his son lay down too, and fell asleep again.

There was no fish for breakfast, and not much of anything else. Mr. Cruncher was out of spirits, and out of temper, and kept an iron pot-lid by him as a projectile for the correction of Mrs. Cruncher, in case he should observe any symptoms of her saying Grace. He was brushed and washed at the usual hour, and set off with his son to pursue his ostensible calling.

Young Jerry, walking with the stool under his arm at his father's side along sunny and crowded Fleet Street, was a very different young Jerry from him of the previous night, running home through darkness and solitude from his grim pursuer. His cunning was fresh with the day, and his qualms were gown with the night—in which particulars it is not improbable that he had compeered in Fleet Street and the City of London, that fine morning.

'Father,' said young Jerry, as they walked along, taking care to keep at arm's length and to have the stool well between them, 'what's a Resurrection Man?'

Mr. Cruncher came to a stop on the pavement before he answered, 'How should I know?'

'I thought you knowed everything father,' said the artless boy.

'Hem! Well,' returned Mr. Cruncher, going on again, and lifting off his hat to give his spikes free play, 'he's a tradesman.'

'What's his goods, father?' asked the brisk young Jerry.

'His goods,' said Mr. Cruncher, after turning it over in his mind, 'is a branch of Scientific goods.'

'Person's bodies, ain't it, father?' asked the lively boy.

'I believe it is something of that sort,' said Mr. Cruncher.

'Oh, father, I should so like to be a Resurrection Man when I'm quite growed up!'

Mr. Cruncher was soothed, but shook his head in a dubious and moral way. 'It depends upon how you dewelop your talents. Be careful to dewelop your talents, and never to say no more than you can help to nobody, and there's no telling at the present time what you may not come to be fit for.' As young Jerry, thus encouraged, went on a few yards in advance, to plant the stool in the shadow of the Bar, Mr. Cruncher added to himself: 'Jerry, you honest tradesman, there's hopes wot that boy will yet be a blessing to you, and a recompense to you for his mother!'

CHAPTER XV

KNITTING

THERE had been earlier drinking than usual in the wine shop of Monsieur Defarge. As early as six o'clock in the morning, sallow faces peeping through its barred windows had described other faces within, bending over measures of wine. Monsieur Defarge sold a very thin wine at the best of times, but it would seem to have been an unusually thin wine that he sold at this time. A sour wine, moreover, or a souring, for its influence on the mood of those who drank it was to make them gloomy. No vivacious Bacchanalian flame leaped out of the pressed grape of Monsieur Defarge: but, a smouldering fire that burnt in the dark, lay hidden in the dregs of it.

This had been the third morning in succession, on which there had been early drinking at the wine shop of Monsieur Defarge. It had been begun on Monday, and here was Wednesday come. There had been more of early brooding than drinking; for, many men had listened and whispered and slunk about there from there from the time of the opening of the door, who could not have laid a piece of money on the counter to save their souls. These were to the full as interested in the place, however, as if they could have commanded whole barrels of wine; and they glided from seat to seat, and from corner to corner, swallowing talk in lieu of drink, with greedy looks.

Notwithstanding an unusual flow of company, the master of the wine shop was not visible. He was not missed; for, nobody who crossed the threshold looked for him, nobody asked for him, nobody wondered to see only Madame Defarge in her seat, presiding over the distribution of wine, with a bowl of battered small coins before her, as much defaced and beaten out of their original impress as the small coinage of humanity from whose ragged pockets they had come.

A suspended interest and a prevalent absence of mind, were perhaps observed by the spies who looked in at the wine shop, as they looked in at every place, high and low, from the king's palace to the criminal's jail. Games at cards languished, players at dominoes musingly built towers with them, drinkers drew figures on the tables with spilt drops of wine, Madame Defarge herself picked out the pattern on her sleeve with her toothpick, and saw and heard something inaudible and invisible a long way off.

Thus, Saint Antoine in this vinous feature of his, until midday. It was high noontide, when two dusty men passed through his streets and under his swinging lamps: of whom, one was Monsieur Defarge: the other a mender of roads in a blue cap. All adjust and athirst, the two entered the wine shop. Their arrival had lighted a kind of fire in the breast of Saint Antoine, fast spreading as they came along, which stirred and flickered in flames of faces at most doors and windows. Yet, no one had followed them, and no man spoke when they entered the wine shop, though the eyes of every man there were turned upon them.

'Good day, gentlemen!' said Monsieur Defarge.

It may have been a signal for loosening the general tongue. It elicited an answering chorus of 'Good day!'

'It is bad weather, gentlemen,' said Defarge, shaking his head.

Upon which, every man looked at his neighbour, and then all cast down their eyes and sat silent. Except one man, who got up and went out.

'My wife,' said Defarge aloud, addressing Madame Defarge: 'I have travelled certain leagues with this good mender of roads, called Jacques. I met him—by accident—a day and half's journey out of Paris. He is a good child, this mender of roads, called Jacques. Give him to drink, my wife!'

A second man got up and went out.

Defarge refreshed himself with a draught of wine—but, he tooks less than was given to the stranger, as being himself a man to whom it was no rarity—and stood waiting until the countryman had made his breakfast. He looked at no one present, and no one now looked at him; not even Madame Defarge, who had taken up her knitting, and was at work.

'Have you finished your repast, friend?' he asked, in due season.

'Yes, thank you.'

'Come, then! You shall see the apartment that I told you could occupy. It will suit you to a marvel.'

Out of the wine shop into the street, out of the street into a courtyard, out of the courtyard up a steep staircase, out of the staircase into a garret—formerly the garret where a white-haired man sat on a low bench, stooping forward and very busy, making shoes.

No white-haired man was there now, but, the three men were there who had gone out of the wine shop singly. And between them and the white-haired man afar off, was the one small link, that they had once looked in at him through the chinks in the wall.

Defarge closed the door carefully, and spoke in a subdued voice:

'Jacques One, Jacques Two, Jacques Three! This is the witness encountered by appointment, by me, Jacques Four. He will tell you all. Speak, Jacques Five!'

The mender of roads, blue cap in hand, wiped his swarthy forehead with it, and said, 'Where shall I commence, monsieur?'

'Commence,' was Monsieur Defarge's not unreasonable reply, 'at the commencement.'

'I saw him then, messieurs,' began the mender of roads, 'a year ago this running summer, underneath the carriage of the Marquis, hanging by the chain. Behold the manner of it. I leaving my work on the road, the sun going to bed, the carriage of the Marquis slowly ascending the hill, he hanged by the chain–like this.'

Again the mender of roads went through the whole performance; in which he ought to have been perfect by that time, seeing that it had been the infallible resource and indispensable entertainment of his village during a whole year.

Jacques One struck in, and asked if he had ever seen the man before?

'Never,' answered the mender of roads, recovering his perpendicular.

Jacques Three demanded how he afterwards recognized him then?

'By his tall figure,' said the mender of roads, softly, and with his finger at his nose. 'When Monsieur the Marquis demands that evening, "Say, what is he like?" I make response, "Tall as a spectre."'

'You should have said, short as a dwarf,' returned Jacques Two.

'But what did I know? The deed was not then accomplished, neither did he confide in me. Observe! Under those circumstances even, I do not offer my testimony. Monsieur the Marquis indicates me with his finger, standing near our little fountain, and says, "To me! Bring that rascal!" My faith, messieurs, I offer nothing.'

'He is right there, Jacques,' murmured Defarge, to him who had interrupted.

'Good!' said the mender of roads, with an air of mystery. 'The tall man is lost, and he is sought–how many months? Nine, ten, eleven?'

'No matter, the number,' said Defarge. 'He is well hidden, but at last he is unluckily found. Go on!'

'I am again at work upon the hillside, and the sun is again about to go to bed. I am collecting my tools to descend to my cottage down in the village below, where it is already dark, when I raise my eyes, and see coming over the hill six soldiers. In the midst of them is a tall man with his arms bound–tied to his sides–like this!'

With the aid of his indispensable cap, he represented a man with his elbows bound fast at his lips, with cords that were knotted behind him.

'I stand aside, messieurs, by my heap of stones, to see the soldiers and their prisoner pass (for it is a solitary road, that, where any spectacle is well worth looking at), and at first, as they approach, I see no more than that they are six soldiers with a tall man bound, and that they are almost black to my sight-except on the side of the sun going to bed, where they have a red edge, messieurs. Also, I see that their long shadows are on the hollow ridge on the opposite side of the road, and are on the hill above it, and are like the shadows of giants. Also, I see that they are covered with dust, and that the dust moves with them as they come, tramp, tramp! But when they advance quite near to me, I recognize the tall man, and he recognizes me. Ah, but he would be well content to precipitate himself over the hillside once again, as on the evening when he and I first encountered, close to the same spot!'

He described it as if he were there, and it was evident that he saw it vividly, perhaps he had not seen much in his life.

'I do not show the soldiers that I recognize the tall man; he does not shoe the soldiers that he recognizes me; we do it, and we know it, with our eyes. "Come on!" says the chief of that company, pointing to the village, "bring him fast to his tomb!" and they bring him faster. I follow. His arms are swelled because of being bound so tight, his wooden shoes are large and clumsy, and he is lame; because he is lame, and consequently slow, they drive him with their guns–like this!'

He imitated the action of a man's being impelled forward by the butt-ends of muskets.

'As they descend the hill like madmen running a race, he falls. They laugh and pick him up again. His face is bleeding and covered with dust, but he cannot touch it; thereupon they laugh again. They bring him into the village; all the village runs to look; they take him past the mill, and up to the prison; all the villages sees the prison gate open in the darkness of the night, and swallow him–like this!'

He opened his mouth as wide as he could, and shut it with a sounding snap of his teeth. Observant of his unwillingness to mar the effect by opening it again, Defarge said, 'Go on, Jacques.'

'All the village,' pursued the mender of roads, on tiptoe and in a low voice, 'withdraws; all the village whispers by the fountain; all the village sleeps; all the village dreams of that unhappy one, with the locks and bars of the prison on the crag, and never to come out of it, except to perish. In the morning, with my tools upon my shoulder, eating my morsel of black bread as I go, I make a circuit by the prison, on my way to my work. Then I see him, high up, behind the bars of a lofty iron cage, bloody and dusty as last night, looking through. He has no free hand, to wave to me; I dare not call to him; he regards me like a dead man.'

Defarge and the three glanced darkly at one another. The looks of all of them were dark, repressed, and revengeful, as they listened to the country-man's story; the manner of all of them, while it was secret, was authoritative too. They had the air of a rough tribunal; Jacques One and Two sitting on the old pallet-bed, each with his chin resting on his hand, and his eyes intent on the road-mender; Jacques Three, equally intent, on one knee behind them, with his agitated hand always gliding over the network of fine nerves about his mouth and nose; Defarge standing between them and the narrator, whom he had stationed in the light of the window, by turns looking from him to them, and from them to him.

'Go on, Jacques,' said Defarge.

'He remains up there in his iron cage some days. The village looks at him by stealth, for it is afraid. But it always looks up, from a distance, at the prison on the crag; and in the evening, when the work of the day is achieved and it assembles to gossip at the fountain, all faces are turned towards the prison. They whisper at the fountain, that although condemned to death he will not be executed; they say that petitions have been presented in Paris, showing that he was enraged and made mad by the death of his child; they say that a petition has been presented to the king himself. What do I know? It is possible. Perhaps yes, perhaps no.'

'Listen then, Jacques,' Number One of that name sternly interposed. 'Know that a petition was presented to the king and queen. All here, your-self excepted, saw the king take it, in his carriage in the street, sitting beside the queen. It is Defarge whom you see here, who, at the hazard of his life, darted out before the horses, with the petition in his hand.'

'And once again listen, Jacques!' said the kneeling Number Three: his fin-gers ever wandering over and over those fine nerves, with a striking greedy air, as if he hungered for something–that was neither food nor drink; 'the guard, horse and foot, surrounded the petitioner, and struck him blows. You hear?'

'I hear, messieurs.'

'Go on then,' said Defarge.

'Again; on the other hand, they whisper at the fountain,' resumed the countryman, 'that he is brought down into our country to be executed on the spot, and that he will very certainly be executed. They even whisper that because he has slain Monseigneur, and because Monseigneur was the fa-ther of his tenants–serfs–what you will–he will be executed as a parricide. One old man says at the fountain, that his right hand, armed with the knife, will be burnt off before his face; that, into wounds which will be made in his arms, his breast, and his legs, there will be poured boiling oil, melted lead, hot resin, wax, and sulphur; finally, that he will be torn limb from limb by four strong horses. That old man says, all this was actually done to a pris-oner who made an attempt on the life of the late king, Louis Fifteen. But how do I know if he lies? I am not a scholar.'

'Listen once again then, Jacques!' said the man with the restless hand and the craving air. 'The name of that prisoner was Damiens, and it was all done in open day, in the open streets of this city of Paris; and nothing was more noticed in the vast concourse that saw it done, than the crowd of ladies of quality and fashion, who were full of eager attention to the last–to the last, Jacques, prolonged until nightfall, when he had lost two legs and an arm, and still breathed! And it was done–why, how old are you?'

'Thirty-five,' said the mender of roads, who looked sixty.

'It was done when you were more than ten years old; you might have seen it.'

'Enough!' said Defarge, with grim impatience. 'Long live the Devil! Go on.'

'Well! Some whispers this, some whisper that; they speak of nothing else, even the fountain appears to fall to that tune. At length, on Sunday night when all the village is asleep, come soldiers, winding down from the prison, and their guns ring on the stones of the little street. Workmen dig, workmen hammer, soldiers laugh and sing; in the morning, by the fountain, there is raises a gallows forty feet high, poisoning the water.'

The mender of roads looked *through* rather than *at* the low ceiling, and pointed as if he saw the gallows somewhere in the sky.

'All work is stopped, all assemble there, nobody leads the cows out, the cows are there with the rest. At midday, the roll of drums. Soldiers have marched into the prison in the night, and he is in the midst of many soldiers. He is bound as before, and in his mouth there is a gag–tied so, with a tight string, making him look almost as if he laughed.' He suggested it, by creasing his face with his two thumbs, from the corners of his mouth to his ears.

'On the top of the gallows is fixed the knife, blade upwards, with its point in the air. He is hanged there forty feet high–and is left hanging, poisoning the water.

They looked at one another, as he used his blue cap to wipe his face, on which the perspiration had started afresh while he recalled the spectacle.

'It is frightful, messieurs. How can the woman and the children draw water! Who can gossip of an evening, under that shadow! Under it, have I said? When I left the village, Monday evening as the sun was going to bed, and looked back from the hill, the shadow struck across the church, across the mill, across the prison–seemed to strike across the earth, messieurs, to where the sky rests upon it!'

The hungry man gnawed one of his fingers as he looked at the other three, and his finger quivered with the craving that was on him.

'That's all, messieurs. I left at sunset (as I had been warned to do), and I walked on, that night and half next day, until I met (as I was warned I should) this comrade. With him, I came on, now riding and now walking, through the rest of yesterday and through last night. And here you see me!'

After a gloomy silence, the first Jacques said, 'Good! You have acted and recounted faithfully. Will you wait for us a little, outside the door?'

'Very willingly,' said the mender of roads. Whom Defarge escorted to the top of the stairs, and, leaving seated there, returned.

The three had risen, and their heads were together when he came back to the garret.

'How say you, Jacques?' demanded Number One. 'To be registered?'

'To be registered, as doomed to destruction,' returned Defarge.

'Magnificent!' croaked the man with the craving.

'The château, and all the race?' inquired the first.

'The château and all the race,' returned Defarge. 'Extermination.'

The hungry man repeated, in a rapturous croak, 'Magnificent!' and began gnawing another finger.

'Are you sure,' asked Jacques Two, of Defarge, 'that no embarrassment can arise from our manner of keeping the register? Without doubt it is safe, for no one beyond ourselves can decipher it; but shall we always be able to decipher it–or, I ought to say, will she?'

'Jacques,' returned Defarge, drawing himself up, 'if madame my wife undertook to keep the register in her memory alone, she would not lose a word of it–not a syllable of it. Knitted, in her own stitches and her own symbols, it will always be as plain to her as the sun. Confide in Madame Defarge. It would be easier for the weakest poltroon that lives, to erase himself from existence, than to erase one letter of his name or crimes from the knitted register of Madame Defarge.'

There was a murmur of confidence and approval, and then the man who hungered, asked: 'Is this rustic to be sent back soon? I hope so. He is very simple; is he not a little dangerous?'

'He knows nothing,' said Defarge; 'at least nothing more than would easily elevate himself to a gallows of the same height. I charge myself with him; let him remain with me; I will take care of him, and set him on his road. He wishes to see the fine world–the king, the queen, and court; let him see them on Sunday.'

'What?' exclaimed the hungry man, staring. 'Is it a good sign, that he wishes to see royalty and nobility?'

'Jacques,' said Defarge; 'judiciously show a cat milk, if you wish her to thirst for it. Judiciously show a dog his natural prey, if you wish him to bring it down one day.'

Nothing more was said, and the mender of roads, being found already dozing on the topmost stair, was advised to lay himself down on the pallet-bed and take some rest. He needed no persuasion, and was soon asleep.

Worse quarters than Defarge's wine shop, could easily have been found in Paris for a provincial slave of that degree. Saving for a mysterious dread of madame by which he was constantly haunted, his life was very new and agreeable. But, madame sat all day at her counter, so expressly unconscious of him, and so particularly determined not to perceive that his being there had any connection with anything below the surface, that he shook in his wooden shoes whenever his eye lighted on her. For, he contended with himself that it was impossible to foresee what that lady might pretend next; and he felt assured that if she should take into her brightly ornamented head to pretend that she had seen him do a murder and afterwards flay the victim, she would infallibly go through with it until the play was played out.

Therefore, when Sunday came, the mender of roads was not enchanted (though he said he was) to find that madame was to accompany monsieur and himself to Versailles. It was additionally disconcerting to have madame knitting all the way there, in a public conveyance; it was additionally disconcerting yet, to have madame in the crowd in the afternoon, still with her knitting in her hands as the crowd waited to see the carriage of the king and queen.

'You work hard, madame,' said a man near her.

'Yes,' answered Madame Defarge, 'I have a good deal to do.'

'What do you make, madame?'

'Many things.'

'For instance—'

'For instance,' returned Madame Defarge, composedly, 'shrouds.'

The man moved a little further away, as soon as he could, and the mender of the roads fanned himself with his blue cap: feeling it mightily close and oppressive. If he needed a king and queen to restore him, he was fortunate in having his remedy at hand; for, soon the large-faced king and the fair-faced queen came in their golden coach, attended by the shining Bull's Eye of their court, a glittering multitude of laughing ladies and fine lords; and in jewels and silks and powder and splendour and elegantly spurning figures and handsomely disdainful faces of both sexes, the mender of roads bathed himself, so much to his temporary intoxication, that he cried Long live the king, Long live the queen, Long live everybody and everything! as if he had never heard a ubiquitous Jacques in his time. Then, there were gardens, courtyards, terraces, fountains, green banks, more king and queen, more Bull's Eye, more lords and ladies, more Long live they all! until he absolutely wept with sentiment. During the whole of this scene, which lasted some three hours, he had plenty of shouting and weeping and sentimental company, and throughout Defarge held him by the collar, as if to restrain him from flying at the objects of his brief devotion and tearing them to pieces.

'Bravo!' said Defarge, clapping him on the back when it was over, like a patron; 'you are a good boy!'

The mender of roads was now coming to himself, and was mistrustful of having made a mistake in his late demonstrations; but no.

'You are the fellow we want,' said Defarge, in his ear; 'you make these fools believe that it will last for ever. Then, they are the more insolent, and it is the nearer ended.'

'Hey,' cried the mender of roads, reflectively; 'that's true.'

'These fools know nothing. While they despise your breath, and would stop it for ever and ever, in you or in a hundred like you rather than in one of their own horses or dogs, they only know what your breath tells them. Let it deceive them, then, a little longer; it cannot deceive them too much.'

Madame Defarge looked superciliously at the client, and nodded in confirmation.

'As to you,' said she, 'you would shout and shed tears for anything, if it made a show and a noise. Say! Would you not?'

'Truly, madame, I think so. For the moment.'

'If you were shown a great heap of dolls, and were set upon them to pluck them to pieces and despoil them for your own advantage, you would pick out the richest and gayest. Say! Would you not?'

'Truly yes, madame.'

'Yes. And if you were shown a flock of birds, unable to fly, and were set upon them to strip them of their feathers for your own advantage, you would set upon the birds of the finest feathers: would you not?'

'It is true, madame.'

'You have seen both dolls and birds to-day,' said Madame Defarge, with a wave of her hand towards the place where they had last been apparent; 'now, go home!'

CHAPTER XVI

STILL KNITTING

MADAME defarge and monsieur her husband returned amicably to the bosom of Saint Antoine, while a speck of a blue cap toiled through the darkness, and through the dust, and down the weary miles of avenue by the wayside, slowly tending towards that point of the compass where the château of Monsieur the Marquis, now in his grave, listened to the whispering trees. Such ample leisure had the stone faces, now, for listening to the trees and to the fountain, that the few village scarecrows who, in their quest for herbs to eat and fragments of dead stick to burn, strayed within sight of the great stone courtyard and terrace staircase, had it borne in upon their starved fancy that the expression of the faces was altered. A rumour just lived in the village–had a faint and bare existence there, as its people had–that when the knife struck home, the faces changed, from faces of pride to faces of anger and pain; also, that when that dangling figure was hauled up forty feet above the fountain, they changed again, and bore a cruel look of being avenged, which they would henceforth bear for ever. In the stone face over the great window of the bed-chamber where the murder was done, two fine dints were pointed out in the sculptured nose, which everybody recognized, and which nobody had seen of old; and on the scarce occasions when two or three ragged peasants emerged from the crowd to take a hurried peep at Monsieur the Marquis petrified, as skinny finger would not have pointed to it for a minute, before they all started away among the moss and leaves, like the more fortunate hares who could find a living there.

Château and hut, stone face and dangling figure, the red stain on the stone floor, and the pure water in the village well–thousands of acres of land–a whole province of France–all France itself–lay under the night sky, concentrated into a faint hairbreadth line. So does the whole world, with all its greatnesses and littlenesses, lie in a twinkling star. And as mere human knowledge can split a ray of light and analyse the manner of its composition, so, sublimer intelligences may read in the feeble shining of this earth of ours, every thought and act, every nice and virtue, of every responsible creature on it.

The Defarges, husband and wife, came lumbering under the starlight, in their public vehicle, to the gate of Paris whereunto their journey naturally tended. There was the usual stoppage at the barrier guard-house, and the usual lanterns came glancing forth for the usual examination and inquiry. Monsieur Defarge alighted; knowing one or two of the soldiery there, and one of the police. The latter he was intimate with, and affectionately embraced.

When Saint Antoine had again enfolded the Defarges in his dusky wings, and they, having finally alighted near the Saint's boundaries, were picking their way on foot through the black mud and offal of his streets, Madame Defarge spoke to her husband:

'Say then, my friend; what did Jacques of the police tell thee?'

'Very little, to-night, but all he knows. There is another spy commissioned for our quarter. There may be many more, for all that he can say, but he knows of one.'

'Eh well!' said Madame Defarge, raising her eyebrows with a cool business air. 'It is necessary to register him. How do they call that man?'

'He is English.'

'So much the better. His name?'

'Barsad,' said Defarge, making it French by pronunciation. But, he had been so careful to get it accurately that he then spelt it with perfect correctness.

'Barsad,' repeated madame. 'Good. Christian name?'

'John.'

'John Barsad,' repeated madame, after murmuring it once to herself. 'Good. His appearance; is it known?'

'Age, about forty years; height, about five feet nine; black hair; complexion dark; generally, rather handsome visage; eyes dark; face thin, long, and sallow; nose aquiline, but not straight, having a peculiar inclination towards the left cheek; expression, therefore, sinister.'

'Eh my faith. It is a portrait!' said madame, laughing. 'He shall be registered to-morrow.'

They turned into the wine shop, which was closed (for it was midnight), and where Madame Defarge immediately took her post at her desk, counting the small moneys that had been taken during her absence, examined the stock, went through the entries in the book, made other entries of her own, checked the serving man in every possible way, and finally dismissed him to bed. Then she turned out the contents of the bowl of money for the second time, and began knotting them up in her handkerchief, in a chain of separate knots, for safe keeping through the night. All this while, Defarge, with his pipe in his mouth, walked up and down, complacently admiring, but never interfering; in which condition, indeed, as to the business and his domestic affairs, he walked up and down through life.

The night was hot, and the shop, close shut and surrounded by so foul a neighbourhood, was ill-smelling. Monsieur Defarge's olfactory sense was by no means delicate, but the stock of wine smelt much stronger than it ever tasted, and so did the stock of rum and brandy and aniseed. He whiffed the compound of scents away, as he put down his smoked-out pipe.

'You are fatigued,' said madame, rasing her glance as she knotted the money. 'There are only the usual odours.'

'I am a little tired,' her husband acknowledged.

'You are a little depressed too,' said madame, whose quick eyes had never been so intent on the accounts, but they had had a ray or two for him. 'Oh, the men, the men!'

'But, my dear!' began Defarge.

'But, my dear!' repeated madame, nodding firmly; 'but, my dear! You are faint of heart to-night, my dear!'

'Well, then,' said Defarge, as if a thought were wrung out of his breast, 'it *is* a long time.'

'It is a long time,' repeated his wife; 'and when is it not a long time? Vengeance and retribution require a long time; it is the rule.'

'It does not take a long time to strike a man with lightning,' said Defarge.

'How long,' demanded madame, composedly, 'does it take to make and store the lightning? Tell me.'

Defarge raised his head thoughtfully, as if there were something in that too.

'It does not take a long time,' said madame, 'for an earthquake to swallow a town. Eh well! Tell me how long it takes to prepare the earthquake?'

'A long time, I suppose,' said Defarge.

'But when it is ready, it takes place, and grinds to pieces everything before it. In the meantime, it is always preparing, though it is not seen or heard. That is your consolation. Keep it.'

She tied a knot with flashing eyes, as if it throttled a foe.

'I tell thee,' said madame, extending her right hand, for emphasis, 'that although it is a long time on the road, it is on the road and coming. I tell thee it never retreats, and never stops. I tell thee it is always advancing. Look around and consider the lives of all the world that we know, consider the rage and discontent to which the Jacquerie addresses itself with more and more of certainty every hour. Can such things last? Bah! I mock you.'

'My brave wife,' returned Defarge, standing before her with his head a little bent, and his hands clasped at his back, like a docile and attentive pupil before his catechist, 'I do not question all this. But it has lasted a long time, and it is possible–you know well, my wife, it is possible–that it may not come, during our lives.'

'Eh well! How then?' demanded madame, tying another knot, as if there were another enemy strangled.

'Well!' said Defarge, with a half complaining and half apologetic shrug. 'We shall not see the triumph.'

'We shall have helped it,' returned madame, with her extended hand in strong action. 'Nothing that we do, is done in vain. I believe, with all my soul, that we shall see the triumph. But even if not, even if I knew certainly not, show me the neck of an aristocrat and tyrant, and still I would—'

Then madame, with her teeth set, tied a very terrible knot indeed.

'Hold!' cried Defarge, reddening a little as if he felt charged with cowardice; 'I too, my dear, will stop at nothing.'

'Yes! But it is your weakness that you sometimes need to see your victim and your opportunity, to sustain you. Sustain yourself without that. When the time comes, let loose a tiger and a devil; but wait for the time with the tiger and the devil chained–not shown–yet always ready.'

Madame enforced the conclusion of this piece of advice by striking her little counter with her chain of money as if she knocked its brains out, and then gathering the heavy handkerchief under her arm in a serene manner, and observing that it was time to go to bed.

Next noontide saw the admirable woman in her usual place in the wine shop, knitting away assiduously. A rose lay beside her, and if she now and then glanced at the flower, it was with no infraction of her usual preoccupied air. There were a few customers, drinking or not drinking, standing or seated, sprinkled about. The day was very hot, and heaps of flies, who were extending their inquisitive and adventurous perquisitions into all the glutinous little glasses near madame, fell dead at the bottom. Their decease made no impression on the other flies out promenading, who looked at them in the coolest manner (as if they themselves were elephants, or something as far removed), until they met the same fate. Curious to consider how heedless flies are!–perhaps they thought as much at Court that sunny summer day.

A figure entering at the door threw a shadow on Madame Defarge which she felt to be a new one. She laid down her knitting, and began to pin her rose in her head-dress, before she looked at the figure.

It was curious. The moment Madame Defarge took up the rose, the customers ceased talking, and began gradually to drop out of the wine shop.

'Good day, madame,' said the newcomer.

'Good day, monsieur.'

She said it aloud, but added to herself, as she resumed her knitting: 'Hah! Good day, age about forty, height about five feet nine, black hair, generally rather handsome visage, complexion dark, eyes dark, thin, long, and sallow face, aquiline nose but not straight, having a peculiar inclination towards the left cheek which imparts a sinister expression! Good day, one and all!'

'Have the goodness to give me a little glass of old cognac, and a mouthful of cool fresh water, madame.'

Madame complied with a polite air.

'Marvellous cognac this, madame!'

It was the first time it had ever been so complimented, and Madame Defarge knew enough of its antecedents to know better. She said, however, that the cognac was flattered, and took up her knitting. The visitor watched her fingers for a few moments, and took the opportunity of observing the place in general.

'You knit with great skill, madame.'

'I am accustomed to it.'

'A pretty pattern too!'

'*You* think so?' said madame, looking at him with a smile.

'Decidedly. May one ask what it is for?'

'Pastime,' said madame, still looking at him with a smile, while her fingers moved nimbly.

'Not for use?'

'That depends. I may find a use for it one day. If I do—well,' said madame, drawing a breath and nodding her head with a stern kind of coquetry, 'I'll use it!'

It was remarkable; but, the taste of Saint Antoine seemed to de decidedly opposed to a rose on the head-dress of Madame Defarge. Two men had entered separately, and had been about to order drink, when, catching sight of that novelty, they faltered, made a pretence of looking about as it for some friend who was not there, and went away. Nor, of those who had been there when this visitor entered, was there one left. They had all dropped off. The spy had kept his eyes open, but had been able to detect no sign. They had lounged away in a poverty-stricken, purposeless, accidental manner, quite natural and unimpeachable.

'JOHN,' thought madame, checking off her work as her fingers knitted, and her eyes looked at the stranger. 'Stay long enough, and I shall knit 'BARSAD' before you go.'

'You have a husband, madame?'

'I have.'

'Children?'

'No children.'

'Business seems bad?'

'Business is very bad; the people are so poor.'

'Ah, the unfortunate, miserable people! So oppressed, too—as you say.'

'As *you* say,' madame retorted, correcting him, and deftly knitting an extra something into his name that boded him no good.

'Pardon me; certainly it was I who said so, but you naturally think so. Of course.'

'*I* think?' returned madame, in a high voice. 'I and my husband have enough to do to keep this wine shop open, without thinking. All we think, here, is how to live. That is the subject *we* think of, and it gives us, from morning to night, enough to think about, without embarrassing our heads concerning others. *I* think for others? No, no.'

The spy, who was there to pick up any crumbs he could find or make, did not allow his baffled state to express itself in his sinister face; but stood with an air of gossiping gallantry, leaning his elbow on Madame Defarge's little counter, and occasionally sipping his cognac.

'A bad business this, madame, of Gaspard's execution. Ah! the poor Gaspard!' With a sigh of great compassion.

'My faith!' returned madame, coolly and lightly, 'if people use knives for such purposes, they have to pay for it. He knew beforehand what the price of his luxury was; he has paid the price.'

'I believe,' said the spy, dropping his soft voice to a tone that invited confidence, and expressing an injured revolutionary susceptibility in every muscle of his wicked face: 'I believe there is much compassion and anger in this neighbourhood, touching the poor fellow? Between ourselves.'

'Is there?' asked madame, vacantly.

'Is there not?'

'Here is my husband!' said Madame Defarge.

As the keeper of the wine shop entered at the door, the spy saluted him by touching his hat, and saying, with an engaging smile, 'Good day, Jacques!' Defarge stopped short, and stared at him.

'Good day, Jacques,' the spy repeated; with not quite so much confidence, or quite so easy a smile under the stare.

'You deceive yourself, monsieur,' returned the keeper of the wine shop. 'You mistake me for another. That is not my name. I am Ernest Defarge.'

'It is all the same,' said the spy, airily, but discomfited too: 'good day!'

'Good day!' answered Defarge, dryly.

'I was saying to madame, with whom I had the pleasure of chatting when you entered, that they tell me there is–and no wonder!–much sympathy and anger in Saint Antoine, touching the unhappy fate of poor Gaspard.'

'No one has told me so,' said Defarge, shaking his head. 'I know nothing of it.'

Having said it, he passed behind the little counter, and stood with his hand on the back of his wife's chair, looking over that barrier at the person to whom they were both opposed, and whom either of them would have shot with the greatest satisfaction.

The spy, well used to his business, did not change his unconscious attitude, but drained his little glass of cognac, took a sip of fresh water, and asked for another glass of cognac. Madame Defarge poured it out for him, took to her knitting again, and hummed a little song over it.

'You seem to know the quarter well; that is to say, better than I do?' observed Defarge.

'Not at all, but I hope to know it better. I am so profoundly interested in its miserable inhabitants.'

'Hah!' muttered Defarge.

'The pleasure of conversing with you, Monsieur Defarge, recalls to me,' pursued the spy, 'that I have the honour of cherishing some interesting associations with your name.'

'Indeed!' said Defarge, with much indifference.

'Yes, indeed. When Doctor Manette was released, you, his old domestic, had the charge of him, I know. He was delivered to you. You see I am informed of the circumstances?'

'Such is the fact, certainly,' said Defarge. He had had it conveyed to him, in an accidental touch of his wife's elbow as she knitted and warbled, that he would do best to answer, but always with brevity.

'It was to you,' said the spy, 'that his daughter came; and it was from your care that his daughter took him, accompanied by a neat brown monsieur; how is he called?

Having made, at least, this one hit, whatever it might prove to be worth, and no customers coming in to help him to any other, Mr. Barsad paid for what he had drunk, and took his leave: taking occasion to say, in a genteel manner, before he departed, that he looked forward to the pleasure of seeing Monsieur and Madame Defarge again. For some minutes after he had emerged into the outer presence of Saint Antoine, the husband and wife remained exactly as he had left them, lest he should come back.

'Can it be true,' said Defarge, in a low voice, looking down at his wife as he stood smoking with his hand on the back of her chair: 'what he has said of Ma'mselle Manette?'

'As he has said it,' returned madame, lifting her eyebrows a little, 'it is probably false. But it may be true.'

'If it is—' Defarge began, and stopped.

'If it is?' repeated his wife.

'—And if it does come, while we live to see it in triumph—I hope, for her sake, Destiny will keep her husband out of France.'

'Her husband's destiny,' said Madame Defarge, with her usual composure, 'will take him where he is to go, and will lead him to the end that is to lead him. That is all I know.'

'But it is very strange—now, at least, is it not very strange,' said Defarge, rather pleading with his wife to indice her to admit it, 'that, after all our sympathy for Monsieur her father, and herself, her husband's name should be proscribed under your hand at this moment, by the side of that infernal dog's who hast just left us?'

'Stranger things than that will happen when it does come,' answered madame. 'I have them both here, of a certainty; and they are both here for their merits; that is enough.'

She rolled up her knitting when she had said those words, and presently took the rose out of the handkerchief that was wound about her head. Either Saint Antoine had an instinctive sense that the objectionable decoration was gone, or Saint Antoine was on the watch for its disappearance; howbeit, the Saint took courage to lounge in, very shortly afterwards, and the wine shop recovered its habitual aspect.

In the evening, at which season of all others Saint Antoine turned himself inside out, and sat on door-steps and window-ledges, and came to the corners of vile streets and courts, for a breath of air, Madame Defarge with her work in her hand was accustomed to pass from place to place and from group to group: a Missionary—there were many like her—such as the world will do well never to breed again. All the women knitted. They knitted worthless things, but, the mechanical work was a mechanical substitute for eating and drinking; the hands moved for the jaws and the digestive apparatus: if the bony fingers had been still, the stomachs would have been more famine-pinched.

But, as the fingers went, the eyes went, and the thoughts. And as Madame Defarge moved on from group to group, all three went quicker and fiercer among very little knot of women that she had spoken with, and left behind.

Her husband smoked at his door, looking after her with admiration. 'A great woman,' said he, 'a strong woman, a grand woman, a frightfully grand woman!'

Darkness closed around, and then came the ringing of church bells and the distant beating of the military drums in the palace courtyard, as the women sat knitting, knitting. Darkness encompassed them. Another darkness was closing in as surely, when the church bells, then ringing pleasantly in many an airy steeple over France, should be melted into thundering cannon; when the military drums should be beating to drown a wretched voice, that night all potent as the voice of Power and Plenty, Freedom and Life. So much was closing in about the women who sat knitting, knitting, that they their very selves were closing in around a structure yet unbuilt, where they were to sit knitting, knitting, counting dropping heads.

CHAPTER XVII

ONE NIGHT

NEVER did the sun go down with a brighter glory on the quiet corner in Soho, than one memorable evening when the Doctor and his daughter sat under the plane-tree together. Never did the moon rise with a milder radiance over great London, than on that night when it found them still seated under the tree, and shone upon their faces through its leaves.

Lucie was to be married to-morrow. She had reserved this last evening for her father, and they sat alone under the plane-tree.

"You are happy, my dear father?"

"Quite, my child."

They had said little, though they had been there a long time. When it was yet light enough to work and read, she had neither engaged herself in her usual work, nor had she read to him. She had employed herself in both ways, at his side under the tree, many and many time; but, this time was not quite like any other, and nothing could make it so.

"And I am very happy to-night, dear father. I am deeply happy in the love that Heaven has so blessed-my love for Charles, and Charles's love for me. But, if my life were not to be, still consecrated to you, or if my marriage were so arranged as that it would part us, even by the length of a few of these streets, I should be more unhappy and self-reproachful now, than I can tell you. Even as it is-,"

Even as it was, she could not command her voice.

In the sad moonlight, she clasped him by the neck, and laid her face upon his breast. In the moonlight which is always sad, as the light of the sun itself is —as the light called human life is —at its coming and its going.

"Dearest dear! Can you tell me, this last time, that you feel quite, quite sure no new affections of mine, and no new duties of mine, will ever interpose between us? I know it well, but do you know it? In your own heart, do you feel quite certain?"

Her father answered, with a cheerful firmness of conviction he could scarcely have assumed, "Quite sure, my darling! More than that," he added, as he tenderly kissed her: "my future is far brighter, Lucie, seen through your marriage, than it could have been – nay, than it ever was – without it."

"If I could hope that, my father!-"

"Believe it, love! Indeed, it is so. Consider how natural and how plain it is, my dear, that it should be so. You, devoted and young, cannot freely appreciate the anxiety I have felt that your life should not be wasted –"

She moved her hand towards his lips, but he took it in his, and repeatd the word.

"- wasted, my child- should not be wasted, struck aside from the natural order of things, for my sake. Your unselfishness cannot entirely comprehend how much my mind has gone on this; but, only ask yourself, how could my happiness be perfect, while yours was incomplete?"

"If I had never seen Charles, my father, I should have been quite happy with you."

He smiled at her unconscious admisión that she would have been unhappy without Charles, having seen him, and replied:

"My child, you did see him, and it is Charles. If it had not been Charles, it would have been another. Or, if it had been no other, I shoud have been the cause, and than the dark part of my life would have cast its shadow beyond myself, and would have fallen on you."

It was the first time, except at the trial, of her even hearing him refer to the period of his suffering. It gave her a strange and new sensation while his words were in her ears; and she remembered it long afterwards.

"See! Said the Doctor of Beauvais, raising his hand towards the moon. "I have looked at her, in a state so dulled and lethargic, that I have thought of nothing but the number of horizontal lines I could draw across her at the full, and the number of perpendicular lines with which I could intersect them." He added in his inward and pondering manner, as he looked at the moon, "It was twenty either way, I remember, and the twentieth was difficult to squeeze in."

The strange thrill with which she heard him go back to that time, deepened as he dwelt upon it; but, there was nothing to shock her in the manner of his reference. He only seemed to contrast his present cheerfulness and felicity with the dire endurance that was over.

'I have looked at her, speculating thousand of times upon the unborn child from whom I had been rent. Whether it was alive. Whether it had been born alive, or the poor mother's shock had killed it. Whether it was a son who would some day avenge his father. (There was a time in my imprisonment, when my desire for vengeance was unbearable.) Whether it was a son who would never know his father's story; who might even live to weigh the possibility of his father's having disappeared of his own will and act. Whether it was a daughter who would grow to be a woman.'

She drew closer to him, and kissed his cheek and his hand.

'I have pictured my daughter, to myself, as perfectly forgetful of me–rather, altogether ignorant of me, and unconscious of me. I have cast up the years of her age, year after year. I have seen her married to a man who knew nothing of my fate. I have altogether perished from the remembrance of the living, and in the next generation my place was a blank.'

'My father! Even to hear that you had such thoughts of a daughter who never existed, strikes to my heart as if I had been that child.'

'You, Lucie? It is out of the consolation and restoration you have brought to me, that these remembrances arise, and pass between us and the moon on his last night.–What did I say just now?'

'She knew nothing of you. She cared nothing for you.'

'So! But on the other moonlight nights, when the sadness and the silence have touched me in a different way–have affected me with something as like a sorrowful sense of peace, as any emotion that had pain for its foundations could–I have imagined her as coming to me in my cell, and leading me out into the freedom beyond the fortress. I have seen her image in the moonlight often, as I now see you, except that I never held her in my arms; it stood between the little grated window and the door. But you understand that that was not the child I am speaking of?'

'The figure was not; the–the–image; the fancy?'

'No. That was another thing. It stood before my disturbed sense of sight, but it never moved. The phantom that my mind pursued, was another and more real child. Of her outward appearance I know no more than that she was like her mother. The other had that likeness too–as you have–but was not the same. Can you follow me, Lucie? Hardly, I think? I doubt you must have been a solitary prisoner to understand these perplexed distinctions.'

His collected and calm manner could not prevent her blood from running cold, as he thus tried to anatomize his old condition.

'In that more peaceful state, I have imagined her, in the moonlight, coming to me and taking me out to show me that the home of her married life was full of her loving remembrance of her lost father. My picture was in her room, and I was in her prayers. Her life was active, cheerful, useful; but my poor history pervaded it all.'

'I was that child, my father. I was not half so good, but in my love that was I.'

'And she showed me her children,' said the Doctor of Beauvais, 'and they had heard of me, and had been taught to pity me. When they passed a prison of the State, they kept far from its frowning walls, and looked up at its bars, and spoke in whispers. She could never deliver me; I imagined that she always brought me back after showing me such things. But then, blessed with the relief of tears, I fell upon my knees, and blessed her.'

'I am that child, I hope, my father. O my dear, my dear, will you bless me as fervently to-morrow?'

'Lucie, I recall these old troubles in the reason that I have to-night for loving you better than words can tell, and thanking God for my great happiness. My thoughts, when they were wildest, never rose near the happiness that I have known with you, and that we have before us.'

He embraced her, solemnly commended her to Heaven, and humbly thanked Heaven for having bestowed her on him. By and by, they went into the house.

There was no one bidden to the marriage but Mr. Lorry; there was even to be no bridesmaid but the gaunt Miss Pross. The marriage was to make no change in their place of residence; they had been able to extend it, by taking to themselves the upper rooms formerly belonging to the apocryphal invisible lodger, and they desired nothing more.

Doctor Manette was very cheerful at the little supper. They were only three at table, and Miss Pross made the third. He regretted that Charles was not there; was more than half disposed to object to the loving little plot that kept him away; and drank to him affectionately.

So, the time came for him to bid Lucie good night, and they separated. But, in the stillness of the third hour of the morning, Lucie came downstairs again, and stole into his room; not free from unshaped fear, beforehand.

All things, however, were in their places; all was quiet; and he lay asleep, his white hair picturesque on the untroubled pillow, and his hands lying quiet on the coverlet. She put her needless candle in the shadow at a distance, crept up to his bed, and put her lips to this; then, leaned over him, and looked at him.

Into his handsome face, the bitter waters of captivity had worn; but, he covered up their tracks with a determination so strong, that he held the mastery of them even in his sleep. A more remarkable face in its quiet, resolute, and guarded struggle with an unseen assailant, was not to be beheld in all the wide dominions of sleep, that night.

She timidly laid her hand on his dear breast, and put up a prayer that she might ever be as true to him as her love aspired to be, and as his sorrows deserved. Then, she withdrew her hand, and kissed his lips once more, and went away. So, the sunrise came, and the shadows of the leaves of the plane-tree moved upon his face, as softly as her lips had moved in praying for him.

CHAPTER XVIII

NINE DAYS

THE marriage day was shining brightly, and they were ready outside the closed door of the Doctor's room, where he was speaking with Charles Darnay. They were ready to go to church; the beautiful bride, Mr. Lorry, and Miss Pross—to whom the event, through a gradual process of reconcilement to the inevitable, would have been on of absolute bliss, but for the yet lingering consideration that her brother Solomon should have been the bridegroom.

'And so,' said Mr. Lorry, who could not sufficiently admire the bride, and who had been moving round her to take in every point of her quiet, pretty dress; 'and so it was for this, my sweet Lucie, that I brought you across the Channel, such a baby! Lord bless me! How little I thought what I was doing! How lightly I valued the obligation I was conferring on my friend Mr. Charles!'

'You didn't mean it,' remarked the matter-of-fact Miss Pross, 'and therefore how could you know it? Nonsense!'

'Really? Well; but don't cry,' said the gentle Mr. Lorry.

'I am not crying,' said Miss Pross; '*you* are.'

'I, my Pross?' (By this time, Mr. Lorry dared to be pleasant with her, on occasion.)

'You were, just now; I saw you do it, and I don't wonder at it. Such a present of plate as you have made 'em, is enough to bring tears into any-body's eyes. There's not a fork or a spoon in the collection,' said Miss Pross, 'that I didn't cry over, last night after the box came, till I couldn't see it.'

'I am highly gratified,' said Mr. Lorry, 'though upon my honour, I had no intention of rendering those trifling articles of remembrance invisible to any one. Dear me! This is an occasion that makes a man speculate on all he has lost. Dear, dear, dear! To think that there might have been a Mrs. Lorry, any time these fifty years almost!'

'Not at all!' From Miss Pross.

'You think there never might have been a Mrs. Lorry?' asked the gentleman of that name.

'Pooh!' rejoined Miss Pross; 'you were a bachelor in your candle.'

'Well!' observed Mr. Lorry, beamingly adjusting his little wig, 'that seems probable, too.'

'And you were cut out for a bachelor,' pursued Miss Pross, 'before you were put in your cradle.'

'Then, I think,' said Mr. Lorry, 'that I was very unhandsomely dealt with, and that I ought to have had a voice in the selection of my pattern. Enough! Now, my dear Lucie,' drawing his arm soothingly round her waist, 'I hear them moving in the next room, and Miss Pross and I, as two formal folks of business, are anxious not to lose the final opportunity of saying something to you that you wish to hear. You leave your good father, my dear, in hands as earnest and as loving as your own; he shall be taken every conceivable care of; during the next fortnight, while you are in Warwickshire and thereabouts, even Tellson's shall go to the wall (comparatively speaking) before him. And when, at the fortnight's end, he comes to join you and your beloved husband, on your other fortnight's trip in Wales, you shall say that we have sent him to you in the best health and in the happiest frame. Now, I hear somebody's step coming to the door. Let me kiss my dear girl with an old-fashioned bachelor blessing, before Somebody comes to claim his own.'

For a moment, he held the fair face from him to look at the well-remembered expression on the forehead, and then laid the bright golden hair against his little brown wig, with a genuine tenderness and delicacy which, if such things be old-fashioned, were as old as Adam.

The door of the Doctor's room opened, and he came out with Charles Darnay. He was so deadly pale–which had not been the case when they went in together–that no vestige of colour was to be seen in his face. But, in the composure of his manner he was unaltered, except that to the shrewd glance of Mr. Lorry it disclosed some shadowy indication that the old air of avoidance and dread had lately passed over him, like a cold wind.

He gave his arm to his daughter, and took her down stairs to the chariot which Mr. Olry had hired in honour of the day. The rest followed in another carriage, and soon, in a neighbouring church where no strange eyes looked on, Charles Darnay and Lucie Manette were happily married.

Besides the glancing tears that shone among the smiles of the little group when it was done, some diamonds, very bright and sparkling, glanced on the bride's hand, which were newly released from the dark obscurity of one of Mr. Lorry's pockets. Thay returned home to breakfast, and all went well, and in due course the golden hair that had mingled with the poor shoemaker's white locks in the Paris garret, were mingling with them again in the morning sunlight, on the threshold of the door at parting.

It was a hard parting, though it was not for long. But, her father cheered her, and said at last, gently disengaging himself from her enfolding arms, "Take her, Charles! She is yours!" And her agitated hand waved to them from a chaise window, and she was gone.

The corner being out of the way of the idle and curious, and the preparations having been very simple and few, the Doctor, Mr Lorry , and Miss Pross, were left quite alone. It was when they turned into the welcome shade of the cool old hall, that Mr Lorry observed a great change to have come over the Doctor; as if the golden arm uplifted there, had struck him a poisoned blow.

He had naturally repressed much, and some revulsion might have been expected in him when the ocasión for repression was gone. But, it was the old scared lost look that troubled Mr Lorry; and through his absent manner of clasping his head and drearily wandering away into his own room when they got up-stairs, Mr Lorry was reminded of Defarge the wine-shop keeper, and the starlight ride.

"I think." He whispered to Miss Pross, after anxious consideration, "I think we had best not speak to him just now, or at all disturb him. I must look in at Tellson's: so I will go there at once and come back presently. Than, we will take him a ride into the country, and dine there, and all will be well."

It was easier for Mr. Lorry to look in at Tellson's, than to look aout at Tellson's. He was detained two hours. When he came back, he ascended the old staircase alone, having asked no question of the servant; going tus into the Doctor's romos, he was sotpped by a low sound of knocking.

'Good God!' he said, with a start. 'What's that?'

Miss Pross, with a terrified face, was at his ear. 'O me, O me! All is lost!' cried she, wringing her hands. 'What is to be told to Ladybird? He doesn't know me, and is making shoes!'

Mr. Lorry said what he could to calm her, and went himself into the Doctor's room. The bench was turned towards the light, as it had been when he had seen the shoemaker at his work before, and his head was bent down, and he was very busy.

'Doctor Manette. My dear friend, Doctor Manette!'

The Doctor looked at him for a moment–half inquiringly, half as if he were angry at being spoken to–and bent over his work again.

He had laid aside his coat and waistcoat; his shirt was open at the throat, as it used to be when he did that work; and even the old haggard, faded surface of face had come back to him. He worked hard–impatiently–as if in some sense that was lying by him, and asked what it was?

'A young lady's walking shoe,' he muttered, without looking up. 'It ought to have been finished long ago. Let it be.'

'But, Doctor Manette. Look at me!'

He obeyed, in the old mechanically submissive manner, without pausing in his work.

'You know me, my dear friend? Think again. This is not your proper occupation. Think, dear friend!'

Nothing would induce him to speak more. He looked up, for an instant at a time, when he was requested to do so; but, no persuasion would extract a word from him. He worked, and worked, in silence, and words fell on him as they would have fallen on an echoless wall, or on the air. The only ray of hope that Mr. Lorry could discover, was, that he sometimes furtively looked up without being asked. In that, there seemed a faint expression of curiosity or perplexity–as though he were trying to reconcile some doubts in his mind.

Two things at once impressed themselves on Mr. Lorry, as important above all others; the first, that this must be kept secret from Lucie; the second that it must be kept secret from all who knew him. In conjunction with Miss Pross, he took immediate steps towards the latter precaution, by giving out that the Doctor was not well, and required a few days of complete rest. In aid of the kind deception to be practised on his daughter, Miss Pross was to write, describing his having been called away professionally, and referring to an imaginary letter of two or three hundred lines in his own hand, represented to have been addressed to her by the same post.

These measures, advisable to be taken in any case, Mr. Lorry took in the hope of his coming to himself. If that should happen soon, he kept another course in reserve; which was, to have a certain opinion that he thought the best, on the Doctor's case.

In the hope of his recovery, and of resort to this third course being thereby rendered practicable, Mr. Lorry resolved to watch him attentively, with as little appearance as possible of doing so. He therefore made arrangements to absent himself from Tellson's for the first time in his life, and took his post by the window in the same room.

He was not long in discovering that it was worse than useless to speak to him, since, on being pressed, he became worried. He abandoned that attempt on the first day, and resolved merely to keep himself always before him, as a silent protest against the delusion into which he had fallen, or was falling. He remained, therefore, in his seat near the window, reading and writing, and expressing in as many pleasant and natural ways as he could think of, that it was a free place.

Doctor Manette took what was given to him to eat and drink, and worked on, that first day, until it was too dark to see—worked on, half an hour after Mr. Lorry could not have seen, for his life, to read or write. When he put his tools aside as useless, until morning, Mr. Lorry rose and said to him:

'Will you go out?'

He looked down at the floor on either side of him in the old manner, looked up in the old manner, and repeated in the old low voice:

'Out?'

'Yes; for a walk with me. Why not?'

He made no effort to say why not, and said not a word more. But, Mr. Lorry thought he saw, as he leaned forward on his bench in the dusk, with his elbows on his knees and his head in his hands, that he was in some misty way asking himself, 'Why not?' The sagacity of the man of business perceived an advantage here, and determined to hold it.

Miss Pross and he divided the night into two watches, and observed him at intervals from the adjoining room. He paced up and down for a long time before he lay down; but, when he did finally lay himself down, he fell asleep. In the morning, he was up betimes, and went straight to his bench and to work.

On this second day, Mr. Lorry saluted his cheerfully by his name, and spoke to him on topics that had been of late familiar to them. He returned no reply, but it was evident that he heard what was said, and that he thought about it, however confusedly. This encouraged Mr. Lorry to have Miss Pross in with her work, several times during the day; at those times they spoke quietly of Lucie, and of her father then present, precisely in the same manner, and as if there were nothing amiss. This was done without any demonstrative accompaniment, not long enough, or often enough to harass him; and it lightened Mr. Lorry's friendly heart to believe that he looked up oftener, and that he appeared to be stirred by some perception of inconsistencies surrounding him.

When it fell dark again, Mr. Lorry asked him as before:

'Dear Doctor, will you go out?'

As before, he repeated, 'Out?'

'Yes; for a walk with me. Why not?'

This time, Mr. Lorry feigned to go out when he could extract no answer from him, and, after remaining absent for an hour, returned. In the meanwhile, the Doctor had removed to the sea in the window, and had sat there looking down at the plane-tree; but on Mr. Lorry's return, he slipped away to his bench.

The time went very slowly on, and Mr. Lorry's hope darkened, and his heart grew heavier again, and grew yet heavier and heavier every day. The third day came and went, the fourth, the fifth. Five days, six days, seven days, eight days, nine days.

With a hope ever darkening, and with a heart always growing heavier and heavier, Mr. Lorry passed through this anxious time. The secret was well kept, and Lucie was unconscious and happy; but he could not fail to observe that the shoemaker, whose hand had been a little out at first, was growing dreadfully skilful, and that he had never been so intent on his work, and that his hands had never been so nimble and expert, as in the dusk of the ninth evening.

CHAPTER XIX

AN OPINION

WORN out by anxious watching, Mr. Lorry fell asleep at his post. On the tenth morning of his suspense, he was startled by the shining of the sun into the room where a heavy slumber had overtaken him when it was dark night.

He rubbed his eyes and roused himself; but he doubted, when he had done so, whether he was not still asleep. For, going to the door of the Doctor's room and looking in, he perceived that the shoemaker's bench and tools were put aside again, and that the Doctor himself sat reading at the window. He was in his usual morning dress, and his face (which Mr. Lorry could not distinctly see), though still very pale, was calmly studious and attentive.

Even when he had satisfied himself that he was awake, Mr. Lorry felt giddily uncertain for some few moments whether the late shoemaking might not be a disturbed dream of his own; for, did not his eyes show him his friend before him in his accustomed clothing and aspect, and employed as usual; and was there any sign within their range, that the change of which he had so strong an impression had actually happened?

It was but the inquiry of his first confusion and astonishment, the answer being obvious. If the impression were not produced by a real corresponding and sufficient cause, how came he, Jarvis Lorry, there? How came he to have fallen asleep, in his clothes, on the sofa in Doctor Manette's consulting-room, and to be debating these points outside the Doctor's bedroom door in the early morning.

Within a few minutes, Miss Pross stood whispering at his side. If he had any particle of doubt left, her talk would of necessity have resolved it; but he was by that time clear-headed, and had none. He advised that they should let the time go by until the regular breakfast hour, and should then meet the Doctor as if nothing unusual had occurred. If he appeared to be in his customary state of mind, Mr. Lorry would then cautiously proceed to seek direction and guidance from the opinion he had been, in his anxiety, so anxious to obtain.

Miss Pross, submitting herself to his judgment, the scheme was worked out with care. Having abundance of time for his usual methodical toilet, Mr. Lorry presented himself at the breakfast hour in his usual white linen, and with his usual neat leg. The Doctor was summoned in the usual way, and came to breakfast.

So far as it was possible to comprehend him without overstepping those delicate and gradual approaches which Lorry felt to be the only safe advance, he at first supposed that his daughter's marriage had taken place yesterday. An incidental allusion, purposely thrown out, to the day of the week, and the day of the month, set him thinking and counting, and evidently made him uneasy. In all other respects, however he was so composedly himself, that Mr. Lorry determined to have the aid he sought. And that aid was his own.

Therefore, when the breakfast was done and cleared away, and he and the Doctor were left together, Mr. Lorry said, feelingly:

'My dear Manette, I am anxious to have your opinion, in confidence, on a very curious case in which I am deeply interested; that is to say, it is very curious to me; perhaps to your better information it may be less so.'

Glancing at his hands, which were discoloured by his late work, the Doctor looked troubled, and listened attentively. He had already glanced at his hands more than once.

'Doctor Manette,' said Mr. Lorry, touching him affectionately on the arm, 'the case is the case of a particularly dear friend of mine. Pray give your mind to it, and advise me well for his sake–and above all, for his daughter's–his daughter's, my dear Manette.'

'If I understand,' said the Doctor, in a subdued tone, 'some mental shock—?'

'Yes!'

'Be explicit,' said the Doctor. 'Spare no detail.'

Mr. Lorry saw that they understood one another, and proceeded.

'My dear Manette, it is the case of an old a prolonged shock, of great acuteness and severity to the affections, the feelings, the–the–as you express it–the mind. The mind. It is the case of a shock under which the sufferer was borne down, one cannot say for how long, because I believe he cannot calculate the time himself, and there are no other means of getting at it. It is the case of a shock from which the sufferer recovered, by a process that he cannot trace himself–as I once heard him publicly relate in a striking manner. It is the case of a shock from which he has recovered, so completely, as to be a highly intelligent man, capable of close application of mind, and great exertion of body, and of constantly making fresh additions to his stock of knowledge, which was already very large. But, unfortunately, there has been'–he paused and took a deep breath–'a slight relapse.'

The Doctor, in a low voice, asked, 'Of how long duration?'

'Nine days and rights.'

'How did it show itself? I infer'–glancing at his hands again–'in the resumption of some old pursuit connected with the shock?'

'That is the fact.'

'Now, did you ever see him,' asked the Doctor, distinctly and collectedly, though in the same low voice, 'engaged in that pursuit originally?'

'Once.'

'And when the relapse fell on him, was in he most respects–or in all respects–as he was then?'

'I think in all respects.'

'You spoke of his daughter. Does his daughter know of the relapse?'

'No. It has been kept from her, and I hope will always be kept from her. It is known only to myself, and to one other who may be trusted.'

The Doctor grasped his hand, and murmured, 'That was very kind. That was very thoughtful!' Mr. Lorry grasped his hand in return, and neither of the two spoke for a little while.

'Now, my dear Manette,' said Mr. Lorry, at length, in his most considerate and most affectionate way, 'I am a mere man of business, and unfit to cope with such intricate and difficult matters. I do not possess the kind of intelligence; I want guiding. There is no man in this world on whom I could so rely for right guidance, as on you. Tell me, how does this relapse come about? Is there danger of another? Could a repetition of it be prevented? How should a repetition of it be treated? How does it come about at all? What can I do for my friend? No man ever can have been more desirious in his heart to serve a friend, than I am to serve mine, if I knew how. But I don't know how to originate, in such a case. If your sagacity, knowledge, and experience, could put me on the right track, I might be able to do so much; unenlightened and undirected, I can do so little. Pray discuss it with me; pray enable me to see it a little more clearly, and teach me how to be a little more useful.'

Doctor Manette sat meditating after these earnest words were spoken, and Mr. Lorry did not press him.

'I think it probable,' said the Doctor, breaking silence with an effort, 'that the relapse you have described, my dear friend, was not quite unforeseen by its subject.'

'Was it dreaded by him?' Mr. Lorry ventured to ask.

'Very much.' He said it with an involuntary shudder.

'You have no idea how such an apprehension weighs on the sufferer's mind, and how difficult–now almost impossible–it is, for him to force himself to utter a word upon the topic that oppresses him.'

'Would he,' asked Mr. Lorry, 'be sensibly relieved if he could prevail upon himself to impart that secret brooding to any one, when it is on him?'

'I think so. But it is, as I have told you, next to impossible. I even believe it–in some cases–to be quite impossible.'

'Now,' said Mr. Lorry, gently laying his hand on the Doctor's arm again, after a short silence on both sides, 'to what would you refer this attack?'

'I believe,' returned Doctor Manette, 'that there had been a strong and extraordinary revival of the train of thought and remembrance that was the first cause of the malady. Some intense associations of the most distressing nature were vividly recalled, I think. It is probable that there had long been a dread lurking in his mind, that those associations would be recalled–say, under certain circumstances–say, on a particular occasion. He tried to prepare himself in vain; perhaps the effort to prepare himself made him less able to bear it.'

'Would he remember what took place in the relapse?' asked Mr. Lorry with natural hesitation.

The Doctor looked resolutely round the room, shook his head, and answered, in a low voice, 'Not at all.'

'Now, as to the future,' hinted Mr. Lorry.

'As to the future,' said the Doctor, recovering firmness, 'I should have great hope. As it pleased Heaven in its mercy to restore him so soon, I should have great hope. He, yielding under the pressure of a complicated something, long dreaded and long vaguely foreseen and contended against, and recovering after the cloud had burst and passed, I should hope that the worst was over.'

'Well, well! That's good comfort. I am thankful!' said Mr. Lorry.

'I am thankful!' repeated the Doctor, bending his head with reverence.

'There are two other points,' said Mr. Lorry, 'on which I am anxious to be instructed. I may go on?'

'You cannot do your friend a better service.' The Doctor gave him his hand.

'To the first, then. He is of a studious habit, and unusually energetic; he applies himself with great ardour to the acquisition of professional knowledge, to the conducting of experiments, to many things. Now, does he do too much?'

'I think not. It may be the character of his mind, to be always in singular need of occupation. That may be, in part, natural to it; in part the result of affliction. The less it was occupied with healthy things, the more it would be in danger of turning in the unhealthy direction. He may have observed himself, and made the discovery.'

'You are sure that he is not under too great a strain?'

'I think I am quite sure of it.'

'My dear Manette, if he were overworked now—'

'My dear Lorry, I doubt if that could easily be. There has been a violent stress in one direction, and it needs a counterweight.'

'Excuse me, as a persistent man of business. Assuming for a moment, that he *was* overworked; it would show itself in some renewal of this disorder?'

'I do not think so. I do not think,' said Doctor Manette with a firmness of self-conviction, 'that anything but the one train of association would renew it. I think that henceforth, nothing but some extraordinary jarring of that chord could renew it. After what has happened, and after his recovery, I find it difficult to imagine any such violent sounding of that string again. I trust, and I almost believe, that the circumstances likely to renew it are exhausted.'

He spoke with the diffidence of a man who had slowly won his assurance out of personal endurance and distress. It was not for his friend to abate that confidence. He professed himself more relieved and encouraged than he really was, and approached his second and last point. He felt it to be the most difficult of all; but, remembering his old Sunday morning conversation with Miss Pross, and remembering what he had seen in the last nine days, he knew that he must face it.

'The occupation resumed under the influence of this passing affliction so happily recovered from,' said Mr. Lorry, clearing his throat,' we will call–Blacksmith's work, Blacksmith's work. We will say, to put a case and for the sake of illustration, that he had been used, in his bad time, to work at a little forge. We will say that he was unexpectedly found at his forge again. Is it not a pity that he should keep it by him?'

The Doctor shaded his forehead with his hand, and beat his foot nervously on the ground.

'He has always kept it by him,' said Mr. Lorry, with an anxious look at his friend. 'Now, would it not be better that he should let it go?'

Still, the Doctor, with shaded forehead, beat his foot nervously on the ground.

'You do not find it easy to advise me?' said Mr. Lorry. 'I quite understand it to be a nice question. And yet I think—' And there he shook his head, and stopped.

'You see,' said Doctor Manette, turning to him after an uneasy pause, it is very hard to explain, consistently, the innermost workings of this poor man's mind. He once yearned so frightfully for that occupation, and it was so welcome when it came; no doubt it relieved his pain so much, by substituting the perplexity of the fingers for the perplexity of the brain, and by substituting, as he became more practised, the ingenuity of the hands, for the ingenuity of the mental torture; that he has never been able to bear the thought of putting it quite out of his reach. Even now, when I believe he is more hopeful of himself than he has ever been, and even speaks of himself with a kind of confidence, the idea that he might need that old employment, and not find it, gives him a sudden sense of terror, like that which one may fancy strikes to the heart of a lost child.'

He looked like his illustration, as he raised his eyes to Mr. Lorry's face.

'But may not–mind! I ask for information, as a plodding man of business who only deals with such material objects as guineas, shillings, and bank-notes–may not the retention of the thing involve the retention of the idea? If the thing were gone, my dear Manette, might not the fear go with it? In short, is it not a concession to the misgiving, to keep the forge?'

There was another silence.

'You see, too,' said the Doctor, tremulously, 'it is such an old companion.'

'I would not keep it,' said Mr. Lorry, shaking his head; for he gained in firmness as he saw the Doctor disquieted. 'I would recommend him to sacrifice it. I only want your authority. I am sure it does no good. Come! Give me your authority, like a dear good man. For his daughter's sake, my dear Manette!'

Very strange to see what a struggle there was within him!

'In her name, then, let it be done; I sanction it. But, I would not take it away while he was present. Let it be removed when he is not there, let him miss his old companion after an absence.'

Mr. Lorry readily engaged for that, and the conference was ended. They passed the day in the country, and the Doctor was quite restored. On the three following days he remained perfectly well, and on the fourteenth day he went away to join Lucie and her husband. The precaution that had been taken to account for his silence, Mr. Lorry had previously explained to him, and he had written to Lucie in accordance with it, and she had no suspicions.

On the night of the day on which he felt the house, Mr. Lorry went into his room with a chopper, saw, chisel, and hammer, attended by Miss Pross carrying a light. There, with closed doors, and in a mysterious and guilty manner, Mr. Lorry hacked the shoemaker's bench to pieces, while Miss Pross held the candle as if she were assisting at a murder–for which, indeed, in her grimness, she was no unsuitable figure. The burning of the body (previously reduced to pieces convenient for the purpose) was commenced without delay in the kitchen fire; and the tools, shoes, and leather, were buried in the garden. So wicked do destruction and secrecy appear to honest minds, that Mr. Lorry and Miss Pross, while engaged in the commission of their deed and in the removal of its traces, almost felt, and almost looked, like accomplices in a horrible crime.

CHAPTER XX

A PLEA

WHEN the newly married pair came home, the first person who appeared, to offer his congratulations, was Sydney Carton. They had not been at home many hours, when he presented himself. He was not improved in habits, or in looks, or in manner; but there was a certain rugged air of fidelity about him, which was new to the observation of Charles Darnay.

He watched his opportunity of taking Darnay aside into a window, and of speaking to him when no one overheard.

'Mr. Darnay,' said Carton, 'I wish we might be friends.'

'We are already friends, I hope.'

'You are good enough to say so, as a fashion of speech; but, I don't mean any fashion of speech. Indeed, when I say I wish we might be friends, I scarcely mean quite that, either.'

Charles Darnay–as was natural–asked him, in all good-humour and good-fellowship, what he did mean.

'Upon my life,' said Carton, smiling, 'I find that easier to comprehend in my own mind, than to convey to yours. However, let me try. You remember a certain famous occasion when I was more drunk than-than the usual?'

'I remember a certain famous occasion, when you forced me to confess that you had been drinking.'

'I remember it too. The curse of those occasions is heavy upon me, for I always remember them. I hope it may be taken into account one day, when all days are at an end for me! Don't be alarmed; I am not going to preach.'

'I am not at all alarmed. Earnestness in you, is anything but alarming to me.'

'Ah!' said Carton, with a careless wave of his hand, as if he waved that away. 'On the drunken occasion in question (one of a large number as you know), I was insufferable about liking you, and not liking you. I wish you would forget it.'

'I forgot it long ago.'

'Fashion of speech again! But, Mr. Darnay, oblivion is not so easy to me, as you represent it to be to you. I have by no means forgotten it, and a light answer does not help me to forget it.'

'If it was a light answer,' returned Darnay, 'I beg your forgiveness for it. I had no other object than to turn a slight thing, which, to my surprise, seems to trouble you too much, aside. I declare to you, on the faith of a gentleman, that I have long dismissed it from my mind. Good Heaven, what was there to dismiss! Have I had nothing more important to remember, in the great service you rendered me that day?'

'As to the great service,' said Carton, 'I am bound to avow to you, when you speak of it in that way, that it was mere professional claptrap. I don't know that I cared what became of you, when I rendered it. Mind! I say when I rendered it; I am speaking of the past.'

'You make light of obligation,' returned Darnay, 'but I will not quarrel with *your* light answer.'

'Genuine truth, Mr. Darnay, trust me! I have gone aside from my purpose; I was speaking about our being friends. Now, you know me; you know I am incapable of all the higher and better flights of men. If you doubt it, ask Stryver, and he'll tell you so.'

'I prefer to form my own opinion, without the aid of his.'

'Well! At any rate you know me as a dissolute dog, who has never done any good, and never will.'

'I don't know that you "never will."'

'But I do, and you must take my word for it. Well! If you could endure to have such a worthless fellow, and a fellow of such indifferent reputation, coming and going at odd times, I should ask that I might be permitted to come and go as a privileged person here; that I might be regarded as a useless (and I would add, if it were not for the resemblance I detected between you and me), an unornamental, piece of furniture, tolerated for its old service, and taken no notice of. I doubt if I should abuse the permission. It is a hundred to one if I should avail myself of it four times in a year. It would satisfy me, I dare say, to know that I had it.'

'Will you try?'

'That is another way of saying that I am placed on the footing I have indicated. I thank you, Darnay. I may use that freedom with your name?'

'I think so, Carton, by this time.'

They shook hands upon it, and Sydney turned away. Within a minute afterwards, he was, to all outward appearance, as unsubstantial as ever.

When he was gone, and in the course of an evening passed with Miss Pross, the Doctor, and Mr. Lorry, Charles Darnay made some mention of this conversation in general terms, and spoke of Sydney Carton as a problem of carelessness and recklessness. He spoke of him, in short, not bitterly or meaning to bear hard upon him, but as anybody might who saw him as he showed himself.

He had no idea that this cloud dwell in the thoughts of his fair young wife; but, when he afterwards joined her in their own rooms, he found her waiting for him with the old pretty lifting of the forehead strongly marked.

'We are thoughtful to-night!' said Darnay, drawing his arm about her.

'Yes, dearest Charles,' with her hands on his breast, and the inquiring and attentive expression fixed upon him; 'we are rather thoughtful to-night, for we have something on our mind to-night.'

'What is it, my Lucie?'

'Will you promise? What will I not promise to my Love?'

What, indeed, with his hand putting aside the golden hair from the cheek, and his other hand against the heart that beat for him!

'I think, Charles, poor Mr. Carton deserves more consideration and respect than you expressed for him to-night.'

'Indeed, my own? Why so?'

'That is what you are not to ask me. But I think–I know–he does.'

'If you know it, it is enough. What would you have me do, my Life?'

'I would ask you, dearest, to be very generous with him always, and very lenient on his faults when he is not by. I would ask you to believe that he has a heart he very, very seldom reveals, and that there are deep wounds in it. My dear, I have seen it bleeding.'

'It is a painful reflection to me,' said Charles Darnay, quite astounded, 'that I should have done him any wrong. I never thought this of him.'

'My husband, it is so. I fear he is not to be reclaimed; there is scarcely a hope that anything in his character or fortunes is reparable now. But, I am sure that he is capable of good things, gentle things, even magnanimous things.'

She looked so beautiful in the purity of her faith in this lost man, that her husband could have looked at her as she was for hours.

'And, O my dearest Love!' she urged, clinging nearer to him, laying her head upon his breast, and raising her eyes to his, 'remember how strong we are in our happiness, and how weak he is in his misery!'

The supplication touched him home. 'I will always remember it, dear Heart! I will remember it as long as I live.'

He bent over her golden head, and put the rosy lips to his, and folded her in his arms. If one forlorn wanderer then pacing the dark streets, could have heard her innocent disclosure, and could have seen the drops of pity kissed away by her husband from the soft blue eyes so loving of that husband, he might have cried to the night–and the word would not have parted from his lips for the first time–

'God bless her for her sweet compassion!'

CHAPTER XXI

ECHOING FOOTSTEPS

A WONDERFUL corner for echoes, it has been remarked, that corner where the Doctor lived. Every busily winding the golden thread which bound her husband, and her father, and herself, and her old directress and companion, in a life of quiet bliss, Lucie sat in the still house in the tranquilly resounding corner, listening to the echoing footsteps of years.

At first, there were times, though she was a perfectly happy young wife, when her work would slowly fall from her hands, and her eyes would be dimmed. For, there was something coming in the echoes, something light, afar off, and scarcely audible yet, that stirred her heart too much. Fluttering hopes and doubts–hopes, of a love as yet unknown to her: doubts, of her remaining upon earth, to enjoy that new delight–divided her breast. Among the echoes then, there would arise the sound of footsteps at her own early grave, and thoughts of the husband who would be left so desolate, and who would mourn for her so much, swelled to her eyes, and broke like waves.

That time passed, and her little Lucie lay on her bosom. Then, among the advancing echoes, there was the tread of her tiny feet and the sound of her prattling words. Let greater echoes resound as they would, the young mother at the cradle side could always hear those coming. They came, and the shady house was sunny with a child's laugh, and the Divine friend of children, to whom in her trouble she had confided hers, seemed to take her child in His arms, a He took the child of old, and made it a sacred joy to her.

Ever busily winding the golden thread that bound them all together, weaving the service of her happy influence through the tissue of all their lives, and making it predominate nowhere, Lucie heard in the echoes of years none but friendly and soothing sounds. Her husband's step was strong and prosperous among them; her father's firm and equal. Lo, Miss Pross, in harness of string, awakening the echoes, as an unruly charger, whip-corrected, snorting and pawing the earth under the plane-tree in the garden!

Even when there were sounds of sorrow among the rest, they were not hash nor cruel. Even when golden hair, like her own, lay in a halo on a pillow round the worn face of a little boy, and he said, with a radiant smile, 'Dear papa and mamma, I am very sorry to leave you both, and to leave my pretty sister; but I am called, and I must go!' those were not tears all of agony that wetted his young mother's cheek as the spirit departed from her embrace that had been entrusted to it. Suffer them and forbid them not. They see my Father's face. O Father, blessed words!

Thus, the rustling of an Angel's wings got blended with the other echoes, and they were not wholly of earth, but had in them that breath of Heaven. Sighs of the winds that blew over a little garden tomb were mingled with them also, and both were audible to Lucie, in a hushed murmur–like the breathing of a summer sea asleep upon a sandy shore–as the little Lucie, comically studious at the task of the morning, or dressing a doll at her mother's footstool, chattered in the tongues of the Two Cities that were blended in her life.

The echoes rarely answered to the actual tread of Sydney Carton. Some half-dozen times a year, at most, he claimed his privilege of coming in uninvited, and would sit among them through the evening, as he had once done often. He never came there heated with wine. And one other thing regarding him was whispered in the echoes, which has been whispered by all true echoes for ages and ages.

No man ever really loved a woman, lost her, and knew her with a blameless though an unchanged mind, when she was a wife and a mother, but her children had a strange sympathy for him–an instinctive delicacy of pity for him. When fine hidden sensibilities are touched in such a case, no echoes tell; but it is so, and it was so here. Carton was the first stranger to whom little Lucie held out her chubby arms, and he kept his place with her as she grew. The little boy had spoken of him, almost at the last. 'Poor Carton! Kiss him for me!'

Mr. Stryver shouldered his way through the law, like some great engine forcing itself through turbid water, and dragged his useful friend in his wake, like a boat towed astern. As the boat so favoured is usually in a rough plight, and mostly under water, so, Sydney had a swamped life of it. But, easy and strong custom, unhappily so much easier and stronger in him than any stimulating sense of desert or disgrace, made it the life he was to lead; and he no more thought of emerging from his state of lion's jackal, than any real jackal may be supposed to think of rising to be a lion. Stryver was rich; had married a florid widow with property and three boys, who had nothing particularly shining about them but the straight hair of their dumpling heads.

These three young gentlemen, Mr. Stryver, exuding patronage of the most offensive quality from every pore, had walked before him like three sheep to the quiet corner in Soho, and had offered as pupil to Lucie's husband: delicately saying, 'Halloa! here are three lumps of bread-and-cheese had quite bloated Mr. Stryver with indignation, which he afterwards turned to account in the training of the young gentlemen, by directing them to beware of the pride of Beggars, like that tutor fellow. He was also in the habit of declaiming to Mrs. Stryver, over his full-bodied wine, on the arts Mr. Darnay had once put in practicle to 'catch' him, and on the diamond-cut-diamond arts in himself, madam, which had rendered him 'not to be caught.' Some of his King's Bench familiars, who were occasionally parties to the full-bodied wine and the lie, excused him for the latter by saying that he had told it so often, that he believed it himself–which is surely such an incorrigible aggravation of an originally bad offence, as to justify any such offender's being carried off to some suitably retired spot, and there hanged out of the way.

These were among the echoes to which Lucie, sometimes pensive, sometimes amused and laughing, listened in the echoing corner, until her little daughter was six years old. How near to her heart the echoes of her child's tread came, and those of her own dear father's, always active and self-possessed, and those of her dear husband's, need not be told. Nor, how the lightest echo of their united home, directed by herself with such a wise and elegant thrift that it was more abundant than any waste, was music to her. Nor, how there were echoes all about her, sweet in her ears of the many times her father had told her that he found her more devoted to him married (if that could be) than single, and of the many times her husband had said to her that no cares and duties seemed to divide her love for him or her help to him, and asked her 'What is the magic secret, my darling, of your being everything to all of us, as if there were only one of us, yet never seeming to be hurried, or to have too much to do?'

But, there were other echoes, from a distance, that rumbled menacingly in the corner all through this space of time. And it was now, about little Lucie's sixth birthday, that they began to have an awful sound, as of a great storm in France with a dreadful sea rising.

On a night in mid July, one thousand seven hundred and eighty-nine, Mr. Lorry came in late, from Tellson's, and sat himself down by Lucie and her husband in the dark window. It was a hot, wild night, and they were all three reminded of the old Sunday night when they had looked at the lightning from the same place.

'I began to think,' said Mr. Lorry, pushing his brown wig back, 'that I should have to pass the night at Tellson's. We have been so full of business all day, that we have not known what to do first, or which way to turn. There is such an uneasiness in Paris, that we have actually a run of confidence upon us! Our customers over there, seem not to be able to confide their property to us fast enough. There is positively a mania among some of them for sending it to England.'

'That has a bad look,' said Darnay.

'A bad look, you say, my dear Darnay? Yes, but we don't know what reason there is in it. People are so unreasonable! Some of us at Tellson's are getting old, and we really can't be troubled out of the ordinary course without due occasion.'

'Still,' said Darnay, 'you know how gloomy and threatening the sky is.'

'I know that, to be sure,' assented Mr. Lorry, trying to persuade himself that his sweet temper was soured, and that he grumbled, 'but I am determined to be peevish after my long day's botheration. Where is Manette?'

'Here he is,' said the Doctor, entering the dark room at the moment.

'I am quite glad you are at home; for these hurries and forebodings by which I have been surrounded all day long, have made me nervous without reason. You are not going out, I hope?'

'No; I am going to play backgammon with you, if you like,' said the Doctor.

'I don't think I do like, if I may speak my mind. I am not fit to be pitted against you to-night. Is the teaboard still there, Lucie? I can't see.'

'Of course, it has been kept for you.'

'Thank ye, my dear. The precious child is safe in bed?'

'And sleeping soundly.'

'That's right; all safe and well! I don't know why anything should be otherwise than safe and well here, thank God; but I have been so put out all day, and I am not as young as I was! My tea, my dear! Thank ye. Now, come and take your place in the circle, and let us sit quiet and hear the echoes about which you have your theory.'

'Not a theory; it was a fancy.'

'A fancy, then my wise pet,' said Mr. Lorry, patting her hand. 'They are very numerous and very loud, though, are they not? Only hear them!'

Headlong, mad and dangerous footsteps to force their way into anybody's life, footsteps not easily made clean again if once stained red, the footsteps raging in Saint Antoine afar off, as the little circle sat in the dark London window.

Saint Antoine had been, that morning, a vast dusky mass of scarecrows heaving to and fro, with frequent gleams of light above the billowy heads, where steel blades and bayonets shone in the sun. A tremendous roar arose from the throat of Saint Antoine, and a forest of naked arms struggled in the air like shrivelled branches of trees in a winter wind: all the fingers convulsively clutching at every weapon or semblance of a weapon that was thrown up from the depths below, no matter how far off.

Who gave them out, whence they last came, where they began, through what agency they crookedly quivered and jerked, scores at a time, over the heads of the crowd, like a kind of lightning, no eye in the throng could have told; but, muskets were being distributed—so were cartridges, powder and ball, bars of iron and wood, knives, axes, pikes, every weapon that distracted ingenuity could discover or devise. People who could lay hold of nothing else, set themselves with bleeding hands to force stones and bricks out of their places in walls. Every pulse and heart in Saint Antoine was on high-fever strain and at high-fever heat. Every living creature there held life as of no account, and was demented with a passionate readiness to sacrifice it.

As a whirlpool of boiling waters has a centre point, so, all this raging circled round Defarge's wine shop, and every human drop in the cauldron had a tendency to be sucked towards the vortex where Defarge himself, already begrimed with gunpowder and sweat, issued orders, issued arms, thrust this man back, dragged this man forward, disarmed not to arm another, laboured and strove in the thickest of the uproar.

'Keep near to me, Jacques Three,' cried Defarge; 'and do you, Jacques One and Two, separate and put yourselves at the head of as many of these patriots as you can. Where is my wife?'

'Eh, well! Here you see me!' said madame, composed as ever, but not knitting to-day. Madame's resolute right hand was occupied with an axe, in place of the usual softer implements, and in her girdle were a pistol and a cruel knife.

'Where do you go, my knife?'

'I go,' said madame, 'with you at present. You shall see me at the head of women, by and by.'

'Come then!' cried Defarge, in a resounding voice. 'Patriots and friends, we are ready! The Bastille!'

With a roar that sounded as if all the breath in France had been shaped into the detested word, the living sea rose, wave on wave, depth on depth, and overflowed the city to that point. Alarm-bells ringing, drums beating, the sea raging and thundering on its new beach, the attack begun.

Deep ditches, double drawbridge, massive stone walls, eight great towers, cannon, muskets, fire and smoke. Through the fire and through the smoke–in the fire and in the smoke, for the sea cast him up against a cannon, and on the instant he became a cannonier–Defarge of the wine shop worked like a manful soldier, Two fierce hours.

Deep ditch, single drawbridge, massive stone walls, eight great towers, cannon, muskets, fire and smoke. One drawbridge down! 'Work, comrades all, work! Work, Jacques One, Jacques Two, Jacques One Thousand, Jacques Two Thousand, Jacques Five-and-Twenty Thousand; in the name of all the Angels or the Devils–which you prefer–work!' Thus Defarge of the wine shop, still at his gun, which had long grown hot.

'To me, women!' cried madame his wife. 'What! We can kill as well as the men when the place is taken!' And to her, with a shrill thirsty cry, trooping women variously armed, but all armed alike in hunger and revenge.

Cannon, muskets, fire and smoke; but, still the deep ditch, the single drawbridge, the massive stone walls, and the eight great towers. Slight displacements of the raging sea, made by the falling wounded. Flashing weapons, blazing torches, smoking wagon-loads of wet straw, hard work at neighbouring barricades in all directions, shrieks, volleys, execrations, bravery without stint, boom smash and rattle, and the furious sounding of the living sea; but, still the deep ditch, and the single drawbridge, and the massive stone walls, and the eight great towers, and still Defarge of the wine shop at his gun, grown doubly hot by the service of Four fierce hours.

A white flag from within the fortress, and a parley–this dimly perceptible through the raging storm, nothing audible in it–suddenly the sea rose immeasurably wider and higher and swept Defarge of the wine shop over the lowered drawbridge, past the massive stone outer walls, in among the eight great towers surrendered!

So resistless was the force of the ocean bearing him on, that even to draw his breath or turn his head was as impracticable as if he had been struggling in the surf at the South Sea, until he was landed in the outer courtyard of the Bastille. There, against an angle of a wall, he made a struggle to look about him. Jacques Three was nearly at his side; Madame Defarge, still heading some of her women, was visible in the inner distance, and her knife was in her hand. Everywhere was tumult, exultation, deafening and maniacal bewilderment, astounding noises, yet furious dumb-show.

'The prisoners!'

'The records!'

'The secret cells!'

'The instrument of torture!'

'The prisoners!'

Of all these cries, and ten thousand incoherencies, 'The prisoners!' was the cry most taken up by the sea that rushed in, as if there were an eternity of people, as well as of time and space. When the foremost billows rolled past, bearing the prison officers with them, and threatening them all with instant death if any secret nook remained undisclosed, Defarge laid his strong hand on the breast of one of these men–a man with a grey head, who had a lighted torch in his hand–separated him from the rest, and got him between himself and the wall.

'Show me the North Tower!' said Defarge. 'Quick!'

'I will faithfully,' replied the man, 'if you will come with me. But there is no one there.'

'What is the meaning of One Hundred and Five, North Tower?' asked Defarge. 'Quick!'

'The meaning, monsieur?'

'Does it mean a captive, or a place of captivity? Or do you mean that I shall strike you dead?'

'Kill him!' croaked Jacques Three, who had come close up.

'Monsieur, it is a cell.'

'Show it to me!'

'Pass this way, then.'

Jacques Three, with his usual craving on him, and evidently disappointed by the dialogue taking a turn that did not seem to promise bloodshed, held by Defarge's arm as he held by the turnkey's. Their three heads had been close together during this brief discourse, and it had been as much as they could do to hear one another, even then: so tremendous was the noise of the living ocean, in its irruption into the fortress, and its inundation of the courts and passages and staircases. All around outside, too, it beat the walls with a deep, hoarse roar, from which, occasionally, some partial shouts of tumult broke and leaped into the air like spray.

Through gloomy vaults where the light of day had never shone, past hideous doors of dark dens and cages, down cavernous flights of steps, and again up steep rugged ascents of stone and brick, more like dry waterfalls than staircases, Defarge, the turnkey, and Jacques Three, linked hand and arm, went with all the speed they could make. Here and there, especially at first, the inundation started on them and swept by; but when they had done descending, and were winding and climbing up a tower, they were alone.

Hemmed in here by the massive thickness of walls and arches, the storm within the fortress and without was only audible to them in a dull, subdued way, as if the noise out of which they had come had almost destroyed their sense of hearing.

The turnkey stopped at a low door, put a key in a clashing lock, swung the door slowly open, and said, as they all bent their heads and passed in—

'One hundred and five, North Tower!'

There was a small, heavily grated, unglazed window high in the wall, with a stone screen before it, so that the sky could be only seen by stooping low and looking up. There was a small chimney, heavily barred across, a few feet within. There was a heap of old feathery wood-ashes on the hearth. There was a stool, and table, and a straw bed. There were the four blackened walls, and a rusted iron ring in on of them.

'Pass that torch slowly along these walls, that I may see them,' said Defarge to the turnkey.

The man obeyed, and Defarge followed the light closely with his eyes.

'Stop!—Look here, Jacques!'

'A. M!' croaked Jacques Three, as he read greedily.

'Alexandre Manette,' said Defarge in his ear, following the letters with his swart forefinger, deeply engrained with gunpowder. 'And here he wrote "a poor physician." And it was he, without doubt, who scratched a calendar on this stone. What is that in your hand? A crowbar? Give it me!'

He had still the linstock of his gun in his own hand. He made a sudden exchange of the two instruments, and turning on the worm-eaten stool and table, beat them to pieces in a few blows.

'Hold the light higher!' he said, wrathfully, to the turnkey. 'Look among those fragments with care, Jacques. And see! Here is my knife'—throwing it to him—'rip open that bed, and search the straw. Hold the light higher, you!'

With a menacing look at the turnkey he crawled upon the hearth, and, peering up the chimney, struck and prised at its sides with the crowbar, and worked at the iron grating across it. In a few minuted, some mortar and dust came dropping down, which he averted his face to avoid; and in it, and in the old wood-ashes, and in a crevice in the chimney into which his weapon had slipped or wrought itself, he groped with a cautious touch.

'Nothing in the wood, and nothing in the straw, Jacques?'

'Nothing.'

'Let us collect them together, in the middle of the cell. So! Light them, you!'

The turnkey fired the little pile, which blazed high and hot. Stooping again to come out at the low-arched door, they left it burning, and retraced their way to the courtyard; seeming to recover their sense of hearing as they came down, until they were in the raging flood once more.

They found it surging and tossing, in quest of Defarge himself. Saint Antoine was clamorous to have its wine-shop keeper foremost in the guard upon the governor who had defended the Bastille and shot the people. Otherwise, the governor would not be marched to the *Hôtel de ville* for judgment. Otherwise, the governor would escape, and the people's blood (suddenly of some value, after many years of worthlessness) be unavenged.

In the howling universe of passion and contention that seemed to en-compass this grim old officer conspicuous in his grey coat and red decora-tion, there was but one quite steady figure, and that was a woman's. 'See, there is my husband!' she cried, pointing him out. 'See Defarge!' She stood immovable close to the grim old officer, and remained immovable close to him; remained immovable close to him through the streets, as Defarge and the rest bore him along; remained immovable close to him when he was got near his destination, and began to be struck at from; remained immovable close to him when the long-gathering rain of stabs and blows fell heavy; was so close to him when he dropped dead under it, that, suddenly animat-ed, she put her foot upon his neck, and with her cruel knife–long ready–hewed off his head.

The hour was come, when Saint Antoine was to execute his horrible idea of hoisting up men for lamps to show what he could be and do. Saint Antoine's blood was up, and the blood of tyranny and domination by the iron hand was down–down on the steps of the *Hôtel de ville* where the gov-ernor's body lay–down on the sole of the shoe of Madame Defarge where she had trodden on the body to steady it for mutilation. 'Lower the lamp yonder!' cried Saint Antoine, after glaring round for a new means of death; 'here is one of his soldiers to be left on guard!' The swinging sentinel was posted, and the sea rushed on.

The sea of black and threatening waters, and of destructive upheaving of wave against wave, whose depths were yet unfathomed and whose forces were yet unknown. The remorseless sea of turbulently swaying shapes, voic-es of vengeance, and faces hardened in the furnaces of suffering until the touch of pity could make no mark on them.

But, in the ocean of faces where every fierce and furious expression was in vivid life, there were two groups of faces–each seven in number–so fixedly contrasting with the rest, that never did sea roll which bore more memorable wrecks with it. Seven faces of prisoners, suddenly released by the storm that had burst their tomb were carried high overhead; all scared, all lost, all wandering and amazed, as if the Last Day were come, and those who rejoiced around them were lost spirits. Other seven faces there were, car-ried higher, seven dead faces, whose drooping eyelids and half-seen eyes awaited the Last Day. Impassive faces, yet with a suspended–not yet abol-ished–expression on them; faces rather, in a fearful pause, as having yet to raise the dropped lids of the eyes, and bear witness with the bloodless lips 'THOU DIDST IT!'

Seven prisoners released, seven gory heads on pikes, the keys of the ac-cursed fortress of the eight strong towers, some discovered letters and other memorials of prisoners of old time, long dead of broken hearts–such, a such-like, the loudly echoing footsteps of Saint Antoine escort through the Paris streets in mid July, one thousand seven hundred and eighty-nine. Now, Heaven defeat the fancy of Lucie Darnay, and keep these feet far out of her life! For, they are headlong, mad, and dangerous; and in the years so long after the breaking of the cask at Defarge's wine-shop door, they are not easily purified when once stained red.

CHAPTER XXII

THE SEA STILL RISES

HAGGARD Saint Antoine had had only one exultant week in which to soften his modicum of hard and bitter bread to such extent as he could, with the relish of fraternal embraces and congratulations, when Madame Defarge sat at her counter, as usual, presiding over the customers. Madame Defarge wore no rose in her head, for the great brotherhood of Spies had become, even in one short week, extremely chary of trusting themselves to the saint's mercies. The lamps across his streets had a portentously elastic swing with them.

Madame Defarge, with her arms folded, sat in the morning light and heat, contemplating the wine shop and the street. In both, there were several knots of loungers, squalid and miserable, but now with a manifest sense of power enthroned on their distress. The raggedest nightcap, awry on the wretchedest head, had this crooked significance in it: 'I know how hard it has grown for me, the wearer of this, to support life in myself; but do you know how easy it has grown for me, the wearer of this, to destroy life in you?' Every lean bare arm, that had been without work before, had this work always ready for it now, that it could strike. The fingers of the knitting women were vicious, with the experience that they could tear. There was a change in the appearance of Saint Antoine; the image had been hammering into this for hundreds of years, and the last finishing blows had told mightily on the expression.

Madame Defarge sat observing it, with such suppressed approval as was to be desired in the leader of the Saint Antoine women. One of her sisterhood knitted beside her. The short, rather plump wife of a starved grocer, and the mother of two children withal, this lieutenant had already earned the complimentary name of The Vengeance.

'Hark!' said The Vengeance. 'Listen, then! Who comes?'

As if a train of powder lain from the outermost bound of the Saint Antoine Quarter to the wine-sho'door, had been suddenly fired, a fast-spreading murmur came rushing along.

'It is Defarge,' said madame. 'Silence, patriots!'

Defarge came in breathless, pulled off a red cap he wore and looked around him! 'Listen, everywhere!' said madame again. 'Listen to him!' Defarge stood, panting, against a background of eager eyes and open mouths, formed outside the door; all those within the wine shop had sprung to their feet.

'Say then, my husband. What is it?'

'New from the other world!'

'How, then?' cried madame, contemptuously. 'The other world?'

'Does everybody here recall old Foulon, who told the famished people that they might eat grass, and who died, and went to Hell?'

'Everybody!' from all throats.

'The new is of him. He is among us!'

'Among us!' from the universal throat again. 'And dead?'

'Not dead! He feared us so much—and with reason—that he caused himself to be represented as dead, and had a grand mock-funeral. But they have found him alive, hiding in the country, and have brought him in. I have seen him but now, on his way to the *Hôtel de ville*, a prisoner. I have said that he had reason to fear us. Say all! *Had* he reason?'

Wretched old sinner of more than threescore years and ten, if he had never known it yet, he would have known it in his heart of hearts if he could have heard answering cry.

A moment of profound silence followed. Defarge and his wife looked steadfastly at one another. The Vengeance stooped, and the jar of a drum was heard as she moved it at her feet behind the counter.

'Patriots!' said Defarge, in a determined voice, 'are we ready?'

Instantly Madame Defarge's knife was in her girdle; the drum was beating in the streets, as if it and a drummer had flown together by magic; and The Vengeance, uttering terrific shrieks, and flinging her arms about her head like all the forty Furies at once, was tearing from house to house, rousing the women.

The men were terrible, in the bloody-minded anger with which they looked from windows, caught up what arms they had, and came pouring down into the streets; but, the women were a sight to chill the boldest. From such household occupations as their bare poverty yielded, from their children, from their aged and their sick crouching on the bare ground famished and naked, they ran out with streaming hair, urging one another, and themselves, to madness with the wildest cries and actions. Villain Foulon taken, my sister! Old Foulon taken, my mother! Miscreant Foulon taken, my daughter! Then, a score of others ran into the midst of these, beating their breasts, tearing their hair, and screaming, Foulon alive! Foulon who told the starving people they might eat grass! Foulon who told my old father that he might eat grass, when I had no bread to give him! Foulon who told my baby it might suck grass, when these breasts were dry with want! O mother of God, this Foulon! O Heaven, our suffering! Hear me, my dead baby and my withered father: I swear on my knees, on these stones, to avenge you on Foulon! Husbands, and brothers, and young men, Give us the blood of Foulon, Give us the head of Foulon, Give us the heart of Foulon, Give us the body and soul of Foulon, Rend Foulon to pieces, and dif him into the ground, that grass may grow from him! With these cries, numbers of the women, lashed into blind frenzy, whirled about, striking and tearing at their own friends until they dropped into a passionate swoon, and were only saved by the men belonging to them from being trampled under foot.

Nevertheless, not a moment was lost; not a moment!

This Foulon was at the *Hôtel de ville*, and might be loosed. Never, if Saint Antoine knew his own sufferings, insults, and wrongs! Armed men and women flocked out of the Quarter so fast, and drew even these last dregs after them with such a force of suction, that within a quarter of an hour there was not a human creature in Saint Antoine's bosom but a few old crones and the wailing children.

No. They were all by that time chocking the Hall of Examination, where this old man, ugly and wicked, was, and overflowing into the adjacent open space and streets. The Defarges, husband and wife, The Vengeance, and Jacques Three, were in the first press, and at no great distance from him in the Hall.

'See!' cried madame, pointing with her knife. 'See the old villain bound with ropes. That was well done to tie a bunch of grass upon his back. Ha, ha! That was well done. Let him eat it now!' Madame put her knife under her arm, and clapped her hands as at a play.

The people immediately behind Madame Defarge, explaining the cause of her satisfaction to those behind them, and those again explaining to others, and those to others, the neighbouring streets resounded with the clapping of hands. Similarly, during two or three hours of drawl, and the winnowing of many bushels of words, Madame Defarge's frequent expressions of impatience were taken up, with marvellous quickness, at a distance: the more readily, because certain men who had by some wonderful exercise of agility climbed up the external architecture to look in from the windows, knew Madame Defarge well, and acted as a telegraph between her and the crowd outside the building.

At length the sun rose so high that it struck a kindly ray as of hope or protection, directly down upon the old prisoner's head. The favour was too much to bear; in an instant the barrier of dust and chaff that had stood surprisingly long, went to the winds, and Saint Antoine had got him!

It was known directly, to the furthest confines of the crowd. Defarge had but sprung over a railing and a table, and folded the miserable wretch in a deadly embrace– Madame Defarge had but followed and turned her hand in one of the ropes with which he was tied–The Vengeance and Jacques Three were not yet up with them, and the men at the windows had not yet swooped into the hall, like birds of prey from their high perches–when the cry seemed to go up, all over the city, 'Bring him out! Bring him to the lamp!'

Down, and up, and head foremost on the steps of the building; now, on his knees; now, on his feet; now, on his back; dragged, and struck at, and stifled by the bunches of grass and straw that were thrust into his face by hundreds of hands; torn, bruised, panting, bleeding, yet always entreating and beseeching for mercy; now full of vehement agony of action, with a small clear space about him as the people drew one another back that they might see; now, a long of dead wood drawn through a forest of legs; he was hauled to the nearest street corner where one of the fatal lamps swung, and there Madame Defarge let him go–as a cat might have done to a mouse–and

silently and composedly looked at him while they made ready, and while
he besought her: the women passionately screeching at him all the time,
and the men sternly calling out to have him killed with grass in his mouth.
Once, he went aloft, and the rope broke, and they caught him shrieking;
then, the rope was merciful, and held him, and his head was soon upon a
pike, with grass enough in the mouth for all Saint Antoine to dance at the
sight of.

Nor was this the end of the day's bad work, for Saint Antoine so
shouted and danced his angry blood up, that it boiled again, on hearing
when the day closed in that the son-in-law of the dispatched, another of
the people's enemies and insulters, was coming into Paris under a guard
five hundred strong, in cavalry alone. Saint Antoine wrote his crimes on
flaring sheets of paper, seized him—would have torn him out of the breast
of an army to bear Foulon company—set his head and heart on pikes,
and carried the three spoils of the day, in Wolf-procession through the
streets.

Not before dark night did the men and women come back to the children, wailing and breadless. Then, the miserable baker's shops were beset
by long files of them, patiently waiting to buy bad bread; and while they
waited with stomachs faint and empty, they beguiled the time by embracing one another on the triumphs of the day, and achieving them again in
gossip. Gradually, these strings of ragged people shortened and frayed
away; and then poor lights began to shine in high windows, and slender
fires were made in the streets, at which neighbours cooked in common,
afterwards supping at their doors.

Scanty and insufficient suppers those, and innocent of meat, as of
most other sauce to wretched bread. Yet, human fellowship infused some
nourishment into the flinty viands, and struck some sparks of cheerfulness
out of them. Fathers and mothers who had had their full share in the worst
of the day, played gently with their meagre children; and lovers, with such
a world around them and before them, loved and hoped.

It was almost morning, when Defarge's wine shop parted with its last
knot of customers, and Monsieur Defarge said to madame his wife, in
husky tones, while fastening the door:

'At last it is come, my dear!'

'Eh well! returned madame. 'Almost.'

Saint Antoine slept, the Defarges slept: even The Vengeance slept
with her starved grocer, and the drum was at rest. The drum's was the
only voice in Saint Antoine that blood and hurry had not changed. The
Vengeance, as custodian of the drum, could have awakened him up and had
the same speech out of him as before the Bastille fell, or old Foulon was
seized; not so with the hoarse tones of the men and women in Saint
Antoine's bosom.

CHAPTER XXIII

FIRE RISES

THERE was a change on the village where the fountain fell, and where the mender of roads went forth daily to hammer out of the stones on the highway such morsels of bread as might serve for patches to hold his poor ignorant soul and his poor reduced body together. The prison on the crag was not so dominant as you of yore; there were soldiers to guard it, but not many; there were officers to guard the soldiers, but not one of them knew what his men would do–beyond this: that it would probably not be what he was ordered.

Far and wide lay a ruined country, yielding nothing but desolation. Every green leaf, every blade of grass and blade of grain, was as shrivelled and poor as the miserable people. Everything was bowed down, dejected, oppressed, and broken. Habitations, fences, domesticated animals, men, women, children, and the soil that bore them–all worn out.

Monseigneur (often a most worthy individual gentleman) was a national blessing, gave a chivalrous tone to things, was a polite example of luxurious and shining life, and a great deal more to equal purpose; nevertheless, Monseigneur as a class had, somehow or other, brought things to this. Strange that Creation, designed expressly for Monseigneur, should be so soon wrung dry and squeezed out! There must be something shortsighted in the eternal arrangements, surely! Thus it was, however; and the last drop of blood having been extracted from the flints, and the last screw of the rack having been turned so often that its purchase crumbled, and it now turned and turned with nothing to bite, Monseigneur began to run away from a phenomenon so low and unaccountable.

But, this was not the change on the village, and on many a village like it. For scores of years gone by, Monseigneur had squeezed it and wrung it, and had seldom graced it with his presence except for the pleasures of the chase–now, found in hunting the people; now, found in hunting the beasts, for whose preservation Monseigneur made edifying spaces of barbarous and barren wilderness. No. The change consisted in the appearance of strange faces of low caste, rather than in the disappearance of the high-caste, chiseled, and otherwise beatified and beatifying features of Monseigneur.

For, in these times, as the mender of roads worked, solitary, in the dust, not often troubling himself to reflect that dust he was and to dust he must return, being for the most part too much occupied in thinking how little he had for supper and how much more he would eat if he had it–in these times, as he raised his eyes from his lonely labour, and viewed the prospect, he would see some rough figure approaching on foot, the like of which was once a rarity in those parts, but was now a frequent presence. As it advanced, the mender of roads would discern without surprise, that it was a shaggy-haired man, of almost barbarian aspect, tall, in wooden shoes that were clumsy even to the eyes of a mender of roads, grim, rough, swart, steeped in the mud and dust of many highways, dank with the marshy moisture of many low grounds, sprinkled with the thorns and leaves and moss of many byways through woods.

Such a man came upon him, like a ghost, at noon in the July weather, as he sat on his heap of stones under a bank, taking such shelter as he could get from a shower of hail.

The man looked at him, looked at the village in the hollow, at the mill, and at the prison on the crag. When he had identified these objects in what benighted mind he had, he said, in a dialect that was just intelligible:

'How goes it, Jacques?'

'All well, Jacques.'

'Touch then!'

They joined hands, and the man sat down on the heap of stones.

'No dinner?'

'Nothing but supper now,' said the mender of roads, with a hungry face.

'It is the fashion,' growled the man. 'I meet no dinner anywhere.'

He took out a blackened pipe, filled it, lighted it with flint and steel, pulled at it until it was in a bright glow: then, suddenly held it from him and dropped something into it from between his finger and thumb, that blazed and went out in a puff of smoke.

'Touch then.' It was the turn of the mender of roads to say it this time, after observing these operations. They again joined hands.

'To-night?' said the mender of roads.

'To-night,' said the man, putting the pipe in his mouth.

'Where?'

'Here.'

He and the mender of roads set on the heap of stones looking silently at one another, with the hail driving in between them like a pygmy charge of bayonets, until the sky began to clear over the village.

'Show me!' said the traveller then, moving to the brow of the hill.

'See!' returned the mender of roads, with extended finger. 'You go down here, and straight through the street, and past the fountain—'

'To the Devil with all that!' interrupted the other, rolling his eye over the landscape. '*I* go through no streets and past no fountains. Well?'

'Well! About two leagues beyond the summit of that hill above the village.'

'Good. When do you cease to work?'

'At sunset.'

'Will you wake me before departing! I have walked two nights without resting. Let me finish my pipe, and I shall sleep like a child. Will you wake me?'

'Surely.'

The wayfarer smoked his pipe out, put it in his breast, slipped off his great wooden shoes, and lay down on his back on the heap of stones. He was fast asleep directly.

As the road-mender plied his dusty labour, and the hail clouds, rolling away, revealed bright bars and streaks of sky which were responded to by silver gleams upon the landscape, the little man (who wore a red cap now, in place of his blue one) seemed fascinated by the figure on the heap of stones. His eyes were so often turned towards it, that he used his tools mechanically, and, one would have said, to very poor account. The bronze face, the shaggy black hair and beard, the coarse woolen red cap, the rough medley dress of home-spun stuff and hairy skins of beasts, the powerful frame attenuated by spare living, and the sullen and desperate compression of the lips in sleep, inspired the mender of roads with awe. The traveller had travelled far, and his feet were footsore, and his ankles chafed and bleeding; his great shoes, stuffed with leaves and grass, had been heavy to drag over the many long leagues and his clothes were chafed into holes, as he himself went into sores. Stooping down beside him, the road mender tried to get a peep at secret weapons in his breast or where not; but, in vain, for he slept with his arms crossed upon him, and set as resolutely as his lips. Fortified towns with their stockades, guard-houses, gates, trenches, and drawbridges, seemed to the mender of roads, to be so much air as against this figure. And when he lifted his eyes from it to the horizon and looked around, he saw in his small fancy similar figures, stopped by no obstacle, tending to centres all over France.

The man slept on, indifferent to showers of hail and intervals of brightness, to sunshine on his face and shadow, to the pattering lumps of dull ice on his body and the diamonds into which the sun changed them, until the sun was low in the west, and the sky was glowing. Then, the mender of roads having got his tools together and all things ready to go down into the village, roused him.

'Good!' said the sleeper, rising on his elbow. 'Two leagues beyond the summit of the hill?'

'About.'

'About. Good!'

The mender of roads went home, with the dust going on before him according to the set of the wind, and was soon at the fountain, squeezing himself in among the lean kine brought there to drink, and appearing even to whisper to them in his whispering to all the village. When the village had taken its poor supper, it did not creep to bed, as it usually did, but came out of doors again, and remained there. A curious contagion of whispering was upon it, and also, when it gathered together at the fountain in the dark, another curious contagion of looking expectantly at the sky in one direction only. Monseigneur Gabelle, chief functionary of the place, became uneasy; went out on his house-top alone, and looked in that direction too; glanced down from behind his chimneys at the darkening faces by the fountain below, and sent word to the sacristan who kept the keys of the church, that there might be need to ring the tocsin by and by.

The night deepened. The trees environing the old château, keeping its solitary state apart, moved in a rising wind, as though they threatened the pile of building massive and dark in the gloom. Up the two terrace flights of steps the rain ran wildly, and beat at the great door, like a swift messenger rousing those within; uneasy rushes of wind went through the hall, among the old spears and knives, and passed lamenting up the stairs, and shook the curtains of the bed where the last Marquis had slept. East, West, North, and South, through the woods, four heavy-treading, unkempt figures crushed the high grass and cracked the branches, striding on cautiously to come together in the courtyard. Four lights broke out there, and moved away in different directions, and all was black again.

But, not for long. Presently, the château began to make itself strangely visible by some light of its own, as though it were growing luminous. Then, a flickering streak played behind the architecture of the front, picking out transparent places, and whowing where balustrades, arches, and windows were. Then it soared higher, and grew broder and brighter. Soon, from a score of the great windows, flames burst forth, and the stone faces awakened, stared out of fire.

A faint murmur arose about the house from the few people who were left there, and there was a saddling of a horse and riding away. There was spurring and splashing through the darkness, and bridle was drawn in the space by the village fountain, and the horse in a foam stood at Monseigneur Gabelle's door. 'Help, Gabelle! Help, every one!' The tocsin rang impatiently, but other help (if there were any) there was none. The mender of roads, and two hundred and fifty particular friends, stood with folded arms at the fountain, looking at the pillar of fire in the sky. 'It must be forty feet high,' said they, grimly; and never moved.

The rider from the château, and the horse in a foam, clattered away through the village, and galloped up the stony steep, to the prison on the crag. At the gate, a group of officers were looking at the fire; removed from them, a group of soldiers. 'Help, gentleman-officers! The château is on fire; valuable objects may be saved from the flames by timely aid! Help, help!' The officers looked towards the soldier who looked at the fire; gave no orders; and answered, with shrugs and biting of lips, 'It must burn.'

As the rider rattled down the hill again and through the street, the village was illuminating. The mender of roads, and two hundred and fifty particular friends, inspired as one man and woman by the idea of lighting up, had darted into their houses, and were putting candles in every dull little pane of glass. The general scarcity of everything occasioned candles to be borrowed in a rather peremptory manner of Monseigneur Gabelle; and in a moment of reluctance and hesitation on that functionary's part, the mender of roads, once so submissive to authority, had remarked that carriages were good to make bonfires with, and that post-horses would roast.

The château was left to itself to flame and burn. In the roaring and raging of the conflagration, a red-hot wind, driving straight from the infernal regions, seemed to be blowing the edifice away. With the rising and falling of the blaze, the stone faces showed as if they were in torment. When great masses of stone and timber fell, the face with the two dints in the nose became obscured: anon struggled out of the smoke again, as if it were the face of the cruel Marquis, burning at the stake and contending with the fire.

The château burned; the nearest trees, laid hold of by the fire, scorched and shrivelled; trees at a distance, fired by the four fierce figures, begirt the blazing edifice with a new forest of smoke. Molten lead and iron boiled in the marble basin of the fountain; the water ran dry; the extinguisher tops of the towers vanished like ice before the heat, and trickled down into four rugged wells of flame. Great rents and splits branched out in the solid walls, like crystallization; stupefied birds wheeled about and dropped into the furnace; four fierce figures trudged away, East, West, North, and South, along the night-enshrouded roads guided by the beacon they had lighted, towards their next destination. The illuminated village had seized hold of the tocsin, and, abolishing the lawful ringer, rang for joy.

Not only that; but the village, light-headed with famine, fire, and bell-ringing, and bethinking itself that Monsieur Gabelle had to do with the collection of rent and taxes–though it was but a small installment of taxes, and no rent at all, that Gabelle had got in those latter days–became impatient for an interview with him, and, surrounding his house, summoned him to come forth for personal conference. Whereupon, Monsieur Gabelle did heavily bar his door, and retire to hold counsel with himself. The result of that conference was, that Gabelle again withdrew himself to his house-top behind his stack of chimneys; this time resolved, if his door was broken in (he was a small Southern man of retaliative temperament), to pitch himself head foremost over the parapet, and crush a man or two below.

Probably, Monsieur Gabelle passed a long night up there, with the distant château for fire and candle, and the beating at his door, combined with the joy-ringing, for music; not to mention his having an ill-omened lamp slung across the road before his posting-house gate, which the village showed a lively inclination to displace in his favour. A trying suspense, to be passing the whole summer night on the brink of the black ocean, ready to take that plunge into it upon which Monsieur Gabelle had resolved! But, the friendly dawn appearing at last, and the rush-candles of the village guttering out, the people happily dispersed, and Monsieur Gabelle came down bringing his life with him for that while.

Within a hundred miles, and in the light of other fires, there were other functionaries less fortunate, that night and other nights, whom the rising sun found hanging across once peaceful streets, where they had been born and bred; also, there were other villagers and townspeople less fortunate than the mender of roads and his fellows, upon whom the functionaries and soldiery turned with success, and whom they strung up in their turn. But, the fierce figures were steadily wending East, West, North, and South, be that as it would; and whosoever hung, fire burned. The altitude of the gallows that would turn to water and quench it, no functionary, by any stretch of mathematics, was able to calculate successfully.

CHAPTER XXIV

DRAWN TO THE LOADSTONE ROCK

IN such risings of fire and risings of sea—the firm earth shaken by the rushes of an angry ocean which had now no ebb, but was always on the flow, higher and higher, to the terror and wonder of the beholders on the shore—three years of tempest were consumed. Three more birthdays of little Lucie had been woven by the golden thread into the peaceful issue of the life of her home.

Many a night and many a day had its inmates listened to the echoes in the corner, with hearts that failed them when they heard the thronging feet. For, the footsteps had become to their minds as the footsteps of a people, tumultuous under a red flag and with their country declared in danger, changed into wild beasts, by terrible enchantment long persisted in.

Monseigneur, as a class, had dissociated himself from the phenomenon of his not being appreciated: of his being so little wanted in France, as to incur considerable danger of receiving his dismissal from it, and this life together. Like the fabled rustic who raised the Devil with infinite pains, and was so terrified at the sight of him that he could ask the Enemy no question, but immediately fled; so, Monseigneur, after boldly reading the Lord's Prayer backwards for a great number of years, and performing many other potent spells for compelling the Evil One, no sooner beheld him in his terrors than he took to his noble heels.

The shining Bull's Eye of the court was gone, or it would have been the mark for a hurricane of national bullets. It had never been a good eye to see with—had long had the note in it of Lucifer's pride, Sardanapalus's luxury, and a mole's blindness—but it had dropped out and was gone. The court, from that exclusive inner circle to its outermost rotten ring of intrigue, corruption, and dissimulation, was all gone together. Royalty was gone; had been besieged in its palace and 'suspended,' when the last tidings came over.

The August of the year one thousand seven hundred and ninety-two was come, and Monseigneur was by this time scattered far and wide.

As was natural, the headquarters and great gathering-place of Monseigneur, in London, was Tellson's Bank. Spirits are supposed to haunt the places where their bodies most resorted, and Monseigneur without a guinea haunted the spot where his guineas used to be. Moreover, it was the spot to which such French intelligence as was most to be relied upon, came quickest. Again: Tellson's was a munificent house, and extended great liberality to old customers who had fallen from their high estate. Again: those nobles who had seen the coming storm in time, and anticipating plunder or confiscation, had made provident remittances to Tellson's, were always to be heard of there by their needy brethren. To which it must be added that every new comer from France reported himself and his tidings at Tellson's, almost as a matter of course. For such variety of reasons, Tellson's was at that time, as to French intelligence, a kind of High Exchange; and this was so well known to the public, and the inquiries made there were in consequence so numerous, that Tellson's sometimes wrote the latest news out in a line or so and posted it in the bank windows, for all who ran through Temple Bar to read.

On a steaming, misty afternoon, Mr. Lorry sat at his desk, and Charles Darnay stood leaning on it, talking with him in a low voice. The penitential den once set apart for interviews with the House, was now the News Exchange, and was filled to overflowing. It was within half an hour or so of the time of closing.

'But, although you are the youngest man that ever lived,' said Charles Darnay, rather hesitating, 'I must still suggest to you—'

'I understand. That I am too old?' said Mr. Lorry.

'Unsettled weather, a long journey, uncertain means of travelling, a disorganized country, a city that may not be even safe for you.'

'My dear Charles,' said Mr. Lorry, with cheerful confidence, 'you touch some of the reasons for my going: not for my staying away. It is safe enough for me; nobody will care to interfere with an old fellow of hard upon fourscore when there are so many people there so much better worth interfering with. As to its being a disorganized city, if it were not a disorganized city there would be no occasion to send somebody from our House here to our House there, who knows the city and the business, of old, and is in Tellson's confidence. As to the uncertain travelling, the long journey, and the winter weather, if I were not prepared to submit myself to a few inconveniences for the sake of Tellson's, after all these years, who ought to be?'

'I wish I were going myself,' said Charles Darnay, somewhat restlessly, and like one thinking aloud.

'Indeed! You are a pretty fellow to object and advise!' exclaimed Mr. Lorry. 'You wish you were going yourself? And you a Frenchman born? You are a wise counsellor.'

'My dear Mr. Lorry, it is because I am a Frenchman born, that the thought (which I did not mean to utter here, however) had passed through my mind often. One cannot help thinking, having had some sympathy for the miserable people, and having abandoned something to them'–he spoke here in his former thoughtful manner–'that one might be listened to, and might have the power to persuade to some restraint. Only last night, after you had left us, when I was talking to Lucie—'

'When you were talking to Lucie,' Mr. Lorry repeated. 'Yes. I wonder you are not ashamed to mention the name of Lucie! Wishing you were going to France at this time of day!'

'However, I am not going,' said Charles Darnay, with a smile. 'It is more to the purpose that you say you are.'

'And I am, in plain reality. The truth is, my dear Charles'–Mr. Lorry glanced at the distant House, and lowered his voice–'you can have no conception of the difficulty with which our business is transacted, and of the peril in which our books and papers over yonder are involved. The Lord above knows what the compromising consequences would be to numbers of people, if some of our documents were seized or destroyed; and they might be, at any time, you know, for who can say that Paris is not set a-fire to-day, or sacked to-morrow! Now, a judicious selection from these with the least possible delay, and the burying of them, or otherwise getting of them out of harm's way is within the power (without loss of precious time) of scarcely any one but myself, if any one. And shall I hang back, when Tellson's knows this and says this–Tellson's, whose bread I have eaten these sixty years–because I am a little stiff about the joints? Why, I am a boy, sir, to half a dozen old codgers here!'

'How I admire the gallantry of your youthful spirit, Mr. Lorry.'

'Tut! Nonesense, sir!–And, my dear Charles,' said Mr. Lorry, glancing at the House again, 'you are to remember, that getting things out of Paris at this present time, no matter what things, is next to an impossibility. Papers and precious matters were this very day brought to us here (I speak in strict confidence; it is not business-like to whisper it, even to you), by the strangest bearers you can imagine, every one of whom had his head hanging on by a single hair as he passed the barriers. At another time, our parcels would come and go, as easily as in business-like Old England; but now, everything is stopped.'

'And do you really go to-night?'

'I really go to-night, for the case has become too pressing to admit of delay.'

'And do you take no one with you?'

'All sorts of people have been proposed to me, but I will have nothing to say to any of them. I intend to take Jerry. Jerry has been my bodyguard on Sunday nights for a long time past, and I am used to him. Nobody will suspect Jerry of being anything but an English bulldog, or of having any design in his head but to fly at anybody who touches his master.'

'I must say again that I heartily admire your gallantry and youthfulness.'

'I must say again, nonsense, nonsense! When I have executed this little commission, I shall, perhaps, accept Tellson's proposal to retire and live at my ease. Time enough, then, to think about growing old.'

This dialogue had taken place at Mr. Lorry's usual desk, with Monseigneur swarming within a yard or two of it, boastful of what he would do to avenge himself on the rascal-people before long. It was too much the way of Monseigneur under his reserves as a refugee, and it was much too much the way of native British orthodoxy, to talk of this terrible Revolution as if it were the one only harvest ever known under the skies that had not been sown–as if nothing had ever been done, or omitted to be done, that had led to it–as if observers of the wretched millions in France, and of the misused and perverted resources that should have made them prosperous, had not seen it inevitably coming, years before, and had not in plain words recorded what they saw. Such vapouring, combined with the extravagant plots of Monseigneur for the restoration of a state of things that had utterly exhausted itself, and worn out Heaven and earth as well as itself, was hard to be endured without some remonstrance by any sane man who knew the truth. And it was such vapouring all about his ears, like a troublesome confusion of blood in his own head, added to a latent uneasiness in his mind, which had already made Charles Darnay restless, and which still kept him so.

Among the talkers, was Stryver, of the King's Bench Bar, far on his way to state promotion, and, therefore, loud on the theme: broaching to Monseigneur, his devices for blowing the people up and exterminating them from the face of the earth, and doing without them; and for accomplishing many similar objects akin to their nature to the abolition of eagles by sprinkling salt on the tails of the race. Him, Darnay heard with a particular feeling of objection; and Darnay stood divided between going away that he might hear no more, and remaining to interpose his word, when the thing that was to be, went on the shape itself out.

The House approached Mr. Lorry, and laying a soiled and unopened letter before him, asked if he had yet discovered any traces of the person to whom it was addressed? The House laid the letter down so close to Darnay that he saw the direction—the more quickly because it was his own right name. The address, turned into English, ran:

'Very pressing. To Monsieur heretofore the Marquis St. Evrémonde, of France. Confided to the cares of Messrs. Tellson and Co., Bankers, London, England.'

On the marriage morning, Doctor Manette had made it his one urgent and express request to Charles Darnay, that the secret of this name should be—useless he, the Doctor, dissolved the obligation—kept inviolate between them. Nobody else knew it to be his name; his own wife had no suspicion of the fact; Mr. Lorry could have none.

'No,' said Mr. Lorry, in reply to the House; 'I have referred it, I think, to everybody now here, and no one can tell me where this gentleman is to be found.'

The hands of the clock verging upon the hour of closing the bank, there was a general set of the current of talkers past Mr. Lorry's desk. He held the letter out inquiringly; and Monseigneur looked at it, in the person of this plotting and indignant refugee; and This, That, and The Other, all had something disparaging to say, in French or in English, concerning the Marquis who was not to be found.

'Nephew, I believe—but in any case degenerate successor—of the polished Marquis who was murdered,' said one. 'Happy to say, I never knew him.'

'A craven who abandoned his post,' said another—this Monseigneur had been got out of Paris, legs uppermost and half suffocated, in a load of hay—'some years ago.'

'Infected with the new doctrines,' said the third, eyeing the direction through his glass in passing; 'set himself in opposition to the last Marquis, abandoned the estates when he inherited them, and left them to the ruffian herd. They will recompense him now, I hope, as he deserves.'

'Hey?' cried the blatant Stryver. 'Did he thought? Is that the sort of fellow? Let us look at his infamous name. D—n the fellow!'

Darnay, unable to restrain himself any longer, touched Mr. Stryver on the shoulder, and said:

'I know the fellow.'

'Do you, by Jupiter?' said Stryver. 'I am sorry for it.'

'Why?'

'Why, Mr. Darnay? D'ye hear what he did? Don't ask, why, in these times.'

'But I do ask why?'

'Then I tell you again, Mr. Darnay, I am sorry for it. I am sorry to hear you putting any such extraordinary questions. Here is a fellow, who, infected by the most pestilent and blasphemous code of devilry that ever was known, abandoned his property to the vilest scum of the earth that ever did murder by wholesale, and you ask me why I am sorry that a man who instructs youth knows him? Well, but I'll answer you. I am sorry because I believe there is contamination in such a scoundrel. That's why.'

Mindful of the secret, Darnay with great difficulty checked himself, and said: 'You may not understand the gentleman.'

'I understand how to put *you* in a corner, Mr. Darnay,' said Bully Stryver, 'and I'll do it. If this fellow is a gentleman, I *don't* understand him. You may tell him so, with my compliments. You may also tell him, from me, that after abandoning his worldly goods and position to this butcherly mob, I wonder he is not at the head of them. But, no, gentlemen,' said Stryver, looking all round, and snapping his fingers, 'I know something of human nature, and I tell you that you'll never find a fellow like this fellow, trusting himself to the mercies of such precious *protégés*. No, gentlemen; he'll always show 'em a clean pair of heels very early in the scuffle, and sneak away.'

With those words, and a final snap of his fingers, Mr. Stryver shouldered himself into Fleet Street, amidst the general approbation of his hearers. Mr. Lorry and Charles Darnay were left alone at the desk, in the general departure from the bank.

'Will you take charge of the letter?' said Mr. Lorry. 'You know where to deliver it?'

'I do.'

'Will you undertake to explain, that we suppose it to have been addressed here, on the chance of our knowing where to forward it, and that it has been here some time?'

'I will do so. Do you start for Paris from here?'

'From here, at eight.'

'I will come back, to see you off.'

Very ill at ease with himself, and with Stryver and most other men, Darnay made the best of his way into the quiet of the Temple, opened the letter, and read it. These were its contents:

'Prison of the Abbaye, Paris.
'June 21, 1792.

'MONSIEUR HERETOFORE THE MARQUIS.

'After having long been in danger of my life at the hands of the village, I have been seized, with great violence and indignity, and brought a long journey on foot to Paris. On the road I have suffered a great deal. Nor is that all; my house has been destroyed-razed to the ground.

'The crime for which I am imprisoned, Monsieur heretofore the Marquis, and for which I shall be summoned before the tribunal, and shall lose my life (without your so generous help), is, they tell me, treason against the majesty of the people, in that I have acted against them for an emigrant. It is in vain I represent that I have acted for them, and not against, according to your commands. It is in vain I represent that, before the sequestration of emigrant property, I had remitted the imposts they had ceased to pay; that I had collected no rent; that I had had recourse to no process. The only response is, that I have acted for an emigrant, and where is that emigrant?

'Ah! most gracious Monsieur heretofore the Marquis, where is that emigrant? I cry in my sleep where is he? I demand of Heaven, will he not come to deliver me? No answer. Ah, Monsieur heretofore the Marquis, I send my desolate cry across the sea, hoping it may perhaps reach your ears through the great bank of Tilson known at Paris!

'For the love of Heaven, of justice, of generosity, of the honour of your noble name, I supplicate you, Monsieur heretofore the Marquis, to succour and release me. My fault is, that I have been true to you. Oh, Monsieur heretofore the Marquis, I pray you be you true to me!

'From this prison here of horror, whence I every hour tend nearer and nearer to destruction, I send you, Monsieur heretofore the Marquis, the assurance of my dolours and unhappy service.

> 'Your afflicted,
> GABELLE.'

The latent uneasiness in Darnay's mind was roused to vigorous life by this letter. The peril of an old servant and a good one, whose only crime was fidelity to himself and his family, stared him so reproachfully in the face, that, as he walked to and fro in the Temple considering what to do, he almost hid his face from the passers-by.

He knew very well, that in his horror of the deed which had culminated the bad deeds and bad reputation of the old family house, in his resentful suspicions of his uncle, and in the aversion with which his conscience regarded the crumbling fabric that he was supposed to uphold, he had acted imperfectly. He knew very well, that in his love for Lucie, his renunciation of his social place, though by no means new to his own mind, had been hurried and incomplete. He knew that he ought to have systematically worked it out and supervised it, and that he had meant to do it, and that it had never been done.

The happiness of his own chosen English home, the necessity of being always actively employed, the swift changes and troubles of the time which had followed on one another so fast, that the events of this week annihilated the immature plans of last week, and the events of the week following made all new again; he knew very well, that to the force of these circumstances he had yielded–not without disquiet, but still without continuous and accumulating resistance. That he had watched the times for a time of action, and that they had shifted and struggled until the time had gone by, and the nobility were trooping from France by every highway and byway, and their very names were blotting out, was as well known to himself as it could be to any new authority in France that might impeach him for it.

But, he had oppressed no man, he had imprisoned no man; he was so far from having harshly exacted payment of his dues, that he had relinquished them of his own will, thrown himself on a world with no favour in it, won his own private place there, and earned his own bread. Monsieur Gabelle had held the impoverished and involved estate on written instructions, to spare the people, to give them what little there was to give–such fuel as the heavy creditors would let them have in the winter, and such produce as could be saved from the same grip in the summer–and no doubt he had put the fact in plea and proof, for his own safety, so that it could not but appear now.

This favoured the desperate resolution Charles Darnay had begun to make, that he would go to Paris.

Yes. Like the mariner in the old story, the winds and streams had driven him within the influence of the Loadstone Rock, and it was drawing him to itself, and he must go. Everything that arose before his mind drifted him on, faster and faster, more and more steadily, to the terrible attraction. His latent uneasiness had been, that bad aims were being worked out in his own unhappy land by bad instruments, and that he who could not fail to know that he was better than they, was not there, trying to do something to stay bloodshed, and assert the claims of mercy and humanity. With this uneasiness half stifled, and half reproaching him, he had been brought to the pointed comparison of himself with the brave old gentleman in whom duty was so strong; upon that comparison (injurious to himself) had instantly followed the sneers of Monseigneur, which had stung him bitterly, and those of Stryver, which above all were coarse and galling, for old reasons. Upon those, had followed Gabelle's letter: the appeal of an innocent prisoner, in danger of death, to his justice, honour, and good name.

His resolution was made. He must go to Paris.

Yes. The Loadstone Rock was drawing him, and he must sail on, until he struck. He knew of no rock; he saw hardly any danger. The intention with which he had done what he had done, even although he had left it incomplete, presented it before him in an aspect that would be gratefully acknowledged in France on his presenting himself to assert it. Then, that glorious vision of doing good, which is so often the sanguine mirage of so many good minds, arose before him, and he even saw himself in the illusion with some influence to guide this raging Revolution that was running so fearfully wild.

As he walked to and fro with his resolution made, he considered that neither Lucie nor her father must know of it until he was gone. Lucie should be spared the pain of separation; and her father, always reluctant to turn his thoughts towards the dangerous ground of old, should come to the knowledge of the step, as a step taken, and not in the balance of suspense and doubt. How much of the incompleteness of his situation was referable to her father, through the painful anxiety to avoid reviving old associations of France in his mind, he did not discuss with himself. But, that circumstance, too, had had its influence in his course.

He walked to and fro, with thoughts very busy, until it was time to return to Tellson's and take leave of Mr. Lorry. As soon as he arrived in Paris he would present himself to this old friend, but he must say nothing of his intention now.

A carriage with post-horses was ready at the bank door, and Jerry was booted and equipped.

'I have delivered that letter,' said Charles Darnay to Mr. Lorry. 'I would not consent to your being charged with any written answer, but perhaps you will take a verbal one?'

'That I will, and readily,' said Mr. Lorry, 'if it is not dangerous.'

'Not at all. Though it is to a prisoner in the Abbaye.'

'What is his name?' said Mr. Lorry, with his open pocket-book in his hand.

'Gabelle.'

'Gabelle. And what is the message to the unfortunate Gabelle in prison?'

'Simply, "that he had received the letter, and will come."'

'Any time mentioned?'

'He will start upon his journey to-morrow night.'

'Any person mentioned?'

'No.'

He helped Mr. Lorry to wrap himself in a number of coats and cloaks, and went out with him from the warm atmosphere of the old bank, into the misty air of Fleet Street. 'My love to Lucie, and to little Lucie,' said Mr. Lorry at parting, 'and take precious care of them till I come back.' Charles Darnay shook his head and doubtfully smiled, as the carriage rolled away.

That night–it was the fourteenth of August–he sat up late, and wrote two fervent letters; one was to Lucie, explaining the strong obligation he was under to go to Paris, and showing her, at length, the reasons that he had, for feeling confident that he could become involved in no personal danger there; the other was to the Doctor, confiding Lucie and their dear child to his care, and dwelling on the same topics with the strongest assurances. To both, he wrote that he would dispatch letters in proof of his safety, immediately after his arrival.

It was a hard day, that day of being among them, with the first reservation of their joint lives on his mind. It was a hard matter to preserve the innocent deceit of which they were profoundly unsuspicious. But, and affectionate glance at his wife, so happy and busy, made him resolute not to tell her what impended (he had been half moved to do it, so strange it was to him to act in anything without her quiet aid), and the day passed quickly. Early in the evening he embraced her, and her scarcely less dear namesake, pretending that he would return by and by (an imaginary engagement took him out, and he had secreted a valise of clothes ready), and so he emerged into the heavy mist of the heavy streets, with a heavier heart.

The unseen force was drawing him fast to itself, now, and all the tides and winds were setting straight and strong towards it. He left his two letters with a trusty porter, to be delivered half an hour before midnight, and no sooner; took horse for Dover; and began his journey. 'For the love of Heaven, of justice, of generosity, of the honour of your noble name!' was the poor prisoner's cry with which he strengthened his sinking heart, as he felt all that was dear on earth behind him, and floated away for the Loadstone Rock.

THE END OF THE SECOND BOOK

BOOK THE THIRD. THE TRACK OF A STORM

CHAPTER I

IN SECRET

THE traveller fared slowly on his way, who fared towards Paris from England in the autumn of the year one thousand seven hundred and ninety-two. More than enough of bad roads, bad equipages, and bad horses, he would have encountered to delay him, though the fallen and unfortunate King of France had been upon his throne in all his glory; but, the changed times were fraught with other obstacles than these. Every town gate and village taxing-house had its band of citizen patriots, with their national muskets in a most explosive state of readiness, who stopped all comers and goers, cross-questioned them, inspected their papers, looked for their names in lists of their own, turned them back, or sent them on, or stopped them and laid them in hold, as their capricious judgment or fancy deemed best for the dawning Republic One and Indivisible, of Liberty, Equality, Fraternity, or Death.

A very few French leagues of his journey were accomplished, when Charles Darnay began to perceive that for him along these country roads there was no hope of return until he should have been declared a good citizen at Paris. Whatever might befall now, he must on to his journey's end. Not a mean village closed upon him, not a common barrier dropped across the road behind him, but he knew it to be another iron door in series that was barred between him and England. The universal watchfulness so encompassed him, that if he had been taken in a net, or were being forwarded to his destination in a cage, he could not have felt his freedom more completely gone.

This universal watchfulness not only stopped him on the highway twenty times in a stage, but retarded his progress twenty times in a day, by riding after him and taking him back, riding before him and stopping him by anticipation, riding with him and keeping him in charge. He had been days upon his journey in France alone, when he went to bed tired out, in a little town on the high road, still a long way from Paris.

Nothing but the production of the afflicted Gabelle's letter from his prison of the Abbaye would have got him on so far. His difficulty at the guard-house in this small place had been such, that he felt his journey to have come to a crisis. And he was, therefore, as little surprised as a man could be, to find himself awakened at the small inn to which he had been remitted until morning, in the middle of the night.

Awakened by a timid local functionary and three armed patriots in rough red caps and with pipes in their mouths, who sat down on the bed.

'Emigrant,' said the functionary, 'I am going to send you on to Paris, under an escort.'

'Citizen, I desire nothing more than to get to Paris, though I could dispense with the escort.'

'Silence!' growled a red-cap, striking at the coverlet with the butt-end of his musket. 'Peace, aristocrat!'

'It is as the good patriot says,' observed the timid functionary. 'You are an aristocrat, and must have an escort–and must pay for it.'

'I have no choice,' said Charles Darnay.

'Choice! Listen to him!' cried the same scowling red-cap. 'As if it was not a favour to be protected from the lamp-iron.'

'It is always as the good patriot says,' observed the functionary. 'Rise and dress yourself, emigrant.'

Darnay complied, and was taken back to the guard-house, where other patriots in rough red caps were smoking, drinking, and sleeping, by a watch-fire. Here he paid a heavy price for his escort, and hence he started with it on the wet, wet roads at three o'clock in the morning.

The escort were two mounted patriots in red caps and tricoloured cockades, armed with national muskets and sabres, who rode one on either side of him. The escorted governed his own horse, but a loose line was attached to his bridle, the end of which one of the patriots kept girded round his wrist. In this state they set forth with the sharp rain driving in their faces: clattering at a heavy dragoon trot over the uneven town pavement, and out upon the mire-deep roads. In this state they traversed without change, except of horses and pace, all the mire-deep leagues that lay between them and the capital.

They travelled in the night, halting an hour or two after daybreak, and lying by until the twilight fell. The escort were so wretchedly clothed, that they twisted straw round their bare-legs, and thatched their ragged shoulders to keep the wet off. Apart from the personal discomfort of being so attended, and apart from such considerations of present danger as arose from one of the patriots being chronically drunk, and carrying his musket very recklessly, Charles Darnay did not allow the restraint that was laid upon him to awaken any serious fears in his breast; for, he reasoned with himself that it could have no reference to the merits of an individual case that was not yet stated, and of representations, confirmable by the prisoner in the Abbaye, that were not yet made.

But when they came to the town of Beauvais–which they did at eventide, when the streets were filled with people–he could not conceal from himself that the aspect of affairs was very alarming. Am ominous crowd gathered to see him dismount at the posting-yard, and many voices called out loudly, 'Down with the emigrant!'

He stopped in the act of swinging himself out of his saddle, and, resuming it as his safest place, said:

'Emigrant, my friends! Do you not see me here, in France, of my own will?'

'You are a cursed emigrant,' cried a farrier, making at him in a furious manner through the press, hammer in hand; 'and you are cursed aristocrat!'

The postmaster interposed himself between this man and the rider's bridle (at which he was evidently making), and soothingly said, 'Let him be; let him be! He will be judged at Paris.'

'Judged!' repeated the farrier, swinging his hammer.

'Ay! and condemned as a traitor.' At this the crowd roared approval.

Checking the postmaster, who was for turning his horse's head to the yard (the drunken patriot sat composedly in his saddle looking on, with the line around his wrist), Darnay said, as soon as he could make his voice heard:

'Friends, you deceive yourselves, or your are deceived. I am not a traitor.'

'He lies,' cried the smith. 'He is a traitor since the decree. His life is forfeit to the people. His cursed life is not his own!'

At the instant when Darnay saw a rush in the eyes of the crowd, which another instant would have brought upon him, the postmaster turned his horse into the yard, the escort rode in close upon his horse's flanks, and the postmaster shut and barred the crazy double gates. The farrier struck a blow upon them with his hammer, and the crowd groaned; but, no more was done.

'What is this decree that the smith spoke of?' Darnay asked the postmaster, when he had thanked him, and stood beside him in the yard.

'Truly, a decree for selling the property of emigrants.'

'When passed?'

'On the fourteenth.'

'The day I left England!'

'Everybody says it is but one of several, and that there will be others—if there are not already—banishing all emigrants, and condemning all to death who return. That is what he meant when he said your life was not your own.'

'But there are no such decrees yet?'

'What do I know!' said the postmaster, shrugging his shoulders; 'there may be, or there will be. It is all the same. What would you have?'

They rested on some straw in a loft until the middle of the night, and then rode forward again when all the town was asleep. Among the many wild changes observable on familiar things which made this wild ride unreal, not the least was the seeming rarity of sleep. After long and lonely spurring over dreary roads, they would come to a cluster of poor cottages, not steeped in darkness, but all glittering with lights, and would find the people, in a ghostly manner in the dead of the night, circling hand in hand around a shrivelled tree of Liberty, or all drawn up together singing a Liberty song. Happily, however, there was sleep in Beauvais that night to help them out of it, and they passed on once more into solitude and loneliness: jingling through the untimely cold and wet, among impoverished fields that had yielded no fruits of the earth that year, diversified by the blackened remains of burnt houses, and by the sudden emergence from ambuscade, and sharp reining up across their way, of patriot patrols on the watch on all the roads.

Daylight at last found them before the wall of Paris. The barrier was closed and strongly guarded when they rode up to it.

'Where are the papers of this prisoner?' demanded a resolute-looking man in authority, who was summoned out by the guard.

Naturally struck by the disagreeable word, Charles Darnay requested the speaker to take notice that he was a free traveller and a French citizen, in charge of an escort which the disturbed state of the country had imposed upon him, and which he had paid for.

'Where,' repeated the same personage, without taking any heed of him whatever, 'are the papers of this prisoner?'

The drunken patriot had them in his cap, and produced them. Casting his eyes over Gabelle's letter, the same personage in authority showed some disorder and surprise, and looked at Darnay with a close attention.

He left escort and escorted without saying a word, however, and went into the guard-room; meanwhile they sat upon their horses outside the gate. Looking about him while in this state of suspense, Charles Darnay observed that the gate was held by a mixed guard of soldiers and patriots, the latter far outnumbering the former; and that while ingress into the city for peasants' carts bringing in supplies, and for similar traffic and traffickers, was easy enough, egress, even for the homeliest people, was very difficult. A numerous medley of men and women, not to mention beasts and vehicles of various sorts, was waiting to issue forth; but the previous identification was so strict, that they filtered through the barrier very slowly. Some of these people knew their turn for examination to be so far off, that they lay on the ground to sleep or smoke, while others talked together, or loitered about. The red cap and tricolour cockade were universal, both among men and women.

When he had sat in his saddle some half-hour, taking note of these things, Darnay found himself confronted by the same man in authority, who directed the guard to open the barrier. Then he delivered to the escort, drunk and sober, a receipt for the escorted, and requested him to dismount. He did so, and the two patriots, leading his tired horse, turned and rode away without entering the city.

He accompanied his conductor into a guard-room, smelling of common wine and tobacco, where certain soldiers and patriots, asleep and awake, drunk and sober, and in various neutral states between sleeping and waking, drunkenness and sobriety, were standing and lying about. The light in the guard-house, half derived from the waning oil lamps of the night, and half from the overcast day, was in a correspondingly uncertain condition. Some registers were lying open on a desk, and an officer of a coarse, dark aspect, presided over these.

'Citizen Defarge,' said he to Darnay's conductor, as he took a slip of paper to write on. 'Is this the emigrant Evrémonde?'

'This is the man.'

'You age, Evrémonde?'

'Thirty-seven.'

'Married, Evrémonde?'

'Yes.'

'Where married?'

'In England.'

'Without doubt.' Where is your wife, Evrémonde?'

'In England.'

'Without doubt. You are consigned, Evrémonde, to the prison of La Force.'

'Just Heaven!' exclaimed Darnay. 'Under what law, and for what offence?'

The officer looked up from his slip of paper for a moment.

'We have new laws, Evrémonde, and new offences, since you were here.' He said it with a hard smile, and went on writing.

'I entreat you to observe that I have come here voluntarily, in response to that written appeal of a fellow-countryman which lies before you. I demand no more than the opportunity to do so without delay. Is not that my right?'

'Emigrants have no rights, Evrémonde,' was the stolid reply. The officer wrote until he had finished, read over to himself what he had written, sanded it, and handed it to Defarge, with the words 'In secret.'

Defarge mentioned with the paper to the prisoner that he must accompany him. The prisoner obeyed, and a guard of two armed patriots attended them.

'Is it you,' said Defarge, in a low voice, as they went down the guard-house steps and turned into Paris, 'who married the daughter of Doctor Manette, once a prisoner in the Bastille that is no more?'

'Yes,' replied Darnay, looking at him with surprise.

'My name is Defarge, and I keep a wine shop in the Quarter Saint Antoine. Possibly you have heard of me.'

'My wife came to your house to reclaim her father? Yes!'

The word 'wife' seemed to serve as a gloomy reminder to Defarge, to say with sudden impatience, 'In the name of that sharp female newly born and called La Guillotine, why did you come to France?'

'You heard me say why, a minute ago. Do you not believe it is the truth?'

'A bad truth for you,' said Defarge, speaking with knitted brows, and looking straight before him.

'Indeed I am lost here. All here is so unprecedented, so changed, so sudden and unfair, that I am absolutely lost. Will you render me a little help?'

'None.' Defarge spoke, always looking straight before him.

'Will you answer me a single question?'

'Perhaps. According to its nature. You can say what it is.'

'In this prison that I am going to so unjustly, shall I have some free communication with the word outside?'

'You will see.'

'I am not to be buried there, prejudged, and without any means of presenting my case?'

'You will see. But, what then? Other people have been similarly buried in worse prisons, before now.'

'But never by me, Citizen Defarge.'

Defarge glanced darkly at him for answer, and walked on in a steady and set silence. The deeper he sank into this silence, the fainter hope there was—or so Darnay thought—of his softening in any slight degree. He, therefore, made haste to say:

'It is the utmost importance to me (you know, citizen, even better than I, of how much importance), that I should be able to communicate to Mr. Lorry of Tellson's Bank, an English gentleman who is now in Paris, the simple fact, without comment, that I have been thrown into the prison of La Force. Will you cause that to be done for me?'

'I will do,' Defarge doggedly rejoined, 'nothing for you. My duty is to my country and the people. I am the sworn servant of both, against you. I will do nothing for you.'

Charles Darnay felt it hopeless to entreat him further, and his pride was touched besides. As they walked on in silence, he could not but see how used the people were to the spectacle of prisoners passing along the streets. The very children scarcely noticed him. A few passers turned their heads, and a few shook their fingers at him as an aristocrat; otherwise that a man in good clothes should be going to prison, was no more remarkable than that a labourer in working clothes should be going to work. In one narrow, dark, and dirty street through which they passed, and excited audience on the crimes against the people, of the king and the royal family. The few words that he caught from this man's lips, first made it known to Charles Darnay that the king was in prison, and that the foreign ambassadors had one and all left Paris. On the road (except at Beauvais) he had heard absolutely nothing. The escort and the universal watchfulness had completely isolated him.

That he had fallen among far greater dangers than those which had developed themselves when he left England, he of course knew now. That perils had thickened about him fast, and might thicken faster and faster yet, he of course knew now. He could not but admit to himself that might not have made this journey, if he could have foreseen the events of a few days. And yet his misgivings were not so dark as, imagined by the light of this later time, they would appear. Troubled as the future was, it was the unknown future, and in its obscurity there was ignorant hope. The horrible massacre, days and nights long, which, within a few rounds of the clock, was to set a great mark of blood upon the blessed garnering time of harvest, was as far out of his knowledge as if it had been a hundred thousand years away. The 'sharp female newly born, and called La Guillotine,' was hardly known to him, or to the generality of people, by name. The frightful deeds that were to be soon done, were probably unimagined at that time in the brains of the doers. How could they have a place in the shadowy conceptions of a gentle mind?

Of unjust treatment in detention and hardship, and in cruel separation from his wife and child, he foreshadowed the likelihood, or the certainty; but, beyond this, he dreaded nothing distinctly. With this on his mind, which was enough to carry him into a dreary prison courtyard, he arrived at the prison of La Force.

A man with a bloated face opened the strong wicket, to whom Defarge presented 'the emigrant Evrémonde.'

'What the Devil! How many more of them!' exclaimed the man with the bloated face.

Defarge took his receipt without noticing the exclamation, and withdrew, with his two fellow-patriots.

'What the Devil, I say again!' exclaimed the jailer, left with his wife. 'How many more!'

The jailer's wife, being provided with no answer to the question, merely replied, 'One must have patience, my dear! Three turnkeys who entered responsive to a bell she rang, echoed the sentiment and one added, 'For the love of Liberty'; which sounded in that place like an inappropriate conclusion.

The prison of La Force was a gloomy prison, dark and filthy, and with a horrible smell of foul sleep in it. Extraordinary how soon the noisome flavour of imprisoned sleep, becomes manifest in all such places that are ill cared for!'

'In secret, too,' grumbled the jailer, looking at the written paper. 'As if it was not already full to bursting!'

He stuck the paper on a file, in an ill-humour, and Charles Darnay awaited his further pleasure for half an hour: sometimes, pacing to and fro in the strong arched room: sometimes, resting on a stone seat: in either case detained to be imprinted on the memory of he chief and his subordinates.

'Come! said the chief, at length taking up his keys, 'come with me, emigrant.'

Through the dismal prison twilight, his new charge accompanied him by corridor and staircase, many doors clanging and locking behind them, until they came into a large, low, vaulted chamber, crowded with prisoners of both sexes. The women were seated at a long table, reading and writing, knitting, sewing, and embroidering; the men were for the most part standing behind their chairs, or lingering up and down the room.

In the instinctive association of prisoners with shameful crime and disgrace, the new comer recoiled from this company. But the crowing unreality of his long unreal ride, was, their all at once rising to receive him, with every refinement of manner known to the time, and with all the engaging graces and courtesies of life.

So strangely clouded were these refinements by the prison manners and gloom, so spectral did they become in the inappropriate squalor and misery through which they were seen, that Charles Darnay seemed to stand in a company of the dead. Ghosts all! The ghost of beauty, the ghost of stateliness, the ghost of elegance, the ghost of pride, the ghost of frivolity, the ghost of wit, the ghost of youth, the ghost of age, all waiting their dismissal from the desolate shore, all turning on him eyes that were changed by the death they had died in coming there.

It struck him motionless. The jailer standing at his side, and the other jailers moving about, who would have been well enough as to appearance in the ordinary exercise of their functions, looked so extravagantly coarse contrasted with sorrowing mothers and blooming daughters who were there–with the apparitions of the coquette, the young beauty, and the mature woman delicately bred–that the inversion of all experience and likelihood which the scene of shadows presented, was heightened to its utmost. Surely, ghosts all. Surely, the long unreal ride some progress of disease that had brought him to these gloomy shades!

'In the name of the assembled companions in misfortune,' said a gentleman of courtly appearance and address, coming forward, 'I have the honour of giving you welcome to La Force, and of condoling with you on the calamity that has brought you among us. May it soon terminate happily! It would be an impertinence elsewhere, but it is not so here, to ask your name and condition?'

Charles Darnay roused himself, and gave the required information, in words as suitable as he could find.

'But I hope,' said the gentleman, following the chief jailer with his eyes, who moved across the room, 'that you are not in secret?'

'I do not understand the meaning of the term, but I have heard them say so.'

'Ah, what a pity! We so much regret it! But take courage; several numbers of our society have been in secret, at first, and it had lasted but a short time.' Then he added, raising his voice, 'I grieve to inform the society–in secret.'

There was a murmur of commiseration as Charles Darnay crossed the room to a grated door where the jailer awaited him, and many voices–among which, the soft and compassionate voices of women were conspicuous–gave him good wishes and encouragement. He turned at the grated door, to render the thanks of his heart; it closed under the jailer's hand; and the apparitions vanished from his sight for ever.

The wicket opened on a stone staircase, leading upward. When they had ascended forty steps (the prisoner of half an hour already counted them), the jailer opened a low black door, and they passed into a solitary cell. It struck cold and damp, but was not dark.

'Yours,' said the jailer.

'Why am I confident alone?'

'How do I know!'

'I can buy pen, ink, and paper?'

'Such are not my orders. You will be visited, and can ask then. At present, you may buy your food, and nothing more.'

There were in the cell, a chair, a table, and a straw mattress. As the jailer made a general inspection of these objects, and of the four walls, before going out, a wandering fancy wandered through the mind of the prisoner leaning against the wall opposite to him, that this jailer was so unwholesomely bloated, both in face and person, as to look like a man who had been drowned and filled with water. When the jailer was gone, he thought in the same wandering way, 'Now am I left, as if I were dead.' Stopping then, to look down at the mattress, he turned from it with a sick feeling, and thought, 'And here in these crawling creatures in the first condition of the body after death.'

'Five paces by four and a half, five paces by four and a half, five paces by four and a half.' The prisoner walked to and fro in his cell, counting its measurement, and the roar of the city arose like muffled drums with a wild swell of voices added to them. 'He made shoes, he made shoes, he made shoes.' The prisoner counted the measurement again, and paced faster, to draw his mind with him from the latter repetition. 'The ghost that vanished when the wicket closed. There was one among them, the appearance of a lady dressed in black, who was leaning in the embrasure of a window, and she had a light shining upon her golden hair, and she looked like... Let us ride on again, for God's sakem through the illuminated villages with the people all awake!... He made shoes, he made shoes, he made shoes... Five paces by four and a half.' With such scraps tossing and rolling upward from the depths of his mind, the prisoner walked faster and faster, obstinately counting and counting; and the roar of the city changed to this extent–that is still rolled in like muffled drums, but with a wail of voices that he knew, in the swell that rose above them.

CHAPTER II

THE GRINDSTONE

TELLSON'S bank, established in the Saint Germain Quarter of Paris, was in the wing of a large house, approached by a courtyard and shut off from the street by a high wall and a strong gate. The house belonged to a great nobleman who had lived in it until he had made a flight from the troubles, in his own cook's dress, and got across the borders. A mere beast of the chase flying from hunters, he was still in his metempsychosis no other than the same Monseigneur, the preparation of whose chocolate for whose lips had once occupied three strong men besides the cook in question.

Monseigneur gone, and the three strong men absolving themselves from the sin of having drawn his high washes, by being more than ready and willing to cut his throat on the alter of the dawning Republic one and indivisible of Liberty, Equality, Fraternity, or Death, Monseigneur's house had been first sequestrated, and then confiscated. For, all things move so fast, and decree followed decree with that fierce precipitation, that now upon the third night of the autumn month of September, patriot emissaries of the law were in possession of Monseigneur's house, and had marked it with the tricolour, and were drinking brandy in its state apartments.

A place of business in London like Tellson's place of business in Paris, would soon have driven the House out of its mind and into the Gazette. For, what would staid British responsibility and respectability have said to orange-trees in boxes in a bank courtyard, and even to a Cupid over the counter? Yet such things were. Tellson's had whiteshaded the Cupid, but he was still to be seen on the ceiling, in the coolest linen, aiming (as he very often does) at money from morning to night. Bankruptcy must inevitably have come of this young Pagan, in Lombard Street, London, and also of a curtained alcove in the rear of the immortal boy, and also of a looking-glass let into the wall, and also of clerks not at all old, who danced in public on the slightest provocation. Yet, a French Tellson's could get on with these things exceedingly well, and, as long as the times held together, no man had taken fright at them, and drawn out his money.

What money would be drawn out of Tellson's henceforth, and what would lie there, lost and forgotten; what plate and jewels would tarish in Tellson's hiding-places, while the depositors rusted in prisons, and when they should have violently perished; how many accounts with Tellson's never to be balanced in this world, must be carried over into the next; no man could have said, that night, any more than Mr. Jarvis Lorry could, though he thought heavily of these questions. He sat by a newly lighted wood fire (the blighted and unfruitful year was prematurely cold), and on his honest and courageous face there was a deeper shade than the pendent lamp could throw, or any object in the room distortedly reflect–a shade of horror.

He occupied rooms in the bank, in his fidelity to the House of which he had grown to be a part, like strong rootivy. It chanced that they derived a kind of security from the patriotic occupation of the main building, but the true-hearted old gentleman never calculated about that. All such circumstances were indifferent to him, so that he did his duty. On the opposite side of the courtyard, under a colonnade, was extensive standing for carriages–where, indeed, some carriages of Monseigneur yet stood. Against two of the pillars were fastened two great flaring flambeaux, and in the light of these, standing out in the open air, was a large grindstone: a roughly mounted thing which appeared to have hurriedly been brought there from some neighbouring smithy, or other workshop. Rising and looking out of the window at these harmless objects, Mr. Lorry shivered, and retired to his seat by the fire. He had opened, not only the glass window, but the lattice blind outside it, and he had closed both again, and he shivered through his frame.

From the streets beyond the high wall and the strong gate, there came the usual night hum of the city, with now and then an indescribable ring in it, weird and unearthly, as if some unwonted sounds of a terrible nature were going up to Heaven.

'Thank God,' said Mr. Lorry, clasping his hands, 'that no one near and dear to me is this dreadful town to-night. May He have mercy on all who are in danger!'

Soon afterwards, the bell at the great gate sounded, and he thought. 'They have come back!' and sat listening. But, there was no loud irruption into the courtyard, as he had expected, and he heard the gate clash again, and all was quiet.

The nervousness and dread that were upon him inspired that vague uneasiness respecting the bank, which a great change would naturally awaken, with such feelings roused. It was well guarded, and he got up to go among the trusty people who were watching it, when his door suddenly opened, and two figured rushed in, at sight of which he fell back in amazement.

Lucie and her father! Lucie with her arms stretched out to him, and with that old look of earnestness so concentrated and intensified, that it seemed as though it had been stamped upon her face expressly to give force and power to it in this one passage of her life.

'What is this?' cried Mr. Lorry, breathless and confused. 'What is the matter? Lucie! Manette! What has happened? What has brought you here? What is it?'

With the look fixed upon him, in her paleness and wildness, she panted out in his arms, imploringly, 'O my dear friend! My husband!'

'Your husband, Lucie?'

'Charles.'

'What of Charles?'

'Here.'

'Here, in Paris?'

'Has been here some days—three or four—I don't know how many—I can't collect my thoughts. An errand of generosity brought him here unknown to us; he was stopped at the barrier, and sent to prison.'

The old man uttered an irrepressible cry. Almost at the same moment, the bell of the great gate rang again, and a loud noise of feet and voices came pouring into the courtyard.

'What is that noise?' said the Doctor, turning towards the window.

'Don't look!' cried Mr. Lorry. 'Don't look out! Manette, for your life, don't touch the blind!'

The Doctor turned, with his hand upon the fastening of the window, and said, with a cool, bold smile:

'My dear friend, I have a charmed life in this city. I have been a Bastille prisoner. There is no patriot in Paris—in Paris? In France—who, knowing me to have been prisoner in the Bastille, would touch me, except to overwhelm me with embraces, or carry me in triumph. My old pain has given me a power that has brought us through the barrier, and gained us news of Charles there, and brought us here. I knew it would be so; I knew I could help Charles out of all danger; I told Lucie so.—What is that noise?' His hand was again upon the window.

'Don't look!' cried Mr. Lorry, absolutely desperate. 'No, Lucie, my dear, nor you!' He got his arm around her, and held her. 'Don't be so terrified, my love. I solemnly swear to you that I know of no harm having happened to Charles; that I had no suspicion even of his being in this fatal place. What prison is he in?'

'La Force!'

'La Force! Lucie, my child, if ever you were brave and serviceable in your life–and you were always both–you will compose yourself now, to do exactly as I bid you; for more depends upon it than you can think, or I can say. There is no help for you in any action on your part to-night; you cannot possibly stir out. I say this, because what I must bid you to do for Charle's sake, is the hardest thing to do of all. You must let me put you in a room at the back here. You must leave your father and me alone for two minutes, and as there are Life and Death in the world you must not delay.'

'I will be submissive to you. I see in your face that you know I can do nothing else than this. I know you are true.'

The old man kissed her, and hurried her into his room, and turned the key; then, came hurrying back to the Doctor, and opened the window and partly opened the blind, and put his hand upon the Doctor's arm, and looked out with him into the courtyard.

Looked out upon a throng of men and women: not enough in number, or near enough, to fill the courtyard: not more than forty or fifty in all. The people in possession of the house had let them in at the gate, and they had rushed in to wok at the grindstone; it had evidently been set up there for their purpose, as in a convenient and retired spot.

But such awful workers, and such awful work!

The grindstone had a double handle, and, turning at it madly were two men, whose faces, as their long hair flapped back when the whirlings of the grindstone brought their faces up, were more horrible and cruel than the visages of the wildest savages in their most barbarous disguise. False eyebrows and false moustaches were stuck upon them, and their hideous countenances were all bloody and sweaty, and all awry with howling, and all staring and glaring with beastly excitement and want of sleep. As these ruffians turned and turned, their matted locks now flung forward over their eyes, now flung backward over their necks, some women held wine to their mouths that they might drink; and what with dropping blood, and what with dropping wine, and what with the stream of sparks struck out of the stone, all their wicked atmosphere seemed gore and fire. The eye could not detect one creature in the group free from the smear of blood. Shouldering one another to get next at the sharpening-stone, were men stripped to the waist, with the stain all over their limbs and bodies; men in all sorts of rags with the stain upon those rags; men devilishly set off with spoils of women's lace and silk and ribbon, with the stain dyeing those trifles through and through. Hatches, knives, bayonets, swords, all brought to be sharpened, were all red with it. Some of the hacked swords were tied to the wrists of those who carried them, with strips of linen and fragments of dress: ligatures various in kind, but all deep of the one colour. And as the frantic wielders of these weapons snatched them from the stream of sparks and tore away into the streets, the same red blue was red in their frenzied eyes—eyes which any unbrutalized beholder would have given twenty years of life, to petrify with a well-directed gun.

All this was seen in a moment, as the vision of a drowning man, or of any human creature at any very great pass, could see a word if it were there. They drew back from the window, and the Doctor looked for explanation in his friend's ashy face.

'They are'—Mr. Lorry whispered the words, glancing fearfully round at the locked room—'murdering the prisoners. If you are sure of what you say; if you really have the power you think you have—as I believe you have—make yourself known to these devils, and get taken to La Force. It may be too late, I don't know, but let it not be a minute later!'

Doctor Manette pressed his hand, hastened bareheaded out of the room, and was in the courtyard when Mr. Lorry regained the blind.

His streaming white hair, his remarkable face, and the impetuous confidence of his manner, as he put the weapons aside like water, carried him in an instant to the heart of the concourse at the stone. For a few moments there was a pause, and a hurry, and a murmur, and the unintelligible sound of his voice; and then Mr. Lorry saw him, surrounded by all, and in the midst of a line of twenty men long, all linked shoulder to shoulder, and hand to shoulder, hurried out with cries of—'Live the Bastille prisoner! Help for the Bastille prisoner's kindred in La Force! Room for the Bastille prisoner in front there! Save the prisoner Evrémonde at La Force!' and a thousand answering shouts.

He closed the lattice again with a fluttering heart, closed the window and the curtain, hastened to Lucie, and told her that her father was assisted by the people, and gone in search of her husband. He found her child and Miss Pross with her; but, it never occurred to him to be surprised by their appearance until a long time afterwards, when he sat watching them in such quiet as the night knew.

Lucie had, by that time, fallen into a stupor on the floor at his feet, clinging to his hand. Miss Pross had laid the child down on his own bed, and her head had gradually fallen on the pillow beside her pretty charge. O the long, long night, with the moans of the poor wife! And O the long, long night with no return of her father and no tidings!

Twice more in the darkness the bell at the great gate sounded, and the irruption was repeated, and the grindstone whirled and spluttered. 'What is it?' cried Lucie, affrighted, 'Hush! The soldiers' swords are sharpened there,' said Mr. Lorry. 'This place is national property now, and used as a kind of armoury, my love.'

Twice more in all; but, the last spell of work was feeble and fitful. Soon afterwards the day began to dawn, and he softly detached himself from the clasping hand, and cautiously looked out again. A man, so besmeared that he might have been a sorely wounded soldier creeping back to consciousness on a field of slain, was rising from the pavement by the side of the grindstone, and looking about him with a vacant air. Shortly, this worn-out murderer descried in the imperfect light one of the carriages of Monseigneur, and, staggering to that gorgeous vehicle, climbed in at the door, and shut himself up to take his rest on its dainty cushions.

The great grindstone, Earth, had turned when Mr. Lorry looked out again, and the sun was red on the courtyard. But, the lesser grindstone stood alone there in the calm morning air, with a red upon it that the sun had never given, and would never take away.

CHAPTER III

THE SHADOW

ONE of the first considerations which arose in the business mind of Mr. Lorry when business hours came round, was this: that he had no right to imperil Tellson's by sheltering the wife of an emigrant prisoner under the bank roof. His own possessions, safety, life, he would have hazarded for Lucie and her child, without a moment's demur; but the great trust he held was not his own, and as to that business charge he was a strict man of business.

At first, his mind reverted to Defarge, and he thought of finding out the wine shop again and taking counsel with its master in reference to the safest dwelling-place in the distracted state of the city. But, the same consideration that suggested him, repudiated him; he lived in the most violent Quarter, and doubtless was influential there, and deep in its dangerous workings.

Noon coming, and the Doctor not returning, and every minute's delay tending to compromise Tellson's, Mr. Lorry advised with Lucie. She said that her father had spoken of hiring a lodging for a short term, in that Quarter, near the banking-house. As there was no business objection to this, and he foresaw that even if it were all well with Charles, and he were to be released, he could not hope to leave the city, Mr. Lorry went out in quest of such a lodging, and found a suitable one, high up in a removed by-street where the closed blinds in all other windows of a high melancholy square of buildings marked deserted homes.

To this lodging he at once removed Lucie and her child, and Miss Pross: giving them what comfort he could, and much more than he had himself. He left Jerry with them, as a figure to fill a doorway that would bear considerable knocking on the head, and returned to his own occupations. A disturbed and doleful mind he brought to bear upon them, and slowly and heavily the day lagged on with him.

It wore itself out, and wore him out with it, until the bank closed. He was again alone in his room of the previous night, considering what to do next, when he heard a foot upon the stair. In a few moments, a man stood in his presence, who, with a keenly observant look at him, addressed him by his name.

'Your servant,' said Mr. Lorry. 'Do you know me?'

He was a strongly made man with dark curling hair, from forty-five to fifty years of age. For answer he repeated, without any change of emphasis, the words:

'Do you know me?'

'I have seen you somewhere.'

'Perhaps at my wine shop?'

Much interested and agitated, Mr. Lorry said: 'You come from Doctor Manette?'

'Yes, I come from Doctor Manette.'

'And what says he? What does he send me?'

Defarge gave into his anxious hand, an open scrap of paper. It bore the words in the Doctor's writing:

'Charles is safe, but I cannot safely leave this place yet. I have obtained the favour that the bearer has a short note from Charles to his wife. Let the bearer see his wife.'

It was dated from La Force, within an hour.

'Will you accompany me,' said Mr. Lorry, joyfully relieved after reading this note aloud, 'to where his wife resides?'

'Yes,' returned Defarge.

Scarcely noticing as yet, in what a curiously reserved bad mechanical way Defarge spoke, Mr. Lorry put on his hat and they went down into the court yard. There, they found two women; one knitting.

'Madame Defarge, surely! said Mr. Lorry, who had left her in exactly the same attitude some seventeen years ago.

'It is she,' observed her husband.

'Does madame go with us?' inquired Mr. Lorry, seeing that she moved as they moved.

'Yes. That she may be able to recognize the faces and know the persons. It is for their safety.'

Beginning to be struck by Defarge's manner, Mr. Lorry looked dubiously at him, and led the way. Both the women followed; the second woman being The Vengeance.

They passed through the intervening streets as quickly as they might, ascended the staircase of the new domicile, were admitted by Jerry, and found Lucie weeping, alone. She was thrown into a transport by the tidings Mr. Lorry gave her of her husband, and clasped the hand that delivered his note-little thinking what it had been doing near him in the night, and might, but for a chance, have done to him.

'DEAREST,–Take courage. I am well, and your father has influence around me. You cannot answer this. Kiss our child for me.'

That was all the writing. It was so much, however, to her who received it, that she turned from Defarge to his wife, and kissed one of the hands that knitted. It was a passionate, loving, thankful, womanly action, but the hand made no response–dropped cold and heavy, and took to its knitting again.

There was something in its touch that gave Lucie a check. She stopped in the act of putting the note in her bosom, and, with her hands yet at her neck, looked terrified at Madame Defarge. Madame Defarge met the lifted eyebrows and forehead with a cold, impassive stare.

'My dear,' said Mr. Lorry, striking in to explain; 'there are frequent risings in the streets; and, although it is not likely they will ever trouble you, Madame Defarge wishes to see those whom she has the power to protect at such times, to the end that she may know them—that she my identify them. I believe,' said Mr. Lorry, rather halting in his reassuring words, as the stony manner of all the three impressed itself upon him more and more, 'I state the case, Citizen Defarge?'

Defarge looked gloomily at his wife, and gave no other answer than a gruff sound of acquiescence.

'You had better, Lucie,' said Mr. Lorry, doing all he could to propitiate, by tone and manner, 'have the dear child here, and our good Pross. Our good Pross, Defarge, is an English lady, and knows no French.'

The lady in question, whose rooted conviction that she was more than a match for any foreigner, was not to be shaken by distress and danger, appeared with folded arms, and observed in English to The Vengeance, whom her eyes first encountered, 'Well, I am sure, Boldface! I hope *you* are pretty well!' She also bestowed a British cough on Madame Defarge; but, neither of the two took much heed of her.

'Is that his child?' said Madame Defarge, stopping in her work for the first time, and pointing her knitting-needle at little Lucie as if it were the finger of Fate.

'Yes, madame,' answered Mr. Lorry; 'this is our poor prisoner's darling daughter, and only child.'

The shadow attendant on Madame Defarge and her party seemed to fall so threatening and dark on the child, that her mother instinctively kneeled on the ground beside her, and held her to her breast. The shadow attendant on Madame Defarge and her party seemed then to fall, threatening and dark, on both the mother and the child.

'It is enough, my husband,' said Madame Defarge. 'I have seen them. We may go.'

But, the suppressed manner had enough of menace in it—not visible and presented, but indistinct and withheld—to alarm Lucie into saying, as she laid her appealing hand on Madame Defarge's dress:

'You will be good to my poor husband. You will do him no harm. You will help me to see him if you can?'

'Your husband is not my business here,' returned Madame Defarge, looking down at her with perfect composure. 'It is the daughter of your father who is my business here.'

'For my sake, then, be merciful to my husband. For my child's sake! She will put her hands together and pray you to be merciful. We are more afraid of you than of these others.'

Madame Defarge received it as a compliment, and looked at her husband. Defarge, who had been uneasily biting his thumb-nail and looking at her, collected his face into a sterner expression.

'What is that your husband says in that little letter?' asked Madame Defarge, with a lowering smile. 'Influence; he says something touching influence?'

'That my father,' said Lucie, hurriedly taking the paper from her breast, but with her alarmed eyes on her questioner and not on it, 'has much influence around him.'

'Surely it will release him!' said Madame Defarge. 'Let it do so.'

'As a wife and mother,' cried Lucie, most earnestly, 'I implore you to have pity on me and not to exercise any power that you possesses, against my innocent husband, but to use it on his behalf. O sister-woman, think of me. As a wife and mother!'

Madame Defarge looked, coldly as ever, at the suppliant, and said, turning to her friend The Vengeance:

'The wives and mothers we have been used to see, since we were as little as this child, and much less, have not been greatly considered? We have known *their* husbands and fathers laid in prison and kept from them, often enough? All our lives, we have seen our sister-women suffer, in themselves and in their children, poverty, nakedness, hunger, thirst, sickness, misery, oppression, and neglect of all kinds?'

'We have seen nothing else,' returned The Vengeance.

'We have borne this a long time,' said Madame Defarge, turning her eyes again upon Lucie. 'Judge you! Is it likely that the trouble of one wife and mother would be much to us now?'

She resumed her knitting and went out. The Vengeance followed. Defarge went last, and closed the door.

'Courage, my dear Lucie,' said Mr. Lorry, as he raised her. 'Courage, courage! So far all goes well with us—much, much better than it has of late gone with many poor souls. Cheer up, and have a thankful heart.'

'I am not thankless, I hope, but that dreadful woman seems to throw a shadow on me and on all my hopes.'

'Tut, tut!' said Mr. Lorry; 'what is this despondency in the brave little breast? A shadow indeed! No substance in it, Lucie.'

But the shadow of the manner of these Defarges was dark upon himself, for all that, and in his secret mind it troubled him greatly.

CHAPTER IV

CALM IN STORM

DOCTOR Manette did not return until the morning of the fourth day of his absence. So much of what had happened in that dreadful time as could be kept from the knowledge of Lucie was so well concealed from her, that

that not until long afterwards, when France and she were far apart, did she know that eleven hundred defenceless prisoners of both sexes and all ages had been killed by the populace; that four days and nights had been darkened by this deed of horror; and that the air around her had been tainted by the slain. She only knew that there had been tainted by the slain. She only knew that there had been an attack upon the prisons, that all political prisoners had been in danger, and that some had been dragged out by the crowd and murdered.

To Mr. Lorry, the Doctor communicated under an injunction of secrecy on which he had no need to dwell, that the crowd had taken him through a scene of carnage to the prison of La Force. That, in the prison he had found a self-appointed Tribunal sitting, before which the prisoners were brought singly, and by which they were rapidly ordered to be put forth to be massacred, or to be released, or (in a few cases) to be sent back to their cells. That, presented by his conductors to this Tribunal, he had announced himself by name and profession as having been for eighteen years a secret and unaccused prisoner in the Bastille; that, one of the body so sitting in judgment had risen and identified him, and that this man was Defarge.

That, hereupon he had ascertained, through the registers on the table, that his son-in-law was among the living prisoners, and had pleaded hard to the Tribunal—of whom some members were asleep and some awake, some dirty with murder and some clean, some sober and some not—for his life and liberty. That, in the first frantic greetings lavished on himself as a notable sufferer under the overthrown system, it had been accorded to him to have Charles Darnay brought before the lawless Court, and examined. That, he seemed on the point of being at once released, when the tide in his favour met with some unexplained check (not intelligible to the Doctor), which led to a few words of secret conference. That, the man sitting as President had then informed Doctor Manette that the prisoner must remain in custody, but should, for his sake, be held inviolate in safe custody. That, immediately, on a signal, the prisoner was removed to the interior of the prison again; but, that he, the Doctor, had then so strongly pleaded for permission to remain and assure himself that his son-in-law was, through no malice or mischance, delivered to the concourse whose murderous yells outside the gate had often drowned the proceedings, that he had obtained the permission, and had remained in that Hall of Blood until the danger was over.

The sights he had seen there, with brief snatches of food and sleep by intervals, shall remain untold. The mad joy over the prisoners who were saved, had astounded him scarcely less than the mad ferocity against those who were cut to pieces. One prisoner there was, he said, who had been discharged into the street free, but at whom a mistaken savage had thrust a pike as he passed out. Being besought to go to him and dress the wound, the Doctor had passed out at the same gate, and had found him in the arms of a company of Samaritans, who were seated on the bodies of their victims. With an inconsistency as monstrous as anything in this awful nightmare, they had helped the healer, and tended the wounded man with the gentlest solicitude—had made a litter for him and escorted him carefully from the spot–had then caught up their weapons and plunged anew into a butchery so dreadful, that the Doctor had covered his eyes with his hands, and swooned away in the midst of it.

As Mr. Lorry received these confidences, and as he watched the face of his friend now sixty-two years of age a misgiving arose within him that such dread experiences would revive the old danger. But, he had never seen his friend in his present character. For the first time the Doctor felt now, that his suffering was strength and power. For the first time he felt that in that sharp fire, he had slowly forged the iron which could break the prison door of his daughter's husband, and deliver him. 'It all tended to a good end, my friend; it was not mere waste and ruin. As my beloved child was helpful in restoring me to myself, I will be helpful now in restoring the dearest part of herself to her; by the aid of Heaven I will do it!' Thus, Doctor Manette. And when Jarvis Lorry saw the kindled eyes, the resolute face, the calm strong look and bearing of the man whose life always seemed to him to have been stopped, like a clock, for so many years, and then set going again with an energy which had lain dormant during the cessation of its usefulness, he believed.

Greater things than the Doctor had at that time to contend with, would have yielded before his persevering purpose. While he kept himself in his place, as a physician whose business was with all degrees of mankind, bond and free, rich and poor, bad and good, hi used his personal influence so wisely, that he was soon the inspecting physician of three prisons, and among them of La Force. He could now assure Lucie that her husband was no longer confined alone, but was mixed with the general body of prisoners; he saw her husband weekly, and brought sweet messages to her, straight from his lips; sometimes her husband himself sent a letter to her (though never by the Doctor's hand), but she was not permitted to write to him: for, among the many wild suspicions of plots in the prisons, the wildest of all pointed at emigrants who were known to have made friends or permanent connections abroad.

This new life of the Doctor's was an anxious life, no doubt; still, the sagacious Mr. Lorry saw that there was a new sustaining pride in it. Nothing unbecoming tinged the pride; it was a natural and worthy one; but he observed it as a curiosity. The Doctor knew, that up to that time, his imprisonment had been associated in the minds of his daughter and his friend, with his personal affliction, deprivation, and weakness. Now that this was changed, and he knew himself to be invested through that old trial with forces to which they both looked for Charle's ultimate safety and deliverance, he became so far exalted by the change, that he took the lead and direction, and required them as the weak, to trust to him as the strong. The preceding relative positions of himself and Lucie were reversed, yet only as the liveliest gratitude and affection could reverse them, for he could have had no pride but in rendering some service to her who had rendered so much to him. 'All curious to see,' thought Mr. Lorry, in his amiably shrewd way, 'but all natural and right; so, take the lead, my dear friend, and keep it; it couldn't be in better hands.'

But, though the Doctor tried hard, and never ceased trying, to get Charles Darnay set at liberty, or at least to get him brought to trial, the public current of the time set too strong and fast for him. The new era began; the king was tried, doomed, and beheaded; the Republic of Liberty, Equality, Fraternity, or Death, declared for victory or death against the world in arms; the black flag waved night and day from the great towers of Notre Dame; three hundred thousand men, summoned to rise against the tyrants of the earth, rose from all the varying soils of France, as if the dragon's teeth had been sown broadcast, and had yielded fruit equally on hill and plain, on rock, in gravel, and alluvial mud, under the bright sky of the South and under the clouds of the North, in fell and forest, in the vineyards and the olive-grounds and among the cropped grass and the stubble of the corn, along the fruitful banks of the broad rivers, and in the sand of the seashore. What private solicitude could rear itself against the deluge of the Year One of Liberty—the deluge rising from below, not falling from above, and with the windows of Heaven shut, not opened!

There was no pause, no pity, no peace, no interval of relenting rest, no measurement of time. Though days and nights circled as regularly as when time was young, and the evening and morning were the first day, other count of time there was none. Hold of it was lost in the raging fever of a nation, as it is in the fever of one patient. Now, breaking the unnatural silence of a whole city, the executioner showed the people the head of the king—and now, it seemed almost in the same breath, the head of his fair wife which had had eight weary months of imprisoned widowhood and misery, to turn it grey.

And yet, observing the strange law of contradiction which obtains in all such cases, the time was long, while it flamed by so fast. A revolutionary tribunal in the capital, and forty or fifty thousand revolutionary committees all over the land; a law of the Suspected, which struck away all security for liberty or life, and delivered over any good and innocent person to any bad and guilty one; prisons gorged with people who had committed no offence, and could obtain no hearing; these things became the established order and nature of appointed things, and seemed to be ancient usage before they were many weeks old. Above all, one hideous figure grew as familiar as if it had been before the general gaze from the foundations of the world—the figure of the sharp female called La Guillotine.

It was the popular theme for jests; it was the best cure for headache, it infallibly prevented the hair from turning grey, it imparted a peculiar delicacy to the complexion, it was the National Razor which shaved close: who kissed La Guillotine looked through the little window and sneezed into the sack. It was the sign of regeneration of the human race. It superseded the Cross. Models of it were worn on breasts from which the Cross was discarded, and it was bowed down to and believed in where the Cross was denied.

It sheared off heads so many, that it, and the ground it most polluted, were a rotten red. It was taken to pieces, like a toy puzzle for a young Devil, and was put together again when the occasion wanted it. It hushed the eloquent, struck down the powerful, abolished the beautiful and good. Twenty-two friends of high public mark, twenty-one living and one dead, it had lopped the heads off, in one morning, in as many minutes. The name of the strong man of Old Scripture had descended to the chief functionary who worked it; but, so armed, he was stronger than his namesake, and blinder, and tore away the gates of God's own Temple every day.

Among these terrors, and the brood belonging to them, the Doctor walked with a steady head: confident in his power, cautiously persistent in his end, never doubting that he would save Lucie's husband at last. Yet the current of the swept by, so strong and deep, and carried the time away so fiercely, that Charles had lain in prison one year and three months when the Doctor was thus steady and confident. So much more wicked and distracted had the Revolution grown in that December month, that the rivers of the South were encumbered with the bodies of the violently drowned by night, and prisoners were shot in lines and squares under the southern wintry sun. Still, the Doctor walked among the terrors with a steady head. No man better known than he, in Paris at that day; no man in a stranger situation. Silent, humane, indispensable in hospital and prison, using his art equally among assassins and victims, he was a man apart. In the exercise of his skill, the appearance and the story of the Bastille captive removed him from all other men. He was not suspected or brought in question, any more than if he had indeed been recalled to life some eighteen years before, or were a Spirit moving among mortals.

CHAPTER V

THE WOOD-SAWYER

ONE year and three months. During all that time Lucie was never sure, from hour to hour, but that the Guillotine would strike off her husband's head next day. Every day, through the stony streets, the tumbrils now jolted heavily, filled with Condemned. Lovely girls; bright women, brown-haired, black-haired, and grey; youths; stalwart men and old, gentle born and peasant born; all red wine for La Guillotine, all daily brought into light from the dark cellars of the loathsome prisons, and carried to her through the streets to slake her devouring thirst. Liberty, Equality, Fraternity, or Death—the last, much the easiest to bestow, O Guillotine!

If the suddenness of her calamity, and the whirling wheels of the time, had stunned the Doctor's daughter into awaiting the result in idle despair, it would but have been with her as it was with many. But, from the hour when she had taken the white head to her fresh young bosom in the garret of Saint Antoine, she had been true to her duties. She was truest to them in the season of trial, as all the quietly loyal and good will always be.

As soon as they were established in their new residence and her father had entered on the routine of his avocations, she arranged the little household as exactly as if her husband had been there. Everything had its appointed place and its appointed time. Little Lucie she taught, as regularly as if they had all been united in their English home. The slight devices with which she cheated herself into the show of a belief that they would soon be reunited–the little preparations for his speedy return, the setting aside of his chair and his books–these, and the solemn prayer at night for one dear prisoner especially, among the many unhappy souls in prison and the shadow of death–were almost the only outspoken reliefs of her heavy mind.

She did not greatly alter in appearance. The plain dark dresses, akin to mourning dresses, which she and her child wore, were as neat and as well attended to as the brighter clothes of happy days. She lost her colour, and the old and intent expression was a constant, not an occasional, thing; otherwise, she remained very pretty and comely. Sometimes, at night on kissing her father, she would burst into the grief she had repressed all day, and would say that her sole reliance, under Heaven, was on him. He always resolutely answered: 'Nothing can happen to him without my knowledge, and I know that I can save him, Lucie.'

They had not made the round of their changed life many weeks, when her father said to her, on coming home one evening:

'My dear, there is an upper window in the prison, to which Charles can sometimes gain access at three in the afternoon. When he can get to it–which depends on many uncertainties and incidents–he might see you in the street, he thinks, if you stood in a certain place that I show you. But you will not be able to see him, my poor child, and even if you could, it would be unsafe for you to make a sign of recognition.'

'O show me the place, my father, and I will go there every day.'

From that time, in all weathers, she waited there two hours. As the clock struck two, she was there, and at four she turned resignedly away. When it was not too wet or inclement for her child to be with her, they went together; at other times she was alone; but, she never missed a single day.

It was the dark and dirty corner of a small winding street. The hovel of a cutter of wood into lengths for burning, was the only house at that end; all else was wall. On the third day of her being there, he noticed her.

'Good day, citizeness.'

'Good day, citizen.'

This mode of address was now prescribed by decree. It had been established voluntarily some time ago, among the more through patriots; but, was now law for everybody.

'Walking here again, citizeness?'

'You see me, citizen!'

The wood-sawyer, who was a little man with a redundancy of gesture (he had once been a mender of roads), cast a glance at the prison, pointed at the prison, and putting his ten fingers before his face to represent bars, peeped through them jocosely.

'But it's not my business,' said he. And went on sawing his wood.

Next day he was looking out for her, and accosted her the moment she appeared.

'What? Walking here again, citizeness?'

'Yes, citizen.'

'Ah! A child too! Your mother, is it not, my little citizeness?'

'Do I say yes, mamma?' whispered little Lucie, drawing close to her.

'Yes, dearest.'

'Yes, citizen.'

'Ah! But it's not my business. My work is my business. See my saw! I call it my Little Guillotine. La, la, la; La, la, la! And off his head comes!'

The billet fell as he spoke, and he threw it into a basket.

'I call myself the Samson of the firewood guillotine. See here again! Loo, loo, loo; Loo, loo, loo! And off *her* head comes! Now, a child. Tickle, tickle; Pickle, pickle! And off *its* head comes. All the family!'

Lucie shuddered as he threw two more billets into his basket, but it was impossible to be there while the wood-sawyer was at work, and not be in his sight. Thenceforth, to secure his goodwill, she always spoke to him first, and often gave him drink money, which he readily received.

He was an inquisitive fellow, and sometimes when she had quite forgotten him in gazing at the prison roof and grates, and in lifting her heart up to her husband, she would come to herself to find him looking at her, with his knee on his bench and his saw stopped in its work. 'But it's not my business!' he would generally say at those times, and would briskly fall to his sawing again.

In all weathers, in the snow and frost of winter, in the bitter winds of spring, in the hot sunshine of summer, in the rains of autumn, and again in the snow and frost of winter, Lucie passed two hours of every day at this place; and every day on leaving it, she kissed the prison wall. Her husband saw her (so he learned from her father) it might be once in five or six times: it might be twice or thrice running: it might be, not for a week or a fortnight together. It was enough that he could and did see her when the chances served, and on that possibility she would have waited out the day, seven days a week.

These occupations brought her round to the December month, wherein her father walked among the terrors with a steady head. On a lightly snowing afternoon she arrived at the usual corner. It was a day of some wild rejoicing, and a festival. She had seen the houses, as she came along, decorated with little pikes, and with little red caps stuck upon them; also, with tricoloured ribbons; also, with the standard inscription (tricoloured letters were the favourite), Republic One and Indivisible, Liberty, Equality, Fraternity, or Death.

The miserable shop of the wood-sawyer was so small, that its whole surface furnished very indifferent space for this legend. He had got somebody to scrawl it up for him, however, who had squeezed Death in with most inappropriate difficulty. On his house-top, he displayed pike and cap, as a good citizen must, and in a window he had stationed his saw inscribed as his 'Little Sainte Guillotine'–for the great sharp female was by that time properly canonized. His shop was shut and he was not there, which was a relief to Lucie, and left her quite alone.

But, he was not far off, for presently she heard a troubled movement and a shouting coming along, which filled her with fear. A moment afterwards, and a throng of people came pouring round the corner by the prison wall, in the midst of whom was the wood-sawyer hand in hand with The Vengeance. There could not be fewer than five hundred people, and they were dancing like five thousand demons. There was no other music than their own singing. They danced to the popular Revolution song, keeping a ferocious time that was like a gnashing of teeth in unison. Men and women danced together, women danced together, men danced together, as hazard had brought them together. At first, they were a mere storm of coarse red caps and coarse woolen rags; but, as they filled the place, and stopped to dance about Lucie, some ghastly apparition of a dance-figure gone raving mad arose among them. They advanced, retreated, struck at one another's hands, clutched at one another's heads, spun round alone, caught one another and spun round in pairs, until many of them dropped. While those were down, the rest linked hand in hand, and all spun round together: then the ring broke, and in separate rings of two and four they turned and turned until they all stopped at once, began again, struck, clutched, and tore, and then reversed the spin, and all spun round another way. Suddenly they stopped again, paused, struck out the time afresh, formed into lines the width of the public way, and, with their heads low down and their hands high up, swooped screaming off. No fight could have been half so terrible as this dance. It was so emphatically a fallen sport–a something, once innocent, delivered over to all devilry–a healthy pastime changed into a means of angering the blood, bewildering the senses, and steeling the heart. Such graces as was visible in it, made it the uglier, showing how warped and perverted all things good by nature were become. The maidenly bosom bared to this, the pretty almost child's head thus distracted, the delicate foot mincing in this slough of blood and dirt, were types of the disjointed time.

This was the Carmagnole. As it passed, leaving Lucie frightened and bewildered in the doorway of the wood-sawyer's house, the feathery snow fell as quietly and lay as white and soft, as if it had never been.

'O my father!' for he stood before her when she lifted up the eyes she had momentarily darkened with her hand; 'such a cruel, bad sight.'

'I know, my dear, I know. I have seen it many times. Don't be frightened. Not one of them would harm you.'

'I am not frightened for myself, my father. But when I think of my husband, and the mercies of these people—'

'We will set him above their mercies very soon. I left him climbing to the window, and I came to tell you. There is no one here to see. You may kiss your hand towards that highest shelving roof.'

'I do so, father, and I send him my Soul with it!'

'You cannot see him, my poor dear?'

'No, father,' said Lucie, yearning and weeping as she kissed her hand, 'no.'

A footstep in the snow. Madame Defarge. 'I salute you, citizeness,' from the Doctor. 'I salute you, citizen.' This in passing. Nothing more. Madame Defarge gone, like a shadow over a white road.

'Give me your arm, my love. Pass from here with an air of cheerfulness of courage, for his sake. That was well done'; they had left the spot; 'it shall not be in vain. Charles is summoned for to-morrow.'

'For to-morrow!'

'There is no time to lose. I am well prepared, but there are precautions to be taken, that could not be taken until he was actually summoned before the Tribunal. He has not received the notice yet, but I know that he will presently be summoned for to-morrow, and removed to the Conciergerie; I have timely information. You are not afraid?'

She could scarcely answer, 'I trust in you.'

'Do so implicity. Your suspense is nearly ended, my darling; he shall be restored to you within a few hours; I have encompassed him with every protection. I must see Lorry.'

He stopped. There was a heavy lumbering of wheels within hearing. They both knew too well what it meant. One. Two. Three. Three tumbrils faring away with their dread loads over the hushing snow.

'I must see Lorry,' the Doctor repeated, turning her another way.

The staunch old gentleman was still in his trust; had never left it. He and his books were in frequent requisitions as to property confiscated and made national. What he could save for the owners, he saved. No better man living to hold fast by what Tellson's had in keeping, and to hold his peace.

A murky red and yellow sky, and a rising mist from the Seine, denoted the approach of darkness. It was almost dark when they arrived at the bank. The stately residence of Monseigneur was altogether blighted and deserted. Above a heap of dust and ashes in the court, ran the letters: National Property. Republic One and Indivisible. Liberty, Equality, Fraternity, or Death!

Who could that be with Mr. Lorry—the owner of the riding-coat upon the chair—who must not be seen? From whom newly arrived, did he come out, agitated and surprised, to take his favourite in his arms? To whom did he appear to repeat her faltering words, when, raising his voice and turning his head towards the door of the room from which he had issued, he said: 'Removed to the Conciergerie, and summoned for to-morrow'?

CHAPTER VI

TRIUMPH

THE dread Tribunal of five Judges, Public Prosecutor, and determined Jury, sat every day. Their lists went forth every evening, and were read put by the jailers of the various prisons to their prisoners. The standard jailer-joke was, 'Come out and listen to the Evening Paper, you inside there!'

'Charles Evrémonde, called Darnay!'

So at last began the Evening Paper at La Force.

When a name was called, its owner stepped apart into a spot reserved for those who were announced as being thus fatally recorded. Charles Evrémonde, called Darnay, had reason to know the usage; he had seen hundreds pass away so.

His bloated jailer, who wore spectacles to read with, glanced over them to assure himself that he had taken his place, and went through the list, making a similar short pause at each name. There were twenty-three names, but only twenty were responded to; for one of the prisoners so summoned had died in jail and been forgotten. The list was read, in the vaulted chamber where Darnay had seen the associated prisoners on the night of his arrival. Every one of those had perished in the massacre; every human creature he had since cared for and parted with, had died on the scaffold.

There were hurried words of farewell and kindness, but the parting was soon over. It was the incident of every day, and the society of La Force were engaged in the preparation of some games of forfeits and a little concert, for that evening. They crowded to the grates and shed tears there; but, twenty places in the projected entertainments had to be refilled, and the time was, at best, short to the lock-up hour, when the common rooms and corridors would be delivered over to the great dogs who kept watch there through the night. The prisoners were far from insensible or unfeeling; their ways arose out of the condition of the time. Similarly, though with a subtle difference, a species of fervour or intoxication, known, without doubt, to have led some persons to brave the guillotine unnecessarily, and to die by it, was not mere boastfulness, but a wild inflection of the wildly shaken public mind. In seasons of pestilence, some of us will have a secret attraction to the disease–a terrible passing inclination to die of it. And all of us have like wonders hidden in our breasts, only needing circumstances to evoke them.

The passage to the Conciergerie was short and dark; the night in its vermin-haunted cells was long and cold. Next day, fifteen prisoners were put to the bar before Charles Darnay's name was called. All the fifteen were condemned, and the trials of the whole occupied an hour and a half.

'Charles Evrémonde, called Darnay,' was at length arraigned.

His judges sat upon the Bench in feathered hats; but the rough red caps and tricoloured cockade was the head-dress otherwise prevailing. Looking at the Jury and the turbulent audience, he might have thought that the usual order of things was reversed, and that the felons were trying the honest men. The lowest, cruelest, and worst populace of a city, never without its quantity of low, cruel, and bad, were the directing spirits of the scene: noisily commenting, applauding, dissapproving, anticipating, and precipitating the result, without a check. Of the men, the greater part were armed in various ways; of the women, some wore knives, some daggers, some ate and drank as they looked on, many knitted. Among these last, was one, with a spare piece of knitting under her arm as she worked. She was in a front row, by the side of a man whom he had never seen since his arrival at the barrier, but whom he directly remembered as Defarge. He noticed that she once or twice whispered in his ear, and that she seemed to be his wife; but, what he most noticed in the two figures was, that although they were posted as close to himself as they could be, they never looked towards him. They seemed to be waiting for something with a dogged determination, and they looked at the Jury, but at nothing else. Under the President sat Doctor Manette, in his usual quiet dress. As well as the prisoner could see, he and Mr. Lorry were the only men there, unconnected with the Tribunal, who wore their usual clothes, and had not assumed the coarse garb of the Carmagnole.

Charles Evrémonde, called Darnay, was accused by the Public Prosecutor as an emigrant, whose life was forfeit to the Republic, under the decree which banished all emigrants on pain of death. It was nothing that the decree bore date since his return to France. There he was, and there was the decree; he had been taken in France, and his head was demanded.

'Take off his head!' cried the audience. 'An enemy to the Republic!'

The President rang his bell to silence those cries, and asked the prisoner whether it was not true that he had lived many years in England?

Undoubtedly it was.

Was he not an emigrant then? What did he call himself?

Not an emigrant, he hoped, within the sense and spirit of the law.

Why not? the President desired to know.

Because he had voluntarily relinquished a title that was distasteful to him, and a station that was distasteful to him, and had left his country–he submitted before the word emigrant in the present acceptation by the Tribunal was in use–to live by his own industry in England, rather than on the industry of the overladen people of France.

What proof had he of this?

He handed in the names of two witnesses; Théophile Gabelle, and Alexandre Manette.

But he had married in England? the President reminded him.

True, but not an English woman.

A citizeness of France?

Yes. By birth.

Her name and family?

'Lucie Manette, only daughter of Doctor Manette, the good physician who sits there.'

This answer had a happy effect upon the audience. Cries in exaltation of the well-known good physician rent the hall. So capriciously were the people moved, that tears immediately rolled down several ferocious countenances which had been glaring at the prisoner a moment before, as if with impatience to pluck him out into the streets and kill him.

On these few steps of his dangerous way, Charles Darnay had set his foot according to Doctor Manette's reiterated instructions. The same cautious counsel directed every step that lay before him, and had prepared every inch of his road.

The President asked, why had he returned to France when he did, and not sooner?

He had not returned sooner, he replied, simply because he had no means of living in France, save those he had resigned; whereas, in England, he lived by giving instruction in the French language and literature. He had returned when he did, on the pressing and written entreaty of a French citizen, who represented that his life was endangered by his absence. He had come back, to save a citizen's life, and to bear his testimony, at whatever personal hazard, to the truth. Was that criminal in the eyes of the Republic?

The populace cried enthusiastically, 'No!' and the President rang his bell to quiet them. Which it did not, for they continued to cry 'No!' until they left off, of their own will.

The President required the name of that citizen. The accused explained that the citizen was his first witness. He also referred with confidence to the citizen's letter, which had been taken from him at the barrier, but which he did not doubt would be found among the papers then before the President.

The Doctor had taken care that it should be there–had assured him that it would be there–and at this stage of the proceedings it was produced and read. Citizen Gabelle was called to confirm it, and did so. Citizen Gabelle hinted, with infinite delicacy and politeness, that in the pressure of business imposed on the Tribunal by the multitude of enemies of the Republic with which it had to deal, he had been slightly overlooked in his prison of the Abbaye–in fact had rather passed out of the Tribunal's patriotic remembrance–until three days ago; when he had been summoned before it, and had been set at liberty on the Jury's declaring themselves satisfied that the accusation against him was answered, as to himself, by the surrender of the citizen Evrémonde, called Darnay.

Doctor Manette was next questioned. His high personal popularity, and the clearness of his answers, made a great impression: but, as he proceeded, as he showed that the accused was his first friend on his release from his long imprisonment; that, the accused had remained in England, always faithful and devoted to his daughter and himself in their exile; that, so far from being in favour with the Aristocrat government there, he had actually been tried for his life by it, as the foe of England and friend of the United States–as he brought these circumstances into view, with the greatest discretion and with the straightforward force of truth and earnestness, the Jury and the populace became one. At last, when he appealed by name to Monsieur Lorry, and English gentleman then and there present, who, like himself, had been a witness on that English trial and could corroborate his account of it, the Jury declared that they had heard enough, and that they were ready with their votes if the President were content to receive them.

At every vote (the Jurymen voted aloud and individually), the populace set up a shout of applause. All the voices were in the prisoner's favour, and the President declared him free.

Then, began one of those extraordinary scenes with which the populace sometimes gratified their fickleness, or their better impulses towards generosity and mercy, or which they regarded as some set-off against their swollen account of cruel rage. No man can decide now to which of these motives such extraordinary scenes were referable; it is probable, to a blending of all the three, with the second predominating. No sooner was the acquittal pronounced, than tears were shed as freely as blood at another time, and such fraternal embraces were bestowed upon the prisoner by as many of both sexes as could rush at him, that after his long and unwholesome confinement he was in danger of fainting from exhaustion; none the less because he knew very well, that the very same people, carried by another current, would have rushed at him with the very same intensity, to rend him to pieces and strew him over the streets.

His removal, to make way for other accused persons who were to be tried, rescued him from these caresses for the moment. Five were to be tried together, next, as enemies of the Republic, forasmuch as they had not assisted it by word or deed. So quick was the Tribunal to compensate itself and the nation for a chance lost, that these five came down to him before he left the place, condemned to die within twenty-four hours. The first of them told him so, with the customary prison sign of death–a raised finger–and they added in words, 'Long live the Republic!'

The five had had, it is true, no audience to lengthen their proceedings, for when he and Doctor Manette emerged from the gate, there was a great crowd about it, in which there seemed to be every face he had seen in court, except two, for which he looked in vain. On his coming out, the concourse made at him anew, weeping, embracing, and shouting, all by turns and all together, until the very tide of the river on the bank of which the mad scene was acted, seemed to run mad, like the people on the shore.

They put him into a great chair they had among them, and which they had taken either out of the court itself, or one of its rooms or passages. Over the chair they had thrown a red flag, and to the back of it they had bound a pike with a red cap on its top. In this car of triumph, not even the doctor's entreaties could prevent his being carried to his home on men's shoulders, with a confused sea of red caps heaving about him, and casting up to sight from the stormy deep such wrecks of faces, that he more than once misdoubted his mind being in confusion, and that he was in the tumbril on his way to the Guillotine.

In wild dreamlike procession, embracing whom they met and pointing him out, they carried him on. Reddening the snowy streets with the prevailing Republican colour, in winding and tramping through them, as they had reddened them below the snow with a deeper dye, they carried him, thus into the courtyard of the building where he lived. Her father had gone on before, to prepare her, and when her husband stood upon his feet, she dropped insensible in his arms.

As he held her to his heart and turned her beautiful head between his face and the brawling crowd, so that his tears and her lips might come together unseen, a few of the people fell to dancing. Instantly, all the rest fell to dancing, and the courtyard overflowed with the Carmagnole. Then, they elevated into the vacant chair a young woman from the crowd to be carried as the Goddess of Liberty, and then swelling and overflowing out into the adjacent streets, and along the river's bank, and over the bridge, the Carmagnole absorbed them every one and whirled them away.

After grasping the Doctor's hand, as he stood victorious and proud before him; after grasping the hand of Mr. Lorry, who came panting in breathless from his struggle against the waterspout of the Carmagnole; after kissing little Lucie, who was lifted up to clasp her hands round his neck; and after embracing the ever zealous and faithful Pross who lifted her; he took his wife in his arms, and carried her up to their rooms.

'Lucie! My own! I am safe.'

'O dearest Charles, let me thank God for this on my knees as I have prayed to Him.'

They all reverently bowed their heads and hearts. When she was again in his arms, he said to her–

'And now speak to your father, dearest. No other man in all this France could have done what he has done for me.'

She laid her head upon her father's breast, as she had laid his poor head on her own breast, long, long ago. He was happy in the return he had made her, he was recompensed for his suffering, he was proud of his strength. 'You must not be weak, my darling,' he remonstrated; 'don't tremble so. I have saved him.'

CHAPTER VII

A KNOCK AT THE DOOR

'I HAVE saved him.' It was not another of the dreams in which he had often come back; he was really here. And yet his wife trembled, and a vague but heavy fear was upon her.

All the air around was so thick and dark, the people were so passionately revengeful and fitful, the innocent were so constantly put to death on vague suspicion and black malice, it was so impossible to forget that many as blameless as her husband and as dear to others as he was to her, every day shared the fate from which he had been clutched, that her heart could not be as lightened of its load as she felt it ought to be. The shadows of the wintry afternoon were beginning to fall, and even now the dreadful carts were rolling through the streets. Her mind pursued them, looking for him among the condemned; and then she clung closer to his real presence and trembled more.

Her father, cheering her, showed a compassionate superiority to this woman's weakness, which was wonderful to see. No garret, no shoemaking, no One Hundred and Five, North Tower, now! He had accomplished the task he had set himself, his promise was redeemed, he had saved Charles. Let them all lean upon him.

Their housekeeping was of a very frugal kind: not only because that was the safest way of life, involving the least offence to the people, but because they were not rich, and Charles, throughout his imprisonment, had had to pay heavily for his bad food, and for his guard, and towards the living of the poorer prisoners. Partly on this account, and partly to avoid a domestic spy, they kept no servant; the citizen and citizeness who acted as porters at the courtyard gate, rendered them occasional service; and Jerry (almost wholly transferred to them by Mr. Lorry) had become their daily retainer, and had his bed there every night.

It was the ordinance of the Republic One and Indivisible of Liberty, Equality, Fraternity, or Death, that on the door or doorpost of every house, the name of every inmate must be legibly inscribed in letters of a certain size, at a certain convenient height from the ground. Mr. Jerry Cruncher's name, therefore, duly embellished the door-post down below; and, as the afternoon shadows deepened, the owner of that name himself appeared from overlooking a painter whom Doctor Manette had employed to add to the list the name of Charles Evrémonde, called Darnay.

In the universal fear and distrust that darkened the time, all the usual harmless ways of life were changed. In the Doctor's little household, as in very many others, the articles of daily consumption that were wanted were purchased every evening, in small quantities and at various small shops. To avoid attracting notice, and to give as little occasion as possible for talk and envy, was the general desire.

For some months past, Miss Pross and Mr. Cruncher had discharged the office of purveyors; the former carrying the money; the latter, the basket. Every afternoon at about the time when the public lamps were lighted, they fared forth on this duty, and made and brought home such purchases as were needful. Although Miss Pross, through her long association with a French family, might have known as much of their language as of her own, if she had had a mind, she had no mind in that direction; consequently she knew no more of that 'nonsense' (as she was pleased to call it) than Mr. Cruncher did. So her manner of marketing was to plump a noun-substantive at the head of a shop-keeper without any introduction in the nature of an article, and, if it happened not to be the name of the thing she wanted, to look round for that thing, lay hold of it, and hold on by it until the bargain was concluded. She always made a bargain for it, by holding up, as a statement of its just price, one finger less than the merchant held up, whatever his number might be.

'Now, Mr. Cruncher,' said Miss Pross, whose eyes were red with felicity; 'if you are ready, I am.'

Jerry hoarsely professed himself at Miss Pross's service. He had worn all his rust off long ago, but nothing would file his spiky head down.

'There's all manner of things wanted,' said Miss Pross, 'and we shall have a precious time of it. We want wine, among the rest. Nice toasts these Redheads will be drinking, wherever we buy it.'

'It will be much the same to your knowledge, miss, I should think,' retorted Jerry, 'whether they drink your health or the Old Un's.'

'Who's he?' said Miss Pross.

Mr. Cruncher, with some diffidence, explained himself as meaning 'Old Nick's.'

'Ha!' said Miss Pross, 'it doesn't need an interpreter to explain the meaning of these creatures. They have but one, and it's Midnight Murder, and Mischief.'

'Hush, dear! Pray, pray, be cautious!' cried Lucie.

'Yes, yes, yes, I'll be cautious,' said Miss Pross; 'but I may say among ourselves, that I do hope there will be no oniony and tobaccoey smotherings in the form of embracings all round, going on in the streets. Now, Ladybird, never you stir from that fire till I come back! Take care of the dear husband you have recovered, and don't move your pretty head from his shoulder as you have it now, till you see me again! May I ask a question, Doctor Manette, before I go?'

'I think you may take that liberty,' the Doctor answered, smiling.

'For gracious sake, don't talk about Liberty; we have quite enough of that,' said Miss Pross.

'Hush, dear! Again?' Lucie remonstrated.

'Well, my sweet,' said Miss Pross, nodding her head emphatically, 'the short and the long of it is, that I am a subject of His Most Gracious Majesty King George the Third'—Miss Pross curtsied at the name—'and as such, my maxim is, Confound their politics, Frustrate their knavish tricks, On him our hopes we fix, God save the King!'

Mr. Cruncher, in an access of loyalty, growlingly repeated the words after Miss Pross, like somebody at church.

'I am glad you have so much of the Englishman in you, though I wish you had never taken that cold in your voice,' said Miss Pross, approvingly. 'But the question, Doctor Manette. Is there'—it was the good creature's way to affect to make light of anything that was a great anxiety with them all, and to come at it in this chance manner—'is there any prospect yet, of our getting out of this place?'

'I fear not yet. It would be dangerous for Charles yet.'

'Heigh-ho-hum!' said Miss Pross, cheerfully repressing a sigh as she glanced at her darling's golden hair in the light of the fire, 'then we must have patience and wait; that's all. We must hold up our heads and fight low, as my brother Solomon used to say. Now, Mr. Cruncher! Don't you move, Ladybird!'

They went out, leaving Lucie and her husband, her father and the child, by a bright fire. Mr. Lorry was expected back presently from the banking house. Miss Pross had lighted the lamp, but had put it aside in a corner, that they might enjoy the fire-light undisturbed. Little Lucie sat by her grandfather with her hands clasped through his arm: and he, in a tone not rising much above a whisper, began to tell her a story of a great and powerful Fairy who had opened a prison wall and let out a captive who had once done the Fairy a service. All was subdued and quiet, and Lucie was more at ease than she had been.

'What is that?' she cried, all at once.

'My dear!' said her father, stopping in his story, and laying his hand on hers, 'command yourself. What a disordered state you are in! The least thing—nothing—startles you! *You*, your father's daughter!'

'I thought, my father,' said Lucie, excusing herself, with a pale face and in a faltering voice, 'that I heard strange feet upon the stairs.'

'My love, the staircase is as still as death.'

As he said the word, a blow was struck upon the door.

'Oh, father, father. What can this be! Hide Charles. Save him!'

'My child,' said the Doctor, rising, and laying his hand upon her shoulder, 'I have *saved* him. What weakness is this, my dear! Let me go to the door.'

He took the lamp in his hand, crossed the two intervening outer rooms, and opened it. A rude clattering of feet over the floor, and four rough men in red caps, armed with sabres and pistols, entered the room.

'The Citizen Evrémonde, called Darnay,' said the first.

'Who seeks him?' answered Darnay.

'I see him. We seek him. I know you, Evrémonde; I saw you before the Tribunal to-day. You are again the prisoner of the Republic.'

The four surrounded him where he stood with his wife and child clinging to him.

'Tell me how and why am I again a prisoner?'

'It is enough that you return straight to the Conciergerie, and will know to-morrow. You are summoned for to-morrow.'

Doctor Manette, whom this visitation had so turned into stone, that he stood with the lamp in his hand, as if he were a statue made to hold it, moved after these words were spoken, put the lamp down, and confronting the speaker, and taking him, not urgently, by the loose front of his red woollen shirt, said:

'You know him, you have said. Do you know me?'

'Yes, I know you, Citizen Doctor.'

'We all know you, Citizen Doctor,' said the other three.

He looked abstractedly from one to another, and said, in a lower voice, after a pause:

'Will you answer his question to me then? How does this happen?'

'Citizen Doctor,' said the first, reluctantly, 'he has been denounced to the Section of Saint Antoine. This citizen'—pointing out the second who had entered—'is from Saint Antoine.'

The citizen here indicated nodded his head, and added:

'He is accused by Saint Antoine.'

'Of what?' asked the Doctor.

'Citizen Doctor,' said the first, with his former reluctance, 'ask no more. If the Republic demands sacrifices from you, without doubt you as a good patriot will be happy to make them. The Republic goes before all. The People is supreme. Evrémonde, we are pressed.'

'One word,' the Doctor entreated. 'Will you tell me who denounced him?'

'It is against rule,' answered the first; 'but you can ask him of Saint Antoine here.'

The Doctor turned his eyes upon that man. Who moved uneasily on his feet, rubbed his beard a little, and at length said:

'Well! Truly it is against rule. But he is denounced–and gravely–by the Citizeness Defarge. And by one other.'

'What other?'

'Do you ask, Citizen Doctor?'

'Yes.'

'Then,' said he of Saint Antoine, with a strange look. 'you will be answered to-morrow. Now, I am dumb!'

CHAPTER VIII

A HAND AT CARDS

HAPPILY unconscious of the new calamity at home, Miss Pross threaded her way along the narrow streets and crossed the river by the bridge of the Pont-Neuf, reckoning in her mind the number of indispensable purchases she had to make. Mr. Cruncher, with the basket, walked at her side. They both looked to the right and to the left into most of the shops they passed, had a wary eye for all gregarious assemblages of people, and turned out of their road to avoid any very excited group of talkers. It was a raw evening, and the misty river, blurred to the eye with blazing lights and to the ear with harsh noises, showed where the barges were stationed, in which the smiths worked, making guns for the Army of the Republic. Woe to the man who played tricks with *that* Army, or got undeserved promotion in it! Better for him that his beard had never grown, for the National Razor shaved him close.

Having purchased a few small articles of grocery, and a measure of oil for the lamp, Miss Pross bethought herself of the wine they wanted. After peeping into several wine shops, she stopped at the sign of The Good Republican Brutus of Antiquity, not far from the National Palace, once (and twice) the Tuileries, where the aspect of things rather took her fancy. It had a quieter look than any other place of the same description they had passed, and, though red with patriotic caps, was not so red as the rest. Sounding Mr. Cruncher, and finding him of her opinion, Miss Pross restored to The Good Republican Brutus of Antiquity, attended by her cavalier.

Slightly observant of the smoky lights; of the people, pipe in mouth, playing, with limp cards, and yellow dominoes; of the one bare-breasted, bare-armed, soot-begrimed workman reading a journal aloud, and of the others listening to him; of the weapons worn, or laid aside to be resumed; of the two or three customers fallen forward asleep, who in the popular high-shouldered shaggy black spencer looked, in that attitude, like slumbering bears or dogs; the two outlandish customers approached the counter, and showed what they wanted.

As their wine was measuring out, a man parted from another man in a corner, and rose to depart. In going, he had to face Miss Pross. No sooner did he face her, than Miss Pross uttered a scream, and clapped her hands.

In a moment, the whole company were on their feet. That somebody was assassinated by somebody vindicating a difference of opinion was the likeliest occurrence. Everybody looked to see somebody fall, but only saw a man and a woman standing staring at each other; the man with all the outward aspect of a Frenchman and a thorough Republican; the woman, evidently English.

What was said in this disappointing anti-climax, by the disciples of The Good Republican Brutus of Antiquity, except that it was something very voluble and loud, would have been as so much Hebrew or Chaldean to Miss Pross and her protector, though they had been all ears. But, they had no ears for anything in their surprise. For, it must be recorded, that not only was Miss Pross lost in amazement and agitation, but, Mr. Cruncher–though it seemed on his own separate and individual account–was in a state of the greatest wonder.

'What is the matter?' said the man who had caused Miss Pross to scream; speaking in a vexed, abrupt voice (though in a low tone), and in English.

'Oh, Solomon, dear Solomon!' cried Miss Pross, clapping her hands again. 'After not setting eyes upon you or hearing of you for so long a time, do I find you here!'

'Don't call me Solomon. Do you want to be the death of me?' asked the man, in a furtive, frightened way.

'Brother, brother!' cried Miss Pross, bursting into tears. 'Have I ever been so hard with you that you ask me such a cruel question?'

'Then hold your meddlesome tongue,' said Solomon, 'and come out, if you want to speak to me. Pay for your wine, and come out. Who's this man?'

Miss Pross, shaking her loving and dejected head at her by no means affectionate brother, said through her tears, 'Mr. Cruncher.'

'Let him come out too,' said Solomon. 'Does he think me a ghost?'

Apparently, Mr. Cruncher did, to judge from his looks. He said not a word, however, and Miss Pross, exploring the depths of her reticule through her tears with great difficulty, paid for her wine. As she did so, Solomon turned to the followers of The Good Republican Brutus of Antiquity, and offered a few words of explanations in the French language, which caused them all to relapse into their former places and pursuits.

'Now,' said Solomon, stopping at the dark street corner, 'what do you want?'

'How dreadfully unkind in a brother nothing has ever turned my love away from!' cried Miss Pross, 'to give me such a greeting, and show me no affection.'

'There. Confound it! There,' said Solomon, making a dab at Miss Pross's lips with his own. 'Now are you content?'

Miss Pross only shook her head and wept in silence.

'If you expect me to be surprised,' said her brother Solomon, 'I am not surprised; I knew you were here; I know of most people who are here. If you really don't want to endanger my existence–which I half believe you do–go your ways as soon as possible, and let me go mine. I am busy. I am an official.'

'My English brother Solomon,' mourned Miss Pross, casting up her tear-fraught eyes, 'that had the makings in him of one of the best and greatest of men in his native country, an official among foreigners, and such foreigners! I would almost sooner have seen the dear boy lying in his—'

'I said so!' cried her brother, interrupting. 'I knew it. You want to be the death of me. I shall be rendered Suspected, by my own sister. Just as I am getting on!'

'The gracious and merciful Heavens forbid!' cried Miss Pross. 'Far rather would I never see you again, dear Solomon, though I have ever loved you truly, and ever shall. Say but one affectionate word to me, and tell me there is nothing angry or estranged between us, and I will detain you no longer.'

Good Miss Pross! As if the estrangement between them had come of any culpability of hers. As if Mr. Lorry had not known it for a fact, years ago, in the quiet corner in Soho, that this precious brother had spent her money and left her!

He was saying the affectionate word, however, with a far more grudging condescension and patronage than he could have shown if their relative merits and positions had been reversed (which is invariably the case, all the world over), when Mr. Cruncher, touching him on the shoulder, hoarsely and unexpectedly interposed with the following singular question:

'I say! Might I ask the favour? As to whether your name is John Solomon, or Solomon John?'

The official turned towards him with a sudden distrust. He had not previously uttered a word.

'Come!' said Mr. Cruncher. 'Speak out, you know.' (Which, by the way, was more than he could do himself.) 'John Solomon, or Solomon John? She calls you Solomon, and she must know, being your sister. And I know you're John, you know. Which of the two goes first? And regarding the name of Pross, likewise. That warn't your name over the water.'

'What do you mean?'

'Well, I don't know all I mean, for I can't call to mind what your name was, over the water.'

'No?'

'No. But I'll swear it was a name of two syllables.'

'Indeed?'

'Yes. T'other one's was one syllable. I know you. You was a spy witness at the Bailey. What, in the name of the Father of Lies, own father to yourself, was you called at that time?'

'Barsad,' said another voice, striking in.

'That's the name for a thousand pound!' cried Jerry.

The speaker who struck in, was Sydney Carton. He had his hands be-hind him under the skirts of his riding-coat, and he stood at Mr. Cruncher's elbow as negligently as he might have stood at the Old Bailey itself.

'Don't be alarmed, my dear Miss Pross. I arrived at Mr. Lorry's, to his surprise, yesterday evening; we agreed that I would not present myself else-where until all was well, or unless I could be useful; I present myself here, to beg a little talk with your brother. I wish you had a better employed brother than Mr. Barsad. I wish for your sake Mr. Barsad was not a Sheep of the Prisons.'

Sheep was a cant word of the time for a spy, under the jailers. The spy, who was pale, turned paler, and asked him how he dared—

'I'll tell you,' said Sydney. 'I lighted on you, Mr. Barsad, coming out of the prison of the Conciergerie while I was contemplating the walls, an hour or more ago. You have a face to be remembered, and I remember faces well. Made curious by seeing you in that connection, and having a reason, to which you are no stranger, for associating you with the misfortunes of a friend now very unfortunate, I walked in your direction. I walked into the wine shop here, close after you, and sat near you. I had no difficulty in de-ducing from your unreserved conversation, and the rumour openly going about among your admirers, the nature of your calling. And gradually, what I had done at random, seemed to shape itself into a purpose, Mr. Barsad.'

'What purpose?' the spy asked.

'It would be troublesome, and might be dangerous, to explain in the street. Could you favour me, in confidence, with some minutes of your company–at the office of Tellson's Bank, for instance?'

'Under a threat?'

'Oh! Did I say that?'

'Then, why should I go there?'

'Really, Mr. Barsad, I can't say, if you can't.'

'Do you mean that you won't say, sir?' the spy irresolutely asked.

'You apprehend me very clearly, Mr. Barsad. I won't.'

Carton's negligent recklessness of manner came powerfully in aid of his quickness and skill, in such a business as he had in his secret mind, and with such a man as he had to do with. His practised eye saw it, and made the most of it.

'Now, I told you so,' said the spy, casting a reproachful look at his sis-ter; 'if any trouble comes of this, it's your doing.'

'Come, come, Mr. Barsad!' exclaimed Sydney. 'Don't be ungrateful. But for my great respect for your sister, I might not have led up so pleasant-ly to a little proposal that I wish to make for our mutual satisfaction. Do you go with me to the bank?'

'I'll hear what you have got to say. Yes, I'll go with you.'

'I propose that we first conduct your sister safely to the corner of her own street. Let me take your arm, Miss Pross. This is not a good city, at this time, for you to be out in, unprotected; and as your escort knows Mr.

Barsad, I will invite him to Mr. Lorry's with us. Are we ready? Come then!'

Miss Pross recalled soon afterwards, and to the end of her life remembered, that as she pressed her hands on Sydney's arm and looked up in his face, imploring him to do no hurt to Solomon, there was a braced purpose in the arm and a kind of inspiration in the eyes, which not only contradicted his light manner, but changed and raised the man. She was too much occupied then with fears for the brother who so little deserved her affection, and with Sydney's friendly reassurances, adequately to heed what she observed.

They left her at the corner of the street, and Carton led the way to Mr. Lorry's, which was within a few minutes' walk. John Barsad, or Solomon Pross, walked at his side.

Mr. Lorry had just finished his dinner, and was sitting before a cheery little log or two of fire–perhaps looking into their blaze for the picture of that younger elderly gentleman from Tellson's, who had looked into the red coals at the 'Royal George' at Dover, now a good many years ago. He turned his head as they entered, and showed the surprise with which he saw a stranger.

'Miss Pross's brother, sir,' said Sydney. 'Mr. Barsad.'

'Barsad?' repeated the old gentleman. 'Barsad? I have an association with the name–and with the face.'

'I told you you had a remarkable face, Mr. Barsad,' observed Carton, coolly. 'Pray sit down.'

As he took a chair himself, he supplied the link that Mr. Lorry wanted, by saying to him with a frown, 'Witness at that trial.' Mr. Lorry immediately remembered, and regarded his new visitor with an undisguised look of abhorrence.

'Mr. Barsad has been recognized by Miss Pross as the affectionate brother you have heard of,' said Sydney, 'and has acknowledged the relationship. I pass to worse news. Darnay has been arrested again.'

Struck with consternation, the old gentleman exclaimed 'What do you tell me! I left him safe and free within these two hours, and am about to return to him!'

'Arrested for all that. When was it done, Mr. Barsad?'

'Just now, if at all.'

'Mr. Barsad is the best authority possible, sir,' said Sydney, 'and I have it from Mr. Barsad's communication to a friend and brother Sheep over a bottle of wine, that the arrest has taken place. He left the messengers at the gate, and saw them admitted by the porter. There is no earthly doubt that he is retaken.'

Mr. Lorry's business eye read in the speaker's face that it was loss of time to dwell upon the point. Confused, but sensible that something might depend on his presence of mind, he commanded himself, and was silently attentive.

'Now, I trust,' said Sydney to him, 'that the name and influence of Doctor Manette may stand him in as good stead to-morrow–you said he would be before the Tribunal again to-morrow, Mr. Barsad?—'

'Yes; I believe so.'

'–In as good stead to-morrow as to-day. But it may not be so. I own
to you, I am shaken, Mr. Lorry, by Doctor Manette's not having had the
power to prevent this arrest.'

'He may not have known it beforehand,' said Mr. Lorry.

'But that very circumstance would be alarming, when we remember
how identified he is with his son-in-law.'

'That's true,' Mr. Lorry acknowledged, with his troubled hand at his
chin, and his troubled eyes on Carton.

'In short,' said Sydney, 'this is a desperate time, when desperate games
are played for desperate stakes. Let the Doctor play the winning game; I will
play the losing one. No man's life here is worth purchase. Any one carried
home by the people to-day, may be condemned to-morrow. Now, the stake
I have resolved to play for, in case of the worst, is a friend in the
Conciergerie. And the friend I purpose to myself to win, is Mr. Barsad.'

'You need have good cards, sir,' said the spy.

'I'll run them over. I'll see what I hold–Mr. Lorry, you know what a
brute I am; I wish you'd give me a little brandy.'

It was put before him, and he drank off a glassful–drank off another
glassful–pushed the bottle thoughtfully away.

'Mr. Barsad,' he went on, in the tone of one who really was looking
over a hand at cards: 'Sheep of the prisons, emissary of republican committees, now turnkey, now prisoner, always spy and secret informer, so much
the more valuable here for being English that an Englishman is less open to
suspicion of subordination in those characters than a Frenchman, repre-
sents himself to his employers under a false name. That's a very good card.
Mr. Barsad, now in the employ of the republican French government, was
formerly in the employ of the aristocratic English government, the enemy of
France and freedom. That's an excellent card. Inference clear as day in this
region of suspicion, that Mr. Barsad, still in the pay of the aristocratic
English government, is the spy of Pitt, the treacherous foe of the Republic
crouching in its bosom, the English traitor and agent of all mischief so much
spoken of and so difficult to find. That's a card not be beaten. Have you followed my hand, Mr. Barsad?'

'Not to understand you play,' returned the spy, somewhat uneasily.

'I play my Ace, Denunciation of Mr. Barsad to the nearest Section
Committee. Look over your hand, Mr. Barsad, and see what you have.
Don't hurry.'

He drew the bottle near, poured out another glassful of brandy, and
drank it off. He saw that the spy was fearful of his drinking himself into a
fit state for the immediate denunciation of him. Seeing it, he poured out and
drank another glassful.

'Look over your hand carefully, Mr. Barsad. Take time.'

It was a poorer hand than he suspected. Mr. Barsad saw losing cards
in it that Sydney Carton knew nothing of. Thrown out of his honourable
employment in England, through too much unsuccessful hard swearing
there–not because he was not wanted there; our English reasons for vaunt-
ing our superiority to secrecy and spies are of very modern date–he knew

that he had crossed the Channel, and accepted service in France: first, as a tempter and an eavesdropper among his own countrymen there: gradually, as a tempter and an eavesdropper among the natives. He knew that under the overthrown government he had been a spy upon Saint Antoine and Defarge's wine shop; had received from the watchful police such heads of information concerning Doctor Manette's imprisonment, release, and history, as should serve him for an introduction to familiar conversation with the Defarges; and tried them on Madame Defarge, and had broken down with them signally. He always remembered with fear and trembling, that that terrible woman had knitted when he talked with her, and had looked ominously at him as her fingers moved. He had since seen her, in the Section of Saint Antoine, over and over again produce her knitted registers, and denounce people whose lives the guillotine then surely swallowed up. He knew, as every one employed as he was did, that he was never safe; that flight was impossible; that he was tied fast under the shadow of the axe; and that in spite of his utmost tergiversation and treachery in furtherance of the reigning terror, a word might bring it down upon him. Once denounced, and on such grave grounds that had just now been suggested to his mind, he foresaw that the dreadful woman of whose unrelenting character he had seen many proofs, would produce against him that fatal register, and would quash his last chance of life. Besides that all secret men are men soon terrified, here were surely cards enough of one black suit, to justify the holder in growing rather livid as he turned them over.

'You scarcely seem to like your hand,' said Sydney, with the greatest composure. 'Do you play?'

'I think, sir,' said the spy, in the meanest manner, as he turned to Mr. Lorry, 'I may appeal to a gentleman of your years and benevolence, to put it to this other gentleman, so much your junior, whether he can under any circumstances reconcile it to his station to play that Ace of which he has spoken. I admit that *I* am a spy, and that it is considered a discreditable station-though it must be filled by somebody; but this gentleman is no spy, and why should he so demean himself as to make himself one?'

'I play my Ace, Mr. Barsad,' said Carton, taking the answer on himself, and looking at his watch, 'without any scruple, in a very few minutes.'

'I should have hoped, gentlemen both,' said the spy, always striving to hook Mr. Lorry into the discussion, 'that your respect for my sister—'

'I could not better testify my respect for your sister than by finally relieving her of her brother,' said Sydney Carton.

'You think not, sir?'

'I have thoroughly made up my mind about it.'

The smooth manner of the spy, curiously in dissonance with his ostentatiously rough dress, and probably with his usual demeanour, received such a check from the inscrutability of Carton-who was a mystery to wiser and honester men than he-that it faltered here and failed him. While he was at loss, Carton said, resuming his former air of contemplating cards:

'And indeed, now I think again, I have a strong impression that I have another good card here, not yet enumerated. That friend and fellow-Sheep, who spoke of himself as pasturing in the country prisons; who was he?'

'French. You don't know him,' said the spy, quickly.

'French, eh?' replied Carton, musing, and not appearing to notice him at all, though he echoed his word. 'Well, he may be.'

'Is, I assure you,' said the spy; 'though it's not important.'

'Though it's not important,' repeated Carton, in the same mechanical way—'though it's not important— No, it's not important. No. Yet I know the face.'

'I think not. I am sure not. It can't be,' said the spy.

'It–can't–be,' muttered Sydney Carton, retrospectively, and filling his glass (which fortunately was a small one) again. 'Can't–be. Spoke good french. Yet like a foreigner, I thought?'

'Provincial,' said the spy.

'No. Foreign!' cried Carton, striking his open hand on the table, as a light broke clearly on his mind. 'Cly! Disguised, but the same man. We had that man before us at the Old Bailey.'

'Now, there you are hasty, sir,' said Barsad, with a smile that gave his aquiline nose an extra inclination to one side; 'there you really give me an advantage over you. Cly (who I will unreservedly admit, at this distance of time, was a partner of mine) has been dead several years. I attended him in his last illness. He was buried in London, at the church of Saint Pancras-in-the-Fields. His unpopularity with the blackguard multitude at the moment prevented my following his remains, but I helped to lay him in his coffin.'

Here, Mr. Lorry became aware, from where he sat, of a most remarkable goblin shadow on the wall. Tracing it to its source, he discovered it to be caused by a sudden extraordinary rising and stiffening of all the risen and stiff hair on Mr. Cruncher's head.

'Let us be reasonable,' said the spy,' and let us be fair. To show you how mistaken you are, and what an unfounded assumption yours is, I will lay before you a certificate of Cly's burial, which I happen to have carried in my pocketbook'–with a hurried hand he produced and opened it–'ever since. There it is. Oh, look at it, look at it! You may take it in your hand; it's no forgery.'

Here Mr. Lorry perceived the reflection on the wall to elongate, and Mr. Cruncher rose and stepped forward. His hair could not have been more violently on end, if it had been that moment dressed by the cow with the crumpled horn in the house that Jack built.

Unseen by the spy, Mr. Cruncher stood at his side, and touched him on the shoulder like a ghostly bailiff.

'That there Roger Cly, master,' said Mr. Cruncher, with a taciturn and iron-bound visage. 'So *you* put him in his coffin?'

'I did.'

'Who took him out of it?'

Barsad leaned back on his chair, and stammered, 'What do you mean?'

'I mean,' said Mr. Cruncher, 'that he warn't never in it. No! Not he! I'll have my head took off, if he was ever in it.'

The spy looked round at the two gentlemen; they both looked in unspeakable astonishment at Jerry.

'I tell you,' said Jerry, 'that you buried paving-stones and earth in that there coffin. Don't go and tell *me* that you buried Cly. It was a take in. Me and two more knows it.'

'How do you know it?'

'What's that to you? Ecod!' growled Mr. Cruncher, 'it's you I have got an old grudge again, is it, with your shameful impositions upon tradesmen! I'd catch hold of your throat and choke you for half a guinea.'

Sydney Carton, who, with Mr. Lorry, had been lost in amazement at this turn of the business, here requested Mr. Cruncher to moderate and explain himself.

'At another time, sir,' he returned, evasively, 'the present time is ill-conwenient for explainin'. What I stand to, is that he knows well wot that there Cly was never in that there coffin. Let him say he was, in so much as a word of one syllable, and I'll either catch hold of his throat and choke him for half a guinea'– Mr. Cruncher dwelt upon this as quite a liberal offer–'or I'll out and announce him.'

'Humph! I see one thing,' said Carton. 'I hold another card, Mr. Barsad. Impossible, here in raging Paris, with Suspicion filling the air, for you to outlive denunciation, when you are in communication with another aristocratic pay of the same antecedents as yourself, who, moreover, has the mystery about him of having feigned death and come to life again! A plot in the prisons, of the foreigner against the Republic. A strong card–a certain Guillotine card! Do you play?'

'No!' returned the spy. 'I throw up. I confess that we were so unpopular with the outrageous mob, that I only got away from England at the risk of being ducked to death, and that Cly was so ferreted up and down, that he never would have got away at all but for that sham. Though how this man knows it was a sham, is a wonder of wonders to me.'

'Never you trouble your head about this man,' retorted the contentious Mr. Cruncher; 'you'll have trouble enough with giving your attention to that gentleman. And look here! Once more!'– Mr. Cruncher could not be restrained from making rather an ostentatious parade of his liberality–'I'd catch hold of your throat and choke you for half a guinea.'

The Sheep of the prisons turned from him to Sydney Carton, and said, with more decision, 'It has come to a point. I go on duty soon, and can't overstay my time. You told me you had a proposal; what is it? Now, it is of no use asking too much of me. Ask me to do anything in my office, putting my head in great extra danger, and I had better trust my life to the chances of a refusal than the chances of consent. In short, I should make that choice. You talk of desperation. We are all desperate here. Remember! I may denounce you if I think proper, and I can answer my way through stone walls, and so can others. Now, what do you want with me?'

'Not very much. You are a turnkey at the Conciergerie?'

'I tell you once for all, there is no such thing as an escape possible,' said the spy firmly.

'Why need you tell me what I have not asked? You are a turnkey at the Conciergerie?'

'I am sometimes.'

'You can be when you choose.'

Sydney Carton filled another glass with brandy, poured it slowly out upon the hearth, and watched it as it dropped. It being all spent, he said, rising:

'So far, we have spoken before these two, because it was as well that the merits of the cards should not rest solely between you and me. Come into the dark room here, and let us have one final word alone.'

CHAPTER IX

THE GAME MADE

WHILE Sydney Carton and the Sheep of the prisons were in the adjoining dark room, speaking so low that not a sound was heard, Mr. Lorry looked at Jerry in considerable doubt and mistrust. That honest tradesman's manner of receiving the look, did not inspire confidence; he changed the leg on which he rested, as often as if he had fifty of those limbs, and were trying them all; he examined his finger-nails with a very questionable closeness of attention; and whenever Mr. Lorry's eye caught his, he was taken with that peculiar kind of short cough requiring the hollow of a hand before it, which is seldom, if ever, known to be an infirmity attendant on perfect openness of character.

'Jerry,' said Mr. Lorry. Come here.'

Mr. Cruncher came forward sideways, with one of his shoulders in advance of him.

'What have you been, besides a messenger?'

After some cogitation, accompanied with an intent look at his patron, Mr. Cruncher conceived the luminous idea of replying, 'Agricultooral character.'

'My mind misgives me much,' said Mr. Lorry, angrily shaking a forefinger at him, 'that you have used the respectable and great house of Tellson's as a blind, and that you have had an unlawful occupation of an infamous description. If you have, don't expect me to befriend you when you get back to England. If you have, don't expect me to keep your secret. Tellson's shall not be imposed upon.'

'I hope, sir,' pleaded the abashed Mr. Cruncher, 'that a gentleman like yourself wot I've had the honour of odd jobbing till I'm grey at it, would think twice about harming of me, even if it wos so—I don't say it is, but even if it wos. And which is to be took into account that if it wos, it wouldn't, even then, be all o' one side. There'd be two sides to it. There might be medical doctors at the present hour, a picking up their guineas where a honest tradesman don't pick up his fardens–fardens! no, nor yet his half-fardens–half-fardens! no, nor yet his quarter–a banking away like smoke at Tellson's, and a cocking their medical eyes at that tradesman on the sly, a going in and going out to their own carriages–ah! equally like smoke, if not more so. Well, that 'ud be imposing, too, on Tellson's. For you cannot sarse the goose and not the gander. And here's Mrs. Cruncher, or leastways wos in the Old England times, and would be to-morrow, if cause given, a floppin' again the business to that degree as is ruinating–stark ruinating! Whereas them medical doctors' wives don't flop–catch 'em at it! Or, if they flop, their floppings goes in favour of more patients, and how can you rightly have one without the t'other? Then, wot with undertakers, and wot with parish clerks, and wot with sextons, and wot with private watchmen (all awarocious and all in it), a man wouldn't get much by it, even if it wos so. And wot little a man did get, would never prosper with him, Mr. Lorry. He'd never have no good of it; he'd want all along to be out of the line, if he could see his way out, being once in–even if it wos so.'

'Ugh!' cried Mr. Lorry, rather relenting, nevertheless. 'I am shocked at the sight of you.'

'Now, what I would humbly offer to you, sir,' pursued Mr. Cruncher, 'even if it wos so, which I don't say it is—'

'Don't prevaricate,' said Mr. Lorry.

'No, I will *not*, sir,' returned Mr. Cruncher, as if nothing were further from his thoughts or practice–'which I don't say it is–wot I would humbly offer to you, sir, would be this. Upon that there stool, at that there Bar, sets that there boy of mine, brought up and growed up to be a man wot will errand you, message you, general-light-job you, till your heels is where your head is, if such should be your wishes. If it was so, which I still don't say it is (for I will not prewaricate to you, sir), let that there boy keep his father's place, and take care of his mother; don't blow upon that boy's father–do not do it, sir–and let that father go into the line of the reg'lar diggin,' and make amends for what he would have un-dug–if it was so–by diggin' of 'em in with a will, and with conwictions respectin' the future keepin' of 'em safe. That, Mr. Lorry,' said Mr. Cruncher wiping his forehead with his arm, as an announcement that he had arrived at the peroration of his discourse, 'is wot would respectfully offer to you, sir. A man don't see all this here a goin' on dreadful round him, in the way of Subjects without heads, dear me, plentiful enough fur to bring the price down to porterage and hardly that, without havin' his serious thoughts of things. And there here would be mine, if it wos so, entreatin' of you fur to bear in mind that wot I said just now, I up and said in the good cause when I might have keep' it back.'

'That at least is true,' said Mr. Lorry. 'Say no more now. It may be that I shall yet stand your friend, if you deserve it, and repent in action–not in words. I want no more words.'

Mr. Cruncher knuckled his forehead, as Sydney Carton and the spy returned from the dark room. 'Adieu, Mr. Barsad,' said the former; 'our arrangement thus made, you have nothing to fear from me.'

He sat down in a chair on the hearth, over against Mr. Lorry. When they were alone, Mr. Lorry asked him what he had done.

'Not much. If it should go ill with the prisoner, I have ensured access to him, once.'

Mr. Lorry's countenance fell.

'It is all I could do,' said Carton. 'To propose too much, would be to put this man's head under the axe, and, as he himself said, nothing worse could happen to him if he were denounced. It was obviously the weakness of the position. there is no help of it.'

'But access to him,' said Mr. Lorry, 'if it should go ill before the Tribunal, will not save him.'

'I never said it would.'

'Mr. Lorry's eyes gradually sought the fire; his sympathy with his darling, and the heavy disappointment of this second arrest gradually weakened them; he was an old man now, overborne with anxiety of late, and his tears fell.

'You are a good man and a true friend,' said Carton, in an altered voice. 'Forgive me if I notice that you are affected I could not see my father weep, and sit by, careless. And I could not respect your sorrow more, if you were my father. You are free from that misfortune, however.'

Though he said the last words, with a slip into his usual manner, there was a true feeling and respect both in his tone and in his touch, that Mr. Lorry, who had never seen the better side of him, was wholly unprepared for. He gave him his hand, and Carton gently pressed it.

'To return to poor Darnay,' said Carton. 'Don't tell Her of this interview, or this arrangement. It would not enable Her to go to see him. She might think it was contrived, in case of the worst, to convey to him the means of anticipating the sentence.'

Mr. Lorry had not thought of that, and he looked quickly at Carton to see if it were in his mind. It seemed to be; he returned the look, and evidently understood it.

'She might think a thousand things,' Carton said, 'and any of them would only add to her trouble. Don't speak of me to her. As I said to you when I first came, I had better not see her. I can put my hand out, to do any little helpful work for her that my hand can find to do, without that. You are going to her, I hope? She must be very desolate to-night.'

'I am going now, directly.'

'I am glad of that. She has such a strong attachment to you and reliance on you. How does she look?'

'Anxious and unhappy, but very beautiful.'

'Ah!'

It was a long, grieving sound, like a sigh—almost like a sob. It attracted Mr. Lorry's eyes to Mr. Carton's face, which was turned to the fire. A light, or a shade (the old gentleman could not have said which) passed from it as swiftly as a change will sweep over a hillside on a wild bright day, and he lifted his foot to put back one of the little flaming logs, which was tumbling forward. He wore the white riding-coat and top-boots, then in vogue, and the light of the fire touching their light surfaces made him look very pale, with his long brown hair, all untrimmed, hanging loose about him. His indifference to fire was sufficiently remarkable to elicit a word of remonstrance from Mr. Lorry: his boot was still upon the hot embers of the flaming log, when it had broken under the weight of his foot.

'I forgot it,' he said.

Mr. Lorry's eyes were again attracted to his face. Taking note of the wasted air which clouded the naturally handsome features, and having the expression of prisoner's faces fresh in his mind, he was strongly reminded of that expression.

'And your duties here have drawn to an end, sir?' said Carton, turning to him.

'Yes. As I was telling you last night, when Lucie came in so unexpectedly, I have at length done all that I can do here. I hoped to have left them in perfect safety, and then to have quitted Paris. I have my Leave to Pass. I was ready to go.'

They were both silent.

'Yours is a long life to look back upon, sir?' said Carton, wistfully.

'I am in my seventy-eighth year.'

'You have been useful all your life; steadily and constantly occupied; trusted, respected, and looked up to?'

'I have been a man of business, ever since I have been a man. Indeed, I may say that I was a man of business when a boy.'

'See what a place you fill at seventy-eight. How many people will miss you when you leave it empty!'

'A solitary old bachelor,' answered Mr. Lorry, shaking his head. 'There is nobody to weep for me.'

'How can you say that! Wouldn't She weep for you? Wouldn't her child?'

'Yes, yes, thank God. I didn't quite mean what I said.'

'It *is* a thing to thank God for; is it not?'

'Surely, surely.'

'It could say, with truth, to your own solitary heart, to-night, "I have secured to myself the love and attachment, the gratitude or respect, of no human creature; I have won myself a tender place in no regard; I have done nothing good or serviceable to be remembered by!" your seventy-eight years would be seventy-eight heavy curses; would they not?'

'You say truly, Mr. Carton; I think they would be.'

Sydney turned his eyes again upon the fire, and, after a silence of a few moments, said:

'I should like to ask you: Does your childhood seem far off? Do the days when you sat at your mother's knee, seem days of very long ago?'

Responding to his softened manner, Mr. Lorry answered:

'Twenty years back, yes; at this time of my life, no. For, as I draw closer and closer to the end, I travel in the circle, nearer and nearer to the beginning. It seems to be one of the kind smoothings and preparings of the way.

My heart is touched now, by many remembrances that had long fallen asleep, of my pretty young mother (and I so old!), and by many associations of the days when what we call the World was not so real with me, and my faults were not confirmed in me.'

'I understand the feeling!' exclaimed Carton, with a bright flush. 'And you are the better for it?'

'I hope so.'

Carton terminated the conversation here, by rising to help him on with his outer coat; 'but you,' said Mr. Lorry, reverting to the theme, 'you are young.'

'Yes,' said Carton. 'I am not old but my young way was never the way to age. Enough of me.'

'And of me, I am sure,' said Mr. Lorry. 'Are you going out?'

'I'll walk with you to her gate. You know my vagabond and restless habits. If I should prowl about the streets a long time, don't be uneasy; I shall reappear in the morning. You go to the court to-morrow?'

'Yes, unhappily.'

'I shall be there, but only as one of the crowd. My Spy will find a place for me. Take my arm, sir.'

Mr. Lorry did so, and they went downstairs and out in the streets. A few minutes brought them to Mr. Lorry's destination. Carton left him there; but lingered at a little distance, and turned back to the gate again when it was shut, and touched it. He had heard of her going to the prison every day. 'She came out here,' he said, looking about him, 'turned this way, must have trod on these stones often. Let me follow in her steps.'

It was ten o'clock at night when he stood before the prison of La Force, where she had stood hundreds of times. A little wood-sawyer, having closed his shop, was smoking his pipe at his shop door.

'Good night, citizen,' said Sydney Carton, pausing in going by; for, the man eyed him inquisitively.

'Good night, citizen.'

'How goes the Republic?'

'You mean the Guillotine. Not ill. Sixty-three to-day. We shall mount to a hundred soon. Samson and his men complain sometimes, of being exhausted. Ha, ha, ha! He is so droll, that Samson. Such a Barber!'

'Do you often go to see him—'

'Shave? Always. Every day. What a barber! You have seen him at work?'

'Never.'

'Go and see him when he has a good batch. Figure this to yourself, citizen; he shaved the sixty-three to-day, in less than two pipes! Less that two pipes. Word of honour!'

As the grinning little man held out the pipe he was smoking, to explain how he timed the execution, Carton was so sensible of a rising desire to strike the life out of him, that he turned away.

'But you are not English.' said the wood-sawyer, 'though you wear English dress?'

'Yes,' said Carton, pausing again, and answering over his shoulder.

'You speak like a Frenchman.'

'I am old student here.'

'Aha, a perfect Frenchman! Good night, Englishman.'

'Good night, citizen.'

'But go and see that droll dog,' the little man persisted, calling after him. 'And take a pipe with you!'

Sydney had gone far out of sight, when he stopped in the middle of the street under a glimmering lamp, and wrote with his pencil on a scrap of paper. Then, traversing with the decided step of one who remembered the way well, several dark and dirty streets—much dirtier than usual, for the best public thoroughfares remained uncleansed in those times of terror—he stopped at a chemist's shop, which the owner was closing with his own hands. A small, dim, crooked shop, kept in a torturous, up-held thoroughfare, by a small, dim, crooked man.

Giving this citizen, too, good night, as he confronted him at his counter, he laid the scrap of paper before him. 'Whew.' The chemist whistled softly, as he read it. 'Hi! hi! hi!'

Sydney Carton took no heed, and the chemist said:

'For you, citizen?'

'For me.'

'You will be careful to keep them separate, citizen. You know the consequences of mixing them?'

'Perfectly.'

Certain small packets were made and given to him. He put them, one by one, in the breast of his inner coat, counted out the money for them, and deliberately left the shop. 'There is nothing more to do,' said he, glancing upward at the moon, 'until to-morrow. I can't sleep.'

It was not a reckless manner, the manner in which he said these words aloud under the fast-sailing clouds, nor was it more expressive of negligence than defiance. It was the settled manner of a tired man, but who at length struck into his road and saw its end.

Long ago, when he had been famous among his earliest competitors as a youth of great promise, he had followed his father to the grave. His mother had died, years before. These solemn words, which had been read at his father's grave, arose in his minds as he went down the dark streets, among the heavy shadows, with the moon and the clouds sailing on high above him. 'I am the resurrection and the life, saith the Lord: he that believeth in me, though he were dead, yet shall he live: and whosoever liveth and believeth in me, shall never die.'

In a city dominated by the axe, alone at night, with natural sorrow rising in him for the sixty-three who had been that day put to death, and for to-morrow's victims then awaiting their doom in the prisons, and still of to-morrow's and tomorro's, the chain of association that brought the words home, like a rusty old ship's anchor from the deep, might have been easily found. He did not seek it, but repeated them and went on.

With a solemn interest in the lighted windows where the people were going to rest, forgetful through a few calm hours of the horrors surrounding them; in the towers of the churches, where no prayers were said, for the popular revulsion had even travelled that length of self-destruction from years of priestly impostors, plunderers, and profligates; in the distant burial-places, reserved, as they wrote upon the gates, for Eternal Sleep; in the abounding jails; and in the streets along which the sixties rolled to a death which had become so common and material, that no sorrowful story of a haunting Spirit ever arose among the people out of all the working of the Guillotine; with a solemn interest in the whole life and death of the city settling down to its short nightly pause in fury; Sydney Carton crossed the Seine again for the lighter streets.

Few coaches were abroad, for riders in coaches were liable to be suspected, and gentility hid its head in red night-caps, and put on heavy shoes, and trudged. But, the theatres were all well filled, and the people poured cheerfully out as he passed, and went chatting home. At one of the theatre doors, there was a little girl with a mother, looking for a way across the street through the mud. He carried the child over, and before the timid arm was loosed from his neck asked her for a kiss.

'I am the resurrection and the life, saith the Lord: he that believeth in me, though he were dead, yet shall he live: and whosoever liveth and believeth in me, shall never die.'

Now, that the streets were quiet and the night wore on, the words were in the echoes of his feet, and were in the air. Perfectly calm and steady, he sometimes repeated them to himself as he walked; but, he heard them always.

The night wore out, and, as he stood upon the bridge listening to the water as it splashed the river-walls of the Island of Paris, where the picturesque confusion of houses and cathedral shone bright in the light of the moon, the day came coldly, looking like a dead face out of the sky. Then, the night, with the moon and the stars, turned pale and died, and for a little while it seemed as if Creation were delivered over to Death's dominion.

But, the glorious sun, rising, seemed to strike those words, that burden of the night, straight and warm to his heart in its long bright rays. And looking along them, with reverently shaded eyes, a bridge of light appeared to span the air between him and the sun, while the river sparkled under it.

The strong tide, so swift, so deep, and certain, was like a congenial friend, in the morning stillness. He walked by the stream, far from the houses, and in the light and warmth of the sun fell asleep on the bank. When he awoke and was afoot again, he lingered there yet a little longer, watching an eddy that turned and turned purposeless, until the stream absorbed it, and carried it on to the sea. 'Like me!'

A trading-boat, with a sail of the softened colour of a dead leaf, then glided into his view, floated by him, and died away. As its silent track in the water disappeared, the prayer that had broken up out of his heart for a merciful consideration of all his poor blindnesses and errors, ended in the words, 'I am the resurrection and the life.'

Mr. Lorry was already out when he got back, and it was easy to sur-mise where the good old man was gone. Sydney Carton drank nothing but a little coffee, ate some bread, and, having washed and changed to refresh him-self, went out to the place of trial.

The court was ill astir and a-buzz, when the black sheep–whom many fell away from in dread–pressed him into an obscure corner among the crowd. Mr. Lorry was there, and Doctor Manette was there. She was there, sitting beside her father.

When her husband was brought in, she turned a look upon him, so sustaining, so encouraging, so full of admiring love, and pitying tenderness, yet so courageous for his sake, that it called the healthy blood into his face, brightened his glance, and animated his heart. If there had been any eyes to notice the influence of her look, on Sydney Carton, it would have been seen to be the same influence exactly.

Before that injust Tribunal, there was little or no order of procedure, ensuring to any accused person any reasonable hearing. There could have been no such Revolution, if all laws, forms, and ceremonies, had not first been so monstrously abused, that the suicidal vengeance of the Revolution was to scatter them all to the winds.

Every eye was turned to the Jury. The same determined patriots and good republicans as yesterday and the day before, and to-morrow and the day after. Eager and prominent among them, one man with a craving face, and his fingers perpetually hovering about his lips, whose appearance gave great satisfaction to the spectators. A life-thirsting, cannibal-looking, bloody-minded juryman, the Jacques Three of Saint Antoine. The whole Jury, as a Jury of dogs empannelled to try the deer.

Every eye then turned to the five Judges and the Public Prosecutor. No favourable aning in that quarter to-day. A fell. Uncompromising, murderous business meaning there. Every eye then sought some other eye in the crowd, and gleamed at it approvingly; and heads nodded at one another, before bending forward with a strained attention.

Charles Evrémonde, called Darnay. Released yesterday. Reaccused and retaken yesterday. Indictment delivered to him last night. Suspected and Denounced enemy of the Republic, Aristocrat, one of a family of tyrants, one of a race proscribed, for that they had used their abolished privileges to the infamous oppression of the people. Charles Evrémonde, called Darnay, in right of such proscription, absolutely Dead in Law.

To this effect, in as few or fewer words, the Public Prosecutor.

The President asked, was the Accused openly denounced or secretly?

'Openly, President.'

'By whom?'

'Three voices. Ernest Defarge, wine vendor of Saint Antoine.'

'Good.'

'Thérèse Defarge, his wife.'

'Good.'

'Alexandre Manette, physician.'

A great uproar took place in the court, and in the midst of it, Doctor

Manette was seen, pale and trembling, standing where he had been seated.

'President, I indignantly protest to you that this is a forgery and a fraud. You know the accused to be the husband of my daughter. My daughter, and those dear to her, are far dearer to me than my life. Who and where is the false conspirator who says that I denounce the husband of my child!'

'Citizen Manette, be tranquil. To fail in submission to the authority of the Tribunal would be to put yourself out of Law. As to what is dearer to you than life, nothing can be so dear to a good citizen as the Republic.'

Loud acclamations hailed this rebuke. The President rang his bell, and with warmth resumed.

'If the Republic should demand of you the sacrifice of your child herself, you would have no duty but to sacrifice her. Listen to what is to follow. In the meanwhile, be silent!'

Frantic acclamations were again raised. Doctor Manette sat down, with his eyes looking around, and his lips trembling; his daughter drew closer to him. The craving man on the Jury rubbed his hands together, and restored the usual hand to his mouth.

Defarge was produced, when the court was quiet enough to admit of his being heard, and rapidly expounded the story of the imprisonment, and of his having been a mere boy in the Doctor's service, and of the release, and of the state of the prisoner when released and delivered to him. This short examination followed, for the court was quick with its work.

'You did good service at the taking of the Bastille, citizen?'

'I believe so.'

Here an excited woman screeched from the crowd: 'You were one of the best patriots there. Why not say so? You were one of the best patriots there. Why not say so? You were a cannonier that day there, and you were among the first to enter the accursed fortress when it fell. Patriots, I speak the truth!'

It was the Vengeance who, amidst the warm commendations of the audience, thus assisted the proceedings. The President rang his bell; but, The Vengeance, warming with encouragement, shrieked, 'I defy that bell!' wherein she was likewise much commended.

'Inform the Tribunal of what you did that day within the Bastille, citizen.'

'I knew,' said Defarge, looking down at his wife, who stood at the bottom of the steps on which he was raised looking steadily up at him; 'I knew that this prisoner, of whom I speak, had been confined in a cell known as one hundred and five, North Tower. I knew it from himself. He knew himself by no other name than One Hundred and Five, North Tower, when he made shoes under my care. As I serve my gun that day, I resolve, when the place shall fall, to examine that cell. It falls. I mount to the cell, with a fellow-citizen who is one of the Jury, directed by a jailer. I examine it, very closely. In the hole in the chimney, where a stone has been worked out and replaced, I find a written paper. This is that written paper. I have made it my business to examine some specimens of the writing of Doctor Manette. This is the writing of Doctor Manette. I confide this paper, in the writing of Doctor Manette, to the hands of the President.'

'Let it be read.'

In a dead silence and stillness–the prisoner under trial looking lovingly at his wife, his wife only looking from him to look with solicitude at her father, Doctor Manette keeping his eyes fixed on the reader, Madame Defarge never taking hers from the prisoner, Defarge never taking his from his feasting wife, and all the other eyes there intent upon the Doctor, who saw none of them–the paper was read, as follows.

CHAPTER X

THE SUBSTANCE OF THE SHADOW

'I, ALEXANDRE Manette, unfortunate physician, native of Beauvais, and afterwards resident in Paris, write this melancholy paper in my doleful cell in the Bastille, during the last month of the year, 1767. I write it at a stolen intervals, under every difficulty. I design to secrete it in the wall of the chimney, where I have slowly and laboriously made a place of concealment for it. Some pitying hand may find it there, when I and my sorrows are dust.

'These words are formed by the rusty iron point with which I write with difficulty in scrapings of soot and charcoal from the chimney, mixed with blood, in the last month of the tenth year of my captivity. Hope has quite departed from my breast. I know from terrible warnings I have noted in myself that my reason will not long remain unimpaired, but I solemnly declare that I am at this time in the possession of my right mind–that my memory is exact and circumstantial–and that I write the truth as I shall answer for these my last recorded words, whether they be ever read by men or not, at the Eternal Judgment Seat.

'One cloudy moonlight night, in the third week of December (I think the twenty-second of the month) in the year 1757, I was walking on a retired part of the quay by the Seine for the refreshment of the frosty air, at an hour's distance from my place of residence in the Street of the School of Medicine, when a carriage came along behind me, driven very fast. As I stood aside to let that carriages pass, apprehensive that it might otherwise run me down, a head was put out at the window, and a voice called to the driver to stop.

'The carriage stopped as soon as the driver could rein in his horses, and the same voice called to me by my name. I answered. The carriage was then so far in advance of me that two gentlemen had time to open the door and alight before I came up with it. I observed that they were both wrapped in cloaks, and appeared to conceal themselves. As they stood side by side near the carriage door, I also observed that they both looked of about my own age, or rather younger, and that they were greatly alike, in stature, manner, voice, and (as far as I could see) face too.

'"You are Doctor Manette?" said one.

'"I am."

'"Doctor Manette, formerly of Beauvais," said the other; "the young physician, originally an expert surgeon, who within the last year or two has made a rising reputation in Paris?"

'"Gentlemen," I returned, "I am that Doctor Manette of whom you speak so graciously."

'"We have been to your residence," said the first, "and not being so fortunate as to find you there, and being informed that you were probably walking in this direction, we followed, in the hope of overtaking you. Will you please to enter the carriage?"

'The manner of both was imperious, and they both moved, as these words were spoken, so as to place me between themselves and the carriage door. They were armed. I was not.

'"Gentlemen," said I, "pardon me; but I usually inquire who does me the honour to seek my assistance, and what is the nature of the case to which I am summoned."

'The reply to this was made by him who had spoken second. "Doctor, your clients are people of condition. As to the nature of your case, our confidence in your skill assures us that you will ascertain it for yourself better than we can describe it. Enough. Will you please to enter the carriage?"

'I could do nothing but comply, and I entered it in silence. They both entered after me—the last springing in, after putting up the steps. The carriage turned about, and drove on at its former speed.

'I repeat this conversation exactly as it occurred. I have no doubt that it is, word for word, the same. I describe everything exactly as it took place, constraining my mind not to wander from the task. When I make the broken marks that follow here, I leave off for the time, and put my paper in its hiding-place...

'The carriage left the streets behind, passed the North Barrier, and emerged upon the country road. At two-thirds of a league from the barrier—I did not estimate the distance at that time, but afterwards when I traversed it—it struck out of the main avenue, and presently stopped at a solitary house. We all three alighted, and walked, by a damp soft footpath in a garden where a neglected fountain had overflowed, to the end of the house. It was not opened immediately, in answer to the ringing of the bell, and one of my two conductors struck the man who opened it, with his heavy riding-glove, across the face.

'There was nothing in this action to attract my particular attention, for I had seen common people struck more commonly than dogs. But, the other of two, being angry likewise, struck the man in like manner with his arm; the look and bearing of the brothers were then so exactly alike, that I then first perceived them to be twin brothers.

'From the time of our alighting from the outer gate (which we found locked, and which one of the brothers had opened to admit us, and had re-locked), I had heard cries proceeding from an upper chamber. I was con-

ducted an upper chamber. I was conducted to this chamber straight, the cries
growing louder as we ascended the stairs, and I found a patient in a high
fever of the brain, lying on a bed.

'The patient was a woman of great beauty, and young; assuredly not
much past twenty. Her hair was torn and ragged, and her arms were bound
to her sides with sashes and handkerchiefs. I noticed that these bonds were
all portions of a gentleman's dress. On one of them, which was a fringed
scarf for a dress of ceremony, I saw the armorial bearings of a noble, and the
letter E.

'I saw this, within the first minute of my contemplation of the patient;
for, in her restless strivings she had turned over on her face on the edge of the
bed, had drawn the end of the scarf into her mouth, and was in danger of
suffocation. My first act was to put out my hand to relieve her breathing;
and in moving the scarf aside, the embroidery in the corner caught my sight.

'I turned her gently over, placed my hands upon her breast to calm
her and keep her down, and looked into her face. Her eyes were dilated and
wild, and she constantly uttered piercing shrieks, and repeated the words,
"My husband, my father, and my brother!" and then counted up to twelve,
and said, "Hush!" There was no variation in the order, or the manner. There
was no cessation, but the regular moment's pause, in the utterance of these
sounds.

'"How long," I asked, "has this lasted?"

'To distinguish the brothers, I will call them the elder and the younger;
by the elder I mean him who exercised the most authority. It was the elder
who replied, "Since about this hour last night."

'"She has a husband, a father, and a brother?"

'"A brother."

'"I do not address her brother?"

'He answered with great contempt, "No."

'"She has some recent association with the number twelve?"

'The younger brother impatiently rejoined, "With twelve o'clock."

'"See, gentlemen," said I, still keeping my hands upon her breast, "how
useless I am, as you have brought me! If I had known what I was coming to
see, I could have come provided. As it is, time must be lost. There are no
medicines to be obtained in this lonely place."

'The elder brother looked to the younger, who said haughtily, "There
is a case of medicines here"; and brought it from a closet, and put it on the
table...

'I opened some of the bottles, smelt them, and put the stoppers to my
lips. If I had wanted to use anything save narcotic medicines that were poi-
sons in themselves, I would not have administered any of those.

'"Do you doubt them?" asked the younger brother.

'"You see, monsieur, I am going to use them," I replied, and said no
more.

'I made the patient swallow, with great difficulty, and after many efforts, the dose that I desired to give. As I intended to repeat it after a while,
and as it was necessary to watch its influence, I then sat down by the side of

the bed. There was a timid and suppressed woman in attendance (wife of the man downstairs), who had retreated into a corner. The house was damp and decayed, indifferently furnished–evidently, recently occupied and temporarily used. Some thick old hangings had been nailed up before the windows, to deaden the sound of the shrieks. They continued to be uttered in their regular succession, with the cry, "My husband, my father, and my brother!" the counting up to twelve, and "Hush!" The frenzy was so violent, that I had not unfastened the bandages restraining the arms; but, I had looked to them, to see that they were not painful. The only spark of encouragement in the case, was, that my hand upon the sufferer's breast had this much soothing influence, that for minutes at a time it tranquilized the figure. It had no effect upon the cries; no pendulum could be more regular.

'For the reason that my hand had this effect (I assume), I had sat by the side of the bed for half an hour, with the two brothers looking on, before the elder said:

'"There is another patient."

'I was startled, and asked, "Is it a pressing case?"

'"You had better see," he carelessly answered; and took up a light...

'The other patient lay in a back room across the second staircase, which was a species of loft over a stable. There was a low plastered ceiling to a part of it; the rest was open, to the ridge of the tiled roof, and there were beams across. Hay and straw were stored in that portion of the place, faggots for firing, and a heap of apples in sand. I had to pass through that part, to get at the other. My memory is circumstantial and unshaken. I try it with these details, and I see them all, in this my cell in the Bastille, near the close of the tenth year of my captivity, as I saw them all that night.

'On some hay on the ground, with a cushion thrown under his head, lay a handsome peasant boy–a boy of not more than seventeen at the most. He lay on his back, with his teeth set, his right hand clenched on his breast, and his glaring eyes looking straight upward. I could not see where his wound was, as I kneeled on one knee over him; but, I could see that he was dying of a wound from a sharp point.

'"I am a doctor, my poor fellow," said I. "Let me examine it."

'"I do not want it examined," he answered; "let it be."

'It was under his hand, and I soothed him to let me move his hand away. The wound was a sword-thrust, received from twenty to twenty-four hours before, but no skill could have saved him if it had been looked to without delay He was then dying fast. As I turned my eyes to the elder brother, I saw him looking down at this handsome boy whose life was ebbing out, as if he were a wounded bird, or hare, or rabbit; not at all as if he were a fellow-creature.

'"How has this been done, monsieur?" said I.

'"A crazed young common dog! A serf! Forced my brother to draw upon him, and has fallen by my brother's sword–like a gentleman."

'There was no touch of pity, sorrow, or kindred humanity, in this answer. The speaker seemed to acknowledge that it was inconvenient to have that different order of creature dying there, and that it would have been better if he had died in the usual obscure routine of his vermin kind. He was quite incapable of any compassionate feeling about the boy, or about his fate.

'The boy's eyes had slowly moved to him as he had spoken, and they now slowly moved to me.

'"Doctor, they are very proud, these nobles; but we common dogs are proud too, sometimes. They plunder us, outrage us, beat us, kill us; but we have a little pride left, sometimes. She–have you seen her, Doctor?"

'The shrieks and the cries were audible there, though subdued by the distance. He referred to them, as if she were lying in our presence.

'I said, "I have seen her."

'"She is my sister, Doctor. They have had their shameful rights, these nobles, in the modesty and virtue of our sisters, many years, but we have had good girls among us. I know it, and have heard my father say so. She was a good girl. She was betrothed to a good young man, too: a tenant of his. We were all tenant of his–that man's who stands there. The other is his brother, the worst of a bad race."

'It was with the greatest difficulty that the boy gathered bodily force to speak; but, his spirit spoke with a dreadful emphasis.

'"We were robbed by that man who stands there, as all we common dogs are by those superior beings–taxed by him without mercy, obliged to work for him without pay, obliged to grind our corn at his mill, obliged to feed scores of his tame birds on our wretched crops, and forbidden for our lives to keep a single tame bird of our own, pillaged and plundered to that degree that when we chanced to have a bit of meat, we ate it in fear, with the door barred and the shutters closed, that his people should not see it and take it from us–I say, we were so robbed, and hunted, and we were made so poor, that our father told us it was a dreadful thing to bring a child into the world, and that what we should most pray for, was, that our women might be barren and our miserable race die out!"

'I had never before seen the sense of being oppressed, bursting forth like a fire. I had supposed that it must be latent in the people somewhere; but, I had never seen it break out, until I saw it in the dying boy.

'"Nevertheless, Doctor, my sister married. He was ailing at that time, poor fellow, and she married her lover, that she might tend and comfort him in our cottage–our dog-hut, as that man would call it. She had not been married many weeks, when that man's brother saw her and admired her, and asked that man to lend her to him–for what are husbands among us! He was willing enough, but my sister was good and virtuous, and hated his brother with a hatred as strong as mine. What did the two then, to persuade her husband to use his influence with her, to make her willing?"

'The boy's eyes, which had been fixed on mine, slowly turned to the looker-on, and I saw in the two faces that all he said was true. The two opposing kinds of pride confronting one another, I can see, even in this Bastille; the gentleman's, all negligent indifference; the peasant's, all trodden-down sentiment, and passionate revenge.

'"You know, Doctor, that it is among the Rights of these noble to harness us common dogs to carts, and drive us. They so harnessed him and drove him. You know that it is among their Rights to keep us in their grounds all night, quieting the frogs, in order that their noble sleep may not be disturbed. They kept him out in the unwholesome mists at night, and ordered him back into his harness in the day. But he was not persuaded. No! Taken out of harness one day at noon, to feed–if he could find food–he sobbed twelve times, once for every stroke of the bell, and died on her bosom."

'Nothing human could have held life in the boy but his determination to tell all his wrong. He forced back the gathering shadows of death, as he forced his clenched right hand to remain clenched, and to cover his wound.

'"Then, with that man's permission and even with his aid, his brother took her away; in spite of what I know she must have told his brother–and what that is, will not be long unknown to you, Doctor, if it now is–his brother took her away–for his pleasure and diversion, for a little while. I saw her pass me on the road. When I took the tidings home, our father's heart burst; he never spoke one of the words that filled it. I took my young sister (for I have another) to a place beyond the reach of this man, and where, at least, she will never be his vassal. Then, I tracked the brother here, and last night climbed in–a common dog, but sword in hand.–Where is the loft window? It was somewhere here?"

'The room was darkening to his sight; the world was narrowing around him. I glanced about me, and saw that the hay and straw were trampled over the floor, as if there had been a struggle.

'"She heard me, and ran in. I told her not to come near us till he was dead. He came in and first tossed me some pieces of money; then struck at me with a whip. But I, though a common dog, so struck at him as to make him draw. Let him break into as many pieces as he will, the sword that he had stained with my common blood; he drew to defend himself–thrust at me with all his skill for his life."

'My glance had fallen, but a few moments before, on the fragments of a broken sword, lying among the hay. That weapon was a gentleman's. In another place, lay an old sword that seemed to have been a soldier's.

'"Now lift me up, Doctor; lift me up. Where is he?"

'"He is not here," I said, supporting the boy, and thinking that he referred to the brother.

'"He! Proud as these noble are, he is afraid to see me. Where is the man who was here? Turn my face to him."

'I did so, raising the boy's head against my knee. But, invested for the moment with extraordinary power, he raised himself completely: obliging me to rise too, or I could not have still supported him.

'"Marquis," said the boy, turned to him with his eyes opened wide, and his right hand raised, "in the days when all these things are to be answered for, I summon you and yours, to the last of your bad race, to answer for them. I mark this cross of blood upon you, as a sign that I do it. In the days when all these things are to be answered for, I summon you and yours, to the last of your bad race, to answer for them. I mark this cross of blood upon you, as a sign that I do it. In the days when all these things are to be answered for, I summon your brother, the worst of the bad race, to answer for them separately. I mark this cross of blood upon him, as a sign that I do it."

'Twice, he put his hand to the wound in his breast, and with his forefinger drew a cross in the air. He stood for an instant with his finger yet araised, and, as it dropped, he dropped with it, and I laid down dead...

'When I returned to the bedside of the young woman, I found her raving in precisely the same order and continuity. I knew that this might last for many hours, and that it would probably end in the silence of the grave.

'I repeated the medicines I had given her, and I sat at the side of the bed until the night was far advanced. She never abated the piercing quality of her shrieks, never stumbled in the distinctness or the order of her words. They were always "My husband, my father, and my brother! One, two, three, four, five, six, seven, eight, nine, ten, eleven, twelve. Hush!"

'This lasted twenty-six hours from the time when I first saw her. I had come and gone twice, and was again sitting by her. I had come and gone twice, and was again sitting by her, when she began to falter. I did what little could be done to assist that opportunity, and by and by she sank into a lethargy, and lay like the dead.

'It was as if the wind and rain had lulled at last, after a long and fearful storm. I released her arms, and called the woman to assist me and to compose her figure and the dress she had torn. It was then that I knew her condition to be that of one in whom the first expectations of being a mother have arisen; and it was then that I lost the little hope I had had of her.

'"Is she dead?" asked the Marquis, whom I will still describe as the elder brother, coming booted into the room from his horse.

'"Not dead," said I; "but like to die."

'"What strength there is in these common bodies!" he said, looking down at her with some curiosity.

'"There is prodigious strength," I answered him, "in sorrow and despair."

'He first laughed at my words, and then frowned at them. He moved a chair with his foot near to mine, ordered the woman away, and said in a subdued voice,

'"Doctor, finding my brother in this difficulty with these hinds, I recommend that your aid should be invited. Your reputation is high, and, as a young man with your fortune to make, you are probably mindful of your interest. The things that you see here, are things to be seen, and not spoken of."

'I listened to the patient's breathing, and avoided answering.

'"Do you honour me with your attention, Doctor?"

'"Monsieur," said I, "in my profession, the communications of patients are always received in confidence." I was guarded in my answer, for I was troubled in my mind with what I had heard and seen.

'Her breathing was so difficult to trace, that I carefully tried the pulse and the heart. There was life, and no more. Looking round as I resumed my seat. I found both the brothers intent upon me...

'I write with so much difficulty, the cold is so severe, I am so fearful of being detected and consigned to an underground cell and total darkness, that I must abridge this narrative. There is no confusion or failure in my memory; it can recall, and could detail, every word that was ever spoken between me and those brothers.

'She lingered for a week. Towards the last, I could understand some few syllables that she said to me, by placing my ear close to her lips. She asked me where she was, and I told her; who I was, and I told her. It was in vain that I asked her for her family name. She faintly shook her head upon the pillow, and kept her secret, as the boy had done.

'I had no opportunity of asking her any question, until I had told the brothers she was sinking fast, and could not live another day. Until then, though no one was ever presented to her consciousness save the woman and myself, one or other of them had always jealously sat behind the curtain at the head of the bed when I was there. But when it came to that, they seemed careless what communication I might hold with her; as if–the thought passed through my mind–I were dying too.

'I always observed that their pride bitterly resented the younger brother's (as I call him) having crossed swords with a peasant, and that peasant a boy. The only consideration that appeared to affect the mind of either of them was the consideration that this was highly degrading to the family, and was ridiculous. As often as I caught the younger brother's eyes, their expression reminded me that he disliked me deeply, for knowing what I knew from the boy. He was smoother and more polite to me than the elder; but I saw this. I also saw that I was an encumbrance in the mind of the elder, too.

'My patient died, two hours before midnight–at a time, by my watch, answering almost to the minute when I had first seen her. I was alone with her, when her forlorn young head dropped gently on one side, and all her earthly wrongs and sorrows ended.

'The brothers were waiting in a room downstairs, impatient to ride away. I had heard them, alone at the bedside, striking their boots with their riding-whips, and loitering up and down.

'"At last she is dead?" said the elder, when I went in.

'"She is dead," said I.

'"I congratulate you, my brother," were his words as he turned round.

'He had before offered me money, which I had postponed taking. He now gave me a rouleau of gold. I took it from his hand, but laid it on the table. I had considered the question, and had resolved to accept nothing.

'"Pray excuse me," said I. "Under the circumstances, no."

'They exchanged looks, but bent their heads to me as I bent mine to them, and we parted without another word on either side...

'I am weary, weary, weary–worn down by misery; I cannot read what I have written with this gaunt hand.

'Early in the morning, the rouleau of gold was left at my door in a little box, with my name on the outside. From the first, I had anxiously considered what I ought to do. I decided, that day, to write privately to the minister, stating the nature of the two cases to which I had been summoned, and the place to which I had gone: in effect stating all the circumstances. I knew what court influence was, and what the immunities of the nobles were, and I expected that the matter would never be heard of; but, I wished to relieve my own mind. I had kept the matter a profound secret, even from my wife; and this, too, I resolved to state in my letter. I had no apprehension whatever of my real danger; but I was conscious that there might be danger for others, if others were compromised by possessing the knowledge that I possessed.

'I was much engaged that day, and could not complete my letter that night. I rose long before my usual time next morning to finish it. It was the last day of the year. The letter was lying before me just completed, when I was told that a lady waited, who wished to see me...

'I am growing more and more unequal to the task I have set myself. It is so cold, so dark, my senses are so benumbed and the gloom upon me is so dreadful.

'The lady was young, engaging, and handsome, but not marked for long life. She was in great agitation. She presented herself to me as the wife of the Marquis St. Evrémonde. I connected the little by which the boy had addressed the elder brother, with the initial letter embroidered on the scarf, and had no difficulty in arriving at the conclusion that I had seen that nobleman very lately.

'My memory is still accurate, but I cannot write the words of our conversation. I suspect that I am watched more closely than I was, and I know not at what times I may be watched. She had in part suspected, and in part discovered, the main facts of the cruel story, of her husband's share in it, and my being restored to. She did not know that the girl was dead. Her hope had been, she said in great distress, to show her, in secret, a woman's sympathy. Her hope had been to avert the wrath of Heaven from a House that had long been hateful to the suffering many.

'She had reasons for believing that there was a young sister living, and her greatest desire was, to help that sister. I could tell her nothing but that there was such a sister; beyond that, I knew nothing. Her inducement to come to me, relying on my confidence, had been the hope that I could tell her the name and place of abode. Whereas, to this wretched hour I am ignorant of both...

'These scraps of paper fail me. One was taken from me, with a warning, yesterday. I must finish my record to-day.

'She was a good, compassionate lady, and not happy in her marriage. How could she be! The brother distrusted and disliked her, and his influence was all opposed to her; she stood in dread of him, and in dread of her husband too. When I handed her down to the door, there was a child, a pretty boy from two or three years old, in her carriage.

'"For his sake, Doctor," she said, pointing to him in tears, "I would do all I can to make what poor amends I can. He will never prosper in his inheritance otherwise. I have a presentiment that if no other innocent atonement is made for this, it will one day be required of him. What I have left to call my own–it is little beyond the worth of a few jewels–I will make it the first charge of his life to bestow, with the compassion and lamenting of his dead mother, on this injured family, if the sister can be discovered."

'She kissed the boy, and said, caressing him, "It is for thine own dear sake. Thou wilt be faithful, little Charles?" The child answered her bravely, "Yes!" I kissed her hand, and she took him in her arms, and went away caressing him. I never saw her more.

'As she had mentioned her husband's name in the faith that I knew it, I added no mention of it to my letter. I sealed my letter, and, not trusting it out of my own hands, delivered it myself that day.

'That night, the last night of the year, towards nine o'clock, a man in a black dress rang at my gate, demanded to see me, and softly followed my servant, Ernest Defarge, a youth, upstairs. When my servant came into the room where I sat with my wife–O my wife, beloved of my heart! My fair young English wife!–we saw the man, who was supposed to be at the gate, standing silent behind him.

'"An urgent case in the rue St. Honoré," he said. It would not detain me, he had a coach in waiting.

'It brought me here, it brought me to my grave. When I was clear of the house, a black muffler was drawn tightly over my mouth from behind, and my arms were pinioned. The two brothers crossed the road from a dark corner, and identified me with a single gesture. The Marquis took from his pocket the letter I had written, showed it me, burnt it in the light of a lantern that was held, and extinguished the ashes with his foot. Not a word was spoken. I was brought here, I was brought to my living grave.

'If it had pleased GOD to put it in the hard heart of either of the brothers, in all these frightful years, to grant me any tidings of my dearest wife–so much as to let me know by a word whether alive or dead–I might have thought that He had not quite abandoned them. But, now I believe that the mark of the red cross is fatal to them, and that they have no part in His mercies. And them and their descendants, to the last of their race, I, Alexandre Manette, unhappy prisoner, do this last night of the year 1767, in my unbearable agony, denounce to the times when all these things shall be answered for. I denounce them to Heaven and to earth.'

A terrible sound arose when the reading of this document was done. A sound of craving and eagerness that had nothing articulate in it but blood. The narrative called up the most revengeful passions of the time, and there was not a head in the nation but must have dropped before it.

Little need, in presence of that Tribunal and that auditory, to show how the Defarges had not made the paper public, with the other captured Bastille memorials borne in procession, and had kept it, biding their time. Little need to show that this detested family name had long been anathematized by Saint Antoine, and was brought into the fatal register. The man never trod ground whose virtues and services would have sustained him in that place that day, against such denunciation.

And all the worse for the doomed man, that the denouncer was a well-known citizen, his own attached friend, the father of his wife. One of the frenzied aspirations of the populace was, for imitations of the questionable public virtues of antiquity, and for sacrifices and self-immolations on the people's altar. Therefore when the President said (else had his own head quivered on his shoulders), that the good physician of the Republic would deserve better still of the Republic by rooting out an obnoxious family of Aristocrats, and would doubtless feel a sacred glow and joy in making his daughter a widow and her child an orphan, there was wild excitement, patriotic fervour, not a touch of human sympathy.

'Much influence around him, has that Doctor?' murmured Madame Defarge, smiling to the Vengeance. 'Save him now, my Doctor, save him!'

At every juryman's vote, there was a roar. Another and another. Roar and roar.

Unanimously voted. At heart and by descent an Aristocrat, an enemy of the Republic, a notorious oppressor of the People. Back to the Conciergerie, and death within four-and-twenty hours!

CHAPTER XI

DUSK

THE wretched wife of the innocent man thus doomed to die, fell under the sentence, as if she had been mortally stricken. But, she uttered no sound; and so strong was the voice within her, representing that it was she of all the world' who must uphold him in his misery and not augment it, that it quickly raised her, even from that shock.

The Judges having to take part in a public demonstration out of doors, the Tribunal adjourned. The quick noise and movement of the court's emptying itself by many passages had not ceased, when Lucie stood stretching out her arms towards her husband, with nothing in her face but love and consolation.

'If I might touch him! If I might embrace him once! O good citizens, if you would have so much compassion for us!'

There was but a jailer left, along with two of the four men who had taken him last night, and Barsad. The people had all poured out to the show in the streets. Barsad proposed to the rest, 'Let her embrace him then; it is but a moment.' It was silently acquiesced in, and they passed her over the seats in the hall to a raised place, where he, by leaning over the dock, could fold her in his arms.

'Farewell, dear darling of my soul. My parting blessing on my love. We shall meet again, where the weary are at rest!'

They were her husband's words, as he held her to his bosom.

'I can bear it, dear Charles. I am supported from above: don't suffer for me. A parting blessing for our child.'

'I send it to her by you. I kiss her by you. I say farewell to her by you.'

'My husband. No! A moment!' He was tearing himself apart from her. 'We shall not be separated long. I feel that this will break my heart by and by; but I will do my duty while I can, and when I leave her, GOD will raise up friends for her, as He did for me.'

Her father had followed her, and would have fallen on his knees to both of them,but that Darnay put out a hand and seized him, crying:

'No, no! What have you done, what have you done, that you should kneel to us! We know now, what a struggle you made of old. We know now, what you underwent when you suspected my descent, and when you knew it. We know now, the natural antipathy you strove against, and conquered, for her dear sake. We thank you with all our hearts, and all our love and duty. Heaven be with you!'

Her father's only answer was to draw his hands through his white hair, and wring them with a shriek of anguish.

'It could not be otherwise,' said the prisoner. 'All things have worked together as they have fallen out. It was the always vain endeavour to discharge my poor mother's trust that first brought my fatal presence near you. Good could never come of such evil, a happier wnd was not in nature to so unhappy a beginning. Be comforted, and forgive me. Heaven bless you!'

As he was drawn away, his wife released him, and stood looking after him with her hands touching one another in the attitude of prayer, and with a radiant look upon her face, in which there was even a comforting smile. As he went out at the prisoners' door, she turned, laid her head lovingly on her father's breast, tried to speak to him, and fell at his feet.

Then, issuing from the obscure corner from which he had never moved, Sydney Carton came and took her up. Only her father and Mr. Lorry were with her. His arm trembled as it raised her, and supported her head. Yet, there was an air about him that was not all of pity—that had a flush of pride in it.

'Shall I take her to a coach? I shall never feel her weight.'

He carried her lightly to the door, and laid her tenderly down in a coach. Her father and their old friend got into it, and he took his seat beside the driver.

When they arrived at the gateway where he had paused in the dark not many hours before, to picture to himself on which of the rough stones of the street her feet had trodden, he lifted her again, and carried her up the staircase to their rooms. There, he laid her down on a couch, where her child and Miss Pross wept over her.

'Don't recall her to herself,' he said, softly, to the latter; 'she is better so. Don't revive her to consciousness, while she only faints.'

'Oh, Carton, Carton, dear Carton!' cried little Lucie, springing up and throwing her arms passionately round him, in a burst of grief. 'Now that you have come, I think you will do something to help mamma, something to save papa! Oh, look at her, dear Carton! Can you, of all the people who love her, bear to see her so?'

He bent over the child, and laid her blooming cheek against his face. He put her gently from him, and looked at her unconscious mother.

'Before I go,' he said, and paused—'I may kiss her?'

It was remembered afterwards that when he bent down and touched her face with his lips, he murmured some words. The child, who was nearest to him, told them afterwards, and told her grandchildren when she was a handsome old lady, that she heard him say, 'A life you love.'

When he had gone out into the next room, he turned suddenly on Mr. Lorry and her father, who were following, and said to the latter:

'You had great influence but yesterday, Doctor Manette; let it at least be tried. These Judges, and all the men in power, are very friendly to you, and very recognisant of your services; are they not?'

'Nothing connected with Charles was concealed from me. I had the strongest assurances that I should save him; and I did.' He returned the answer in great trouble, and very slowly.

'Try them again. The hours between this and tomorrow afternoon are few and short, but try.'

'I intend to try. I will not rest a moment.'

'That's well. I have known such energy as yours do great things before now—thougyh never,' he added, with a smile and a sigh together, 'such great things as this. But try! Of little worth as life is when we missue it, it is worth that effort. It would cost nothing to lay down if it were not.'

'I will go,' said Doctor Manette, 'to the Prosecutor and the President straight, and I will go to others whom it is better not to name. I will write too, and— But stay! There is a celebration in the streets, and no one will be accessible until dark.'

'That's true. Well! It is a forlorn hope at the best and not much the forloner for being delayed till dark. I should like to know how you speed; though mind! I expect nothing! Where are you likely to have seen these dread powers, Doctor Manette?'

'Immediately after dark, I should hope. Within an hour or two from this.'

'I will be dark soon after four. Let us stretch the hour or two. If I go to Mr. Lorry's at nine, shall I hear what you have done, either from our friend or from yourself?'

'Yes.'

'May you prosper!'

Mr. Lorry followed Sydney to the outer door, and, touching him on the shoulder as he was going away, caused him to turn.

'I have no hope,' said Mr. Lorry, in a low and sorrowful whisper.

'Nor have I.'

'If any one of these men, or all of these men, were disposed to spare him—which is a large supposition; for what is his life, or any man's to them!—I doibt if they durst spare him after the demonstration in the court.'

'And so do I. I heard the fall of the axe in that sound.'

Mr. Lorry leaned his arm upon the door post and bowed his face upon it.

'Don't despond,' said Carton, very gently; 'don't grieve. I encouraged Doctor Manette in this idea, because I felt that it might one day be consolatory to her. Otherwise, she might think "his wife wantonly thrown away or wasted," and that might trouble her.'

'Yes, yes, yes,' returned Mr. Lorry, drying his eyes, 'you are right. But he will perish; there is no real hope.'

'Yes. He will perish: there is no real hope,' echoed Carton. And walked with a settled step, downstairs.

CHAPTER XII

DARKNESS

SYDNEY Carton paused in the street, not quite decided where to go. 'At Tellson's banking-house at nine,' he said, with a musing face. 'Shall I do well, in the meantime, to show myself? I think so. It is best that these people should know there is such a man as I here; it is a sound precaution, and may be a necessary preparation. But care, care, care! Let me think it out!'

Cheking his steps which had begun to tend towards an object, he took a turn or two in the already darkening street, and traced the thought in his mind to its possible consequences. His first impression was confirmed. 'It is best,' he said, finally resolved, 'that these people should know there is such a man as I here.' And he turned his face towards Saint Antoine.

Defarge had described himself, that day, as the keeper of a wine shop in the Saint Antoine suburb. It was not difficult for one who knew the city well, to find his house without asking any question. Having ascertained its situation, Carton came out of those closer streets again, and dined at a place of refreshment and fell sound asleep after dinner. For the first time in many years, he had no strong drink. Since last night he had taken nothing but a little light thin wine, and last night he had dropped the brandy slowly down on Mr. Lorry's hearth like a man who had done with it.

It was as late as seven o'clock when he awoke refreshed, and went out into the streets again. As he passed along towards Saint Antoine, he stopped at a shop window where there was a mirror, and slightly altered the disordered arrangement of his loose cravant, and his coat collar, and his wild hair. This done, he went on direct to Defarge's, and went in.

There happened to be no customer in the shop but Jacques Three, of the restless fingers and the croaking voice. This man, whom he had seen upon the Jury, stood drinking at the little counter, in conversation with the Defarges, man and wife. The Vengeanace assisted in the conversation, like a regular member of the establishment.

As Carton walked in, took his seat and asked (in very indifferent French) for a small measure of wine, Madame Defarge cast a careless glance at him, and then a keener, and then a keener, and then advanced to him herself, and asked him what it was he had ordered.

He repeated what he had already said.

'English?' asked Madame Defarge, inquisitively raising her dark eyebrows.

After looking at her, as if the sound of even a single French word were slow to express itself to him, he answered, in his former strong foreign accent. 'Yes, madame, yes. I am English!'

Madame Defarge returned to her counter to get the wine, and, as he took up a Jacobin journal and feigned to pore over its puzzling out its meaning, he heard her say, 'I swear to you, like Evrémonde!'

Defarge brought him the wine, and gave him Good Evening.

'How?'

'Good evening.'

'Oh! Good evening, citizen,' filling his glass. 'Ah! and good wine. I drink to the Republic.'

Defarge went back to the counter, and said, 'Certainly, a little like.' Madame sternly retorted, 'I tell you a good deal like.' Jacques Three pacifically remarked, 'He is so much in your mind, see you, madame.' The amiable Vengeance added, with a laugh, 'Yes, my faith! And you are looking forward with so much pleasure to seeing him once more to-morrow!'

Carton followed the lines and words of his paper, with a slow forefinger, and with a studious and absorbed face. They were all leaning their arms on the counter close together, speaking low. After a silence of a few moments, during which they all looked towards him without disturbing his outward attention from the Jacobin editor, they resumed their conversation.

'It is true what madame says,' observed Jacques Three. Why stop? There is great force in that. Why stop?'

'Well, well,' reasoned Defarge, 'but one must stop somewhere. After all, the quiestion is still where?'

'At extermination,' said madame.

'Magnificent!' croaked Jacques Three. The Vengeance, also, highly approved.

'Extermination is a good doctrine, my wife,' said Defarge, rather troubled; 'in general, I say nothing against it. But this Doctor has suffered much; you have seen him to-day; you have observed his face when the paper was read.'

'I have observed his face!' repeated madame, contemtuously and angrily. 'Yes. I have observed his face. I have observed his face to be not the face of a true friend of the Republic. Let him take care of his face!'

'And you have observed, my wife,' said Defarge, in a deprecatory manner, 'the anguish of his daughter, which must be a dreadful anguish to him!'

'I have observed his daughter,' repeated madame; 'yes, I have observed his daughter,' repeated madame; 'yes, I have observed her to-day, and I have observed her other days. I have observed her in the court, and I have observed her in the street by the prison. Let me but lift my finger—!' She seemed to raise it (the listener's eyes were always on his paper), and let it fall with a rattle on the ledge before her, as if the axe had dropped.

'The citizeness is suberb!' croaked the Juryman.

'She is an Angel!' said The Vengeance, and embraced her.

'As to thee, pursued madame, implaxably, addressing her husband, 'if it depended on thee—which, happily, it does not—thou wouldst rescue this man even now.'

'No!' protested Defarge. 'Not if to lift this glass would do it! But I would leave the matter there. I say, stop there.'

'See you then, Jacques,' said Madame Defarge, wrathfully; 'and see you, too, my little Vengeance: see you both! Listen! For other crimes as tyrants and oppressors, I have this race a long time on my register, doomed to destruction and extermination. Ask my husband, is that so.'

'It is so,' assented Defarge, without being asked.

'In the beginning of the great days, when the Bastille falls, he finds this paper of to-day, and he brings it home, and in the middle of the night when this place is clear and shut, we read it, here on this spot, by the light of this lamp. Ask him, is that so.'

'It is so,' assented Defarge.

'That night, I tell him, when the paper is read through, and the lamp is burnt out, and the day is gleaming in above those shutters and between those iron bars, that I have now a secret to communicate. Ask him, is that so.'

'It is so,' assented Defarge again.

'I communicate to him that secret. I smite this bosom with these two hands as I smite it now, and I tell him, "Defarge, I was brought up among the fishermen of the sea-shore, and that peasant family so injured by the two Evrémonde brothers, as that Bastille paper describes, is my family. Defarge, that sister of the mortally wounded biy upon the ground was my sister, that husband was my sister's husband, that unborn child was their child, that brother was my brother, that father was my father, those dead are my dead, and that summons to answer for those things descends to me!" Ask him, is that so.'

'It is so,' assented Defarge once more.

'Then tell Wind and Fire where to stop,' returned madame; 'but don't tell me.'

Both her hearers derived a horrible enjoyment from the deadly nature of her wrath—the listener could feel how white she was, without seeing her—and both highly comended it. Defarge, a weak minority, interposed a few words for the memory of the compassionate wife of the Marquis; but only elicited from his own wife a repetition of her last reply. 'Tell the Wind and the Fire where to stop; not me!'

Customers entered, and the group was broken up. The English customer paid for what he had had, perplexedly counted his change, and asked, as a stranger, to be directed towards the National Palace. Madame Defarge took him to the door, and put her arm on his, in pointing out the road. The

English customer was not without his reflections then, that it might be a good deed to seize that arm, lift it, and strike under it sharp and deep.

But, he went his way, and was soon swallowed up in the shadow of the prison wall. At the appointed hour, he emerged from it to present himself in Mr. Lorry's room again, where he found the old gentleman walking to and fro in restless anxiety. He said he had been with Lucie until just now, and had only left her for a few minutes, to come and keep his appointment. Her father had not been seen, since he quitted the banking-house towards four o'clock. She had some faint hopes that his mediation might save Charles, but they were very slight. He had been more than five hours gone: where could he be?

Mr. Lorry waited until ten; but, Doctor Manette not returning, and he being unwilling to leave Lucie any longer, it was arranged that he should go back to her, and come to the banking-house again at midnight. In the meanwhile, Carton could wait alone by the fire for the Doctor.

He waited and waited, and the clock struck twelve; but Doctor Manette did not come back. Mr. Lorry returned, and found no tidings of him, and brought none. Where could he be?

They were discussing this question, and were almost building up some weak structure of hope on his prolonged absence, when they heard him on the stairs. The instant he entered the room, it was plain that all was lost.

Whether he had really been to any one, or whether he had been all that time traversing the streets, was never known. As he stood staring at them, they asked him no question, for his face told them everything.

'I cannot find it,' said he, 'and I must have it. Where is it?'

His head and throat were bare, and, as he spoke with a helpless look straying all around, he took his coat off, and let it drop on the floor.

'Where is my bench? I have been looking everywhere for my bench, and I can't find it. What have they done with my work? Time presses: I must finish those shoes.'

They looked at one another, and their hearts died within them.

'Come, come!' said he, in a whimpering miserable way; 'let me get to work. Give me my work.'

Receiving no answer, he tore his hair, and beat his feet upon the ground, like a distracted child.

'Don't tortue a poor forlorn wretch,' he implored them, with a dreadful cry; 'but give me my work! What is to become of us, if those shoes are not done to-night?'

Lost, utterly lost!

It was so clearly beyond hope to reason with him, or try to restore him, that–as if by agreement–they each put a hand upon his shoulder, and soothed him to sit down before the fire, with a promise that he should have his work presently. He sank into the chair, and brooded over the embers, and shed tears. As if all that had happened since the garret time were a momentary fancy, or a dream, Mr. Lorry saw him shrink into the exact figure that Defarge had had in keeping.

Affected, and impressed with terror as they both were, by the spectacle of ruin, it was not a time to yield to such emotions. His lonely daughter, bereft of her final hope and reliance, appealed to them both too strongly. Again, as if by agreement, they looked at one another with one meaning in their faces. Carton was the first to speak:

'The last chance is gone: it was not much. Yes; he had better taken to her. But, before you go, will you, for a moment, steadily attend to me? Don't ask me why I make the stipulations I am going to make, and exact the promise I am going to exact; I have a reason—a good one.'

'I do not doubt it,' answered Mr. Lorry. 'Say on.'

The figure in the chair between them, was all the time monotonously rocking itself to and fro, and moaning. They spoke in such a tone as they would have used if they had been watching by a sick-bed in the night.

Carton stooped to pick up the coat, which lay almost entangling his feet. As he did so, a small case in which the Doctor was accustomed to carry the list of his day's duties, fell lightly on the floor. Carton took it up, and there was a folded paper in it. 'We should look at this!' he said. Mr. Lorry nodded his consent. He opened it, and exclaimed 'Thank GOD!'

'What is it?' asked Mr. Lorry, eagerly.

'A moment! Let me speak of it in its place. First—' he put his hand in his coat, and took another paper from it—'that is the certificate which enables me to pass out of this city. Look at it. You see—Sydney Carton, an Englishman?'

Mr. Lorry held it open in his hand, gazing in his earnest face.

'Keep it for me until to-morrow. I shall see him tomorrow, you remember, and I had better not take it into the prison.'

'Why not?'

'I don't know; I prefer not to do so. Now, take this paper that Doctor Manette has carried about him. It is a similar certificate, enabling him and his daughter and her child, at any time, to pass the barrier and the frontier. You see?'

'Yes!'

'Perhaps he obtained it as his last and utmost precaution against evil, yesterdy. When is it dated? But no matter; don't stay to look; put it carefully with mine and your own. Now, observe! I never doubted until within this hour or two, that he had, or could have such a paper. It is good, until recalled. But it may be soon recalled, and I have reason to think, will be.'

'They are not in danger?'

'They are in great danger. They are in danger of denunciation by Madame Defarge. I know it from her own lips. I have overhead words of that woman's, to-night, which have presented their danger to me in strong colours. I have lost no time, and since then I have seen the spy. He confirms me. He knows that a wood-sawyer, living by the prison wall, is under the control of the Defarges, and has been rehearsed by Madame Defarge as to his having seen Her'—he never mentioned Lucie's name—'making signs and signals to prisoners. It is easy to foresee that the pretence will be the common one, a prison plot, and that it will involve her life—and perhaps her child's—and perhaps her father's—for both have been seen with her at that place.'

'Heaven grant I may, Carton! But how?'

'I am going to tell you how. It will depend on you, and it could depend on no better man. This new denunciation will certainly not take place until after to-morrow; probably not until two or three days afterwards; more probably a week afterwards. You know it is a capital crime, to mourn for, or sympathize with, a victim of the Guillotine. She and her father would unquestionably be guilty of this crime, and this woman (the inveteracy of whose pursuit cannot be described) would wait to add that strength to her case, and make herself doubly sure. You follow me?'

'So attentively, and with so much confidence in what you say, that for the moment I lose sight'—touching the back of the Doctor's chair—'even of this distress.'

'You have money, and can buy the means of travelling to the sea coast as quickly as the journey can be made. Your preparations have been completed for some days, to return to England. Early to-morrow have your horses ready, so that they may be in starting trim at two o'clock in the afternoon.'

'It shall be done!'

His manner was so fervent and inspiring, that Mr. Lorry caught the flame, and was quick as youth.

'You are a noble heart. Did I say we coulkd depend upon no better man? Tell her, to-night, what you know of her danger as involving her child and her father. Dwell upon that, for she would lay her own fair head beside her husband's cheerfully.' He faltered for an instant; then went on as before. 'For the sake of her child and her father, press upon her the necessity of leaving Paris, with them and you, at that hour. Tell her that it was her husband's last arrangement. Tell her that more depends upon it than she dare believe, or hope. You think that her father, even in this sad state, will submit himself to her; do you not?'

'I am sure of it.'

'I thought so. Quietly and steadily have all these arrangements made in the courtyard here, even to the taking of your own seat in the carriage. The moment I come to you, take me in, and drive away.'

'I understand that I wait for you under all circumstances?'

'You have my certificate in your hand with the rest, you know, and will reserve my place. Wait for nothing but to have my place occupied, and then for England!'

'Why, then,' said Mr. Lorry, grasping his eager but so firm and steady hand, 'it does not all depend on one old man, but I shall have a young and ardent man at my side.'

'By the help of Heaven you shall! Promise me solemnly that nothing will influence you to alter the course on which we now stand pledged to one another.'

'Nothing, Carton.'

'Remember these words to-morrow: change the course, or delay in it—for any reason—and no life can possibly be saved, and many lives must inevitably be sacrificed.'

'I will remember them. I hope to do my part faithfully.'

'And I hope to do mine. Now, good-bye!'

Though he said it with a grave smile of earnestness, and though he even put the old man's hand to his lips, he did not part from him then. He helped him so far to arouse the rocking figure before the dying embers, as to get a cloak and hat upon it, and to tempt it forth to find where the bench and work were hidden that it still moaningly besought to have. He walked on the other side of it and protected it to the courtyard of the house where the afflicted heart—so happy in the memorable time when he had revealed his own desolate heart to it—outwatched the awful night. He entered the courtyard and remained there for a few moments alone, looking up at the light in the window of her room. Before he went away, he breathed a blessing towards it, and a Farewell.

CHAPTER XIII

FIFTY-TWO

IN the black prison of the Conciergerie, the doomed of the day awaited their fate. They were in number as the weeks of the year. Fifty-two were to roll that afternoon on the life-tide of the city to the boundless everlasting sea. Before their cells were quit of them, new occupants were appointed; before their blood that was to mingle with theirs tomorrow was already set apart.

Two score and twelve were told off. From the farmer-general of seventy, whose riches could not buy his life, to the seamstress of twenty, whose poverty and obscurity could not save her. Physical diseased, engendered in the vices and neglects of men, will seize on victims of all degrees; and the frightful moral disorder, born of unspeakable suffering, intolerable oppression, and heartless indifference, smote equally without distinction.

Charles Darnay, alone in a cell, had sustained himself with no flattering delusion since he came to it from the Tribunal. In every line of the narrative he had heard his condemnation. He had fully comprehended that no personal influence could possibly save him, that he was virtually sentenced by the millions, and that units could avail him nothing.

Nevertheless, it was not easy, with the face of his beloved wife fresh before him, to compose his mind to what it must bear. His hold on life was strong, and it was very, very hard, to loosen; by gradual efforts and degrees unclosed a little here, it clenched the tighter there; and when he brought his strength to ebar on that hand and it yielded, this was closed again. There was a hurry, too, in all his thoughts, a turbulent and heated working of his heart, that contended against resignation. If, for a moment, he did feel resigned, then his wife and child who had to live after him, seemed to protest and to make it a selfish thing.

But, all this was at first. Before long, the consideration that there was no disgrace in the fate he must meet, and that numbers went the same road wrongfully, and trod it firmly every day, sprang up to stimulate him. Next followed the thought that much of the future peace of mind enjoyable by the dear ones, depended on his quiet fortitude. So, by degrees he calmed into the better state, when he could raise his thoughts much higher, and draw comfort down.

Before it had sent in dark on the night of his condemnation, he had travelled thus for on his last way. Being allowed to purchase the means of writing, and a light, he sat down to write until such time as the prison lamps should be extinguished.

He wrote a long letter to Lucie, showing her that he had known nothing of her father's imprisonment, until he had heard of it from herself, and that he had been as ignorant as she of his father's and uncle's responsability for that misery, until the paper had been read. He had already explained to her that his concealment from her herself of the name he had relinquished, was the one condition–fully intelligible now–that her father had attached to their betrothal, and was the one promise he had still exacted on the morning of their marriage. He entreated her, for her father's sake, never to seek to know whether her father had become oblivious of the existence of the paper, or had had it recalled to him (for the moment or, for good), by the story of the Tower, on that old Sunday under the dear old plane-tree in the garden. If he had preserved any definite remembrance of it, there could be no doubt that he had supposed it destroyed with the Bastille, when he had found no mention of it among the relics of prisoners which the populace had discovered there, and which had been described to all the world. He besought her–though he added that he knew it was needless–to console her father, by impressing him through every tender means she could think of, with the truth that he had done nothing for which he could justly reproach himself, but had uniformly forgotten himself for their joint sakes. Next to her preservation of his own last grateful love and blessing, and her overcoming of her sorrow, to devote herself to their dear child, he adjured her, as they would meet in Heaven, to comfort her father.

To her father himself, he wrote in the same strain; but, he told her father that he expressly confided his wife and child to his care. And he told him this, very strongly, with the hope of rousing him from any despondency or dangerous retrospect towardds which he foresaw he might be tending.

To Mr. Lorry, he commended them all, and explained his worldly affairs. That done, with many added sentences of grateful friendship and warm attachment, all was done. He never thought of Carton. His mind was so full of the others, that he never once thought of him.

He had time to finish these letters before the lights were put out. When he lay down on his straw bed, he thought he had done with this world.

But, it beckoned him back in his sleep, and showed itself in shining forms. Free and happy, back in the old house in Soho (though it had nothing in it like the real house), unaccountably released and light of heart, he was with Lucie again, and she told him it was all a dream, and he had never gone away. A pause of forgetfulness, and then he had even suffered, and had come back to her, dead and at peace, and yet there was no difference in him. Another pause of oblivion, and he awoke in the sombre morning, unconscious where he was or what had happened, until it flashed upon his mind, 'This is the day of my death!'

Thus, he had come through the hours, to the day when the fifty-two heads were to fall. And now, while he was composed, and hoped that he could meet the end with quiet heroism, a new action began in his waking thoughts, which was very difficult to master.

He had never seen the instrument that was to terminate his life. How high it was from the ground, how many steps it had, where he would be stood, how he would be touched, whether the touching hands would be dyed red, which way his face would be turned, whether he would be the first, or might be the last: these and many similar questions, in no wise directed by his will, obtruded themselves over and over again, countless times. Neither were they connected with fear: he was conscious of no fear. Rather, they originated in a strange besetting desire to know what to do when the time came; a desire gigantically disproportionate to the few swift moments to which it referred; a wondering that was more like the wondering of some other spirit within his, than his own.

The hours went on as he walked to and fro, and the clocks struck the numbers he would never hear again. Nine gone for ever, ten gone for ever, eleven gone for ever, twelve coming on to pass away. After a hard contest with that eccentric action of thought which had last perplexed him, he had got the better of it. He walked up and down softly repeating their names to himself. The worst of the strife was over. He could walk up and down, free from distracting fancies, praying for himself and for them.

Twelve gone for ever.

He had been apprised that the final hour was Three, and he knew he would be summoned some time earlier, inasmuch as the tumbrils jolted heavily and slowly through the streets. Therefore, he resolved to keep Two before his mind, as the hour, and so to strengthen himself in the interval that he might be able, after that time, to strengthen others.

Walking regularly to and fro with his arms folded on his breast, a very different man from the prisoner, who had walked to and fro at La Force, he heard One struck away from him, without surprise. The hour had measured like most others hours. Devoutly thankful to Heaven for his recovered self-possession, he thought, 'There is but another now,' and turned to walk again.

Footsteps in the stone passage outside the door. He stopped.

The key was put in the lock, and turned. Before the door was opened, or as it opened, a man said in a low voice, in English: 'He has never seen me here; I have kept out of his way. Go you in alone; I wait near. Lose no time!'

The door was quickly opened and closed, and there stood before him face to face, quiet, intent upon him, with the light of a smile on his features, and cautionary finger on his lip, Sydney Carton.

There was something so bright and remarkable in his look, that, for the first moment, the prisoner misdoubted him to be an apparition of his own imagining. But, he spoke, and it was his voice; he took the prisoner's hand, and it was his real grasp.

'Of all the people upon earth, you least expected to see me?' he said.

'I could not believe it to be you. I can scarcely believe it now. You are not'–the apprehension came suddenly into his mind–'a prisoner?'

'No. I am accidentally possessed of a power over one of the keepers here, and in virtue of it I stand before you. I come from her–your wife, dear Darnay.'

The prisoner wrung his hand.

'I bring you a request from her.'

'What is it?'

'A most earnest, pressing, and emphatic entreaty, addressed to you in the most pathetic tones of the voice so dear to you, that you well remember.'

The prisoner turned his face partly aside.

'You have no time to ask me why I bring it, or what it means; I have no time to tell you. You must comply with it–take off those boots you wear, and draw on these of mine.'

There was a chair against the wall of the cell, behind the prisoner. Carton, pressing forward, had already, with the speed of lightning, got him down into it, and stood over him, barefoot.

'Draw on these boots of mine. Put your hands to them; put your will to them. Quick!'

'Carton, there is no escaping from this place; it never can be done. You will only die with me. It is madness.'

'It would be madness if I asked you to escape; but do I? When I ask you to pass out at that door, tell me it is madness and remain here. Change that cravat for this of mine, that coat for this of mine. While you do it, let me take this ribbon from your hair, and shake out your hair like this of mine!'

With wonderful quickness, and with strength both of will and action, that appeared quite supernatural, he forced all these changes upon him. The prisoner was like a young child in his hands.

'Carton! Dear Carton! It is madness. It cannot be accomplished, it never can be done, it has been attempted and has always failed. I implore you not to add your death to the bitterness of mine.'

'Do I ask you, my dear Darnay, to pass the door? When I ask that, refuse. There are pen and ink and paper on this table. Is your hand steady enough to write?'

'It was when you came in.'

'Steady it again, and write what I shall dictate. Quick, friend, quick!'

Pressing his hand to his bewildered head, Darnay sat down at the table. Carton, with his right hand in his breast, stood close beside him.

'Write exactly as I speak.'

'To whom do I address it?'
'To no one.' Carton still had his hand in his breast.
'Do I date it?'
'No.'

The prisoner looked up at each question. Carton, standing over him with his hand in his breast, looked down.

'"If you remember,"' said Carton, dictating, '"the words that passed between us, long ago, you will readily comprehend this when you see it. You do remember them, I know. It is not in your nature to forget them."'

He was drawing his hand from his breast; the prisoner chancing to look up in his hurried wonder as he wrote, the hand stopped, closing upon something.

'Have you written "forget them"?' Carton asked.
'I have. Is that a weapon in your hand?'
'No; I am not armed.'
'What is it in your hand?'
'You shall know directly. Write on; there are but a few words more.' He dictated again. '"I am thankful that the time has come, when I can prove them. That I do so is no subject for regret or grief."' As he said these words with his eyes fixed on the writer, his hand slowly and soflty moved down close to the writer's face.

The pen dropped from Darnay's fingers on the table, and he looked about his vacantly.

'What vapour is that?' he asked.
'Vapour?'
'Something that crossed me?'
'I am conscious of nothing; there can be nothing here. Take up the pen and finish. Hurry, hurry!'

As if this memory were impaired, or his faculties disordered, the prisoner made an effort to rally his attention. As he looked at Carton with clouded eyes and with an altered manner of breathing, Carton–his hand again in his breast–looked steadily at him.

'Hurry, hurry!'

The prisoner bent over the paper, once more.

'"If it had been otherwise"'–Carton's hand was again watchfully and softly stealing down–'"I never should have used the longer opportunity. If it had been otherwise"'–the hand was at the prisoner's face–'"I should but have had so much the more to answer for. If it had been otherwise—."' Carton looked at the pen and saw it was trailing off into unintelligible signs.

Carton's hand moved back to his breast no more. The prisoner sprang up with a reproachful look, but Carton's hand was close and firm to his nostrils, and Carton's left arm caught him round the waist. For a few seconds he faintly struggled with the man who had come to lay down his life for hiim; but, within a minute or so, he was stretched insensible on the ground.

Quickly, but with hands as true to the purpose as his heart was, Carton dressed himself in the clothes the prisoner had laid aside. Combed back his hair, and tied it with the ribbon the prisoner had worn. Then, he softly called, 'Enter there! Come in!' and the spy presented himself.

'You see?' said Carton, looking up, as he kneeled on one knee beside the insensible figure, putting the paper in the breast; 'is your hazard very great?'

'Mr. Carton,' the spy answered, with a timid snap of his fingers, 'my hazard is not that, in the thick of business here, if you are true to the whole of your bargain.'

'Don't fear me. I will be true to the death.'

'You must be, Mr. Carton, if the tale of fifty-two is to be right. Being made right by you in that dress, I shall have no fear.'

'Have no fear! I shall soon be out of the way of harming you, and the rest will soon be far from here, please God! Now, get assistance and take me to the coach.'

'You?' said the spy nervously.

'Him, man, with whom I have exchanged. You go out at the gate by which you brought me in?'

'Of course.'

'I was weak and faint when you brought me in, and I am fainter now you to take me out. The parting interview has overpowed me. Such a thing has happened here, often, and too often. Your life is in your own hands. Quick! Call assistance!'

'You swear not to betray me?' said the trembling spy, as he paused for a last moment.

'Man, man!' returned Carton, stamping his foot; 'have I sworn by no solemn vow already, to go through with this, that you waste the precious moments now? Take him yourself to the courtyard you know of, place him yourself in the carriage, show him yourself to Mr. Lorry, tell him yourself to give him to restorative but air, and to remember my words of last night, and his promises of last night, and drive away!'

The spy withdrew, and Carton seated himself at the table, rsting his forehead on his hands. The spy returned immediately, with two men.

'How, then?' said one of them, contemplating the fallen figure. 'So afflicted to find that his friend has drawn a prize in the lottery of Sainte Guillotine?'

'A good patriot,' said the other, 'could hardly have been more afflicted if the Aristocrat had drawn a blank.'

They raised the unconscious figure, placed it on a litter they ahd brought to the door, and bent to carry it away.

'The time is short, Evrémonde,' said the spy, in a warning voice.

'I know it well,' answered Carton. 'Be careful of my friend, I entreat you, and leave me.'

'Come, then, my children,' said Barsad. 'Lift him, and come away!'

The door closed, and Carton was left alone. Straining his powers of listening to the utmost, he listened for any sound that might denote suspicion or alarm. There was none. Keys turned, doors clashed, footsteps passed along distant passages: no cry was raised, or hurry made, that seemed unusual. Breathing more freely in a little while, he sat down at the table, and listened again until the clock struck Two.

Sounds that he was not afraid of, for he divined their meaning, then began to be audible. Several doors were opened in succession, and finally his own. A jailer, with a list in his hand, looked in, merely saying, 'Follow me, Evrémonde!' and he followed him into a large dark room, at a distance. It was a dark winter, and what with the shadows within, and what with the shadows without, he could but dimly discern the others who were brought there to have their arms bound. Some were standing; some seated. Some were lamenting, and in restless motion; but, these were few. The great majority were silent and still, looking fixedly at the ground.

As he stood by the wall in a dim corner, while some of the fifty-two were brought in after him, one man stopped in passing, to embrace him, as having a knowledge of him. It thrilled him with a great dread of discovery; but the man went on. A very few moments after that, a young woman, with a slight girlish form, a sweet spare face in which there was no vestige of colour, and large widely opened patient eyes, rose from the seat where he had observed her sitting, and came to speak to him.

'Citizen Evrémonde,' she said, touching him with her cold hand. 'I am a poor little seamstress, who was with you in La Force.'

He murmured for answer: 'True. I forget what you were accused of?'

'Plots. Though the just Heaven knows I am innocent of any. Is it likely? Who would think of plotting with a poor little weak creature like me?'

The forlorn smile with which she said it, so touched him, that tears started from his eyes.

'I am not afraid to die, Citizen Evrémonde, but I have done nothing. I am not unwilling to die, if the Republic which is to do so much good to us poor, will profit by my death; but I do not know how that can be, Citizen Evrémonde. Such a poor weak little creature!'

As the last night on earth that his heart was to warm and soften to, it warmed and softened to this pitiable girl.

'I heard you were released, Citizen Evrémonde. I hoped it was true?'

'It was. But, I was again taken and condemned.'

'If I may ride with you, Citizen Evrémonde, will you let me hold your hand? I am not afraid, but I am little and weak, and it will give me more courage.'

As the patient eyes were lifted to his face, he saw a sudden doubt in them, and then astonishment. He pressed the work-worn, hunger-worn young fingers, and touched his lips.

'Are you dying for him?' she whispered.

'And his wife and child. Hush! Yes.'

'Oh, you will let me hold your brave hand, stranger?'

'Hush! Yes, my poor sister; to the last.'

The same shadows that are falling on the prison, are falling, in that same hour of the early afternoon, on the barrier with the crowd about it, when a coach going out of Paris drives up to be examined.

'Who goes here? Whom have we within? Papers!'

The papers are handed out, and read.

'Alexandre Manette. Physician. French. Which is he?'

This is he; this helpless, inarticulately murmuring, wandering old man pointed out.

'Apparently the Citizen Doctor is not in his right mind? The Revolution-fever will have been too much for him?'

Greatly too much for him.

'Hah! Many suffer with it. Lucie. His daughter. French. Which is she?'

This is she.

'Apparently it must be. Lucie, the wife of Evrémonde; is it not?'

It is.

'Hah! Evrémonde has an assignation elsewhere. Lucie, her child. English. This is she?'

She and no other.

'Kiss me, child of Evrémonde. Now, thou has kissed a good Republican; something new in thy family; remember it! Sydney Carton. Advocate. English. Where is he?'

He lies here, in this corner of the carriage. He, too, is pointed out.

'Apparently the English advocate is in a swoon?'

It is hoped he will recover in the fresher air. It is represented that he is not in strong health, and has separated sadly from a friend who is under the displeasure of the Republic.

'Is that all? It is not a great deal that! Many are under the displeasure of the Republic, and most look out at the little window. Jarvis Lorry. Banker. English. Which is he?'

'I am he. Necessarily, being the last.'

It is Jarvis Lorry who has replied to all the previous questions. It is Jarvis Lorry who had alighted and stands with his hand on the coach door, replying to a group of officials. They leisurely walked round the carriage and leisurely mount the box, to look at what little luggage it carries on the roof; the country people hanging about, press nearer to the coach doors and greedily stare in; a little child, carried by its mother, has its short arm held out for it, that it may touch the wife of an aristocrat who has gone to the Guillotine.

'Behold your papers, Jarvis Lorry, counter-signed.'

'One can depart, citizen?'

'One can depart. Forward, my postillions! A good journey!'

'I salute you, citizens.–And the first danger passed!'

These are again the words of Jarvis Lorry, as he clasps his hands, and looks upwards. There is terror in the carriage, there is weeping, there is the heavy breathing of the insensible traveller.

'Are we not going too slowly? Can they not be induced to go faster?' asks Lucie, clinging to the old man.

'It would seem like flight, my darling. I must not urge them too much; it would rouse suspicion.'

'Look back, look back, and see if we are pursued!'

'The road is clear, my dearest. So far, we are not pursued.'

Houses in twos and threes pass by us, solitary farms, ruinous buildings, dye-works, tanneries, and the like, open country, avenues of leafless trees. The hard uneven pavement is under us, the soft deep mud is on either side. Sometimes we strike into the skirting mud, to avoid the stones that clatter us and shake us, sometimes we stick in ruts and sloughs there. The agony of our impatience is then so great, that in our wild alarm and hurry we are for getting out and running–hiding–doing anything but stopping.

Out of the open country, in again among the ruinous buildings, solitary farms, dye-works, tanneries, and the like, cottages in twos and threes, avenues of leafless trees. Have these men deceived us, and taken us back by another road? Is not this the same place twice over? Thank Heaven, no. A village Look back, look back, and see if we are pursued! Hush! the posting-house.

Leisurely, our four horses are taken out; leisurely, the coach stands in the little street, bereft of horses, and with no likelihood upon it of ever moving again; leisurely, the new horses come into visible existence, one by one; leisurely, the new postillions follow, sucking and plaiting the lashes of their whips; leisurely, the old postillions count their money, make wrong additions, and arrive at dissatisfied results. All the time, our overfraught hearts are beating at a rate that would far outstrip the fastest gallop of the fastest horses ever foaled.

At length the new postillions are in their saddles, and the old are left behind. We are through the village, up the hill, and down the hill, and on the low watery grounds. Suddenly, the postillions exchange speech with animated grsticulation, and the horses are pulled up, almost on their hanuches. We are pursued?

'Ho! Within the carriage there. Speak then!'

'What is it?' asks Mr. Lorry, looking out at window.

'How many did they say?'

'I do not understand you.'

'–At the last post. How many to the Guillotine to-day?'

'Fifty-two.'

'I said so! A brave number! My fellow-citizen here would have it forty-two; ten more heads are worth having. The Guillotine goes handsomely. I love it. Hi, forward. Whoop!'

The night comes on dark. He moves more; he is beginning to revive, and to speak intelliglibly; he thinks they are still together; he asks him, by his name, what he has in his hand. Oh, pity us, kind Heaven, and help us! Look out, look out, and see if we are pursued.

The wind is rushing after us, and the clouds are flying after us, and the moon is plunging after us, and the whole wild night is in pursuit of us; but, so far, we are pursued by nothing else.

CHAPTER XIV

THE KNITTING DONE

IN that same juncture of time when the fifty-two awaited their fate, Madame Defarge held darkly ominous council with The Vengeance and Jacques Three of the Revoultionary Jury. Not in the wine shop did Madame Defarge confer with these ministers, but in the shed of the wood-sawyer, erst a mender of roads. The sawyer himself did not participate in the conference, but abided at a little distance, like an outer satellite who was not to speak until required, or to offer an opinion until invited.

'But our Defarge,' said Jacques Three, 'is undoubtedly a good Republican? Eh?'

'There is no better,' the voluble Vengeance protested in her shrill notes, 'in France.'

'Peace, little Vengeance,' said Madame Defarge, laying her hand with a slight frown on her lieutenant's lips; 'hear me speak. My husband, fellow-citizen, is a good Republican and a bold man; he has deserved well of the Republic, and possesses its confidence. But my husband had his weaknesses, and he is so weak as to relent towards this Doctor.'

'It is a great pity,' croaked Jacques Three, dubiously shaking his head, with his cruel fingers at his hungry mouth; 'it is not quite like a good citizen; it is a thing to regret.'

'See you,' said madame, 'I care nothing for this Doctor, I. He may wear his head or lose it, for any interest I have in him; it is all one to me. But, the Evrémonde people are to be exterminated, and the wife and child must follow the husband and father.'

'She has a fine head for it,' croaked Jacque Three. 'I have seen blue eyes and golden hair there, and they looked charming when Samson held them up.' Ogre that he was, he spoke like an epicure.

Madame Defarge cast down her eyes, and reflected a little.

'The child also,' observed Jacques Three, with a meditative enjoyment of his words, 'has golden hair and blue eyes. And was seldom have a child there. It is a pretty sight!'

'In a word,' said Madame Defarge, coming out of her short abstraction, 'I cannot trust my husband in this matter. Not only do I feel, since last night, that I dare not confide to him the details of my prjects; but also I feel that if I delay, there is danger of his giving warning, and then they might escape.'

'That must never be,' croaked Jacques Three; no one must escape. We have not half enough as it is. We ought to have six score a day.

'In a word,' Madame Defarge went on, 'my husband has not my reason for pursuing this family to annihilation, and I have not his reason for regarding this Doctor with any sensibility. I must act for myself, therefore. Come hither, little citizen.'

The wood-sawyer, who held her in the respect, and himself in the submission, of mortal fear, advanced with his hand to his red cap.

'Touching those signals, little citizen,' said Madame Defarge, sternly, 'that she made to the prisoners; you are ready to bear witness to them this very day?'

'Ay, ay, why not!' cried the sawyer. 'Every day, in all weathers, from two to four, always signalling, sometimes with the little one, sometimes without. I know what I know. I have seen with my eyes.'

He made all manner of gestures while he spoke, as if in incidental imitation of some few of the great diversity of signals that he had never seen.

'Clearly plots,' said Jacques Three. 'Transparently!'

'There is no doubt of the Jury?' inquired Madame Defarge, letting her eyes turn to him with a gloomy smile.

'Rely upon the patriotic Jury, dear citizeness. I answer for my fellow-jurymen.'

'Now, let me see,' said Madame Defarge, pondering again. 'Yet once more! Can I spare this Doctor to my husband? I have no feeling either way. Can I spare him?'

'He would count as one head,' observed Jacques Three, in a low voice. 'We really have not heads enough; it would be a pity, I think.'

'He was signalling with her when I saw her,' argued Madame Defarge; 'I cannot speak of one without the other; and I must not be silent, and trust the case wholly to him, this little citizen here. For I am not a bad witness.'

The Vengeance and Jacques Three vied with each other in their fervent protestations that she was the most admirable and marvellous of witnesses. The little citizen, not to be outdone, declared her to be a celestial witness.

'He must take his chance,' said Madame Defarge. 'No, I cannot spare him! You are engaged at three o'clock; you are going to see the batch of to-day executed.–You?'

The question was addressed to the wood-sawyer, who hurriedly replied in the affirmative: seizing the occasion to add that he was the most ardent of Republicans, and that he would be in effect the most desolate of Republicans, if anything prevented him from enjoying the pleasure of smoking his afternoon pipe in the contemplation of the droll national barber. He was so very demonstrative herein, that he might have been suspected (perhaps was, by the dark eyes that looked contemptuously at him out of Madame Defarge's head) of having his small individual fears for his own personal safety, every hour in the day.

'I,' said madame, 'am equally engaged at the same place. After it is over–say at eight to-night–come you to me, in Saint Antoine, and we will give information against these people at my Section.'

The wood-sawyer said he would be proud and flattered to attend the citizeness. The citizeness looked at him, he became embarrassed, evaded her glance as a small dog would have done, retreated among his wood, and hid his confusion over the handle of his saw.

Madame Defarge beckoned the Juryman and The Vengeance a little nearer to the door, and there expounded her further views to them thus:

'She will now be at home, awaiting the moment of his death. She will be mourning and grieving. She will be in a state of mind to impeach the justice of the Republic. She will be full of sympathy with its enemies. I will go to her.'

'What an admirable woman; what an adorable woman!' exclaimed Jacques Three, rapturously. 'Ah, my cherished!' cried The Vengeance; and embraced her.

'Take you my knitting,' said Madame Defarge, placing it in her lieutenant's hands, 'and have it ready for me in my usual seat. Keep me my usual chair. Go you there, straight, for there will probably be a greater concourse than usual, to-day.'

'I willingly obey the orders of my Chief,' said The Vengeance with alacrity, and kissing her cheek. 'You will not be late?'

'I shall be there before the commencement.'

'And before the tumbrils arrive. Be sure you are there, my soul,' said The Vengeance, calling after her, for she had already turned into the street, 'before the tumbrils arrive!'

Madame Defarge slightly waved her hand, to implu that she heard, and might be relied upon to arrive in good time, and so went through the mud, and round the corner of the prison wall. The Vengeance and the Juryman, looking after her as she walked away, were highly appreciative of her fine figure, and her superb moral endowments.

There were many women at that time, upon whom the time laid a dreadfully disfiguring hand; but there was not one among them more to be dreaded than this ruthless woman, now taking her way along the streets. Of a strong and fearless character, of shrewd sense and readiness, of great determination, of that kind of beauty which not only seems to impart to its possessor firmness and animosity, but to strike into others an instinctive recognition of those qualities; the troubled time would have heaved her up, under any circumstances. But, imbued from her childhood with a brooding sense of wrong, and an inveterate hatred of a class, opportunity had developed her into a tigress. She was absolutely without pity. If she had ever had the virtue in her, it had quite gone out of her.

It was nothing to her, than an innocent man was to die for the sins of his forefathers; she saw, not him, but them. It was nothing to her, that his wife was to be made a widow and his daughter an orphan; that was insufficient punishment, because they were her natural enemies and her prey, and as such had no right to live. To appeal to her, was made hopeless by her having no sense of pity, even for herself. If she had been laid low in the streets, in any of the many encounters in which she had been engaged, she would not have pitied herself; nor, if she had been ordered to the axe to-morrow, would she have gone to it with any softer feeling than a fierce desire to change places with the man who sent her there.

Such a heart Madame Defarge carried under her rough robe. Carelessly worn, it was becoming robe enough, in a certain weird way, and her dark hair looked rich under her coarse red cap. Lying hidden in her bosom, was a loaded pistol. Lying hidden at her waist, was a sharpened dagger. Thus accoutred, and walking with with the confident tread of such a character, and with the supple freedom of a woman who had habitually walked in her girlhood, bare-foot and bare-legged, on the brown sea-sand, Madame Defarge took her way along the streets.

Now, when the journey of the travelling coach, at that very moment waiting for the completion of its load, had been planned out last night the difficulty of taking Miss Pross in it had much engaged Mr. Lorry's attention. It was not merely desirable to avoid overloading the coach, but it was of the highest importance that the time occupied in examining it and its passengers, should be reduced to the utmost; since their escape might depend on the saving of only a few seconds here and there. Finally, he had proposed, after anxious consideration, that Miss Pross and Jerry, who were at liberty to leave the city, should leave it at three o'clock in the lightest-wheeled conveyance known to that period. Unencumbered with luggage, they would soon overtake the coach, and, passing it and preceding it on the road, would order its horses in advance, and greatly facilitate its progress during the precious hours of the night, when delay was the most to be dreaded.

Seeing in this arrangement the hope of rendering real service in that pressing emergency, Miss Pross hailed it with joy. She and Jerry had beheld the coach start, had known who it was that Solomon brought, had passed some ten minutes in torture of suspense, and were now concluding their arrangements to follow the coach, even as Madame Defarge, taking her way through the streets, now drew nearer and nearer to the else-deserted lodging in which they held their consultation.

'Now what do you think, Mr. Cruncher,' said Miss Pross, whose agitation was so great that she could hardly speak, or stand, or move, or live: 'what do you think of our not starting from this courtyard? Another carriage having already gone from here to-day, it might awaken suspicion.'

'My opinion, miss,' returned Mr. Cruncher, 'is as you're right. Likewise wot I'll stand by you, right or wrong.'

'I am so distracted with fear and hope for our precious creatures,' said Miss Pross, wildly crying, 'that I am incapable of forming any plan. Are you capable of forming any plan, my dear good Mr. Cruncher?'

'Respectin' a future spear o' life, miss,' returned Mr. Cruncher, 'I hope so. Respectin' any present use o' this here blessed old head o' mine, I think not. Would you do me the favour, miss, to take notice o' two promises and wows wot it is my wished fur to record in this here crisis?'

'Oh, for gracious sake!' cried Miss Pross, still wildly crying, 'record them at once, and get them out of the way, like an excellent man.'

'First,' said Mr. Cruncher, who was all in a tremble, and who spoke with an ashy and solemn visage, 'them poor things well out o' this, never no more will I do it, never no more!'

'I am quite sure, Mr. Cruncher,' returned Miss Pross, 'that you will never do it again, whatever it is, and I beg you not to think it necessary to mention more particularly what it is.'

'No, miss,' returned Jerry, 'it shall not be named to you. Second: them poor things well out o' this, and never no more will I interfere with Mrs. Cruncher's flooping, never no more!'

'Whatever housekeeping arrangement that may be,' said Miss Pross, striving to dry her eyes and compose herself, 'I have no doubt it is best that Mrs. Cruncher shoud have it entirely under her own superintendence.–Oh, my poor darlings!'

'I go so far as to say, miss, morehover,' proceeded Mr. Cruncher, with a most alarming tendency to hold forth as from a pulpit–'and let my words be took down and took to Mrs. Cruncher through yourself–that wot my opinions respectin' flooping has undergone a change, and that wot I only hope with all my heart, as Mrs. Cruncher may be a flooping at the present time.'

'There, there, there! I hope she is, my dear man,' cried the distracted Miss Pross, 'and I hope she finds it answering her expectations.'

'Forbid it,' proceeded Mr. Cruncher, with additional solemnity, additional slowness, and additional tendency to hold forth and hold out, 'as anything wot I have ever said or done should be wisited on my earnest wished for them poor creeturs now! Forbid it as we shouldn't all flop (if it was anyways conwenient) to get 'em out o' this here dismal risk! Forbid it, miss! Wot I say, for–BID it!' This was Mr. Cruncher's conclusion after a protracted but vain endeavour to find a better one.'

And still Madame Defarge, pursuing her way along the streetsm came nearer and nearer.

'If we ever get back to our native land,' said Miss Pross, 'you may rely upon my telling Mrs. Cruncher as much as I may be able to remember and understand of what you have so impressively said; and at all events you may be sure that I shall bear witness to your being thoroughly in earnest at this dreadful time. Now, pray let us think! My esteemed Mr. Cruncher, let us think!'

Still, Madame Defarge, pursuing her way along the streets, came nearer and nearer.

'If you were to go before,' said Miss Pross, 'and stop the vehicle and horses from coming here, and were to wait somewhere for me; wouldn't that be best?'

Mr. Cruncher thought it might be best.

'Where could you wait for me?' asked Miss Pross.

Mr. Cruncher was so bewildered that he could think of no locality but Temple Bar. Alas! Temple Bar was hundreds of miles away, and Madame Defarge was drawing very near indeed.

'By the cathedral door,' said Miss Pross. 'Would it be much out of the way, to take me in, near the great cathedral door between the two towers?'

'No, miss,' answered Mr. Cruncher.

'Then, like the best of men,' said Miss Pross, 'go to the posting-house straight, and make that change.'

'I am doubtful,' said Mr. Cruncher, hesitating and shaking his head, 'about leaving of you, you see. We don't know what may happen.'

'Heaven knows we don't,' returned Miss Pross, 'but have no fear for me. Take me in at the cathedral, at three o'clock, or as near it as you can, and I am sure it will be better that our going from here. I feel certain of it. There! Bless you, Mr. Cruncher! Think—not of me, but of the lives that may depend on both of us!'

The exordium, and Miss Pross's two hands in quite agonized entreaty clasping his decided Mr. Cruncher. With an encouraging nod or two, he immediately went out to alter the arrangements, and left her by herself to follow as she had proposed.

The having originated a precaution which was already in course of execution, was a great relief to Miss Pross. The necessity of composing her appearance so that it should attract no special notice in the streets, was another relief. She looked at her watch, and it was twenty minutes past two. She had no time to lose, but must get ready at once.

Afraid, in her extreme perturbation, of the loneliness of the deserted rooms, and of half-imagined faces peeping from behind every open door in them, Miss Pross got a basin of cold water and began laving her eyes, which were swollen and red. Haunted by her feverish apprehensions, she could not bear to have her sight obscured for a minute at a time by the dripping water, but constantly paused and looked round to see that there was no one watching her. In one of those pauses she recoiled and cried out, for she saw a figure standing in the room.

The basin fell to the ground broken, and the water flowed to the feet of Madame Defarge. By strange stern ways, and through much staining blood, those feet had come to meet that water.

Madame Defarge looked coldly at her, and said, 'The wife of Evrémonde; where is she?'

It flashed upon Miss Pross's mind that the doors were all standing open, and would suggest the flight. Her first act was to shut them. There were four in the room, and she shut them all. She then placed herself before the door of the chamber which Lucie had occupied.

Madame Defarge's dark eyes followed her through this rapid movement, and rested on her when it was finished. Miss Pross had nothing beautiful about her; years had not tamed the wildness, or softened the grimness, of her appearance; but, she too was a determined woman in her different way, and she measured Madame Defarge with her eyes, every inch.

'You might, from your appearance, be the wife of Lucifer,' said Miss Pross, in her breathing. 'Nevertheless, you shall not get the better of me. I am an Englishwoman.'

Madame Defarge looked at her scornfully, but still with something of Miss Pross's own perception that they two were at bay. She was a tight, hard, wiry woman before her, as Mr. Lorry had seen in the same figure a woman with a strong hand, in the years gone by. She knew full well that Miss Pross was the family's devoted friend; Miss Pross knew full well that Madame Defarge was the family's malevolent enemy.

'On my way yonder,' said Madame Defarge, with a slight move-ment of her hand towards the fatal spot, 'where they reserve my chair and my knitting for me, I am come to make my compliments to her in passing. I wish to her.'

'I know that your intentions are evil,' said Miss Pross, 'and you may depend upon it, I'll hold my own against them.'

Each spoke in her own language; neither understood the other's words; both were very watchful, and intent to deduce from look and manner, what the unintelligible words meant.

'It will do her no good to keep herself concealed from me at this moment,' said Madame Defarge. 'Good patriots will know what that means. Let me see her. Go tell her that I wish to see her. Do you hear?'

'If those eyes of yours were bed-winches,' returned Miss Pross, 'and I was an English four-poster, they shouldn't loose a splinter of me. No, you wicked foreign woman; I am your match.'

Madame Defarge was not likely to follow these idiomatic remarks in detail; but, she so far understood them as to perceive that she was set at naught.

'Woman imbecile and pig-like!' said Madame Defarge, frowning. 'I take no answer from you. I demand to see her. Either tell her that I de-mand to see her, or stand out of the way of the door and let me go to her!' This, with an angry explanatory wave of her right arm.

'I litle thought,' said Miss Pross, 'that I should ever want to un-derstand you nonesensical language; but I would give all I have, except the clothes I wear, to know whether you suspect the truth, or any part of it.'

Neither of them for a singe moment released the other's eyes. Madame Defarge had not moved from the spot where she stood when Miss Pross first became aware of her; but, she now advanced one step.

'I am a Briton,' said Miss Pross, 'I am desperate. I don't care an English Twopence for myself. I know that the longer I keep you here, the greater hope there is for my Ladybird. I'll not leave a handful of that dark hair upon your head, if you lay a finger on me!'

Thus Miss Pross, with a shake of her head and a flash of her eyes be-tween every rapid sentence, and every rapid sentence a whole breath. Thus Miss Pross, who had neevr struck a blow in her life.

But, her courage was of that emotional nature that it brought the ir-repressible tears into her eyes. This was a courage that Madame Defarge so little comprehended as to mistake for weakness. 'Ha, ha!' she laughed, 'you poor wretch! What are you worth! I address myself to that Doctor.' Then she raised her voice and called out, 'Citizen Doctor! Wife of Evrémonde! Child of Evrémonde! Any person but this miserable fool, answer the Citizeness Defarge!'

Perhaps the following silence, perhaps some latent disclosure of the expression of Miss Pross's face, perhaps a sudden misgiving apart from either suggestion, whispered to Madame Defarge that they were gone. Three of the doors she opened swiftly, and looked in.

'Those rooms are all in disorder, there has been hurried packing, there are odds and ends upon the ground. There is no one in that room behind you! Let me look.'

'Never!' said Miss Pross, who understood the request as perfectly as Madame Defarge understood the answer.

'If they are not in that room, they are gone, and can be pursued and brought back,' said Madame Defarge to herself.

'As long as you don't know whether they are in that room or not, you are uncertain what to do,' said Miss Pross to *her*self; 'and you shall not know that, if I can prevent your knowing it; and know that, or not know that, you shall not leave her while I can hold you.'

'I have been in the streets from the first, nothing had stopped me, I will tear you to pieces, but I will have you from that door,' said Madame Defarge.

'We are alone at the top of a high house in a solitary courtyard, we are not likely to be heard, and I pray for bodily strength to keep you here, while every minute you are here is worth a hundred thousand guineas to my darling,' said Miss Pross.

Madame Defarge made at the door. Miss Pross, on the instinct of the moment, seized her round the waist in both her arms, and held her tight. It was in vain for Madame Defarge to struggle and to strike; Miss Pross, with the vigorous tenacity of love, always so much stronger than hate, clasped her tight, and even lifted her from the floor in the struggle that they had. The two hands of Madame Defarge buffeted and tore her face; but, Miss Pross, with her head down, held her round the waist, and clung to her with more than the hold of a drowning woman.

'Soon, Madame Defarge's hands ceased to strike, and felt at her encircled waist. 'It is under my arm,' said Miss Pross, in smothered tones; 'you shall not draw it. I am stronger than you, I bless Heaven for it. I'll hold you till one or other of us faints or dies!'

Madame Defarge's hands were at her bosom. Miss Pross looked up, saw what it was, struck at it, struck out a flash and a crash, and stood alone–blinded with smoke.

All this was in a second. As the smoke cleared, leaving an awful stillness, it passed out in the air, like the soul of the furious woman whose body lay lifeless on the ground.

In the first fright and horror of the situation, Miss Pross passed the body as far from it as she could, and ran down the stairs to call for fruitless help. Happily, she bethought herself of the consequences of what she did, in time to check herself and go back. It was dreadful to go in at the door again; but, she did go in, and even went near it, to get the bonnet and other things that she must wear. These she put on, out on the staircase, first shutting and locking the door and taking away the key. She then sat down on the stairs a few moments to breathe and to cry, and then got up and hurried away.

By good fortune she had a veil on her bonnet, or she could hardly have gone along the streets without being stopped. By good fortune, too, she was naturally so peculiar in appearance as not to show disfigurement like any other woman. She needed advantages, for the marks of griping fingers were deep in her face, and her hair was torn, and her dress (hastily composed with unsteady hands) was clutched and dragged a hundred ways.

In crossing the bridge, she dropped the door key in the river. Arriving at the cathedral some few minutes before her escort, and waiting there, she thought, what if the key were already taken in a net, what if it were identified, what if the door were opened and the remains discovered, what if she were stopped at the gate, sent to prison, and charged with murder! In the midst of these fluttering thoughts, the escort appeared, took her in, and took her away.

'Is there any noise in the streets?' she asked him.

'The usual noises,' Mr. Cruncher replied; and looked surprised by the question and by her aspect.

'I don't hear you,' said Miss Pross. 'What do you say?'

It was in vain for Mr. Cruncher to repeat what he said; Miss Pross could not hear him. 'So I'll nod my head,' thought Mr. Cruncher, amazed; 'at all events she'll see that.' And she did.

'Is there any noise in the streets now?' asked Miss Pross again, presently.

Again Mr. Cruncher nodded his head.

'I don't hear it.'

'Gone deaf in an hour?' said Mr. Cruncher, ruminating, with his mind much disturbed; 'wot's come to her?'

'I feel,' said Miss Pross, 'as if there had been a flash and a crash, and that crash was the last thing I should ever hear in this life.'

'Blest if she ain't in a queer condition!' said Mr. Cruncher, more and more disturbed. 'What can she have been a takin', to keep her courage up? Hark! There's the roll of them dreadful carts! You can hear that, miss?'

'I can hear,' said Miss Pross, seeing that he spoke to her, 'nothing. Oh, my good man, there was first a great crash, and then a great stillness, and that stillness seems to be fixed and unchangeable, neve to broken any more as long as my life lasts.'

'If she don't hear the roll of those dreadful carts, now very high their journey's end,' said Mr. Cruncher, glancing over his shoulder, 'it's my opinion that indeed she never will hear anything else in this world.'

And indeed she never did.

CHAPTER XV

THE FOOTSTEPS DIE OUT FOR EVER

ALONG the Paris streets, the death-carts rumble, hollow and harsh. Six tumbrils carry the day's wine to La Guillotine. All the devouring and insatiate Monsters imagined since imagination could record itself, are fused in the one realization, Guillotine. And yet there is not in France, with its rich variety of soil and climate, a blade, a leaf, a root, a sprig, a peppercorn, which will grow to maturity under conditions more certain than those that have produced this horror. Crush humanity out of shape once more, under similar hammers, and it will twist itself into the same tortured forms. Sow the same seed of rapacious licence and oppression over again, and it will surely yield the same fruit according to its kind.

Six tumbrils roll along the streets. Change these back again to what they were, thou powerful enchanter, Time, and they shall be seen to be the carriages of absolute monarchs, the equipages of feudal nobles, the toilettes of flaring Jezebels, the churches that are not my Father's house but dens of thieves, the huts of millions of starving peasants! No; the great magician who majestically works out the appointed order of the Creator, never reverses his transformations. 'If thou be changed into this shape by the will of God,' say the seers to the enchanted, in the wise Arabian stories, 'then remain so! But, if thou wear this form through mere passing conjuration, then resume thy former aspect!' Changeless and hopeless, the tumbrils roll along.

As the sombre wheels of the six carts go round, they seem to plough up a long crooked furrow among the populace in the streets. Ridges of faces are throw to this side and to that, and the ploughs go steadily onward. So used are the regukar inhabitants of the houses to the spectacle, that in many windows there are no people, and in some the occupation of the hands is not so much as suspended, while the eyes aurvey the faces in the tumbrils. Here and there, the inmate has visitors to see the sight; then he points his finger, with something of the complacency of a curator or authorized exponent, to this cart and to this, and seems to tell who at here yesterday, and who there the day before.

Of the riders in the tumbrils, some observe these things, and all things on their last roadside, with an impassive stare; others, with a lingering interest in the ways of life and men. Some seated with drooping heads, are sunk in silent despair; again, there are some so heedful of their looks that they cast upon the multitude such glances as they have seen in theatres, and in pictures. Several close their eyes, and think, or try to get their straying thoughts together. Only one, and he is a miserable creature, of a crazed aspect, is so shattered and made drunk by horror, that he sings, and tries to dance. Not one of the whole number appeals by look or gesture, to the pity of the people.

There is a guard of sundry horsemen riding abreast of the tumbrils, and faces are often turned up to some of them, and they are asked some questions. It would seem to be always the same question, for, it is always followed by a press of people towards the third cart. The horsemen abreast of that cart, frequently point out one man in it with their swords. The leading curiosity is, to know which is he; he stands at the back of the tumbril with his head bent down, to converse with a mere girl who sits on the side of the cart, and holds his hand. He has no curiosity or care for the scene about him, and always speaks to the girl. Here and there in the long street of St. Honoré, cries are raised against him. If they move him at all, it is only to a quiet smile, as he shakes his hair a little more loosely about his face. He cannot easily touch his face, his arms being bound.

On the steps of a church, awaiting the coming-up of the tumbrils, stands the spy and prison sheep. He looks into the first of them: not there. He looks into the second: not there. He already asks himself, 'Has he sacrificed me?' when his face clears, as je looks into the third.

'Which is Evrémonde? says a man behind him.

'That. At the back there.'

'With his hand in the girl's?'

'Yes.'

The man cries, 'Down, Evrémonde! To the Guillotine, all aristocrats! Down, Evrémonde!'

'Hush, hush!' the spy entreats him, timidly.

'And why not, citizen?'

'He is going to pay the forfeit: it will be paid in five minutes more. Let him be at peace.'

But the man continuing to exclaim, 'Down, Evrémonde!' the face of Evrémonde is for a moment turned towards him. Evrémonde then sees the spy, and looks attentively at him, and goes his way.

The clocks are on the stroke of three, and the furrow ploughed among the populace is turning round, to come on into the place of execution, and end. The ridges thrown to this side and to that, now crumble in and close behind the last plough as it passes on, for all are following to the Guillotine. In front of it, seated in chairs, as in a garden of public diversion, are a number of women, busily knitting. On one of the foremost chairs, stands The Vengeance, looking about for her friend.

'Thérèse!' she cries, in her shrill tones 'Who has seen her? Thérèse Defarge!'

'She never missed before,' says a knitting-woman of the sisterhood.

'No: nor will she miss now,' cries The Vengeance petulantly. Thérèse.'

'Louder,' the woman recommends.

Ay! Louder, Vengeance, much louder, and still she will scarcely hear thee. Louder yet, Vengeance, with a little oath or so added, and yet it will hardly bring her. Send other women up and down to seek her, lingering somewhere; and yet, although the messengers have done dread deeds, it is questionable whether of their own wills they will go far enough to find her!

'Bad Fortune!' cries The Vengeance, stamping her foot in the chair, 'and here are the tumbrils! And Evrémonde will be dispatched in a wink, and she not here! See her knitting in my hand, and her empty chair ready for her. I cry with vexation and disappointment!'

As The Vengeance descends from her elevation to do it, the tumbrils begin to discharge their loads. The ministers of Saint Guillotine are robed and ready. Crash!–a head is held up, and the knitting-women, who scarcely lifted their eyes to look at it a moment ago when it could think and speak, count One.

The second tumbril empties and moves on; the third comes up. Crash!–and the knitting-women, never faltering or pausing in their work, count Two.

The supposed Evrémonde descends, and the seamstress is lifted out next after him. He has not relinquished her patient hand in getting out, but still holds it as he promised. He gently places her with her back to the crashing engine that constantly whirrs up and falls, and she looks into his face and thanks him.

'But for you, dear stranger, I should not be so composed, for I am naturally a poor little thing, faint of heart; nor should I have been able to raise my thoughts to Him who was put to death, that we might have hope and comfort here to-day. I think you were sent to me by Heaven.'

'Or you to me,' says Sydney Carton. 'Keep your eyes upon me, dear child, and mind no other object.'

'I mind nothing while I hold your hand. I shall mind nothing when I let it go, if they are rapid.'

'They will be rapid. Fear not!'

The two stand in the fast-thinning throng of victims, but they speak as if they were alone. Eye to eye, voice to voice, hand to hand, heart to heart, these two children of the Universal Mother, else so wide apart and differing, have come together on the dark highway, to repair home together, and to rest in her bosom.

'Brave and generous friend, you will let me ask you one lst question? I am very ignorant, and it troubles me–just a little.'

'Tell me what it is.'

'I have a cousin, an only relative and an orphan, like myself, whom I love very dearly. She is five years younger than I, and she lives in a farmer's house in the south country. Poverty parted us, and she knows nothing of my fate–for I cannot write–and if I could, how should I tell her! It is better as it is.'

'Yes, yes, better as it is.'

'What I have been thinking as we came along, and what I am still thinking now, as I look into your kind strong face which gives me so much support, is this: If the Republic really does good to the poor, and they come to be less hungry, and in all ways to suffer less, and she may live a long time: she may even live to be old.'

'What then, my gentle sister?'

'Do you think'–the uncomplaining eyes in which there is so much endurance, fill with tears, and the lips part a little more and tremble–' that it will seem long to me, while I wait for her in the better land where I trust both you and I will be mercifully sheltered?'

'It cannot be, my child, there is no Time there, and no trouble there.'

'You comfort me so much! I am so ignorant. Am I to kiss you now? Is the moment come?'

'Yes.'

She kisses his lips; he kisses hers; they solemnly bless each other. The spare hand does not tremble as he releases it; nothing worse than a sweet, bright constancy is in the patient face. She goes next before him–is gone; the knitting-women count Twenty-two.

'I am the Resurrection and the Life, saith the Lord: he that believeth in me, though he were dead, yet shall he live: and whosoever liveth and believeth in me shall never die!'

The murmuring of many voices, the upturning of many faces, the pressing on of many footsteps in the outskirts of the crowd, so that it swells forward in mass, like one great heave of water, all flashes away. Twenty-three.

They said of him, about the city that night, that it was the peace-fullest man's face ever beheld there. Many added that he looked sublime and prophetic.

One of the most remarkable sufferers by the same axe–a woman–had asked at the foot of the same scaffold, not long before, to be allowed to write down the thoughts that were inspiring her. If he had given any utterance to his, and they were prophetic, they would have been these:

'I see Barsad, and Cly, Defarge, The Vengeance, the Juryman, the Judge, long ranks of the new oppressors who have risen on the destruction of the old, perishing by this retributive instrument, before it shall cease out of its present use. I see a beautiful city and a brilliant people rising from this abyss, and, in their struggles to be truly free, in their triumphs and defeats, through long long years to come, I see the evil of this time and of the previous time of which this is the natural birth, gradually making expiation for itself and wearing out.

'I see the lives for which I lay down my life, peaceful, useful, prosperous and happy, in that England which I shall see no more. I see Her with a child upon her bosom, who bears my name. I see her father, aged and bentm but otherwise restored, and faithful to all men in his healing office, and at peace. I see the good old man, so long their friend, in ten years' time enriching them with all he has, and passing tranquilly to his reward.

'I see that I hold a sanctuary in their hearts, and in the hearts of their descendants, generations hence. I see her, an old woman, weeping for me on the anniversary of this day. I see her and her husband, their course done, lying side by side in their last earthly bed, and I know that each was not more honoured and held sacred in the other's soul, than I was in the souls of both.

'I see that child who lay upon her bosom and who bore my name, a man winning his way up in that path of life which once was mine. I see him winning it so well, that my name is made illustrious there by the light of his. I see the blots I threw upon it, faded away. I see him, foremost of just judges and honoured men, bringing a boy of my name, with a forehead that I know and golden hair, to this place–then fair to look upon, with not a trace of this day's disfigurement–and I hear him tell the child my story, with a tender and a faltering voice.

'It is a far, far better thing that I do, than I have ever done; it is a far, far better rest that I go to, than I have ever known.'

THE END

INDEX